BIRDS
of
MINNESOTA
and
WISCONSIN

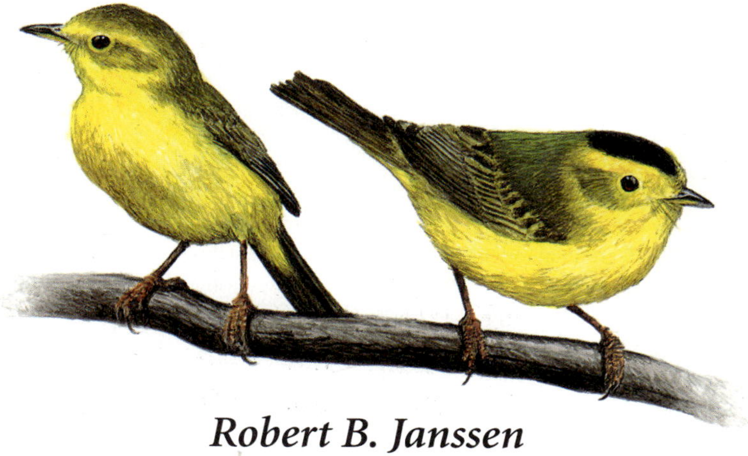

Robert B. Janssen
Daryl D. Tessen
Gregory Kennedy

with contributions from Greg Butcher,
Chris Fisher & Andy Bezener

LONE PINE

Lone Pine Publishing

First printed in 2003 10 9 8 7 6 5 4 3 2
Printed in Canada

The Publisher: Lone Pine Publishing
1808 B Street NW, Suite 140
Auburn, WA, USA 98001

10145 – 81 Avenue Edmonton, AB, Canada T6E 1W9

Website: www.lonepinepublishing.com

National Library of Canada Cataloguing in Publication Data
Janssen, Robert B.
Birds of Minnesota and Wisconsin / Robert B. Janssen, Daryl D. Tessen, Gregory Kennedy.

Includes bibliographical references and index.

ISBN 1-55105-324-1

1. Birds—Minnesota—Identification. 2. Birds—Wisconsin—Identification. I. Tessen, Daryl, D., 1939– II. Kennedy, Gregory, 1956– III. Title.
QL684.M6J36 2003 598'.07'234776 C2003-910253-X

Editorial Director: Nancy Foulds
Project Editor: Nicholle Carriere
Editorial: Nicholle Carriere, Genevieve Boyer
Illustrations Coordinator: Carol Woo
Production Manager: Gene Longson
Layout & Production: Arlana Anderson-Hale
Cover Design: Gerry Dotto
Cover Illustration: Common Loon, by Gary Ross
Illustrations: Gary Ross, Ted Nordhagen
Maps: Volker Bodegom, Elliot Engley, Arlana Anderson-Hale
Separations & Film: Elite Lithographers Co.

We acknowledge the financial support of the Government of Canada through the Book Publishing Industry Development Program (BPIDP) for our publishing activities.

PC: P1

CONTENTS

Acknowledgments 4
Reference Guide 5
Introduction 17

Loons, Grebes, Pelicans, Cormorants 34

Bitterns, Herons, Egrets, Vultures 45

Geese, Swans, Ducks 56

Ospreys, Eagles, Hawks, Falcons 89

Partridges, Pheasants, Grouse, Prairie-Chickens, Turkeys 107

Rails, Soras, Moorhens, Coots, Cranes 115

Plovers, Sandpipers, Phalaropes 122

Jaegers, Gulls, Terns 157

Doves, Cuckoos 174

Owls 178

Nighthawks, Swifts, Hummingbirds, Kingfishers 188

Woodpeckers, Sapsuckers, Flickers 193

Flycatchers, Wood-Pewees, Phoebes, Kingbirds 203

Shrikes, Vireos 214

Jays, Magpies, Crows, Ravens 223

Larks, Martins, Swallows 228

Chickadees, Nuthatches, Creepers, Wrens 235

Kinglets, Gnatcatchers, Bluebirds, Thrushes, Robins 246

Mimics, Starlings, Pipits, Waxwings 259

Warblers, Redstarts, Waterthrushes, Yellowthroats, Tanagers 266

Towhees, Sparrows, Juncos, Longspurs, Buntings, Grosbeaks 305

Blackbirds, Meadowlarks, Grackles, Cowbirds, Orioles 335

Grosbeaks, Finches, Crossbills, Redpolls, Old World Sparrows 346

Appendix of Occasional Bird Species 357
Select References 361
Glossary 362
Checklist 364
Index 369

ACKNOWLEDGMENTS

Thanks are extended to the growing family of ornithologists and dedicated birders who have offered their inspiration and expertise to help build Lone Pine's expanding library of field guides. Thanks also go to John Acorn, Chris Fisher, Andy Bezener and Eloise Pulos for their contributions to previous books in this series. In addition, thank you to Gary Ross, Ted Nordhagen and Ewa Pluciennik, whose skilled illustrations have brought each page to life.

DIVING BIRDS

Red-throated Loon
size 25 in • p. 34

Pacific Loon
size 26 in • p. 35

Common Loon
size 32 in • p. 36

Pied-billed Grebe
size 13 in • p. 37

Horned Grebe
size 13 in • p. 38

Red-necked Grebe
size 20 in • p. 39

Eared Grebe
size 13 in • p. 40

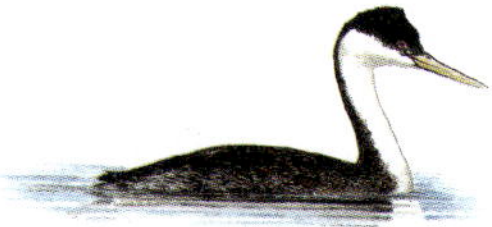
Western Grebe
size 22 in • p. 41

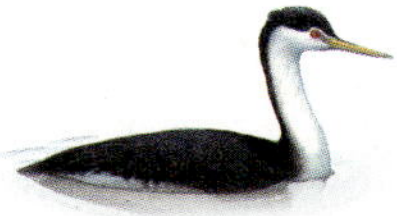
Clark's Grebe
size 22 in • p. 42

American White Pelican
size 62 in • p. 43

Double-crested Cormorant
size 29 in • p. 44

HERONLIKE BIRDS

American Bittern
size 25 in • p. 45

Least Bittern
size 13 in • p. 46

Great Blue Heron
size 52 in • p. 47

Great Egret
size 39 in • p. 48

Snowy Egret
size 24 in • p. 49

Little Blue Heron
size 24 in • p. 50

Cattle Egret
size 20 in • p. 51

Green Heron
size 18 in • p. 52

Black-crowned Night-Heron
size 25 in • p. 53

Yellow-crowned Night-Heron
size 24 in • p. 54

Turkey Vulture
size 29 in • p. 55

WATERFOWL

Greater White-fronted Goose
size 30 in • p. 56

Snow Goose
size 31 in • p. 57

Ross's Goose
size 23 in • p. 58

Canada Goose
size 36 in • p. 59

Mute Swan
size 60 in • p. 60

Trumpeter Swan
size 65 in • p. 61

Tundra Swan
size 54 in • p. 62

Wood Duck
size 18 in • p. 63

Gadwall
size 20 in • p. 64

American Wigeon
size 20 in • p. 65

American Black Duck
size 22 in • p. 66

Mallard
size 24 in • p. 67

Blue-winged Teal
size 15 in • p. 68

Cinnamon Teal
size 16 in • p. 69

Northern Shoveler
size 19 in • p. 70

Northern Pintail
size 23 in • p. 71

Green-winged Teal
size 14 in • p. 72

Canvasback
size 20 in • p. 73

Redhead
size 20 in • p. 74

Ring-necked Duck
size 16 in • p. 75

Greater Scaup
size 18 in • p. 76

Lesser Scaup
size 16 in • p. 77

Harlequin Duck
size 16 in • p. 78

Surf Scoter
size 18 in • p. 79

WATERFOWL

White-winged Scoter
size 21 in • p. 80

Black Scoter
size 19 in • p. 81

Long-tailed Duck
size 19 in • p. 82

Bufflehead
size 14 in • p. 83

Common Goldeneye
size 18 in • p. 84

Hooded Merganser
size 17 in • p. 85

Common Merganser
size 25 in • p. 86

Red-breasted Merganser
size 22 in • p. 87

Ruddy Duck
size 15 in • p. 88

BIRDS OF PREY

Osprey
size 24 in • p. 89

Bald Eagle
size 36 in • p. 90

Northern Harrier
size 20 in • p. 91

Sharp-shinned Hawk
size 13 in • p. 92

Cooper's Hawk
size 17 in • p. 93

Northern Goshawk
size 23 in • p. 94

Red-shouldered Hawk
size 19 in • p. 95

Broad-winged Hawk
size 16 in • p. 96

Swainson's Hawk
size 21 in • p. 97

Red-tailed Hawk
size 21 in • p. 98

Ferruginous Hawk
size 24 in • p. 99

Rough-legged Hawk
size 22 in • p. 100

Golden Eagle
size 35 in • p. 101

American Kestrel
size 8 in • p. 102

Merlin
size 11 in • p. 103

Gyrfalcon
size 22 in • p. 104

BIRDS OF PREY

Peregrine Falcon
size 17 in • p. 105

Prairie Falcon
size 16 in • p. 106

GROUSE & ALLIES

Gray Partridge
size 13 in • p. 107

Ring-necked Pheasant
size 30 in • p. 108

Ruffed Grouse
size 17 in • p. 109

Spruce Grouse
size 15 in • p. 110

Sharp-tailed Grouse
size 17 in • p. 111

Greater Prairie-Chicken
size 17 in • p. 112

Wild Turkey
size 39 in • p. 113

Northern Bobwhite
size 10 in • p. 114

RAILS, COOTS & CRANES

Yellow Rail
size 7 in • p. 115

King Rail
size 15 in • p. 116

Virginia Rail
size 10 in • p. 117

Sora
size 9 in • p. 118

Common Moorhen
size 13 in • p. 119

American Coot
size 14 in • p. 120

Sandhill Crane
size 45 in • p. 121

SHOREBIRDS

Black-bellied Plover
size 12 in • p. 122

American Golden-Plover
size 10 in • p. 123

Semipalmated Plover
size 7 in • p. 124

Piping Plover
size 7 in • p. 125

Killdeer
size 10 in • p. 126

American Avocet
size 17 in • p. 127

Greater Yellowlegs
size 14 in • p. 128

Lesser Yellowlegs
size 10 in • p. 129

Solitary Sandpiper
size 8 in • p. 130

Willet
size 15 in • p. 131

Spotted Sandpiper
size 7 in • p. 132

Upland Sandpiper
size 11 in • p. 133

Whimbrel
size 18 in • p. 134

Hudsonian Godwit
size 14 in • p. 135

Marbled Godwit
size 18 in • p. 136

Ruddy Turnstone
size 9 in • p. 137

Red Knot
size 10 in • p. 138

Sanderling
size 8 in • p. 139

Semipalmated Sandpiper
size 6 in • p. 140

Western Sandpiper
size 6 in • p. 141

Least Sandpiper
size 5 in • p. 142

White-rumped Sandpiper
size 7 in • p. 143

Baird's Sandpiper
size 7 in • p. 144

Pectoral Sandpiper
size 9 in • p. 145

Purple Sandpiper
size 9 in • p. 146

Dunlin
size 8 in • p. 147

Stilt Sandpiper
size 8 in • p. 148

Buff-breasted Sandpiper
size 8 in • p. 149

Ruff
size 10 in • p. 150

Short-billed Dowitcher
size 11 in • p. 151

Long-billed Dowitcher
size 11 in • p. 152

Wilson's Snipe
size 11 in • p. 153

American Woodcock
size 11 in • p. 154

Wilson's Phalarope
size 9 in • p. 155

Red-necked Phalarope
size 7 in • p. 156

Parasitic Jaeger
size 18 in • p. 157

Laughing Gull
size 16 in • p. 158

Franklin's Gull
size 14 in • p. 159

Little Gull
size 10 in • p. 160

Bonaparte's Gull
size 13 in • p. 161

REFERENCE GUIDE

GULLS & ALLIES

Mew Gull
size 16 in • p. 162

Ring-billed Gull
size 19 in • p. 163

Herring Gull
size 24 in • p. 164

Thayer's Gull
size 23 in • p. 165

Iceland Gull
size 22 in • p. 166

Lesser Black-backed Gull
size 21 in • p. 167

Glaucous Gull
size 27 in • p. 168

Great Black-backed Gull
size 30 in • p. 169

Caspian Tern
size 21 in • p. 170

Common Tern
size 15 in • p. 171

Forster's Tern
size 15 in • p. 172

Black Tern
size 9 in • p. 173

DOVES & CUCKOOS

Rock Dove
size 12 in • p. 174

Mourning Dove
size 12 in • p. 175

Black-billed Cuckoo
size 12 in • p. 176

Yellow-billed Cuckoo
size 12 in • p. 177

OWLS

Eastern Screech-Owl
size 8 in • p. 178

Great Horned Owl
size 21 in • p. 179

Snowy Owl
size 23 in • p. 180

Northern Hawk Owl
size 16 in • p. 181

Barred Owl
size 20 in • p. 182

Great Gray Owl
size 28 in • p. 183

Long-eared Owl
size 15 in • p. 184

Short-eared Owl
size 14 in • p. 185

Boreal Owl
size 10 in • p. 186

Northern Saw-whet Owl
size 8 in • p. 187

Common Nighthawk
size 9 in • p. 188

Whip-poor-will
size 9 in • p. 189

Chimney Swift
size 5 in • p. 190

Ruby-throated Hummingbird
size 4 in • p. 191

Belted Kingfisher
size 12 in • p. 192

Red-headed Woodpecker
size 9 in • p. 193

Red-bellied Woodpecker
size 10 in • p. 194

Yellow-bellied Sapsucker
size 8 in • p. 195

Downy Woodpecker
size 6 in • p. 196

Hairy Woodpecker
size 8 in • p. 197

Three-toed Woodpecker
size 8 in • p. 198

Black-backed Woodpecker
size 9 in • p. 199

Northern Flicker
size 13 in • p. 200

Pileated Woodpecker
size 17 in • p. 201

Olive-sided Flycatcher
size 7 in • p. 203

Eastern Wood-Pewee
size 6 in • p. 204

Yellow-bellied Flycatcher
size 6 in • p. 205

Acadian Flycatcher
size 6 in • p. 206

Alder Flycatcher
size 6 in • p. 207

Willow Flycatcher
size 6 in • p. 208

Least Flycatcher
size 6 in • p. 209

Eastern Phoebe
size 7 in • p. 210

Great Crested Flycatcher
size 8 in • p. 211

Western Kingbird
size 8 in • p. 212

Eastern Kingbird
size 8 in • p. 213

Loggerhead Shrike
size 9 in • p. 214

Northern Shrike
size 10 in • p. 215

White-eyed Vireo
size 5 in • p. 216

Bell's Vireo
size 5 in • p. 217

SHRIKES & VIREOS

Yellow-throated Vireo
size 5 in • p. 218

Blue-headed Vireo
size 5 in • p. 219

Warbling Vireo
size 5 in • p. 220

Philadelphia Vireo
size 5 in • p. 221

Red-eyed Vireo
size 6 in • p. 222

JAYS & CROWS

Gray Jay
size 12 in • p. 223

Blue Jay
size 12 in • p. 224

Black-billed Magpie
size 20 in • p. 225

American Crow
size 18 in • p. 226

Common Raven
size 20 in • p. 227

LARKS & SWALLOWS

Horned Lark
size 7 in • p. 228

Purple Martin
size 7 in • p. 229

Tree Swallow
size 5 in • p. 230

Northern Rough-winged Swallow
size 5 in • p. 231

Bank Swallow
size 5 in • p. 232

Cliff Swallow
size 5 in • p. 233

Barn Swallow
size 7 in • p. 234

CHICKADEES, NUTHATCHES & WRENS

Black-capped Chickadee
size 5 in • p. 235

Boreal Chickadee
size 5 in • p. 236

Tufted Titmouse
size 5 in • p. 237

Red-breasted Nuthatch
size 5 in • p. 238

White-breasted Nuthatch
size 6 in • p. 239

Brown Creeper
size 5 in • p. 240

Carolina Wren
size 5 in • p. 241

House Wren
size 5 in • p. 242

Winter Wren
size 4 in • p. 243

Sedge Wren
size 4 in • p. 244

Marsh Wren
size 5 in • p. 245

Golden-crowned Kinglet
size 4 in • p. 246

Ruby-crowned Kinglet
size 4 in • p. 247

Blue-gray Gnatcatcher
size 5 in • p. 248

Eastern Bluebird
size 7 in • p. 249

Mountain Bluebird
size 7 in • p. 250

Townsend's Solitaire
size 8 in • p. 251

Veery
size 7 in • p. 252

Gray-cheeked Thrush
size 7 in • p. 253

Swainson's Thrush
size 7 in • p. 254

Hermit Thrush
size 7 in • p. 255

Wood Thrush
size 8 in • p. 256

American Robin
size 10 in • p. 257

Varied Thrush
size 9 in • p. 258

Gray Catbird
size 9 in • p. 259

Northern Mockingbird
size 10 in • p. 260

Brown Thrasher
size 11 in • p. 261

European Starling
size 8 in • p. 262

American Pipit
size 6 in • p. 263

Bohemian Waxwing
size 8 in • p. 264

Cedar Waxwing
size 7 in • p. 265

Blue-winged Warbler
size 5 in • p. 266

Golden-winged Warbler
size 5 in • p. 267

Tennessee Warbler
size 5 in • p. 268

Orange-crowned Warbler
size 5 in • p. 269

Nashville Warbler
size 5 in • p. 270

Northern Parula
size 5 in • p. 271

Yellow Warbler
size 5 in • p. 272

Chestnut-sided Warbler
size 5 in • p. 273

Magnolia Warbler
size 5 in • p. 274

Cape May Warbler
size 5 in • p. 275

Black-throated Blue Warbler
size 5 in • p. 276

Yellow-rumped Warbler
size 5 in • p. 277

Black-throated Green Warbler
size 5 in • p. 278

Blackburnian Warbler
size 5 in • p. 279

Yellow-throated Warbler
size 5 in • p. 280

Pine Warbler
size 5 in • p. 281

Prairie Warbler
size 5 in • p. 282

Palm Warbler
size 5 in • p. 283

Bay-breasted Warbler
size 5 in • p. 284

Blackpoll Warbler
size 5 in • p. 285

Cerulean Warbler
size 5 in • p. 286

Black-and-white Warbler
size 5 in • p. 287

American Redstart
size 5 in • p. 288

Prothonotary Warbler
size 5 in • p. 289

Worm-eating Warbler
size 5 in • p. 290

Ovenbird
size 6 in • p. 291

Northern Waterthrush
size 6 in • p. 292

Louisiana Waterthrush
size 6 in • p. 293

Kentucky Warbler
size 5 in • p. 294

Connecticut Warbler
size 5 in • p. 295

Mourning Warbler
size 5 in • p. 296

Common Yellowthroat
size 5 in • p. 297

Hooded Warbler
size 5 in • p. 298

Wilson's Warbler
size 5 in • p. 299

Canada Warbler
size 5 in • p. 300

Yellow-breasted Chat
size 7 in • p. 301

Summer Tanager
size 7 in • p. 302

Scarlet Tanager
size 7 in • p. 303

Western Tanager
size 7 in • p. 304

Spotted Towhee
size 8 in • p. 305

Eastern Towhee
size 8 in • p. 306

American Tree Sparrow
size 6 in • p. 307

Chipping Sparrow
size 6 in • p. 308

Clay-colored Sparrow
size 6 in • p. 309

Field Sparrow
size 6 in • p. 310

Vesper Sparrow
size 6 in • p. 311

Lark Sparrow
size 6 in • p. 312

Savannah Sparrow
size 6 in • p. 313

Grasshopper Sparrow
size 5 in • p. 314

Henslow's Sparrow
size 5 in • p. 315

Le Conte's Sparrow
size 5 in • p. 316

Nelson's Sharp-tailed Sparrow
size 5 in • p. 317

Fox Sparrow
size 7 in • p. 318

Song Sparrow
size 6 in • p. 319

Lincoln's Sparrow
size 5 in • p. 320

Swamp Sparrow
size 6 in • p. 321

White-throated Sparrow
size 7 in • p. 322

Harris's Sparrow
size 7 in • p. 323

White-crowned Sparrow
size 6 in • p. 324

Dark-eyed Junco
size 6 in • p. 325

Lapland Longspur
size 6 in • p. 326

Smith's Longspur
size 6 in • p. 327

Chestnut-collared Longspur
size 6 in • p. 328

Snow Bunting
size 7 in • p. 329

SPARROWS, GROSBEAKS & BUNTINGS

Northern Cardinal
size 8 in • p. 330

Rose-breasted Grosbeak
size 8 in • p. 331

Blue Grosbeak
size 7 in • p. 332

Indigo Bunting
size 5 in • p. 333

Dickcissel
size 6 in • p. 334

BLACKBIRDS & ORIOLES

Bobolink
size 7 in • p. 335

Red-winged Blackbird
size 9 in • p. 336

Eastern Meadowlark
size 9 in • p. 337

Western Meadowlark
size 9 in • p. 338

Yellow-headed Blackbird
size 9 in • p. 339

Rusty Blackbird
size 9 in • p. 340

Brewer's Blackbird
size 9 in • p. 341

Common Grackle
size 12 in • p. 342

Brown-headed Cowbird
size 7 in • p. 343

Orchard Oriole
size 7 in • p. 344

Baltimore Oriole
size 7 in • p. 345

FINCHLIKE BIRDS

Pine Grosbeak
size 9 in • p. 346

Purple Finch
size 6 in • p. 347

House Finch
size 6 in • p. 348

Red Crossbill
size 6 in • p. 349

White-winged Crossbill
size 6 in • p. 350

Common Redpoll
size 5 in • p. 351

Hoary Redpoll
size 5 in • p. 352

Pine Siskin
size 5 in • p. 353

American Goldfinch
size 5 in • p. 354

Evening Grosbeak
size 8 in • p. 355

House Sparrow
size 6 in • p. 356

INTRODUCTION

BIRDING IN MINNESOTA AND WISCONSIN

Yellow-bellied Sapsucker

In recent decades, birding has evolved from an eccentric pursuit practiced by a few dedicated individuals to a continent-wide activity that boasts millions of professional and amateur participants. There are many good reasons why birding has become so popular. Many people find it simple and relaxing, while others enjoy the outdoor exercise that it affords. Some see it as a rewarding learning experience, an opportunity to socialize with like-minded people and a way to monitor the health of the local environment. Still others watch birds to reconnect with nature. These days, a visit to any of our region's premier birding locations, such as Duluth and the North Shore region of Lake Superior in Minnesota, or Wisconsin Point (Superior) in Wisconsin, would doubtless uncover still more reasons why people watch birds.

We are truly blessed by the geographical and biological diversity of our region. In addition to supporting a wide range of breeding birds and year-round residents, this area hosts a large number of spring and fall migrants that move through our area on their way to breeding and wintering grounds. In all, 427 bird species have been seen and recorded in Minnesota and 421 in Wisconsin. Out of these, more than 320 species make annual appearances in the whole region.

Christmas bird counts, breeding bird surveys, nest box programs, migration monitoring and birding lectures and workshops all provide a chance for novice, intermediate and expert birders to interact and share their enthusiasm for the splendor of birds. So, whatever your level, there is ample opportunity for you to get involved!

BIRDING BY HABITAT

The USDA Forest Service classifies the Minnesota-Wisconsin area into three ecological regions or "ecoregions":

Mixed Deciduous-Coniferous Forest, which has mixed stands of coniferous and deciduous trees, as well as areas that are purely coniferous or purely deciduous.

Eastern Broadleaf Forest, which consists primarily of deciduous tree species.

Prairie Parkland, which is characterized by areas of prairie interspersed with strips or groves of deciduous trees.

Each of these can be further broken down into smaller regions, based on soil type, elevation, land use or human influences.

Snowy Owl

The large surface area of the two Great Lakes and their shorelines arguably form yet another ecoregion. Each ecoregion is composed of a number of different habitats. Each habitat is a community of plants and animals supported by the infrastructure of water and soil and regulated by the constraints of topography, climate and elevation.

Simply put, a bird's habitat is the place in which it normally lives. Some birds prefer the open water, some birds are found in cattail marshes, others like mature coniferous forest, and still others prefer abandoned agricultural fields overgrown with tall grass and shrubs. Knowledge of a bird's habitat increases the chances of identifying the bird correctly. Only in migration, especially during inclement weather, do some birds leave their usual habitat.

BIRD CONSERVATION

Minnesota and Wisconsin abound with bird life. There are still large areas of wilderness here, including parks, wildlife refuges and public lands. Nevertheless, agriculture and forestry and development for housing are threatening viable bird habitat throughout the region. We hope that more people will learn to appreciate nature in the form of birding, and that those people will do their best to protect the natural areas that remain. Many bird enthusiasts support groups such as the Nature Conservancy and Ducks Unlimited, which help birds by buying and managing tracts of good habitat.

Landscaping your own property to provide native plant cover and natural foods for birds is an immediate and personal way to ensure the conservation of bird habitat. The cumulative effects of such urban "nature-scaping" can be significant. If your yard is to become a bird sanctuary, you may want to keep the neighborhood cats out; every year, millions of birds are killed by cats. Check with the local Humane Society for methods of protecting both your feline friends and wild birds.

BIRD FEEDING

Many people set up backyard bird feeders to attract birds to their yard or plant native berry- or seed-producing plants in their garden. The kind of food available will determine which birds visit your yard. Staff at birding stores can suggest which foods will attract specific birds. Hummingbird feeders are popular in summer and are filled with a simple sugar solution made from one part sugar and four parts water.

Contrary to popular opinion, birds do not become dependent on feeders, nor do they subsequently forget to forage naturally. Winter is when birds appreciate feeders the most, but it is also difficult to find food in spring before flowers bloom, seeds develop and insects hatch.

NEST BOXES

Another popular way to attract birds is to set out nest boxes, especially for wrens, bluebirds and swallows. Not all birds will use nest boxes: only species that normally use cavities in trees are comfortable in such confined spaces. Larger nest boxes can attract kestrels, owls and cavity-nesting ducks.

CLEANING FEEDERS AND NEST BOXES

Nest boxes and feeding stations must be kept clean to prevent birds from becoming ill or spreading disease. Old nesting material may harbor parasites, as well as their eggs. Once the birds have left for the season, remove the old nesting material and wash and scrub the nest box with detergent or a 10 percent bleach solution (1 part bleach to 9 parts water). You can also scald the nest box with boiling water. Rinse it well and let it dry thoroughly before you remount it.

Feeding stations should be cleaned monthly. Feeders can become moldy and any seed, fruit or suet that is moldy or spoiled must be removed. Unclean bird feeders can also be contaminated with salmonellosis and possibly other avian diseases. Clean and disinfect feeding stations with a 10 percent bleach solution, scrubbing thoroughly. Rinse the feeder well and allow it to dry completely before refilling it. Discarded seed and feces on the ground under the feeding station should also be removed.

We advise that you wear rubber gloves and a mask when cleaning nest boxes or feeders.

BIRDING ACTIVITIES

Birding Groups

We recommend that you join in on such activities as Christmas bird counts, birding festivals and the meetings of your local birding or natural history club. If you are interested in bird conservation and environmental issues, natural history groups and conscientious birding stores can keep you informed about the situation in your area and what you can do to help. Bird hotlines provide up-to-date information on the sightings of rarities, which are often easier to relocate than you might think. We have included a brief list of contacts that will help you get involved.

American Kestrel

Minnesota
Organizations

Minnesota Ornithologists' Union
J.F. Bell Museum of Natural History
University of Minnesota
10 Church Street SE
Minneapolis, MN 55455-0104
http://biosci.cbs.umn.edu/˜7

Minnesota Audubon
Suite 207, 26 East Exchange Street
St. Paul, MN 55101
651-225-1830
http://www.audubon.org/chapter/mn/mn/index.html

Minnesota Department of Natural Resources–State Parks
(has bird checklists for all Minnesota state parks)
DNR Information Center
500 Lafayette Road
St. Paul, MN 55155-4040
651-296-6157
1-888-MINNDNR
http://www.dnr.state.mn.us/state_parks/index.html

The Nature Conservancy of Minnesota
Suite 314, 1313 Fifth Street SE
Minneapolis, MN 55414-1588
612-331-0700
http://nature.org/wherewework/northamerica/states/minnesota

Hotlines
Statewide
763-780-8890
1-800-657-3700
Duluth and Northeastern Minnesota
218-728-5030
Northwestern Minnesota
1-800-433-1888

Wisconsin
Organizations

Wisconsin Society for Ornithology
W330, N8275 West Shore Drive
Hartland, WI 53029
262-966-1072
http://www.uwgb.edu/birds/wso

Madison Audubon Society
Suite 1, 222 S Hamilton
Madison, WI 53703-3201
608-255-BIRD
608-255-2473
http://madisonaudubon.org/audubon

Wisconsin Department of Natural Resources
101 S Webster Street
Madison, WI 53703
608-266-2621
http://www.dnr.state.wi.us/org/land/parks

The Nature Conservancy of Wisconsin
Madison Field Office
633 West Main Street
Madison, WI 53703
608-251-8140
http://nature.org/wherewework/northamerica/states/wisconsin

Hotlines
Statewide 414-352-3857
Green Bay 920-391-3686
Madison 608-255-2476

Marsh Wren

TOP BIRDING SITES IN MINNESOTA AND WISCONSIN

The following areas have been selected to represent a broad range of bird communities and habitats, with an emphasis on accessibility. Common birds are included in these accounts, as well as exciting rarities.

Minnesota's Top 10 Birding Sites

Duluth Area

The Duluth area is Minnesota's premier birding location. Lake Superior and adjacent landforms attract migrant shorebirds, waterfowl of all types, warblers, raptors, flycatchers, thrushes, vireos and sparrows. Hawk Ridge Nature Reserve is world famous for raptor watching. Fall is the best time to see large numbers of hawks, especially in September. However, it is now becoming a place to watch raptors during their spring migration. Minnesota Point and the adjacent harbor and lake area are excellent places to view shorebirds and waterfowl. In winter, the harbor area normally features Snowy Owls and the rare Gyrfalcon, plus other raptors. Interstate Island in the harbor hosts the largest Common Tern colony in the state. Over 350 species of birds have been recorded in the Duluth area, an incredible total for the Midwest. This list includes many rarities and vagrants not usually seen anywhere else in the state, including three jaeger species, the Red-throated Loon, Common Ground-Dove, Mew Gull, Band-tailed Pigeon, Black Vulture and Gray-crowned Rosy Finch.

Grand Marais–Cook County

Cook County is one of the best birding counties in Minnesota, as well as being one of the most scenic. There are numerous birding localities along the North Shore of Lake Superior, and especially in the city of Grand Marais. From October to May, Good Harbor Bay, just to the east of Grand Marais, is the most reliable place to see Long-tailed Ducks. Scoters, loons and Whimbrels are also often seen in the bay. The Grand Marais harbor and city streets are the places to watch for vagrant birds, especially during spring and fall migration. The list of vagrants is incredible and includes the King Eider, Barrow's Goldeneye, Sage Thrasher, Rock Ptarmigan, McCown's Longspur, Painted Bunting, Black-headed Grosbeak, Anna's Hummingbird, a number of gull species and Minnesota's most unusual bird, the Fieldfare. Grand Marais in the fall is the place to see Bohemian Waxwings, Common Redpolls, Hoary Redpolls and Townsend's Solitaire. Up the shore, Five Mile Rock and Paradise Beach are good places for waterfowl such as loons and scoters. There are four magnificent state parks near Grand Marais: Grand Portage, Judge C. R. Magney, Cascade River and Temperance River—all excellent places for bird observation.

Sherburne National Wildlife Refuge

Sherburne National Wildlife Refuge is located within easy driving distance of the Twin Cities metropolitan area. The refuge offers good birding opportunities in spring, summer and fall on the Prairie's Edge Wildlife Drive and the Mahnomen and Blue Hill hiking trails. There are a variety of habitats to enjoy, including woodlands, oak savanna, grasslands and wetlands. Along the Wildlife Drive you will see most of these habitats and their associated birds. In the many wetlands, migrating waterfowl are plentiful in the spring and fall, shorebirds frequent the pool edges, and resident wetland birds such as rails and bitterns remain through the seasons. Wetland pools harbor numerous nesting waterfowl and marsh birds, including nesting Black Terns,

Sora and Virginia Rails. Several pairs of Bald Eagles also nest on the refuge. Migrating songbirds and resident woodland edge species can be observed in the scattered patches of trees along the Drive and on its Woodland Trail. In addition, fields of native prairie grasses and wildflowers provide habitat and viewing opportunities for grassland birds. The habitats along the Mahnomen and Blue Hill trails are predominantly upland, but also provide some opportunity for viewing wetland species. Upland birds seen on these trails range from grassland birds such as the Eastern Meadowlark, Grasshopper Sparrow and Savannah Sparrow, to the deeper forest birds such as the Ovenbird, American Redstart, Golden-winged Warbler, Blue-winged Warbler and Yellow-throated Vireo. Sherburne is noted for its nesting flock of Sandhill Cranes, which is increasing on an annual basis.

Frontenac State Park

Located on the bluffs overlooking the Mississippi River, Frontenac State Park and the surrounding area is an outstanding birding location. Over 260 species have been recorded and there are more than 100 potential breeding species in the park. The bottomland hardwood forests along the river provide excellent habitat and food sources for migrating warblers, thrushes, vireos, flycatchers, sparrows and other species. These same forests provide nesting habitat for Prothonotary Warblers, Blue-gray Gnatcatchers, Yellow-throated Vireos, Wood Thrushes, American Redstarts and many species of woodpeckers and flycatchers. The beaches at Sand Point and Lake Pepin are excellent places to observe shorebirds, gulls, terns and numerous waterfowl. The bluffs overlooking the river provide good viewing areas for the observation of migrating hawks, eagles, vultures and waterfowl. In November, a spectacular migration of Common Mergansers passes through Lake Pepin. Prairie areas located within the park provide opportunities to observe the rare Henslow's Sparrow, plus Savannah, Clay-colored, Grasshopper and Field sparrows. In addition, Bobolinks, Sedge Wrens and Eastern Meadowlarks are common in the grasslands. The wooded and brushy edges are habitat for Orchard Orioles and Bell's Vireos. The upland forests provide opportunities to observe Cardinals, Eastern Towhees and Yellow-bellied Sapsuckers.

Itasca State Park

Itasca State Park, home to the headwaters of the Mississippi River, also provides habitat for over 225 species of birds and potentially 140 or more breeding species. The extensive stands of virgin, boreal-type forests and mixed woodlands provide excellent habitat for many northern species such as crossbills, Gray Jays, finches, thrushes and Black-backed Woodpeckers. Twenty-seven species of warblers have been recorded in the park during migration periods, the majority of these remaining to nest. Many rarities have been documented in Itasca, a few examples being the Magnificent Frigatebird, Magnificent Hummingbird, Williamson's Sapsucker, Parasitic Jaeger, Lark Bunting and Prothonotary Warbler. Common Loons nest regularly at lakes in the park, as do Bald Eagles and Ospreys. Itasca State Park is also the location of the University of Minnesota's Biological Field Station, where ornithology students at the university study the bird life of this region.

Big Stone National Wildlife Refuge

Located on the upper reaches of the Minnesota River, Big Stone National Wildlife Refuge contains 10,795 acres of very diverse birding habitat, from the wet world of river and reservoir areas to the dry world of granite outcrops. As a result, the region offers excellent birding opportunities throughout the year. A recent program at the refuge concerns the maintenance of shorebird habitat on a permanent basis at one of the reservoirs, making it one of the only places in the state where a birder can reliably view shorebirds. As well, a program to reintroduce the Greater Prairie-Chicken on the refuge has been successful. The dam on the Minnesota River has created an additional 4250 acres of wetlands that provide a stopping-off place for migrating waterfowl and a summer home for species such as the Great Egret, Great Blue Heron, Double-crested Cormorant and many species of ducks. American White Pelicans are common in the summer and Western Grebes can also be seen. Low-lying woodlands support migrating warblers and other songbirds. Flooded woodlands support cavity-nesting species such as woodpeckers, Wood Ducks and Hooded Mergansers. Seventeen species of ducks have been recorded on the refuge as well as many Canada, Snow and White-fronted geese. The refuge also contains over 1700 acres of native prairie, where Bobolinks, Clay-colored Sparrows and Sedge Wrens are common.

Blue Mounds State Park

Geographically located in the southwestern corner of the state in Rock County, Blue Mounds State Park is in a region known as the Coteau des Prairies, meaning highland or upland prairie. Over 230 species of birds have been recorded in this 1800-acre park, including a potential 81 breeding species. Many migrants stop in the park to feed and rest, and 29 species of warblers and vireos, 10 species of flycatchers and 17 species of sparrows have been documented. It is the only reliable place in the state to record the Blue Grosbeak and the only area in the state where the Brewer's Sparrow has been seen. Other interesting species in the park include the Swainson's Hawk, Mountain Bluebird, Say's Phoebe, Orchard Oriole, Black-headed Grosbeak and Lark Bunting. The Northern Mockingbird has nested in the park, one of only two or three localities that this species has nested in the state. There are two small lakes in the park, created by dams across Mound Creek, that attract waterbirds. The park's extensive, unplowed grasslands, which support a bison herd, are attractive to many grassland birds. The vista from the high prairie of endless skies and horizons is a beautiful sight, with Western Meadowlarks, Grasshopper Sparrows, Bobolinks and Upland Sandpipers adding their voices to the landscape.

McGregor Marsh–Aitkin County

McGregor Marsh is famous all over the United States in birding circles because of the presence of Yellow Rails. The rhythmic, ticking calls of the rails can be heard in many areas of the marsh, usually at night. June is the best month of the year to see and hear these birds. The marsh area is also known for Nelson's Sharp-tailed Sparrows and Le Conte's Sparrows.

Just to the north of McGregor Marsh are several very good birding areas. Rice Lake National Wildlife Refuge is known for the presence of Sharp-tailed Grouse and concentrations of waterfowl in the fall. The refuge is a good place for Black-billed Cuckoos, Alder Flycatchers, Sedge Wrens, Golden-winged Warblers, Clay-colored Sparrows and Le Conte's Sparrows. In the heavier woods of the refuge there are Ruffed Grouse, Barred Owls, Pileated and other woodpeckers, as well as many songbird species.

A little farther along Aitkin County Roads 5 and 18, the birding gets even better. Just off County Road 18 is Pietz's Road, which has been the most reliable place in the state to find Great Gray Owls at any time of the year. In winter, County Road 18 is a good area for Northern Shrikes, Pine Grosbeaks, Northern Hawk Owls, White-winged Crossbills, Rough-legged Hawks and Northern Goshawks. Yellow-bellied Flycatchers, Connecticut Warblers, Le Conte's Sparrows and Sedge Wrens are found here during the breeding season.

To the south of McGregor Marsh is Mille Lacs Lake, a concentration point for Common Loons and Bonaparte's Gulls in October and November. The list of rarities and vagrants for the lake is a very long one.

Agassiz National Wildlife Refuge

Containing 61,500 acres, Agassiz National Wildlife Refuge is a unit in a chain of National Wildlife Refuges in the Mississippi Flyway extending from Canada to Mexico. Marshall County Highway 7 passes through the southern portion of the refuge, providing an excellent cross-section of the local habitat types. The terrain is flat and open water and freshwater marshes occupy 40,000 acres of the refuge. Shallow-water marshes and emergent plants attract breeding waterfowl and many other waterbirds and provide optimum habitat conditions for nesting. Over 280 species of birds have been recorded on the refuge, including 27 species of swans, geese and ducks, and 29 species of shorebirds, many of which are present especially when water levels are controlled. Warblers and vireos are well represented with over 30 species recorded. Yellow Rails and Nelson's Sharp-tailed Sparrows are seen each year. Western, Eared and Red-necked grebes nest on the refuge and the Clark's Grebe has been recorded here. Agassiz National Wildlife Refuge is probably most famous for its breeding colony of Franklin's Gulls. In some years, as many as 50,000 birds are present in the breeding colony, and it is an incredible sight to see tens of thousands of these birds flying about the colony on a warm evening in June.

Sax-Zim Bog

Bird Watcher's Digest, in its September–October 2002 issue, listed the Sax-Zim Bog as one of the "25 Must-See Birding Hotspots in North America." Named for its proximity to two small towns in St. Louis County, the Sax-Zim Bog covers over 200 square miles and includes a number of different habitats. A nice variety of breeding and wintering bird species are found in the area and year-round specialties include the Ruffed Grouse, Sharp-tailed Grouse, Great Gray Owl, Black-backed Woodpecker, Gray Jay, Black-billed Magpie, Boreal Chickadee and Evening Grosbeak. In late May and early June, look and listen for nesting species. Winter possibilities include the Northern Goshawk, Snowy Owl, Northern Hawk Owl, Northern Shrike, Snow Bunting, Pine Grosbeak, White-winged Crossbill, Common Redpoll and Hoary Redpoll.

Wisconsin's Top 10 Birding Sites

Wisconsin Point–Superior

Wisconsin Point is a two-mile-long peninsula that juts into Lake Superior and is considered one of the state's premier birding sites. During migration, bad weather can ground hundreds, even thousands, of migrant birds, often including rare species. Thus foggy conditions and cold fronts can make for exciting birding. Loons, ducks, grebes, gulls, terns and shorebirds use the lake and Allouez Bay while hawks, flycatchers, vireos, warblers, sparrows and finches are found in the wooded and grassy sections. Rarities include all three species of jaegers and scoters, Smew, Harlequin Ducks, Arctic Terns, Sabine's Gulls, Black-legged Kittiwakes, Pacific Loons, Buff-breasted Sandpipers, Piping Plovers and Gyrfalcons.

Crex Meadows Wildlife Area

Located just north of Grantsburg in western Burnett County, the Crex Meadows Wildlife Area comprises over 30,000 acres and is known not only for its nesting species and rarities, but also for its accessibility. Two county highways and over 40 miles of town roads allow birders access to many of the dikes and flowages. Habitat includes wetlands and brush-prairie that is constantly being expanded. The refuge headquarters, where birders can secure maps and inquire about recent bird sightings, are located just east of the junction of County Highways D and F. Highly recommended stops include Phantom Lake Flowage for Trumpeter Swans, Ospreys, Common Loons, Soras, Virginia Rails, Red-necked Grebes and Black Terns; the refuge, located in the center of the area, for views of Sharp-tailed Grouse and Bald Eagles; and the pumphouse section of Reed's Lake sedge marsh from mid-May to early July for Yellow Rails, Le Conte's Sparrows, Nelson's Sharp-tailed Sparrows, American Bitterns and Sandhill Cranes. Nearby Fish Lake Wildlife Area, located three miles south of Grantsburg, has similar habitats, birds and accessibility.

Nicolet National Forest–Hiles–Three Lakes

Nicolet National Forest dominates this northern area and is characterized by coniferous, deciduous and mixed forests. In addition, there are numerous lakes, swamps, bogs and marshes that dot the landscape. Some of these wet areas are thickly overgrown with black spruce, cedar, tamarack, alder and willow. During summer, over 22 warbler species are present. Other interesting resident birds include the Black-backed Woodpecker, Spruce Grouse, Boreal Chickadee, Gray Jay and varying numbers of finches. "Must-stops" in this extensive area include Thunder Lake Marsh, Three Lakes (Old A) Bog, Pine, Shelp and Scott lakes and various forestry roads (2174, 2178, 2182, 2183, 2414) that bisect the forest to the north of Hiles and east of Three Lakes. Any season can produce memorable birding, but care must be taken when driving the forestry roads in winter—it is a long hike for help!

Green Bay Area

Situated at the end of its namesake, the city of Green Bay is probably best known for its football team. However, birders also recognize the area for quality birding, particularly during migration, when its location at the end of the bay makes it a "migrant trap." The diversity of habitat—open water, marshes, swamps, woods and fields—ensures an excellent variety of birds. Depending upon the season, expect to see Snowy Owls, Lapland Longspurs, Snow Buntings, Gray Partridge, Peregrine Falcons, American White Pelicans, egrets, various shorebirds, gulls, terns and songbirds. Unusual sightings can include species such as the Curlew Sandpiper, Black-legged Kittiwake, Little Gull and Gyrfalcon. Recommended stops include the Bay Beach Wildlife Sanctuary, the mouth of the Fox River, Atkinson Marsh, L. H. Barkhausen Waterfowl Preserve and the Sensiba Wildlife Area.

Horicon Marsh

Horicon Marsh is the largest cattail wetland in the country. Encompassing 32,000 acres, the southern third of Horicon Marsh is managed by the state, while the remainder is a national wildlife refuge. While the marsh is most famous for its fall concentration of Canada Geese, numbering over 200,000 birds, it is also famous for its diversity of migrant and nesting bird species. Breeding species include bitterns, herons, waterfowl, rails, pelicans, cormorants, terns and various songbirds. When water levels are controlled for shorebirds, the number and variety can be impressive. Rarities include the White-faced Ibis, Curlew Sandpiper, Blue Grosbeak, Tricolored Heron, Little Blue Heron, Black-necked Stilt, Ruff, Buff-breasted Sandpiper and Pomarine Jaeger. Accessibility is limited and highly controlled in the wildlife refuge and some areas are closed or designated for restricted use only. Birding sites include points along Highway 49, which bisects the northern part of the marsh (care must be taken because there is fast-moving traffic on the highway), the Auto Tour Route and hiking trails, Old Marsh Road (currently open only on weekends for hiking and biking), Ledge Road, the main dike, the DNR Field Office and trails, and nearby Ledge Park.

Wyalusing State Park

Wyalusing State Park overlooks the confluence of the Mississippi and Wisconsin Rivers. Encompassing nearly 2700 acres, it includes hardwood forests, pine plantations and wetlands. An outstanding site, this area is a gem for birders, particularly from late April to late October. Nesting species include Kentucky, Cerulean, Hooded, Prothonotary, Yellow-throated and Worm-eating warblers, Louisiana Waterthrushes, Acadian Flycatchers, Red-shouldered Hawks, Blue-gray Gnatcatchers, Pileated Woodpeckers and Bell's Vireos. The songbird migration can be outstanding, especially during May, with lesser numbers in September, and the hawk migration is often quite good during September and October. Visitors can stop at the park office to secure a map and bird the immediate area. All roads and trails are potentially good for birding, but the Homestead and Wisconsin Ridge campgrounds and Long Valley Road to the boat landing should be checked out. Drive the latter slowly or, better, walk its length to truly enjoy the May chorus of migrants or the summer serenade of nesting species.

Devil's Lake State Park and Baxter's Hollow

Nestled in the Baraboo Range, Devil's Lake State Park and adjacent gorge give birders a blend of the southern and northern nesters. The park is mainly oak forest with a red maple understory, but because of the bluffs that abut Devil's Lake there is also sugar maple forest interspersed with birch, pine and cedar groves, areas of dry prairie on the bluff tops, plus marshes and abandoned farmlands. Summer residents include the Broad-winged Hawk, Turkey Vulture, Wood Thrush, Yellow-throated Vireo, Winter Wren and Scarlet Tanager. Migrations can produce excellent songbird waves. During almost every winter it is possible to find Townsend's Solitaires residing along the eastern bluff.

Baxter's Hollow is a wooded, rocky gorge that follows Otter Creek, with a deciduous forest on its northern edge that is an important nesting area for many forest-dwelling birds. A narrow paved road provides access to most of the area, although it is best to walk the entire length. The road is not maintained during the winter.

Summer residents include the Acadian Flycatcher, Louisiana Waterthrush, Pileated Woodpecker, Yellow-throated Warbler, Worm-eating Warbler and Winter Wren. The gorge is best birded between May and September.

Madison Area

Besides being the state capital, Madison beckons to birders with its diverse habitat. Birding is excellent at the University of Wisconsin Arboretum that borders Lake Mendota—in particular Picnic Point, which extends out into the lake—plus University Bay and Marshall Park, Lake Monona, the Yahara River flowing into Lower Mud Lake, Nine Springs sewage ponds and Cherokee Marsh. Migration is the optimum time for viewing waterfowl and songbirds, especially during spring. Exciting sightings include Pacific Loons, Western Grebes, Ross's Geese, Buff-breasted Sandpipers, Scissor-tailed Flycatchers, Fork-tailed Flycatchers, Northern Mockingbirds, Carolina Wrens, White-eyed Vireos, Worm-eating Warblers, Prairie Warblers, Yellow-breasted Chats and Spotted Towhees.

Eastern Ozaukee County

Eastern Ozaukee County, bordering Lake Michigan, has excellent areas for watching migrants and wintering birds. Songbirds can be found in the wooded areas, while waterfowl, gulls and terns use the lake. During fall, the hawk flight can be impressive along the bluffs that border the lake. Important birding sites include Virmond Park for waterfowl and songbirds, Concordia University for hawks and waterfowl, Port Washington Harbor for waterfowl and gulls and Harrington Beach State Park for waterfowl, shorebirds, gulls, terns and songbirds. Depending upon the season, sightings may include the Red-throated Loon, Pacific Loon, various grebes including the Western Grebe, scoters, King Eider, Barrow's Goldeneye, Harlequin Duck, Purple Sandpiper, Parasitic Jaeger and various gulls, including some rarities. It is also possible to see the Black-legged Kittiwake, Yellow-throated Warbler, Prairie Warbler, Orchard Oriole and Northern Mockingbird.

Milwaukee Area

The state's largest metropolitan area lays claim to quality birding within its boundaries despite a sea of people and vehicles. Most of the best birding sites are concentrated along or near Lake Michigan. During migration, waterfowl, shorebirds, gulls, terns and songbirds often rest here during their treks. In winter the lake harbor and break walls hold varying numbers of waterfowl and gulls. The 225-acre Schlitz Audubon Nature Center and adjacent Doctor's Park offer excellent birding opportunities. Also worth a visit are various parks such as Lake and South Shore, as well as Bradford Beach, North Point, McKinley Marina, and Milwaukee Harbor and Coast Guard Impoundment. Besides the normal spring and fall migrants and winter birds, interesting sightings include all scoter species, various rare gull species, the Western Grebe, Harlequin Duck, King Eider, Red Phalarope, White-eyed Vireo, Summer Tanager, Mountain Bluebird, Worm-eating Warbler, Piping Plover, Black Rail, Yellow Rail, Nelson's Sharp-tailed Sparrow and Le Conte's Sparrow.

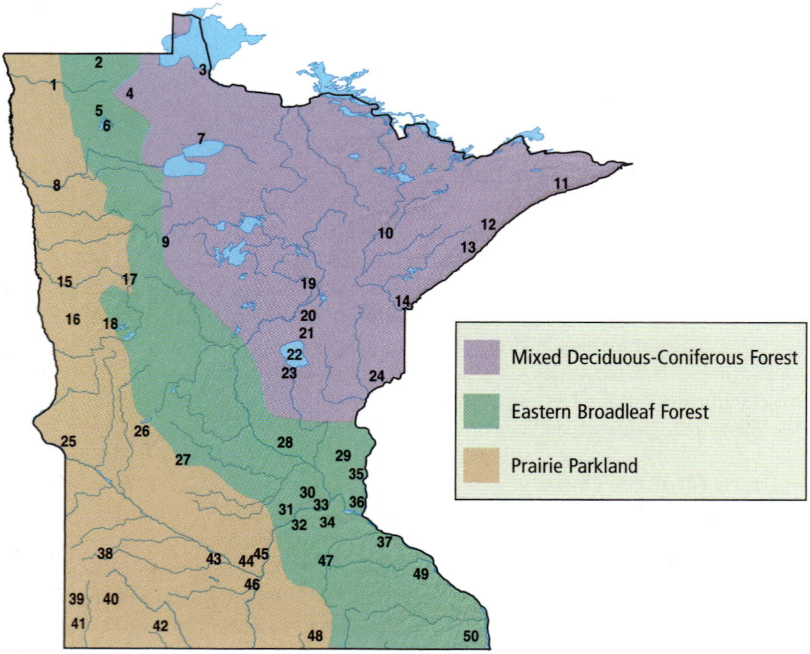

MINNESOTA'S TOP 50 BIRDING SITES

1. Lake Bronson SP
2. Roseau Bog
3. Pine and Curry Island
4. Hayes Lake SP
5. Thief Lake WMA
6. Agassiz NWR
7. Big Bog State Recreation Area
8. Crookston sewage ponds
9. Itasca SP
10. Sax-Zim Bog
11. Grand Marais
12. Tettegouche SP
13. Gooseberry Falls SP
14. Duluth
15. Felton Prairie–Buffalo River SP
16. Rothsay Prairie
17. Tamarac NWR
18. Maplewood SP
19. County Road 18 (Aitkin Co.)
20. Rice Lake NWR
21. McGregor Marsh
22. Mille Lacs Lake
23. Mille Lacs Kathio SP
24. St. Croix SP
25. Big Stone NWR
26. Glacial Lakes SP
27. Sibley SP
28. Sherburne NWR
29. Carlos Avery WMA
30. Wood Lake Nature Reserve
31. Carver Park Reserve
32. Minnesota River Valley State Recreation Area
33. Minnesota Valley NWR
34. Murphy-Hanrehan Park Reserve
35. William O'Brien SP
36. Afton SP
37. Frontenac SP
38. Camden SP–Black Rush Lake
39. Pipestone NM
40. Lake Shetek SP
41. Blue Mounds SP
42. Heron Lake (Jackson Co.)
43. Flandrau SP
44. Swan Lake (Nicollet Co.)
45. Seven Mile Creek
46. Minneopa SP
47. Nerstrand–Big Woods SP
48. Myre–Big Island SP
49. Whitewater SP
50. Beaver Creek Valley SP

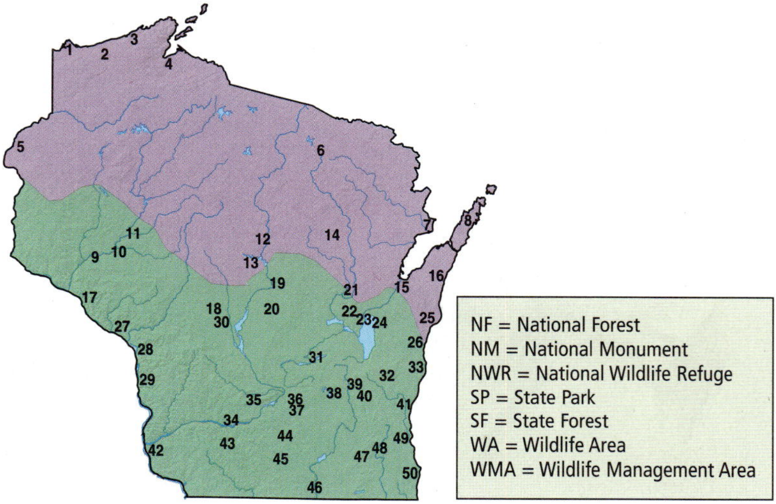

WISCONSIN'S TOP 50 BIRDING SITES

1. Wisconsin Point–Superior
2. Brule River
3. Port Wing–Herbster–Cornucopia
4. Ashland–Fish Creek
5. Crex Meadows WA and Fish Lake WA
6. Nicolet NF–Hiles–Three Lakes
7. Seagull Bar–Red Arrow Park
8. Northern Door County
9. Meridean area
10. Eau Claire area
11. Lake Wissota SP
12. Wausau area
13. Mead Wildlife Area
14. Stockbridge-Munsee and Menominee Reservations
15. Green Bay area
16. Eastern Kewaunee County
17. Western Buffalo County
18. Bear Bluff area
19. Stevens Point area
20. Buena Vista Grasslands
21. Shiocton–Black Creek–New London
22. Rat River WA
23. Fox Cities area
24. High Cliff SP
25. Manitowoc–Two Rivers
26. Cleveland–Fischer Creek County Park
27. Trempealeau NWR
28. LaCrosse area
29. Upper Mississippi NWR
30. Necedah NWR
31. Green Lake County
32. Kettle Moraine SF–North Unit
33. Sheboygan area
34. Spring Green Reserve
35. Devil's Lake SP–Baxter's Hollow
36. Mud Lake WA and Grassy Lake WA
37. Arlington ponds
38. Beaver Dam ponds
39. Horicon Marsh
40. Theresa Marsh
41. Eastern Ozaukee County
42. Wyalusing SP
43. Governor Dodge SP
44. Madison area
45. Brooklyn WA
46. Sugar River–Beloit–Janesville
47. Kettle Moraine SF–South Unit
48. Vernon Marsh
49. Milwaukee area
50. Racine area

ABOUT THE SPECIES ACCOUNTS

Eastern Bluebird

This book gives detailed accounts of the 322 species of birds that are listed as regular by either or both the *Minnesota Ornithologists' Union* and the *Wisconsin Society for Ornithology;* these species can be expected on a fairly regular basis. Thirty-four occasional species are briefly mentioned in an appendix (pp. 357–60). These species can be expected to be seen in small numbers every year or every few years because of anticipated range expansion, migration or well-documented wandering tendencies. The order of the birds and their common and scientific names follow the American Ornithologists' Union's *Check-list of North American Birds* (7th edition, July 1998, and *The Forty-third Supplement, 2002*).

ID: It is difficult to describe the features of a bird without being able to visualize it, so this section is best used in combination with the illustrations. Where appropriate, the description is subdivided to highlight the differences between male and female birds, breeding and nonbreeding plumages and immature and adult birds. The descriptions use as few technical terms as possible, and favor easily understood language. Birds may not have "eyebrows" or "chins," but these and other terms are easily understood by all readers, in spite of their scientific inaccuracy. Some of the most common features of birds are pointed out in the Glossary illustration (p. 363).

Size: The average length of the bird's body from bill to tail, as well as wingspan, are approximate measurements of the bird as it is seen in nature. The size is sometimes given as a range, because there is variation between individuals, or between males and females. Please note that birds with long tails often have large measurements that do not necessarily reflect "body" size.

Red-breasted Nuthatch

Status: A general comment, such as "common," "uncommon" or "rare," is usually sufficient to describe the relative abundance of a species. Situations are bound to vary somewhat since migratory pulses, seasonal changes and centers of activity tend to concentrate or disperse birds.

Habitat: The habitats we have listed describe where each species is most commonly found. In most cases, it is a generalized description, but if a bird is restricted to a specific habitat, the habitat is described precisely. Because of the freedom flight gives them, birds can turn up in almost any type of habitat. However, they will usually be found in environments that provide the specific food, water, cover and, in some cases, nesting habitat that they need to survive.

Cliff Swallow

Nesting: In each species account, nest location and structure, clutch size, incubation period and parental duties are discussed. Remember that birding ethics discourage the disturbance of active bird nests. The nesting behavior of birds that do not nest in our region is not described.

Feeding: Birds spend a great deal of time foraging for food. If you know what a bird eats and where the food is found, you will have a good chance of finding that bird. Birds are frequently encountered while they are foraging.

Voice: You will hear many birds, particularly songbirds, which may remain hidden from view. Memorable paraphrases of distinctive sounds will aid you in identifying a species by ear. Please note that these paraphrases only loosely resemble the call, song or sound produced by the bird.

Similar Species: Easily confused species are discussed briefly. If you concentrate on the most relevant field marks, the subtle differences between species can be reduced to easily identifiable traits. You might find it useful to consult this section when finalizing your identification; knowing the most relevant field marks will speed up the identification process. Even experienced birders can mistake one species for another.

Best Sites: If you are looking for a particular bird, you will have more luck in some places than in others, even within the range shown on the range map. We have listed places that, besides providing a good chance of seeing a species, are easily accessible. As a result, many conservation sites, national wildlife refuges and state parks are mentioned.

Range Maps: The range map for each species represents the overall range of the species in an average year. Most birds will confine their annual movements to this range, although each year some birds wander beyond their traditional boundaries. These small maps do not show differences in abundance within the range. These maps also cannot show small pockets within the range where the species

Cedar Waxwing

may actually be absent, or how the range may change from year to year. Every effort has been made to ensure that the maps are as accurate as possible, and occasional discrepancies at the Minnesota-Wisconsin border result from differences in the availability and interpretation of data.

Unlike most other field guides, we have attempted to show migratory pathways. The representations of the pathways do not distinguish high-use migration corridors from areas that are seldom used. Although most migratory birds will travel over the Great Lakes, usually at high altitude, their migration patterns over these large expanses of water are not well known. Some species spend much of their time on the water in winter or during migration, and this is shown on the maps by having the colored area extend out onto the water and gradually fading out. Bird activity far out on the Great Lakes is not well documented. Birding in our region is generally done from land, and the maps reflect this.

Red-winged Blackbird

Range Map Symbols

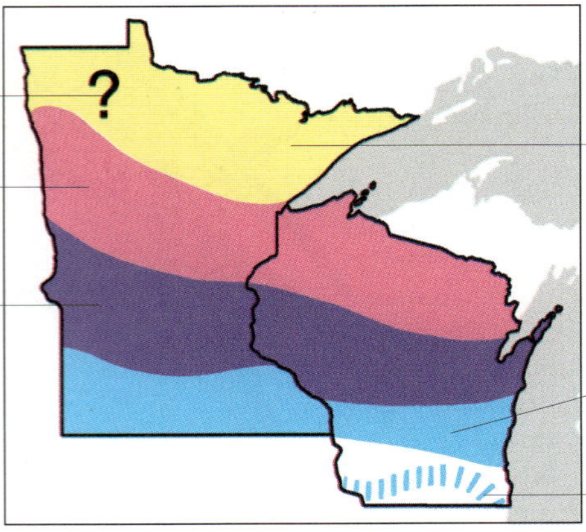

NONPASSERINES

Northern Hawk Owl

Nonpasserine birds represent 17 of the 18 orders of birds that are found in Minnesota and Wisconsin, but only about 55% of the total bird species in our region. They are grouped together and called "nonpasserines" because, with few exceptions, they are easily distinguished from the "passerines," or "perching birds," which make up the 18th order. Being from 17 different orders, however, means that nonpasserines vary considerably in their appearance and habits—they include everything from the 5-foot-tall Great Blue Heron to the 3-inch-long Calliope Hummingbird.

Generally speaking, nonpasserines do not "sing." Instead, their vocalizations are referred to as "calls." There are also other morphological differences. For example, the muscles and tendons in the legs of passerines are adapted to grip a perch, and the toes of passerines are never webbed. Many nonpasserines are large, so they are among our most notable birds. Waterfowl, raptors, gulls, shorebirds and woodpeckers are easily identified by most people. Some of the smaller nonpasserines, such as doves, swifts and hummingbirds, are frequently thought of as passerines by novice birders, and can cause those beginners some identification problems. With a little practice, however, they will become recognizable as nonpasserines. By learning to separate the nonpasserines from the passerines at a glance, birders effectively reduce by half the number of possible species for an unidentified bird.

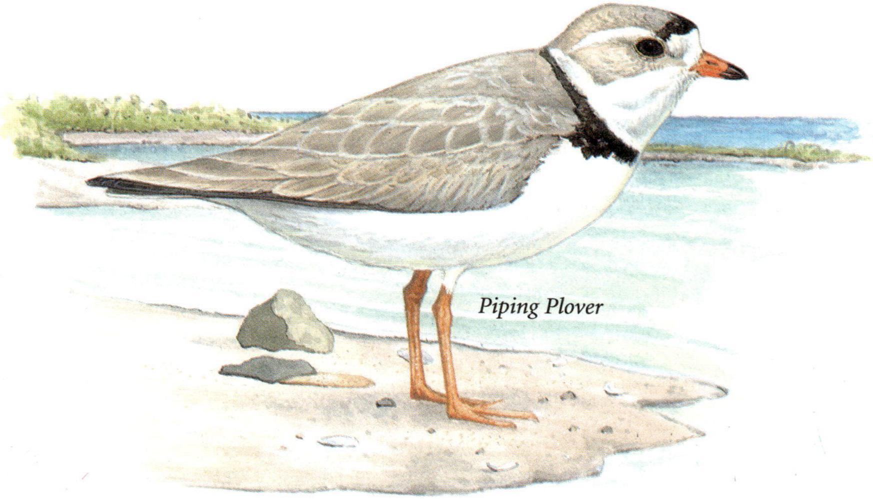

Piping Plover

RED-THROATED LOON

Gavia stellata

The Red-throated Loon is an easy bird to identify because it typically swims low in the water with its bill held high. Our smallest loon, the Red-throat is able to leap up from the water directly into flight, stand upright on land and even take off from land. No other loon has these abilities—other loons require 300 feet or more of runway on open water in order to gain flight. As a result, Red-throated Loons can nest on smaller bodies of water than their larger, less agile relatives. • The Red-throated Loon is an unparalleled diver and obtains most of its food underwater. It can dive to depths of 70 feet, though most dives are shallower, and can vary its buoyancy, making it easier to stay below the surface. While underwater, the bird's heart rate drops to conserve oxygen. • Native peoples have long considered Red-throated Loons as meteorologists—these birds often become very noisy before the onset of foul weather, possibly sensing changes in barometric pressure. • The scientific name *stellata* refers to the starlike, white speckles on this bird's back in its nonbreeding plumage.

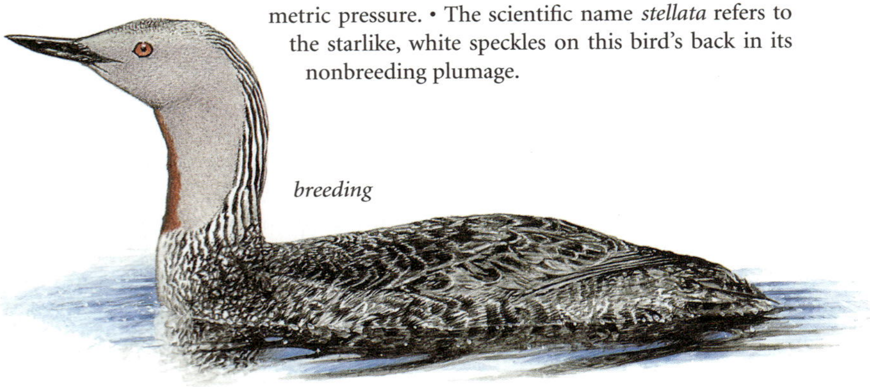

breeding

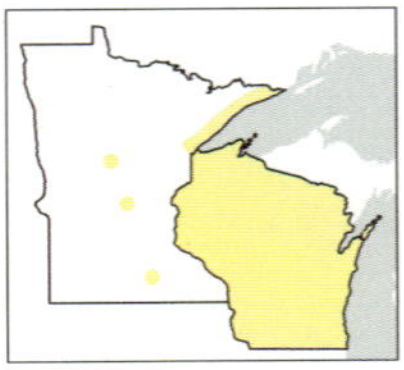

ID: slim bill is held upward. *Breeding:* red throat; gray face and neck; black and white stripes from nape to back of head; plain, brownish back. *Nonbreeding:* white-speckled back; white face; dark gray on crown and back of head. *In flight:* hunched back; legs trail behind tail; rapid wingbeats.

Size: *L* 23–27 in; *W* 3½ ft.

Status: ***MN:*** rare and local, usually on L. Superior in late May and into June and occasionally in October; very few records elsewhere in the state. ***WI:*** uncommon migrant from March to May and from September to December, especially on L. Michigan and L. Superior; limited inland sightings.

Habitat: large freshwater lakes.

Nesting: does not nest in our region.

Feeding: dives deeply to capture small fish; sometimes eats aquatic insects and amphibians; occasionally eats aquatic vegetation in early spring.

Voice: Mallard-like *kwuk-kwuk-kwuk-kwuk* in flight; distraction call is a loud *gayor-work*.

Similar Species: *Common Loon* (p. 36): larger; heavier bill; lacks white speckling on back in nonbreeding plumage. *Pacific Loon* (p. 35): larger; purple throat and white speckling on back in breeding plumage; all-dark back in nonbreeding plumage.

Best Sites: ***MN:*** L. Superior; Duluth. ***WI:*** Virmond Park, Harrington Beach SP and Cleveland area (L. Michigan); Wisconsin Pt. (L. Superior).

PACIFIC LOON

Gavia pacifica

With extreme luck you may discover a Pacific Loon on one of the Great Lakes or on a large inland lake. Though sightings have increased in recent years, this bird is a very rare migrant through the region. Usually only seen as individual birds, Pacific Loons pause here for only a short period of time in their trek between nesting grounds in northern Canada and Alaska and wintering grounds to the south. • The Pacific Loon is not afraid of getting its head wet, and will swim along with only its head underwater before choosing to dive beneath the surface in pursuit of fish or invertebrates. • Loons have weak legs that are placed far back on the body. They are clumsy and awkward on land, but powerful and agile in water. Unlike other waterbirds, loons rely solely on their feet for propulsion when diving, using their wings only for balance and turning. Loons find their prey using sight, and their eyes are adapted to allow the bird to see well both in air and underwater.

nonbreeding

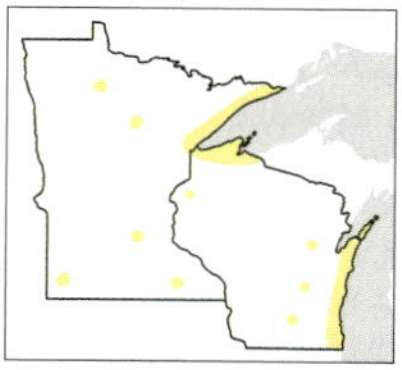

ID: *Breeding:* silver gray crown and nape; dark throat is framed by white stripes; white breast; dark back with large, bold, white spots. *Nonbreeding:* pale, well-defined "cheek" and throat; dark upperparts; dark "chin" stripe. *In flight:* hunched back; legs trail behind tail; rapid wingbeats.

Size: *L* 23–$28\frac{1}{2}$ in; *W* $3\frac{1}{2}$–4 ft.

Status: ***MN:*** rare migrant, mainly on L. Superior; found on larger lakes in October and occasionally in spring. ***WI:*** very rare migrant from March to early May and from September to December.

Habitat: large freshwater lakes.

Nesting: does not nest in our region.

Feeding: dives deeply for fish and occasionally aquatic invertebrates; average dive is 45 seconds; may eat aquatic vegetation.

Voice: calls include a doglike yelp, a catlike meow and a ravenlike croak.

Similar Species: breeding plumage is distinctive. *Common Loon* (p. 36): larger; lacks sharp definition between black and white on face and neck; often has pale "collar" in nonbreeding plumage. *Red-throated Loon* (p. 34): tilts its bill upward; extensive white spotting on back in nonbreeding plumage.

Best Sites: ***MN:*** L. Superior; Duluth. ***WI:*** Virmond Park, Concordia University and Harrington Beach SP (L. Michigan); Wisconsin Pt. (L. Superior); inland lakes, including L. Mendota, Green L. and Shawano L.

COMMON LOON

Gavia immer

Most summer cottagers and wilderness explorers recognize and delight in this loon's haunting songs and elegant, black-and-white breeding plumage. Loons float very low on the water, disappearing behind swells, then reappearing like ethereal guardians of the lakes. • The Common Loon is well adapted to its aquatic lifestyle: its nearly solid bones make it less buoyant (most birds have hollow bones), and its feet are placed well back on its body for underwater propulsion. Small bass, perch, sunfish, pike and whitefish are all fair game for this excellent underwater hunter. On land, the rear-placed legs make walking seem difficult, and this bird's heavy body and small wing size means that it requires a lengthy sprint over water before taking off. • It is thought that the name "loon" is derived from the Scandinavian word *lom*, meaning "clumsy person," in reference to this bird's awkwardness on land.

breeding

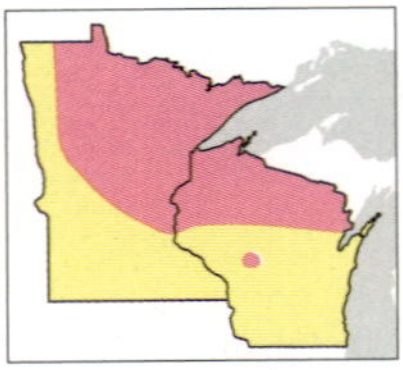

ID: *Breeding:* green black head; stout, thick, black bill; white "necklace"; white breast and underparts; black-and-white "checkerboard" upperparts; red eyes. *Nonbreeding:* much duller plumage; sandy brown back; light underparts. *In flight:* long wings beat constantly; hunchbacked appearance; legs trail behind tail.

Size: *L* 28–35 in; *W* 4–5 ft.

Status: ***MN:*** common migrant and breeder from late March to early November. ***WI:*** common migrant and breeder from late March to November.

Habitat: *Breeding:* large rivers and lakes, often with islands that provide undisturbed shorelines for nesting. *Winter:* lakes with open water.

Nesting: on a muskrat lodge, small island or projecting shoreline; always very near water; nest mound is built from aquatic vegetation; pair incubates 1–3 dark-spotted, olive eggs for 24–31 days; pair shares all parental duties, including nest building, egg incubation and rearing of the young.

Feeding: pursues small fish underwater to depths of 180 ft; occasionally eats large, aquatic invertebrates and larval and adult amphibians.

Voice: alarm call is a quavering tremolo, often called "loon laughter"; contact call is a long but simple wailing note: *where aaare you?;* breeding notes are soft, short hoots; male territorial call is an undulating, complex yodel.

Similar Species: *Red-throated Loon* (p. 34): smaller; slender bill; red throat in breeding plumage; sharply defined white face and white-spotted back in nonbreeding plumage. *Pacific Loon* (p. 35): smaller; dusty gray head often looks silver; dark "cap" extends down over eye and is lighter than back in nonbreeding plumage.

Best Sites: ***MN:*** Mille Lacs L. (over 2500 are sometimes seen in October); Boundary Waters Canoe Area Wilderness; Leech L.; Lake of the Woods; L. Superior; L. Winnibigoshish. ***WI:*** *Breeding:* lakes in the northern counties plus a few in central regions. *In migration:* large inland lakes, L. Michigan and L. Superior.

PIED-BILLED GREBE

Podilymbus podiceps

The secretive Pied-billed Grebe is the most widely distributed of any grebe in the Americas, breeding from northern Canada through Central America to southern South America. • The Pied-billed Grebe is a wary bird, and is far more common than encounters would lead you to believe. It is seldom seen in flight because it migrates nocturnally, landing before or at dawn on the nearest body of water. The Pied-billed Grebe also tends to swim inconspicuously in the shallow waters of quiet bays and rivers, only occasionally voicing its strange chuckle or whinny. • These grebes build their floating nests among sparse vegetation, so that they can see predators approaching from far away. When frightened by an intruder, they cover their eggs and slide underwater, leaving a nest that looks like nothing more than a mat of debris. • A Pied-billed Grebe can slowly submerge up to its head, so that only its nostrils and eyes remain above the water.

breeding

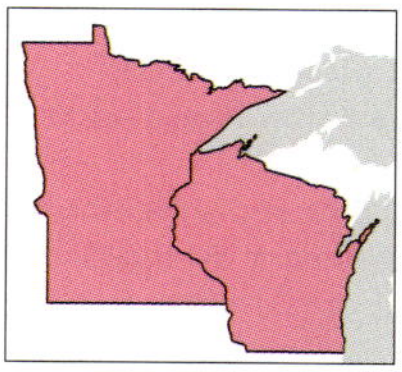

ID: *Breeding:* all-brown body; black ring on pale bill; laterally compressed "chicken bill"; black throat; very short tail; white undertail coverts; pale belly; pale eye ring. *Nonbreeding:* yellow eye ring; yellow bill lacks black ring; white "chin"and throat; brownish crown.

Size: *L* 12–15 in; *W* 16 in.

Status: ***MN:*** common migrant and breeder from April to October; occasionally lingers into winter. ***WI:*** common migrant and breeder from March to December.

Habitat: ponds, marshes and backwaters with sparse emergent vegetation.

Nesting: among sparse vegetation in a sheltered bay, pond or marsh; floating platform nest, made of wet and decaying plants, is anchored to or placed among emergent vegetation; pair incubates 4–5 white to buff eggs for about 23 days and raises the striped young together.

Feeding: makes shallow dives and gleans the water's surface for aquatic invertebrates, small fish and adult and larval amphibians; occasionally eats aquatic plants.

Voice: loud, whooping call that begins quickly, then slows down: *kuk-kuk-kuk cow cow cow cowp cowp cowp.*

Similar Species: *Eared Grebe* (p. 40): red eyes; black-and-white head; golden "ear" tufts and chestnut brown flanks in breeding plumage. *Horned Grebe* (p. 38): red eyes; black-and-white head; golden "ear" tufts and red neck in breeding plumage. *American Coot* (p. 120): all-black body; pale bill extends onto forehead.

Best Sites: ***MN:*** wetlands, marshes and lakes, especially Agassiz NWR. ***WI:*** marshes and wetlands in summer; lakes in migration.

HORNED GREBE

Podiceps auritus

Cold, mucky wetlands might not seem very inviting, but nothing is more appealing to Horned Grebes than quiet, well-vegetated marshes. Their propensity for these habitats starts early in life, before the birds are born—Horned Grebe eggs often lie in a shallow pool of water in their floating nest. The wet vegetation and tea-colored water stain the eggs, improving their camouflage. When an incubating parent is frightened off its nest, it will frequently attempt to cover the eggs with soggy vegetation before leaving them. • Unlike the fully webbed front toes of many swimming birds, grebe toes are individually webbed, or "lobed"—the three forward-facing toes have individual flanges that are not connected to the other toes. • This bird's common name and its scientific name, *auritus* (eared), refer to the golden feather tufts, or "horns," that these grebes acquire in breeding plumage.

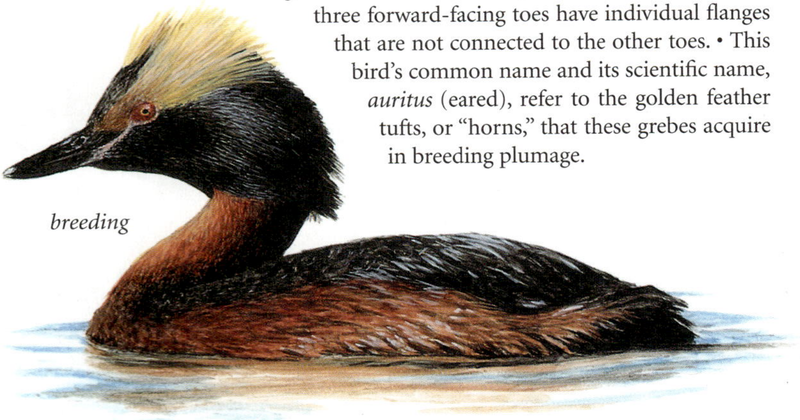

breeding

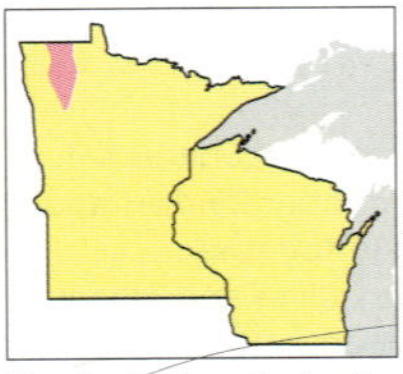

ID: *Breeding:* rufous neck and flanks; black head; golden "ear" tufts ("horns"); black back; white underparts; red eyes; flat crown. *Nonbreeding:* lacks "ear" tufts; black upperparts; white "cheek," foreneck and underparts. *In flight:* wings beat constantly; hunchbacked appearance; legs trail behind tail.

Size: *L* 12–15 in; *W* 18 in.

Status: ***MN:*** common migrant from mid-March to early June; uncommon migrant from mid-August to mid-December; very rare breeder; rare in early winter. ***WI:*** common migrant from March to May and from September to December; casual breeder with only 2 records in over 60 years; rare summer and winter visitor.

Habitat: *Breeding:* shallow, weedy wetlands. *In migration:* wetlands and larger lakes.

Nesting: usually singly or in groups of 2–3 pairs; in thick vegetation along the edges of lakes, ponds, marshes and reservoirs; pair incubates 4–7 white eggs for 22–25 days and raises the young together.

Feeding: makes shallow dives and gleans the water's surface for aquatic insects, crustaceans, mollusks, small fish and adult and larval amphibians.

Voice: loud series of croaks and shrieking notes and a sharp *keark keark* during courtship; usually quiet outside the breeding season.

Similar Species: *Eared Grebe* (p. 40): black neck in breeding plumage; black "cheek" and darker neck in nonbreeding plumage. *Pied-billed Grebe* (p. 37): thicker, stubbier bill; mostly brown body. *Red-necked Grebe* (p. 39): larger; dark eyes; lacks "ear" tufts; white cheek in breeding plumage; generally louder.

Best Sites: ***MN:*** most larger and medium-sized lakes; L. Superior; Duluth; Mille Lacs L.; Sturgeon L. (Pine Co.), especially in April. ***WI:*** L. Michigan and L. Superior, plus various inland lakes during migration.

RED-NECKED GREBE

Podiceps grisegena

As spring evenings settle over lakes and ponds, the enthusiastic laughing calls of courting Red-necked Grebes punctuate the beginning of a new breeding season. Although Red-necked Grebes are not as vocally refined as loons, few loons can match the verbal vigor of a pair of Red-necks romancing the passions of spring. Typically, their wild laughter lasts through the nights in late May. Although their whinnylike calls are a raucous part of spring evenings, Red-necks are usually quiet and retiring when they are away from their breeding grounds. • All grebes feed, sleep and court on water, and they even carry their newly hatched young on their backs. The striped young are able to stay aboard even when the parents dive underwater. • The Red-necked Grebe is one of the largest North American grebes. The scientific name *grisegena* means "gray cheek"—a distinctive field mark of this bird in nonbreeding plumage.

breeding

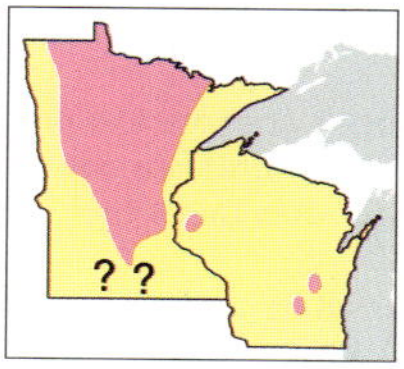

ID: *Breeding:* rusty neck; whitish "cheek"; black crown; straight, heavy bill is dark above and yellow underneath; black upperparts; light underparts; dark eyes. *Nonbreeding:* grayish white foreneck, "chin" and "cheek."

Size: *L* 17–22 in; *W* 24 in.

Status: ***MN:*** uncommon to occasionally common migrant from early April to late May, especially on L. Superior; uncommon migrant from late August to early December; uncommon breeder in the north-central region; expanding as a breeder in central and south-central regions. ***WI:*** endangered; uncommon migrant from April to May, with smaller numbers migrating from late September to November; rare breeder.

Habitat: *Breeding:* emergent vegetation zone of lakes and ponds. *In migration:* open, deep lakes.

Nesting: usually singly, but occasionally in loosely scattered colonies; floating platform nest of aquatic vegetation is anchored to submerged plants; pair incubates 4–5 white eggs for 20–23 days.

Feeding: dives and gleans the water's surface for small fish, aquatic invertebrates and amphibians.

Voice: often-repeated, whinnylike, excited *ah-ooo ah-ooo ah-ooo ah-ah-ah-ah-ah.*

Similar Species: *Horned Grebe* (p. 38): dark "cheek" and golden "horns" in breeding plumage; red eyes, all-dark bill and bright white "cheek" in nonbreeding plumage. *Eared Grebe* (p. 40): black neck in breeding plumage; black "cheek" in nonbreeding plumage. *Pied-billed Grebe* (p. 37): thicker, stubbier bill; mostly brown body. *Western Grebe* (p. 41): red eyes; black-and-white neck in breeding plumage.

Best Sites: ***MN:*** L. Superior; lakes in Otter Tail, Todd, Douglas, Beltrami and Hubbard Counties; Thief Lake WMA; Agassiz NWR; Swan L. (Nicollet Co.). ***WI:*** *Breeding:* Rush L. (Winnebago Co.); Grassy L. (Columbia Co.); a few lakes in Polk Co. and St. Croix Co. *In migration:* L. Michigan; L. Superior; assorted inland lakes.

EARED GREBE

Podiceps nigricollis

This little grebe is typically found farther west, but each year small numbers find their way into our region in every season except winter. The Eared Grebe also inhabits parts of Europe, Asia, Central Africa and South America, making it the most abundant grebe not only in North America, but also the world. • Eared Grebes undergo cyclical periods of atrophy and hypertrophy throughout the year, meaning that their internal organs and pectoral muscles shrink or swell, depending on whether or not the birds need to migrate. This strategy leaves Eared Grebes flightless for a longer period—nine to ten months per year—than any other flying bird in the world. • Like other grebes, the Eared Grebe eats feathers. The feathers pack the digestive tract, and it is thought that they protect the stomach lining and intestines from sharp fish bones or parasites, or perhaps slow the passage of food, allowing more time for complete digestion.

breeding

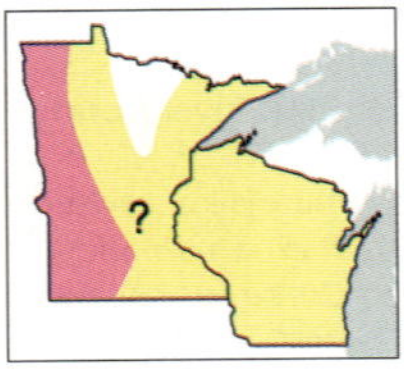

ID: *Breeding:* black neck, "cheek," forehead and back; red flanks; fanned-out, golden "ear" tufts; white underparts; thin, straight bill; red eyes; slightly raised crown. *Nonbreeding:* dark "cheek" and upperparts; light underparts; dusky upper foreneck and flanks. *In flight:* wings beat constantly; hunchbacked appearance; legs trail behind tail.

Size: *L* 11½–14 in; *W* 16 in.

Status: ***MN:*** uncommon migrant and local breeder from May to November, mainly in the west. ***WI:*** uncommon migrant from mid-April to early June and from late September to mid-November; rare summer resident with 1 breeding record.

Habitat: *Breeding:* shallow, weedy wetlands. *In migration:* wetlands and lakes.

Nesting: usually colonial; in thick vegetation on lake edges, ponds and marshes; shallow, flimsy, floating platform nest of wet and decaying plants is anchored to or placed among emergent vegetation; pair incubates 3–5 white eggs and raises the young together.

Feeding: makes shallow dives and gleans the water's surface for aquatic insects, crustaceans, mollusks, small fish and larval and adult amphibians.

Voice: mellow *poo-eee-chk* during courtship; usually quiet outside the breeding season.

Similar Species: *Horned Grebe* (p. 38): rufous neck in breeding plumage; white "cheek" in nonbreeding plumage. *Pied-billed Grebe* (p. 37): thicker, stubbier bill; mostly brown body. *Red-necked Grebe* (p. 39): larger; longer bill; red neck and whitish "cheek" in breeding plumage; dusky white "cheek" in nonbreeding plumage.

Best Sites: ***MN:*** Swan L. (Nicollet Co.); Swan L. (Sibley Co.); Agassiz NWR; Thief Lake WMA. ***WI:*** inland lakes; L. Michigan and L. Superior in migration.

WESTERN GREBE

Aechmophorus occidentalis

As its name implies, the Western Grebe breeds mostly in the western half of North America, though its breeding range extends into our region. • This bird's courtship display is one of the most elaborate breeding rituals found in the bird world. These performances occur in May on medium to large wetlands and lakes. During the "rushing" phase of the display, the birds glance briefly at one another before exploding into a sprint across the surface of the water. Both grebes stand high, feet paddling furiously, with their wings held back and heads and necks rigid, until the race ends with the pair breaking the water's surface in a headfirst dive. Then, during the "weed dance," the male and female gently raise their torsos out of the water, caressing each other with aquatic vegetation held in their long, rapierlike bills. To make their bond even stronger, the pair will mimic each other by preening, bobbing their heads and cleaning each other. • The Western Grebe is unique among grebes in having the heronlike ability to thrust its head forward like a spear. The genus name *Aechomophorus* is derived from Greek words meaning "spear bearer."

breeding

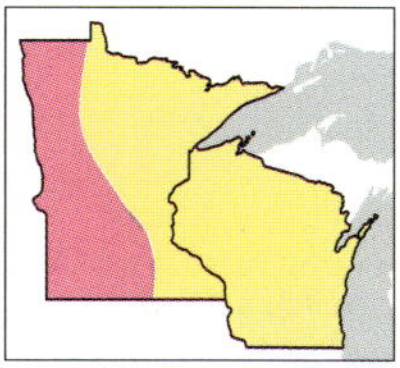

ID: long, slender neck; black upperparts from base of bill to tail; white underparts from "chin" through belly; long, thin, yellow bill; white "cheek"; black on face extends down around red eyes.

Size: *L* 20–24 in; *W* 24 in.

Status: ***MN:*** uncommon to common migrant from mid-April to early June and from late August to mid-November in western and central regions; uncommon migrant in the east; local breeder in the west; range is expanding eastward. ***WI:*** rare migrant; 1 breeding record; a limited number of summer sightings.

Habitat: *Breeding:* large lakes with dense areas of emergent vegetation or thick mats of floating aquatic plants. *In migration:* large, deep lakes.

Nesting: colonial; pair builds a floating nest of aquatic vegetation anchored to submerged plants; pair incubates 2–4 pale bluish white eggs for about 24 days; young are carried on adult's back.

Feeding: gleans the water's surface and dives for small fish and aquatic invertebrates.

Voice: high-pitched, froglike *crreeet-crreeet.*

Similar Species: *Clark's Grebe* (p. 42): eyes are surrounded by white; yellow orange bill. *Double-crested Cormorant* (p. 44): all-black body. *Common Loon* (p. 36): shorter, stocky neck. *Eared Grebe* (p. 40) and *Horned Grebe* (p. 38): much smaller. *Red-necked Grebe* (p. 39): rusty neck; white "cheek."

Best Sites: ***MN:*** Swan L. (Nicollet Co.); Long L. (Meeker Co.); L. Traverse; L. Osakis; Agassiz NWR; French L. (Hennepin Co.). ***WI:*** L. Michigan; L. Superior; various inland lakes.

CLARK'S GREBE

Aechmophorus clarkii

Until 1985, the Clark's Grebe and the Western Grebe were thought to be color phases of one species, not two separate species. Clark's Grebes look and act like Western Grebes and are most often found among them. Slight physical and behavioral differences prevent these two grebe species from interbreeding, but it is a challenge for human observers to tell them apart. One way to do this is by their calls: the Clark's Grebe gives a one-syllable call, while the Western Grebe gives a two-syllable call. There are also differences in bill color and facial patterns. This pair of grebes is a perfect example in the debate of "what makes a species a species." • The Clark's Grebe was named in honor of John Henry Clark, a mathematician, surveyor and bird collector who obtained the first scientific specimen of this grebe from Mexico in 1858.

breeding

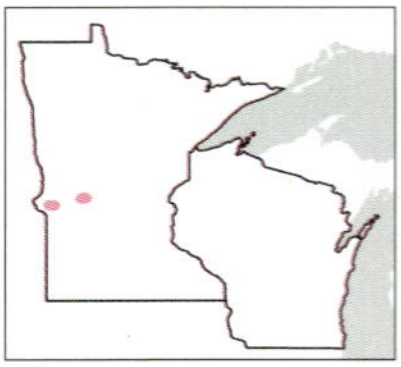

ID: long, slender neck; long, slender, yellow orange bill; white on face surrounds the red eyes; black upperparts; white underparts; short tail.

Size: *L* 20–23 in; *W* 24 in.

Status: most often encountered as individuals in association with Western Grebes. ***MN:*** rare and local migrant and breeder; little is known about its migration routes in the state. ***WI:*** casual or accidental migrant.

Habitat: large lakes, marshes and reservoirs with shallow, vegetated margins.

Nesting: colonial; pair builds a floating nest of wet or decaying vegetation anchored to submerged plants; pair incubates 2–4 pale bluish white eggs for about 24 days; young climb onto adult's back within minutes of hatching.

Feeding: surface dives for small fish, aquatic invertebrates and amphibians; often ingests feathers.

Voice: high-pitched, froglike, prolonged *creeet.*

Similar Species: *Western Grebe* (p. 41): black plumage on face surrounds eyes; yellow to olive bill.

Best Sites: ***MN:*** L. Osakis (Todd Co. and Douglas Co.); Thielke L. (Big Stone Co.). ***WI:*** no consistent sites.

AMERICAN WHITE PELICAN

Pelecanus erythrorhynchos

Pelicans are a majestic wetland presence with a wingspan only a foot shy of the height of a basketball hoop. Their porous, bucketlike bills are dramatically adapted for feeding. Groups of foraging pelicans deliberately herd fish into schools, then dip their bills and scoop up the prey. In a single scoop, a pelican can hold over 3 gallons of water and fish, which is about two to three times as much as its stomach can hold. This impressive feat confirms Dixon Lanier Merritt's quotation: "A wonderful bird is a pelican, His bill will hold more than his belican!" White Pelicans eat about 4 pounds of fish per day, but because they prefer nongame fish they do not pose a threat to the potential catches of fishermen. • All other large, white birds with black wing tips fly with their necks extended, while the Amercian White Pelican is the only one to fly with its neck pulled back toward its wings.

nonbreeding

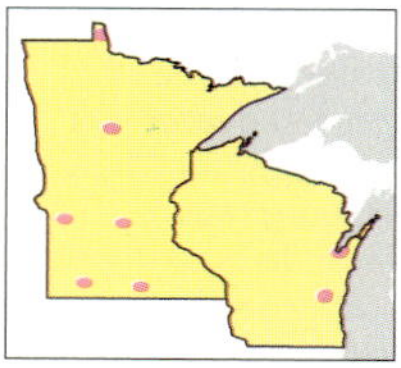

ID: very large, stocky, white bird; long, orange bill and throat pouch; black primary and secondary wing feathers; short tail; naked, orange skin patch around eye. *Breeding:* small, keeled plate develops on upper mandible; pale yellow crest on back of head. *Nonbreeding* and *immature:* white plumage is tinged with brown.

Size: *L* 4½–6 ft; *W* 9 ft.

Status: ***MN:*** special concern; common migrant from early April to early June and from late August to mid-November in central and western regions, uncommon migrant in the east; numbers are increasing; at least 6 breeding colonies; post-breeding dispersal in fall to many areas in the state. ***WI:*** uncommon migrant from April to May and from October to November; locally common breeder.

Habitat: large lakes or rivers.

Nesting: colonial; on a bare, low-lying island; nest scrape is lined with pebbles and debris or is completely unlined; pair incubates 2 dull white eggs for 29–36 days; young hatch at different times and differ in size; young are fed by regurgitation.

Feeding: surface dips for small fish and amphibians; small groups of pelicans often feed cooperatively by herding fish into large concentrations.

Voice: generally quiet; adults rarely issue piglike grunts; nestlings may give grunts and piercing screams.

Similar Species: no other large, white bird has a long bill with a pouch.

Best Sites: ***MN:*** Lake of the Woods; Leech L.; Marsh L. (Lac Qui Parle Co.); Minnesota L. (Faribault Co.); Pigeon L. (Meeker Co.); Heron L. (Jackson Co.). ***WI:*** along the western shore and on the southern tip of Green Bay (breeds on Cat I.); Mississippi R. between Crawford Co. and Buffalo Co.; breeds at Horicon Marsh.

DOUBLE-CRESTED CORMORANT

Phalacrocorax auritus

breeding

The slick-feathered Double-crested Cormorant is the only North American cormorant that occurs inland in large numbers. Though these birds are seldom seen out of sight of land, their mastery of the aquatic environment is virtually unsurpassed. The Double-crested Cormorant does not have oil glands for waterproofing its feathers, which helps it during underwater dives by decreasing the bird's buoyancy. Instead of floating on the water after a bout of diving, this bird is often seen perched on a rock or in a tree with its wings partially spread, a posture thought to aid in drying wet feathers. The cormorant's long, rudderlike tail, excellent underwater vision and sealed nostrils also contribute to the success of its aquatic lifestyle. Once believed to compete with fishermen for the same fish, it is now known that cormorants take undesirables such as alewives, smelt and yellow perch. • Cormorants nest in trees or on the ground, in colonies often interpersed with Great Blue Herons, Great Egrets and American White Pelicans.

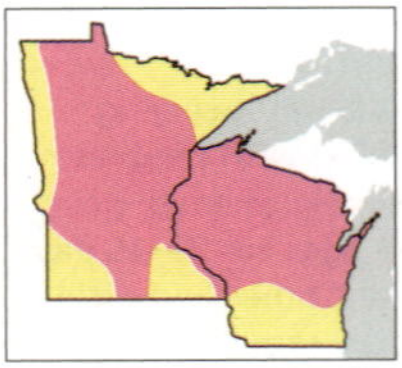

ID: all-black body; long, crooked neck; thin bill, hooked at tip; blue eyes. *Breeding:* throat pouch becomes intense yellow orange; fine, black plumes trail from eyebrows. *Immature:* brown upperparts; buff throat and breast; yellowish throat patch. *In flight:* rapid wingbeats; kinked neck.

Size: *L* 26–32 in; *W* 4½ ft.

Status: ***MN:*** common migrant from late March to mid-May and from mid-September to early December; common breeder in local colonies throughout the state, increasing in recent years but scarce or absent over most of the north-central and northeastern regions. ***WI:*** common migrant and breeder from April to late November.

Habitat: large lakes and large, meandering rivers.

Nesting: colonial; on a low-lying island, often with pelicans, terns and gulls, or precariously high in a tree; nest platform is made of sticks, aquatic vegetation and guano; pair incubates 3–6 bluish white eggs for 25–33 days; young are fed by regurgitation.

Feeding: long underwater dives to depths of 30 ft or more when after small schooling fish or, rarely, amphibians and invertebrates; uses bill to grasp prey and bring it to the surface to swallow.

Voice: generally quiet; may issue piglike grunts or croaks, especially near nesting colonies.

Similar Species: *Common Loon* (p. 36): shorter neck; black bill lacks hooked tip; spotted back in breeding plumage; white underparts in nonbreeding plumage. *Canada Goose* (p. 59): white "cheek"; brown overall.

Best Sites: ***MN:*** Lake of the Woods; Leech L.; Minnesota L. (Faribault Co.); Pigeon L. (Meeker Co.). ***WI:*** Green Bay; Horicon Marsh; Mississippi R.; L. Michigan; L. Superior.

AMERICAN BITTERN

Botaurus lentiginosus

The American Bittern's mysterious booming call is as characteristic of a spring marsh as the sound of croaking frogs, winnowing snipes and nighttime showers. This bittern is common around productive marsh habitat, but it's uncommon or rare to actually see one. Even honed and patient eyes are no match for this elusive bird. • At the approach of an intruder, a bittern's first reaction is to freeze with its bill pointed skyward—its vertically streaked, brown plumage blends perfectly with the surroundings. An American Bittern will always face an intruder, moving ever so slowly to keep its camouflaged breast toward danger. In most cases, intruders simply pass by without ever noticing the cryptic bird. This defensive reaction can sometimes result in an unfortunate comical turn for the bittern—it will try to mimic a reed even in an entirely open field. • American Bittern populations declined in our region in the latter part of the 20th century, but seem to be stable or increasing at present.

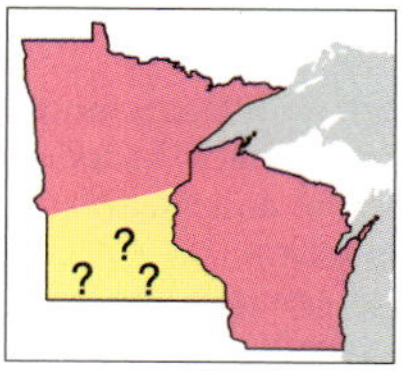

ID: brown upperparts; brown streaking from "chin" through breast; straight, stout bill; yellow legs and feet; brownish black outer wings; black streaks from bill down neck to shoulder; short tail.

Size: *L* 23–27 in; *W* 3½ ft.

Status: ***MN:*** uncommon migrant from April to May and from August to November; rare summer resident and breeder in larger marshes, mainly in the north. ***WI:*** common migrant and breeder from April to early November.

Habitat: marshes, wetlands and lake edges with tall, dense grasses, sedges, bulrushes and cattails.

Nesting: singly; above the waterline in dense vegetation; nest platform is made of grass, sedges and dead reeds; nest often has separate entrance and exit paths; female incubates 3–5 pale olive or buff eggs for 24–28 days.

Feeding: patient stand-and-wait predator; strikes at small fish, crayfish, amphibians, reptiles, mammals and insects.

Voice: deep, slow, resonant, repetitive *pomp-er-lunk* or *onk-a-BLONK;* most often heard in the evening or at night.

Similar Species: *Black-crowned Night-Heron* (p. 53), *Yellow-crowned Night-Heron* (p. 54), *Least Bittern* (p. 46) and *Green Heron* (p. 52): immatures lack dark streaks from bill to shoulder; immature night-herons have white-flecked upperparts.

Best Sites: ***MN:*** Agassiz NWR; Southwick Marsh WMA (Murray Co.); Big Stone NWR; Tamarac NWR; Hampden Slough NWR. ***WI:*** marshes such as Horicon, Vernon, Mead, Crex Meadows, Powell and Rat River.

LEAST BITTERN

Ixobrychus exilis

The Least Bittern is the smallest of the herons and one of the most seclusive marsh birds in North America. It inhabits freshwater marshes where tall, impenetrable stands of cattails conceal most of its movements. This bird moves about with ease, its slender body passing freely and unnoticed through dense marshland habitat. An expert climber, it can be seen 3 feet or more above water, clinging to vertical stems and hopping about without getting its feet wet. • In our region, where this species approaches the northern limit of its North American range, the Least Bittern pushes the boundaries of its adaptability, particularly its tolerance to chilly summer nights. Least Bitterns are uncommon here and sightings are rare, owing in part to this bird's secretive behavior and solitary lifestyle.

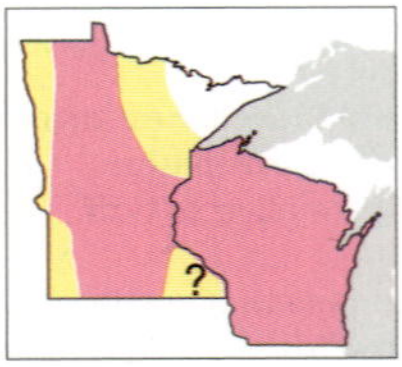

ID: rich buff flanks and sides; streaking on foreneck; white underparts; mostly pale bill; yellowish legs; short tail; dark primary and secondary feathers. *Male:* black crown and back. *Female* and *immature:* chestnut brown head and back; immature has darker streaking on breast and back. *In flight:* large, buffy shoulder patches.

Size: *L* 11–14½ in; *W* 17 in.

Status: ***MN:*** uncommon and local; seldom seen in migration; uncommon breeder in central regions; rare breeder elsewhere. ***WI:*** common migrant and breeder from late April to early October.

Habitat: freshwater marshes with cattails and other dense emergent vegetation.

Nesting: mostly the male constructs a platform of dry plant stalks on top of bent marsh vegetation; nest site is usually well concealed within dense vegetation; pair incubates 4–5 pale green or blue eggs for 17–20 days; pair feeds the young by regurgitation.

Feeding: stabs prey with its bill; eats mostly small fish; also takes large insects, tadpoles, frogs, small snakes, leeches and crayfish; may build a hunting platform.

Voice: *Male:* guttural *uh-uh-uh-oo-oo-oo-ooah*. *Female:* a ticking sound. Both issue a *tut-tut* call or a *koh* alarm call.

Similar Species: *American Bittern* (p. 45): larger; bold, brown streaking on underparts; dark streaks from bill to shoulder. *Black-crowned Night-Heron* (p. 53) and *Yellow-crowned Night-Heron* (p. 54): immatures have dark brown upperparts with white flecking. *Green Heron* (p. 52): immature has dark brown upperparts.

Best Sites: ***MN:*** Wood Lake Nature Center (Hennepin Co.); Agassiz NWR; Swan L. (Nicollet Co.). ***WI:*** marshes such as Horicon, Sensiba, Crex Meadows, Mead, Rat River, Powell, Vernon and Collins.

GREAT BLUE HERON

Ardea herodias

The sight of a Great Blue Heron is always memorable. Whether you are observing this heron as it stealthily hunts, or tracking its graceful wingbeats as it returns to its feeding site or nest, it is difficult not to notice this bird's majesty. • The Great Blue Heron nests in large colonies. Its communal treetop nests, known as rookeries, are sensitive to human disturbance, so if you are fortunate enough to discover a colony, it is best to observe the birds' behavior from a distance. • It is rare, but not unheard of, for a few Great Blue Herons to successfully survive a winter in this region. • Unlike a crane, which holds its neck outstretched in flight, the Great Blue Heron folds its neck back over its shoulders in an S-shape.

breeding

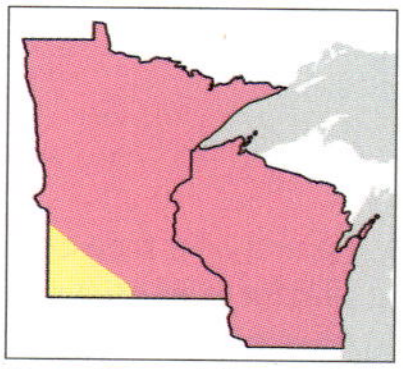

ID: large, blue gray bird; long, curving neck; long, dark legs; blue gray wing coverts and back; straight, yellow bill; chestnut brown thighs. *Breeding:* richer colors; plumes streak from crown and throat. *In flight:* neck folds back over shoulders; legs trail behind body; slow, steady wingbeats.

Size: *L* 4–4½ ft; *W* 6 ft.

Status: ***MN:*** common migrant and breeder from March to October; less common in heavily wooded areas of northern regions. ***WI:*** common migrant and breeder from mid-March to mid-November.

Habitat: forages along the edges of rivers, lakes and marshes; also seen in fields and wet meadows.

Nesting: colonial; usually in a tree but occasionally on the ground; stick-and-twig platform is added onto, often over years, and can be up to 4 ft in diameter; pair incubates 4–7 pale blue eggs for about 28 days.

Feeding: patient stand-and-wait predator; strikes at small fish, amphibians, small mammals, aquatic invertebrates and reptiles; rarely scavenges.

Voice: usually quiet away from the nest; occasionally a deep, harsh *frahnk frahnk frahnk,* usually during takeoff.

Similar Species: *Green Heron* (p. 52), *Black-crowned Night-Heron* (p. 53) and *Yellow-crowned Night-Heron* (p. 54): much smaller; shorter legs. *Great* (p. 48), *Snowy* (p. 49) and *Cattle* (p. 51) *egrets:* all are predominately white. *Sandhill Crane* (p. 121): red "cap"; flies with neck outstretched. *Little Blue Heron* (p. 50): smaller; dark overall; purplish head; lacks yellow on bill. *Tricolored Heron* (p. 357): darker upperparts; white underparts.

Best Sites: ***MN:*** Minnesota L. (Faribault Co.); Pigeon L. (Meeker Co.); Long L. (Kandiyohi Co.); Howard L. (Anoka Co.); Pelican L. (Grant Co.). ***WI:*** Horicon Marsh; Green Bay; Collins Marsh; Mississippi R.; Mead WA.

GREAT EGRET

Ardea alba

breeding

Great Egrets reappeared in Minnesota in 1932 after having been absent since the late 19th century, when this species was a straggler to southern portions of the state. In Wisconsin, these birds were common in the southeastern part of the state in the mid-1800s. They became virtually nonexistent through the 1920s, beginning a gradual recovery after 1929. This bird is now a fairly common breeder in certain areas of Wisconsin and Minnesota. • The plumes of the Great Egret and Snowy Egret were widely used to decorate hats in the early 20th century. An ounce of egret feathers cost as much as $32—more than an ounce of gold at that time—and, as a result, egret populations began to disappear. Some of the first conservation legislation in North America was enacted to outlaw the hunting of Great Egrets. • Egrets are actually herons, but were given their name for their impressive breeding plumes, referred to as "aigrettes." • The Great Egret is the symbol for the National Audubon Society, one of the oldest conservation organizations in the U.S.

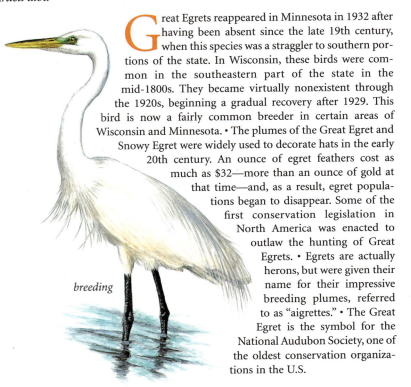

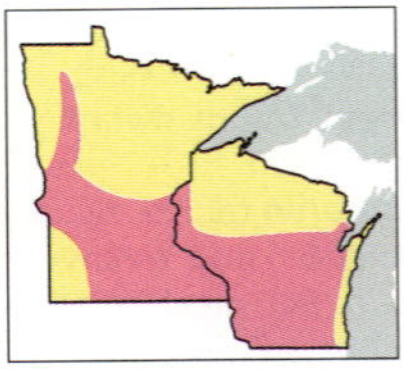

ID: all-white plumage; black legs; yellow bill. *Breeding:* white plumes trail from throat and rump; green skin patch between eyes and base of bill. *In flight:* neck folds back over shoulders; legs extend backward.

Size: *L* 3–3½ ft; *W* 4 ft.

Status: ***MN:*** common migrant and breeder from April to September across the southern half of the state; casual migrant and breeder in the north. ***WI:*** threatened; fairly common migrant and breeder from late March to mid-November.

Habitat: marshes, open riverbanks, irrigation canals and lakeshores.

Nesting: colonial, often with Great Blue Herons and Double-crested Cormorants, but may nest in isolated pairs; in a tree or tall shrub; pair builds a platform of sticks and incubates 3–5 pale blue green eggs for 23–26 days.

Feeding: patient stand-and-wait predator; occasionally stalks slowly, stabbing at frogs, lizards, snakes and small mammals.

Voice: rapid, low-pitched, loud *cuk-cuk-cuk*.

Similar Species: *Snowy Egret* (p. 49): smaller; black bill; yellow feet. *Cattle Egret* (p. 51): smaller; stockier; orange bill and legs. *Whooping Crane* (p. 358): much larger; red crown; black-and-red "mask"; black primaries; extremely rare.

Best Sites: ***MN:*** locally abundant in the Minnesota R. valley in late summer and early fall; Minnesota L. (Faribault Co.); New Germany (Carver Co.). ***WI:*** Horicon Marsh; Green Bay; Mississippi R.

SNOWY EGRET

Egretta thula

The Snowy Egret is distinguished by its small size and spotless white plumage. When it reaches adulthood, its black legs and yellow feet make it stand out even more. • The Snowy Egret was more affected by plume hunters than the Great Egret, because its plumes were softer and more delicate. After staging a comeback in the 1960s and 1970s, there were widespread population declines in the late 20th century, likely attributable to the Snowy Egret's sensitivity to a variety of conservation threats. • Herons and egrets, particularly Snowy Egrets, use a variety of foraging techniques. By poking their bright yellow feet in the muck of shallow wetlands, these birds spook potential prey out of hiding places. In an even more devious hunting strategy, Snowy Egrets are known to create shade by extending their wings over open water. When a fish succumbs to the attraction of the cooler shaded spot, it is promptly seized and eaten. Some paleontologists have even suggested that this was one of the original functions of bird wings!

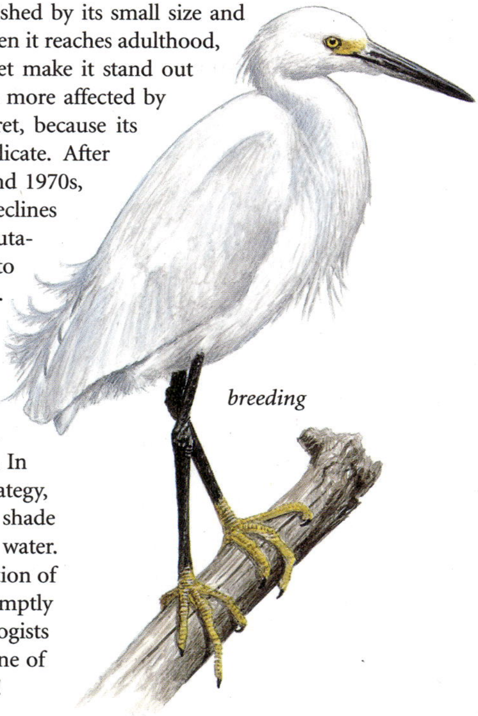

breeding

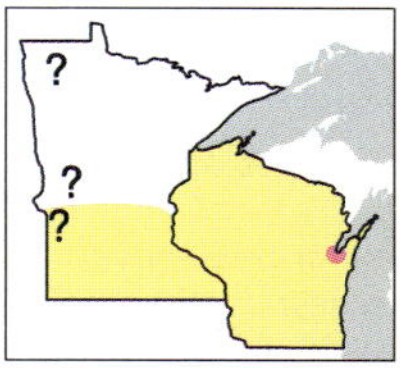

ID: white plumage; black bill and legs; bright yellow feet. *Breeding:* long plumes on throat and rump; erect crown; orange red lores. *Immature:* similar to adult but with more yellow on legs. *In flight:* yellow feet are obvious.

Size: *L* 22–26 in; *W* 3½ ft.

Status: ***MN:*** occasional to rare spring migrant and rare fall migrant; breeding status unknown. ***WI:*** endangered; uncommon migrant from April to May and from mid-July to September; rare breeder and summer resident.

Habitat: open edges of rivers, lakes and marshes.

Nesting: colonial, often among other herons; in a tree or tall shrub; pair builds a platform of sticks and incubates 3–5 pale blue green eggs for 20–24 days.

Feeding: stirs wetland muck with its feet; stands and waits with wings held open; occasionally hovers and stabs; eats small fish, amphibians and invertebrates.

Voice: low croaks; bouncy *wulla-wulla-wulla* on breeding grounds.

Similar Species: *Great Egret* (p. 48): larger; yellow bill; black feet. *Cattle Egret* (p. 51): yellow orange legs and bill. *Little Blue Heron* (p. 50): juvenile has pale, bluish gray legs and 2-tone bill.

Best Sites: ***MN:*** no consistent sites. ***WI:*** Green Bay; Horicon Marsh.

LITTLE BLUE HERON

Egretta caerulea

breeding

Because of its dark plumage and lack of aigrette plumes, the Little Blue Heron was only occasionally taken by plume hunters in the early 20th century and did not suffer the same population decimation as many of its close relatives. • Although adults of the species look quite different from Snowy Egrets, the white-plumaged young of the two species can be easily confused. It takes two years for Little Blue Herons to reach the completely dark plumage of adult birds. • Feeding behavior is often the best way to distinguish herons. Larger herons seem graceful even while lunging for a fish, whereas the Little Blue Heron often seems tentative and stiff in its hunting maneuvers, as it awkwardly jabs at prey. • The Little Blue Heron nests in colonies, often composed of many heron species. At other times of the year, the herons gather nightly at communal roosting sites.

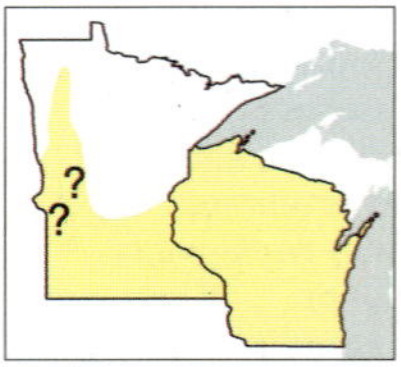

ID: medium-sized heron; slate blue overall. *Breeding:* shaggy, maroon-colored head and neck; black legs and feet. *Nonbreeding:* smooth, purple head and neck; dull green legs and feet.

Size: *L* 24 in; *W* 3½ ft.

Status: ***MN:*** rare migrant in southern regions; has been declining since the 1980s; breeding status unknown. ***WI:*** irregular yearly sightings; rare migrant from April to May; summer visitor.

Habitat: marshes, ponds, lakes, streams and meadows.

Nesting: nests in a shrub or tree above water; pair builds large nest of sticks; pair incubates 3–5 pale greenish blue eggs for 22–24 days.

Feeding: patient stand-and-wait predator but may also wade slowly to stalk prey; eats mostly fish, crabs and crayfish; also eats grasshoppers and other insects, frogs, lizards, snakes and turtles.

Voice: generally silent.

Similar Species: none.

Best Sites: ***MN:*** no consistent sites. ***WI:*** marshes and swamps, such as Horicon, Trempealeau and Vernon.

CATTLE EGRET

Bubulcus ibis

Over the last century—and without help from humans—the Cattle Egret has dispersed from Africa to inhabit every continent except Antarctica. Like most herons, the Cattle Egret is a natural wanderer, but it was probably not until North American forests had been sufficiently cleared—about 100 years ago—that Cattle Egrets were truly able to colonize the New World. This bird has become common in many regions in the last 50 years, but populations in our region declined in the late 20th century. • The Cattle Egret gets its name from its habit of following grazing animals. Unlike other egrets, its diet consists primarily of terrestrial invertebrates—it feeds on the insects and other small creatures found around ungulates. When foraging, Cattle Egrets sometimes use a "leapfrog" feeding strategy in which birds leapfrog over one another, stirring up insects for the birds that follow.

breeding

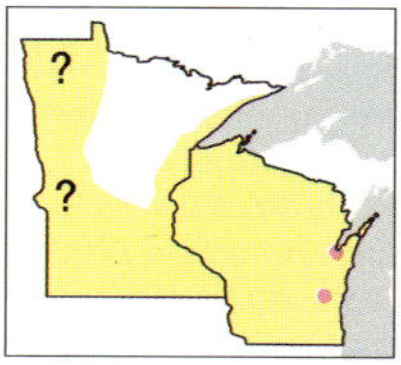

ID: mostly white; yellow orange bill and legs. *Breeding:* long plumes on throat and rump; buff orange throat, rump and crown; orange red legs and bill; purple lores. *Immature:* similar to adult, but with black feet and dark bill.

Size: *L* 19–21 in; *W* 3 ft.

Status: ***MN:*** rare spring and fall migrant; does not currently breed in the state (formerly bred in the 1980s in western regions). ***WI:*** special concern; uncommon migrant from mid-April to late May and from mid-September to November; uncommon summer resident; uncommon to rare breeder.

Habitat: agricultural fields and marshes.

Nesting: colonial; often among other herons; in a tree or tall shrub; male supplies sticks for female who builds a platform or shallow bowl; pair incubates 3–4 pale blue eggs for 21–26 days.

Feeding: picks grasshoppers, other insects, worms, small vertebrates and spiders from fields; often associated with livestock.

Voice: generally silent.

Similar Species: *Great Egret* (p. 48): larger; black legs and feet. *Snowy Egret* (p. 49): black legs; yellow feet; black bill.

Best Sites: ***MN:*** Coon Creek WMA (Lyon Co. and Lincoln Co.). ***WI:*** Green Bay; Horicon Marsh.

GREEN HERON

Butorides virescens

This crow-sized heron is far less conspicuous than its Great Blue cousin. The Green Heron eats primarily small fish and prefers to hunt in shallow, weedy wetlands, where it often perches just above the water's surface. While hunting, Green Herons sometimes drop small debris, including twigs, vegetation and feathers, onto the water's surface as a form of bait to attract fish within striking range. • If the light is just right, you may be fortunate enough to see a glimmer of green on the back and outer wings of this bird. Most of the time, however, this magical shine is not apparent, especially when the Green Heron stands frozen under the shade of dense marshland vegetation. • Unlike most herons, Green Herons generally nest singly rather than communally, although they can sometimes be found in loose colonies.

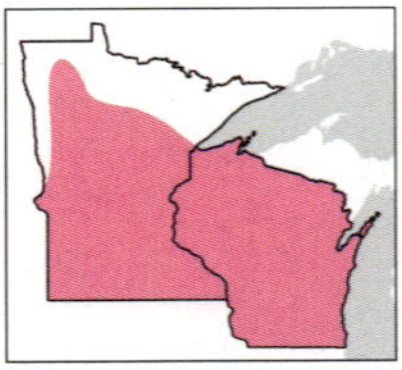

ID: stocky; green black crown; chestnut brown face and neck; white foreneck and belly; blue gray back and wings mixed with iridescent green; relatively short, yellow green legs; bill is dark above and greenish below; short tail. *Breeding male:* bright orange legs. *Immature:* heavy streaking along neck and underparts; dark brown upperparts.

Size: *L* 15–22 in; *W* 26 in.

Status: ***MN:*** common migrant and breeder from April to September. ***WI:*** common migrant and breeder from April to October.

Habitat: marshes, lakes and streams with dense shoreline or emergent vegetation.

Nesting: nests singly or in small, loose groups; male begins and female completes construction of a stick platform in a tree or shrub, usually very close to water; pair incubates 3–5 pale blue green to green eggs for 19–21 days; young are fed by regurgitation.

Feeding: stabs prey with its bill after slowly stalking or standing and waiting; eats mostly small fish; also takes frogs, tadpoles, crayfish, aquatic and terrestrial insects, small rodents, snakes, snails and worms.

Voice: generally silent; alarm and flight call are a loud *kowp, kyow* or *skow;* aggression call is a harsh *raah.*

Similar Species: *Black-crowned Night-Heron* (p. 53): larger; white "cheek"; pale gray and white neck; 2 long, white plumes trail down from crown; immature has streaked face and white flecking on upperparts. *Least Bittern* (p. 46): buffy yellow shoulder patches, sides and flanks. *American Bittern* (p. 45): larger; more tan overall; dark streaks from bill to shoulder.

Best Sites: ***MN:*** wetlands across southern and central regions; Goose L. (Ramsey Co.); L. Minnetonka (Hennepin Co.); Sherburne NWR. ***WI:*** marshy areas, especially near trees; Horicon Marsh; Sensiba WA; Trempealeau NWR; Crex Meadows WA.

BLACK-CROWNED NIGHT-HERON

Nycticorax nycticorax

When the setting sun has sent most wetland waders to their nightly roosts, Black-crowned Night-Herons arrive to hunt the marshy waters and to voice their hoarse squawks. These herons patrol the shallows for prey, which they can see in the dim light with their large, light-sensitive eyes. They remain alongside water until morning, when they flap off to treetop roosts. • During the breeding season or in unusual weather, Black-crowned Night-Herons sometimes forage during the day. A popular hunting strategy for day-active birds is to sit motionless atop a few bent-over cattails. Anything passing below the perch becomes fair game—even ducklings, small shorebirds or young muskrats. • Because of their heavily streaked underparts, young night-herons are easily confused with other immature herons and American Bitterns.

breeding

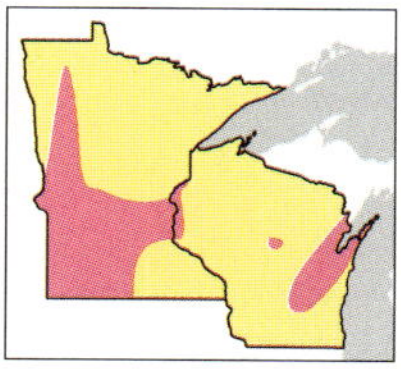

ID: black "cap" and back; white "cheek," foreneck and underparts; gray neck and wings; dull yellow legs; stout black bill; large, red eyes. *Breeding:* 2 white plumes trail down from crown. *Immature:* lightly streaked underparts; brown upperparts with white flecking.

Size: *L* 23–26 in; *W* 3½ ft.

Status: ***MN:*** common but erratic migrant, mainly from April to May and from September to November, in central and southwestern regions; expanding northwestward; rare and local breeder; absent over wide areas, especially the southeast and northeast. ***WI:*** common migrant and breeder from April to November.

Habitat: shallow cattail and bulrush marshes, lakeshores and along slow rivers.

Nesting: colonial, often with Great Blue Herons and Great Egrets; in a tree or shrub; male gathers the nest material; female builds a loose nest platform of twigs and sticks and lines it with finer materials; pair incubates 3–4 pale green eggs for 21–26 days.

Feeding: often at dusk; patient stand-and-wait predator; stabs for small fish, amphibians, aquatic invertebrates, reptiles, young birds and small mammals.

Voice: deep, guttural *quark* or *wok,* often heard as the bird takes flight.

Similar Species: *Great Blue Heron* (p. 47): much larger; longer legs; blue gray back. *Yellow-crowned Night-Heron* (p. 54): white plumes; white crown and "cheek" patch on otherwise black head; gray back; immature is very similar to Black-crowned immature. *Green Heron* (p. 52): chestnut brown face and neck; blue gray back with green iridescence; immature has heavily streaked underparts. *American Bittern* (p. 45): similar to immature Black-crowned Night-Heron, but bittern has dark streaks from bill to shoulder and is lighter tan overall.

Best Sites: ***MN:*** L. Minnetonka. ***WI:*** Green Bay; Horicon Marsh; Trempealeau NWR; Crex Meadows WA.

YELLOW-CROWNED NIGHT-HERON

Nyctanassa violacea

The Yellow-crowned Night-Heron's partiality for crustaceans has earned it the name "Crab Eater" in some parts of its range. While in our region, its diet is more varied and also includes frogs, insects and fish. In the fall, a return to subtropical and tropical locales will find this heron hunting primarily crabs once again. The Yellow-crowned Night Heron will typically grab a crab by its legs or pinchers and shake vigorously until these fall off, making the crab more manageable. • Like many other herons, this bird is a patient predator—it stands and waits for prey to glide underneath its still body. Despite its name, the Yellow-crowned Night-Heron commonly feeds by day as well as by night, although poor lighting is a standard criterion for suitable breeding and hunting habitat. • During the breeding season, pairs greet each other with their crests raised and delicately preen each other's feathers.

breeding

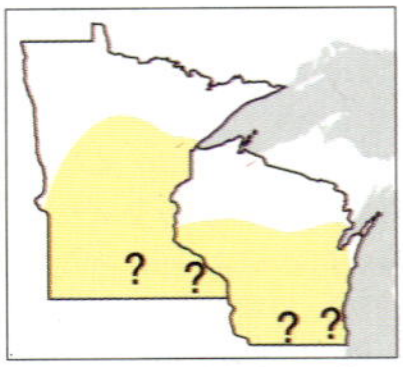

ID: gray overall; heavy bill; black head with buffy white crown and white "cheek." *Breeding:* long, white head plumes. *In flight:* feet extend well beyond tail.

Size: *L* 24 in; *W* $3\frac{1}{2}$ ft.

Status: ***MN:*** rare and very local migrant and visitor across southern regions of the state; breeding status unknown.

WI: threatened; rare migrant from April to May and from August to September; rare summer resident; very rare breeder.

Habitat: in wetlands and along lowland rivers.

Nesting: singly or in colonies; in a tree or shrub near water; pair builds a nest of heavy twigs and lines it with finer twigs, rootlets and sometimes leaves; pair incubates 2–4 pale greenish blue eggs for 21–25 days.

Feeding: stands and waits or wades slowly in shallow water to catch crabs, crayfish, other freshwater invertebrates, fish, frogs and insects; forages alone or in small groups.

Voice: a loud *quok!* that is less harsh and slightly higher in pitch than the Black-crowned Night-Heron's call.

Similar Species: *Black-crowned Night-Heron* (p. 53): black crown and back; shorter legs; thinner bill.

Best Sites: ***MN:*** no consistent sites.

WI: scarce and unpredictable; along wooded rivers in the south, such as the Sugar, Rock and Wisconsin; Horicon Marsh; swamps along the Mississippi R.

TURKEY VULTURE

Cathartes aura

Turkey Vultures are unmatched at using updrafts and thermals—they can tease lift from the slightest pocket of rising air and patrol the skies when other soaring birds are grounded. • The Turkey Vulture eats carrion almost exclusively, so its bill and feet are not nearly as powerful as those of hawks and falcons, which kill live prey. Its red, featherless head may appear grotesque, but this adaptation allows it to remain relatively clean while feeding on messy carcasses. • Vultures seem to have mastered the art of regurgitation. This ability allows parents to transport food over long distances to their young and also enables engorged birds to repulse an attacker or "lighten up" for an emergency takeoff. • Recent studies have shown that American vultures are most closely related to storks, not to hawks and falcons as was previously thought.

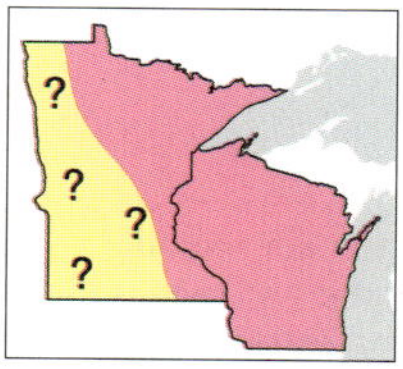

ID: black overall; bare, red head. *Immature:* gray head. *In flight:* head appears small; silver gray flight feathers; black wing linings; wings are held in a shallow "V"; rocks from side-to-side when soaring.

Size: *L* 26–32 in; *W* 5½–6 ft.

Status: ***MN:*** uncommon to common migrant and breeder from April to October. ***WI:*** common migrant from March to May and from September to November; uncommon breeder.

Habitat: usually seen flying over open country, shorelines or roads; rarely seen over forested areas.

Nesting: in a cave crevice or among boulders; rarely in a hollow stump or log; no nest material is used; female lays 2 dull white eggs, spotted and blotched with reddish brown, on bare ground; pair incubates the eggs for 41 days; young are fed by regurgitation.

Feeding: entirely on carrion (mostly mammalian); not commonly seen at roadkills.

Voice: generally silent; occasionally produces a hiss or grunt if threatened.

Similar Species: *Golden Eagle* (p. 101) and *Bald Eagle* (p. 90): lack silvery gray wing linings; wings are held flat in flight; do not rock when soaring; head is more visible in flight. *Rough-legged Hawk* (p. 100): dark morph has multi-banded tail with black, subterminal tip and whitish wing linings with dark bars. *Black Vulture:* rare visitor; gray head; silvery tips on otherwise black wings.

Best Sites: ***MN:*** Hawk Ridge (Duluth); Minnesota R. valley; St. Croix R. valley; lower Mississipi R. valley. ***WI:*** Devil's Lake SP; Baxter's Hollow; Wyalusing SP; L. Michigan bluffs and Mississippi R. bluffs in migration.

GREATER WHITE-FRONTED GOOSE

Anser albifrons

Greater White-fronted Geese breed on the arctic tundra and winter in the southern U.S. and Mexico. They can be seen in our region, especially during spring migration, when they stop to refuel on aquatic plants in shallow ponds and marshes or on freshly sprouted grains in fields and pastures. They often travel among flocks of Canada Geese. The slightly smaller White-fronted Geese can best be distinguished by their bright orange feet, which shine like beacons as the birds stand on frozen spring wetlands and fields. • The Greater White-fronted Goose has an almost circumpolar arctic distribution and, of the five species of gray geese found in Eurasia, it is the only one that also occurs in North America. Like most geese, White-fronts are long-lived birds that mate for life, with both parents caring for the young. • This goose is probably most familiar to hunters, who know it as "Speckle Belly."

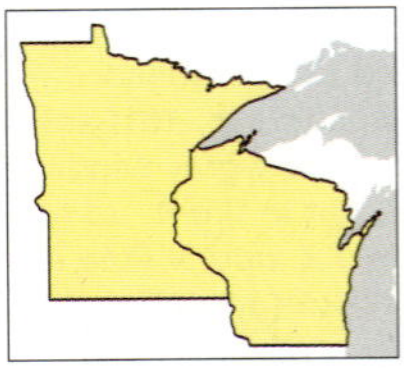

ID: brown overall; black speckling on belly; pinkish bill; white around bill and on forehead; white hindquarters; black band on upper tail; orange feet. *Immature:* pale belly lacks speckling; little or no white on face.

Size: *L* 27–33 in; *W* $4\frac{1}{2}$–5 ft.

Status: ***MN:*** common migrant from March to April; rare fall migrant; a few summer and winter records. ***WI:*** uncommon migrant from late February to April; rare migrant from September to November.

Habitat: croplands, fields, open areas and shallow marshes in migration.

Nesting: does not nest in our region.

Feeding: dabbles in water and gleans the ground for grass shoots, sprouting and waste grain and occasionally aquatic invertebrates.

Voice: high-pitched "laugh."

Similar Species: *Canada Goose* (p. 59): white "chin strap"; black neck; lacks speckling on belly. *Snow Goose* (p. 57): blue morph has white head and upper neck and all-dark breast and belly.

Best Sites: ***MN:*** Big Stone NWR; L. Traverse; Mud L.; Salt L. (Lac Qui Parle Co.); Nobles Co.; Lincoln Co. and Lyon Co. in spring. ***WI:*** Arlington area (Goose, V, DM, I and Schumacher ponds); Mud Lake WA; Horicon Marsh; Beaver Dam area; Shiocton–Black Creek.

SNOW GOOSE

Chen caerulescens

Minnesota and Wisconsin do not receive the staggering numbers of migrating Snow Geese found in other areas, but these birds are still sure to come in spring and fall. Landing in farmers' fields, these cackling geese fuel up on waste grain from the previous year's crops. In recent years, Snow Goose populations have increased dramatically in North America, as they take advantage of human-induced changes in the landscape and in the food supply. • Snow Geese grub for their food, often targeting the belowground parts of plants. Their strong, serrated bills are well designed for pulling up the root stalks of marsh plants and gripping slippery grasses. • Unlike Canada Geese, which fly in "V" formations, migrating Snow Geese usually form oscillating, wavy lines. • Snow Goose plumage, like that of Sandhill Cranes, is often stained rusty red from iron in the water. • Until 1983, this species' two color morphs, a white and a blue, were considered different species.

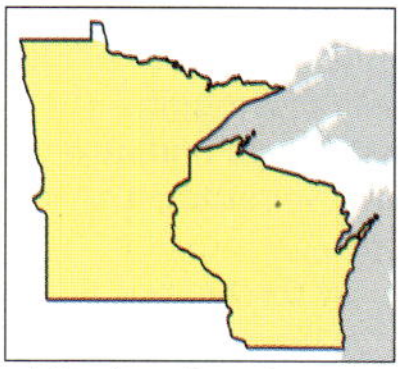

ID: white overall; black wing tips; pink feet and bill; dark "grinning patch" on bill; plumage is sometimes stained rusty red. *Blue morph:* white head and upper neck; dark blue gray body. *Immature:* gray or dusty white plumage; dark bill and feet.

Size: *L* 28–33 in; *W* 4½–5 ft.

Status: ***MN:*** common to at times abundant migrant from mid-March to late May and from mid-September to early December, especially in western regions. ***WI:*** common migrant from late February to April and from late September to November.

Habitat: shallow wetlands, lakes and fields.

Nesting: does not nest in our region.

Feeding: grazes on waste grain and new sprouts; also eats aquatic vegetation, grasses, sedges and roots.

Voice: loud, constant, nasal *houk-houk* in flight.

Similar Species: *Ross's Goose* (p. 58): smaller; shorter neck; lacks black "grinning patch." *Tundra* (p. 62), *Trumpeter* (p. 61) and *Mute* (p. 60) *swans:* larger; white wing tips. *American White Pelican* (p. 43): much larger bill and body.

Best Sites: ***MN:*** L. Traverse; Mud L. (Traverse Co.); Marsh L. (Lac Qui Parle Co.); Agassiz NWR; Nobles Co.; Lincoln Co.; Lyon Co. ***WI:*** Horicon Marsh; Shiocton–Black Creek; Arlington ponds; Crex Meadows WA; Collins Marsh.

ROSS'S GOOSE

Chen rossii

The Ross's Goose is the smallest of the three varieties of white, or snow, geese that breed in North America. It looks so similar to the Snow Goose that inexperienced birders can easily get the two confused. The Ross's Goose is often overlooked, particularly when a few individuals are mixed in with large flocks of migrating Snow Geese. Although the Ross's Goose is often found among breeding colonies and migrating flocks of Lesser Snow Geese, it is seldom found associating with the Greater Snow Goose. • Approximately 95 percent of all Ross's Geese nest in the Queen Maud Gulf Migratory Bird Sanctuary in the central Canadian Arctic. The population of Ross's Geese in our region has been increasing rapidly since the 1990s. • This bird was named after Bernard Rogan Ross, a naturalist and anthropologist who was a fellow of the National Geographic Society and a contributor of specimens to the Smithsonian Institute and the British Museum.

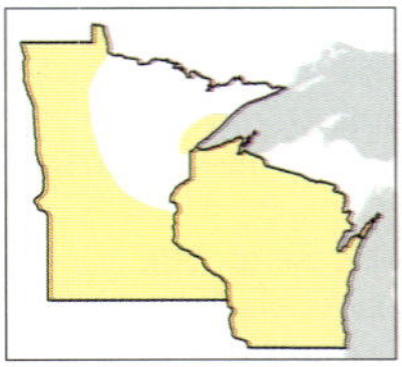

ID: white overall; black wing tips; dark pink feet and bill; lacks "grinning patch"; small bluish or greenish "warts" on base of bill; plumage is occasionally stained rusty red by iron in the water. *Blue morph:* very rare; white head; blue gray body plumage. *Immature:* gray plumage; dark bill and feet.

Size: *L* 21–26 in; *W* 4 ft.

Status: ***MN:*** uncommon migrant from March to April; rare fall migrant. ***WI:*** uncommon migrant from March to April; very uncommon migrant from October to November.

Habitat: shallow wetlands, lakes and fields.

Nesting: does not nest in our region.

Feeding: grazes on waste grain and new sprouts; also eats aquatic vegetation, grasses, sedges and roots.

Voice: similar to the Snow Goose, but higher pitched.

Similar Species: *Snow Goose* (p. 57): larger; longer neck; dark "grinning patch" on bill. *Tundra* (p. 62), *Trumpeter* (p. 61) and *Mute* (p. 60) *swans:* much larger; white wing tips. *American White Pelican* (p. 43): much larger bill and body.

Best Sites: ***MN:*** western regions of the state, especially Lincoln, Nobles, Lyon and Jackson Counties. ***WI:*** Shiocton–Black Creek; Arlington ponds; Horicon Marsh.

CANADA GOOSE

Branta canadensis

Canada Geese are among the most recognizable birds in our region, but they are also among the least valued. Few people realize that at one time these birds were hunted almost to extinction. Populations have since been reestablished and, in recent decades, these large, bold geese have inundated urban waterfronts, picnic sites, golf courses and city parks. Today, many people even consider them pests. • Many geese overwinter in more sheltered locations where food is available year-round. Canada Goose pairs mate for life and, unlike most birds, the parents do not sever bonds with their young until the start of the next year's nesting, almost a year after the young are born, thus increasing the chance for survival for young birds. • Fuzzy goslings seem to compel people, especially children, to get closer. Unfortunately, goose parents can cause harm to unwelcome strangers. Hissing sounds and low, outstretched necks are signs that you should give these birds some space.

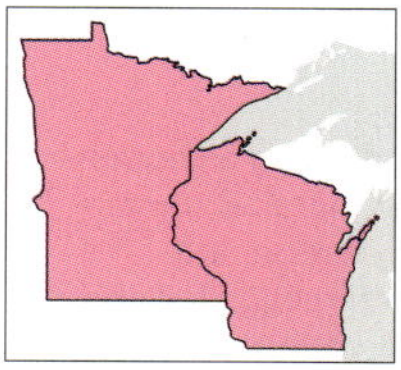

ID: long, black neck; white "chin strap"; white undertail coverts; light brown underparts; dark brown upperparts; short, black tail.

Size: *L* 25–45 in; *W* $3\frac{1}{2}$–5 ft.

Status: ***MN:*** increasingly abundant migrant and breeder from March to November; winters in large numbers where there is open water in southern and central regions. ***WI:*** abundant migrant and breeder from March to December; common to uncommon winter visitor depending on the severity of the season.

Habitat: lakeshores, riverbanks, ponds, farmlands and city parks.

Nesting: on an island or shoreline; usually on the ground or on a muskrat lodge; may use a heron rookery; female builds a nest of plant material lined with down; female incubates 3–8 white eggs for 25–28 days while the male stands guard.

Feeding: grazes on new sprouts, aquatic vegetation, grass and roots; tips up for aquatic roots and tubers.

Voice: loud, familiar *ah-honk,* often answered by other Canada Geese.

Similar Species: *Greater White-fronted Goose* (p. 56): brown neck and head; lacks white "chin strap"; orange legs; white around base of bill; dark speckling on belly. *Brant* (p. 357): lacks white "chin strap"; white "necklace"; black upper breast. *Snow Goose* (p. 57): blue morph has white head and upper neck. *Double-crested Cormorant* (p. 44): lacks white "chin strap" and undertail coverts; crooked neck in flight.

Best Sites: ***MN:*** Lac Qui Parle WMA; Chippewa Co.; Big Stone Co. ***WI:*** Horicon Marsh; Arlington ponds; Crex Meadows WA; Shiocton–Black Creek; Theresa Marsh; Grand River Marsh.

MUTE SWAN

Cygnus olor

Admired for its grace and beauty, this Eurasian native was introduced to eastern North America in the mid-1800s to adorn estates and city parks. Over the years, Mute Swans have adapted well to the North American environment. They have continued to expand their feral populations, and although they are not usually migratory, more northerly nesters have established short migratory routes to milder wintering areas. • Like many nonnative species, Mute Swans are often fierce competitors for nesting areas and food sources. They can be very aggressive toward geese and ducks, often displacing native species. Of particular concern is the negative influence Mute Swans have on the Common Loon and Trumpeter Swan—both native species in our area. • A reliable long-distance characteristic for distinguishing a Mute Swan from a native swan is the way a Mute Swan holds its neck in a graceful curve with its orange bill hanging down.

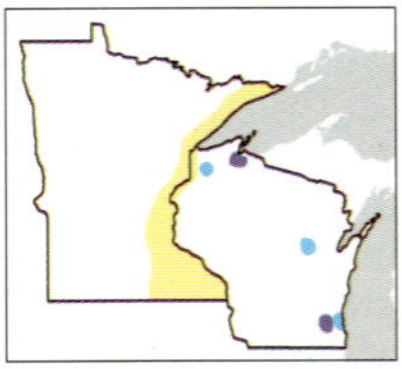

ID: all-white plumage; orange bill with down-turned tip; black, bulbous knob at base of bill; neck is usually held in an S-shape; wings are often held in an arch over back while swimming. *Immature:* plumage may be white to grayish brown.

Size: *L* 5 ft; *W* 7½–8 ft.

Status: ***MN:*** wild birds are rare vagrants that may occur in the eastern part of the state at any time; also occurs as a released or escaped bird. ***WI:*** locally common resident at scattered sites in northern and southern regions.

Habitat: marshes, lakes and ponds.

Nesting: on the ground along a shoreline; male helps gather nest material; female builds a mound of vegetation and incubates 5–10 pale green eggs for about 36 days; pair tends the young.

Feeding: tips up or dips its head below the water's surface for aquatic plants; grazes on land.

Voice: generally silent; may hiss or issue hoarse barking notes; loud wingbeats can be heard from up to half a mile away.

Similar Species: *Tundra Swan* (p. 62) and *Trumpeter Swan* (p. 61): lack orange bill with black knob at base; neck is usually held straight.

Best Sites: ***MN:*** no consistent sites. ***WI:*** Ashland; Chequamegon Bay; various lakes in Waukesha Co.

TRUMPETER SWAN

Cygnus buccinator

The Trumpeter Swan was hunted nearly to extinction in the early 20th century. Breeding populations in Alaska and western Canada persisted, but eastern populations were less fortunate and the bird was extirpated in our region. Attempts to reintroduce the Trumpeter Swan to former parts of its breeding range are meeting with success in certain areas. In 1966, Minnesota pioneered the effort to reestablish this bird. By the 1980s, Trumpeter Swan recovery programs had been initiated in Wisconsin, Michigan and Minnesota by state natural resources agencies. • Both "trumpeter" and *buccinator* refer to this bird's loud, bugling voice, which is produced when air is forced through the long windpipe that runs through the keel of the bird's breastbone. • The neck of a Trumpeter Swan is twice the length of its body. This magnificent bird is the world's largest species of waterfowl.

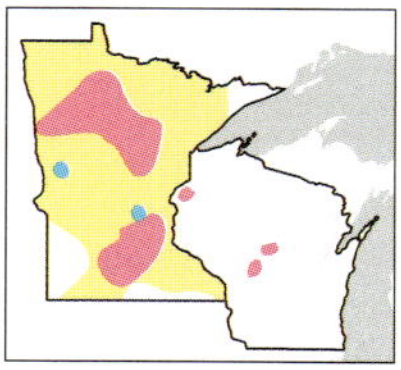

ID: all-white plumage; large, solid black bill; black skin extends from bill to eyes; black feet; neck is kinked at base when standing or swimming. *Immature:* gray brown plumage; gray bill.

Size: *L* 5–6 ft; *W* 6–7 ft.

Status: ***MN:*** reintroduced; threatened; approximately 1500 birds in the state; breeds in widely scattered localities; most winter at Fergus Falls or Monticello. ***WI:*** reintroduced; endangered; uncommon breeder in northern regions and on scattered lakes in the central region; there has been a limited expansion of current nesting areas.

Habitat: lakes and large wetlands; extremely local.

Nesting: on shore, on a small island or on a muskrat or beaver lodge; always close to water; male gathers marsh plants such as cattails, bulrushes, sedges and grasses; female constructs a nest mound and lines it with down; mostly the female incubates 4–6 creamy white to dull white eggs for 32–37 days.

Feeding: tips up, surface gleans and occasionally grazes for vegetation; primarily eats pondweeds, duckweed, aquatic tubers and roots.

Voice: loud, resonant, buglelike *koh-hoh.*

Similar Species: *Tundra Swan* (p. 62): smaller; more common; often shows yellow lores; neck and head are rounder; softer, more nasal voice. *Mute Swan* (p. 60): orange, downpointed bill with black knob on upper base; neck is usually held in an S-shape; wings are often held in an arch over back while swimming. *Snow Goose* (p. 57): smaller; black wing tips; shorter neck; pinkish bill.

Best Sites: ***MN:*** Tamarac NWR; winters in Fergus Falls (Otter Tail Co.) and on the Mississippi R. at Monticello (Wright Co.). ***WI:*** Crex Meadows WA; Mead WA; Bear Bluff area.

TUNDRA SWAN

Cygnus columbianus

Before the last of the winter's snows have melted into the fields, Tundra Swans return to our region, bringing us the first whispers of spring. Massive flocks of these swans soar over cities and fields, stopping to refuel on waste grain and aquatic vegetation before continuing on to their arctic breeding grounds. • Of the three species of swans that may be seen in our region, the Tundra Swan is the most likely to be seen in the wild. Distinguishing among swan species comes down to the bill: the bright orange bill of the Mute Swan is hard to mistake, while the subtle difference in slope between the bills of the Tundra Swan and the Trumpeter Swan, and the yellow at the base of the Tundra's bill, can be more difficult to discern. • Members of the Lewis and Clark expedition found this bird near the Columbia River, thus its scientific name *columbianus.*

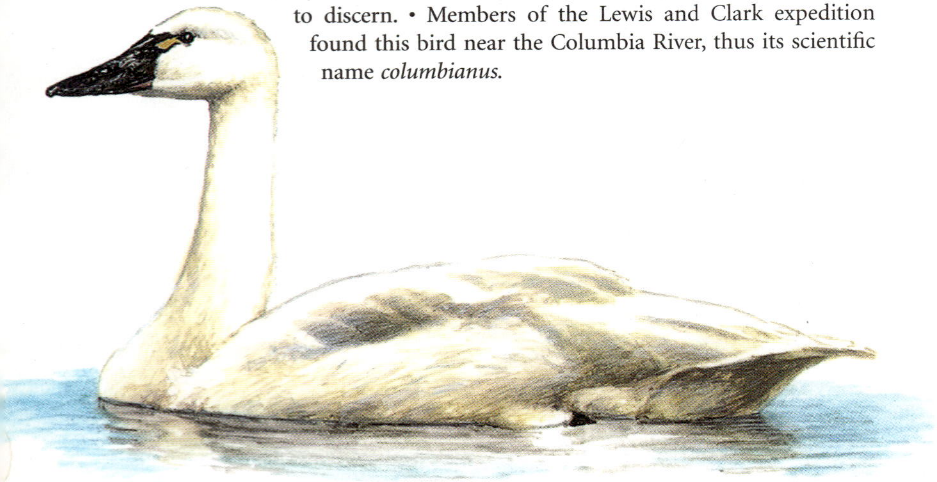

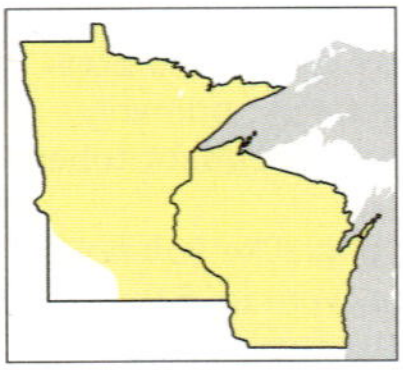

ID: white plumage; large, black bill; black feet; often shows yellow lores; neck is held straight up; neck and head show rounded, slightly curving profile. *Immature:* gray brown plumage; gray bill.

Size: *L* 4–5 ft; *W* 6½ ft.

Status: ***MN:*** common migrant from late March to mid-May and in November; rare migrant in the southwest; a few summer and winter records. ***WI:*** common migrant from March through April and from October to early December.

Habitat: shallow areas of lakes and wetlands, agricultural fields and flooded pastures.

Nesting: does not nest in our region.

Feeding: tips up, dabbles and surface gleans for aquatic vegetation and aquatic invertebrates; grazes for tubers, roots and waste grain.

Voice: high-pitched, quivering *oo-oo-whoo* is constantly repeated by migrating flocks.

Similar Species: *Trumpeter Swan* (p. 61): larger; loud, buglelike voice; lacks yellow lores; neck and head show more angular profile. *Mute Swan* (p. 60): orange bill with black knob on upper base; neck is usually held in an S-shape; downpointed bill; wings are often held in an arch over back while swimming. *Snow Goose* (p. 57): smaller; black wing tips; shorter neck; pinkish bill.

Best Sites: ***MN:*** Weaver Bottoms (Wabasha Co.) in fall; St. Louis R. estuary (Duluth); L. Traverse; Houston Co. ***WI:*** Shiocton–Black Creek and Arlington ponds in spring; along the Mississippi R. north and south of La Crosse in fall.

WOOD DUCK

Aix sponsa

The male Wood Duck is one of the most colorful waterbirds in North America, and books, magazines, postcards and calendars routinely celebrate its beauty. • Truly birds of the forest, Wood Ducks will nest in trees that are a mile or more from the nearest body of water. Forced into the adventures of life at an early age, newly hatched ducklings often jump 20 feet out of their nest cavity in a tree to follow their mother to the nearest body of water. The little bundles of down are not exactly feather light, but they bounce fairly well and seldom sustain injury. • Landowners with a tree-lined beaver pond or other suitable wetland may attract a family of Wood Ducks by building a nest box with a predator guard and lining it with sawdust. The nest box should be erected close to the wetland shoreline at a reasonable height, usually at least 5 feet from the ground. • The scientific name *sponsa* is Latin for "promised bride," suggesting that the male appears formally dressed for a wedding.

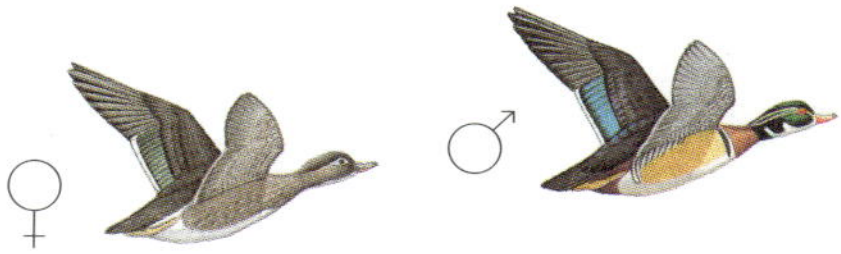

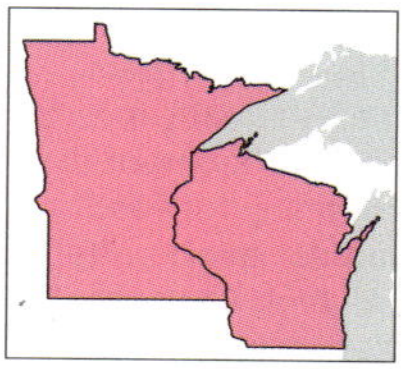

ID: *Male:* glossy green head with some white streaks; crest is slicked back from crown; white "chin" and throat; white-spotted, purplish chestnut breast; black-and-white shoulder slash; golden sides; dark back and hindquarters. *Female:* white, teardrop-shaped eye patch; mottled brown breast is streaked with white; gray brown upperparts; white belly.
Size: *L* 15–20 in; *W* 30 in.
Status: ***MN:*** common migrant and breeder from March to October; occasional in winter. ***WI:*** common migrant and breeder from March to early November; rare winter visitor.
Habitat: beaver ponds, swamps, ponds, marshes and lakeshores with wooded edges.

Nesting: in a hollow or tree cavity (may be 30 ft or more above the ground); also in an artificial nest box; usually near water; cavity is lined with down; female incubates 9–14 white to buff eggs for 25–35 days.
Feeding: gleans the water's surface and tips up for aquatic vegetation, especially duckweed, aquatic sedges and grasses; eats more fruits and nuts than other ducks.
Voice: *Male:* ascending *ter-wee-wee.* *Female:* squeaky *woo-e-e-k.*
Similar Species: *Hooded Merganser* (p. 85): male has black head with white crest patch; slim, black bill; black-and-white breast. *Harlequin Duck* (p. 78): male is blue gray overall with black-and-white patches; female has unstreaked breast and white ear patch.
Best Sites: ***MN:*** wooded habitat along streams, marshes and lakes; Tamarac NWR; Lac Qui Parle WMA. ***WI:*** Horicon Marsh: Rat River WA; Mississippi R.

GADWALL

Anas strepera

Male Gadwalls lack the striking plumage of most other male ducks, but they nevertheless have a dignified appearance and a subtle beauty. Once you learn their field marks, a black rump and white wing patches, Gadwalls are surprisingly easy to identify. • Ducks in the genus *Anas,* the dabbling ducks, are most often observed tipping up their hindquarters and submerging their heads to feed, but Gadwalls dive more frequently than others of this group. These ducks feed equally during the day and night, a strategy that reduces the risk of predation because the birds avoid spending long periods of time sleeping or feeding. • Gadwall numbers have greatly increased in this area since the 1950s, and this duck has expanded its range throughout North America. The majority of Gadwalls winter on the Gulf Coast of the U.S. and Mexico, although increasing numbers overwinter on inland lakes across the country, including the Great Lakes region.

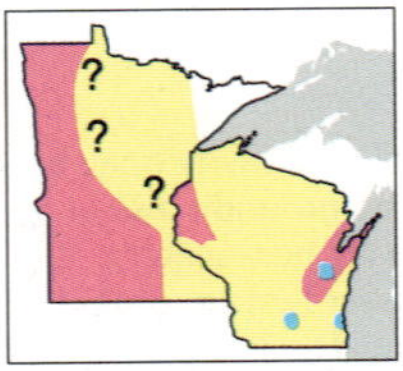

ID: white speculum; white belly. *Male:* mostly gray; black hindquarters; dark bill. *Female:* mottled brown overall; brown bill with orange sides.

Size: *L* 18–22 in; *W* 33 in.

Status: ***MN:*** common migrant from early March to mid-May and from mid-September to early December in central and western regions; expanding northward; uncommon breeder; occasional in winter, especially in east-central and southeastern regions. ***WI:*** common migrant from March to May and from September to November; uncommon breeder; uncommon winter visitor in the south.

Habitat: shallow wetlands, lake borders and beaver ponds.

Nesting: in tall vegetation, sometimes far from water; nest is well concealed in a scraped-out hollow, often with grass arching overhead; nest is made of grass and other dry vegetation and lined with down; female incubates 8–11 white eggs for 24–27 days.

Feeding: dabbles and tips up for water plants; grazes on grass and waste grain during migration; also eats aquatic invertebrates, tadpoles and small fish; one of the few dabblers to dive routinely for food.

Voice: *Male:* simple, singular quack; often whistles harshly. *Female:* high *kaak kaaak kak-kak-kak,* given in series and oscillating in volume.

Similar Species: *American Wigeon* (p. 65): green speculum; male has white forehead and green swipe trailing from eye; female lacks black hindquarters. *Mallard* (p. 67), *Northern Pintail* (p. 71) and *other dabbling ducks* (pp. 63–72): generally lack white speculum and black hindquarters of male Gadwall and orange-sided beak of female.

Best Sites: ***MN:*** Agassiz NWR; Minnesota R. valley (Scott Co.). ***WI:*** Green Bay; Horicon Marsh; Crex Meadows WA; Madison-McFarland, Neenah-Menasha and Milwaukee in winter.

AMERICAN WIGEON

Anas americana

The male American Wigeon's characteristic, piping, three-syllable whistle sets it apart from the wetland orchestra of buzzes, quacks and ticks. • Although this bird frequently dabbles for food, nothing seems to please a wigeon more than the succulent stems and leaves of pond-bottom plants. These plants grow far too deep for a dabbling duck, however, so wigeons often pirate from accomplished divers, such as American Coots, Canvasbacks, Redheads and scaups. In contrast to most ducks, the American Wigeon is a good walker and is commonly observed grazing on shore. • The American Wigeon nests farther north than any other dabbling duck with the exception of the Northern Pintail. Pair bonds are strong and last well into incubation. • The name "wigeon" comes from a French word meaning "whistling duck." Because of the male's bright white crown and forehead, some people call this bird "Baldpate."

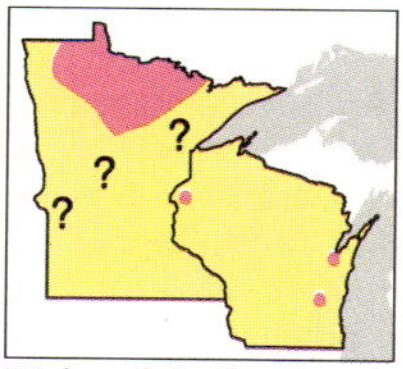

ID: large, white upperwing patch; cinnamon breast and sides; white belly; black-tipped, gray blue bill; green speculum; white "wing pits." *Male:* white forehead; green swipe extends back from eye. *Female:* grayish head; brown underparts.

Size: *L* $18–22\frac{1}{2}$ in; *W* 32 in.

Status: ***MN:*** common migrant from early March to early June and from mid-August to mid-December; uncommon breeder; occasional in winter in the south. ***WI:*** special concern; common migrant from March to May and from late August to November; uncommon to rare breeder; uncommon winter visitor.

Habitat: shallow wetlands, lake edges and ponds.

Nesting: always on dry ground, often far from water; nest is well concealed in tall vegetation and is built with grass, leaves and down; female incubates 8–11 white eggs for 23–25 days.

Feeding: dabbles and tips up for the leaves and stems of aquatic plants; also grazes and uproots young shoots in fields; may eat some invertebrates; occasionally pirates food from other birds.

Voice: *Male:* nasal, frequently repeated whistle: *whee WHEE wheew. Female:* soft, seldom heard quack.

Similar Species: *Gadwall* (p. 64): white speculum; lacks large, white upperwing patch; male lacks green eye swipe; female has orange swipes on bill. *Eurasian Wigeon* (p. 357): gray "wing pits"; male has rufous head, cream forehead and rosy breast; lacks green eye swipe; female usually has browner head.

Best Sites: ***MN:*** Agassiz NWR; Swan L. (Nicollet Co.). ***WI:*** Green Bay; Horicon Marsh; Mississippi R.; Madison-McFarland and Milwaukee in winter.

AMERICAN BLACK DUCK

Anas rubripes

Once a very common duck, the American Black Duck population has decreased in recent years because of habitat loss, plus competition and hybridizing by Mallards. A male Mallard will aggressively pursue a female American Black Duck, and if she is unable to find a mate of her own kind, she will often accept the offer. Hybrid offspring are less fertile and are usually unable to reproduce. To the abundant Mallard it is not a loss, but to the American Black Duck it is a further setback. • This duck usually feeds in shallows where it is able to probe the mud by dabbling, searching below the water's surface with only its rump left exposed. In summer, it will eat aquatic insects, salamanders, small frogs and anything else that it is able to snatch up. • Male and female American Black Ducks are remarkably similar in appearance, which is unusual for waterfowl.

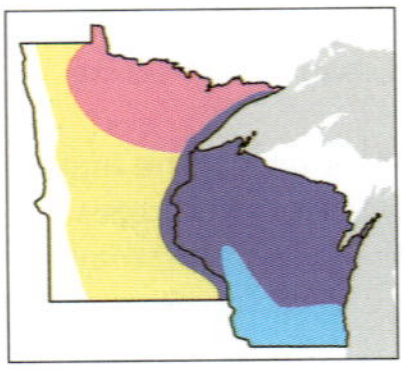

ID: dark brownish black body; light brown head and neck; bright orange feet; violet speculum. *Male:* yellow olive bill. *Female:* dull green bill mottled with gray or black. *In flight:* whitish underwings; dark body.

Size: *L* 20–24 in; *W* 35 in.

Status: ***MN:*** uncommon migrant from March to April and from October to November in eastern and northern regions, rare in other regions; rare and declining breeder in northeastern and north-central regions; regular winter visitor where there is open water. ***WI:*** common migrant from mid-March to May and from mid-September to November; fairly common breeder in the north; uncommon breeder in central and southern areas; fairly common winter visitor.

Habitat: lakes, wetlands, rivers and agricultural areas.

Nesting: usually on the ground among clumps of dense vegetation near water; female fills a shallow depression with plant material and lines it with down; female incubates 7–11 white to greenish buff eggs for 26–28 days; second clutches are common, usually to replace lost broods.

Feeding: tips up and dabbles in shallows for seeds and roots of pondweeds; also eats aquatic invertebrates, larval amphibians and fish eggs.

Voice: *Male:* a croak. *Female:* a loud quack.

Similar Species: *Mallard* (p. 67): white belly; blue speculum bordered with white; female is lighter overall and has white outer tail feathers. *Gadwall* (p. 64): black hindquarters; white speculum.

Best Sites: ***MN:*** Rice Lake NWR; Weaver Bottoms (Wabasha Co.); Agassiz NWR. ***WI:*** Horicon Marsh; Green Bay; Ashland; Green Bay, Neenah-Menasha, Madison and Milwaukee in winter.

MALLARD

Anas platyrhynchos

The male Mallard, with his iridescent, green head and chestnut brown breast, is the classic wild duck. Mallards can be seen almost any day of the year, often in flocks and always near open water. These confident ducks have even been known to take up residence in local swimming pools. • As well as captivating female American Black Ducks, wild Mallards will freely hybridize with domestic ducks, which were originally derived from Mallards in Europe. The resulting offspring are a confusing blend of both parents. • Male ducks molt after breeding, losing much of their extravagant plumage. This "eclipse" plumage camouflages them during their flightless period. They usually molt again into their breeding colors by early fall. • The scientific name *platyrhynchos* means "broad, flat bill" in Greek.

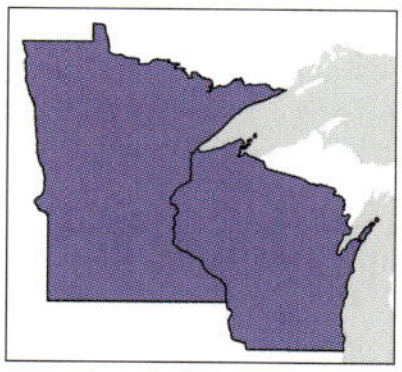

ID: dark blue speculum bordered with white; orange feet. *Male:* glossy, green head; yellow bill; chestnut brown breast; white "necklace"; gray body plumage; black tail feathers curl upward. *Female:* mottled brown overall; orange bill is spattered with black.
Size: *L* 20–27½ in; *W* 35 in.
Status: ***MN:*** abundant migrant and breeder from March to November; common winter visitor where there is open water, mainly in central and southern regions. ***WI:*** abundant year-round resident.
Habitat: lakes, wetlands, rivers, city parks, agricultural areas and sewage lagoons.
Nesting: in tall vegetation or under a bush, often near water; nest of grass and other plant material is lined with down; female incubates 7–10 light green to white eggs for 26–30 days.
Feeding: tips up and dabbles in shallows for the seeds of sedges, willows and pondweeds; also eats insects, aquatic invertebrates, larval amphibians and fish eggs.
Voice: *Male:* deep, quiet quacks. *Female:* loud quacks; very vocal.
Similar Species: *Northern Shoveler* (p. 70): much larger bill; male has white breast. *American Black Duck* (p. 66): darker than female Mallard; purple speculum lacks white border. *Common Merganser* (p. 86): blood red bill and white underparts; male lacks chestnut brown breast.
Best Sites: ***MN:*** Agassiz NWR; Lac Qui Parle WMA. ***WI:*** lakes, ponds and marshes, such as Horicon Marsh, Green Bay and Mead WA.

BLUE-WINGED TEAL

Anas discors

Blue-winged Teals are one of the last ducks to return in spring and the last to establish pair ponds, often waiting until they are on their breeding grounds. Males defend their female partners, but do not establish territories. As a result, Blue-wings have more nests concentrated in a small area than any other waterfowl. • The small, speedy Blue-winged Teal is renowned for its aviation skills. These teals can be identified in flight by their small size and by the sharp twists and turns that they execute with precision. • Despite the similarity of their names, the Green-winged Teal is not the Blue-winged Teal's closest relative. The Blue-winged Teal is more closely related to the Cinnamon Teal and the Northern Shoveler. Female Cinnamon Teals are so similar in appearance to female Blue-winged Teals that even expert birders and ornithologists have difficulty distinguishing them in the field.

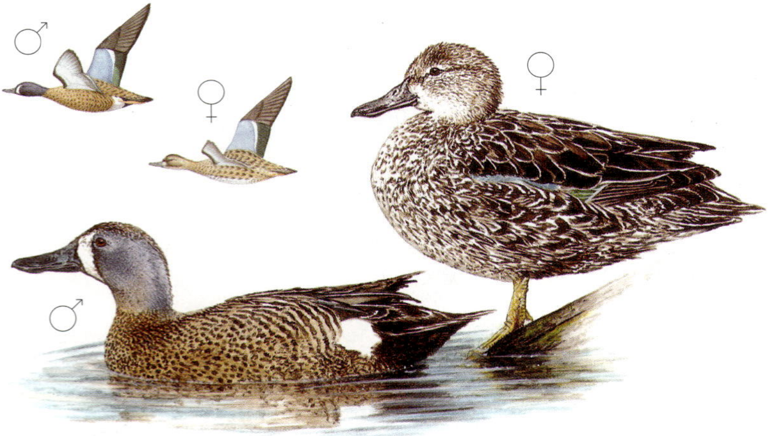

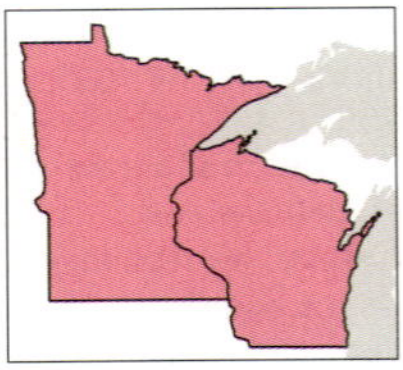

ID: *Male:* blue gray head; white crescent on face; black-spotted breast and sides; round, white patch on rear flank. *Female:* mottled brown overall. *In flight:* blue forewing patch; green speculum.

Size: *L* 14–16 in; *W* 23 in.

Status: ***MN:*** common migrant and breeder from April to September. ***WI:*** special concern; abundant migrant and breeder from late March to October; rare winter visitor.

Habitat: shallow lake edges and wetlands; prefers areas of short but dense emergent vegetation.

Nesting: in grass along a shoreline or in a meadow; nest is built with grass and considerable amounts of down; female incubates 8–13 white eggs, sometimes tinged with olive, for 23–27 days.

Feeding: gleans the water's surface for sedge and grass seeds, pondweeds, duckweeds and aquatic invertebrates.

Voice: *Male:* soft *keck-keck-keck*. *Female:* soft quacks.

Similar Species: *Cinnamon Teal* (p. 69): female is virtually identical to female Blue-winged Teal, but brown is richer and eye line is less distinct. *Green-winged Teal* (p. 72): female has smaller bill, black-and-green speculum and lacks blue forewing patch. *Northern Shoveler* (p. 70): much larger bill with paler base; male has green head and lacks spotting on body.

Best Sites: ***MN:*** Agassiz NWR; Swan L. (Nicollet Co.); wetland areas throughout the state. ***WI:*** marshes, ponds and lakes, such as Horicon Marsh, Mead WA and Crex Meadows WA.

CINNAMON TEAL

Anas cyanoptera

When the morning sun strikes a spring wetland, the male Cinnamon Teal glows upon the water like an ember. The intense reddish brown plumage, accented by ruby red eyes, makes this bird worth admiring at any time of day. • Female ducks of most species are abandoned by their mates during nesting, but female Cinnamon Teals may be accompanied by their partners throughout the nesting cycle. Males have sometimes even been seen accompanying their mates and young. • Cinnamon Teals appear very rarely and irregularly in our region and are usually seen together with Blue-winged Teals and Green-winged Teals, so check each teal carefully. • The scientific name—from *cyano,* "blue," and *pteron,* "wing"—refers to this bird's blue forewing patch, which is easily seen when the bird is in flight. It also reinforces the similarities of this species to the Blue-winged Teal, with which it may occasionally interbreed.

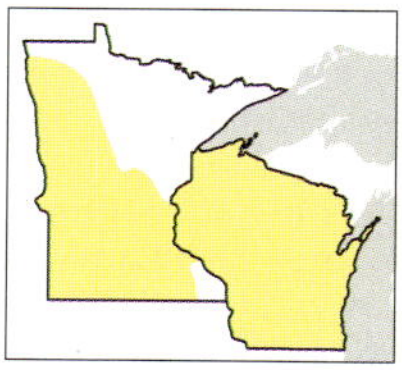

ID: long, broad bill; blue forewing patch; green speculum. *Male:* intense cinnamon red head, neck and underparts; red eyes. *Female:* mottled warm brown overall; dark eyes.
Size: *L* 15–17 in; *W* 22 in.
Status: ***MN:*** rare migrant from mid-April to early June; casual migrant from late August to October, mainly in western regions with a scattering of records in central regions. ***WI:*** rare migrant from mid-April to May; very rare migrant from October to November.
Habitat: shallow wetlands with extensive emergent vegetation and sedge beds.
Nesting: does not nest in our region.
Feeding: dabbles in shallow water for grass and sedge seeds, pondweeds, duckweeds and aquatic invertebrates; occasionally tips up.
Voice: *Male:* whistled *peep. Female:* rough *karr, karr, karr.*
Similar Species: *Ruddy Duck* (p. 88): male has white "cheek," blue bill and stiff, upward-angled tail. *Green-winged Teal* (p. 72): small bill; gray body; white shoulder slash; green streak trails from eye. *Blue-winged Teal* (p. 68): male has white crescent in front of eye.
Best Sites: ***MN:*** no consistent sites, but Salt L. (Lac Qui Parle Co.) is possibly the best location. ***WI:*** no consistent sites.

NORTHERN SHOVELER

Anas clypeata

The initial reaction upon meeting this bird for the first time is often, "Wow, look at the big honker on that Mallard!" A closer look, however, will reveal a completely different bird altogether—the Northern Shoveler. An extra large, spoonlike bill allows this handsome duck to strain small invertebrates from the water and from the mud on the bottom of ponds. The shoveler's specialized feeding strategy means that it is rarely seen tipping up, but is more often found in the shallows of ponds and marshes where the mucky bottom is easiest to access. • During the breeding season, male Northern Shovelers fiercely defend small feeding territories. However, they are remarkably sociable during migration and on their wintering grounds. • The scientific name *clypeata* is Latin for "furnished with a shield," possibly for the chestnut patches on the flanks of the male.

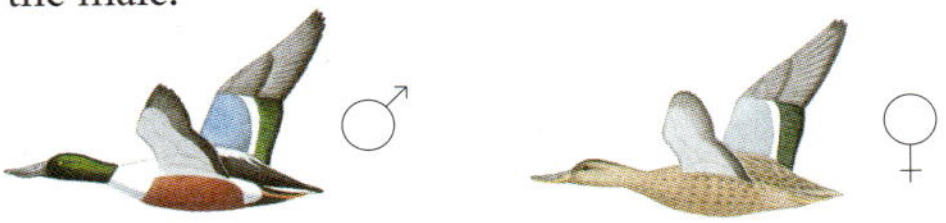

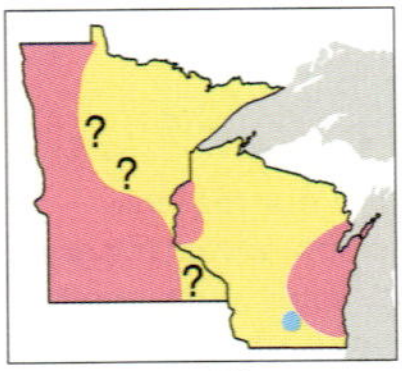

ID: large, spatulate bill; blue forewing patch; green speculum. *Male:* green head; white breast; chestnut brown flanks. *Female:* mottled brown overall; orange-tinged bill.
Size: *L* 18–20 in; *W* 30 in.
Status: ***MN:*** common migrant from early March to mid-May and from August to early December, except in north-central and northeastern regions; increasing rapidly in all regions; uncommon breeder; rare in winter in the south. ***WI:*** common migrant from mid-March to early June and from September to November; uncommon breeder; uncommon winter visitor.
Habitat: shallow marshes, bogs and lakes with muddy bottoms and emergent vegetation, usually in open and semi-open areas.
Nesting: in a shallow hollow on dry ground, usually near water; female builds a nest of dry grass and down and incubates 10–12 pale greenish buff eggs for 21–28 days.
Feeding: dabbles in shallow and often muddy water; strains out plant and animal matter, especially aquatic crustaceans, insect larvae and seeds; rarely tips up.
Voice: generally quiet; occasionally a raspy chuckle or quack; most often heard during spring courtship.
Similar Species: *Mallard* (p. 67): blue speculum bordered by white; lacks pale blue forewing patch; male has chestnut brown breast and white flanks. *Blue-winged Teal* (p. 68): much smaller bill; smaller overall; male has spotted breast and sides.
Best Sites: ***MN:*** Agassiz NWR; Big Stone NWR. ***WI:*** Horicon Marsh; Green Bay; Mead WA; Madison-McFarland and Milwaukee in winter.

NORTHERN PINTAIL

Anas acuta

The trademark of the elegant and graceful male Northern Pintail is its long, tapering tail feathers, which are easily seen in flight and point skyward when he dabbles. In our region, only the male Long-tailed Duck shares this pintail feature. • Migrating pintails are often seen in flocks of 20 to 40 birds, but some flocks have been known to consist of nearly 10,000 individuals. Spring-flooded agricultural fields tend to attract the largest pintail flocks. In the fall, migrating flocks often have almost twice as many males as females, probably the result of summer predation on the fairly open ground nesting sites. • Pintails breed earlier than most waterfowl, and in this region begin nesting in mid-April. Unfortunately, many Northern Pintail nests are destroyed each year by predators and agricultural activity.

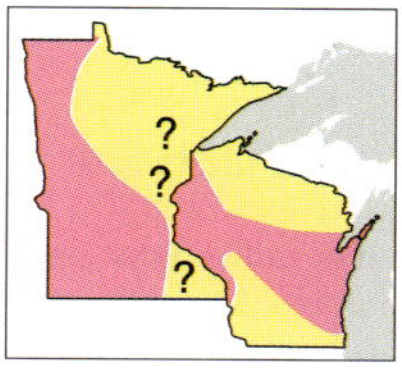

ID: long, slender neck; dark, glossy bill. *Male:* chocolate brown head; long, tapering tail feathers; white on breast extends up sides of neck; dusty gray body plumage; black-and-white hindquarters. *Female:* mottled light brown overall. *In flight:* slender body; brownish speculum with white trailing edge.
Size: *L* 21–25 in; 34 in.
Status: ***MN:*** uncommon migrant from late February to early May and from early September to early December; best represented in western regions; uncommon breeder; occasional in winter in southern regions. ***WI:*** common migrant from March to mid-May and from late August to November; uncommon breeder; rare winter visitor.
Habitat: shallow wetlands, fields and lake edges.

Nesting: in a small depression in low vegetation; nest of grass, leaves and moss is lined with down; female incubates 6–12 greenish buff eggs for 22–25 days.
Feeding: tips up and dabbles in shallows for the seeds of sedges, willows and pondweeds; also eats aquatic invertebrates and larval amphibians; eats waste grain in agricultural areas during migration; diet is more varied than other dabbling ducks.
Voice: *Male:* soft, whistling call. *Female:* rough quack.
Similar Species: male is distinctive. *Mallard* (p. 67) and *Gadwall* (p. 64): females are chunkier, usually with dark or 2-tone bills, and lack tapering tail and long, slender neck. *Blue-winged Teal* (p. 68): green speculum; blue forewing patch; female is smaller. *Long-tailed Duck* (p. 82): head is not uniformly dark; all-dark wings.
Best Sites: ***MN:*** Agassiz NWR; Big Stone NWR; Sherburne NWR. ***WI:*** Shiocton–Black Creek; Horicon Marsh; Arlington ponds; Crex Meadows WA.

GREEN-WINGED TEAL

Anas crecca

Green-winged Teals are among the speediest and most maneuverable of waterfowl. When startled by intruders, these small ducks rocket up from wetlands and circle quickly overhead in tight-flying flocks, returning to the water only when the threat has departed. A predator's only hope of catching a healthy teal is to snatch it from the water or from a nest. Although female Green-winged Teals go to great lengths to conceal their nests among grasses and brush, there are always those that are discovered by predators. • Weighing less than a pound, the Green-winged Teal is the smallest dabbling duck in North America. These lovely little teals often loiter on ponds and marshy wetlands until cold winter weather freezes the water's surface. • The name "teal" possibly originated from the medieval English word *tele* or the old Dutch word *teling,* both of which mean "small" and which originally referred to the Green-winged Teal's Eurasian counterpart.

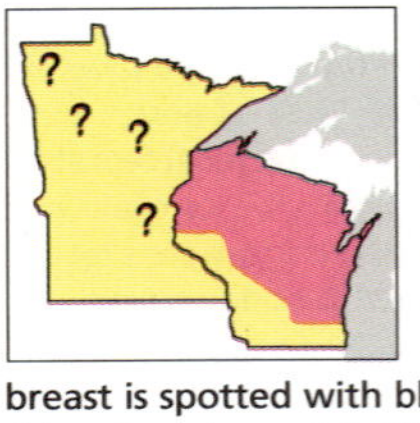

ID: small bill; black-and-green speculum. *Male:* chestnut brown head; green swipe extends back from eye; white shoulder slash; creamy breast is spotted with black; pale gray sides. *Female:* mottled brown overall; light belly.

Size: *L* 12–16 in; *W* 23 in.

Status: ***MN:*** common migrant from early March to mid-May and from late August to early December; rare breeder in the northwest, but pairs can be found almost anywhere in the state; occasional in winter in southern regions. ***WI:*** common migrant from mid-March to early May and from late August to November; uncommon breeder; rare winter visitor.

Habitat: shallow lakes, wetlands, beaver ponds and meandering rivers.

Nesting: well concealed in tall vegetation; nest is built of grass and leaves and lined with down; female incubates 6–14 cream to pale buff eggs for 20–24 days.

Feeding: dabbles in shallows, particularly on mudflats, for aquatic invertebrates, larval amphibians, marsh plant seeds and pondweeds.

Voice: *Male:* crisp whistle. *Female:* soft quack.

Similar Species: *American Wigeon* (p. 65): male lacks white shoulder slash and chestnut brown head. *Blue-winged Teal* (p. 68) and *Cinnamon Teal* (p. 69): female has blue forewing patch.

Best Sites: ***MN:*** Agassiz NWR; Big Stone NWR. ***WI:*** Horicon Marsh; Arlington ponds; Shiocton–Black Creek; Crex Meadows WA.

CANVASBACK

Aythya valisineria

While most male ducks sport richly decorated backs, the male Canvasback has a bright, clean back that, appropriately, appears to be wrapped in white canvas. In profile, the Canvasback casts a noble image—the long bill meets the forecrown with no apparent break in angle, allowing birds of either sex to be distinguished at long range. This bird's back and unique profile are unmistakable field marks. • Canvasbacks are devoted deep divers and seldom stray into areas of wetlands that are too shallow to allow foraging dives. Because these ducks prefer the deepest areas of wetlands, birders often need binoculars to admire the male's wild red eyes and rich mahogany head. Canvasbacks are most likely to be seen during spring and fall migration, when flocks composed of more than 10,000 individuals occasionally converge on a suitable wetland. • The scientific name *valisineria* refers to one of the Canvasback's favorite foods—wild celery *(Vallisneria americana).*

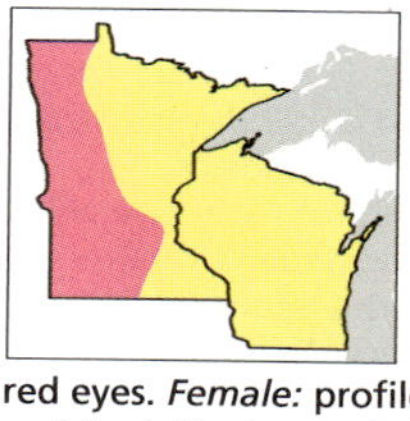

ID: head slopes upward from bill to forehead. *Male:* canvas white back and sides; chestnut brown head and neck; black breast and hindquarters; red eyes. *Female:* profile is similar to male's; duller brown head and neck; grayish back and sides.

Size: *L* 19–22 in; *W* 29 in.

Status: ***MN:*** common migrant from early March to mid-May and from late September to mid-December; uncommon breeder, primarily in the northwest; occasional in winter in southeastern and east-central regions. ***WI:*** common migrant from mid-March to May and especially from October to November; very rare to casual breeder; uncommon to rare winter visitor.

Habitat: marshes, ponds, shallow lakes and other wetlands; large lakes in migration.

Nesting: basket nest of reeds and grass is lined with down and suspended above shallow water in dense stands of cattails and bulrushes; may also nest on dry ground; female incubates 7–9 olive green eggs for up to 29 days.

Feeding: dives to depths of up to 30 ft (average is 10–15 ft); feeds on roots, tubers, the basal stems of plants, including pondweeds and wild celery, and bulrush seeds; occasionally eats aquatic invertebrates.

Voice: generally quiet. *Male:* occasional coos and "growls" during courtship. *Female:* low, soft, "purring" *quack* or *kuck;* also "growls."

Similar Species: *Redhead* (p. 74): rounded rather than sloped forehead; male has gray back and bluish bill.

Best Sites: ***MN:*** L. Christina (Douglas Co.); Reno; Agassiz NWR. ***WI:*** Goose Pond; L. Winnebago; Green L.; Puckaway L.; Shawano L.; Mississippi R. in fall (peaks of 150,000–300,000 birds).

REDHEAD

Aythya americana

Like the Canvasback, the Redhead is an abundant migrant in our region. Unlike the Canvasback, however, the Redhead maintains a more prominent presence in summer among our wetlands. To distinguish a Canvasback from a Redhead, most birders will tell you to contrast the ducks' profiles, but the most obvious difference between them is the color of their backs—the Canvasback has a white back, while the Redhead's is gray. • Redheads prefer large marshes for nesting, where they easily blend into the busy goings-on of summer wetland life. Female Redheads usually incubate their own eggs and brood their young as other ducks do, but they occasionally lay their eggs in the nests of other ducks. In our region, the Blue-winged Teal, Gadwall and Ring-necked Duck may all be victims of Redhead egg dumping, otherwise known as "brood parasitism." • The Redhead is a diving duck, but it will occasionally feed on the surface of a wetland like a dabbler.

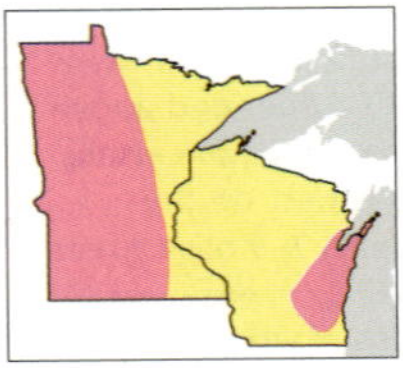

ID: black-tipped, blue gray bill. *Male:* rounded, red head; black breast and hindquarters; gray back and sides. *Female:* dark brown overall; light "chin" and "cheek" patches.
Size: *L* 18–22 in; *W* 29 in.
Status: ***MN:*** common migrant from early March to mid-May and from early September to early December; fairly common breeder primarily in western regions but expanding into central and eastern regions; occasional in winter in the south. ***WI:*** common migrant from mid-March to May and from late September to November; locally common breeder in eastern regions; uncommon winter visitor.
Habitat: large, shallow, well-vegetated wetlands, ponds and lakes; less often bays and rivers.
Nesting: usually in shallow water, sometimes on dry ground; deep basket nest of reeds and grass is suspended over water at the base of emergent vegetation and lined with fine, white down; female incubates 9–14 greenish eggs for 23–29 days; female may lay eggs in other ducks' nests.
Feeding: dives to depths of 10 ft; primarily eats aquatic vegetation, especially pondweeds, duckweeds and the leaves and stems of plants; occasionally eats aquatic invertebrates.
Voice: generally quiet. *Male:* catlike meow in courtship. *Female:* rolling *kurr-kurr-kurr; squak* when alarmed.
Similar Species: *Canvasback* (p. 73): clean white back; bill extends onto forehead. *Ring-necked Duck* (p. 75): female has more prominent white eye ring, white ring on bill and peaked head. *Lesser Scaup* (p. 77) and *Greater Scaup* (p. 76): prominent white wing bar; male has dark head and whiter sides; female has more white at base of bill.
Best Sites: ***MN:*** Agassiz NWR; Tamarac NWR; Big Stone NWR. ***WI:*** L. Michigan; L. Winnebago; Green Bay; Horicon Marsh.

RING-NECKED DUCK

Aythya collaris

The Ring-necked Duck's distinctive white bill markings and angular head are field marks that immediately strike an observer. After seeing the Ring-necked Duck in the wild, you may wonder why it was not named the "Ring-billed Duck," and you would not be the first birder to ponder this perplexing puzzle. The official appellation is derived from the scientific name *collaris* (collar), which originated with an ornithologist looking at an indistinct cinnamon "collar" on a museum specimen, not a birder looking at a live duck through binoculars. • Ring-necked Ducks are generalized feeders, allowing them to capitalize on the low resources found in the subarctic and boreal settings where they commonly nest. Although Ring-necks are diving ducks like scaups, Redheads and Canvasbacks, they behave more like dabbling ducks, frequently tipping up for food, hiding their young in dense vegetation and taking flight directly from the water.

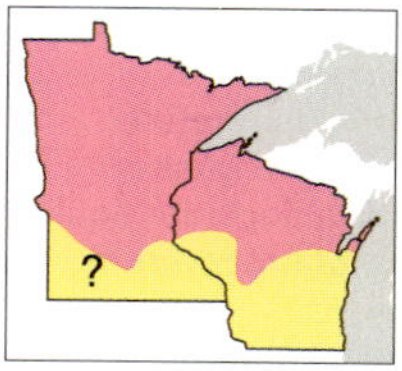

ID: *Male:* angular, dark purple head; black breast, back and hindquarters; white shoulder slash; gray sides; blue gray bill with black and white bands at tip; thin, white border around base of bill. *Female:* dark brown overall; white eye ring; dark bill with black and white bands at tip; pale crescent on front of face.

Size: *L* 14–18 in; *W* 25 in.

Status: ***MN:*** common migrant from early March to late May and from mid-September to early December; common breeder mainly in the north; occasional in winter in the south. ***WI:*** common migrant from mid-March to May and from mid-September to October; locally common breeder; rare winter visitor.

Habitat: reservoirs, shallow wooded ponds, swamps, marshes and sloughs with emergent vegetation.

Nesting: on a floating island or hummock; frequently over water; rarely on a shoreline; bulky nest of grass and moss is lined with down; female incubates 8–10 olive tan eggs for 25–29 days.

Feeding: dives underwater for aquatic vegetation, including seeds, tubers and pondweed leaves; also eats aquatic invertebrates and mollusks.

Voice: seldom heard. *Male:* low-pitched, hissing whistle. *Female:* growling *churr.*

Similar Species: *Lesser Scaup* (p. 77) and *Greater Scaup* (p. 76): lack white ring near tip of bill; male lacks black back; female has broad, clearly defined, white border around base of bill and lacks eye ring. *Redhead* (p. 74): rounded rather than peaked head; less white on front of face; female has less prominent eye ring.

Best Sites: ***MN:*** Rice Lake NWR; Agassiz NWR; Reno. ***WI:*** Crex Meadows WA; Shiocton–Black Creek; Arlington ponds; Horicon Marsh.

GREATER SCAUP

Aythya marila

Substantial flocks of Greater Scaup winter on Lake Michigan, where they can be seen alongside Long-tailed Ducks, scoters and Common Goldeneyes. In addition, this bird is abundant on both Lake Michigan and Lake Superior during migration. • Look for the rounder, not peaked, more greenish head of the Greater Scaup to distinguish it from its Lesser relative. The Lesser Scaup also has a lavender iridescence on its head, making it easy to remember which scaup is which by correlating the color of each duck's head with the corresponding letter of its name. However, scaups usually raft so far out in the water that specific identification is often not possible. • Scaups are diving ducks, which have a heavy bone structure, and as such they require a running start across the surface of the water to gain takeoff. • Both the Greater Scaup and the Lesser Scaup are known by the nickname "Bluebill."

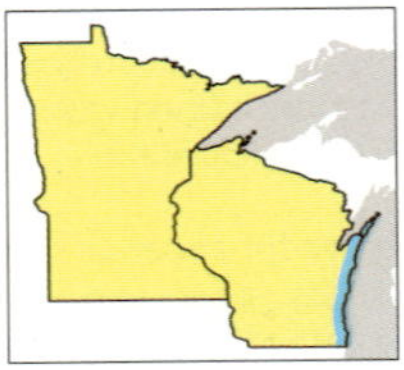

ID: rounded head; golden eyes. *Male:* iridescent, dark green head; black breast; white belly and flanks; light gray back; dark hindquarters; blue bill with black tip. *Female:* brown overall; well-defined white patch at base of bill. *In flight:* white flash through wing extends well into primary feathers.

Size: *L* 16–19 in; *W* 28 in.

Status: ***MN:*** common migrant from late March to early June and from early October to early December, mainly in the Mississippi R. valley, on L. Superior and on lakes in central and north-central regions; uncommon migrant elsewhere in the state. ***WI:*** common migrant from mid-March to May and from late September to December on L. Michigan and L. Superior; uncommon to rare inland migrant; common winter visitor on L. Michigan; rare winter visitor inland.

Habitat: lakes, large marshes and reservoirs, usually far from shore.

Nesting: does not nest in our region.

Feeding: dives underwater to greater depths than other *Aythya* ducks for aquatic invertebrates and vegetation; favors mollusks in winter.

Voice: generally quiet in migration; alarm call is a deep *scaup*. *Male:* may issue a 3-note whistle and a soft *wah-hooo*. *Female:* may give a subtle "growl."

Similar Species: *Lesser Scaup* (p. 77): slightly smaller; shorter white wing flash in flight; slightly smaller bill; male has peaked, purplish head; female usually has peaked head. *Ring-necked Duck* (p. 75): black back; white shoulder slash; white ring around base of bill. *Redhead* (p. 74): female has less white at base of bill; male has red head and darker sides.

Best Sites: ***MN:*** Duluth; L. Superior. ***WI:*** Milwaukee, Virmond Park and Harrington Beach SP (L. Michigan).

LESSER SCAUP

Aythya affinis

The male Lesser Scaup and its close relative, the male Greater Scaup, mirror the color pattern of an Oreo cookie: they are black at both ends and light in the middle. The Lesser Scaup is one of the most abundant and widespread North American ducks and is most at home among the lakes of forested areas. Although the Greater Scaup and Lesser Scaup may occur together on larger lakes during migration, they tend not to mingle. • A member of the *Aythya* genus of diving ducks, the Lesser Scaup leaps up neatly before diving underwater, where it propels itself with powerful strokes of its feet. • The name "scaup" might refer to a preferred winter food of this duck—shellfish beds are called "scalps" in Scotland—or it might be a phonetic imitation of one of this bird's calls.

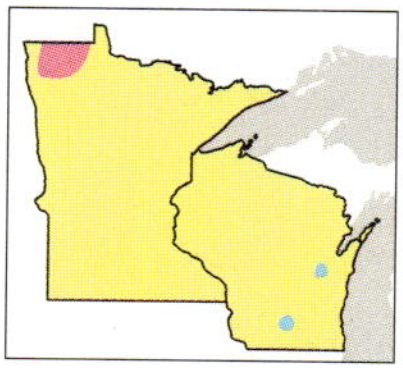

ID: yellow eyes. *Male:* peaked, dark purplish head; black breast and hindquarters; dusty white sides; grayish back; black-tipped, blue gray bill. *Female:* dark brown overall; well-defined white patch at base of bill.

Size: *L* 15–18 in; *W* 25 in.

Status: ***MN:*** common to abundant migrant from late February to late May and from mid-September to mid-December; may be declining; breeds sparingly only in northwestern region; uncommon in winter, mainly in the south. ***WI:*** abundant migrant from mid-March to mid-May and from October to November; uncommon to rare summer resident; casual breeder; uncommon winter visitor.

Habitat: *Breeding:* wetlands and lake edges with grassy margins. *In migration:* lakes, large marshes and rivers.

Nesting: in tall, concealing vegetation, generally close to water and occasionally on an island; nest hollow is built of grass and lined with down; female incubates 8–14 olive buff eggs for 21–27 days; usually nests later than other ducks.

Feeding: dives underwater for aquatic invertebrates, mostly mollusks, amphipods and insect larvae; occasionally eats aquatic vegetation.

Voice: alarm call is a deep *scaup*. *Male:* soft *whee-oooh* in courtship. *Female:* purring *kwah*.

Similar Species: *Greater Scaup* (p. 76): slightly larger bill; longer white wing flash; rounded head; male has greenish head. *Ring-necked Duck* (p. 75): male has white shoulder slash and black back; female has white-ringed bill. *Redhead* (p. 74): female has less white at base of bill; male has red head and darker sides.

Best Sites: ***MN:*** Mississippi R. (Winona Co.); Agassiz NWR; Reno; Sherburne NWR. ***WI:*** L. Winnebago; Arlington ponds; Shiocton–Black Creek; Green Bay; Mead WA; Mississippi R.

HARLEQUIN DUCK

Histrionicus histrionicus

The small, surf-loving Harlequin Duck is a rare migrant and winter visitor to our region, where it occupies the shorelines of the Great Lakes. Eastern Harlequin populations have dwindled to only about 1000 birds, but there seems to have been an increase in sightings, although by only a few each year. Though the length of its stay varies, this duck's dynamic appearance never fails to excite and impress fortunate onlookers. • In eastern North America, Harlequins breed along the northeastern Atlantic Coast of Canada, favoring fast-flowing, coastal mountain streams as breeding habitat. After a short breeding season, flocks of Harlequins move south, wintering primarily along the coast from Newfoundland south to New York State. • This duck is named after a character from traditional Italian comedy and pantomime, the Harlequin, who wore a diamond-patterned costume and performed "histrionics," or tricks. Some people refer to Harlequins as "Lords and Ladies."

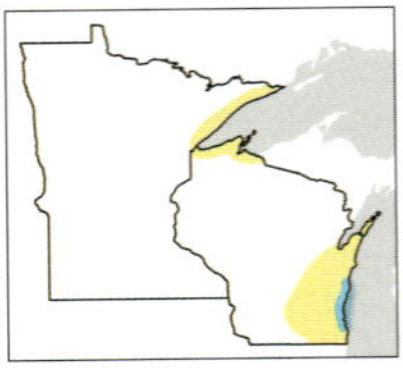

ID: small, rounded duck; blocky head; short bill; raises and lowers its tail while swimming. *Male:* blue gray body; chestnut brown sides; white spots and stripes are outlined in black on head, neck and flanks. *Female:* dusky brown overall; light underparts; 2–3 light-colored patches on head.
Size: *L* 14–19 in; *W* 26 in.
Status: ***MN:*** rare migrant and winter visitor, mainly along the North Shore of L. Superior; a few vagrant summer records. ***WI:*** rare migrant and winter visitor on L. Michigan and L. Superior; casual inland.
Habitat: large freshwater lakes.
Nesting: does not nest in our region.
Feeding: dabbles and dives for aquatic invertebrates, mostly crustaceans and mollusks in lakes.
Voice: generally silent outside the breeding season.
Similar Species: male is distinctive. *Bufflehead* (p. 83): smaller; female lacks white between eye and bill. *Surf Scoter* (p. 79): female has bulbous bill. *White-winged Scoter* (p. 80): female has white wing patch and bulbous bill.
Best Sites: ***MN:*** L. Superior. ***WI:*** Milwaukee, Harrington Beach SP and Sheboygan (L. Michigan); Wisconsin Pt. (L. Superior).

SURF SCOTER

Melanitta perspicillata

When storms whip up whitecaps on our Great Lakes, migrating Surf Scoters ride comfortably among the crashing waves. These scoters are most often seen during fall migration, when tired flocks settle upon open water in large, dark rafts. • The Surf Scoter has the unfortunate distinction of being one of the least-studied waterbirds in North America. Much of the information that is known of its behavior and distribution was documented for the first time only in the latter part of the 20th century. • The Surf Scoter breeds in northern Canada and Alaska and winters along the eastern and western coasts of North America. It is the only scoter that breeds and winters exclusively in North America. The Surf Scoter is generally seen in our area only in migration. • The scientific name *Melanitta* means "black duck"; *perspicillata* is Latin for "spectacular," which refers to this bird's colorful, bulbous bill.

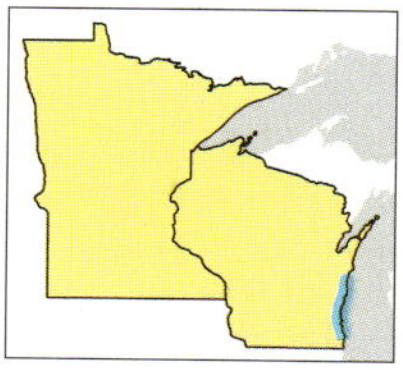

ID: large, stocky duck; large bill; sloping forehead. *Male:* black overall; white forehead and nape; orange bill and legs; black spot, outlined in white, at base of bill. *Female:* brown overall; dark gray bill; 2 whitish patches on sides of head.

Size: *L* 16–20 in; *W* 30 in.

Status: ***MN:*** uncommon migrant from early May to early June and from late September to mid-November; generally found in October along the North Shore of L. Superior, with some birds lingering into January; rare but regular in fall away from L. Superior; rare migrant in spring anywhere in the state. ***WI:*** uncommon migrant from October to November; rare migrant from April to May; rare winter visitor.

Habitat: large, deep lakes.

Nesting: does not nest in our region.

Feeding: dives to depths of 30 ft; eats mostly mollusks; also takes aquatic insect larvae, crustaceans and some aquatic vegetation.

Voice: generally quiet; infrequently utters low, harsh croaks. *Male:* occasionally gives a low, clear whistle. *Female:* guttural *krraak krraak*.

Similar Species: *White-winged Scoter* (p. 80): white wing patches; male lacks white on forehead and nape. *Black Scoter* (p. 81): male is all black; female has well-defined, pale "cheek."

Best Sites: ***MN:*** L. Superior; Mille Lacs L.; L. Winnibigoshish; sewage ponds in most regions. ***WI:*** Milwaukee, Virmond Park, Harrington Beach SP, Sheboygan, Cleveland and Door Co. (L. Michigan); Wisconsin Pt., Bayfield Co. and Ashland (L. Superior); rare inland.

WHITE-WINGED SCOTER

Melanitta fusca

As White-winged Scoters race across lakes, their flapping wings reveal a key identifying feature—the white inner-wing patches that strike a sharp contrast with the bird's otherwise black plumage. The White-winged Scoter is the largest of the three scoter species found in our region. Because scoters have small wings relative to the weight of their bodies, they require long stretches of water for takeoff. However, once in the air their flight is fast and strong. • The White-winged Scoter often eats hard-shelled clams and shellfishes whole. It relies on its remarkably powerful gizzard to crush shells that would require a hammer for us to open. • The name "scoter" may be derived from the way this bird scoots across the water's surface. Scooting can be a means of traveling quickly from one foraging site to another. The name "coot" has also been incorrectly applied to all three species of scoter because of their superficial resemblance to this totally unrelated species.

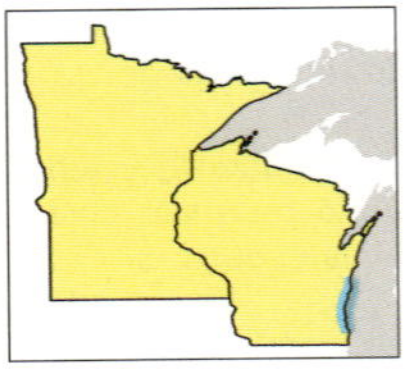

ID: stocky body; large, bulbous bill; sloping forehead; base of bill is fully feathered. *Male:* black overall; white patch below eye. *Female:* brown overall; gray brown bill; 2 whitish patches on sides of head. *In flight:* white wing patches.

Size: *L* 18–24 in; *W* 34 in.

Status: ***MN:*** uncommon migrant from early April to early June and from mid-October to late November on L. Superior; rare to uncommon in other regions in both spring and fall (better represented in fall); casual in winter on L. Superior. ***WI:*** common migrant from March to May and from October to December on the Great Lakes; rare inland; rare winter visitor.

Habitat: large, deep lakes and large rivers.

Nesting: does not nest in our region.

Feeding: deep, underwater dives last up to 1 minute; eats mostly mollusks; may also take crustaceans, aquatic insects and some small fish.

Voice: courting pair produces harsh, guttural noises, between a *crook* and a quack.

Similar Species: *Surf Scoter* (p. 79): lacks white wing patches; male has white forehead and nape. *Black Scoter* (p. 81): lacks white patches on wings and around eyes. *American Coot* (p. 120): whitish bill and nasal shield; lacks white patches on wings and around red eyes.

Best Sites: ***MN:*** L. Superior; Mille Lacs L. ***WI:*** L. Michigan; L. Superior.

BLACK SCOTER

Melanitta nigra

Migration is a lengthy journey, especially after a rigorous breeding season, so many Black Scoters make rest stops on the Great Lakes and other large bodies of water as they travel south through our region. These handsome scoters begin arriving as early as September, but the majority arrive later in fall, just as the frigid cold beckons at our doors. • While floating on the water's surface, Black Scoters tend to hold their heads high, unlike the other scoters, which tend to look downward. The male is the only North American duck that is uniformly black. • Black Scoters are the most vocal of the scoters, and often give away their presence with their plaintive, mellow, whistling calls from far out on open water. • Of the three species of scoters in the region, the Black Scoter is the least common. This rarity belies its earlier designation of "Common Scoter," the name still given to the Eurasian *nigra* subspecies.

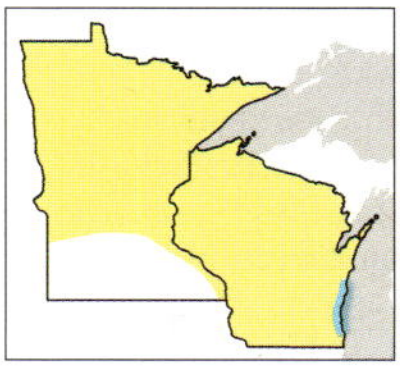

ID: *Male:* black overall; large orange knob on base of bill. *Female:* light "cheek"; dark "cap"; dark brown overall; dark gray bill.

Size: *L* 17–20 in; *W* 28 in.

Status: ***MN:*** rare migrant from late April to early June, mainly on L. Superior; rare to uncommon migrant from early October to late November on L. Superior and Mille Lacs L.; rare migrant elsewhere in the state. ***WI:*** uncommon migrant from October to November; rare migrant from April to May; rare inland; rare winter visitor.

Habitat: large, deep lakes and large rivers.

Nesting: does not nest in our region.

Feeding: dives underwater; eats mostly mollusks and aquatic insect larvae; may eat aquatic vegetation and small fish.

Voice: generally quiet; occasionally an unusual *cour-loo;* wings whistle in flight.

Similar Species: *White-winged Scoter* (p. 80): white wing patches; male has white slash below eye. *Surf Scoter* (p. 79): male has white on head; female has 2 whitish patches on sides of head.

Best Sites: ***MN:*** L. Superior; Mille Lacs L. ***WI:*** L. Michigan; L. Superior.

LONG-TAILED DUCK

Clangula hyemalis

This ancient mariner of the Great Lakes is able to survive violent winter gales like the great storm that scuttled the unfortunate *Edmund Fitzgerald.* Long-tailed Ducks tend to remain in deeper waters, well away from shore, limiting observers to brief glimpses of their winter finery and the long, slender tail feathers for which the bird is named. Some offshore flocks on Lake Michigan range to 40,000 birds. • The breeding and nonbreeding plumages of these arctic-nesting sea ducks are like photo-negatives of each other: their spring breeding plumage is mostly dark with white highlights, while their winter plumage is mostly white with dark patches. • King Eiders and Long-tailed Ducks are among the world's deepest diving waterfowl—both make regular dives to depths of more than 200 feet. • Until recently, this duck was officially called "Oldsquaw," a name that many people still use.

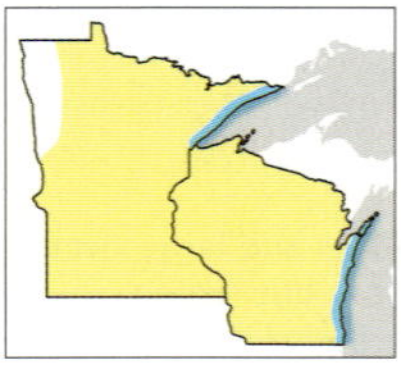

ID: *Breeding male:* dark head with white eye patch; dark neck and upperparts; white belly; dark bill; long, dark central tail feathers. *Breeding female:* short tail feathers; gray bill; dark crown, throat patch, wings and back; white underparts. *Nonbreeding male:* pale head with dark patch; pale neck and belly; dark breast; long, white patches on back; pink bill with dark base; long, dark central tail feathers. *Nonbreeding female:* generally lighter than breeding female, especially on head.

Size: *L* 17–20 in; *W* 28 in.

Status: ***MN:*** uncommon to common migrant and winter visitor from October to March on L. Superior; some linger into early June; rare in northern and central regions away from L. Superior; casual in southern regions in spring and fall, accidental in winter in these areas. ***WI:*** common migrant and winter visitor from October to May in eastern regions; uncommon in the north and rare elsewhere.

Habitat: large, deep lakes.

Nesting: does not nest in our region.

Feeding: dives for mollusks, crustaceans and aquatic insects; occasionally eats roots and young shoots; may also take some small fish.

Voice: courtship call is *owl-owl-owlet*, but is rarely heard outside the breeding range.

Similar Species: *Northern Pintail* (p. 71): thin, white line extends up side of neck; gray sides.

Best Sites: ***MN:*** L. Superior. ***WI:*** Milwaukee, Sheboygan, Port Washington, Two Rivers, Door Co. (L. Michigan); L. Superior.

BUFFLEHEAD

Bucephala albeola

Every winter, dozens of species of waterfowl patrol the waters of Lakes Michigan and Superior in huge flotillas that are often composed of thousands of birds. Winter imposes many limiting factors on birds, so food and suitable habitat may be scarce at times. Fortunately for the tiny Bufflehead, it is right at home on the water amid its larger relatives. • Buffleheads are active birds, spending as much time chasing each other as they do feeding. Rarely do you see a raft of Buffleheads at rest—it is just not their nature. Activity intensifies as spring approaches. Courtship takes place on the wintering grounds, and there is always plenty of competition for mates. • The scientific name *Bucephala,* meaning "ox-headed" in Greek, refers to the shape of this bird's head; *albeola* is Latin for "white," a reference to the male's plumage.

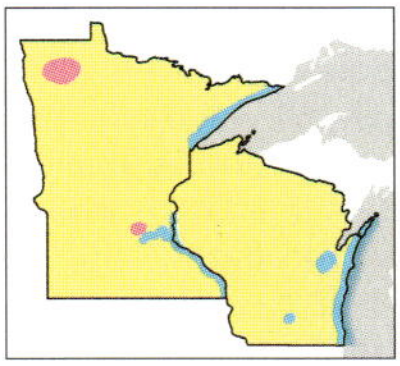

ID: very small, rounded duck; white speculum in flight; short gray bill; short neck. *Male:* white wedge on back of head; head is otherwise iridescent, dark green or purple, usually appearing black; dark back; white neck and underparts. *Female:* dark brown head; white, oval ear patch; light brown sides.

Size: *L* 13–15 in; *W* 21 in.

Status: ***MN:*** common migrant from early March to mid-May and from early October to early December; very rare breeder; occasional in winter. ***WI:*** common migrant from mid-March to mid-May and from October to late December; fairly common winter visitor; very rare summer resident.

Habitat: open water of lakes, large ponds and rivers.

Nesting: in a tree cavity, usually an abandoned woodpecker nest or a natural cavity; often near water; nest chamber may be unlined or filled with down; female incubates 6–12 pale buff to cream eggs for 28–33 days; ducklings leave the nest within 3 days of hatching.

Feeding: dives for aquatic invertebrates; takes water boatmen and mayfly and damselfly larvae in summer; favors mollusks, snails and crustaceans in winter; also eats some small fish and pondweeds.

Voice: *Male:* growling call. *Female:* harsh quack.

Similar Species: *Hooded Merganser* (p. 85): white crest is outlined in black. *Harlequin Duck* (p. 78): female has several light spots on head. *Common Goldeneye* (p. 84) and *Barrow's Goldeneye* (p. 357): males are larger and have white patch between eye and bill. *Other diving ducks* (pp. 73–88): females are much larger.

Best Sites: ***MN:*** L. Superior; Agassiz NWR; Tamarac NWR; large lakes in central and northern regions. ***WI:*** L. Michigan; L. Superior; inland lakes in migration.

COMMON GOLDENEYE

Bucephala clangula

The courtship display of the male Common Goldeneye looks much like an avian slapstick routine, although to the bird itself it is surely a serious matter. The male performs a number of odd postures and vocalizations, often to apparently disinterested females. In one common routine, he arches his puffy, iridescent head backward until his forehead seems to touch his back. Next, he catapults his neck forward like a coiled spring while producing a seemingly painful *peent* sound. • Common Goldeneye females often lay their eggs in the nests of other goldeneyes and cavity-nesting ducks. After hatching, ducklings remain in the nest for one to three days before jumping out of the tree cavity, often falling a long distance to the ground below. • Because the wind whistles through their wings when they fly, Common Goldeneyes are frequently called "Whistlers."

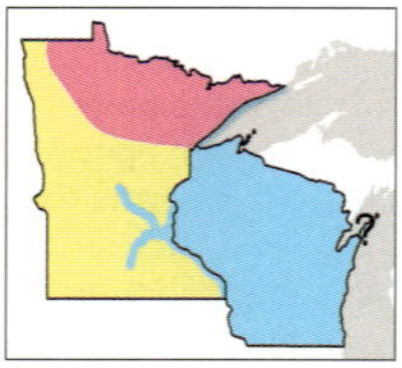

ID: steep forehead with peaked crown; black wings with large, white patches; golden eyes. *Male:* dark, iridescent green head; round, white "cheek" patch; dark bill; dark back; white sides and belly. *Female:* chocolate brown head; lighter breast and belly; gray brown body plumage; dark bill is tipped with yellow in spring and summer.

Size: *L* 16–20 in; *W* 26 in.

Status: ***MN:*** common migrant from late February to late May and from early October to mid-December; least common in western regions; common breeder; common in winter on open rivers and lakes in eastern, central and north-central regions. ***WI:*** common migrant from March to mid-May and from October to mid-December; abundant winter visitor; very rare breeder; a few summer residents.

Habitat: *Breeding:* marshes, ponds, lakes and rivers. *In migration* and *winter:* open water of lakes, large ponds and rivers.

Nesting: in a tree cavity, but will use a nest box; often close to water but occasionally quite far from it; cavity is lined with wood chips and down; female incubates 6–10 blue green eggs for 28–32 days; 2 females may each lay a clutch in the same nest if cavities are in short supply.

Feeding: dives for crustaceans, mollusks and aquatic insect larvae; may also eat tubers, leeches, frogs and small fish.

Voice: *Male:* courtship calls are a nasal *peent* and a hoarse *kraaagh*. *Female:* a harsh croak.

Similar Species: *Barrow's Goldeneye* (p. 357): male has large, white, crescent-shaped "cheek" patch and purplish head; female has more orange on bill and more steeply sloped forehead.

Best Sites: ***MN:*** L. Superior (Houston Co.); Mississippi R.; Leech L.; L. Vermilion. ***WI:*** L. Michigan; L. Superior; inland lakes in migration.

HOODED MERGANSER

Lophodytes cucullatus

Extremely attractive and exceptionally shy, the Hooded Merganser is one of the most sought-after ducks from a birder's perspective. • Most of the time the male Hooded Merganser's crest is held flat, but in moments of arousal or agitation he quickly unfolds his brilliant crest to attract a mate or signal approaching danger. The drake displays his full range of colors and athletic abilities in elaborate, late-winter courtship displays and chases. It is important that he put on an impressive show because there are usually twice as many males as there are females. • All mergansers have thin bills with small, toothlike serrations to help the birds keep a firm grasp on slippery prey. The smallest of the mergansers, Hoodies have a more diverse diet than their larger relatives. They add crustaceans, insects and even acorns to the usual diet of fish.

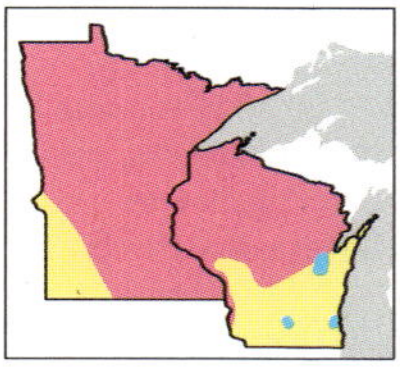

ID: slim body; crested head; dark, thin, pointed bill. *Male:* black head and back; bold, white crest is outlined in black; white breast with 2 black slashes; rusty sides. *Female:* dusky brown body; shaggy, reddish brown crest. *In flight:* small, white wing patches.

Size: *L* 16–18 in; *W* 24 in.

Status: ***MN:*** uncommon to common migrant and breeder from April to November; a few overwinter in the southeastern region. ***WI:*** common migrant and breeder from March to November; uncommon to rare winter visitor.

Habitat: forest-edged ponds, wetlands, lakes and rivers.

Nesting: usually in a tree cavity 15–40 ft above the ground; may also use a nest box; cavity is lined with leaves, grass and down; female incubates 10–12 spherical, white eggs for 29–33 days; some females may lay their eggs in other birds' nests, including the nests of other species.

Feeding: very diverse diet; dives for small fish, caddisfly and dragonfly larvae, snails, amphibians and crayfish.

Voice: low grunts and croaks. *Male:* frog-like *crrrrooo* in courtship display. *Female:* generally quiet; occasionally a harsh *gak* or a croaking *croo-croo-crook*.

Similar Species: *Bufflehead* (p. 83): male lacks black outline to crest and 2 black breast and shoulder slashes. *Red-breasted Merganser* (p. 87) and *Common Merganser* (p. 86): females have much longer, orange bill and gray back. *Other diving ducks* (pp. 73–88): females lack crest.

Best Sites: ***MN:*** Pleasant L. (Ramsey Co.). ***WI:*** *In migration:* lakes, ponds and flooded fields. *Winter:* Madison; Neenah-Menasha; Kaukauna; Milwaukee.

COMMON MERGANSER

Mergus merganser

After a labored takeoff, the Common Merganser flies arrow-straight, low over the water, making broad sweeping turns to follow the meanderings of rivers and lake shorelines. These ducks often gather in large groups over winter and during migration. In winter, any source of open water with a fish-filled shoal may support good numbers of these skilled divers—concentrations of up to 75,000 have been recorded in November. • In our region, Common Mergansers breed among forest-edged waterways wherever there are cool, clear, unpolluted lakes and rivers. These birds are cavity-nesters, but will also nest on the ground in areas with good fishing and an absence of suitable cavities, such as the Great Lakes. • The Common Merganser is the most widespread and abundant merganser in North America.

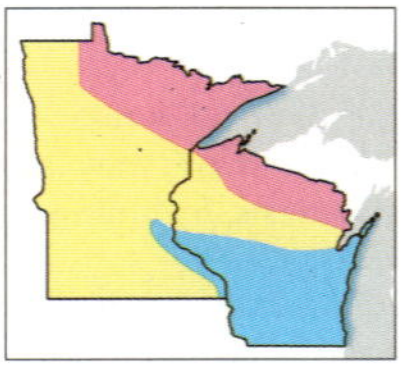

ID: large, elongated body. *Male:* glossy, green head without crest; blood red bill and feet; white body plumage; black stripe on back; dark eyes. *Female:* rusty neck and crested head; clean white "chin" and breast; orange bill; gray body; orangish eyes. *In flight:* shallow wingbeats; body is compressed and arrowlike.
Size: *L* 22–27 in; *W* 34 in.
Status: ***MN:*** common migrant from mid-February to mid-May and from mid-September to mid-December; uncommon migrant in the northwest; uncommon breeder; winters on the Mississippi R. and on L. Superior. ***WI:*** common migrant from March to April and in November; uncommon breeder; common winter visitor.
Habitat: large rivers and deep lakes.
Nesting: often in a tree cavity 15–20 ft above the ground; occasionally on the ground, under a bush or log, on a cliff ledge or in a large nest box; usually not far from water; female incubates 8–11 pale buff eggs for 30–35 days.
Feeding: dives to depths of 30 ft for small fish, usually whitefish, trout, suckers, perch and minnows; young eat insects and aquatic invertebrates before switching to small fish.
Voice: *Male:* harsh *uig-a,* like a guitar twang. *Female:* harsh *karr karr.*
Similar Species: *Red-breasted Merganser* (p. 87): male has shaggy, green crest and spotted, red breast; female lacks cleanly defined white throat. *Mallard* (p. 67): male has chestnut brown breast and yellow bill. *Common Goldeneye* (p. 84): male has white "cheek" patch and stubby, dark bill. *Common Loon* (p. 36): dark bill; white spotting on back.
Best Sites: ***MN:*** L. Pepin (Goodhue Co.). ***WI:*** *In migration:* large inland lakes; L. Michigan; L. Superior. *Winter:* L. Michigan; Neenah-Menasha; Green Bay; Sheboygan; Madison-McFarland.

RED-BREASTED MERGANSER

Mergus serrator

Each spring and fall, the shores of Lakes Michigan and Superior host huge congregations of Red-breasted Mergansers. Their glossy, slicked-back crests and wild red eyes give Red-breasted Mergansers the disheveled, wave-bashed look of adrenalized windsurfers or windswept pirates. • Unlike the other two merganser species, the Red-breast prefers to nest on the ground. This bird's lack of dependence on trees enables it to nest where related cavity-nesting species cannot. • Shortly after their mates have begun incubating, the males fly off to join large offshore rafts for the duration of summer. During this time, a brief molt makes the males largely indistinguishable from their female counterparts. • Red-breasts will sometimes fish cooperatively, funneling fish for easier capture.

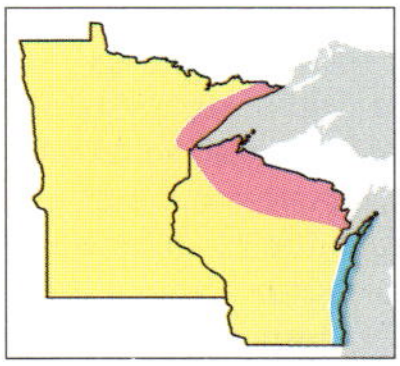

ID: large, elongated body; red eyes; thin, serrated, orange bill; shaggy, slicked-back head crest. *Male:* green head; light rusty breast is spotted with black; white "collar"; gray sides; black-and-white shoulders. *Female:* gray brown overall; reddish head; white "chin," foreneck and breast. *In flight:* male has large, white wing patch crossed by 2 narrow, black bars; female has 1 dark bar separating white speculum from white upperwing patch.

Size: *L* 19–26 in; *W* 30 in.

Status: ***MN:*** common migrant from early March to late May and from early September to mid-December, lingering into January; abundant migrant on L. Superior in spring; uncommon migrant in western regions; uncommon breeder; occasional winter visitor on L. Superior and open areas of the Mississippi R. ***WI:*** common migrant from late February to mid-May and from early October to December; uncommon breeder; common winter visitor.

Habitat: lakes and large rivers, especially those with rocky shorelines and islands.

Nesting: usually on a rocky island or shoreline; on the ground, well concealed under bushes, driftwood or in dense vegetation; female lines a hollow with plant material and down; female incubates 7–10 olive buff eggs for 29–35 days.

Feeding: dives underwater for small fish; also eats aquatic invertebrates, fish eggs and crustaceans.

Voice: generally quiet. *Male:* catlike *yeow* during courtship and feeding. *Female:* harsh *kho-kha*.

Similar Species: *Common Merganser* (p. 86): lacks head crest; male has clean white breast and blood red bill; female's rusty foreneck contrasts with white "chin" and breast.

Best Sites: ***MN:*** Duluth; L. Superior; inland lakes. ***WI:*** L. Michigan; L. Superior; inland lakes as well as the Great Lakes in migration.

RUDDY DUCK

Oxyura jamaicensis

Clowns of the wetlands, male Ruddy Ducks display energetic courtship behavior with comedic enthusiasm. The small males vigorously pump their bright blue bills, almost touching their breasts. The *plap, plap, plap-plap-plap* of the display increases in speed to its hilarious climax: a spasmodic jerk and sputter. In late summer, Ruddies blend into the crowd, their white "cheeks" the only sign that they were once stars of the show. Their behavior in winter is subdued—they spend hours with their heads tucked into their back feathers and their tails flattened against the water. • Female Ruddies lay an average of eight eggs at a time—a remarkable feat, considering that their eggs are bigger than those of a Mallard and that a Mallard is significantly larger than a Ruddy Duck. Females take part in an unusual practice, often dumping eggs in a communal "dummy" nest, which may finally accumulate as many as 60 eggs that will receive no motherly care.

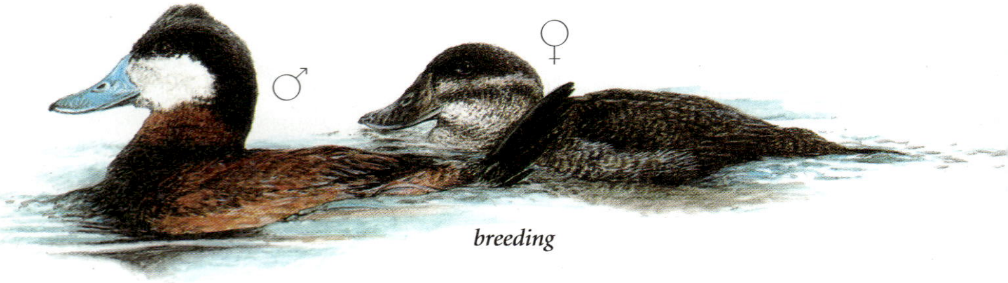

breeding

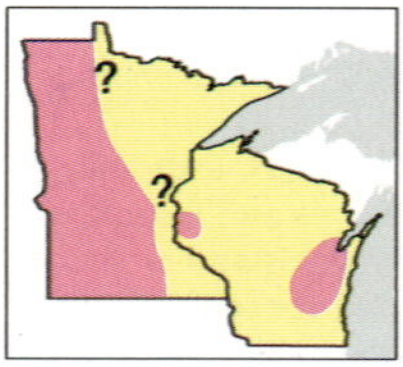

ID: large bill and head; short neck; long, stiff tail feathers (often held upward). *Breeding male:* white "cheek"; chestnut red body; blue bill; black tail and crown. *Female:* brown overall; dark "cheek" stripe; darker crown and back. *Nonbreeding male:* like female but with white "cheek."

Size: *L* 15–16 in; *W* 18½ in.

Status: ***MN:*** common migrant from early March to mid-May and from early September to mid-December, rare in north-central and northeastern regions; uncommon breeder. ***WI:*** common migrant from late March to May and from September to November; uncommon breeder; uncommon winter visitor.

Habitat: *Breeding:* shallow marshes with dense emergent vegetation and muddy bottoms. *In migration* and *winter:* lakes with open, shallow water.

Nesting: in cattails, bulrushes or other emergent vegetation; female suspends a woven platform nest over water; may use an abandoned duck or coot nest, muskrat lodge or exposed log; female incubates 5–10 rough, whitish eggs for 23–26 days; an occasional brood parasite.

Feeding: dives to the bottom of wetlands for the seeds of pondweeds, sedges and bulrushes and for the leafy parts of aquatic plants; also eats a few aquatic invertebrates.

Voice: *Male:* courtship display is *chuck-chuck-chuck-chur-r-r-r. Female:* generally silent.

Similar Species: *Cinnamon Teal* (p. 69): lacks white "cheek" and blue bill. *Other diving ducks* (pp. 73–87): females lack long, stiff tail and dark facial stripe.

Best Sites: ***MN:*** Heron L. (Jackson Co.); Agassiz NWR; Salt L. (Lac Qui Parle Co.); marshes and lakes. ***WI:*** L. Maria; Horicon Marsh; L. Winnebago; L. Michigan; Green Bay.

OSPREY

Pandion haliaetus

The Osprey is the only species in its family and is found on every continent except Antarctica. This raptor eats fish exclusively and is always found near water. • Most fish-eating birds land on water and dive for their food or enter the water headfirst. The Osprey takes the middle ground—it hovers above the water, then folds its wings and hurls itself in a headfirst dive toward a flash of silver or a slowly moving shadow. An instant before striking the water, the Osprey rights itself and thrusts its feet forward to grasp its slippery prey, often striking the water with a tremendous splash. • The Osprey's feet are specialized to prevent its catch from making a squirmy escape. Two toes face forward, two face backward and the toes have sharp spines to help the Osprey clamp tightly onto the slipperiest of fish.

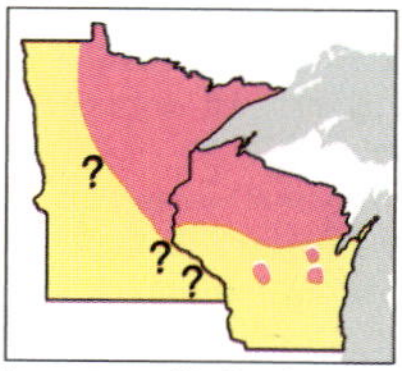

ID: dark brown upperparts; white underparts; dark eye line; light crown; yellow eyes. *Male:* all-white throat. *Female:* fine, dark "necklace." *In flight:* long wings are held in a shallow "M"; dark "wrist" patches; brown and white banded tail.
Size: *L* 22–25 in; *W* 4½–6 ft.
Status: ***MN:*** uncommon migrant from April to late May and from mid-August through October; uncommon and local breeder, extending its range southward. ***WI:*** threatened; common migrant from April to mid-May and from mid-August to mid-October; common breeder in the north; uncommon breeder in the central region.
Habitat: lakes and slowly flowing rivers and streams.
Nesting: on a treetop, usually near water; may also use a specially made platform, utility pole or tower up to 100 ft high; massive stick nest is reused over many years; pair incubates 2–4 yellowish eggs, spotted and blotched with reddish brown, for about 38 days; both adults feed the young, but the male hunts more.
Feeding: dramatic, feet-first dives into water; fish, averaging 2 lbs, make up almost all of the diet.
Voice: series of melodious ascending whistles: *chewk-chewk-chewk;* also an often-heard *kip-kip-kip.*
Similar Species: *Bald Eagle* (p. 90): larger; holds its wings straighter while soaring; larger bill has yellow base; yellow legs; adult has clean white head and tail on otherwise dark body; lacks white underparts and dark "wrist" patches. *Rough-legged Hawk* (p. 100): smaller; hovers with wings in an open "V"; light morph has whitish wing linings and light tail band.
Best Sites: ***MN:*** *Breeding:* large northern lakes. *In migration:* Hawk Ridge (Duluth). ***WI:*** *Breeding:* northern and central lakes. *In migration:* L. Michigan bluffs (Concordia University); Mississippi R. bluffs (Wyalusing SP).

BALD EAGLE

Haliaeetus leucocephalus

The Bald Eagle is a source of inspiration and wonder for anyone longing for a wilderness experience. • Bald Eagles feed mostly on fish and scavenged carrion. Sometimes an eagle will steal food from an Osprey, resulting in a spectacular aerial chase. • Pairs perform dramatic aerial displays. In the most impressive display, the two birds fly to a great height, lock talons and then tumble perilously toward the earth. They break off at the last second, just before crashing into the ground. • Bald Eagles generally mate for life. They renew their pair bonds each year by adding new sticks and branches to their massive nests, the largest of any North American bird.

immature

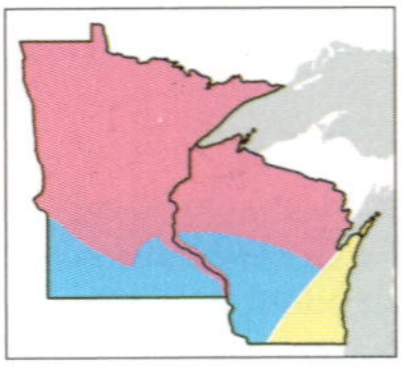

ID: white head and tail; dark brown body; yellow bill and feet; broad wings are held flat in flight. *1st-year:* dark overall; dark bill; some white on underwings. *2nd-year:* dark "bib"; white on underwings. *3rd-year:* mostly white plumage; yellow at base of bill; yellow eyes. *4th-year:* light head with dark facial streak; variable pale and dark plumage; yellow bill; paler eyes. *In flight*: broad wings are held flat.

Size: *L* 30–43 in; *W* 5½–8 ft.

Status: ***MN:*** special concern; common migrant from mid-February to April and from late August to late December; uncommon and local breeder; increasing as a migrant and breeder; main summer range is in north-central and northeastern regions, expanding southward; overwinters in areas with open water. ***WI:*** common migrant from mid-February through April and from October to mid-November; common breeder in the north; uncommon breeder in central regions; common winter visitor, especially along the Wisconsin R. and Mississippi R.

Habitat: large lakes and rivers.

Nesting: usually in a tree near a lake or large river, but may be far from water; huge stick nest, up to 15 ft across, is often reused for many years; pair incubates 1–3 white eggs for 34–36 days; pair feeds the young; young remain in the nest until they can fly.

Feeding: eats waterbirds, small mammals and fish captured at the water's surface; frequently feeds on carrion; sometimes pirates fish from Ospreys.

Voice: thin, weak squeal or gull-like cackle: *kleek-kik-kik-kik* or *kah-kah-kah.*

Similar Species: *Golden Eagle* (p. 101): dark overall except for golden nape; tail may appear faintly banded with white; immature has prominent white patch on wings and at base of tail. *Osprey* (p. 89): similar to 4th-year Bald Eagle, but has M-shaped wings in flight, dark "wrist" patches and dark bill.

Best Sites: ***MN:*** Hawk Ridge (Duluth); L. Pepin; Mississippi R. ***WI:*** *Breeding:* northern lakes and rivers. *In migration:* Mississippi R. bluffs; L. Michigan bluffs. *Winter:* Prairie du Sac–Sauk City; Mississippi R. dams.

NORTHERN HARRIER

Circus cyaneus

The Northern Harrier cruises low over fields, meadows and marshes, grazing the tops of long grasses and cattails, relying on sudden surprise attacks to capture its prey. Although the harrier has excellent vision, its owl-like, parabolic facial disc allows it to hunt by sound as well. • The Northern Harrier was once known as "Marsh Hawk" in North America, and it is still called "Hen Harrier" in Europe. Britain's Royal Air Force was so impressed by this bird's maneuverability that it named its Harrier aircraft after this hawk. • In the perilous courtship flight of the Northern Harrier, the pale-colored male climbs almost vertically in flight and then stalls, sending himself into a reckless dive toward solid ground. At the last second he saves himself with a flight course that sends him skyward again.

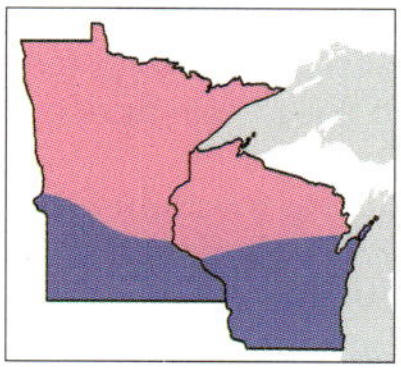

ID: long wings and tail; white rump; black wing tips. *Male:* blue gray to silver gray upperparts; white underparts; indistinct tail bands, except for 1 dark subterminal band. *Female:* dark brown upperparts; streaky brown-and-buff underparts. *Immature:* rich reddish brown plumage; dark tail bands; streaked breast, sides and flanks.

Size: *L* 16–24 in; *W* $3\frac{1}{2}$–4 ft.

Status: ***MN:*** uncommon migrant from mid-February to early May and from August to November; uncommon and local breeder mainly in northern regions; occasional in winter in the south. ***WI:*** special concern; common migrant and breeder from April to November; uncommon winter visitor.

Habitat: open country including fields, wet meadows, cattail marshes, bogs and croplands.

Nesting: on the ground, often on a slightly raised mound; usually in grass, cattails or tall vegetation; shallow depression or platform nest is lined with grass, sticks and cattails; female incubates 4–6 bluish white eggs for 30–32 days.

Feeding: hunts in low, rising and falling flights, often skimming the tops of vegetation; eats small mammals, birds, amphibians, reptiles and some invertebrates.

Voice: most vocal near the nest and during courtship, but generally quiet; high-pitched *ke-ke-ke-ke-ke-ke* near the nest.

Similar Species: *Rough-legged Hawk* (p. 100): broader wings; dark "wrist" patches; black tail with wide, white base; dark belly. *Red-tailed Hawk* (p. 98): lacks white rump and long, narrow tail.

Best Sites: ***MN:*** Hawk Ridge (Duluth); Agassiz NWR. ***WI:*** *Breeding:* Horicon Marsh; Buena Vista Grasslands; Crex Meadows WA; Rat River WA; Powell Marsh; Grand River Marsh. *In migration:* L. Michigan bluffs; Mississippi R. bluffs.

SHARP-SHINNED HAWK

Accipiter striatus

After a successful hunt, the diminutive Sharp-shinned Hawk usually perches on a favorite "plucking post," grasping its meal in its razor-sharp talons. Sharpies prey almost exclusively on small birds, such as chickadees, finches and sparrows, pursuing them in high-speed chases. • Most people never see a Sharpie nest, because the birds are very tight sitters. Disturb one, however, and you will feel the occupants' wrath. These birds are feisty defenders of their nest and young. • When delivering food to his nestlings, a male Sharp-shinned Hawk is cautious around his mate—she is typically one-third larger than he is and notoriously short-tempered. • Accipiters, named after their genus, are woodland hawks. Their short, rounded wings, long, rudderlike tails and flap-and-glide flight pattern give them the maneuverability necessary to negotiate a maze of forest foliage at high speed.

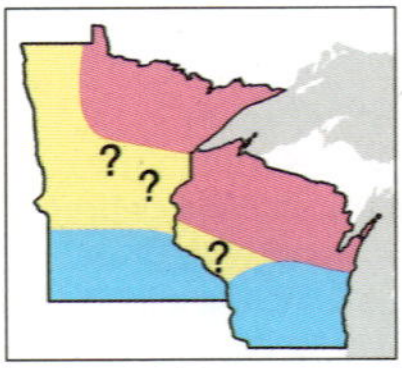

ID: short, rounded wings; long, straight, heavily barred, square-tipped tail; dark barring on pale underwings; blue gray back; red horizontal bars on underparts; red eyes. *Immature:* brown overall; yellow eyes; vertical, brown streaking on breast and belly. *In flight:* flap-and-glide flyer; very agile in wooded areas.

Size: *Male: L* 10–12 in; *W* 20–24 in. *Female: L* 12–14 in; *W* 24–28 in.

Status: ***MN:*** common migrant from March to mid-May and from August to November, especially at Hawk Ridge (Duluth) in September; uncommon breeder; occasional in winter. ***WI:*** common migrant in March and April and from late August to November; uncommon breeder; uncommon winter visitor.

Habitat: dense to semi-open forests and large woodlots; occasionally along rivers; favors bogs and dense, moist coniferous forests.

Nesting: in a conifer; usually builds a new stick nest each year but might remodel an abandoned crow nest; female incubates 4–5 brown-blotched, bluish white eggs for 34–35 days; male feeds the female during incubation.

Feeding: pursues small birds through forests; rarely takes small mammals, amphibians and insects.

Voice: silent, except during the breeding season, when an intense and often repeated *kik-kik-kik-kik* can be heard.

Similar Species: *Cooper's Hawk* (p. 93): larger; tail tip is more rounded and has broader terminal band. *American Kestrel* (p. 102): long, pointed wings; 1 dark "tear streak"; 1 dark "sideburn"; typically seen in open country. *Merlin* (p. 103): pointed wings; rapid wingbeats; 1 dark "tear streak"; brown streaking on buff underparts; dark eyes; usually darker, more obvious tail bands.

Best Sites: ***MN:*** *In migration:* Hawk Ridge (Duluth). ***WI:*** *In migration:* L. Michigan bluffs (Concordia University, Harrington Beach SP); Mississippi R. bluffs (Wyalusing SP).

COOPER'S HAWK

Accipiter cooperii

Larger and heavier than the Sharp-shinned Hawk, the Cooper's Hawk glides silently along forest clearings, using surprise and speed to snatch its prey from midair. Females have the size and build of male Goshawks and can seize and decapitate birds as large as Ruffed Grouse, which they sometimes pursue on the ground like overweight roadrunners. • These birds are now protected by law and the use of DDT has been banned throughout North America, with the result that the Cooper's Hawk is increasing in numbers. • Distinguishing the Cooper's Hawk from the Sharp-shinned Hawk is challenging. In flight, the Cooper's has a shallower, stiffer-winged flight, while the Sharpie has deeper wingbeats with more bending in the wings. Sharp-shins have a square tail, while the Cooper's tail is more rounded.

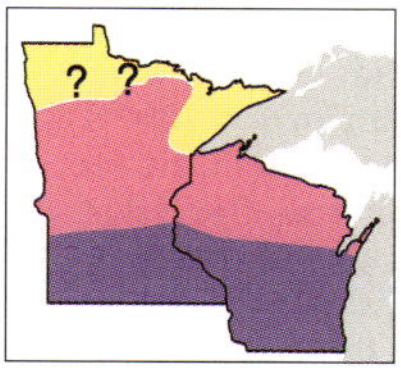

ID: short, rounded wings; long, straight, heavily barred, rounded tail; dark barring on pale undertail and underwings; squarish head; blue gray back; red horizontal barring on underparts; red eyes; white terminal tail band. *Immature:* brown overall; dark eyes; vertical brown streaks on breast and belly. *In flight:* flap-and-glide flyer.

Size: *Male: L* 15–17 in; *W* 27–32 in. *Female: L* 17–19 in; *W* 32–37 in.

Status: ***MN:*** uncommon migrant from late March to mid-May and mid-August through November; numbers are increasing especially in the south; local breeder in most areas except the northeast; occasional in winter. ***WI:*** uncommon but increasing migrant in March and April and from late August to November; uncommon breeder; uncommon but increasing winter visitor, especially in urban areas.

Habitat: mixed woodlands, riparian woodlands and woodlots and, increasingly, urban gardens with feeders.

Nesting: nest of sticks and twigs is built 20–65 ft above the ground in the crotch of a deciduous or coniferous tree; often near a stream or pond; might reuse an abandoned crow nest; female incubates 3–5 bluish white eggs for 34–36 days; male feeds the female during incubation.

Feeding: pursues prey in flights through forests; eats mostly songbirds, squirrels and chipmunks; uses a "plucking post" or nest for eating.

Voice: fast, woodpecker-like *cac-cac-cac-cac.*

Similar Species: *Sharp-shinned Hawk* (p. 92): smaller; less rounded tail tip; thinner terminal tail band. *American Kestrel* (p. 102): smaller; long, pointed wings; 1 dark "tear streak"; 1 dark "sideburn"; typically seen in open country. *Merlin* (p. 103): smaller; pointed wings; rapid wingbeats; 1 dark "tear streak"; brown streaking on buff underparts; dark eyes; usually darker and more obvious tail bands.

Best Sites: ***MN:*** *In migration:* Hawk Ridge (Duluth). ***WI:*** *In migration:* L. Michigan bluffs; Mississippi R. bluffs.

NORTHERN GOSHAWK

Accipiter gentilis

The Northern Goshawk is an agile and powerful predator capable of negotiating lightning-fast turns through dense forest cover. This raptor will prey on any animal it can overtake, dispatching its capture with powerful talons. It has even been known to chase quarry on foot. • Goshawks are devoted parents that ferociously defend their nest sites. Unfortunate souls who wander too close to a goshawk nest are assaulted with an almost deafening, squawking dive-bomb attack. • Northern Goshawks require extensive areas of forest habitat. The clearing of forests for agricultural and residential development has caused goshawk populations to decline significantly throughout their range in Northern Europe, Asia and parts of North America.

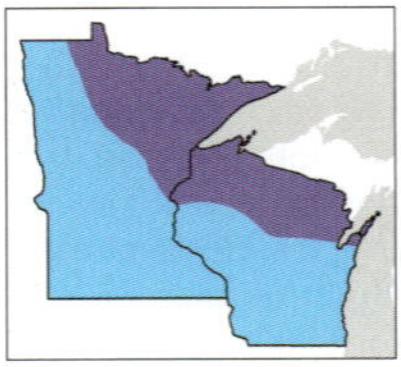

ID: rounded wings; long, banded tail with white terminal band; white "eyebrow"; dark crown; blue gray back; fine, gray, vertical streaking on pale breast and belly; gray barring on pale undertail and underwings; red eyes. *Immature:* brown overall; brown, vertical streaking on whitish breast and belly; brown barring on pale undertail and underwings; grayish yellow eyes.

Size: *Male: L* 21–23 in; *W* 3–3½ ft. *Female: L* 23–25 in; *W* 3½–4 ft.

Status: ***MN:*** uncommon and irruptive migrant from mid-March to early April and from September to November; scattered nesting in northeastern and north-central regions; uncommon to rare in winter, but can be common during invasion years. ***WI:*** uncommon but irruptive migrant in March and April and from September to November; uncommon breeder; rare winter visitor.

Habitat: *Breeding:* mature coniferous, deciduous and mixed woodlands. *Nonbreeding:* forest edges, semi-open parklands and farmlands.

Nesting: in deep woods; male builds a large, bulky stick platform in the crotch of a deciduous or coniferous tree, usually 25–80 ft above the ground; nest is often reused for several years; female incubates 2–4 bluish white eggs for 35–36 days; male feeds the female during incubation.

Feeding: low foraging flights through the forest; feeds primarily on large songbirds, grouse, rabbits and squirrels.

Voice: silent, except during the breeding season, when adults utter a loud, fast, shrill *kak-kak-kak-kak*.

Similar Species: *Cooper's Hawk* (p. 93) and *Sharp-shinned Hawk* (p. 92): smaller; reddish breast bars; lack white "eyebrow" stripe; immatures are smaller and have yellow eyes, which become more orange with age. Buteo *hawks* (pp. 95–100): shorter tails; broader wings; gray or brown eyes. *Gyrfalcon* (p. 104): more pointed wings; dark eyes; often has dark "tear streak."

Best Sites: ***MN:*** *In migration:* Hawk Ridge (Duluth). ***WI:*** *In migration:* L. Michigan bluffs, especially in fall.

RED-SHOULDERED HAWK

Buteo lineatus

The Red-shouldered Hawk is a bird of wetter habitats than the closely related Broad-winged Hawk and Red-tailed Hawk. It nests in mature trees, usually around river bottoms and in lowland tracts of woods alongside creeks. • During the summer months, the dense cover of the Red-shouldered Hawk's forested breeding habitat allows few opportunities for viewing this bird. However, during spring and fall migration, Red-shouldered Hawks can be found hunting from exposed perches. Its seasonal use of telephone poles and fence posts for hunting gives observers a better glimpse into this hawk's otherwise private life. • If left undisturbed, Red-shouldered Hawks will remain faithful to productive nest sites, returning yearly. After the parents die, one of their young will carry on the family nesting tradition.

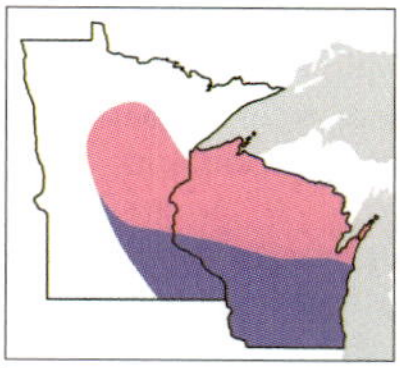

ID: chestnut red shoulders on otherwise dark brown upperparts; reddish underwing linings; narrow, white bars on dark tail; barred, reddish breast and belly; reddish undertail coverts. *Immature*: large, brown streaks on white underparts; whitish undertail coverts. *In flight:* light and dark barring on underside of flight feathers and tail; white crescents or "windows" at base of primaries.
Size: *L* 19 in; *W* $3\frac{1}{2}$ ft.
Status: ***MN:*** special concern; uncommon migrant from mid-March to early May and from September to early December; uncommon breeder, expanding its range northward and westward; rare breeder in other regions; casual in winter. ***WI:*** threatened; uncommon migrant and breeder from late February to November; uncommon to rare winter visitor.
Habitat: mature deciduous and mixed forests, wooded riparian areas, swampy woodlands and large, mature woodlots.

Nesting: pair assembles a bulky nest of sticks and twigs, usually 15–80 ft above the ground in the crotch of a deciduous tree; nest is often reused; female incubates 2–4 darkly blotched, bluish white eggs for about 33 days; both adults raise the young.
Feeding: small mammals, birds, reptiles and amphibians are usually detected from a fence post, tree or telephone pole and caught in a swooping attack; may catch prey flushed by low flight.
Voice: repeated series of high *key-ah* notes.
Similar Species: *Broad-winged Hawk* (p. 96): lacks reddish shoulders; wings are broader, more whitish and dark-edged underneath; wide, white tail bands. *Red-tailed Hawk* (p. 98): lacks barring on tail and light "windows" at base of primaries.
Best Sites: ***MN:*** William O'Brien SP; Camp Ripley (Morrison Co.); Whitewater SP.
WI: *Breeding:* in wooded tracts along rivers in southern and central regions, including Wisconsin R., Wolf R., Embarrass R. and Mississippi R. *In migration:* bluffs along L. Michigan, Mississippi R. and Wisconsin R.

BROAD-WINGED HAWK

Buteo platypterus

The generally shy and secretive Broad-winged Hawk prefers different habitat than most other buteos. Shunning the open fields and forest clearings favored by the Red-tailed Hawk, it secludes itself in dense, often wet, forests. In this habitat, its short, broad wings and highly flexible tail help it to maneuver in the heavy growth. • Most hunting is done from a high perch with a good view and the hawk will return to its perch after being flushed to resume its vigilant search for a meal. • At the end of the nesting season, "kettles" of buteos and other hawks spiral up from their forest retreats, testing thermals for the opportunity to head south. Broad-winged Hawks are often the most numerous species in these flocks. In good flight years, large concentrations of these birds numbering in the tens of thousands can sometimes be seen.

light morph

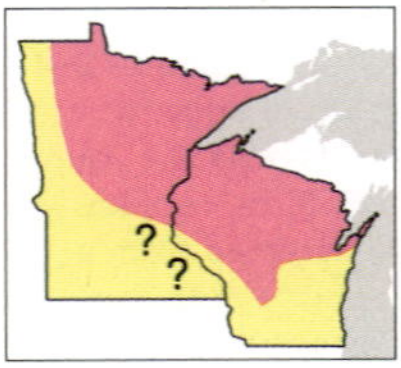

ID: broad, black and white tail bands; broad wings with pointed tips; heavily barred, rufous brown breast; dark brown upperparts. *Immature:* dark brown streaks on white breast, belly and sides; buff and dark brown tail bands. *In flight:* pale underwings are outlined with dark brown.
Size: *L* 14–19 in; *W* 32–39 in.
Status: ***MN:*** common migrant from mid-April to mid-May and from mid-August to early October in eastern and central regions; uncommon migrant in the west; uncommon breeder in eastern and central regions, most common in the north.
WI: abundant to common migrant from April to mid-May and in September; common breeder in the north; uncommon breeder in western and central regions.
Habitat: *Breeding:* dense mixed and deciduous forests and woodlots. *In migration:* escarpments and shorelines; also riparian and deciduous forests and woodland edges.
Nesting: usually in a deciduous tree, often near water; bulky stick nest is built in a crotch 20–40 ft above the ground; usually builds a new nest each year; mostly the female incubates 2–4 brown-spotted, whitish eggs for 28–31 days; both adults raise the young.
Feeding: swoops from a perch for small mammals, amphibians, insects and young birds; often seen hunting from roadside telephone poles.
Voice: high-pitched, whistled *peeeo-wee-ee;* generally silent during migration.
Similar Species: *Other* Buteo *hawks* (pp. 95–100): lack broad banding on tail and dark-edged, broad wings with pointed tips. Accipiter *hawks* (pp. 92–94): long, narrow tails with less distinct banding.
Best Sites: ***MN:*** *In migration:* Hawk Ridge (Duluth). ***WI:*** *In migration:* bluffs along L. Michigan, Mississippi R. and Wisconsin R.

SWAINSON'S HAWK

Buteo swainsoni

The Swainson's Hawk dominates in areas where open country exceeds forests. In this region, it is an uncommon to rare breeder in Minnesota, and is only seen as a very rare migrant in Wisconsin. • Once you learn to look for relatively pointed wing tips, slightly uptilted wings and flight feathers that are darker than the wing lining, you will be able to identify these birds from as far away as you can see them. • Swainson's Hawks undertake long migratory journeys. Traveling up to 12,500 miles in a single year, the Swainson's Hawk is second only to the Peregrine Falcon for long-distance travel among birds of prey. The massive "kettles" of migrating Swainson's Hawks through Central America have been likened to the legendary flocks of Passenger Pigeons that were said to blacken the sky. Unfortunately, many of these hawks are killed by the incautious use of insecticides in Argentina, reminding us that the conservation of migratory species requires international cooperation.

light morph

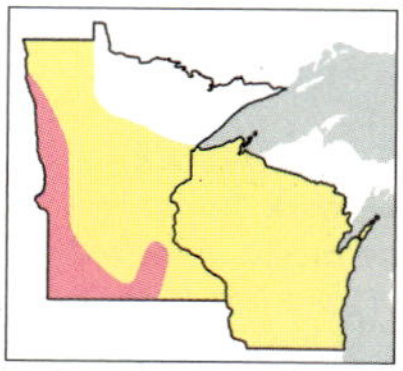

ID: long wings with pointed tips; narrowly banded tail; dark flight feathers. *Light morph:* more common than dark morph; dark "bib"; white belly; white wing linings contrast with dark flight feathers. *Dark morph:* dark overall; brown wing linings blend with flight feathers. *In flight:* holds wings in shallow "V."

Size: *L* 19–22 in; *W* 4½ ft.

Status: ***MN:*** uncommon migrant from April through mid-May and from late August to mid-September mainly in western and south-central regions; rare to casual migrant in other areas; rare to occasionally uncommon breeder; occasional over Hawk Ridge (Duluth). ***WI:*** very rare migrant.

Habitat: open fields, grasslands and agricultural areas.

Nesting: usually in a solitary tree in an open field; may use the abandoned nest of another raptor, crow, raven or magpie; builds a large stick nest; uses the same nest repeatedly; female incubates 2–3 sparsely blotched, white eggs for 28–35 days.

Feeding: dives for voles, mice and ground squirrels; also eats snakes, small birds and large insects, such as grasshoppers and crickets.

Voice: typical hawk call, *keeeaar,* is higher pitched than a Red-tail's.

Similar Species: *Red-tailed Hawk* (p. 98): more rounded wing tips; holds wings flat in flight. *Other* Buteo *hawks* (pp. 95–100): flight feathers are paler than wing lining.

Best Sites: ***MN:*** Lincoln Co.; Murray Co.; Pipestone Co. ***WI:*** no consistent sites.

RED-TAILED HAWK

Buteo jamaicensis

The Red-tailed Hawk is the most commonly seen hawk in the region, and is conspicuous year-round, particularly near agricultural lands. An afternoon drive through the country will reveal Red-tails perching on exposed tree limbs, fence posts or utility poles overlooking open fields and roadsides. • During spring courtship, excited Red-tailed Hawks dive at each other, sometimes locking talons and tumbling through the air together before breaking off to avoid crashing to the ground. • This hawk's tail does not obtain its brick red coloration until the bird matures into a breeding adult. Most eastern birds are light morphs, while dark morphs are more common in western North America.

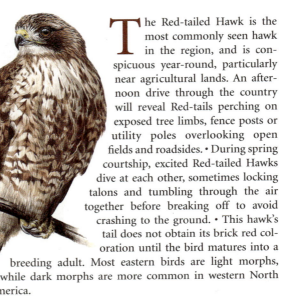

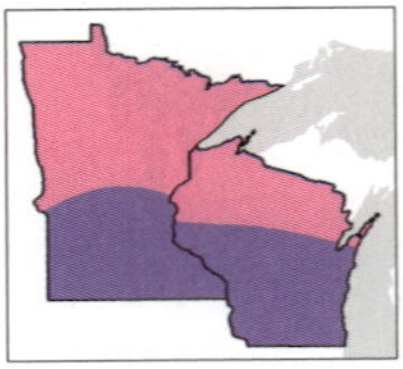

ID: red tail; dark upperparts with some white highlights; dark brown band of streaks across belly. *Immature:* very variable; lacks red tail; generally darker; band of streaks on belly. *In flight:* fan-shaped tail; white or tawny brown underside and underwing linings; dark leading edge on underside of wing; light underwing flight feathers with faint barring.

Size: *Male: L* 18–23 in; *W* 4–5 ft. *Female: L* 20–25 in; *W* 4–5 ft.

Status: ***MN:*** common migrant from mid-February to late April and from mid-August through November; common breeder, least common in the northeast; regular in winter in the south. ***WI:*** very common migrant and breeder from March to December; common winter visitor.

Habitat: open country with some trees; also roadsides, fields, woodlots, hedgerows, mixed forests and moist woodlands.

Nesting: in woodlands adjacent to open habitat; usually in a deciduous tree; rarely on a cliff or in a conifer; bulky stick nest is usually added to each year; pair incubates 2–4 brown-blotched, whitish eggs for 28–35 days; male brings food to the female and young.

Feeding: scans for food while perched or soaring; drops to capture prey; rarely stalks prey on foot; eats voles, mice, rabbits, chipmunks, birds, amphibians and reptiles; rarely takes large insects.

Voice: powerful, descending scream: *keeearrrr.*

Similar Species: *Rough-legged Hawk* (p. 100): white tail base; dark "wrist" patches on underwings; broad, dark terminal tail band. *Broad-winged Hawk* (p. 96): broadly banded tail; broader wings with pointed tips; lacks dark "belt." *Red-shouldered Hawk* (p. 95): reddish wing linings and underparts; reddish shoulders. *Swainson's Hawk* (p. 97): all-dark back; more pointed wing tips; dark flight feathers and pale wing linings in flight; holds wings in shallow "V."

Best Sites: ***MN:*** *In migration:* Hawk Ridge (Duluth) ***WI:*** *In migration:* Concordia University; Harrington Beach SP; Wyalusing SP.

FERRUGINOUS HAWK

Buteo regalis

Coursing the contours of rolling, grassy prairie, circling high above the landscape or sitting alertly in a barren field, the Ferruginous Hawk is a bird of open country. The combination of the Ferruginous Hawk's large size, rich color and real rarity make this a prize buteo for birders in Minnesota and Wisconsin. This grassland hawk spends much of its time perched on a fence post or low in a tree watching for unsuspecting rodents. Hunting from the air, this powerful bird strikes unexpectedly, swooping down on its prey from great heights. • Because the Ferruginous Hawk's diet is composed mostly of rabbits, ground squirrels and mice, this hawk can actually be of service to ranchers and farmers. Rodent control programs and habitat disturbance have adversely affected Ferruginous Hawk populations.

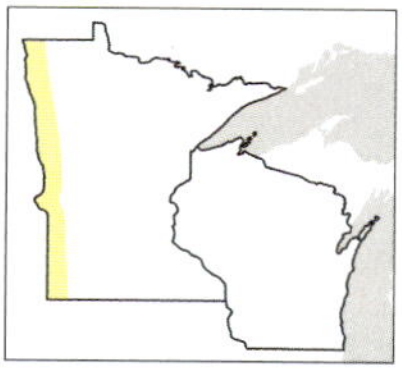

ID: the largest *Buteo* hawk. *Light morph:* rusty red shoulders and back; pale underparts; dark legs; light tail is tipped with rust red. *Dark morph:* less common than light morph; dark underparts; white tail; dark wing linings; light flight feathers. *Immature:* very pale; may have pale legs. *In flight (light morph):* dark reddish brown legs stand out against white belly; mostly white underparts; holds wings in shallow "V" while soaring.

Size: *L* 22–27 in; *W* 4½ ft.

Status: ***MN:*** rare migrant from mid-March through April and from late September to early November in the west; casual or accidental migrant in other regions; no positive breeding evidence; a few June and July records may indicate very rare breeding. ***WI:*** casual migrant.

Habitat: open grasslands and croplands.

Nesting: usually in a solitary tree, on a cliff or on the ground; wide, massive nest of sticks, weeds and cow dung is lined with finer materials; female incubates 2–4 speckled, white to bluish white eggs for 32–33 days; male brings food to the female and young.

Feeding: swoops down on prey spotted while soaring; also hunts from a low perch or from the ground; eats ground squirrels, mice, rabbits and hares; also takes snakes and small birds.

Voice: generally silent; alarm call is a loud, squealing *kaaarr,* dropping at the end.

Similar Species: *Red-tailed Hawk* (p. 98): smaller; darker underparts; dark abdominal "belt"; dark leading edge on underwing near body; usually has red tail. *Swainson's Hawk* (p. 97): dark flight feathers contrast with light wing linings. *Rough-legged Hawk* (p. 100): dark "wrist" patches; dark streaking on breast; dark brown belly band or dark streaking on belly.

Best Sites: no consistent sites.

ROUGH-LEGGED HAWK

Buteo lagopus

♀

light morph

While hunting, the Rough-legged Hawk often "wind-hovers" to scan the ground below, flapping to maintain a stationary position while facing upwind—a hunting technique that serves as an excellent long distance identification tool for birders. This hawk's habit of hovering is necessary because its open country habitat often lacks high perches, though these birds will use fence posts and telephone poles when available. • This hawk is a favorite migratory bird in our region, signifying the changing seasons and adding some spice to the local birding communities' bird lists. • Rough-legged Hawks show great variety in coloration, ranging from a whitish light morph with dark patterning to dark-morph birds that are almost entirely dark with distinctive whitish areas. The light morph is much more common in our region. • The name *lagopus*, meaning "hare's foot," refers to this bird's distinctive feathered legs, which are an adaptation for survival in cold climates.

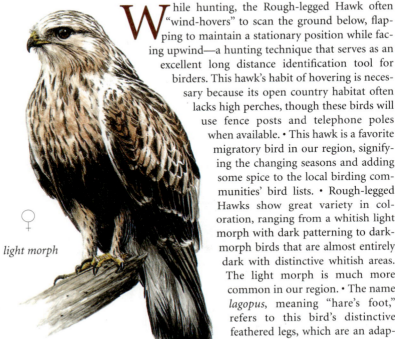

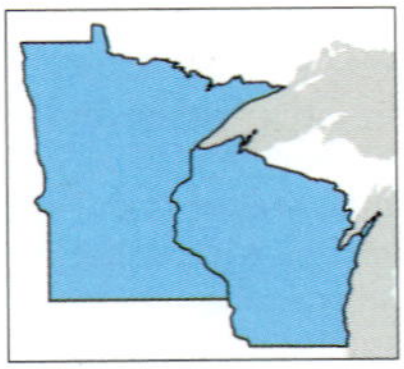

ID: white tail base with 1 wide, dark subterminal band; dark brown upperparts; pale flight feathers; legs are feathered to toes. *Light morph:* wide, dark abdominal "belt"; dark streaks on breast and head; dark "wrist" patches; light underwing linings. *Dark morph:* dark wing linings, head and underparts. *Immature:* lighter streaking on breast; bold belly band; buff leg feathers. *In flight:* frequently hovers; most birds show dark "wrist" patches.

Size: *L* 19–24 in; *W* 4–$4\frac{1}{2}$ ft.

Status: ***MN:*** uncommon to occasionally common migrant and winter visitor from early September to mid-May; best represented in eastern regions; accidental in June. ***WI:*** common migrant and winter visitor from mid-September to early May; very rare in summer.

Habitat: fields, meadows, open bogs and agricultural croplands.

Nesting: does not nest in our region.

Feeding: soars and hovers while searching for prey; primarily eats small rodents; also takes birds, amphibians and large insects.

Voice: alarm call is a catlike *kee-eer,* usually dropping at the end.

Similar Species: *Other* Buteo *hawks* (pp. 95–100): rarely hover; lacks dark "wrist" patches and white tail base. *Northern Harrier* (p. 91): facial disc; lacks dark "wrist" patches and dark belly band; longer, thinner tail lacks broad, dark subterminal band.

Best Sites: ***MN:*** *In migration:* Hawk Ridge (Duluth). ***WI:*** *In migration:* L. Michigan bluffs; Mississippi R. bluffs. *Winter:* Buena Vista Grasslands; Rat River WA; Horicon Marsh; Killsnake WA.

GOLDEN EAGLE

Aquila chrysaetos

The Golden Eagle embodies the wonder and wildness of the North American landscape. With the advent of widespread human settlement and intensive agricultural practices, this noble bird became the victim of a lengthy persecution. In the past, it was perceived as a threat to livestock and bounties were offered, encouraging the shooting and poisoning of this regal bird. • The Golden Eagle is actually more closely related to the *Buteo* hawks than it is to the Bald Eagle. Unlike the Bald Eagle, which feeds mostly on fish and carrion, the Golden Eagle is an active, impressive predator, taking prey as large as foxes, cranes and geese. • Few people ever forget the sight of a Golden Eagle soaring overhead—the average wingspan of an adult exceeds 6 feet! • Although the adult Golden Eagle is uniformly colored except for its tawny head, the immature has a white patch in the center of each wing and at the base of the tail. These patches distinguish it from the smaller immature Bald Eagle.

immature

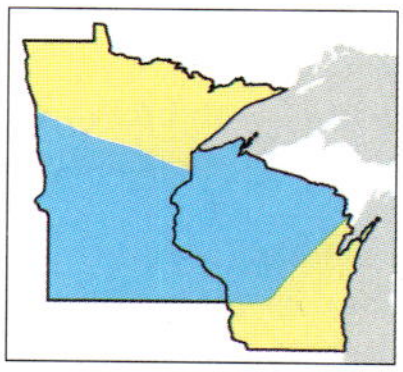

ID: very large; brown overall with golden tint to neck and head; brown eyes; dark bill; brown tail has grayish white bands; yellow feet; fully feathered legs. *Immature:* white tail base; white patch at base of underwing primary feathers. *In flight:* relatively short neck; long tail; long, large, rectangular wings.

Size: *L* 30–40 in; *W* 6½–7½ ft.

Status: ***MN:*** uncommon to rare migrant from mid-February to mid-April and in October and November; casual winter visitor around national wildlife refuges and other areas where large concentrations of waterfowl occur. ***WI:*** uncommon migrant and winter visitor from October to late April.

Habitat: *In migration:* along bluffs and lake shorelines. *Winter:* semi-open woodlands and fields; hilly regions bordering rivers.

Nesting: does not nest in our region.

Feeding: swoops down on prey from soaring flight; eats hares, grouse, rodents, foxes and occasionally young ungulates; often eats carrion.

Voice: generally quiet; rarely a short bark.

Similar Species: *Bald Eagle* (p. 90): longer neck; shorter tail; immature lacks distinct, white underwing patches and tail base. *Turkey Vulture* (p. 55): naked, pink head; pale flight feathers; dark wing linings. *Dark-morph Rough-legged Hawk* (p. 100): pale flight feathers; white tail base.

Best Sites: ***MN:*** Hawk Ridge (Duluth); Agassiz NWR; Whitewater WMA; Tamarac NWR. ***WI:*** *In migration:* bluffs along major rivers and L. Michigan. *Winter:* Bear Bluff area; bluffs along the Mississippi, Kickapoo and Chippewa Rivers.

AMERICAN KESTREL

Falco sparverius

The American Kestrel is the smallest and most common of our falcons. It hunts small rodents in open areas, and a kestrel perched on a telephone wire or fence post along an open field is a familiar sight throughout the region year-round. This bird is attracted to habitats that have been modified by humans, including pastures, parklands and even urban areas. • The kestrel's eyesight is phenomenal and few rodents escape this hunter's vigilance—a kestrel will hover in the wind and wait patiently until the right opportunity presents itself, then swoop down on its prey. • The American Kestrel's diminutive size allows it to nest in tree cavities, which helps to protect defenseless young kestrels from hungry predators. Kestrels that take advantage of nest boxes may also take advantage of the House Sparrows, Starlings and urban rodents that city living offers. • Old field guides and old-time birders refer to this bird as "Sparrow Hawk."

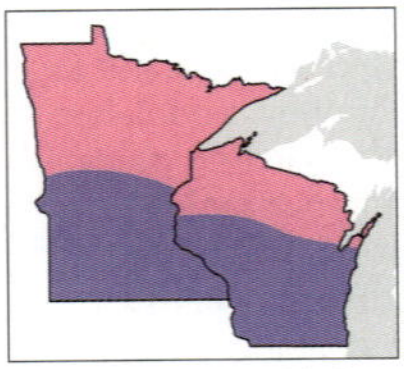

ID: 2 distinctive facial stripes. *Male:* rusty back; blue gray wings; blue gray crown with rusty "cap"; lightly spotted underparts. *Female:* rusty back, wings and breast streaking. *In flight:* frequently hovers; long, rusty tail; buoyant, indirect flight style.

Size: *L* 7½–8 in; *W* 20–24 in.

Status: ***MN:*** common to abundant migrant and breeder from early March to mid-May and from August to late October; least numerous in heavily wooded areas, especially in the northeast; uncommon but regular in winter. ***WI:*** common migrant and breeder from early March to October; common winter visitor.

Habitat: open fields, riparian woodlands, woodlots, forest edges, grasslands and croplands.

Nesting: in a tree cavity (usually an abandoned flicker or woodpecker cavity) or nest box; mostly the female incubates 4–6 white to pale brown eggs, spotted with brown and gray, for 29–30 days; both adults raise the young.

Feeding: swoops from a perch (a tree, fenceline, post, road sign or powerline) or from hovering flight; eats mostly insects and some small rodents, birds, reptiles and amphibians.

Voice: loud, often repeated, shrill *killy-killy-killy* when excited; female's voice is lower pitched.

Similar Species: *Merlin* (p. 103): only 1 facial stripe; less colorful; does not hover; flight is more powerful and direct. *Sharp-shinned Hawk* (p. 92): short, rounded wings; reddish barring on underparts; lacks facial stripes; flap-and-glide flight.

Best Sites: ***MN:*** Hawk Ridge (Duluth). ***WI:*** farmlands and open areas. *In migration:* bluffs along L. Michigan and Mississippi R.

MERLIN

Falco columbarius

Like all its falcon relatives, the main weapons of the Merlin are speed, surprise and sharp, daggerlike talons. This small falcon's sleek body, long, narrow tail and pointed wings increase its aerodynamic efficiency for high-speed songbird pursuits. • Most Merlins migrate to Central and South America each fall, but a few overwinter, capitalizing on the abundance of songbirds that are attracted to suburban ornamental shrubs and backyard feeders. • Medieval falconers termed the Merlin "the lady's hawk," and Catherine the Great and Mary Queen of Scots were among the enthusiasts who would pitch Merlin and Sky Lark *(Alauda arvensis)* into matches of aerial prowess. • The Merlin was formerly known as "Pigeon Hawk," and the scientific name *columbarius* comes from the Latin for "pigeon," which it somewhat resembles in flight.

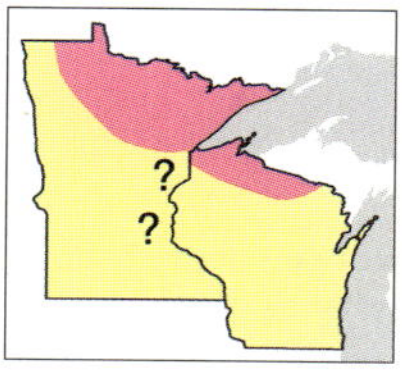

ID: banded tail; heavily streaked underparts; 1 indistinct facial stripe; long, narrow wings and tail. *Male:* blue gray back and crown; rufous leg feathers. *Female:* brown back and crown. *In flight:* very rapid, shallow wingbeats.

Size: *L* 10–12 in; *W* 23–26 in.

Status: ***MN:*** rare to uncommon migrant from late March to mid-May and from mid-August to early November; uncommon at peak migration periods over Hawk Ridge (Duluth); rare breeder; recent (2001) nesting in the Twin Cities; occasional in winter. ***WI:*** uncommon to fairly common migrant from March to April and from late August to November; uncommon breeder; rare but increasing winter visitor.

Habitat: *Breeding:* forests and plantations adjacent to open hunting grounds; sometimes suburban areas. *In migration:* open fields and lakeshores.

Nesting: in a coniferous or deciduous tree, crevice or cliff; usually reuses an abandoned raptor, crow, jay or squirrel nest; mostly the female incubates 4–5 whitish eggs, marked with reddish brown, for 28–32 days; male feeds the female away from the nest; both adults raise the young.

Feeding: overtakes smaller birds in flight; also eats rodents and large insects, such as grasshoppers and dragonflies; may also take bats.

Voice: loud, noisy, cackling cry: *kek-kek-kek-kek-kek* or *ki-ki-ki-ki;* calls in flight or while perched, often around the nest.

Similar Species: *American Kestrel* (p. 102): 2 facial stripes; more colorful; less direct flight style; often hovers. *Peregrine Falcon* (p. 105): larger; well-marked, dark "helmet"; pale, unmarked upper breast; black flecking on light underparts. *Sharp-shinned Hawk* (p. 92) and *Cooper's Hawk* (p. 93): short, rounded wings; reddish barring on breast and belly. *Rock Dove* (p. 174): broader wings in flight; shorter tail; often glides with its wings held in a "V."

Best Sites: ***MN:*** *In migration:* Hawk Ridge (Duluth); North Shore of L. Superior. ***WI:*** *In migration:* L. Michigan bluffs (Concordia University, Harrington Beach SP); Mississippi R. bluffs (Wyalusing SP).

GYRFALCON

Falco rusticolus

Every year, as the days get shorter and the snow begins to fall, birders of our region anxiously await the return of the world's largest falcon. Rarely do Gyrfalcons leave the Hudson Bay Lowlands of Canada and the arctic tundra, but even a brief glimpse of a Gyrfalcon will revive any birder who may have a bad case of the winter blues. • Watching a Gyrfalcon in flight is like watching an expertly piloted fighter plane. Cruising at slow speed, it looks for potential targets and then reacts with lightning swiftness. Unlike the Peregrine Falcon, the Gyrfalcon rarely swoops down from above with its wings closed—it prefers to outfly its prey, often launching a surprise attack from below, and almost any size bird is a potential meal.

gray morph

gray morph

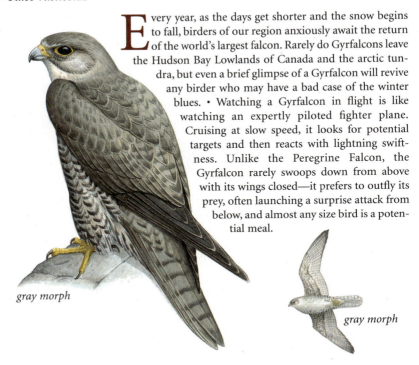

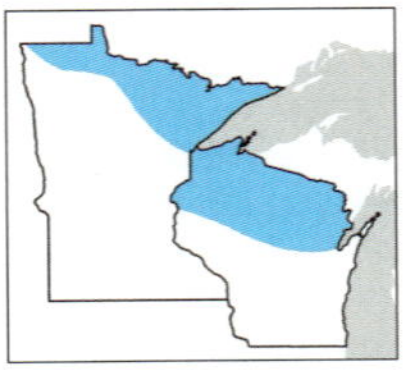

ID: long tail extends beyond wing tips when bird is perched; tail may be barred or unbarred. *Gray morph:* dark gray upperparts; streaking on white underparts. *Brown morph:* dark brown upperparts; streaking on white underparts. *White morph:* pure white head, breast and rump; white back and wings have dark flecking and barring. *Immature:* darker and more heavily streaked than adult; gray (rather than yellow) feet and cere.

Size: *Male: L* 20–22 in; *W* 4 ft. *Female: L* 22–25 in; *W* $4\frac{1}{2}$ ft.

Status: ***MN:*** rare visitor from November to March in the northeast, especially at Duluth; rare to accidental elsewhere in the state. ***WI:*** very rare migrant; rare winter visitor.

Habitat: open and semi-open areas, including fields and open wetlands where prey concentrates.

Nesting: does not nest in our region.

Feeding: locates prey from an elevated perch or by flying low over the ground; takes prey in midair or chases it down; eats mostly birds, especially waterfowl and shorebirds; also takes small mammals.

Voice: loud, harsh *kak-kak-kak*.

Similar Species: *Peregrine Falcon* (p. 105): prominent dark "helmet"; shorter tail; unstreaked upper breast and throat. *Northern Goshawk* (p. 94): similar at times to gray morph; prominent, white "eyebrow"; dark "cap"; rounded wings in flight; grayer underparts with finer streaking; unstreaked, white undertail coverts; eyes are red (adult) or pale yellow (immature).

Best Sites: ***MN:*** *Winter:* Duluth. ***WI:*** *Winter:* Superior; Buena Vista Grasslands.

PEREGRINE FALCON

Falco peregrinus

No bird elicits more admiration than a hunting Peregrine Falcon in full flight. Diving at speeds of up to 220 miles per hour, the Peregrine clenches its feet and then strikes its prey with a lethal blow that often sends both falcon and prey tumbling. • The Peregrine Falcon's awesome speed and hunting skills were little defense against the pesticide DDT. The chemical caused contaminated birds to lay eggs with thin shells, which broke when the adults incubated the eggs. This bird was extirpated in our region by the early 1960s, and completely eradicated east of the Mississippi River by 1964. DDT was banned in North America in 1972 and, in the 1980s, the Midwest Peregrine Falcon Restoration program successfully reintroduced Peregrine Falcons in cities throughout the Midwest. • Peregrine Falcons are a cosmopolitan species, nesting on every continent except Antarctica.

immature

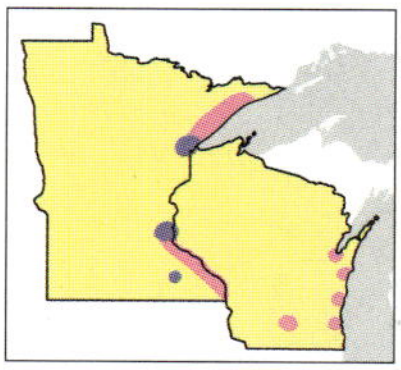

ID: blue gray back; prominent, dark "helmet"; light underparts with fine, dark spotting and flecking. *Immature:* brown where adult is blue gray; heavier breast streaks; gray (rather than yellow) feet and cere. *In flight:* pointed wings; long, narrow, dark-banded tail.
Size: *Male: L* 15–17 in; *W* 3–3½ ft. *Female: L* 17–19 in; *W* 3½–4 ft.
Status: ***MN:*** reintroduced; threatened; rare migrant from early March to late May and from mid-August through November; reintroduction has established populations of both resident and migratory birds.
WI: reintroduced; endangered; fairly common migrant from April to May and from late August to November; uncommon breeder; rare winter visitor.
Habitat: lakeshores, river valleys, river mouths, urban areas and open fields.
Nesting: usually on a rocky cliff or cutbanks; may use a skyscraper ledge; no material is added, but the nest is littered with prey remains, leaves and grass; nest sites are often reused; mostly the female incubates 3–4 creamy to buff eggs, heavily blotched with reddish brown, for 32–34 days.
Feeding: high-speed, diving stoops; strikes birds with clenched feet in midair; takes primarily pigeons, waterfowl, shorebirds, flickers and larger songbirds; rarely eats small mammals or carrion; prey is consumed on a nearby perch.
Voice: loud, harsh, continuous *cack-cack-cack-cack-cack* near the nest site.
Similar Species: *Gyrfalcon* (p. 104): larger; lacks dark "helmet"; longer tail. *Merlin* (p. 103): smaller; lacks prominent dark "helmet"; heavily streaked breast and belly.
Best Sites: ***MN:*** Hawk Ridge (Duluth); North Shore of L. Superior; lower Mississippi R. valley; Twin Cities; Rochester.
WI: *Breeding:* Milwaukee; Racine; Sheboygan; Manitowoc; Green Bay. *In migration:* L. Michigan bluffs; Mississippi R. bluffs.

PRAIRIE FALCON

Falco mexicanus

The Prairie Falcon's preferred habitat is the dry regions of western North America. It is usually found in areas where cliffs or bluffs interrupt open plains and deserts. In our region, the Prairie Falcon is a very rare or casual migrant. • Although Prairie Falcons are about the same size as Peregrines, they are more closely related to Gyrfalcons and hunt in the same manner, initiating high-speed chases close to the ground. Their flying style alternates quick, powerful wingbeats with gliding. • Like any human pilot learning to fly a plane, young falcons only get to keep their wings if they survive flight training. Inexperienced and overeager falcons risk serious injury or death when pushing the limits in early hunting forays. A swooping falcon can easily misjudge its flight speed or its ability to pull out of a dive.

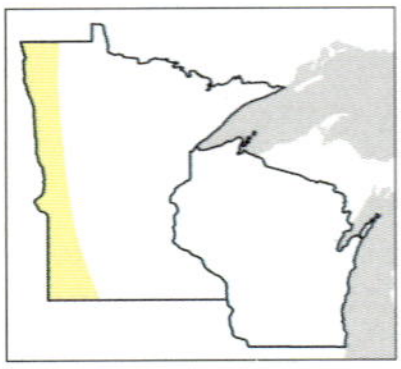

ID: brown upperparts; light face with dark, narrow facial stripe; light underparts with brown spotting. *In flight:* black "wing pits"; pointed wings; long, narrow, banded tail; rapid wingbeats.

Size: *Male: L* 14–15 in; *W* 3 ft. *Female: L* 16½–18 in; *W* 3½ ft.

Status: ***MN:*** casual migrant from mid-March to mid-May and from early August to late October; casual in winter in western regions. ***WI:*** casual migrant.

Habitat: open country, such as fields and grasslands.

Nesting: does not nest in our region.

Feeding: high-speed aerial attack, often overtakes songbirds and shorebirds in midair; also surprises ground squirrels in low, fast attacks.

Voice: alarm call is a rapid, shrill *kik-kik-kik-kik*.

Similar Species: no other falcon has dark "wing pits." *Peregrine Falcon* (p. 105): dark "helmet"; uniformly dark underwing; longer, less rounded wing tips. *Gyrfalcon* (p. 104): larger. *Merlin* (p. 103): much smaller; fainter facial stripe. *Swainson's Hawk* (p. 97): rounded wings in flight; lacks dark "wing pits"; immature may have facial stripe, but is generally heavier.

Best Sites: ***MN:*** Rothsay WMA. ***WI:*** no consistent sites.

GRAY PARTRIDGE

Perdix perdix

Gray Partridges can be seen "graveling" and picking seeds along quiet country roads, particularly during the early morning and late afternoon. Like other seed-eating birds, they regularly swallow small bits of gravel. These small stones accumulate in the bird's gizzard, a muscular pouch in the digestive system, and help to crush the hard grain and other seeds that these birds feed on. • Gray Partridges travel in groups called "coveys." When flushed, the entire covey bursts suddenly from cover, flapping furiously and then gliding to a safe haven nearby. During cold weather, Gray Partridges huddle together in a circle to conserve heat, with each bird facing outward, always ready to burst into flight. • This Eurasian game bird, also known as "Hungarian Partridge" or "Hun," was introduced into our region in the early part of the 20th century.

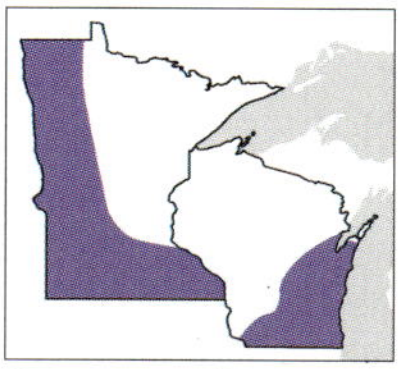

ID: small, rounded body; short tail with chestnut brown outer feathers; chestnut brown barring on flanks; orange brown face and throat; gray breast; mottled brown back; bare, yellowish legs. *Male:* chestnut brown patch on white belly. *Female:* no belly patch; paler face and throat.
Size: *L* 11–14 in; *W* 19 in.
Status: ***MN:*** uncommon and local year-round resident; declining over the past decade. ***WI:*** fairly common to uncommon local year-round resident in eastern regions; uncommon to rare year-round in the south.
Habitat: grassy and weedy fields and agricultural croplands.
Nesting: in hay fields, pastures, grassy fencelines and field margins; on the ground in a scratched-out depression lined with grass; female incubates 15–17 olive-colored eggs for 23–25 days; male helps care for the brood until the following spring.
Feeding: at dawn and dusk during summer; throughout the day during winter; gleans the ground for waste grain and seeds; may also eat leaves and large insects; often seen feeding on manure piles in winter.
Voice: at dawn and dusk; sounds like a rusty gate hinge: *kee-uck* or *scirl;* call is *kuta-kut-kut-kut* when excited.
Similar Species: *Ruffed Grouse* (p. 109): lacks rusty face and outer tail feathers. *Northern Bobwhite* (p. 114): white spots and crescents edged in black on chestnut brown sides and upper breast; male has white throat and long eye line; female has buff throat and eye line.
Best Sites: ***MN:*** Wilkin Co.; Pipestone Co.; Rock Co.; Murray Co.; Sibley Co.; Lyon Co. ***WI:*** country roads in Calumet, Brown, Kewaunee, Manitowoc and Outagamie Counties; best when there is adequate snow cover.

RING-NECKED PHEASANT

Phasianus colchicus

A native of Asia, the spectacular Ring-necked Pheasant was introduced to this region in the early 20th century as a game bird for hunters. Unfortunately, cold, snowy winters are a problem for this Eurasian bird. Unlike native grouse, the Ring-necked Pheasant does not have feathered legs and feet to insulate it through the winter months, and it cannot survive on native plants alone. The availability of grain and corn crops, as well as sheltered hedgerows and woodlots, has allowed this pheasant to survive in our area. Populations fluctuate widely in local areas depending on weather conditions, predation and farming practices. • The male pheasant's loud *ka-squawk* call is recognizable near farmyards, woodlots and brushy suburban parks. The female rarely calls and is more secretive for most of the year. • Ring-necked Pheasants are not very strong long-distance fliers, but are swift runners and are able to fly in explosive bursts over small open areas to escape predators.

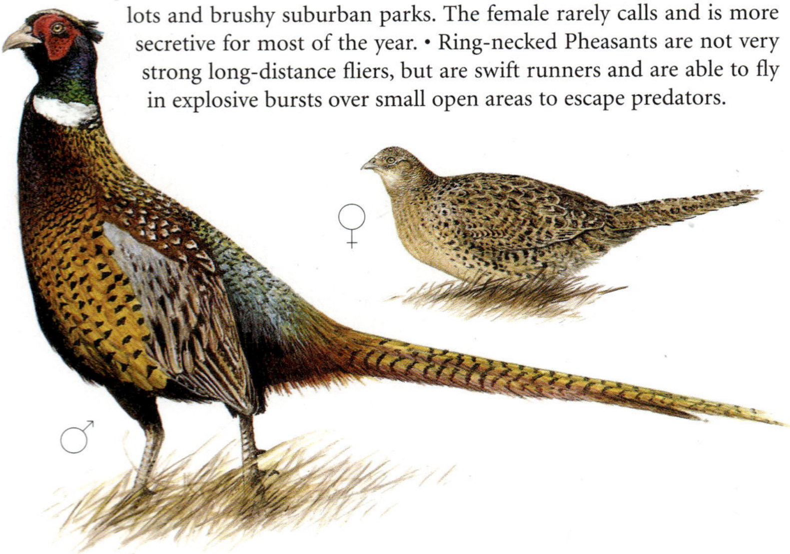

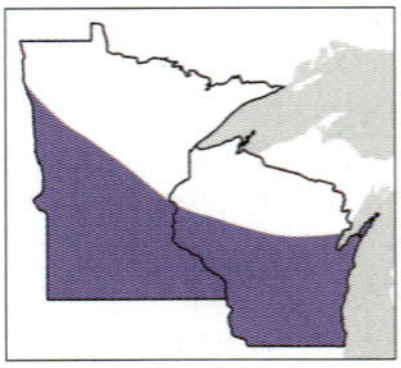

ID: large; long, barred tail; unfeathered legs. *Male:* green head; naked, red face patch; white "collar"; bronze underparts. *Female:* mottled brown overall; light underparts.
Size: *L* 20–36 in (male is noticeably larger than female); *W* 31 in.
Status: ***MN:*** common year-round resident. ***WI:*** fairly common year-round resident.
Habitat: *Breeding:* grasslands, grassy ditches, hay fields and grassy or weedy fields, fencelines, crop margins and woodlot margins. *Nonbreeding:* grain and corn fields in fall; woodlots, cattail marshes and shrubby areas close to croplands in winter.

Nesting: on the ground, among grass or sparse vegetation or next to a log or other natural debris; in a slight depression lined with grass and leaves; female incubates 10–12 olive buff eggs for 23–28 days; male takes no part in parental duties.
Feeding: *Summer:* gleans the ground and vegetation for weed seeds, grains and insects. *Winter:* eats mostly seeds, corn kernels and buds.
Voice: *Male:* loud, raspy, roosterlike, crowing *ka-squawk;* whirring of wings, usually just before sunrise.
Similar Species: male is distinctive. *Other grouselike birds* (pp. 107–14): generally smaller; shorter tails.
Best Sites: ***MN:*** wildlife management areas; wildlife refuges and Conservation Reserve Program lands. ***WI:*** agricultural fields and roads.

RUFFED GROUSE

Bonasa umbellus

Puzzled by the sound of a two-stroke motorcycle or lawnmower engine starting up and stalling in the woods? Actually, what you are hearing is the sound of a "drumming" Ruffed Grouse. Every spring, and occasionally in fall, the male Ruffed Grouse proclaims his territory. He struts along a fallen log with his tail fanned and his neck feathers ruffed, beating the air with accelerating wingstrokes. • The Ruffed Grouse is the most common and widespread grouse in the region, inhabiting a wide variety of woodland habitats ranging from small deciduous woodlots and suburban riparian woodlands to vast expanses of mixedwood forest. • Populations of Ruffed Grouse seem to fluctuate over a 10-year cycle. Many predators such as the Northern Goshawk that rely on this bird as a food source show population fluctuations that closely follow Ruffed Grouse trends. • During winter, scales grow out along the sides of this bird's toes, providing the Ruffed Grouse with temporary snowshoes.

♂ *gray morph*

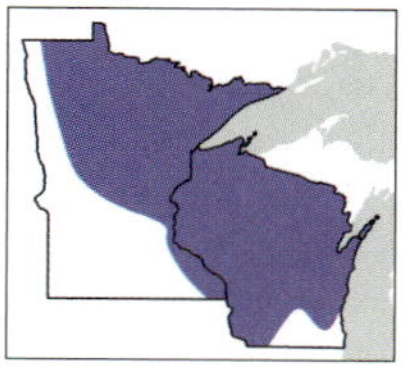

ID: small head crest; mottled gray brown overall; black feathers on sides of lower neck (visible when fluffed out in courtship displays); gray- or reddish-barred tail has broad, dark subterminal band and white tip. *Female:* incomplete subterminal tail band.

Size: *L* 15–19 in; *W* 22 in.

Status: ***MN:*** common year-round resident; absent from southwestern and south-central regions and the Red R. valley. ***WI:*** common year-round resident, except in the southeast.

Habitat: deciduous and mixed forests and riparian woodlands; in many areas favors young second-growth stands with birch and poplar.

Nesting: in a shallow depression among leaf litter; often beside boulders, under a log or at the base of a tree; female incubates 9–12 buff-colored eggs for 23–25 days.

Feeding: gleans from the ground and vegetation; omnivorous diet includes seeds, buds, flowers, berries, catkins, leaves, insects and snails; may take small frogs.

Voice: *Male:* uses his wings to produce a hollow, drumming courtship sound of accelerating, deep booms. *Female:* clucks and "hisses" around her chicks.

Similar Species: *Spruce Grouse* (p. 110): dark tail lacks barring and white tip; lacks head crest; male has red eye combs. *Sharp-tailed Grouse* (p. 111): lacks fan-shaped tail and black feathers on lower neck. *Greater Prairie-Chicken* (p. 112): short, dark tail; found in prairie and grassland habitats, not woods.

Best Sites: ***MN:*** Wild River SP; Chippewa NF; North Shore of L. Superior; mixed woodlands of the north-central region. ***WI:*** roads in forested areas anywhere except the southeastern corner of the state.

SPRUCE GROUSE

Falcipennis canadensis

The secretive, forest-dwelling Spruce Grouse trusts its cryptic plumage to conceal it from view in its dark, damp home. The Northern Goshawk is its most common predator, but the Spruce Grouse must also be wary of many mammalian carnivores. Despite its many predators, this grouse often allows people to approach within a few feet, which is the reason it is often called "Fool Hen." • The Spruce Grouse spends most of its time in upland black spruce stands and young jack pine forests searching for seasonally available food, such as blueberries, flowers, black spruce buds, moss spore capsules and insects. • Spruce Grouse are most conspicuous during April and May, when females issue their vehement calls and strutting males magically appear in open areas along trails, roads and campgrounds. The Spruce Grouse's deep call is nearly undetectable to the human ear, but displaying males attract attention as they transform from their usual dull camouflage to become red-eyebrowed, puff-necked, fan-tailed splendors.

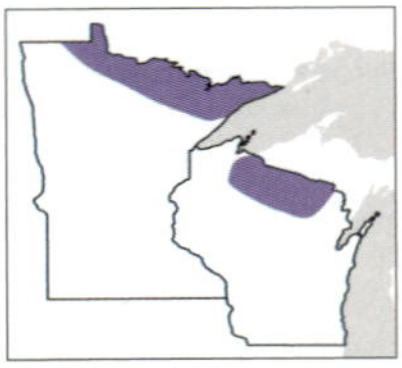

ID: black, unbarred tail with chestnut brown tip; mottled gray, brown and black overall; feathered legs. *Male:* red comb over eye; black throat, neck and breast; white-tipped undertail, lower neck and belly feathers. *Female:* barred, mottled underparts.
Size: *L* 13–16 in; *W* 22 in.
Status: ***MN:*** uncommon year-round resident. ***WI:*** threatened; uncommon year-round resident.
Habitat: conifer-dominated forest; sometimes disperses into deciduous forests.
Nesting: on the forest floor; in a well-hidden, shallow scrape lined with a few grasses and needles; female incubates 4–10 buff eggs, blotched and spotted with brown and chestnut, for up to 21 days.
Feeding: live buds and needles of spruce, pine and fir trees; also eats berries, flowers, seeds and a few insects in summer.
Voice: very low, guttural *krrrk krrrk krrrk*.
Similar Species: *Ruffed Grouse* (p. 109): crested head; tail has broad, dark, subterminal band and white tip; lacks black throat and breast. *Sharp-tailed Grouse* (p. 111): thinner, sharper tail; white throat; yellow eye combs.
Best Sites: ***MN:*** Lake Co.; Cook Co. ***WI:*** forest roads (2174, 2178, 2182, 2183, 2414 and Fire Lane Road) in Forest, Oneida and Vilas Counties.

SHARP-TAILED GROUSE

Tympanuchus phasianellus

From the last weeks of April through most of May, male Sharp-tailed Grouse gather at traditional dancing grounds, known as "leks," to perform courtship dances. With their wings drooping at their sides, their long, thin tails pointed skyward and their purplish pink air sacs fully inflated, males furiously pummel the ground with their feet, vigorously cooing and cackling for a crowd of prospective mates. Each male has a small stage within the larger, circular lek, and the inner, central position features the most virile dancers. • Like other grouse, Sharp-tail numbers rise and fall over time. However, habitat loss has caused this species to decline in numbers rather dramatically over the past decade • The term "lek" is derived from the Swedish word for "play."

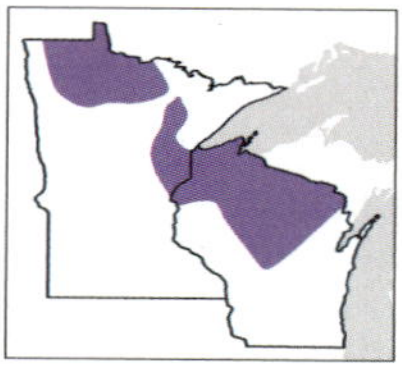

ID: mottled brown-and-black upperparts, neck and breast; dark crescents on white belly; white undertail coverts and outer tail feathers; long central tail feathers; yellow eye combs; white throat; feathered legs. *Male:* purplish pink air sacs on neck are inflated during courtship display.

Size: *L* 15–20 in; *W* 25 in.

Status: ***MN:*** locally common year-round resident in the north; most numerous in the northwest, absent from most of the northeast. ***WI:*** special concern; uncommon year-round resident.

Habitat: grasslands, abandoned pastures, fields and meadows, as well as open bogs, fens and forest clearings with scattered shrubs and trees.

Nesting: on the ground; occasionally under cover; in a depression lined with grass and leaves; female incubates 10–14 buff-colored eggs for 23–24 days.

Feeding: gleans the ground, trees and shrubs for buds, seeds, flowers, green shoots and berries; also eats insects when available.

Voice: rarely heard outside of courtship events: male gives a mournful, cooing call and a cackling call on the lek just before sunrise.

Similar Species: *Ruffed Grouse* (p. 109): slight crest; broad, fan-shaped tail with broad, dark subterminal band; black patches on neck. *Ring-necked Pheasant* (p. 108): female has longer tail and unfeathered legs; paler markings on underparts. *Spruce Grouse* (p. 110): black, fan-shaped tail; black or mottled throat; male has red eye combs. *Greater Prairie-Chicken* (p. 112): short, dark, rounded tail.

Best Sites: ***MN:*** Marshall Co.; Kittson Co.; Aitkin Co. ***WI:*** Crex Meadows WA; eastern Douglas Co. south of CTH S; Bear Bluff–Wood County WA.

GREATER PRAIRIE-CHICKEN

Tympanuchus cupido

From March to May, male Greater Prairie-Chickens congregate on leks, or booming grounds, to win the favor of loitering females. With their tails cocked upward and their wings low at their sides, males rhythmically inflate and deflate their golden air sacs, repeatedly producing a hollow "boom." • Male Greater Prairie-Chickens actively defend their territories from other males. Occasionally, they chase each other with their air sacs inflated and their neck tufts and tails erect, or a male may leap into the air, emitting loud cackles and striking his opponent with feet, wings and beak. • The Greater Prairie-Chicken was common across much of the region in the early 1900s, but populations have declined, primarily as a result of habitat disturbance. One subspecies, known as "Heath Hen," is now extinct.

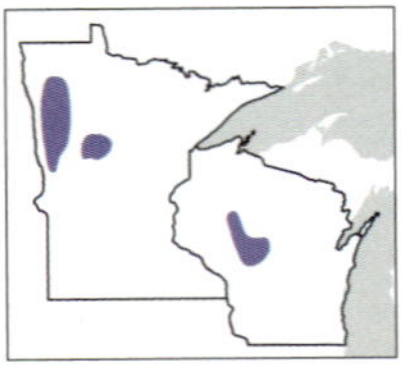

ID: medium-sized; heavily barred with brown, rufous and buff above and below; long, dark neck feathers (longer on male); short, rounded tail. *Male:* yellow "eyebrow"; yellow neck sacs are inflated when displaying (not visible otherwise); dark tail. *Female:* brown-barred tail.

Size: 17–18 in; *W* 28 in.

Status: ***MN:*** special concern; common year-round resident in Wilkin, Clay, Becker, Polk, Red Lake, Wadena and Cass Counties. ***WI:*** threatened; locally common year-round resident in central regions.

Habitat: tall-grass prairie; sometimes found in agricultural areas and brushy fields.

Nesting: on the ground in a shallow scrape lined with grass, feathers and leaves; female incubates 10–12 brown-speckled, olive-colored eggs for 23–26 days.

Feeding: eats mostly seeds, waste grain, leaves and occasionally acorns; supplements its diet in summer with buds, berries and insects; forages on the ground and occasionally in trees.

Voice: *Male:* during courtship produces a series of 3–4 booming notes that do not accelerate in speed; sometimes emits loud cackles.

Similar Species: *Sharp-tailed Grouse* (p. 111): pointed, brown tail with white border.

Best Sites: ***MN:*** Rothsay WMA; Tympanuchus WMA; recent releases at Big Stone NWR. ***WI:*** Buena Vista Grasslands; Mead WA.

WILD TURKEY

Meleagris gallopavo

Reintroduction efforts have reestablished the Wild Turkey as a permanent fixture in our region. Wild Turkeys were once much more common, but by the 1880s, habitat loss and overharvesting had taken a toll on these birds and they were extirpated in Minnesota and Wisconsin. • Although Wild Turkeys prefer to feed on the ground and travel on foot—they can run faster than 19 miles per hour—they are able to fly short distances and roost in trees at night. • This charismatic bird is the only native North American animal that has been widely domesticated. The wild ancestors of most other domestic animals all came from Europe, Asia or Africa. In their natural habitat, Wild Turkeys are wary birds with acute senses and a highly developed social system. • If Congress had taken Benjamin Franklin's advice in 1782, our national emblem would be the Wild Turkey instead of the majestic Bald Eagle.

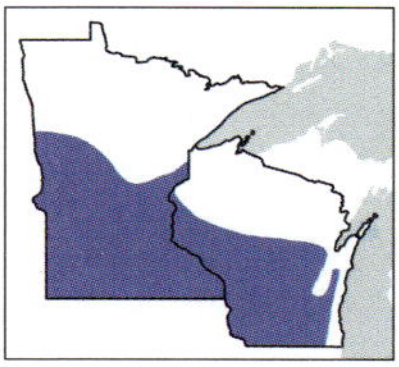

ID: naked, blue red head; dark, glossy, iridescent body plumage; barred, copper-colored tail; largely unfeathered legs. *Male:* long central breast tassel; red wattles. *Female:* smaller; blue gray head; less iridescent body.
Size: *Male: L* 3–3½ ft; *W* 5½ ft. *Female: L* 3 ft; *W* 4 ft.
Status: ***MN:*** reintroduced; local year-round resident in southern (especially southeastern), western and some parts of the central regions; expanding its range northward. ***WI:*** reintroduced; common year-round resident.
Habitat: deciduous, mixed and riparian woodlands; occasionally eats waste grain and corn in late fall and winter.
Nesting: in a woodland or at a field edge; in a depression on the ground under thick cover; nest is lined with grass and leaves; female incubates 10–12 brown-speckled, pale buff eggs for up to 28 days.
Feeding: in fields near protective woods; forages on the ground for seeds, fruits, bulbs and sedges; also eats insects, especially beetles and grasshoppers; may take small amphibians.
Voice: wide array of sounds; courting male gobbles loudly; alarm call is a loud *pert;* gathering call is a *cluck;* contact call is a loud *keouk-keouk-keouk*.
Similar Species: all other grouse and grouselike birds are much smaller. *Ring-necked Pheasant* (p. 108): feathered head and neck; long, narrow tail.
Best Sites: ***MN:*** Whitewater WMA (Winona Co.); Houston Co.; Washington Co. ***WI:*** wood and field borders in the southern half of the state.

NORTHERN BOBWHITE

Colinus virginianus

Throughout fall and winter, Northern Bobwhites typically travel in large family groups called "coveys," collectively seeking out sources of food and huddling together during cold nights. When they huddle, members of the covey all face outward, enabling the group to detect danger from any direction. With the arrival of summer, breeding pairs break away from their coveys to perform elaborate courtship rituals in preparation for another nesting season. • The male's characteristic, whistled *bob-white* call, usually issued in spring, is often the only evidence of this bird's presence among the dense, tangled vegetation of its rural woodland home. Bobwhites benefit from habitat disturbance, using the early successional habitats created by fire, agriculture and forestry. However, as land use has intensified and pesticide use has increased, populations have declined. Severe winters also reduce numbers considerably, with a slow recovery during ensuing years.

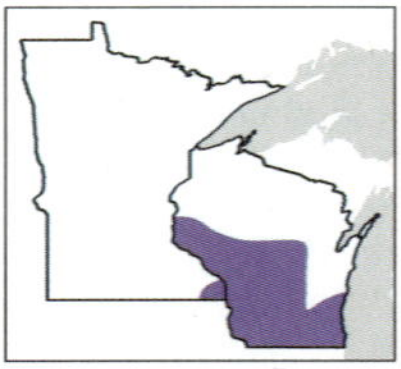

ID: mottled brown, buff-and-black upperparts; white crescents and spots edged in black on chestnut brown sides and upper breast; short tail.
Male: white throat; broad white "eyebrow."
Female: buff throat and "eyebrow."
Immature: smaller and duller overall; lacks black on underparts.
Size: *L* 10 in; *W* 13 in.
Status: ***MN:*** formerly widespread year-round resident across southern regions; probably extirpated as a wild species; a few may remain in Houston Co. and Filmore Co. ***WI:*** fairly common to common year-round resident, numbers fluctuate yearly.
Habitat: farmlands, open woodlands, woodland edges, grassy fencelines, roadside ditches and brushy, open country.

Nesting: in a shallow depression on the ground; often concealed by surrounding vegetation or a woven, partial dome; nest is lined with grass and leaves; pair incubates 12–16 white to pale buff eggs for 22–24 days.
Feeding: eats seasonally available seeds, berries, leaves, roots and nuts; also takes insects and other invertebrates.
Voice: whistled *hoy* is given year-round. *Male:* a whistled, rising *bob-white* given in spring and summer.
Similar Species: *Ruffed Grouse* (p. 109): lacks conspicuous throat patch and broad "eyebrow"; long, fan-shaped tail has wide, dark subterminal band; black patches on sides of neck. *Gray Partridge* (p. 107): orange brown face and throat; gray breast; chestnut brown outer tail feathers.
Best Sites: ***MN:*** Houston Co.; Filmore Co. ***WI:*** roads that bisect grassy fencelines; brushy open country in the southern part of the state.

YELLOW RAIL

Coturnicops noveboracensis

The Yellow Rail might be the most challenging breeding bird to find in this area. Not only is it quite rare and very cryptic, but it is most active at night, when naturalists are dreaming of birds behind closed eyelids. Under a blanket of darkness, this secretive bird slips quietly through tall sedges, grasses and cattails, more like a small mammal than a bird, picking food from the ground and searching for snails and earthworms. By day, the shy Yellow Rail hides behind a cover of dense, marshy vegetation. • With its laterally compressed body, the rail is a master at slipping through tightly packed stands of low vegetation. Its large feet, which distribute the bird's weight and help it to rest atop thin mats of floating plant material, add to its strange appearance. • The rail may have gotten its name because it looks "as thin as a rail."

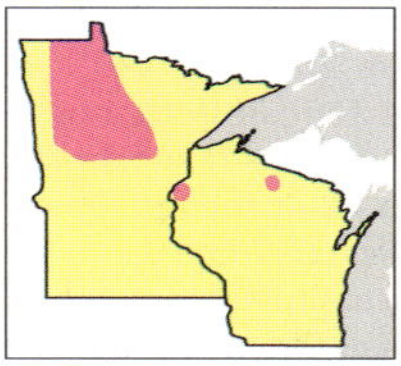

ID: short, pale bill; black and tawny stripes on upperparts (black stripes have fine, white barring); broad, dark line through eye; white throat and belly. *Immature:* darker overall; pattern on upperparts extends onto breast, sides and flanks. *In flight:* white trailing edge on inner wing.

Size: *L* 6½–7½ in; *W* 11 in.

Status: ***MN:*** special concern; probably migrates from late April to mid-May and in September; locally common breeder in the northwest. ***WI:*** threatened; rare migrant from late April to late May and from late August to early October; very rare breeder.

Habitat: sedge marshes and wet sedge meadows.

Nesting: on the ground or low over water; hidden by overhanging plants; shallow cup nest is made of grass or sedges; female incubates 8–10 buff-colored eggs, speckled with reddish brown, for up to 18 days.

Feeding: picks food from the ground and aquatic vegetation; eats mostly snails, aquatic insects, spiders and possibly earthworms; occasionally eats seeds.

Voice: like 2 bones or small stones clicking together: *tik, tik, tik-tik-tik.*

Similar Species: *Sora* (p. 118): lacks stripes on back and white patches on wings; breeding birds have black face and throat and bright yellow bill; distinctly different call. *Virginia Rail* (p. 117): long, reddish bill; rusty breast; gray face; lacks stripes on back and white patches in wings.

Best Sites: ***MN:*** McGregor Marsh; Waubun WMA; Roseau WMA. ***WI:*** Comstock Bog-Meadow; Puchyan Marsh; Crex Meadows WA.

KING RAIL

Rallus elegans

The King Rail is the largest rail in North America, even though it is only roughly the size of a farmyard chicken. Unlike some of the more secretive rails, this bird will wade through shallow water along the edge of a freshwater marsh, stalking its prey within full view of eager onlookers. Prey caught away from the water is usually brought to the water and submerged before eating, and larger prey is usually beaten against debris. • King Rail nests, which are commonly built above shallow water, often include a protective dome of woven vegetation and a well-engineered entrance ramp. Despite these deluxe features, young rails and their attending parents desert the nest mere hours after the eggs hatch. • King Rail populations have declined significantly in the last 40 years throughout large portions of its range, mostly as a result of habitat destruction.

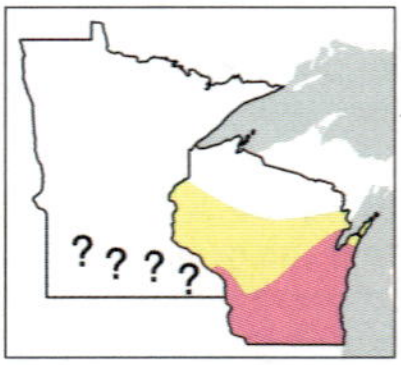

ID: long, slightly downcurved bill; black back feathers have buffy or tawny edges; rufous shoulders and underparts; strongly barred, black-and-white flanks; grayish brown "cheeks." *Immature:* similar plumage patterning with lighter, washed-out colors.

Size: *L* 15 in; *W* 20 in.

Status: ***MN:*** endangered; former breeder across the southern half of the state; only occasional migration and summer records since the 1950s; last recorded in June 1992 (Hennepin Co.). ***WI:*** uncommon migrant and breeder from late April to late September.

Habitat: marshes, shrubby swamps, marshy riparian shorelines and flooded fields with shrubby margins.

Nesting: among clumps of grass or sedge just above the water or ground; male builds most of the platform nest, canopy and entrance ramp using marsh vegetation; pair incubates 10–12 pale buff eggs, lightly spotted with brown, for 21–24 days.

Feeding: aquatic insects, crustaceans and occasionally seeds; small fish and amphibians are caught by foraging in shallow water, often in or near dense plant cover.

Voice: chattering call is 10 or fewer evenly spaced *kek* notes.

Similar Species: *Virginia Rail* (p. 117): much smaller; brown back feathers; gray face; red bill. *Least Bittern* (p. 46): solid black back feathers lack lighter edging; buff orange face and wing patches; thicker bill.

Best Sites: ***MN:*** none known. ***WI:*** Rat River WA; Horicon Marsh; Richard Bong State Recreation Area; Waunakee Marsh.

VIRGINIA RAIL

Rallus limicola

The best way to meet a Virginia Rail is to sit alongside a wetland marsh in spring, clap your hands three or four times to imitate this bird's *kidick* calls and wait patiently. If you are lucky, a Virginia Rail will reveal itself for a brief instant, but on most occasions you will only hear this elusive bird. • When pursued, a rail will almost always attempt to scurry away through dense, concealing vegetation rather than risk exposure in a fluttering getaway flight. Rails are very narrow birds that have modified feather tips and flexible vertebrae, which allow them to squeeze through the narrow confines of their marshy homes. • The Virginia Rail and its relative the Sora are often found living in the same marshes. The secret of their successful coexistence is found in their microhabitat preferences and distinct diets. The Virginia Rail typically favors the dry shoresides of marshes and feeds on invertebrates, while the Sora prefers waterfront property and eats plants and seeds.

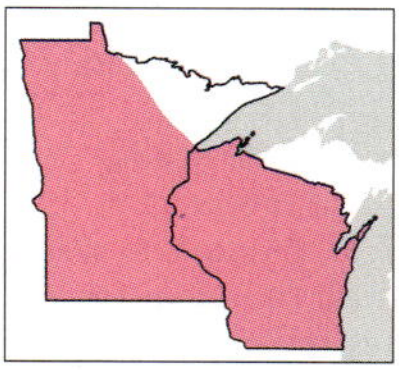

ID: long, downcurved, reddish bill; gray face; rusty breast; barred flanks; chestnut brown wing patch; very short tail. *Immature:* much darker overall; light-colored bill.

Size: *L* 9–11 in; *W* 13 in.

Status: ***MN:*** uncommon migrant from mid-April to late May; gradual exodus in August and September; uncommon breeder; rare or absent in heavily forested areas of northeastern and north-central regions; a few winter records in the south. ***WI:*** common migrant and breeder from mid-April to mid-October.

Habitat: wetlands, especially cattail and bulrush marshes.

Nesting: concealed in emergent vegetation, usually suspended just over the water; loose basket nest is made of coarse grass, cattail stems or sedges; pair incubates 5–13 spotted, pale buff eggs for up to 20 days.

Feeding: probes into soft substrates and gleans vegetation for invertebrates, including beetles, snails, spiders, earthworms, insect larvae and nymphs; also eats some pondweeds and seeds.

Voice: call is an often-repeated, telegraph-like *kidick, kidick;* also "oinks" and croaks.

Similar Species: *King Rail* (p. 116): much larger; dark legs; lacks reddish bill and gray face; immature is mostly pale gray. *Sora* (p. 118): short, yellow bill; black face and throat. *Yellow Rail* (p. 115): short, pale yellowish bill; black-and-tawny-striped back; white trailing edges of wings are seen in flight.

Best Sites: ***MN:*** none known. ***WI:*** Rat River WA; Horicon Marsh; Vernon Marsh; Trempealeau NWR; Mead WA; Sensiba WA; Ken Euers Nature Area.

SORA

Porzana carolina

The Sora is the most common and widespread rail in North America. Its elusive habits and preference for dense marshlands force most would-be observers to settle for a quick look at this small bird. However, if you venture out alone or with suitably silent partners on a calm, clear night in appropriate habitat, your chances of observing this bird are greatly increased. On occasion it has been known to parade around, unconcerned of onlookers, searching the shallows for food. • Even though its feet are not webbed or lobed, the Sora swims quite well over short distances. Though it appears to be a weak and reluctant flyer, the Sora migrates hundreds of miles each year between its breeding and wintering wetlands. • The species name *carolina* means "of Carolina" and this bird is also known as "Carolina Rail."

breeding

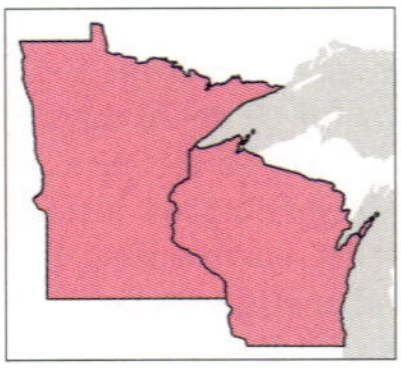

ID: short, yellow bill; black face, throat and foreneck; gray neck and breast; long, greenish legs. *Immature:* no black on face; buffier with paler underparts; bill is more greenish.

Size: *L* 8–10 in; *W* 14 in.

Status: ***MN:*** common migrant from mid-April to mid-May and from mid-August to mid-October; common breeder; uncommon to rare in the northeast. ***WI:*** very common migrant from mid-April to May and from late August to mid-October; very common breeder.

Habitat: wetlands with abundant emergent cattails, bulrushes, sedges and grasses.

Nesting: usually over water, but occasionally in a wet meadow under concealing vegetation; well-built basket nest is made of grass and aquatic vegetation; pair incubates 10–12 buff or olive buff, darkly speckled eggs for 18–20 days.

Feeding: gleans and probes for seeds, plants, aquatic insects and mollusks.

Voice: usual call is a clear, 2-note *coo-wee;* alarm call is a sharp *keek;* courtship song begins *or-Ah or-Ah,* descending quickly in a series of maniacal *weee-weee-weee* notes.

Similar Species: *Virginia Rail* (p. 117) and *King Rail* (p. 116): larger; long, downcurved bill; chestnut brown wing patch; rufous breast. *Yellow Rail* (p. 115): streaked back; tawny upperparts; white throat; white trailing edges of wings are seen in flight.

Best Sites: ***MN:*** Agassiz NWR; Carlos Avery WMA; Anoka Co.; large cattail marshes. ***WI:*** Horicon Marsh; Trempealeau NWR; Rat River WA; Collins Marsh; Sensiba WA; Mead WA.

COMMON MOORHEN

Gallinula chloropus

The Common Moorhen is a curious-looking creature that appears to have been assembled from bits and pieces left over from other birds: it has the bill of a chicken, the body of a duck and the long legs and large feet of a small heron. It strolls around the wetland with its head bobbing back and forth in synchrony with its legs, producing a comical, chugging stride. Its swimming style perpetuates the head bobbing and accentuates the bird's white undertail coverts. • Common Moorhens are fiercely argumentative when nesting, but moderate their bombastic tendencies somewhat in migration, when they will feed with American Coots, grebes and ducks. • For moorhens, the responsibilities of parenthood do not end when their eggs have hatched—parents will feed and shelter their young until they are capable of feeding themselves and flying on their own.

breeding

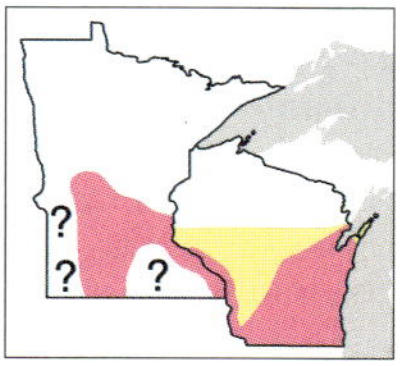

ID: reddish forehead shield; yellow-tipped bill; gray black body; white streak on sides and flanks; long, greenish yellow legs. *Breeding:* brighter bill and forehead shield. *Immature:* paler plumage; duller legs and bill; white throat.

Size: *L* 12–15 in; *W* 21 in.

Status: ***MN:*** special concern; little is known about migration movements; rare breeder; usually encountered on breeding areas in June. ***WI:*** fairly common migrant and breeder from mid-April to mid-October.

Habitat: marshes, ponds, lakes and sewage lagoons.

Nesting: pair builds a platform nest or a wide, shallow cup of bulrushes, cattails and reeds in shallow water or along a shoreline; often built with a ramp leading to the water; pair incubates 6–17 buff-colored, spotted or blotched eggs for 19–22 days.

Feeding: eats mostly aquatic vegetation, berries, fruits, tadpoles, insects, snails, worms and spiders; may take carrion and eggs.

Voice: noisy in summer; various sounds include chickenlike clucks, screams, squeaks and a loud *cup;* courting males give a harsh *ticket-ticket-ticket.*

Similar Species: *American Coot* (p. 120): white bill and forehead shield; lacks white streak on flanks.

Best Sites: ***MN:*** Houston Co.; Kandiyohi Co. ***WI:*** Horicon Marsh; Sensiba WA; Rat River WA; Vernon Marsh; Theresa Marsh; V pond; Schoeneberg Marsh; Mead WA.

AMERICAN COOT

Fulica americana

The American Coot behaves much like both a duck and a grebe. Like a duck, it dives and dabbles in the water and also grazes confidently on land. Like the most accomplished grebe, it swims about skillfully with its lobed feet. • American Coots squabble constantly during the breeding season, not just among themselves, but also with any waterbird that has the audacity to intrude upon their waterfront property. These odd birds can often be seen scooting across the surface of the water, charging rivals with flailing, splashing wings in an attempt to intimidate. Outside the breeding season, coots gather amicably together in large groups. • The American Coot is colloquially known as "Mud Hen," and many people mistakenly believe it is a species of duck.

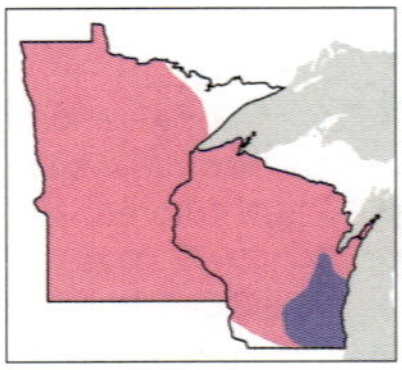

ID: gray black overall; white, chickenlike bill with dark ring around tip; reddish spot on white forehead shield; long, greenish yellow legs; lobed toes; red eyes. *Immature:* lighter body color; darker bill and legs; lacks prominent forehead shield.
Size: *L* 13–16 in; *W* 24 in.
Status: ***MN:*** common to abundant migrant from early March to late April and from mid-September to November; common to abundant breeder; rare to uncommon in the northeast; occasional in winter in the south where open water exists. ***WI:*** abundant migrant and breeder from mid-March to November; uncommon winter visitor.
Habitat: shallow marshes, ponds, lakes and wetlands with open water and emergent vegetation.

Nesting: in emergent vegetation; pair builds a floating nest from cattails and grass; pair incubates 6–11 brown-spotted, buffy white eggs for 21–25 days; regularly produces 2 broods in a season.
Feeding: gleans the water's surface; sometimes dives, tips up or even grazes on land; eats aquatic vegetation, insects, snails, crayfish, worms, tadpoles and fish; may steal food from ducks.
Voice: calls frequently in summer, day and night: *kuk-kuk-kuk-kuk-kuk;* also grunts.
Similar Species: *Ducks* (pp. 63–88): all lack white, chickenlike bill and uniformly black body. *Grebes* (pp. 37–42): lack white forehead shield and all-dark plumage. *Common Moorhen* (p. 119): reddish forehead shield; yellow-tipped bill; white streak on flanks.
Best Sites: ***MN:*** *In migration:* Agassiz NWR; Gun Club L. (Hennepin Co.); L. Minnewaska; L. Christina. ***WI:*** *Breeding:* marshes and swamps. *In migration:* also lakes.

SANDHILL CRANE

Grus canadensis

Deep, resonant, rattling calls announce the approach of a flock of migrating Sandhill Cranes long before they pass overhead. The coiling of their trachea adds harmonies to the notes in Sandhill Crane calls, allowing them to call louder and farther. At first glance, the large, V-shaped flocks look very similar to flocks of Canada Geese, but cranes circle upward on thermal rises, then slowly soar downward until they find another rise, continuing this pattern all the way to their nesting sites. Migrating flocks of Sandhills consist mainly of mated pairs and close family members. • Cranes mate for life, reinforcing pair bonds each spring with an elaborate courtship dance. • Sandhill Cranes are sensitive nesters, so they prefer to raise their young in areas that are isolated from human disturbance.

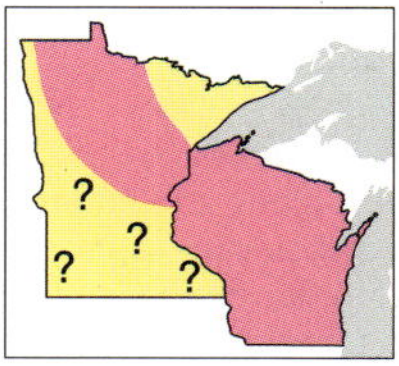

ID: very large, gray bird with long neck and legs; naked, red crown; long, straight bill; plumage is often stained rusty red from iron oxides in water. *Immature:* lacks red crown; reddish brown plumage may appear patchy. *In flight:* extends neck and legs; often glides, soars and circles.

Size: *L* 3½–4 ft; *W* 6–7 ft.

Status: ***MN:*** uncommon to common migrant from late March to early May and from early September to early December in west-central and northwestern regions; expanding its range eastward and southward; uncommon breeder primarily in the northwest but scattered pairs can occur almost anywhere in summer. ***WI:*** common migrant and breeder from mid-March to mid-November.

Habitat: *In migration:* agricultural fields and shorelines. *Breeding:* open marshes.

Nesting: on a large mound of aquatic vegetation in water or along a shoreline; pair incubates 2 brown-splotched, olive buff eggs for 29–32 days; egg hatching is staggered; young fly at about 50 days.

Feeding: probes and gleans the ground for insects, soft-bodied invertebrates, waste grain, shoots and tubers; frequently eats small vertebrates.

Voice: loud, resonant, rattling *gu-rrroo gu-rrroo gurrroo.*

Similar Species: *Great Blue Heron* (p. 47): lacks red forehead patch; neck is folded back over shoulders in flight. *Whooping Crane* (p. 358): all-white plumage; black flight feathers.

Best Sites: ***MN:*** Rothsay WMA; Agassiz NWR; Kittson Co.; Sherburne NWR; Roseau River WMA. ***WI:*** Crex Meadows WA; Rat River WA; Sandhill WA; Necedah NWR.

BLACK-BELLIED PLOVER

Pluvialis squatarola

The Black-bellied Plover's black-and-white breeding plumage is seen briefly in spring as birds race northward to make full use of the short arctic summer. In late summer, after nesting is completed, adults in faded plumage begin to appear. They are followed by juveniles in brighter, gold-flecked dress in September and October. Black-bellies choose a variety of wet habitats in fall migration, such as lakeshores and mudflats, as well as drier habitats, such as grassland pools and farmlands. They are usually encountered as individuals or in small flocks of less than ten. • Black-bellied Plovers forage for small invertebrates with a robinlike run-and-stop technique, frequently pausing to lift their heads for a reassuring scan of their surroundings. • Most plovers have three toes, but the Black-bellied Plover has a fourth toe higher on its leg, like most sandpipers.

breeding

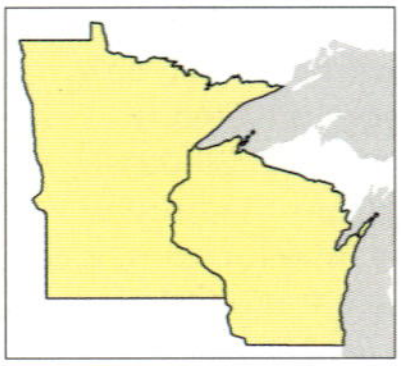

ID: short, black bill; long, black legs. *Breeding:* black face, breast, belly and flanks; white undertail coverts; white stripe leads from crown down to "collar," neck and sides of breast; mottled black-and-white back. *Nonbreeding:* mottled gray brown upperparts; lightly streaked, pale underparts. *In flight:* black "wing pits"; whitish rump; white wing linings.

Size: *L* 11–13 in; *W* 29 in.

Status: ***MN:*** uncommon migrant from late April to early June and from late July to mid-November. ***WI:*** fairly common migrant from April to early June and from July to November.

Habitat: plowed fields, meadows, lakeshores and mudflats along the edges of reservoirs, marshes and sewage lagoons.

Nesting: does not nest in our region.

Feeding: run-and-stop foraging technique; eats insects, mollusks and crustaceans.

Voice: rich, plaintive, 3-syllable whistle: *pee-oo-ee.*

Similar Species: *American Golden-Plover* (p. 123): gold-mottled upperparts; black undertail coverts in breeding plumage; lacks black "wing pits." *Red Knot* (p. 138): nonbreeding birds have longer bills, shorter legs and lack black "wing pits."

Best Sites: ***MN:*** Duluth; any good mudflat habitat. ***WI:*** L. Superior; L. Michigan; Seagull Bar; Green Bay; Shiocton–Black Creek; Arlington ponds; Nine Springs sewage ponds (Madison); Beaver Dam (A and W) ponds; Horicon Marsh.

AMERICAN GOLDEN-PLOVER

Pluvialis dominica

The American Golden-Plover population was among the largest of any bird in the world before they were mercilessly harvested in the late 1800s—a single day's shooting often yielded tens of thousands of birds. Populations have recovered somewhat, but they will likely never return to their former numbers. • In late summer, American Golden-Plovers migrate through our region, fattening up before heading across the western Atlantic to Brazil in one of the longest migrations of any North American bird. Migrating flocks may vary in numbers from 10 or 20 birds to thousands. • Although this bird is boldly marked, the white stripe down its side disrupts the sight of a predator, confusing the hunter as to where the bird's head or tail is. • The Eskimo Curlew *(Numenius borealis),* which is believed to be extinct, once migrated with this bird between the Canadian Arctic and South America. If the Eskimo Curlew does still exist, it may be found traveling alongside the American Golden-Plover.

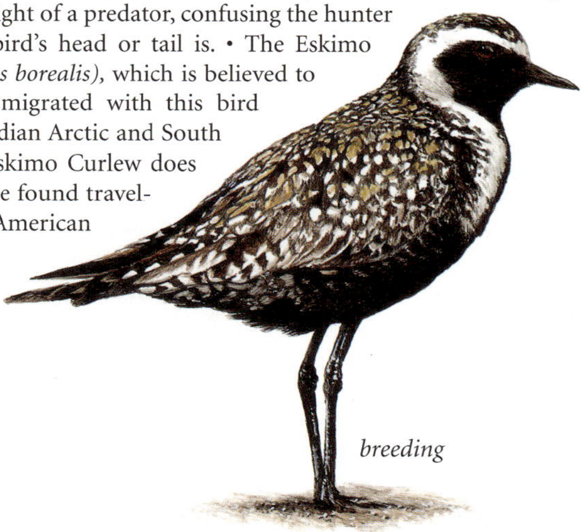

breeding

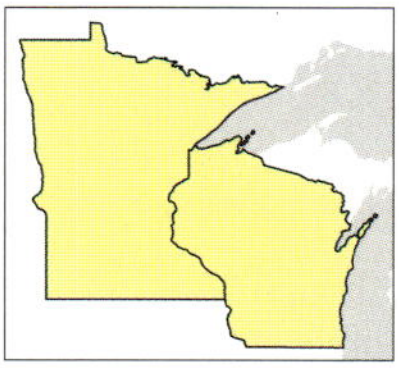

ID: straight, black bill; long, black legs. *Breeding:* black face and underparts; S-shaped, white stripe from forehead down to shoulders; dark upperparts are speckled with gold and white. *Nonbreeding:* broad, pale "eyebrow"; dark streaking on pale neck and underparts; much less gold on upperparts. *Immature:* somewhat brighter than adult; white forehead. *In flight:* gray "wing pits."

Size: *L* 10–11 in; *W* 26 in.

Status: ***MN:*** fairly common migrant from late March through June and from July to early November; most common in central and western regions. ***WI:*** fairly common migrant in April and May and from July to early November.

Habitat: cultivated fields, meadows, sod farms, lakeshores and mudflats along the edges of reservoirs, marshes and sewage lagoons.

Nesting: does not nest in our region.

Feeding: run-and-stop foraging technique; snatches insects, mollusks and crustaceans; also takes seeds and berries.

Voice: soft, melodious whistle: *quee, quee-dle*.

Similar Species: *Black-bellied Plover* (p. 122): white undertail coverts; whitish crown; lacks gold speckling on upperparts; conspicuous black "wing pits." *Buff-breasted Sandpiper* (p. 149): longer, finer bill; lacks black on underparts; flashy, white wing linings.

Best Sites: ***MN:*** Duluth; Big Stone NWR; sod farms. ***WI:*** sod farms at Wind L., Middleton, Stevens Point and Appleton; muddy, flooded fields and areas such as Arlington ponds, Beaver Dam ponds and Horicon Marsh.

SEMIPALMATED PLOVER

Charadrius semipalmatus

On the way to their arctic breeding grounds, small flocks of Semipalmated Plovers touch down on our shorelines and flooded fields from late April until mid-June. Spring migration is a brief, hurried affair because there is tremendous pressure for these long-distance migrants to begin breeding before the end of the short northern summer. After nesting, adults will leave the breeding grounds as early as July to enjoy a prolonged, leisurely migration to the coastlines of the southern U.S. and Central and South America. The young begin their journey as soon as they are strong enough to fly. Semipalmated Plovers are usually encountered in loosely associated groups, but flocks in the hundreds are sometimes seen. • The scientific name *semipalmatus* means "half-webbed" and refers to the slight webbing between the toes of this plover. The partial webbing is thought to give the bird's feet more surface area when it is walking on soft substrates.

♂ *breeding*

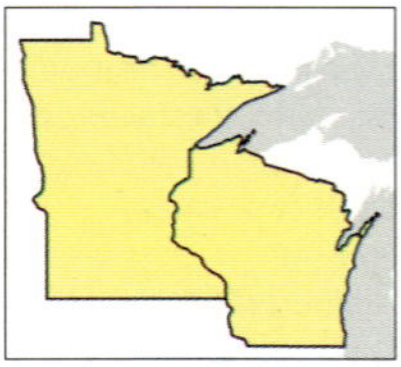

ID: *Breeding:* dark brown back; white breast with 1 black, horizontal band; long, orange legs; stubby, orange, black-tipped bill; white patch above bill; white throat and "collar"; black band across forehead; small, white eyebrow. *Nonbreeding:* duller; mostly dark bill. *Immature:* dark legs and bill; brown banding.

Size: *L* 7 in; *W* 19 in.

Status: ***MN:*** uncommon to sometimes common migrant from mid-April to early June and from late July through October. ***WI:*** fairly common migrant from April to mid-June and from July to October.

Habitat: sandy beaches, lakeshores, river edges and mudflats.

Nesting: does not nest in our region.

Feeding: usually on shorelines and beaches; run-and-stop foraging technique; eats crustaceans, worms and insects.

Voice: crisp, high-pitched, 2-part, rising whistle: *tu-wee*.

Similar Species: *Killdeer* (p. 126): larger; 2 black bands across breast. *Piping Plover* (p. 125): lacks dark band through eyes; much lighter upperparts; narrower breast band is incomplete in females and most males.

Best Sites: ***MN:*** Big Stone NWR; Agassiz NWR; sewage ponds. ***WI:*** Arlington ponds; Horicon Marsh; Green Bay; L. Michigan; L. Superior.

PIPING PLOVER

Charadrius melodus

A master of illusion, the Piping Plover's pale, sand-colored plumage is the perfect camouflage against a sandy beach. As well, from a distance the dark bands across its forehead and neckline resemble scattered pebbles or strips of washed-up vegetation. • This plover's cryptic plumage has done little to protect it from wetland drainage, increased predation and disturbance by humans. The recreational use of beaches during summer, and an increase in human-tolerant predators, such as gulls, raccoons and skunks, has impeded its ability to reproduce successfully. Consequently, the Piping Plover is now considered an endangered species. • On beaches with wave action, these birds often employ a foot-trembling strategy to entice invertebrates to the surface. • If threatened, Piping Plover chicks typically take to the water and swim away, while adults rarely swim at all.

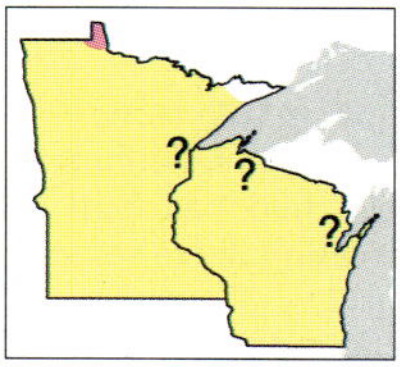

ID: pale, sandy upperparts; white underparts; orange legs. *Breeding:* black-tipped, orange bill; black forehead band; black "necklace" (usually incomplete, especially on females). *Nonbreeding* and *immature:* no breast or forehead band; all-black bill.

Size: *L* 7 in; *W* 19 in.

Status: ***MN:*** endangered; rare migrant from mid-April to mid-May and from late July to early September; formerly more common; very rare breeder; breeds only in the Lake of the Woods area (Pine and Curry I. and possibly along the shores of the Northwest Angle). ***WI:*** endangered; rare migrant from late April to May and from mid-July to October; very rare breeder.

Habitat: sandy beaches, mudflats and open lakeshores.

Nesting: on bare sand along an open shoreline; in a shallow scrape sometimes lined with pebbles and tiny shells; pair incubates 4 pale buff eggs, blotched with dark brown and black, for 26–28 days.

Feeding: run-and-stop foraging technique; eats worms and insects; almost all its food is taken from the ground.

Voice: clear, whistled melody: *peep peep peep-lo*.

Similar Species: *Semipalmated Plover* (p. 124): dark band over eye; much darker upperparts. *Killdeer* (p. 126): larger; 2 breast bands; much darker upperparts.

Best Sites: ***MN:*** Lake of the Woods; Duluth. ***WI:*** L. Michigan; L. Superior.

KILLDEER

Charadrius vociferus

The ubiquitous Killdeer is often the first shorebird a birder learns to identify. Its boisterous *kil-dee-dee* calls rarely fail to catch the attention of people passing through its wide variety of nesting environments. The Killdeer's preference for open fields, gravel driveways, beach edges, golf courses and abandoned industrial areas has allowed it to thrive throughout our rural and urban landscapes. • If you happen to wander too close to a Killdeer nest, the parent will try to lure you away, issuing loud alarm calls, feigning a broken wing and exposing its rufous rump. Most predators take the bait and are led far enough away for the parent to suddenly recover from its injury and fly off, sounding its piercing calls. Similar distraction displays are widespread phenomena in the bird world, but in our region, the Killdeer's broken-wing act is by far the gold medal winner. • The scientific name *vociferus* aptly describes this vocal bird, but double-check all calls in spring, when the Killdeer is often imitated by frisky European Starlings.

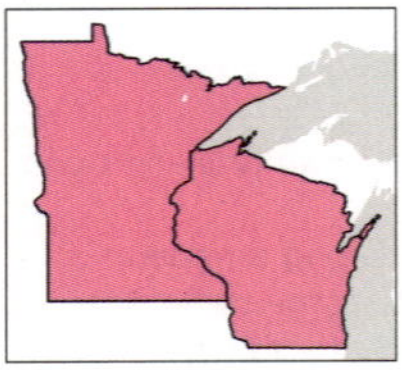

ID: long, dark yellow legs; white upperparts with 2 black breast bands; brown back; white underparts; brown head; white "eyebrow"; white face patch above bill; black forehead band; rufous rump. *Immature:* downy; only 1 breast band.

Size: *L* 9–11 in; *W* 24 in.

Status: ***MN:*** common migrant from late February to late April and from mid-August to December; common breeder; casual in winter in the southern part of the state. ***WI:*** common migrant and breeder from late March to early November; rare winter visitor.

Habitat: open ground, fields, lakeshores, sandy beaches, mudflats, gravel streambeds, wet meadows and grasslands; also urban areas and parks, often at a distance from water.

Nesting: on open ground; in a shallow, usually unlined, depression; pair incubates 4 darkly spotted and blotched, pale buff eggs for 24–28 days; occasionally raises 2 broods.

Feeding: run-and-stop foraging technique; eats mostly insects; also takes spiders, snails, earthworms and marine invertebrates.

Voice: loud, distinctive *kill-dee kill-dee kill-deer* and variations, including *deer-deer.*

Similar Species: *Semipalmated Plover* (p. 124): smaller; only 1 breast band. *Piping Plover* (p. 125): smaller; lighter upperparts; 1 breast band.

Best Sites: widespread throughout both states.

AMERICAN AVOCET

Recurvirostra americana

An American Avocet in full breeding plumage is a strikingly elegant bird, with its long, peachy red neck. Usually by August, the peach-colored "hood" has been replaced by a more subdued winter gray, which the bird will wear for the greater part of the year. It is the only avocet in the world that undergoes a yearly color change. • The American Avocet's upturned bill looks bent out of shape, but is ideal for efficiently skimming aquatic vegetation and invertebrates off the surface of shallow water. • During courtship, the female extends her bill forward and lowers her "chin" until it just clears the water's surface. The male struts around his lovely mate until conditions are just right. Following mating, the pair cross their bills and walk away in unison, celebrating and reinforcing their bond.

♂ breeding

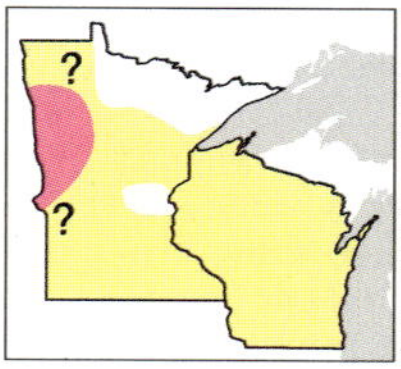

ID: long, upturned, black bill; long, pale blue legs; black wings with wide, white patches; white underparts; female's bill is more upturned and shorter than male's. *Breeding:* peachy red head, neck and breast. *Nonbreeding:* gray head, neck and breast. *In flight:* a "stick with wings"; long, skinny legs and neck; black-and-white wings.

Size: *L* 17–18 in; *W* 31 in.

Status: ***MN:*** uncommon to rare migrant from mid-April to mid-May and from July to October; rare fall migrant; intermittent breeder in a number of western counties. ***WI:*** uncommon migrant in April and May and from July to October; casual breeder.

Habitat: lakeshores, alkaline wetlands and exposed mudflats.

Nesting: semi-colonial; along dried mudflats, exposed shorelines or open areas; always near water; in a shallow depression sparsely lined with vegetation; pair incubates 4 darkly spotted and blotched, pale brownish buff eggs for 22–24 days.

Feeding: sweeps its bill from side to side along the water's surface, picking up aquatic invertebrates, insects and occasionally seeds; male sweeps lower in the water than female; occasionally swims and tips up like a duck.

Voice: harsh, shrill *plee-eek plee-eek.*

Similar Species: *Black-necked Stilt* (p. 358): straight bill; mostly black head. *Willet* (p. 131): grayish overall; straight bill.

Best Sites: ***MN:*** Becker Co.; Traverse Co.; Salt L. (Lac Qui Parle Co.). ***WI:*** Racine, Milwaukee, Sheboygan and Manitowoc (L. Michigan), especially in spring.

GREATER YELLOWLEGS

Tringa melanoleuca

The Greater Yellowlegs is one of the birds that performs the role of lookout among mixed flocks of shorebirds. At the first sign of danger, these large sandpipers bob their heads and call incessantly. If forced to, they will usually retreat into deeper water, becoming airborne only as a last resort. • Many shorebirds, including the Greater Yellowlegs, often stand or hop around beachflats on one leg. These stubborn "one-leggers" may be mistaken for crippled individuals, but this stance is an adaptation that conserves body heat. • Despite its long bill, the Greater Yellowlegs does not probe for its food, but instead picks it off the water's surface, or swings its bill from side to side in the the water like an avocet. • Greater Yellowlegs are the more solitary of the two yellowlegs species, but can be seen in small flocks during migration.

breeding

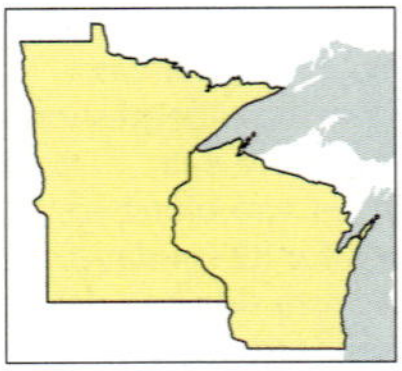

ID: long, bright yellow legs; dark, 2-tone bill is slightly upturned and noticeably longer than head width. *Breeding:* brown black back and upperwing; fine, dense, dark streaking on head and neck; dark barring on breast often extends onto belly; subtle, dark eye line; light lores. *Nonbreeding:* gray overall; fine streaks on breast; clear belly. *Immature:* warmer brown upperparts, spotted with pale buff notches; brown streaks on breast, flanks and undertail.

Size: *L* 13–15 in; *W* 28 in.

Status: ***MN:*** common migrant from late March to early May and from late June to early November. ***WI:*** fairly common migrant from late March to May and from July to early November.

Habitat: almost all wetlands including lakeshores, marshes, flooded fields and river shorelines.

Nesting: does not nest in our region.

Feeding: usually wades in water over its knees; sometimes sweeps its bill from side to side; primarily eats aquatic invertebrates; also takes small fish; occasionally snatches prey from the water's surface.

Voice: quick, whistled series of *tew-tew-tew,* usually 3 notes.

Similar Species: *Lesser Yellowlegs* (p. 129): smaller; straight bill is not noticeably longer than width of head; call is generally a pair of higher notes: *tew-tew.* *Willet* (p. 131): white wing bars; heavier, straighter bill; dark, greenish legs; distinctive, clear *will-will-willet* call.

Best Sites: ***MN:*** Big Stone NWR; Salt L. (Lac Qui Parle Co.); sewage ponds. ***WI:*** Horicon Marsh; Arlington ponds; Shiocton–Black Creek; Green Bay; Beaver Dam ponds.

LESSER YELLOWLEGS

Tringa flavipes

With a series of continuous, rapid-fire *tew-tew* calls, the Lesser Yellowlegs streaks across the surface of wetlands and lakeshores. This bird is usually seen in small flocks, but occasionally large aggregations occur. • Some birders find it a challenge to separate Lesser Yellowlegs and Greater Yellowlegs in the field. However, with practice you will notice that the Lesser's bill is finer, straighter and not noticeably longer than the width of its head, that the Greaters will stray into deeper water and even swim at times, and that the birds' calls are different. • The Lesser Yellowlegs was a popular game bird in the late 1800s. The birds were easy targets because of this species' tendency to return and hover above wounded flockmates. • The scientific name *flavipes* is derived from Latin words meaning "yellow foot."

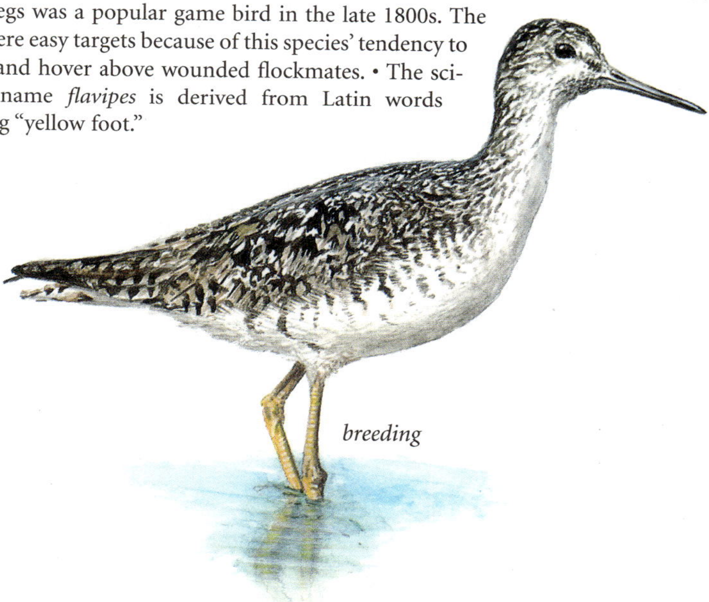

breeding

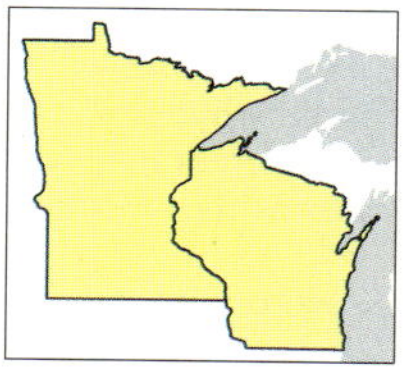

ID: bright yellow legs; all-dark bill is not noticeably longer than width of head. *Breeding:* brown black back and upperwing; fine, dense, dark streaking on head, neck and breast; lacks barring on belly; subtle, dark eye line; light lores. *Nonbreeding:* similar, but gray overall.

Size: *L* 10–11 in; *W* 24 in.

Status: ***MN:*** common to locally abundant migrant from late March to early June and from July to October. ***WI:*** common migrant from late March to May and from July to October.

Habitat: shorelines of lakes, rivers, marshes and ponds.

Nesting: does not nest in our region.

Feeding: snatches prey from the water's surface; frequently wades in shallow water; primarily eats aquatic invertebrates; also takes small fish and tadpoles.

Voice: typically a high-pitched pair of *tew* notes.

Similar Species: *Greater Yellowlegs* (p. 128): larger; bill is slightly upturned and noticeably longer than width of head; *tew* call is usually given in a series of 3 notes. *Solitary Sandpiper* (p. 130): white eye ring; darker upperparts; paler bill; greenish legs. *Willet* (p. 131): much bulkier; black-and-white wings; heavier bill.

Best Sites: ***MN:*** Big Stone NWR; Crookston sewage ponds; Heron L. (Jackson Co.); Salt L. (Lac Qui Parle Co.); sewage ponds throughout the state. ***WI:*** Horicon Marsh; Arlington ponds; Shiocton–Black Creek; Green Bay; Beaver Dam ponds.

SOLITARY SANDPIPER

Tringa solitaria

True to its name, the Solitary Sandpiper is usually seen alone, bobbing its body like a spirited dancer as it forages for insects along stream courses and lakeshores. In addition, Solitary Sandpipers are very aggressive when protecting a nest site or feeding, so breeding pairs are rarely in close proximity to one another. Once in a while, especially during migration, a lucky observer may happen upon a small group of these birds. • The Solitary Sandpiper's nesting strategy remained a mystery until 1903, when a homesteader in western Canada peered into what he thought was a robin's nest, but found a Solitary Sandpiper instead. For years, this wily shorebird had stumped amateur naturalists and professional ornithologists alike. Few thought that a shorebird would nest in an abandoned songbird nest!

breeding

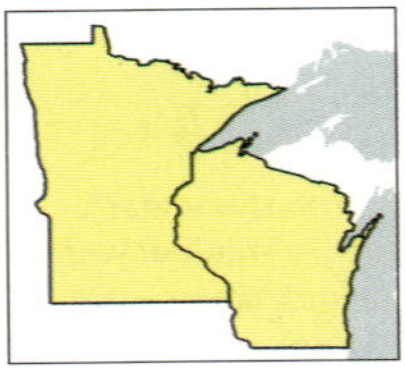

ID: white eye ring; short, green legs; dark yellowish bill with black tip; spotted, gray brown back; white lores; gray brown head, neck and breast have fine, white streaks; dark upper tail feathers with black-and-white barring on sides. *In flight:* dark underwings.

Size: *L* 7½–9 in; *W* 22 in.

Status: ***MN:*** uncommon to common migrant from mid-April to mid-May and from July to mid-August; less common as a migrant in western regions; only 1 confirmed (1982) and 1 possible nesting record (1973). ***WI:*** fairly common migrant in April and May and from July to October.

Habitat: wet meadows, sewage lagoons, muddy ponds, sedge wetlands, beaver ponds and wooded streams.

Nesting: in a coniferous tree in a bog or near near open water; will use the abandoned nest of a thrush, blackbird or other songbird; pair incubates 4 spotted and blotched, pale greenish eggs for 23–24 days.

Feeding: stalks shorelines and wetlands, picking up aquatic invertebrates, such as water boatmen and damselfly nymphs; also gleans for terrestrial invertebrates; occasionally stirs the water with its foot to spook out prey.

Voice: high, thin *peet-wheet* or *wheat wheat wheat.*

Similar Species: *Lesser Yellowlegs* (p. 129): no eye ring; longer, bright yellow legs. *Spotted Sandpiper* (p. 132): incomplete eye ring; spotted breast in breeding plumage; black-tipped, orange bill. *Other sandpipers* (pp. 128–49): black bills and legs; lack white eye ring.

Best Sites: ***MN:*** Big Stone NWR; Carlos Avery WMA; Lewiston sewage ponds; Salt L. (Lac Qui Parle Co.). ***WI:*** Arlington ponds; Green Bay; Beaver Dam ponds; Horicon Marsh; Shiocton–Black Creek.

WILLET

Catoptrophorus semipalmatus

A resting Willet gives the impression of being a rather overweight, underactive yellowlegs. The moment it takes flight or displays, however, its black-and-white wings add sudden color while it calls out a loud, rhythmic *will-will-willet, will-will-willet!* The bright, bold flashes of the Willet's wings may alert other shorebirds to imminent danger. These flashes may also double as a means of intimidating predators during the bird's dive-bombing defense of its young. • Willets are loud, social, easily identified birds—a nice change when dealing with sandpipers. There are two distinct subspecies of the Willet, a western and an eastern, with the western subspecies most likely to be seen here. The eastern race rarely ventures far from the Atlantic Coast, while the western race breeds far inland and winters on the Pacific Coast.

breeding

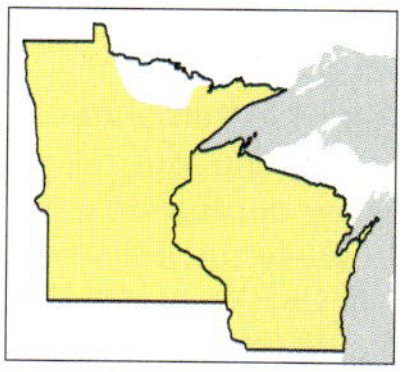

ID: large, plump body; heavy, straight, black bill; light throat and belly. *Breeding:* dark streaking and barring overall. *In flight:* black-and-white wing pattern with white stripe across base of primaires and secondaries.
Size: *L* 14–16 in; *W* 26 in.
Status: ***MN:*** uncommon migrant from mid-April to mid-May; rare migrant from July to late September; best represented in western regions; numbers vary—in some years it may be common in local areas in spring; former breeder in western regions, but has disappeared as a nesting species; a few July records indicate a post-breeding dispersal. ***WI:*** uncommon migrant from mid-April to May and from mid-July to October.

Habitat: wet fields and shorelines of marshes, lakes and ponds.
Nesting: does not nest in our region.
Feeding: feeds by probing muddy areas; also gleans the ground for insects; occasionally eats shoots and seeds.
Voice: loud, rolling *will-will-willet, will-will-willet.*
Similar Species: *Marbled Godwit* (p. 136) and *Hudsonian Godwit* (p. 135): much longer, pinkish yellow bills with dark, slightly upturned tips; larger body; lack black-and-white wing pattern. *Greater Yellowlegs* (p. 128): long, yellow legs; slightly upturned bill; lacks black-and-white wing pattern.
Best Sites: ***MN:*** Salt L. (Lac Qui Parle Co.); Tamarac NWR; Agassiz NWR.
WI: Milwaukee, Manitowoc, Sheboygan and Racine (L. Michigan); Horicon Marsh; Arlington ponds; Eau Claire and Chippewa Falls ponds.

SPOTTED SANDPIPER

Actitis macularia

This diminutive shorebird is a widespread breeder here, and during summer the Spotted Sandpiper is the most frequently encountered sandpiper throughout much of the region. It is usually encountered individually or in small flocks of less than 10 birds. • It was not until 1972 that the unexpected truth about the Spotted Sandpiper's breeding activities was realized. The female defends a territory and mates with more than one male in a single breeding season, leaving the males to tend the nests and eggs. This unusual nesting behavior, known as polyandry, is found in about one percent of all bird species. • Although its breast spots are not noticeable from a distance, the Spotted Sandpiper's stiff-winged, quivering flight pattern and tendency to burst from the shore are easily recognizable. This bird is also known for its continuous teetering behavior as it forages.

breeding

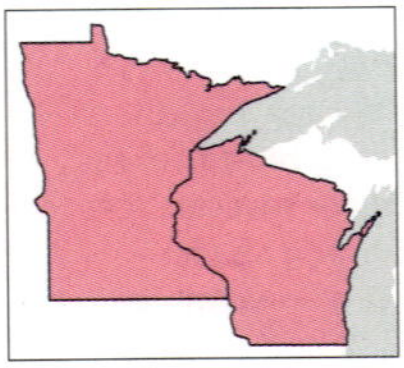

ID: teeters continuously. *Breeding:* white underparts are heavily spotted with black; yellow orange legs; black-tipped, yellow orange bill; white "eyebrow." *Nonbreeding* and *immature:* pure white breast, foreneck and throat; brown bill; dull yellow legs. *In flight:* flies close to the water's surface; rapid, shallow wingbeats; white upperwing stripe.

Size: *L* 7–8 in; *W* 15 in.

Status: ***MN:*** common migrant from mid-April to mid-May and from mid-August to October; common breeder. ***WI:*** common migrant and breeder from mid-April to October.

Habitat: shorelines, gravel beaches, ponds, marshes, alluvial wetlands, rivers, streams, swamps and sewage lagoons; occasionally seen in cultivated fields.

Nesting: usually near water; often under overhanging vegetation among logs or under bushes; in a shallow depression lined with grass; almost exclusively the male incubates 4 creamy buff, heavily blotched and spotted eggs and raises the young.

Feeding: picks and gleans along shorelines for terrestrial and aquatic invertebrates; also snatches flying insects from the air.

Voice: sharp, crisp *eat-wheat, eat-wheat, wheat-wheat-wheat-wheat.*

Similar Species: *Solitary Sandpiper* (p. 130): complete eye ring; lacks spotting on breast; yellowish bill with dark tip. *Other sandpipers* (pp. 128–49): mostly black bills and legs; lack spotting on breast.

Best Sites: ***MN:*** lakes and sewage ponds. ***WI:*** L. Michigan; L. Superior; numerous inland lakes.

UPLAND SANDPIPER

Bartramia longicauda

In spring, Upland Sandpipers are occasionally seen perched atop tall fence posts belting out airy, "wolf-whistle" courtship tunes. Excited males will even launch into the air to perform courtship flight displays, combining song with shallow, fluttering wingbeats. At the height of the breeding season, however, these large-eyed, inland shorebirds are rarely seen, remaining hidden in the tall grass of abandoned fields and ungrazed pastures. • Twice each year, the wide-ranging Upland Sandpiper journeys between Canada and South America. It spends a remarkably short time on its breeding grounds and begins its fall migration unusually early. • During the late 1800s, demand for this bird's meat led to overharvesting and catastrophic declines in its population over much of North America. Its numbers have since improved in our region, but only in limited areas where grassland habitat persists.

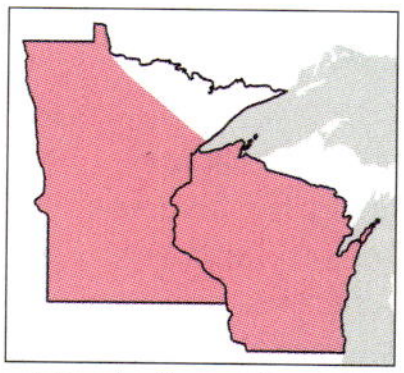

ID: small head; long neck; large, dark eyes; yellow legs; mottled, brownish upperparts; lightly streaked breast, sides and flanks; white belly and undertail coverts; bill is about same length as head.
Size: *L* 11–12½ in; 26 in.
Status: ***MN:*** uncommon migrant in April and May; most have left by early August; common breeder in western regions; uncommon breeder in central and eastern regions; rare in other regions. ***WI:*** special concern; fairly common to uncommon migrant and breeder from mid-April to mid-September.
Habitat: hay fields, ungrazed pastures, grassy meadows, abandoned fields, natural grasslands and airports.
Nesting: in dense grass or along a wetland; in a depression, usually with grass arching over the top; pair incubates 4 pale to pinkish buff eggs, lightly spotted with reddish brown, for 22–27 days; both adults tend the young.
Feeding: gleans the ground for insects, especially grasshoppers and beetles.
Voice: courtship song is an airy, whistled *whip-whee-ee you;* alarm call is *quip-ip-ip.*
Similar Species: *Willet* (p. 131): longer, heavier bill; dark greenish legs; black-and-white wings in flight. *Buff-breasted Sandpiper* (p. 149): shorter neck; larger head; daintier bill; lacks streaking on "cheek" and foreneck. *Pectoral Sandpiper* (p. 145): streaking on breast ends abruptly; smaller eyes; shorter neck; usually seen in larger numbers.
Best Sites: ***MN:*** Rothsay WMA; Big Stone NWR; Becker Co.; Polk Co.; Felton Prairie SNA (Clay Co.). ***WI:*** Buena Vista Grasslands; Crex Meadows WA; Bird Sanctuary Park (Douglas County WA); Door Co.

WHIMBREL

Numenius phaeopus

During spring and fall, wide scatterings of Whimbrels can be seen on expansive mudflats or in large, plowed fields. Each bird forages individually, yet remains in contact with others of its kind, ever prepared to take flight as a flock. • The Whimbrel enjoys a widespread distribution, nesting across northern North America and Eurasia and spending its winters on the shores of six continents. In migration, this bird is primarily coastal and oceanic, though some fly overland and find their way into our region. Here, the Whimbrel is usually found in small flocks, though substantial flocks ranging in the hundreds to thousands of birds are occasionally encountered, if one is lucky. • Both the Whimbrel and the Eskimo Curlew *(N. borealis)* suffered devastating losses to their populations during the commercial hunts of the late 1800s. The Whimbrel population slowly recovered, but the Eskimo Curlew seemed to vanish into thin air—the last confirmed sighting of this bird was in 1963.

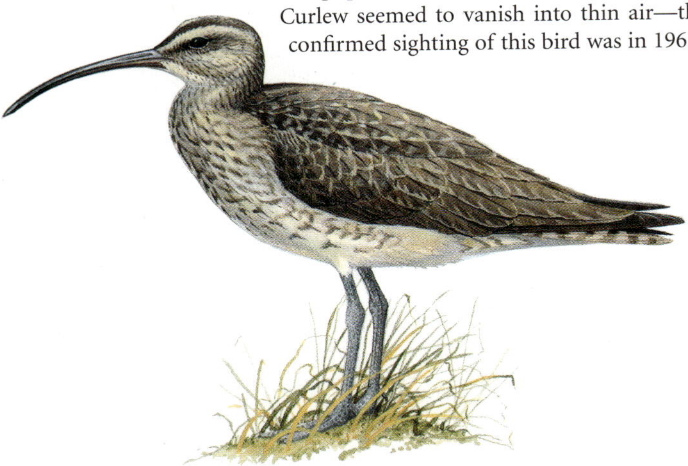

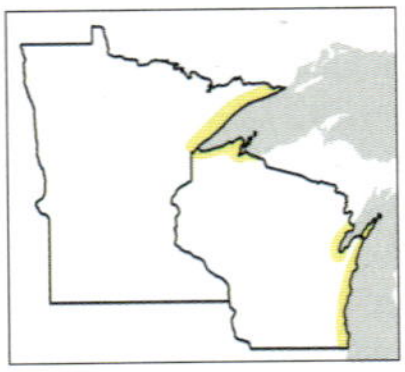

ID: long, downcurved bill; striped crown; dark eye line; mottled, dark brown upperparts; pale underparts. *In flight:* dark underwings.

Size: *L* 17½ in; *W* 32 in.

Status: ***MN:*** uncommon migrant from mid-May to mid-June; very rare migrant from July to September at Duluth and along the North Shore of L. Superior; rare to accidental fall migrant in other regions.
WI: uncommon migrant from mid-May to early June; rare migrant from July to mid-October; during migration is mainly found along the shores of both Great Lakes; rare migrant inland.

Habitat: mudflats, lakeshores, airports and flooded agricultural fields.

Nesting: does not nest in our region.

Feeding: probes and pecks for invertebrates in mud or vegetation; also eats enormous amounts of berries in fall.

Voice: incoming flocks can be heard uttering a distinctive and easily imitated, rippling *bibibibibibibi* long before they come into sight.

Similar Species: *Upland Sandpiper* (p. 133): smaller; straight bill; lacks head markings; yellowish legs. *Long-billed Curlew:* much larger overall; much longer bill; lacks bold striping on head and through eye.

Best Sites: ***MN:*** Duluth; North Shore of L. Superior (Lake Co. and Cook Co.).
WI: Manitowoc–Two Rivers; Baileys Harbor; Milwaukee; Wisconsin Pt.; Seagull Bar; Green Bay.

HUDSONIAN GODWIT

Limosa haemastica

Hudsonian Godwits are attaining their colorful breeding plumage when they arrive in spring. Their flight path takes small flocks of these birds through our region in good numbers. In contrast, they head east in fall, so few typically are found. • Of the world's four godwit species, the Hudsonian Godwit is the least well known. It was considered to be one of the rarest birds in North America until the 1940s, when biologists discovered large flocks along the coastlines of James Bay and Hudson Bay in northern Canada. • The Hudsonian Godwit can be seen probing sandy depths for worms, mollusks and crustaceans, sometimes with its bill buried up to its eyes! Female godwits and curlews have longer bills than males.

♂

breeding

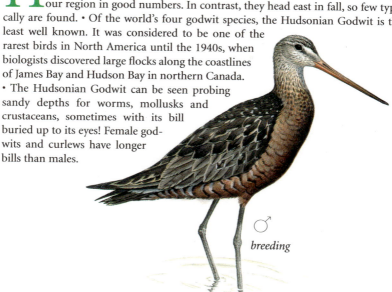

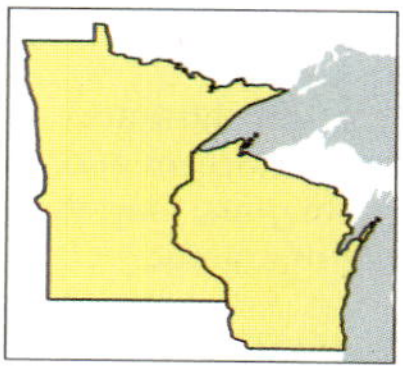

ID: long, yellow orange bill with dark, slightly upturned tip; white rump; black tail; long, blue black legs. *Breeding:* heavily barred, chestnut red underparts; dark grayish upperparts; male is more brightly colored. *Nonbreeding adult:* grayish upperparts; whitish underparts may show a few short, black bars. *Immature:* dark gray brown upperparts fringed pale buff; well-marked scapulars and tertials; underparts faintly washed with brownish buff. *In flight:* white rump; black "wing pits" and wing linings.

Size: *L* 14–15½ in; *W* 29 in.

Status: ***MN:*** uncommon migrant from late April to early June; rare migrant from July to October; mainly found in western regions; rare to uncommon migrant in other regions of the state. ***WI:*** uncommon migrant from late April to early June; rare migrant from late July to late October.

Habitat: flooded fields, marshes, mudflats and lakeshores.

Nesting: does not nest in our region.

Feeding: probes deeply into water or mud; walks into deeper water than most shorebirds but rarely swims; eats mollusks, crustaceans, insects and other invertebrates; also picks earthworms from plowed fields.

Voice: usually quiet in migration; sometimes a sharp, rising *god-WIT!*

Similar Species: *Marbled Godwit* (p. 136): larger; mottled brown overall; lacks white rump. *Greater Yellowlegs* (p. 128): shorter, all-dark bill; bright yellow legs; lacks white rump. *Short-billed Dowitcher* (p. 151) and *Long-billed Dowitcher* (p. 152): smaller; straight, all-dark bills; yellow green legs; mottled rust brown upperparts in breeding plumage.

Best Sites: ***MN:*** Salt L. (Lac Qui Parle Co.); Hamden Slough NWR; Heron L. (Jackson Co.). ***WI:*** Arlington ponds; Beaver Dam (CTH A and W) ponds; Horicon Marsh; Shiocton–Black Creek; Manitowoc; Milwaukee; Sheboygan; Green Bay.

MARBLED GODWIT

Limosa fedoa

The Marbled Godwit's bill looks long enough to reach buried prey, but this bird doesn't seem content with its reach. It is frequently seen with its head submerged beneath the water or with its face pressed into a mudflat. These deep probings seem to pay off for this large, resourceful shorebird, and a godwit looks genuinely pleased with a freshly extracted meal and a face covered in mud. • Unlike the Hudsonian Godwit, which undertakes long migrations from the Arctic to South America, Marbled Godwits breed on the Canadian Prairies and the American Great Plains and migrate only short distances to coastal wintering areas in the southern U.S. and Central America. Sightings of Marbled Godwits are uncommon in our region.

breeding

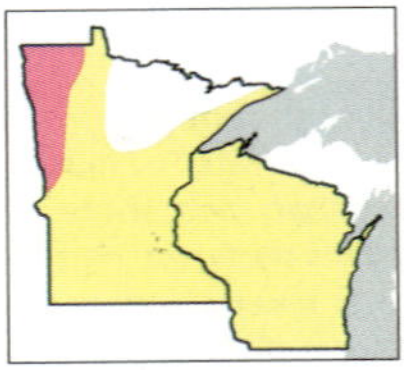

ID: long, yellow orange bill with dark, slightly upturned tip; long neck and legs; mottled buff brown plumage is darkest on upperparts; long, blue black legs. *In flight:* cinnamon wing linings.

Size: *L* 16–20 in; *W* 30 in.

Status: ***MN:*** special concern; uncommon migrant from mid-April to mid-May and from late June to late August; can be a locally common migrant on the prairies of west-central and northwestern regions; local breeder. ***WI:*** uncommon migrant from mid-April to early June; rare migrant from mid-July to October.

Habitat: flooded fields, wet meadows, marshes, mudflats and lakeshores.

Nesting: on dry ground in grass or sedges, usually near water; in a slight depression lined with grass; nest may have a partial canopy; pair probably shares the incubation of 4 brown-spotted, olive buff to greenish eggs for 21–23 days.

Feeding: probes deeply in soft substrates for worms, insect larvae, crustaceans and mollusks; picks insects from grass; may also eat the tubers and seeds of aquatic vegetation.

Voice: loud, ducklike, 2-syllable squawks: *co-rect co-rect* or *god-wit god-wit.*

Similar Species: *Hudsonian Godwit* (p. 135): smaller; chestnut red neck and underparts; white rump. *Greater Yellowlegs* (p. 128): shorter, all-dark bill; bright yellow legs. *Short-billed Dowitcher* (p. 151) and *Long-billed Dowitcher* (p. 152): smaller; straight, all-dark bills; white rump wedge; yellow green legs. *Long-billed Curlew:* long, downcurved bill.

Best Sites: ***MN:*** Felton Prairie SNA (Clay Co.); Rothsay WMA (Wilkin Co.); Salt L. (Lac Qui Parle Co.). ***WI:*** Milwaukee; Manitowoc; Sheboygan; Nine Springs sewage ponds (Madison); Arlington ponds; Horicon Marsh.

RUDDY TURNSTONE

Arenaria interpres

From mid-May to mid-June, flocks of boldly patterned Ruddy Turnstones settle along the shores of Lakes Michigan and Superior to mingle and forage among the other shorebird migrants. Flocks of over a hundred birds have been recorded. These birds' painted faces and eye-catching, black-and-red backs set them apart from the salmon-bellied Red Knots and the multitudes of little brown-and-white sandpipers. • Ruddy Turnstones are truly long-distance migrants. Individuals that nest along the shores of islands in Canada's Arctic routinely fly to South America or western Europe to avoid frosty winters. • The name "turnstone" is appropriate for this bird, which uses its bill to flip over pebbles, shells and washed-up vegetation to expose hidden invertebrates. Its short, stubby, slightly upturned bill is an ideal utensil for this unusual foraging style.

breeding ♂

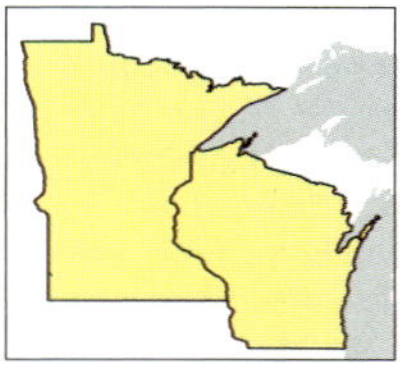

ID: white belly; black "bib" curves up to shoulder; stout, black, slightly upturned bill; red orange legs. *Breeding:* ruddy upperparts (female is slightly paler); white face; black "collar"; dark, streaky crown. *Nonbreeding:* brownish upperparts and face.

Size: *L* 9½ in; *W* 21 in.

Status: ***MN:*** uncommon migrant from mid-May to mid-June and from late July through September, with stragglers into October and November. ***WI:*** common migrant from May to mid-June; uncommon migrant from July to November.

Habitat: lakeshores, reservoirs, marshes and sewage lagoons; also in cultivated fields.

Nesting: does not nest in our region.

Feeding: probes under and flips rocks, weeds and shells for food items; picks, digs and probes for invertebrates from the soil or mud; also eats crabs, fish heads, berries, seeds, spiders and carrion.

Voice: clear, staccato, rattling *cut-a-cut* alarm call and lower, repeated contact notes.

Similar Species: *Other sandpipers* (pp. 128–49): all lack the Ruddy Turnstone's bold patterning and flashy wing markings in flight. *Plovers* (pp. 122–26): equally bold plumage but in significantly different patterns.

Best Sites: ***MN:*** Duluth; Minnesota Pt.; North Shore of L. Superior; larger lakes in the central part of the state such as Mille Lacs L. and Leech L. ***WI:*** Manitowoc–Two Rivers; Sheboygan; Green Bay; Milwaukee; Racine; Wisconsin Pt.; Oshkosh; Seagull Bar.

RED KNOT

Calidris canutus

Small flocks of Red Knots appear for a brief period between mid-May and early June. Never abundant in our region, and usually encountered as individuals, these tubby, red-bellied knots are distinguished from the masses of migrating plovers and sandpipers by their bright rufous plumage. • During the breeding season, their red plumage serves to attract mates and camouflage the birds against the sea of grasses and colorful wildflowers on their arctic nesting grounds. In fall and winter, drab, gray-and-white Red Knots are difficult to distinguish from other migrating and overwintering shorebirds, and they blend in perfectly with the open sandy beaches that they inhabit at this time of year. • Red Knots are another migratory champion, flying up to 19,000 miles in a single year.

breeding

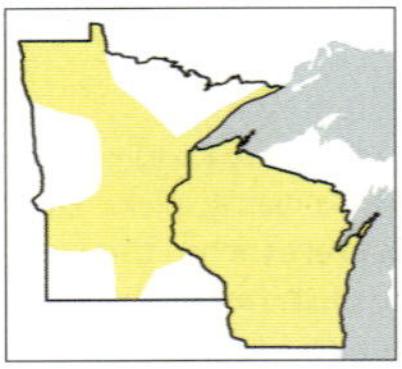

ID: chunky, round body; greenish legs. *Breeding:* rusty face, breast and underparts; brown, black and buff upperparts. *Nonbreeding:* pale gray upperparts; white underparts with some faint streaking on upper breast; faint barring on rump; *Immature:* buffy wash on breast; scaly-looking back. *In flight:* white wing stripe.

Size: *L* 10½ in; *W* 23 in.

Status: ***MN:*** uncommon migrant for short periods from mid-May to mid-June and from late July to late September at Duluth and in the Lake of the Woods area; rare spring migrant elsewhere. ***WI:*** uncommon migrant from May to early June and from August to October in eastern and northern regions; rare migrant in other regions.

Habitat: lakeshores, marshes, mudflats and plowed fields.

Nesting: does not nest in our region.

Feeding: gleans shorelines for insects, crustaceans and mollusks; probes soft substrates, creating lines of small holes.

Voice: usually silent; low, monosyllabic *knut* reminiscent of its name.

Similar Species: *Long-billed Dowitcher* (p. 152) and *Short-billed Dowitcher* (p. 151): much longer bills; barring under tail and on flanks; white wedge on rump and lower back. *Buff-breasted Sandpiper* (p. 149): finer, shorter bill; light buff in color; dark flecking on sides. *Other peeps* (pp. 138–48): smaller; most have black legs; only *Sanderling* (p. 139) and *Curlew Sandpiper* (p. 358): show reddish coloration on undersides in breeding plumage.

Best Sites: ***MN:*** Duluth; Minnesota Pt.; Lake of the Woods. ***WI:*** Manitowoc; Sheboygan; Wisconsin Pt.; Milwaukee; Green Bay; Horicon Marsh; Seagull Bar.

SANDERLING

Calidris alba

A spring or fall stroll along the shores of the Great Lakes is often punctuated by the sight of tiny Sanderlings running and playing in the waves. Their well-known habit of chasing waves has a simple purpose: to snatch washed-up aquatic invertebrates before the next wave rolls onto shore. Sprinting along the beach while foraging, Sanderlings move so fast on their dark legs that they appear to be gliding across the sand. Sanderlings are also expert tweakers of marine worms and other soft-bodied creatures from just below the surface of mudflats. • When resting, Sanderlings often tuck one leg up to preserve body heat. They seek the company of other sandpipers, plovers and turnstones for the same reason. • This sandpiper is one of the world's most widespread birds. It breeds across the Arctic in Alaska, Canada and Russia, and spends the winter running up and down sandy shorelines in North America, South America, Asia, Africa and Australia.

breeding

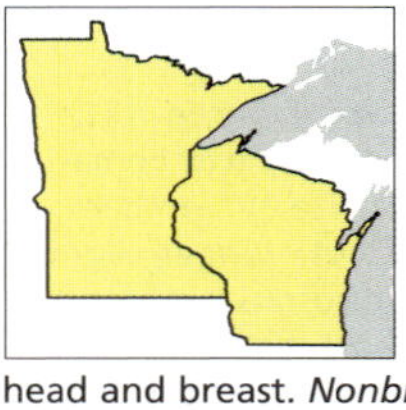

ID: straight, black bill; black legs; white underparts; striking, white wing bar and pale rump. *Breeding:* dark spotting or mottling on rufous head and breast. *Nonbreeding:* pale gray upperparts; black shoulder patch (often concealed).

Size: *L* 7–8½ in; *W* 17 in.

Status: ***MN:*** uncommon migrant from late April to mid-June and from August to November; locally common migrant in the Duluth area in both spring and fall; declining in numbers over the last decade. ***WI:*** common migrant along L. Michigan and L. Superior from late April to mid-June and from mid-July to mid-November; uncommon migrant inland.

Habitat: lakeshores, marshes and reservoirs.

Nesting: does not nest in our region.

Feeding: gleans shorelines for insects, crustaceans and mollusks; probes repeatedly, creating a line of small holes in the sand or mud.

Voice: flight call is a sharp *kip*.

Similar Species: *Dunlin* (p. 147): larger and darker; slightly downcurved bill. *Red Knot* (p. 138): larger; gray-barred, whitish rump; breeding adult has unstreaked, reddish belly. *Least Sandpiper* (p. 142): smaller and darker; yellowish legs; lacks rufous breast in breeding plumage. *Western Sandpiper* (p. 141) and *Semipalmated Sandpiper* (p. 140): lack rufous breast in breeding plumage; sandy upperparts in nonbreeding plumage.

Best Sites: ***MN:*** Duluth; L. Superior. ***WI:*** L. Michigan; L. Superior.

SEMIPALMATED SANDPIPER

Calidris pusilla

The small, plain Semipalmated Sandpiper can be difficult to identify among the swarms of similar-looking *Calidris* sandpipers that appear each spring and fall. Known collectively as "peeps" because of the similarity of their high-pitched calls, these strikingly similar miniatures, which include the Semipalmated, Least, Western, White-rumped and Baird's sandpipers, can make shorebird identification either a complete nightmare or an uplifting challenge. • Each spring and fall, Semipalmated Sandpipers are usually encountered in small numbers on our shorelines, but large concentrations can be found where good habitat exists. Pecking and probing soft substrates in mechanized fury, these birds strive to replenish their body fat for the remainder of their long migratory journey. Semipalmated Sandpipers fly almost the entire length of the Americas during migration, so their staging sites must provide ample food sources.

nonbreeding

breeding

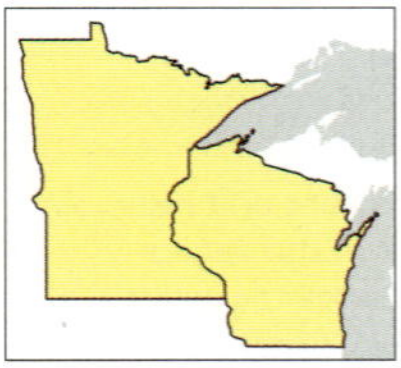

ID: short, straight, black bill; black legs. *Breeding:* mottled upperparts; slight rufous tinge on ear patch, crown and scapulars; faint streaks on upper breast and flanks. *Nonbreeding:* white "eyebrow"; gray brown upperparts; white underparts with light brown wash on sides of upper breast. *Immature:* much like breeding adult but with smudgier markings on upper breast; often washed warm buff; white line above eye; dark brown lores and ear coverts. *In flight:* narrow, white wing stripe; white rump is split by black line.

Size: *L* $5\frac{1}{2}$–7 in; *W* 14 in.

Status: ***MN:*** common migrant from mid-April to late June and from August to late October. ***WI:*** common migrant from May to mid-June and from July to October.

Habitat: mudflats and the shores of ponds and lakes.

Nesting: does not nest in our region.

Feeding: probes soft substrates and gleans for aquatic insects and crustaceans.

Voice: flight call is a harsh *cherk;* sometimes a longer *chirrup* or a chittering alarm call.

Similar Species: *Least Sandpiper* (p. 142): yellowish legs; darker upperparts; immatures have distinctive white "V" on back. *Western Sandpiper* (p. 141): longer, slightly downcurved bill; bright rufous wash on crown and ear patch, sometimes on back. *Sanderling* (p. 139): pale gray upperparts and blackish trailing edge on flight feathers in nonbreeding plumage. *White-rumped Sandpiper* (p. 143): larger; white rump; folded wings extend beyond tail. *Baird's Sandpiper* (p. 144): larger; longer bill; folded wings extend beyond tail.

Best Sites: ***MN:*** Big Stone NWR; Salt L. (Lac Qui Parle Co.); sewage ponds; mudflats. ***WI:*** Arlington ponds; Beaver Dam ponds; Horicon Marsh; Green Bay; Shiocton–Black Creek; Manitowoc; Sheboygan; Milwaukee; Racine; Wisconsin Pt.

WESTERN SANDPIPER

Calidris mauri

Most Western Sandpipers are seen only along the Pacific Coast, but some adventurous individuals traverse the continent, flying through our region on their way to the Atlantic for the winter. • Most identification guides will tell you to look for this bird's downcurved bill, and on paper this seems like a sensible plan. In the field, however, as angles and lighting change, the bills of "peeps" can look downcurved one moment, straight the next, and anything in between when double-checked. To track down this rare shorebird, try calling local birding hotlines to find out the locations of the most recent local sightings. Unless you are a particularly keen birder, there's no reason why you shouldn't let more experienced birders do most of the work for you!

nonbreeding

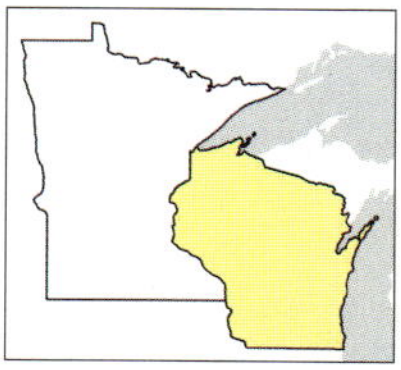

ID: black, slightly downcurved bill; black legs. *Breeding:* rufous patches on crown, ear and scapulars; V-shaped streaking on upper breast and flanks; light underparts. *Nonbreeding:* white "eyebrow"; gray brown upperparts; white underparts; streaky, light brown wash on upper breast. *In flight:* narrow, white wing stripe; white rump is split by black line.

Size: *L* 6–7 in; *W* 14 in.

Status: ***MN:*** little information available; probably occurs as a vagrant, most likely in early August; only 3 documented records from Lac Qui Parle, Hennepin and Marshall Counties. ***WI:*** rare migrant from May to early June and from mid-July to September.

Habitat: pond edges, lakeshores and mudflats.

Nesting: does not nest in our region.

Feeding: gleans and probes mud and shallow water; occasionally submerges its head; primarily eats aquatic insects, worms and crustaceans.

Voice: flight call is a high-pitched *cheep.*

Similar Species: *Semipalmated Sandpiper* (p. 140): shorter, straight bill; less rufous on crown, ear patch and scapulars. *Least Sandpiper* (p. 142): smaller; yellowish legs; darker breast wash in all plumages; lacks rufous patches. *White-rumped Sandpiper* (p. 143): larger; white rump; folded wings extend beyond tail; lacks rufous wing patches. *Baird's Sandpiper* (p. 144): larger; folded wings extend beyond tail; lacks rufous patches. *Dunlin* (p. 147): larger; black belly in breeding plumage; longer bill is thicker at base and droops at tip; grayer, unstreaked back in nonbreeding plumage. *Sanderling* (p. 139): nonbreeding plumage shows pale gray upperparts, blackish trailing edge on flight feathers and bold, white upperwing stripe in flight.

Best Sites: ***MN:*** no consistent sites. ***WI:*** Manitowoc; Milwaukee; Arlington ponds; Green Bay; Horicon Marsh.

LEAST SANDPIPER

Calidris minutilla

The Least Sandpiper is the smallest North American shorebird, but its size does not deter it from performing migratory feats. Like most other "peeps," the Least Sandpiper migrates almost the entire length of the globe twice each year, from the Arctic to the southern tip of South America and back again. • Arctic summers are incredibly short, so shorebirds must maximize their breeding efforts. Least Sandpipers lay large eggs relative to those of other sandpipers, and the entire clutch may weigh over half the weight of the female! The young hatch in an advanced state of development, getting an early start on preparations for the fall migration. These tiny shorebirds begin moving south as early as late June to early July, so they are some of the first fall migrants to arrive in our region. Least Sandpipers are usually encountered in small flocks, but can occur in large concentrations of hundreds, or sometimes thousands, of birds. • The scientific name *minutilla* is Latin for "very small"—apt for the littlest sandpiper.

breeding

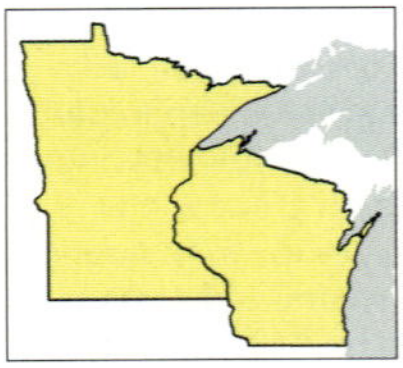

ID: *Breeding:* black bill; yellowish legs; dark, mottled back; buff brown breast, head and nape; light breast streaking; prominent white "V" on back. *Nonbreeding:* much duller; often lacks back stripes; prominent, streaked breast band. *Immature:* similar to breeding adult, but with faintly streaked breast.

Size: *L* 5–6½ in; *W* 13 in.

Status: ***MN:*** common migrant from mid-April to early June and from early July to October. ***WI:*** common migrant in April and May and from early July to October.

Habitat: sandy beaches, lakeshores, sewage lagoons, mudflats and wetland edges.

Nesting: does not nest in our region.

Feeding: probes or pecks for insects, crustaceans, small mollusks and occasionally seeds.

Voice: high-pitched *kreee*.

Similar Species: *Semipalmated Sandpiper* (p. 140): black legs; lighter upperparts; rufous tinge on crown, ear patch and scapulars. *Western Sandpiper* (p. 141): slightly larger; black legs; lighter breast wash in all plumages; rufous patches on crown, ear and scapulars in breeding plumage. *Other peeps* (pp. 138–48): all are larger; dark legs.

Best Sites: ***MN:*** Big Stone NWR; Salt L. (Lac Qui Parle Co.); sewage ponds; mudflats. ***WI:*** Horicon Marsh; Shiocton–Black Creek; Green Bay; Nine Springs sewage ponds (Madison); Arlington ponds; Manitowoc; Sheboygan; Milwaukee; Seagull Bar.

WHITE-RUMPED SANDPIPER

Calidris fuscicollis

Just as a die-hard shorebird watcher is about to go into a peep-induced stupor, small brownish heads emerge from hiding, back feathers are ruffled, wings are stretched and, almost without warning, the birds take flight and flash pure white rumps. There is no doubt that the beautiful White-rumped Sandpiper has been identified! • This sandpiper's white rump may serve as a visual signal to alert other birds when danger threatens. Flocks of White-rumped Sandpipers sometimes collectively rush at a predator, and then suddenly scatter in its face. • In fall, White-rumped Sandpipers migrate to the southern reaches of South America, a journey that these birds make in a few long, nonstop flights, sometimes flying for stretches of 60 hours at a time.

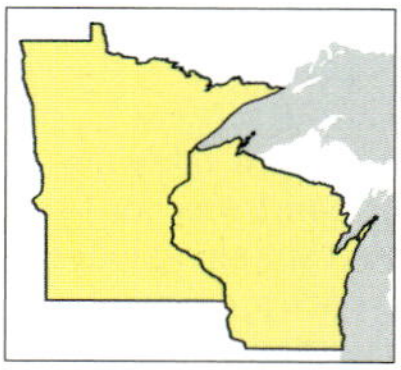

ID: black legs; black bill; wings extend well beyond tail. *Breeding:* mottled brown and rufous upperparts; streaked breast, sides and flanks. *Nonbreeding:* mottled gray upperparts; white "eyebrow." *Immature:* black upperparts edged with white, chestnut and buff. *In flight:* white rump; dark tail; indistinct wing bar.

Size: *L* 7–8 in; *W* 17 in.

Status: ***MN:*** uncommon migrant from late April to mid-June; uncommon to rare migrant from July to October. ***WI:*** fairly common migrant from May to mid-June; uncommon migrant from July to October.

Habitat: lakeshores, marshes, sewage lagoons, reservoirs and flooded fields.

Nesting: does not nest in our region.

Feeding: gleans the ground and shorelines for insects, crustaceans and mollusks.

Voice: flight call is a characteristic, squeal-like *tzeet,* higher than any other peep.

Similar Species: *Other peeps* (pp. 138–48): all have dark line through rump. *Baird's Sandpiper* (p. 144): lacks clean white rump; breast streaking does not extend onto flanks. *Stilt Sandpiper* (p. 148) and *Curlew Sandpiper* (p. 358): much longer legs trail beyond tail in flight.

Best Sites: ***MN:*** Duluth; Big Stone NWR; Agassiz NWR; Salt L. (Lac Qui Parle Co.). ***WI:*** Green Bay; Shiocton–Black Creek; Horicon Marsh; Arlington ponds; Manitowoc; Sheboygan; Milwaukee.

BAIRD'S SANDPIPER

Calidris bairdii

The Baird's Sandpiper is one of the most difficult sandpipers to identify correctly. One clue is that while it often migrates with other sandpipers, it leaves them upon landing and feeds alone. These birds are usually encountered individually or in small flocks of 10 or more birds. • Like all its *Calidris* relatives, this modest-looking shorebird has extraordinary migratory habits—it flies twice annually between South America and the Arctic. The Baird's Sandpiper remains on its northern breeding grounds for only a short time. Soon after the chicks hatch and are able to fend for themselves, the adults flock together to begin their southward migration. After a few weeks of accumulating fat reserves, the young gather in a second wave of southbound migrants.

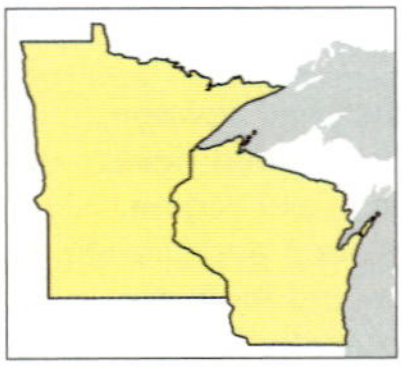

ID: black legs and bill; streaked, gray buff breast; buffy white "eyebrow"; folded wings extend beyond tail. *Breeding:* black, diamondlike pattern on back and wing coverts. *Immature:* brighter and browner; "scaly" appearance to back.

Size: *L* 7–7$\frac{1}{2}$ in; *W* 17 in.

Status: ***MN:*** uncommon migrant from late March to mid-June and from mid-July to October; rare migrant in northeastern and north-central regions (except Duluth). ***WI:*** uncommon migrant from May to early June; fairly common migrant from July to October.

Habitat: sandy beaches, mudflats, meadows and wetland edges.

Nesting: does not nest in our region.

Feeding: gleans aquatic invertebrates, especially larval flies; also eats beetles and grasshoppers; rarely probes.

Voice: soft, rolling *kriit kriit.*

Similar Species: "scaly" back is fairly distinctive. *White-rumped Sandpiper* (p. 143): clean white rump; breast streaking extends onto flanks; head and back are more streaked. *Pectoral Sandpiper* (p. 145): dark breast ends abruptly at edge of white belly. *Least Sandpiper* (p. 142): smaller; yellowish legs. *Western Sandpiper* (p. 141) and *Sanderling* (p. 139): lack streaked, gray buff breast. *Semipalmated Sandpiper* (p. 140): smaller; shorter bill; lacks streaked breast in nonbreeding plumage.

Best Sites: ***MN:*** Big Stone NWR; Salt L. (Lac Qui Parle Co.); Hamden Slough NWR. ***WI:*** Horicon Marsh; Green Bay; Manitowoc; Milwaukee; Sheboygan; Arlington ponds.

PECTORAL SANDPIPER

Calidris melanotos

This widespread traveler may be found in Siberia as well as the Canadian Arctic, and its epic annual migrations include destinations such as South America, Australia and New Zealand. In spring and fall, Pectoral Sandpipers are conspicuous along the shores of lakes and in wet, grassy fields. Though usually encountered in small flocks of 10 or more birds, they are occasionally found in larger concentrations. • Unlike most sandpipers, the Pectoral exhibits sexual dimorphism—the females are only two-thirds the size of the males. • The name "pectoral" refers to the location of the male's prominent air sacs. When agitated, the male inflates these air sacs, causing his feathers to rise. • If threatened, a flock of Pectoral Sandpipers will suddenly launch into the air and converge into a single, swirling mass.

breeding

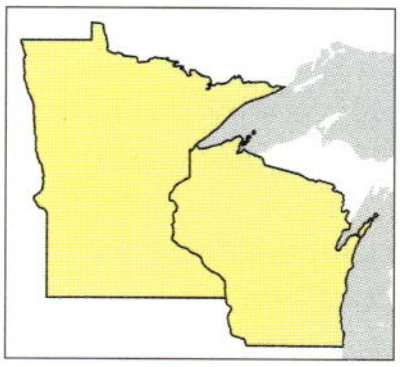

ID: brown breast streaks end abruptly at edge of white belly; white undertail coverts; black bill has slightly downcurved tip; long, yellow legs; mottled upperparts; may have faintly rusty, dark crown and back; folded wings extend beyond tail. *Immature:* less spotting on breast; broader, white feather edges on back form 2 white "V"s.

Size: *L* 8½ in; *W* 18 in. (female is noticeably smaller).

Status: ***MN:*** common migrant from late March to mid-June and from early July to early November; uncommon migrant in northeastern and north-central regions. ***WI:*** common migrant in April and May and from July to early November.

Habitat: lakeshores, marshes, mudflats and flooded fields or pastures.

Nesting: does not nest in our region.

Feeding: probes and pecks for small insects; eats mainly flies, but also takes beetles and some grasshoppers; may eat small mollusks, amphipods, berries, seeds, moss, algae and some plant material.

Voice: sharp, short, low *krrick krrick*.

Similar Species: *Other peeps* (pp. 138–48): lack well-defined, dark "bib" and yellow legs. *Ruff* (p. 150): male is larger and more heavily marked on upperparts and underparts; female has all-dark bill and indistinct "bib."

Best Sites: ***MN:*** Big Stone NWR; Salt L. (Lac Qui Parle Co.); sewage ponds. ***WI:*** Horicon Marsh; Shiocton–Black Creek; Nine Springs sewage ponds (Madison); Green Bay; Arlington ponds; Beaver Dam ponds; Milwaukee.

PURPLE SANDPIPER

Calidris maritima

The Purple Sandpiper is chunky and has no flashy colors or ringing calls to applaud. Unlike most shorebirds, which prefer shallow marshy areas, sand beaches or mudflats, Purple Sandpipers forage perilously close to crashing waves along rocky headlands, piers and breakwaters. These birds expertly navigate their way across rugged, slippery rocks while foraging for crustaceans, mollusks and insect larvae. In fact, they are rarely seen associated with any beach that is not near a rocky area. • Purple Sandpipers winter along the Atlantic Coast and breed in high Arctic coastal regions, so few grace our shores each year. No other shorebird winters as far north along the Atlantic Coast as the Purple Sandpiper. • The name "purple" was given to this sandpiper for the purplish iridescence that is occasionally observed on its shoulders.

nonbreeding

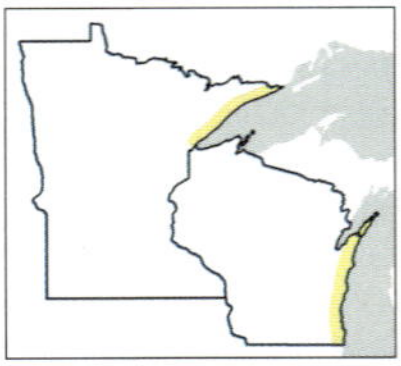

ID: long, slightly drooping, black-tipped bill with yellow orange base; yellow orange legs; dull streaking on breast and flanks. *Breeding:* streaked neck; buff crown with dark streaks; dark back feathers with tawny to rusty brown edges. *Nonbreeding:* unstreaked, gray head, neck and upper breast form a "hood"; gray-spotted, white belly. *Immature:* streaking on head; chestnut brown, white and buff feather edgings on upperparts.

Size: *L* 9 in; *W* 17 in.

Status: ***MN:*** accidental fall migrant with only 4 records for the state (2 from Grand Marais in Cook Co.). ***WI:*** rare migrant from mid-October to early December; casual winter visitor.

Habitat: sand and gravel beaches, rocky shorelines, piers and breakwaters.

Nesting: does not nest in our region.

Feeding: food is found visually and is snatched while moving over rocks and sand; eats mostly mollusks, insects, crustaceans and other invertebrates; also eats a variety of plant material.

Voice: call is a soft *prrt-prrt*.

Similar Species: *Other peeps* (pp. 138–48): all lack bicolored bill, yellow orange legs and unstreaked, gray "hood" in nonbreeding plumage.

Best Sites: ***MN:*** no consistent sites. ***WI:*** Sheboygan; Manitowoc; Kewaunee; Harrington Beach SP; Milwaukee; Racine.

DUNLIN

Calidris alpina

Outside the breeding season, Dunlins form dynamic, synchronous flocks. These tight flocks are generally more exclusive than other shorebird troupes and rarely include other species. Sometimes hundreds of these birds are seen flying wing tip to wing tip. Unlike many of their shorebird relatives, Dunlins overwinter in North America, mostly in coastal areas—few ever cross the equator. They gather in flocks that can number in the tens of thousands. • Dunlins are fairly distinctive in their breeding attire: their black bellies and legs make them look as though they have been wading belly-deep in puddles of ink. • This bird was originally called "Dunling," meaning "little dark one," but with the passage of time, the "g" was dropped.

breeding *nonbreeding*

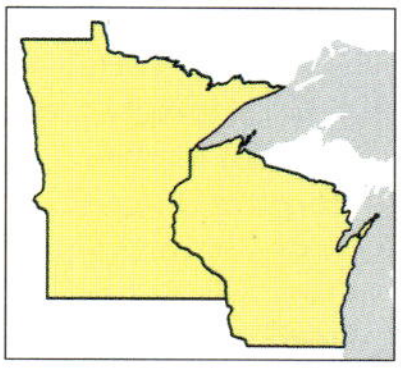

ID: slightly downcurved, black bill; black legs. *Breeding:* black belly; streaked, white neck and underparts; rufous wings, back and crown. *Nonbreeding:* pale gray underparts; brownish gray upperparts; light brown streaking on breast and nape. *Immature:* buffy head and breast; mantle and scapulars fringed chestnut brown and white; whitish "V" on back; blackish brown lines on flanks and sides of belly. *In flight:* white wing stripe.
Size: *L* $7\frac{1}{2}$–9 in; *W* 17 in.
Status: ***MN:*** uncommon migrant from mid-April to mid-June; rare to uncommon fall migrant, not usually seen before September in any region, with stragglers into November. ***WI:*** common migrant from April to mid-June and from August to November.

Habitat: mudflats and the shores of ponds, marshes and lakes; occasionally seen in pastures or sewage lagoons.
Nesting: does not nest in our region.
Feeding: gleans and probes for aquatic crustaceans, worms, mollusks and insects.
Voice: flight call is a grating *cheezp* or *treezp*.
Similar Species: black belly in breeding plumage is distinctive. *Western Sandpiper* (p. 141) and *Semipalmated Sandpiper* (p. 140): smaller; nonbreeding plumage is browner overall; bill tip of female is less downcurved. *Least Sandpiper* (p. 142): smaller; darker upperparts; yellowish legs. *Sanderling* (p. 139): paler; straight bill; usually seen running in the surf. *Stilt Sandpiper* (p. 148): larger; longer bill; yellowish green legs.
Best Sites: ***MN:*** Duluth; Agassiz NWR; Big Stone NWR; Salt L. (Lac Qui Parle Co.). ***WI:*** Manitowoc, Green Bay, Sheboygan, Milwaukee and Racine (L. Michigan); Wisconsin Pt. (L. Superior); Horicon Marsh; Arlington ponds; Beaver Dam ponds.

STILT SANDPIPER

Calidris himantopus

With the silhouette of a small Lesser Yellowlegs and the foraging behavior of a dowitcher—two birds with which the Stilt Sandpiper often associates—this bird is easily overlooked by most birders. Named for its relatively long legs, this shorebird prefers to feed in shallow water, where it digs like a dowitcher, often dunking its head completely underwater. Because its bill is shorter than a dowitcher's, however, it has to lean farther forward than its larger cousin—a characteristic that can aid in identification. This sandpiper will also wade into deep water up to its breast in search of a meal. To snag invertebrates, insect larvae or tiny minnows from just below the water's surface, it may sweep its bill from side to side. • Though Stilt Sandpipers are individualists for the most part, large concentrations of these birds are sometimes encountered.

breeding

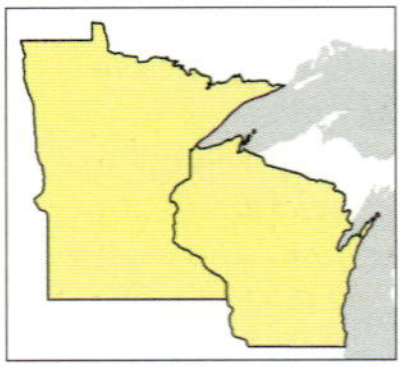

ID: long, greenish legs; long bill droops slightly at end. *Breeding:* chestnut red ear patch; white "eyebrow"; striped crown; streaked neck; barred underparts. *Nonbreeding:* less conspicuous, white "eyebrow"; dirty white neck and breast; white belly; dark brownish gray upperparts. *Immature:* dark brown upperparts, fringed rufous or light buff; buff wash on throat and breast; faintly streaked, white belly. *In flight:* white rump; legs trail behind tail; no wing stripe.

Size: *L* 8–9 in; *W* 18 in.

Status: ***MN:*** uncommon migrant from early May to early June; uncommon to locally common migrant from July to early October. ***WI:*** rare migrant from late April to May; uncommon migrant from July to October.

Habitat: lakeshores, reservoirs, marshes and flooded fields.

Nesting: does not nest in our region.

Feeding: probes deeply in shallow water; eats mostly invertebrates; occasionally picks insects from the water's surface or the ground; also eats seeds, roots and leaves.

Voice: soft, rattling *querp* or *kirr* in flight; clearer *whu.*

Similar Species: *Greater Yellowlegs* (p. 128) and *Lesser Yellowlegs* (p. 129): straight bills; yellow legs; lack red ear patch of breeding adult, chestnut mantle of immature or blotchy back feathers of nonbreeding adult, *Curlew Sandpiper* (p. 358): shorter; bill has more obvious curve; black legs; paler gray upperparts in nonbreeding plumage. *Dunlin* (p. 147): shorter, black legs; dark rump; whitish wing bar.

Best Sites: ***MN:*** Big Stone NWR; Salt L. (Lac Qui Parle Co.); sewage ponds in western and central regions. ***WI:*** Horicon Marsh; Beaver Dam ponds; Arlington ponds; Nine Springs sewage ponds (Madison); Green Bay.

BUFF-BREASTED SANDPIPER

Tryngites subruficollis

Shy in behavior and humble in appearance, the Buff-breasted Sandpiper is a rare visitor to our region. Buff-breasts frequent drier habitats than most other sandpipers, and the peak time to look for this bird is from mid-August to early September, especially on sod farms. • When feeding, this subtly colored bird stands motionless, blending beautifully into a backdrop of furrowed, cultivated fields, mudflats or cured, grassy pastures. Only when it catches sight of moving prey does it become visible, making a short, forward sprint to snatch a fresh meal. • Most adult Buff-breasted Sandpipers migrate through the center of the continent, so the individuals that we see in our region are mainly dispersing juveniles heading south for the first time. They are often found in the company of foraging Pectoral Sandpipers, Black-bellied Plovers and American Golden-Plovers.

breeding

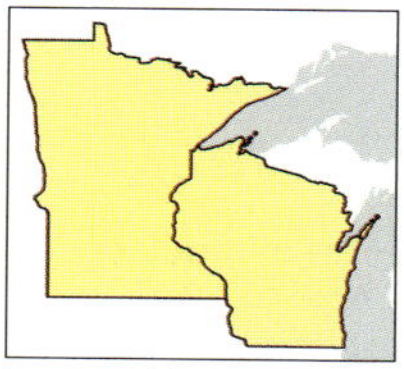

ID: buffy, unpatterned face and foreneck; large, dark eyes; very thin, straight, black bill; buff underparts; small spots on crown, nape, breast, sides and flanks; "scaly" look to back and upperwings; yellow legs. *In flight:* pure white underwings; no wing stripe.

Size: *L* 7½–8 in; *W* 18 in.

Status: ***MN:*** rare migrant from early May to early June in western regions; casual to accidental migrant in spring in other areas; uncommon to rare migrant from late July to late September, best represented in Duluth. ***WI:*** uncommon migrant from August to September.

Habitat: lakeshores, reservoirs and marshes; sod farms and cultivated and flooded fields.

Nesting: does not nest in our region.

Feeding: gleans the ground and shorelines for insects, spiders and small crustaceans; may eat seeds.

Voice: usually silent; calls include *chup* or *tick* notes; *preet* flight call.

Similar Species: *Upland Sandpiper* (p. 133): bolder streaking on breast; longer neck; smaller head; larger bill; streaking on "cheek" and foreneck. *Pectoral Sandpiper* (p. 145): grayer brown on back and breast; white on belly; white ovals at sides of tail. *Ruff* (p. 150): larger and heavier; sloping forehead; less tidy markings; greener legs; white ovals at sides of tail.

Best Sites: ***MN:*** Duluth; sod farms, especially in Dakota Co. ***WI:*** sod farms (Wind L., Stevens Point, Middleton, Appleton); occasionally in grassy areas of Horicon Marsh, Beaver Dam ponds and Arlington ponds.

RUFF

Philomachus pugnax

The Ruff is the most regular and widespread of the Eurasian vagrants that sometimes stray into North America. A rare to casual migrant, it may occasionally be seen in the company of other shorebirds, such as yellowlegs or sandpipers. • The male of this species is called a "Ruff," while the female is known as a "Reeve." In spring, the males are particularly unmistakeable with their prominent neck and "ear" ruffs. It is not known whether the male was named for his neck-feather ruffs, or if ruffs were named after the bird. "Reeve" has even more obscure origins, but some suggest it is linked to the meaning "observer" or "baliff"—the females oversee the tussling males, which, like Sharp-tailed Grouse, gather together in leks on their breeding grounds where they attempt to attract females through elaborate courtship posturing. • The scientific name *pugnax* means "pugnacious," which is an appropriate description of the courting males.

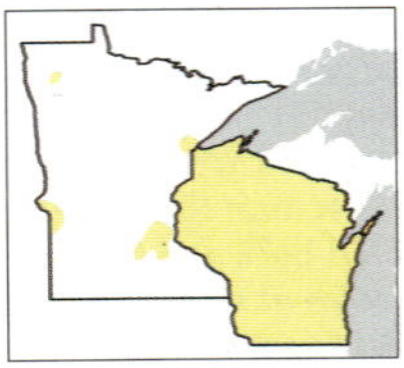

ID: plump body; small head; yellow green to red legs; yellow or black bill; brown gray upperparts. *Breeding male:* black, white or orangy neck ruff, usually flattened, but erected during courtship; dark underparts. *Breeding female:* dark blotches on underparts. *In flight:* thin, white wing stripe; oval, white rump divided by a dark central stripe.

Size: *L* 9–12 in; *W* 21 in.

Status: ***MN:*** casual migrant; 31 records, mostly concentrated in May and August from many scattered areas of the state. ***WI:*** rare migrant from April to mid-June; very rare migrant from late July to mid-October.

Habitat: shallow marshes and wetlands, flooded fields, mudflats and sewage lagoons.

Nesting: does not nest in our region.

Feeding: probes and picks at the surface of mudflats for aquatic invertebrates.

Voice: rarely vocal; call is a short *tu-whit*.

Similar Species: *Greater Yellowlegs* (p. 128) and *Lesser Yellowlegs* (p. 129): slimmer bodies; longer legs; streaked underparts. *Red Knot* (p. 138): shorter legs; "cleaner" breast in nonbreeding plumage.

Best Sites: no consistent sites.

SHORT-BILLED DOWITCHER

Limnodromus griseus

Long before deciduous trees burst into their brilliant fall colors, Short-billed Dowitchers from northern locales arrive on the mudflats, marshes and beaches of the Great Lakes region. These plump shorebirds are seen in good numbers during spring migration, but the largest concentrations are usually seen during the protracted fall migration, which begins as soon as early July. While foraging along shorelines, dowitchers "stitch" up and down into the mud with a rhythm like a sewing machine. This drilling motion liquifies the mud or sand, allowing birds to reach their hidden prey. • The best way to distinguish between Short-billed Dowitchers and the very similar Long-billed Dowitchers is by their flight calls or by listening to them feeding—Long-bills chatter softly while feeding; Short-bills feed silently.

breeding

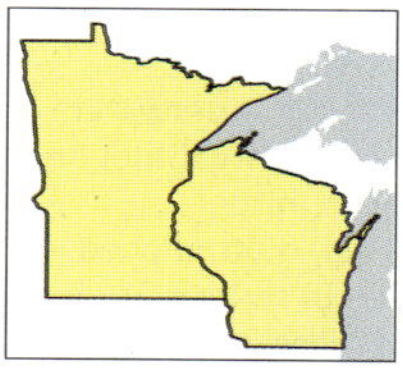

ID: straight, long, dark bill; white "eyebrow"; chunky body; yellow green legs. *Breeding:* white belly; dark spotting on reddish buff neck and upper breast; prominent dark barring on white sides and flanks. *Nonbreeding:* dirty gray upperparts; dirty white underparts. *Immature:* chestnut-edged crown and back; barred or striped tertials; no streaking or spotting on underparts. *In flight:* white wedge on rump and lower back.

Size: *L* 11–12 in; *W* 19 in.

Status: ***MN:*** fairly common migrant in May and from early July to early September. ***WI:*** fairly common migrant from May to early June and from early July to September.

Habitat: lakeshores, mudflats, reservoirs, marshes and flooded fields.

Nesting: does not nest in our region.

Feeding: wades in shallow water or on mud, probing deeply into the substrate with a repeated up-down bill motion; eats aquatic invertebrates, including insects, mollusks, crustaceans and worms; may feed on seeds, aquatic plants and grasses.

Voice: generally silent; flight call is a mellow, repeated *tututu, toodulu* or *toodu*.

Similar Species: *Long-billed Dowitcher* (p. 152): black-and-white barring on red flanks in breeding plumage; very little white on belly; dark spotting on neck and upper breast; alarm call is a high-pitched *keek*. *Red Knot* (p. 138): much shorter bill; unmarked, red breast in breeding plumage; nonbreeding birds lack barring on tail and white wedge on back in flight. *Wilson's Snipe* (p. 153): heavy streaking on neck and breast; bicolored bill; pale median stripe on crown; shorter legs.

Best Sites: ***MN:*** Salt L. (Lac Qui Parle Co.); Big Stone NWR; Heron L. (Jackson Co.). ***WI:*** Horicon Marsh; Arlington ponds; Shiocton–Black Creek; Manitowoc; Milwaukee; Nine Springs sewage ponds (Madison); Beaver Dam ponds.

LONG-BILLED DOWITCHER

Limnodromus scolopaceus

Every spring and especially in late fall, mudflats and marshes host small numbers of enthusiastic Long-billed Dowitchers. These chunky, sword-billed shorebirds diligently forage up and down through shallow water and mud in a quest for invertebrate sustenance. A diet of insects, freshwater shrimp, mussels, clams and snails provides migrating birds with plenty of fuel for flight and essential calcium for bone and egg development. • Dowitchers have shorter wings than most shorebirds that migrate long distances, making it more practical for them to take flight from shallow water, where a series of hops can help them to become airborne. • Mixed flocks of shorebirds demonstrate a variety of foraging styles: some species probe deeply, while others pick at the water's surface or glean the shorelines. Large numbers of shorebird species are able to coexist because of their different foraging styles and specialized diets.

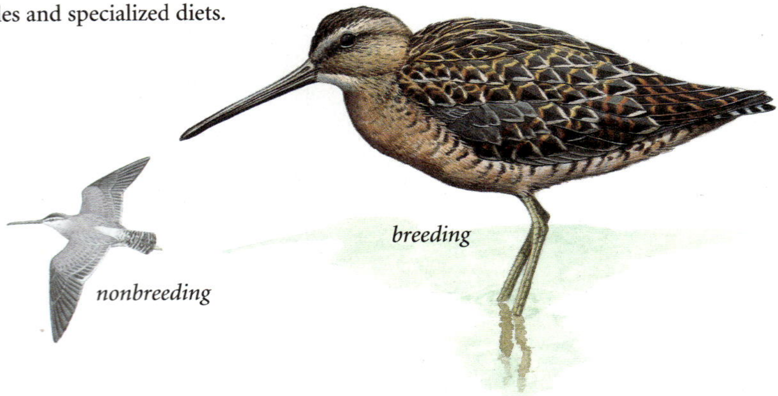

breeding

nonbreeding

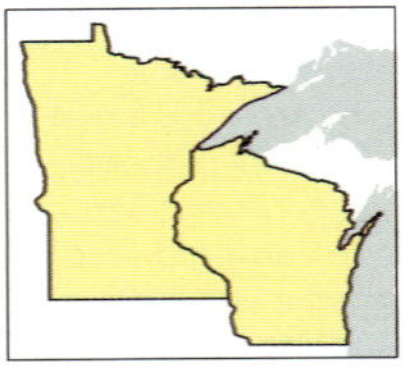

ID: very long, straight, dark bill; dark eye line; white "eyebrow"; chunky body; yellow green legs. *Breeding:* black-and-white barring on reddish underparts; some white on belly; dark, mottled upperparts. *Nonbreeding:* gray overall; dirty white underparts; *In flight:* white wedge on rump and lower back.

Size: *L* 11–12½ in; *W* 19 in.

Status: ***MN:*** uncommon migrant from late April to late May and from September to early November. ***WI:*** uncommon migrant in May; fairly common migrant from August to early November.

Habitat: lakeshores, ponds, reservoirs, shallow marshes and mudflats.

Nesting: does not nest in our region.

Feeding: probes in shallow water and mudflats with a repeated up-down bill motion; frequently plunges its head underwater; eats shrimps, snails, worms, larval flies and other soft-bodied invertebrates.

Voice: alarm call is a loud, high-pitched *keek,* occasionally given in series.

Similar Species: *Short-billed Dowitcher* (p. 151): white sides, flanks and belly; more spots than bars on reddish sides and flanks; brighter feather edges on upperparts; call is a lower-pitched *toodu* or *tututu. Red Knot* (p. 138): much shorter bill; unmarked, red breast in breeding plumage; nonbreeding birds lack barring on tail and white wedge on back in flight. *Wilson's Snipe* (p. 153): shorter legs; heavy streaking on neck and breast; bicolored bill; light median stripe on crown.

Best Sites: ***MN:*** sewage ponds; Big Stone NWR; Salt L. (Lac Qui Parle Co.); Agassiz NWR; Hamden Slough NWR. ***WI:*** Horicon Marsh; Arlington ponds; Beaver Dam ponds; Green Bay; Milwaukee; Manitowoc.

WILSON'S SNIPE

Gallinago delicata

Visit almost any open wetland in spring or early summer and you will hear the eerie, hollow winnowing sound of courting male Wilson's Snipes. Their specialized outer tail feathers vibrate rapidly in the air as they perform daring, headfirst dives high above their marshland habitat. Though evening performances are not uncommon, snipes display most actively in the early morning. • Outside the courtship season, the well-camouflaged Wilson's Snipe enters its shy and secretive mode, remaining concealed in vegetation. Only when an intruder approaches too closely will a snipe flush from cover, performing a series of aerial zigzags—an evasive maneuver designed to confuse predators. Because of this habit, hunters that were skilled enough to shoot a snipe came to be known as "snipers," a term later adopted by the military.

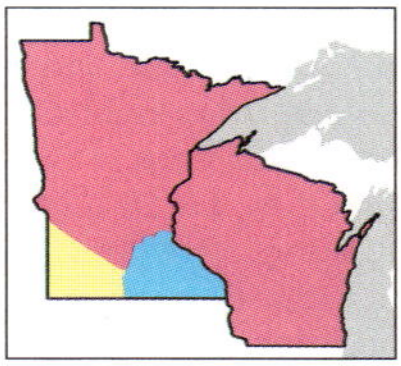

ID: long, sturdy, bicolored bill; relatively short legs; heavily striped head, back, neck and breast; dark eye stripe; dark barring on sides and flanks; unmarked white belly. *In flight:* quick zigzags on takeoff.

Size: *L* 10½–11½ in; *W* 18 in.

Status: ***MN:*** common migrant from March to early May and from early September to early November; common breeder across the northern two-thirds of the state; frequently overwinters in the southeast. ***WI:*** common migrant and breeder from late March to late October; uncommon winter visitor.

Habitat: cattail and bulrush marshes, sedge meadows, poorly drained floodplains, bogs, fens and willow and red osier dogwood tangles.

Nesting: usually in dry grass, often under vegetation; nest is made of grass, moss and leaves; female incubates 4 darkly marked, olive buff to brown eggs for 18–20 days; both parents raise the young, often splitting the brood.

Feeding: probes soft substrates for larvae, earthworms and other soft-bodied invertebrates; also eats mollusks, crustaceans, spiders, small amphibians and some seeds.

Voice: eerie, accelerating courtship song is produced in flight: *woo-woo-woo-woo-woo-woo;* often sings *wheat wheat wheat* from an elevated perch; alarm call is a nasal *scaip.*

Similar Species: *Short-billed Dowitcher* (p. 151) and *Long-billed Dowitcher* (p. 152): lack heavy striping on head, back, neck and breast; longer legs; all-dark bills; usually seen in flocks. *American Woodcock* (p. 154): unmarked, buff underparts; yellowish bill; pale bars on black crown and nape.

Best Sites: ***MN:*** Agassiz NWR; Roscoe Prairie (Stearns Co.); Rothsay WMA; Big Stone NWR. ***WI:*** marshes and swamps in the northern two-thirds of the state, including Horicon Marsh, Rat River WA, Crex Meadows WA, Powell Marsh State WA and Mead WA.

AMERICAN WOODCOCK

Scolopax minor

The American Woodcock's behavior usually mirrors its cryptic and inconspicuous attire. This denizen of moist woodlands and damp thickets usually goes about its business in a quiet and reclusive manner, but during courtship the male woodcock reveals his true character. Just before dawn or just after sunset, the male struts provocatively in an open woodland clearing or a brushy, abandoned field while calling out a series of loud *peeent* notes. He then launches into the air, twittering upward in a circular flight display until, with wings partly folded, he plummets to the ground in the zigzag pattern of a falling leaf, chirping at every turn. At the end of this stunning "sky dance," he lands precisely where he started.

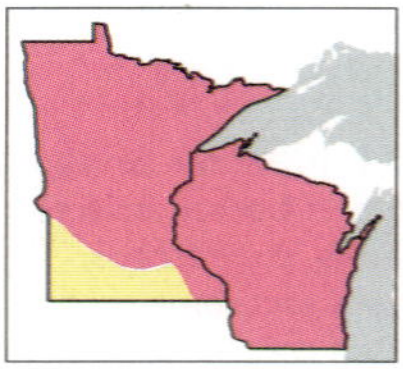

ID: very long, sturdy bill; very short legs; large head; short neck; chunky body; large, dark eyes; unmarked, buff underparts; light-colored bars on black crown and nape. *In flight:* rounded wings; makes a twittering sound when flushed from cover.

Size: *L* 11 in; *W* 18 in.

Status: ***MN:*** uncommon to common migrant from March to early May and from early September to early November, best represented in eastern and central areas; uncommon breeder in southeastern and east-central regions; increasing in numbers northward throughout north-central and northeastern regions; increasing breeder in all western and central regions. ***WI:*** fairly common migrant and breeder from mid-March to early November.

Habitat: moist woodlands and brushy thickets adjacent to grassy clearings or abandoned fields.

Nesting: on the ground in woods or in an overgrown field; female digs a scrape and lines it with dead leaves and other debris; female incubates 4 pinkish buff eggs, blotched with brown and gray, for 20–22 days; female tends the young.

Feeding: probes in soft, moist or wet soil for earthworms and insect larvae; also takes spiders, snails, millipedes and some plant material, including seeds, sedges and grasses.

Voice: nasal *peent;* during courtship dance male produces high-pitched, twittering, whistling sounds.

Similar Species: *Wilson's Snipe* (p. 153): heavily striped head, back, neck and breast; dark barring on sides and flanks. *Short-billed Dowitcher* (p. 151) and *Long-billed Dowitcher* (p. 152): all-dark bills; longer legs; lack light-colored barring on dark crown and nape; usually seen in flocks.

Best Sites: ***MN:*** Rice Lake NWR; Mille Lacs WMA; Sherburne NWR; Black Dog Nature Preserve; Carver Park Reserve; Superior NF; Chippewa NF. ***WI:*** White River WA; Rat River WA; Baraboo Hills; Cedarburg Bog; Crex Meadows WA.

WILSON'S PHALAROPE

Phalaropus tricolor

Of the three North American phalarope species, the Wilson's Phalarope is the only one that breeds here. Phalaropes practice an uncommon mating strategy known as polyandry: each female mates with several males, often producing a clutch of eggs with each mate. After laying a clutch, the female usually abandons her mate, leaving him to incubate the eggs and tend the precocial young. This reversal of gender roles also includes a reversal of plumage characteristics—females are more brightly colored than their male counterparts. Even John James Audubon was fooled by the phalarope's strange breeding habits and unique coloration: he mislabeled the male and female birds in all of his phalarope illustrations.

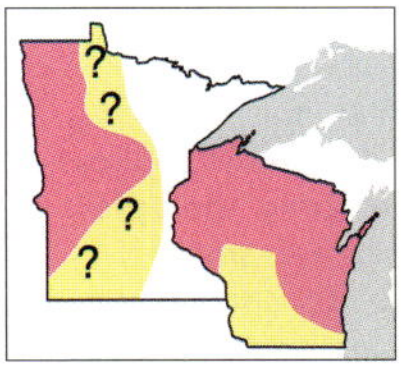

ID: dark, needlelike bill; white "eyebrow," throat and nape; light underparts; black legs. *Breeding female:* gray "cap"; chestnut brown on side of neck; black eye line extends down side of neck and onto back. *Breeding male:* duller overall; dark "cap". *Nonbreeding:* all-gray upperparts; white "eyebrow" and gray eye line; white underparts; dark yellowish or greenish legs.

Size: *L* 9–9½ in; *W* 17 in.

Status: ***MN:*** threatened; common migrant from late April to late May and from July to late September, primarily in western and central regions; uncommon to rare migrant in eastern regions; locally common breeder in the west. ***WI:*** special concern; fairly common migrant in April and May and from July to September; uncommon breeder.

Habitat: *Breeding:* marshes and grass or sedge margins of sewage lagoons. *In migration:* lakeshores, ponds, mudflats, marshes and sewage lagoons.

Nesting: often near water; well concealed in a depression lined with grass and other vegetation; male incubates 4 brown-blotched, buff eggs for 18–27 days; male rears the young.

Feeding: whirls in tight circles to stir up prey, then picks aquatic insects, worms and small crustaceans from the water's surface or just below it; on land makes short jabs to pick up invertebrates.

Voice: deep, grunting *work work* or *wu wu wu,* usually given on the breeding grounds.

Similar Species: *Red-necked Phalarope* (p. 156): rufous stripe down side of neck in breeding plumage; dark nape and line behind eye in nonbreeding plumage. *Red Phalarope* (p. 358): all-reddish neck, breast and underparts in breeding plumage; dark nape and broad, dark line behind eye in nonbreeding plumage; rarely seen inland. *Peeps* (pp. 138–48): less pronounced facial markings; most have streaked underparts.

Best Sites: ***MN:*** sewage ponds; Roseau River WMA; Salt L. (Lac Qui Parle Co.); Heron L. (Jackson Co.). ***WI:*** Horicon Marsh; Shiocton–Black Creek; Arlington ponds; Green Bay; Crex Meadows WA; Nine Springs sewage ponds (Madison).

RED-NECKED PHALAROPE

Phalaropus lobatus

One of the world's smallest seabirds, the Red-necked Phalarope is also the smallest of the three phalarope species. This bird is an inveterate sailor and spends up to nine months of the year at sea. Most Red-necked Phalaropes migrate to and from their arctic wintering grounds via the Atlantic Coast, but every year small flocks of these tiny shorebirds take the inland route through our region. • When foraging on the water with other shorebirds, phalaropes can usually be singled out by their unusual behavior—they spin and whirl about in tight circles, stirring up tiny crustaceans, mollusks and other aquatic invertebrates. As prey funnels toward the water's surface, these birds daintily pluck at them with their needlelike bills.

nonbreeding

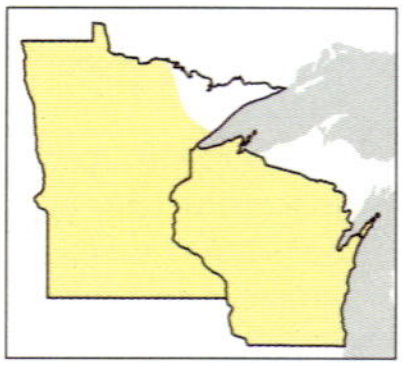

ID: thin, black bill; long, gray legs; lobed toes. *Breeding female:* chestnut brown stripe on neck and throat; white "chin"; blue black head; incomplete, white eye ring; white belly; 2 rusty buff stripes on each upperwing. *Breeding male:* white "eyebrow"; less intense colors than female. *Nonbreeding:* white underparts; dark nape; dark gray "cap"; broad, dark band from eye to ear; whitish stripes on blue gray upperparts.

Size: *L* 7 in; *W* 15 in.

Status: ***MN:*** uncommon migrant from early May to mid-June and from late July to early September; occurs primarily in western regions. ***WI:*** uncommon migrant from May to early June and from mid-July to early November.

Habitat: open water bodies, including ponds, lakes, marshes and sewage lagoons; also flooded fields.

Nesting: does not nest in our region.

Feeding: whirls in tight circles in shallow or deep water to stir up prey, then picks aquatic insects, mollusks and small crustaceans from the water's surface or just below it; on land makes short jabs to pick up invertebrates.

Voice: often noisy in migration; soft *krit krit krit.*

Similar Species: *Wilson's Phalarope* (p. 155): female has gray "cap" and black eye line extending down side of neck and onto back in breeding plumage; dark "cap" in nonbreeding plumage. *Red Phalarope* (p. 358): all-red neck, breast and underparts in breeding plumage; lacks white stripes on upperwing in nonbreeding plumage. *Peeps* (pp. 138–48): less pronounced facial markings; most have streaked underparts.

Best Sites: ***MN:*** sewage ponds in fall; Salt L. (Lac Qui Parle Co.). ***WI:*** Horicon Marsh; Arlington ponds; Beaver Dam ponds; Green Bay; Nine Springs sewage ponds (Madison).

PARASITIC JAEGER

Stercorarius parasiticus

Although "jaeger" means "hunter" in German, "parasitic" more aptly describes this bird's foraging tactics. "Kleptoparasitism" is the scientific term for this jaeger's pirating ways, and these birds are truly relentless. Parasitic Jaegers will harass and intimidate terns and gulls until the victims regurgitate their partially digested meals. As soon as the food is ejected, these aerial pirates snatch it out of midair or pick it from the water's surface in a swooping dive. Less than 25 percent of these encounters are successful, and many Parasitic Jaegers are content to find their own food. • Parasitic Jaegers are the most numerous predatory birds on their arctic breeding grounds. When nesting, adults defend their eggs and young aggressively. Both adults will attack approaching danger in stooping, parabolic dives or aggressive, blazing pursuits. • The Parasitic Jaeger is the most abundant jaeger in the world and the most commonly seen in our region.

light morph

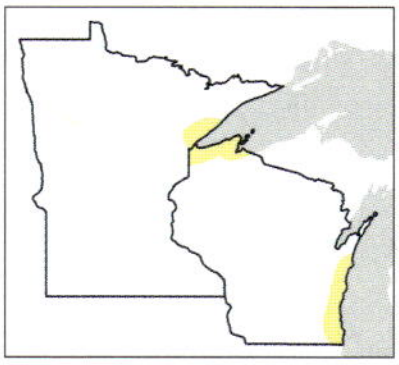

ID: long, dark, pointed wings with 3–5 white feathers on upperwing primaries; long, pointed central tail feathers; brown upperparts; dark "cap"; light underwing tips. *Light morph:* white underparts; white to cream-colored "collar"; light brown neck band. *Dark morph:* all-brown underparts and "collar." *Immature:* barred underparts; central tail feather extends just past tail.

Size: *L* 15–20½ in; *W* 3 ft.

Status: ***MN:*** very rare migrant from late May to early June and from early August to late October on L. Superior, mainly near Duluth; accidental in other areas of the state. ***WI:*** casual migrant in late May; rare migrant from August to November.

Habitat: shorelines of large lakes and rivers and open water.

Nesting: does not nest in our region.

Feeding: pirates, scavenges and hunts for food; eats fish, eggs, large insects and small birds and mammals; also takes carrion and some berries when on land; often pirates food from other birds; may scavenge at landfills.

Voice: generally silent; may make shrill calls in migration.

Similar Species: *Pomarine Jaeger* (p. 358): shorter, blunt, twisted central tail feathers; dark, mottled sides and flanks; white on upperwing primaries. *Long-tailed Jaeger* (p. 358): much smaller; much longer, pointed central tail feathers; only 1–2 white feathers on upperwing primaries; lacks dark neck band.

Best Sites: ***MN:*** Duluth. ***WI:*** Wisconsin Pt. (Superior); Ashland–Chequamegon Bay; Harrington Beach SP; Milwaukee.

LAUGHING GULL

Larus atricilla

The black-hooded Laughing Gull's beautiful plumage and lilting laugh are readily accepted by humans today, but life has not always been so easy for this bird. In the late 19th century, high commercial demand for egg collections and feathers for use in women's headdresses resulted in the extirpation of this gull as a breeding species in many parts of its Atlantic Coast range. Today, East Coast populations are gradually assuming their former abundance, and consequently a few drift over to our region occasionally. • The Laughing Gull's breeding range is primarily along the Atlantic and Gulf coasts of North America and in the Caribbean. It winters in Mexico and Central and South America.

breeding

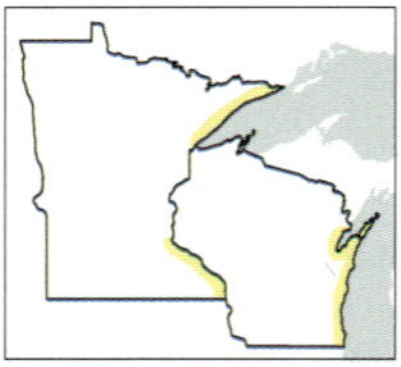

ID: *Breeding:* black head; broken, white eye ring; red bill. *Nonbreeding:* white head with some pale gray bands; black bill. *3rd-year:* white neck and underparts; dark gray back; black-tipped wings; black legs. *Immature:* variable plumage; brown to gray and white overall; broad, black subterminal band on tail.

Size: *L* 15–17 in; *W* 3 ft.

Status: ***MN:*** casual migrant and summer visitor; majority of records are from L. Superior and range from April through October. ***WI:*** rare spring migrant and summer visitor from mid-March to early September.

Habitat: shorelines of lakes and rivers and open water.

Nesting: does not nest in our region.

Feeding: omnivorous; gleans insects, small mollusks, crustaceans, spiders and small fish from the ground or water while flying, wading, walking or swimming; may steal food from other birds; may eat the eggs and nestlings of other birds; often scavenges at landfills

Voice: loud, high-pitched, laughing call: *ha-ha-ha-ha-ha-ha*.

Similar Species: *Franklin's Gull* (p. 159): smaller overall; red legs; shorter, slimmer bill; white on outer primaries; nonbreeding adult has black "mask." *Black-headed Gull* (p. 358) and *Bonaparte's Gull* (p. 161): orange or reddish legs; slimmer bill (Bonaparte's has black bill); lighter mantle; white wedge on upper leading edge of wing; black "hood" on breeding adult does not extend over nape. *Little Gull* (p. 160): much smaller; paler mantle; reddish legs; dainty black bill; no eye ring; lacks black wing tips.

Best Sites: ***MN:*** L. Superior; Duluth. ***WI:*** Manitowoc; Sheboygan; Milwaukee; Racine; Green Bay.

FRANKLIN'S GULL

Larus pipixcan

Twice each year, small flocks of Franklin's Gulls drift into our region from their prairie stronghold. They are usually seen intermingled among large groups of Bonaparte's Gulls and other gull relatives. • The Franklin's Gull is not a typical "seagull." A large part of its life is spent inland, and on its traditional nesting territory on the prairies, it is affectionately known as "Prairie Dove." It has a dovelike profile and often follows tractors across agricultural fields, snatching up insects from the tractor's path in much the same way its cousins follow fishing boats. • Most Franklin's Gulls winter along the Pacific coast of Peru and Chile, and it is one of only two gull species that migrate long distances between breeding and wintering grounds.

breeding

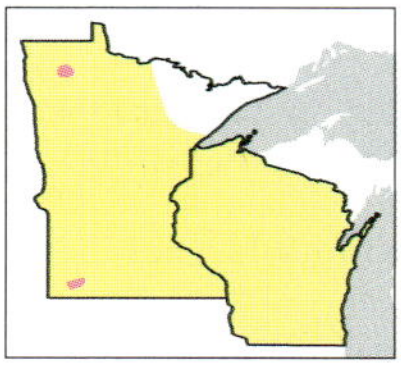

ID: dark gray mantle; broken, white eye ring; white underparts. *Breeding:* black head; orange red bill and legs; breast may have pinkish tinge. *Nonbreeding:* white head; dark patch on side of head. *In flight:* black crescent on white wing tips.

Size: *L* 13–15 in; *W* 3 ft.

Status: ***MN:*** special concern; common migrant from late March to mid-May and at times abundant migrant from late July to late November in western and central regions; irregular migrant in eastern regions; rare to uncommon migrant over most of the northeast and southeast; breeds in a large colony at Agassiz NWR; sporadic breeder at Heron L. (Jackson Co.). ***WI:*** uncommon to rare migrant from late March to late May and from late July to late November.

Habitat: agricultural fields, marshlands, river and lake shorelines, rivermouths and landfills.

Nesting: colonial; in a marsh; both sexes build a large, floating platform from cattails and bulrushes; both adults incubate 2–4 blotched and spotted, greenish to buff-colored eggs for 23–26 days.

Feeding: very opportunistic; gleans agricultural fields and meadows for grasshoppers and insects; often catches dragonflies, mayflies and other flying invertebrates in midair; also eats small fish and some crustaceans.

Voice: mewing, shrill *weeeh-ah weeeh-ah* while feeding and in migration.

Similar Species: *Bonaparte's Gull* (p. 161): black bill; conspicuous white wedge on forewing. *Little Gull* (p. 160): much smaller; paler mantle; lacks black crescent on wing tips; breeding adult lacks broken, white eye ring and white nape; nonbreeding adult lacks black "mask." *Black-headed Gull* (p. 358): paler mantle; conspicuous white wedge on forewing; breeding adult has much more white on back of head; nonbreeding adult lacks black "mask." *Sabine's Gull* (p. 359): large black, white and gray triangles on upperwing; dark, yellow-tipped bill. *Laughing Gull* (p. 158): larger; black legs; longer, heavier bill; nonbreeding adult lacks black "mask."

Best Sites: ***MN:*** Agassiz NWR; Lake of the Woods; Thief Lake WMA; Heron L. (Jackson Co.); Albert Lea L. (Freeborn Co.). ***WI:*** Manitowoc; Milwaukee; Sheboygan; Green Bay; Arlington ponds.

LITTLE GULL

Larus minutus

This common Eurasian bird was first identified in North America around 1820 as a specimen collected on the first expedition of explorer John Franklin. It was considered an exceptionally rare vagrant until 1962, when the first documented nest in the New World was discovered in Ontario, Canada. • Little Gulls never nest in a given site for more than a few years. In North America, they have been found nesting primarily in the Great Lakes region and the Hudson Bay Lowlands in Canada. • Look for the Little Gull's dark underwings when it is in flight. This field mark makes it quite conspicuous among the masses of white-underwinged Bonaparte's Gulls with which it usually mingles. • The Little Gull, true to its name, is the smallest of all gulls.

breeding

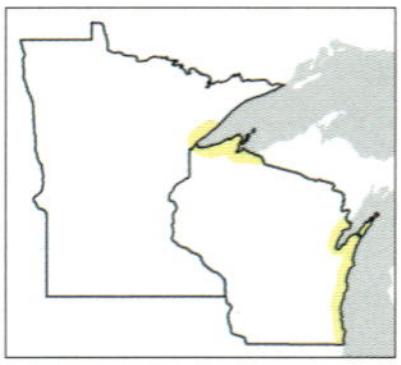

ID: white neck, rump, tail and underparts; gray back and wings; orange red legs. *Breeding:* black head; dark red bill. *Nonbreeding:* black bill; dark ear spot and "cap." *Immature:* pinkish legs; brown and black in wings and tail. *In flight:* white wing tips and trailing edge of wing; dark underwings.

Size: *L* 10–11 in; *W* 24 in.

Status: ***MN:*** rare migrant in May and June and very rare fall migrant on larger lakes, mainly on L. Superior; 1 nesting record (1986) in Jackson Co. ***WI:*** uncommon to rare migrant; casual breeder.

Habitat: larger lakes, freshwater marshes and ponds.

Nesting: colonial, but occasionally in isolated pairs; on the ground near water; pair lines a shallow depression with vegetation or builds a raised mound on a wet site; pair incubates 1–5 olive to buff eggs, marked with brown and gray, for 23–25 days.

Feeding: gleans insects from the ground or from the water's surface while flying, wading, walking or floating; may also take small mollusks, fish, crustaceans, marine worms and spiders.

Voice: repeated *kay-ee* and a low *kek-kek-kek*.

Similar Species: *Bonaparte's Gull* (p. 161): black-tipped primary feathers; breeding adult has broken, white eye ring, larger, black bill and white nape; nonbreeding adult has white "cap." *Black-headed Gull* (p. 358): black-tipped primary feathers; breeding adult has broken, white eye ring, larger bill and white nape; nonbreeding adult has white "cap" and red bill. *Franklin's Gull* (p. 159): larger; black wing tips; darker mantle; breeding adult has broken, white eye ring, white nape and brighter red bill; nonbreeding adult has black "mask." *Laughing Gull* (p. 158): larger; black wing tips; darker mantle; black legs; breeding adult has broken, white eye ring and much larger bill. *Sabine's Gull* (p. 359): black forewing wedge; black legs; yellow-tipped bill.

Best Sites: ***MN:*** L. Superior; Duluth; Mille Lacs L. ***WI:*** Manitowoc; Sheboygan; Green Bay; Wisconsin Pt.; Milwaukee.

BONAPARTE'S GULL

Larus philadelphia

Many people feel great disdain for gulls, but they might change their minds when they meet the Bonaparte's Gull. This graceful, reserved gull is nothing like its contentious, aggressive relatives. Delicate in plumage and behavior, this small gull avoids landfills, preferring to dine on insects caught in midair or plucked from the water's surface. This engaging bird will sometimes even tip up like a dabbling duck to catch small invertebrates in the shallows. Only when a flock of Bonaparte's Gulls spies a school of fish or an intruder do the birds raise their soft, scratchy voices in excitement. • Unlike other gulls and terns, Bonaparte's Gulls nest in coniferous trees. Their nests are usually situated high in the canopy, and they often choose sites that are close to a lake or large beaver pond. • In years when mild winter weather prevails, some of these gulls remain in our region, flying about for hours on end, wheeling and flashing their pale wings.

breeding

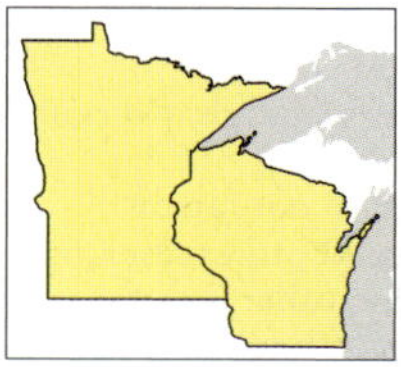

ID: black bill; gray mantle; white underparts. *Breeding:* black head; white eye ring; orange legs. *Nonbreeding:* white head; dark ear patch. *In flight:* white forewing wedge; black wing tips.
Size: *L* 11½–14 in; *W* 33 in.
Status: ***MN:*** common migrant from mid-April to early June and from late July to late November; sometimes abundant in fall at staging areas. ***WI:*** common migrant from late March to early June and from mid-July to late December; fairly common summer resident; rare winter visitor.
Habitat: large lakes, rivers and marshes; flooded fields in spring.
Nesting: does not nest in our region.
Feeding: dabbles and tips up for aquatic invertebrates, small fish and tadpoles; gleans the ground for terrestrial invertebrates; also captures insects in the air.
Voice: scratchy, soft *ear ear* while feeding.
Similar Species: *Franklin's Gull* (p. 159): larger; lacks white upper forewing wedge; breeding adult has orange bill; nonbreeding adult has black "mask." *Little Gull* (p. 160): smaller; daintier bill; adult has white wing tips; black "hood" of breeding adult lacks white eye ring and extends over nape; nonbreeding adult has white "cap." *Black-headed Gull* (p. 358): larger overall; larger, red bill; dark underwing primaries; more red than orange on legs; breeding adult has brownish "hood." *Sabine's Gull* (p. 359): large black, white and gray triangles on upperwings; dark, yellow-tipped bill.
Best Sites: ***MN:*** L. Superior; Mille Lacs L.; L. Winnibigoshish; Grey Cloud I.; larger lakes; sewage ponds. ***WI:*** Racine, Milwaukee, Sheboygan, Manitowoc–Two Rivers, Green Bay (L. Michigan); Wisconsin Pt., Ashland (L. Superior).

MEW GULL

Larus canus

The Mew Gull is the smallest of the typical "white-headed" gulls. This petite and delicate gull is almost always seen in the company of other gulls, so side-by-side comparisons are usually possible. The large eyes and single, subterminal white patch in the black wing tip makes the adult easy to identify. Scanning for a young bird is more challenging—it has the look of a Ring-bill, but with a more dovelike profile. As well, the Mew Gull dives for fish more often than our other gulls. • The soft, "mewing" call for which this gull was named is a pleasant change from the usual screeches of other gulls. Unfortunately, this call is mostly used on the breeding grounds. • This bird's scientific name is very literal—*Larus* is Greek for "gull," and *canus* is Latin for "grayish white."

breeding

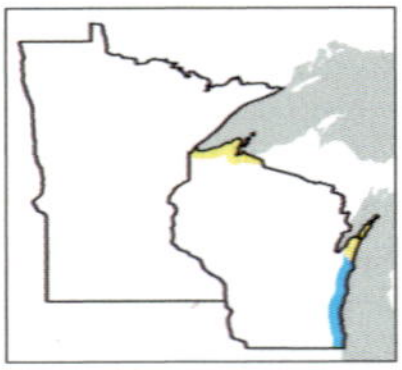

ID: dainty; small, thin bill; wings extend well beyond tail at rest; rapid walking stride. *Breeding:* all-white head; unmarked, yellow bill; gray mantle. *Nonbreeding:* dark eyes; greenish yellow bill (variable) with dark smudge on lower mandible; darker mantle; minimal to extensive dusky streaking or clouding on head, neck and upper breast; noticeable single white area on black wing tips; pale green yellow legs and feet. *1st-winter:* dingy gray brown with grayish back; dark-tipped, pink bill; slightly darker brown outer primaries; broad, blackish terminal tail band.

Size: *L* 15–18 in; *W* $3\frac{1}{2}$ ft.

Status: ***MN:*** accidental; only 3 records for the state from September, November and December (2 from L. Superior and 1 from L. Winnibigoshish). ***WI:*** very rare migrant and winter visitor.

Habitat: lakes, shallow wetlands, rivers and landfills.

Nesting: does not nest in our region.

Feeding: opportunistic; captures small fish, crustaceans, insects and other invertebrates by plunging to the water's surface or picking from the ground; scavenges on carrion and at landfills.

Voice: typical, gull-like *hiyah hiyah hiyah;* distinctive *mee-you mee-you.*

Similar Species: *Ring-billed Gull* (p. 163): paler gray upperparts; heavier yellow bill has distinct black ring; pale eyes; lacks eye-catching, single white wing tip area; less dusky-headed in nonbreeding plumage. *Other white-headed gulls:* larger; heavier bills, marked with black or red or both.

Best Sites: ***MN:*** no consistent sites. ***WI:*** Milwaukee, Manitowoc (L. Michigan); Superior, Ashland (L. Superior).

RING-BILLED GULL

Larus delawarensis

The Ring-billed Gull's tolerance for humans has made it a part of our everyday lives. It wanders almost everywhere and has picked up many of the bad habits associated with its larger relatives. • In the early 1900s, some naturalists were unsure if Ring-billed Gulls were nesting in this area, although others at that time felt certain that there were small colonies nesting here. By 1940, there was no mistaking the rise in the number of breeding Ring-bills in Minnesota and Wisconsin, and by the mid-1960s, the approximately 100,000 birds were impossible to miss. Some people feel that Ring-billed Gulls have become pests—many parks, beaches, golf courses and even fast-food parking lots are often inundated with marauding gulls looking for food handouts. Few species, however, have fared as well as the Ring-billed Gull in the face of human development, which, in itself, is something to appreciate.

breeding

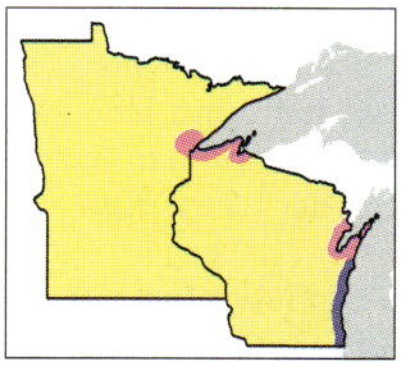

ID: white head; yellow bill and legs; black ring around bill tip; pale gray mantle; yellow eyes; white underparts. *Immature:* gray back; brown wings and breast. *In flight:* black wing tips with a few white spots.
Size: *L* 18–20 in; *W* 4 ft.
Status: ***MN:*** abundant migrant from early March to late May and from mid-August to late December; common breeder at Duluth; increasing breeder near larger lakes. ***WI:*** very common to abundant migrant and breeder from March to December; uncommon winter visitor.
Habitat: *Breeding:* sparsely vegetated natural and human-made islands, open beaches and breakwaters. *In migration* and *winter:* lakes, rivers, landfills, golf courses, fields and parks.
Nesting: colonial; in a shallow scrape on the ground lined with plants, debris, grass and sticks; pair incubates 2–4 brown-blotched, gray to olive eggs for 23–28 days.
Feeding: gleans the ground for human food waste, spiders, insects, rodents, earthworms, grubs and some waste grain; scavenges for carrion; surface-tips for aquatic invertebrates and fish.
Voice: high-pitched *kakakaka-akakaka;* also a low, laughing *yook-yook-yook*.
Similar Species: *Herring* (p. 164), *Thayer's* (p. 165), *Glaucous* (p. 168) and *Iceland* (p. 166) *gulls:* larger; pinkish legs; red spot near tip of lower mandible; lack bill ring. *Mew Gull* (p. 162): less black on wing tips; dark eyes; darker mantle; lacks bill ring. *Lesser Black-backed Gull* (p. 167): larger; much darker mantle; much less white on wing tips; lacks bill ring.
Best Sites: ***MN:*** Duluth; Spring L. (Dakota Co.); L. Calhoun (Hennepin Co.); L. George (Anoka Co.); Lake of the Woods.
WI: L. Michigan; L. Superior; inland lakes and rivers.

HERRING GULL

Larus argentatus

Herring Gulls are skilled hunters, but they are also opportunistic birds that scavenge at landfills and in fast-food restaurant parking lots. • Herring Gulls nest comfortably in large colonies, or a pair may choose a site miles from any other gulls. In some areas, increasing Herring Gull populations have meant decreasing tern numbers owing to this gull's fondness for tern eggs and nestlings. • Like many gulls, Herring Gulls have a small red spot on the lower mandible that serves as a target for nestling young. When a downy chick pecks at the lower mandible, the parent recognizes the cue and regurgitates its meal. Many juveniles continue to beg for food well into winter, with varying success depending on their parents' disposition.

breeding

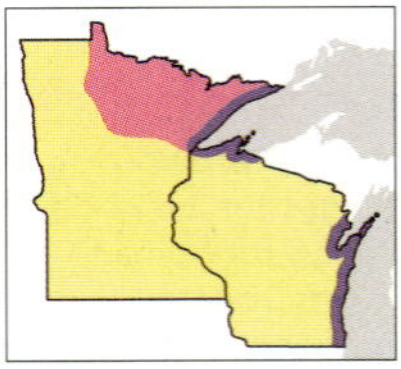

ID: large gull; yellow bill; red spot on lower mandible; light eyes; light gray mantle; pink legs. *Breeding:* white head; white underparts. *Nonbreeding:* white head and nape are washed with brown. *Immature:* mottled brown overall. *In flight:* white-spotted, black wing tips.

Size: *L* 23–26 in; *W* 4 ft.

Status: ***MN:*** common migrant from late February to late May and from early September to early January in eastern and central regions; locally abundant migrant on L. Superior and larger lakes in northeastern and north-central regions; uncommon migrant in the west; locally common breeder; occasional in winter, especially on L. Superior. ***WI:*** very common to abundant migrant and breeder from early March to early December; common winter visitor.

Habitat: large lakes, wetlands, rivers, landfills and urban areas.

Nesting: singly or colonially, often with other gulls, pelicans and cormorants; on an island in a large lake; on the ground in a shallow scrape lined with plants and sticks; pair incubates 3 darkly blotched, olive to buff eggs for 31–32 days.

Feeding: surface-tips for aquatic invertebrates and fish; gleans the ground for insects and worms; scavenges human food waste at landfills; eats other birds' eggs and young.

Voice: loud, buglelike *kleew-kleew;* also an alarmed *kak-kak-kak*.

Similar Species: *California Gull* (p. 359): smaller; dark eyes; yellowish legs; black-and-red spot on lower mandible. *Ring-billed Gull* (p. 163): smaller; black bill ring; yellow legs. *Glaucous Gull* (p. 168): larger; paler mantle; lacks black in wings. *Iceland Gull* (p. 166): smaller; paler mantle; lacks black in wings. *Thayer's Gull* (p. 165): slightly darker mantle; dark eyes. *Lesser Black-backed Gull* (p. 167): darker mantle. *Great Black-backed Gull* (p. 169): larger; black mantle.

Best Sites: ***MN:*** L. Superior; lower Mississippi R. valley; Twin Cities area; larger inland lakes and rivers. ***WI:*** L. Superior; L. Michigan; inland lakes and rivers.

THAYER'S GULL

Larus thayeri

Thayer's Gulls are uncommon in our region, and because many of these visitors are immature birds (the identification of which is beyond the scope of this book), it is often only the most experienced birders who recognize them. These gulls are most often sighted traveling inconspicuously among large flocks of Ring-billed Gulls and Herring Gulls during winter. • The Thayer's Gull belongs to a group of recently evolved gulls that have similar traits, and therefore could potentially still interbreed. It was actually once considered a subspecies of the very similar-looking Herring Gull, and some ornithologists dispute the decision to grant this bird full species status. Alternatively, other ornithologists believe that the Thayer's Gull is actually a subspecies of the Iceland Gull.

nonbreeding

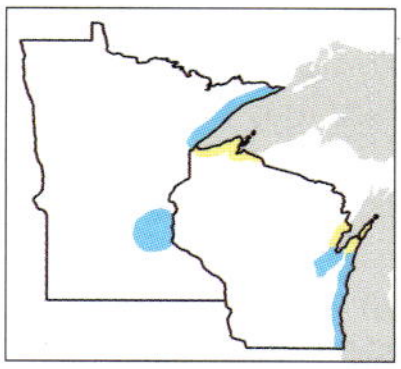

ID: white-spotted, dark gray wing tips; dark eyes; yellow bill has red spot at tip of lower mandible; dark pink legs. *Breeding:* clean white head, neck and upper breast. *Nonbreeding:* brown-flecked head, neck and upper breast. *Immature:* variable, mottled white-and-brown plumage; 1st-year has black bill; 2nd-year has black ring around dusky bill.

Size: *L* 22–25 in; *W* 4½ ft.

Status: ***MN:*** rare migrant from late October to late November and from March to early April; winter visitor in December and January; nearly all records are from L. Superior or lakes in the Twin Cities area; casual elsewhere in the state. ***WI:*** uncommon migrant and winter visitor from early September to mid-May.

Habitat: open water on large lakes and rivers and landfills.

Nesting: does not nest in our region.

Feeding: gleans from the water's surface while in flight; eats small fish, crustaceans, mollusks, carrion and human food waste.

Voice: various raucous and laughing calls are given, much like the Herring Gull's *kak-kak-kak*.

Similar Species: *Herring Gull* (p. 164): black wing tips; light eyes; darker mantle. *Iceland Gull* (p. 166): pale eyes; more white than dark gray on wing tips. *Glaucous Gull* (p. 168): larger; longer, heavier bill; light eyes; white wing tips; lighter pink legs. *Ring-billed Gull* (p. 163): smaller; dark ring on yellow bill; yellow legs. *Lesser Black-backed Gull* (p. 167): darker mantle; black wing tips; yellow feet.

Best Sites: ***MN:*** North Shore of L. Superior; landfills in the Twin Cities area. ***WI:*** L. Michigan and L. Superior harbors; Green Bay; DePere; Neenah-Menasha.

ICELAND GULL

Larus glaucoides

The pale Iceland Gull can be seen each winter in small numbers, usually among larger flocks of more common wintering gulls. This graceful glider spends much of its time searching for fish over icy, open waters. When fishing proves unrewarding, this opportunistic gull has no qualms about digging through a landfill or scavenging in a harbor in search of food. This bird's dirty brown head and breast streaking are not the result of its filthy scavenging habits, but are the natural markings of its nonbreeding plumage. • The Iceland Gull comes in two slightly different forms in our region, although one is more common than the other. Most common is the *kumlieni* subspecies, which has gray on its wing tips. On Baffin Island in Canada, this subspecies interbreeds with the Thayer's Gull, producing fertile hybrids that are also seen here, although only occasionally. Debate continues on the status of these gulls, and some scientists believe that the Thayer's Gull is really just a subspecies of the Iceland Gull.

nonbreeding

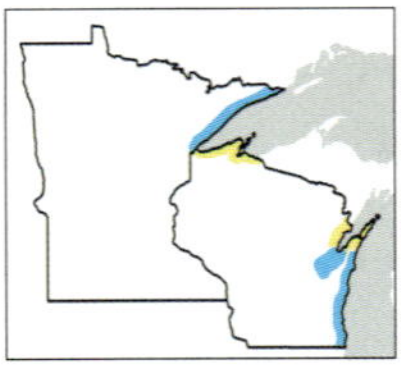

ID: *Breeding:* relatively short, yellow bill has red spot on lower mandible; rounded head; yellow eyes; dark eye ring; white wing tips with some dark gray; pink legs; white underparts; pale gray mantle. *Nonbreeding:* brown-streaked head and breast. *Immature:* dark eyes; black bill; various plumages with varying amounts of gray on upperparts and brown flecking over entire body.

Size: *L* 22 in; *W* 4½ ft.

Status: ***MN:*** rare to uncommon fall migrant and winter visitor from mid-November to mid-May, mainly along the North Shore of L. Superior; rare in the Twin Cities area and the lower Mississippi R. valley. ***WI:*** uncommon to rare migrant and winter visitor from late September to late April.

Habitat: landfills, harbors and open water on large lakes and rivers.

Nesting: does not nest in our region.

Feeding: eats mostly fish; may also take crustaceans, mollusks, carrion, seeds and human food waste; scavenges at landfills and in harbors.

Voice: high, screechy calls, much less bugling than other large gulls.

Similar Species: *Herring Gull* (p. 164): black wing tips; darker mantle. *Thayer's Gull* (p. 165): more dark gray than white on wing tips; dark eyes. *Glaucous Gull* (p. 168): larger; longer, heavier bill; pure white wing tips. *Ring-billed Gull* (p. 163): smaller; dark ring on yellow bill; yellow legs. *Great Black-backed Gull* (p. 169) and *Lesser Black-backed Gull* (p. 167): darker mantle; black wing tips; Lesser has yellow legs.

Best Sites: ***MN:*** L. Superior. ***WI:*** L. Michigan and L. Superior harbors; Green Bay; DePere; Neenah-Menasha.

LESSER BLACK-BACKED GULL

Larus fuscus

Equipped with long wings for long-distance flights, small numbers of Lesser Black-backed Gulls leave their familiar European and Icelandic surroundings each fall to make their way to North America. Most of these gulls settle along the Atlantic Coast during winter, but a few make their way into our region. • The Lesser Black-backed Gull is a relative newcomer to this area. It was first sighted in Wisconsin in October 1980 and in Minnesota in October 1984. In recent years, Lesser Black-backed Gull sightings have increased, and it is possible that this Eurasian species will soon colonize North America. Some Lesser Black-backed Gulls have already been found paired with Herring Gulls, we may see even more puzzling hybrids in the future.

nonbreeding

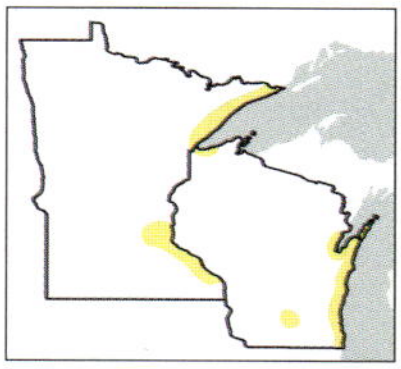

ID: *Breeding:* dark gray or black mantle; mostly black wing tips; yellow bill has red spot on lower mandible; yellow eyes; yellow legs; white head and underparts. *Nonbreeding:* brown-streaked head and neck. *Immature:* black bill or pale, black-tipped bill; eyes may be dark or light; various plumages with varying amounts of gray on upperparts and brown flecking over entire body.

Size: *L* 20½ in; *W* 4½ ft.

Status: ***MN:*** rare migrant from early March to early May; rare to uncommon migrant from early September to late December; found almost exclusively along L. Superior, in the Twin Cities area and in the lower Mississippi R. valley. ***WI:*** rare spring and fall migrant.

Habitat: landfills, harbors and open water on large lakes and rivers.

Nesting: does not nest in our region.

Feeding: eats mostly fish, crustaceans, mollusks, insects, small rodents, carrion, seeds and human food waste; scavenges at landfills and harbors.

Voice: screechy call is like a lower-pitched version of the Herring Gull's.

Similar Species: *Herring Gull* (p. 164): lighter mantle; pink legs. *Thayer's* (p. 165), *Glaucous* (p. 168) and *Iceland* (p. 166) *gulls:* pale gray mantle; white or gray wing tips; pink legs. *Ring-billed Gull* (p. 163): smaller; dark ring on yellow bill; paler mantle. *Great Black-backed Gull* (p. 169): much larger; black mantle; pale pinkish legs.

Best Sites: ***MN:*** Duluth to Grand Marais (L. Superior); Twin Cities area; lower Mississippi R. valley; Black Dog L. (Dakota Co.). ***WI:*** Milwaukee; Sheboygan; Superior; Manitowoc; Two Rivers; Green Bay; Madison; Ashland.

GLAUCOUS GULL

Larus hyperboreus

The Glaucous Gull's white underparts and pale gray mantle camouflage it against the cloud-filled skies of winter as it flies above the open waters of the Great Lakes. Its pale plumage also helps birders to distinguish its ghostly figure from other, more numerous, overwintering gull species. • Glaucous Gulls traditionally fished for their meals or stole food from smaller gulls or even fast-flying Gyrfalcons. More recently, however, wintering Glaucous Gulls have traded the rigors of hunting for the job of defending plots of garbage at various landfills. • Immature birds of this species, though difficult to identify, are light enough to be easily distinguished from other immature gulls, and most have a distinctive, pale pink bill with a dark tip. • In summer, while other gulls are strolling along local beaches or hanging out in fast-food restaurant parking lots, the Glaucous Gull is far away in the arctic wilderness. The scientific name *hyperboreus* means "of the far north."

nonbreeding

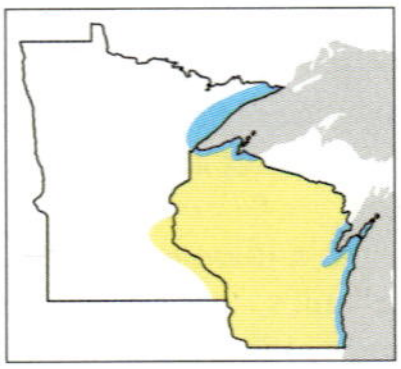

ID: *Breeding:* relatively long, heavy, yellow bill has red spot on lower mandible; pure white wing tips; flattened crown profile; yellow eyes; pink legs; white underparts; very pale gray mantle. *Nonbreeding:* brown-streaked head, neck and breast. *Immature:* dark eyes; pale, black-tipped bill; various plumages have varying amounts of brown flecking on body.

Size: *L* 27 in; *W* 5 ft.

Status: ***MN:*** uncommon to rare migrant and winter visitor from late October to late May along the North Shore of L. Superior and in the lower Mississippi R. valley; casual to accidental elsewhere. ***WI:*** uncommon migrant and winter visitor from early November to early May; rare summer resident.

Habitat: landfills, harbors and open water on large lakes and rivers.

Nesting: does not nest in our region.

Feeding: predator, pirate and scavenger; eats mostly fish, crustaceans, mollusks and some seeds; feeds on carrion and at landfills.

Voice: high, screechy calls similar to Herring Gull's *kak-kak-kak*.

Similar Species: *Thayer's Gull* (p. 165) and *Iceland Gull* (p. 166): smaller; slightly darker mantle; gray on wing tips. *Herring Gull* (p. 164): slightly smaller; black wing tips; much darker mantle. *Great Black-backed Gull* (p. 169): darker in all plumages; young birds have all-dark bills.

Best Sites: ***MN:*** L. Superior; lower Mississippi R. valley. ***WI:*** L. Michigan and L. Superior harbors; Green Bay; DePere; Appleton; Neenah-Menasha.

GREAT BLACK-BACKED GULL

Larus marinus

The Great Black-backed Gull's commanding size and bold, aggressive disposition enable it to dominate other gulls, ensuring that it has first dibs at food, whether it is fresh fish or a meal from a landfill. • In recent years, the Great Black-backed Gull has chosen the Great Lakes as a new nesting location, although nesting in our region is still very casual. These gulls do not tolerate Herring Gulls near their nest sites. As a result, terns, whose nestlings often suffer high mortality because of predation by Herring Gulls, benefit considerably from the presence of this unwitting ally. • The Great Black-backed Gull is a "four-year gull," meaning that it goes through various plumage stages until its fourth winter, when it develops its refined adult plumage. Most immature gulls have dark streaking, spotting or mottling, which helps them to avoid detection by predators.

nonbreeding

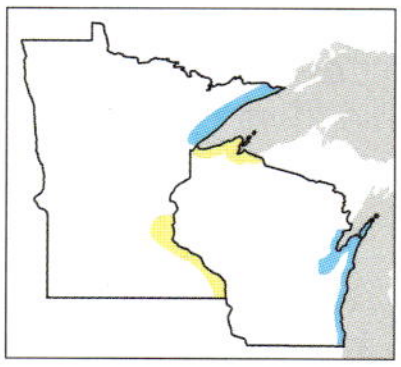

ID: very large gull. *Breeding:* all white except for gray underwings and black mantle; pale pinkish legs; pale eyes; large, yellow bill has red spot on lower mandible. *Nonbreeding:* may have faintly streaked nape. *Immature:* variable plumage; mottled gray brown, white and black; black bill or pale, black-tipped bill.

Size: *L* 30 in; *W* $5\frac{1}{2}$ ft.

Status: ***MN:*** rare visitor in November and December and in March primarily along the North Shore of L. Superior; also found in the Twin Cities area and the lower Mississippi R. valley; accidental elsewhere in the state. ***WI:*** uncommmon migrant and winter visitor from late August to late April; rare summer resident; casual breeder.

Habitat: landfills and open water on large lakes and rivers.

Nesting: usually colonial, but also breeds in isolated pairs; on an island, cliff top or beach; pair builds a mound of vegetation and debris on the ground, often near rocks; pair incubates 2–3 brown-blotched, olive to buff eggs for 27–28 days.

Feeding: opportunistic feeder; finds food by flying, swimming or walking; eats fish, eggs, birds, small mammals, berries, carrion, mollusks, crustaceans, insects and other invertebrates, as well as human food waste; scavenges at landfills.

Voice: a harsh *kyow*.

Similar Species: *Glaucous Gull* (p. 168): paler plumage. *All other gulls:* smaller; most lack black mantle.

Best Sites: ***MN:*** L. Superior. ***WI:*** L. Michigan harbors, especially Kewaunee, Two Rivers, Manitowoc, Sheboygan and Milwaukee.

CASPIAN TERN

Sterna caspia

In size and habits, the mighty Caspian Tern bridges the gulf between the smaller terns and the larger gulls. It is the largest tern in North America, and its wingbeats are slower and more gull-like than those of most other terns. Because of this gull-like flight, many birders confuse the Caspian Tern with a gull until its raucous call gives it away. This tern's distinctive, heavy, red orange bill and forked tail also help to reveal its true identity. • Caspian Terns are often seen together with gulls on shoreline sandbars and mudflats in migration or during the breeding season, when they nest in colonies on exposed islands and protected beaches. • This species was first collected from the Caspian Sea, hence its name. Caspian Terns are found nesting the world over, in Eurasia, Africa and even Australia.

breeding

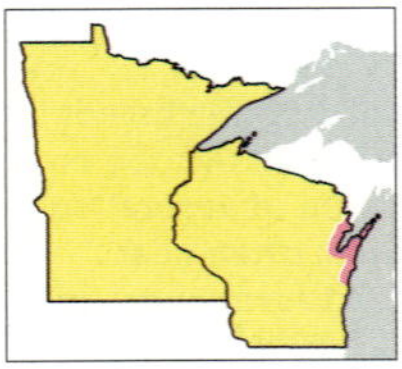

ID: *Breeding:* black "cap"; heavy, red orange bill has faint black tip; light gray mantle; black legs; shallowly forked tail; white underparts; long, frosty, pointed wings; dark gray on underside of outer primaries. *Nonbreeding:* black "cap" is streaked with white.

Size: *L* 19–23 in; *W* 4–4½ ft.

Status: ***MN:*** uncommon migrant from late April to mid-June and from mid-July to mid-October; best represented in eastern and central regions; 1 nesting record (1969). ***WI:*** endangered; common migrant from mid-April to early June and from mid-July to mid-October; uncommon breeder.

Habitat: *Breeding:* usually on islands in lakes and rivers. *In migration:* wetlands and shorelines of large lakes and rivers.

Nesting: in a shallow scrape on bare sand, lightly vegetated soil or gravel; nest is sparsely lined with vegetation, rocks or twigs; pair incubates 1–3 pale buff eggs, spotted with brown or black, for 20–22 days.

Feeding: hovers over water and plunges headfirst after small fish, tadpoles and aquatic invertebrates; also feeds by swimming and gleaning at the water's surface.

Voice: low, harsh *ca-arr;* loud *kraa-uh;* juveniles answer with a high-pitched whistle.

Similar Species: *Common* (p. 171), *Arctic* (p. 359) and *Forster's* (p. 172) *terns:* much smaller; daintier bills; lack dark primary underwing patch.

Best Sites: ***MN:*** L. Superior; Leech L.; Mille Lacs L. ***WI:*** Door Co.; Kewaunee; Manitowoc; Sheboygan; Milwaukee; Racine; Green Bay; Marinette; Superior; Ashland.

COMMON TERN

Sterna hirundo

Common Terns patrol the shorelines of Lakes Michigan and Superior in spring and fall, with a few nesting in small colonies. Both males and females perform aerial courtship dances, and for most pairs the nesting season commences when the female accepts her suitor's gracious fish offerings. • Tern colonies are noisy and chaotic, and are often associated with even noisier gull colonies. Should an intruder approach a tern nest, the parent will dive repeatedly, often defecating on the offender. • In the late 19th century, the Common Tern and other seabirds were slaughtered for the purpose of adorning ladies hats, and this species was extirpated in much of its North American range. With the passage of bird protection legislation, populations quickly recovered and by the 1930s the Common Tern had made a comeback, almost to its original numbers.

breeding

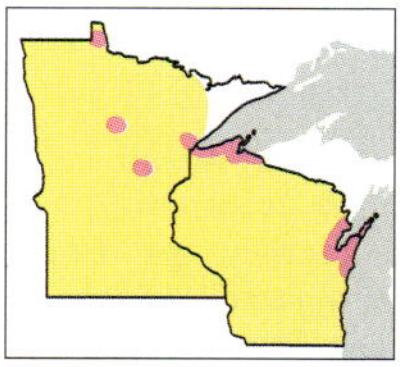

ID: *Breeding:* black "cap"; thin, red, black-tipped bill; red legs; white rump; white tail with gray outer edges; white underparts. *Nonbreeding:* black nape; lacks black "cap." *In flight:* shallowly forked tail; long, pointed wings; dark gray wedge near lighter gray upperwing tips.

Size: *L* 13–16 in; *W* 30 in.

Status: ***MN:*** threatened; uncommon migrant from mid-April to early June and from early August to early October, mainly in eastern and some parts of the central regions; rare migrant in the west; common breeder on a few of the larger lakes and in the Duluth harbor; declining as a nesting species. ***WI:*** endangered; common migrant in mid-April to mid-June and from early August to mid-October; uncommon breeder.

Habitat: *Breeding:* natural and human-made islands, breakwaters and beaches. *In migration:* large lakes.

Nesting: primarily colonial; usually on an island with nonvegetated, open areas; in a small scrape lined sparsely with pebbles, vegetation or shells; pair incubates 1–3 variably marked eggs for up to 27 days.

Feeding: hovers over the water and plunges headfirst after small fish and aquatic invertebrates.

Voice: high-pitched, drawn-out *keee-are* is most commonly heard at colonies but also in foraging flights.

Similar Species: *Forster's Tern* (p. 172): gray tail with white outer edges; upper primaries have silvery look; broad, black eye band in nonbreeding plumage. *Arctic Tern* (p. 359): all-red bill; deeply forked tail; upper primaries lack dark gray wedge; grayer underparts; rare in migration. *Caspian Tern* (p. 170): much larger overall; much heavier, red orange bill; very dark primary underwing patch.

Best Sites: ***MN:*** Duluth; Mille Lacs L.; Leech L.; Lake of the Woods. ***WI:*** *In migration:* L. Michigan harbors (Manitowoc, Sheboygan, Milwaukee, Racine); L. Superior harbors (Ashland, Superior).

FORSTER'S TERN

Sterna forsteri

The Forster's Tern so closely resembles the Common Tern that the two often seem indistinguishable to the eyes of many observers. It is usually not until these terns acquire their distinct fall plumages that birders begin to note the Forster's presence. • Most terns are known for their extraordinary ability to catch fish in dramatic headfirst dives, but the Forster's Tern excels at gracefully snatching flying insects in midair. • The Forster's Tern has an exclusively North American breeding distribution, but it bears the name of a man who never visited this continent: German naturalist Johann Reinhold Forster. Forster examined tern specimens sent from Hudson Bay, Canada, and was the first to recognize this bird as a distinct species. Taxonomist Thomas Nuttall agreed, and in 1832 he named the species "Forster's Tern" in his *Manual of Ornithology*.

breeding

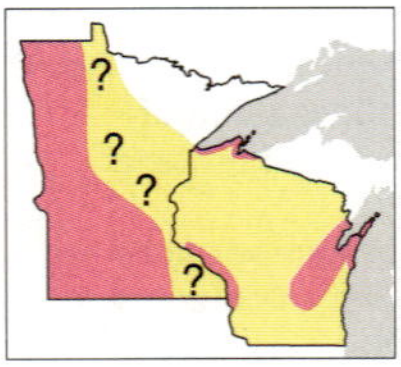

ID: *Breeding:* black cap and nape; thin, orange, black-tipped bill; orange legs; light gray mantle; pure white underparts; white rump; gray tail with white outer edges. *Nonbreeding:* lacks black "cap"; black band through eyes. *In flight:* forked, gray tail; long, pointed wings.

Size: *L* 14–16 in; *W* 31 in.

Status: ***MN:*** special concern; common migrant from early April to mid-May and from August to early October; rare to absent in northeastern and north-central regions; uncommon breeder. ***WI:*** endangered; common migrant from early April to mid-May and from August to mid-October; fairly common breeder.

Habitat: *Breeding:* cattail marshes. *In migration:* lakes and marshes.

Nesting: colonial; in a cattail marsh, atop floating vegetation; occasionally on a muskrat lodge or in an old grebe nest; pair incubates 3 brown-marked, buff to olive eggs for 23–25 days.

Feeding: hovers above the water and plunges headfirst after small fish and aquatic invertebrates; catches flying insects and snatches prey from the water's surface.

Voice: flight call is a nasal, short *keer keer;* also a grating *tzaap*.

Similar Species: *Common Tern* (p. 171): darker red bill and legs; mostly white tail; gray wash on underparts; dark wedge near tip of primaries. *Caspian Tern* (p. 170): much larger overall; much heavier, red orange bill. *Arctic Tern* (p. 359): lacks black-tipped bill; short, red legs; gray underparts; white tail with gray outer edges.

Best Sites: ***MN:*** L. Osaskis; Swan L. (Nicollet Co.); Heron L. (Jackson Co.); Agassiz NWR. ***WI:*** Horicon Marsh; Rush L.; Mississippi R.; Crex Meadows WA; L. Michigan and L. Superior harbors.

BLACK TERN

Chlidonias niger

Wheeling about in foraging flights, Black Terns pick small minnows from the water's surface or catch flying insects in midair. Even in stiff winds, these acrobats slice through the sky with grace. Black Terns may appear frail, but they have dominion over the winds. When they leave our region in August and September, they head for the warmer foreign waters of Central and South America. • Black Terns are finicky nesters, refusing to return to nesting areas that show even slight changes in water level or in the density of emergent vegetation. This selectiveness has contributed to a significant decline in populations of this bird over recent decades. Commitment to restoring and protecting valuable wetland habitats will eventually help the Black Tern to reclaim its once prominent place in our region.

breeding

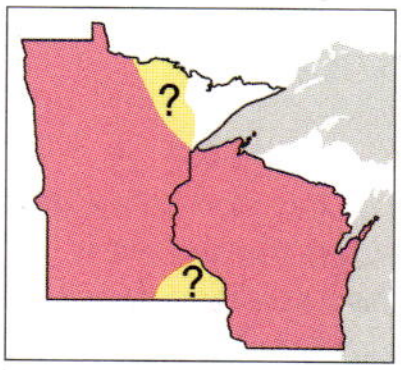

ID: *Breeding:* black head and underparts; gray back, tail and wings; white undertail coverts; black bill; reddish black legs. *Nonbreeding:* white underparts and forehead; molting fall birds may be mottled with brown. *In flight:* long, pointed wings; shallowly forked tail.

Size: *L* 9–10 in; *W* 24 in.

Status: ***MN:*** common migrant and breeder from late April to early October; rare to absent in the northeast; best represented in the west; declining. ***WI:*** common migrant and breeder from late April to late September.

Habitat: shallow cattail marshes, wetlands, lake edges and sewage ponds with emergent vegetation.

Nesting: loosely colonial; flimsy nest of dead plant material is built on floating vegetation, a muddy mound or a muskrat house; pair incubates 3 darkly blotched, olive to pale buff eggs for 21–22 days.

Feeding: snatches insects from the air, tall grass and the water's surface; also eats small fish.

Voice: greeting call is a shrill, metallic *kik-kik-kik-kik-kik;* typical alarm call is *kreea.*

Similar Species: *Other terns* (pp. 170–72): all are light in color, not dark.

Best Sites: ***MN:*** Agassiz NWR; Tamarac NWR; larger marshes in western and central regions. ***WI:*** Horicon Marsh; Rush L.; Mead WA; Crex Meadows WA; Trempealeau NWR; Vernon Marsh; Grassy L.; Powell Marsh; Fish Lake WA.

ROCK DOVE

Columba livia

Brought to North America from Europe by early settlers in the 17th century, Rock Doves have settled wherever there are cities, towns and farms. These birds are commonly referred to as "pigeons," and indeed there is no technical difference between doves and pigeons. • Rock Doves are believed to have been domesticated from Eurasian birds in about 4500 BC as a source of meat. Since their domestication, Rock Doves have been used as message couriers (both Caesar and Napoleon used them), as scientific subjects and even as pets. One of the most intensively studied birds, much of our understanding of bird migration, avian flight mechanics, endocrinology, orientation, navigation and sensory perception derives from experiments involving Rock Doves. • All members of the pigeon family, including doves, feed "milk" to their young. Because birds lack mammary glands, it is not true milk, but a nutritious liquid produced by glands in the bird's crop. The chicks insert their bills down the adult's throat to eat the thick, protein-rich fluid.

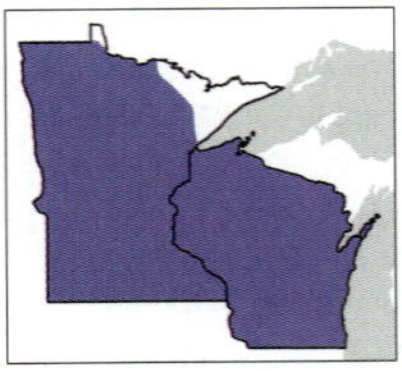

ID: color is highly variable (iridescent blue gray, red, white or tan); usually has white rump and orange feet; dark-tipped tail. *In flight:* holds its wings in a deep "V" while gliding.

Size: *L* 12–13 in; *W* 28 in.

Status: ***MN:*** common to abundant year-round resident; absent in heavily forested areas of the north. ***WI:*** abundant year-round resident.

Habitat: urban areas, railroad yards and agricultural areas; high cliffs provide a more natural habitat for some.

Nesting: on a ledge in a barn or on a cliff, bridge, building or tower; flimsy nest is made of sticks, grass and assorted vegetation; pair incubates 2 white eggs for 16–19 days; pair feeds the young "pigeon milk"; may raise broods year-round.

Feeding: gleans the ground for waste grain, seeds and fruits; occasionally eats insects.

Voice: soft, cooing *coorrr-coorrr-coorrr.*

Similar Species: *Mourning Dove* (p. 175): smaller; slimmer; pale brown plumage; long tail and wings. *Merlin* (p. 103): not as heavy bodied; longer tail; does not hold its wings in a "V"; wings do not clap on takeoff.

Best Sites: near farm buildings and in larger towns and cities.

MOURNING DOVE

Zenaida macroura

The soft cooing of the Mourning Dove that filters through broken woodlands, farmlands and suburban parks and gardens is often confused with the sounds of a hooting owl. Tracking down the source of the calls, however, usually reveals one or two Mourning Doves perched upon a fence, tree branch or utility wire. • The Mourning Dove is one of the most abundant and widespread native birds in North America and one of the most popular game birds. This species has benefited from human-induced changes to the landscape and its numbers and distribution have increased since the continent was settled. It is encountered in both rural and urban habitats, but avoids heavily forested areas. • Despite its fragile look, the Mourning Dove is a swift, direct flier whose wings often whistle as it cuts through the air at high speed. When this bird bursts into flight, its wings clap above and below its body.

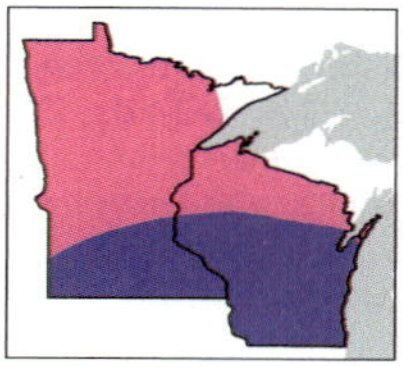

ID: buffy, gray brown plumage; small head; long, white-trimmed, tapering tail; sleek body; dark, shiny patch below ear; dull red legs; dark bill; pale rosy underparts; black spots on upperwing.
Size: *L* 11–13 in; *W* 18 in.
Status: ***MN:*** abundant migrant and breeder from early March to late November; uncommon in northeastern and most of the north-central regions; occasional to regular in winter, especially in the south. ***WI:*** common year-round resident.
Habitat: open or riparian woodlands, woodlots, forest edges, agricultural and suburban areas and open parks; has benefited from human-induced habitat change.
Nesting: occasionally on the ground or in the fork of a shrub or tree; female builds a fragile, shallow platform nest from twigs supplied by the male; pair incubates 2 white eggs for 14 days; young are fed "pigeon milk."
Feeding: gleans the ground and vegetation for seeds; visits feeders.
Voice: mournful, soft, slow *oh-woe-woe-woe.*
Similar Species: *Rock Dove* (p. 174): stockier; white rump; shorter tail; iridescent neck. *Yellow-billed Cuckoo* (p. 177) and *Black-billed Cuckoo* (p. 176): curved bills; long tails with broad, rounded tips; brown upperparts; white underparts.
Best Sites: common in both urban and rural areas.

BLACK-BILLED CUCKOO

Coccyzus erythropthalmus

Shrubby field edges, hedgerows, tangled riparian thickets and abandoned, overgrown fields provide the elusive Black-billed Cuckoo with its preferred nesting haunts. Although this bird can be fairly common in our region, it remains an enigma to many would-be observers. Arriving in late May, this cuckoo quietly hops, flits and skulks through low, dense deciduous vegetation in its ultra-secretive search for sustenance. Only when vegetation is in full bloom will males issue their loud, long, irregular calls, advertising to females that it is time to nest. After a brief courtship, newly joined Black-billed Cuckoo pairs construct a makeshift nest, incubate the eggs and raise their young, after which they promptly return to their covert lives. • The Black-billed Cuckoo is one of the few birds that thrives on hairy caterpillars, particularly tent caterpillars. There is even evidence to suggest that Black-billed Cuckoo populations increase when a caterpillar infestation occurs.

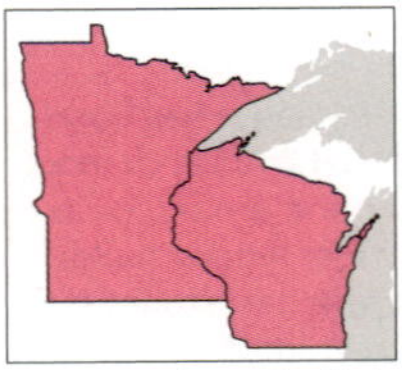

ID: brown upperparts; white underparts; long, white-spotted undertail; downcurved, dark bill; reddish eye ring. *Immature:* buff eye ring; may have buff tinge on throat and undertail coverts.

Size: *L* 11–13 in; *W* 17½ in.

Status: ***MN:*** uncommon migrant and breeder from early May to early October; numbers vary and may be declining. ***WI:*** fairly common migrant and breeder from early May to late September.

Habitat: dense second-growth woodlands, shrubby areas and thickets; often in tangled riparian areas and abandoned farmlands with low deciduous vegetation and adjacent open areas.

Nesting: in a shrub or small deciduous tree; flimsy nest of twigs is lined with grass and other vegetation; may lay eggs in other birds' nests; pair incubates 2–5 blue green, occasionally mottled eggs for 10–14 days.

Feeding: gleans hairy caterpillars from leaves, branches and trunks; also eats other insects and berries.

Voice: fast, repeated *cu-cu-cu* or *cu-cu-cu-cu-cu;* also a series of *ca, cow* and *coo* notes.

Similar Species: *Yellow-billed Cuckoo* (p. 177): yellow bill; rufous tinge to primaries; larger, more prominent, white undertail spots; lacks red eye ring. *Mourning Dove* (p. 175): short, straight bill; pointed, triangular tail; buffy, gray brown plumage; black spots on upperwing.

Best Sites: ***MN:*** widespread but not numerous in wooded edges, groves and thickets. ***WI:*** deciduous forests, especially in northern tracts.

YELLOW-BILLED CUCKOO

Coccyzus americanus

Most of the time, the Yellow-billed Cuckoo skillfully negotiates its tangled home within impenetrable deciduous undergrowth in silence, relying on obscurity for survival. For a short period during nesting, however, the male cuckoo tempts fate, issuing a barrage of loud, rhythmic courtship calls. Because the cuckoo has a propensity for calling on dark, cloudy days in late spring and early summer, it is called "Rain Crow" in some parts of its North American range. • The Yellow-billed Cuckoo's diet is varied. In addition to consuming large quantities of hairy caterpillars, these birds feast on wild berries, young frogs and newts, small bird eggs and insects, including beetles, grasshoppers and cicadas. • Unlike distantly related Eurasian cuckoos, which lay their eggs only in other birds' nests, neither of the North American cuckoos is considered to be a "brood parasite."

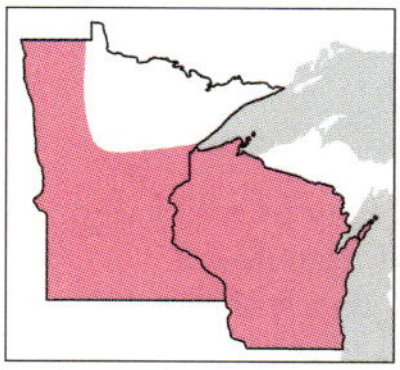

ID: olive brown upperparts; white underparts; downcurved bill with black upper mandible and yellow lower mandible; yellow eye ring; long tail with large white spots on underside; rufous tinge on primaries.
Size: *L* 11–13 in; *W* 18 in.
Status: ***MN:*** uncommon migrant and breeder from early May to early October, mainly in southern and western regions; rare to absent in north-central and northeastern regions. ***WI:*** fairly common migrant and breeder from early May to late September, especially in the south.
Habitat: semi-open deciduous habitats; dense tangles and thickets at the edges of orchards, urban parks, agricultural fields and roadways; sometimes woodlots.
Nesting: on a horizontal branch in a deciduous shrub or small tree, within 7 ft of the ground; builds a flimsy platform of twigs lined with roots and grass; mostly the female incubates 3–4 pale bluish green eggs for 9–11 days.
Feeding: gleans insect larvae, especially hairy caterpillars, from deciduous vegetation; also eats berries, small fruits, small amphibians and occasionally the eggs of small birds.
Voice: long series of deep, hollow *kuks,* slowing near the end: *kuk-kuk-kuk-kuk kuk kop kow kowlp kowlp.*
Similar Species: *Black-billed Cuckoo* (p. 176): all-black bill; lacks rufous tinge on primaries; less prominent, white undertail spots; red eye ring; immature has buff eye ring and may have buff wash on throat and undertail coverts. *Mourning Dove* (p. 175): short, straight bill; pointed, triangular tail; buffy gray brown plumage; black spots on upperwing.
Best Sites: ***MN:*** woodlands, thickets, orchards and streamside groves, mainly in southern regions. ***WI:*** wooded bottom lands, especially in southern and western regions.

EASTERN SCREECH-OWL

Otus asio

The diminutive Eastern Screech-Owl is a year-round resident of deciduous woodlands, but its presence is rarely detected. Most screech-owls sleep away the daylight hours snuggled safely inside a tree cavity or an artificial nest box. An encounter with an Eastern Screech-Owl is usually the result of a sound cue—the noise of mobbing hordes of chickadees or squawking gangs of Blue Jays will occasionally alert you to an owl's presence during daylight hours. The smaller birds that mob screech-owls during the day often do so after losing a family member during the night. More commonly, you will find this owl by listening for the male's eerie, "horse-whinny" courtship calls and loud, spooky trills at night. • Unique among the owls found in our region, Eastern Screech-Owls are polychromatic: they show red or gray color morphs. The red birds are not as common because they are less able to withstand cold winters. Mixed-colored pairs may produce buffy brown, intermediate-colored young.

gray morph

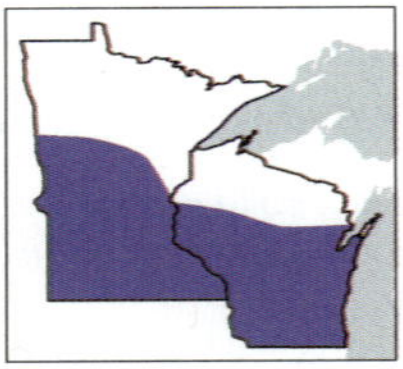

ID: conspicuous "ear" tufts; reddish or grayish overall; dark breast streaking; yellow eyes; yellowish to grayish bill; large feet; feathered toes.

Size: *L* 8–9 in; *W* 20–22 in.

Status: ***MN:*** uncommon year-round resident in the southern one-third of the state; there are records as far north as Duluth, Otter Tail Co. and Marshall Co.; appears to be declining. ***WI:*** common year-round resident in southern and central regions; rare in the north.

Habitat: mature deciduous forests, open deciduous woodlands, riparian woodlands, orchards and shade trees with natural cavities.

Nesting: in a natural cavity or artificial nest box; no lining is added; female incubates 4–5 white eggs for about 26 days; male brings food to the female during incubation.

Feeding: small mammals, earthworms, fish, birds and insects, including moths in flight; feeds at dusk and at night.

Voice: horselike "whinny" that rises and falls.

Similar Species: *Northern Saw-whet Owl* (p. 187): lacks "ear" tufts; long, reddish streaks on white underparts. *Long-eared Owl* (p. 184): much longer, slimmer body; longer, closer-set "ear" tufts; rusty facial disc; grayish, brown white body. *Great Horned Owl* (p. 179): much larger; lacks vertical breast streaks.

Best Sites: ***MN:*** wooded stream valleys in the south; Twin Cities area. ***WI:*** wooded areas in southern and central regions.

GREAT HORNED OWL

Bubo virginianus

This formidable, primarily nocturnal hunter uses its acute hearing and powerful vision to hunt a wide variety of prey. Almost any small creature that moves is fair game for the Great Horned Owl. However, it has a poorly developed sense of smell, which might explain why it is the only consistent predator of skunks. • Great Horned Owls often begin their courtship as early as January, at which time their hooting calls make them quite conspicuous. By February and March, females are already incubating their eggs. The pair continues to feed the young, both in and out of the nest, well into autumn. • The large eyes of an owl are fixed in place, so to look up, down or to the side, the bird must move its entire head—an owl can swivel its neck 180 degrees to either side and 90 degrees up and down!

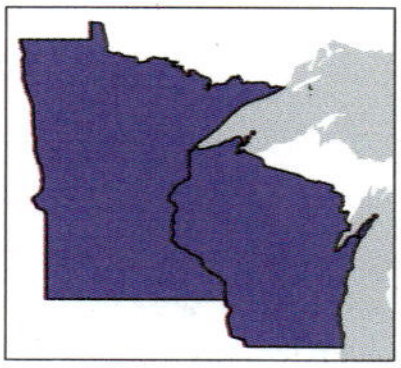

ID: yellow eyes; tall "ear" tufts set wide apart on head; fine, horizontal barring on breast; facial disc is outlined in black and is often rusty orange in color; white "chin"; heavily mottled gray, brown and black upperparts; overall plumage varies from light gray to dark brown.

Size: *L* 18–25 in; *W* 3–5 ft.

Status: ***MN:*** common year-round resident; uncommon in the north-central region and heavily forested portions of the northeast. ***WI:*** common year-round resident.

Habitat: fragmented forests, agricultural areas, woodlots, meadows, riparian woodlands, wooded suburban parks and the wooded edges of landfills and town dumps.

Nesting: in the abandoned stick nest of another bird; may also nest on a cliff; adds little or no material to the nest; mostly the female incubates 2–3 dull whitish eggs for 28–35 days.

Feeding: mostly nocturnal, but also hunts at dusk or by day in winter; usually swoops from a perch; eats small mammals, birds, snakes, amphibians and even fish.

Voice: call during the breeding season is 4–6 deep hoots: *hoo-hoo-hoooo hoo-hoo* or *eat-my-food, I'll-eat you;* male also gives higher-pitched hoots.

Similar Species: *Long-eared Owl* (p. 184): smaller; thinner; vertical breast streaks; "ear" tufts are close together. *Eastern Screech-Owl* (p. 178): much smaller; vertical breast streaks. *Great Gray* (p. 183), *Short-eared* (p. 185) and *Barred* (p. 182) *owls:* no "ear" tufts.

Best Sites: ***MN:*** widespread; mainly in small woodlots in the south and west. ***WI:*** woods, swamps and urban areas; Wyalusing SP; White River WA; Crex Meadows WA; Horicon Marsh; Nicolet NF; Governor Dodge SP.

SNOWY OWL

Nyctea scandiaca

When the mercury drops and the landscape hardens in winter's icy grip, ghostly white Snowy Owls appear on fence posts, utility poles, fields and lakeshores throughout the region. These birds blend in perfectly against almost any flat, open, snow-covered landscape. Snow cover is not a prerequisite for a Snowy Owl visit—many of these birds perch conspicuously on earth-tone fields in snowless portions of our region each winter. • Feathered to the toes, a Snowy Owl can remain active at cold temperatures that often send other owls to the woods for shelter. As Snowy Owls age, their plumage becomes lighter in color—older males are often pure white. • Snowy Owls are annual visitors to our region, but their numbers can fluctuate quite dramatically. When lemming and vole populations in the Arctic crash, large numbers of Snowy Owls often venture south in search of food.

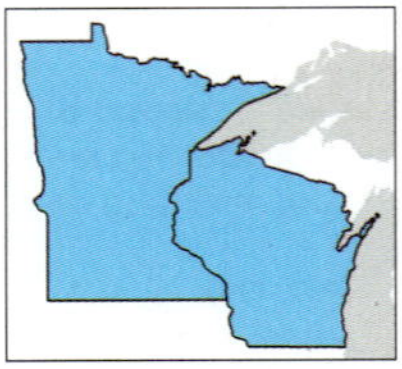

ID: predominantly white; yellow eyes; black bill and talons; no "ear" tufts. *Male:* almost entirely white with very little dark flecking. *Female:* prominent dark barring or flecking on breast and upperparts. *Immature:* heavier barring than adult female.

Size: *L* 20–27 in; *W* $4\frac{1}{2}$–6 ft. (female is noticeably larger).

Status: ***MN:*** generally a rare and local migrant and winter visitor from early October to mid-April in the north; occasionally irruptive, with numbers of birds reaching the southern part of the state in winter; a few may linger until late May or early June. ***WI:*** common migrant and winter visitor from late October to late April.

Habitat: open country, including croplands, meadows, airports and lakeshores; often perches on fence posts, buildings and utility poles.

Nesting: does not nest in our region.

Feeding: swoops from a perch, often punching through the snow to take mice, voles, grouse, hares, weasels and rarely songbirds and waterbirds.

Voice: quiet in winter.

Similar Species: no other owl in the region is largely white and lacks "ear" tufts.

Best Sites: ***MN:*** Duluth; Wilkin, Clay and Norman Counties in early March. ***WI:*** Superior; Green Bay; Freedom; Milwaukee; Manitowoc; Spencer; Kewaunee; Arlington.

NORTHERN HAWK OWL

Surnia ulula

The Northern Hawk Owl has a bold nature and seems unafraid of humans, making its year-round home in the remote boreal forests of northern Canada. Like the Snowy Owl, the Northern Hawk Owl is an "irruptive" winter visitor to our region, meaning that it may be more abundant in some winters than most others. When a "Hawk Owl" year comes around, be sure to make the most of the event—there may not be a repeat performance for many years. • Northern Hawk Owls summer where the days are long, so they are comfortable hunting in daylight. They are by no means the only owls that hunt during the day, but they are the ones most likely to rest on exposed perches, often at the top of a pole or coniferous tree. • With its long, slender, hawklike features and direct flight pattern, it is easy to understand how this bird got its name. Yet no matter how much it behaves like a hawk, this bird is definitely an owl. Its facial disc is a distinctive feature of the owl family that allows these birds to use sound to locate their prey.

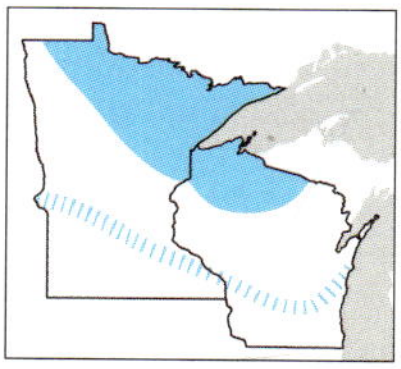

ID: long tail; no "ear" tufts; fine horizontal barring on underparts; white facial disc is bordered with black; yellowish bill; yellow eyes; white-spotted forehead.

Size: *L* 15–17 in; *W* 31–35 in.

Status: ***MN:*** irruptive; rare and local migrant and winter visitor from mid-October to early April, primarily in the far north; a few remain to nest in the remote bogs of northeastern and north-central regions. ***WI:*** irruptive; rare migrant and winter visitor from late October to early April; accidental breeder.

Habitat: black spruce bogs, old burns and tree-bordered clearings.

Nesting: in an abandoned woodpecker cavity or abandoned nest; adds no lining to the nest; female incubates 5–7 whitish eggs for 25–30 days.

Feeding: swoops from a perch; eats mostly voles, mice and birds; also eats some large insects in summer.

Voice: usually quiet; whistled, purring breeding trill; call is an accipiter-like *kee-kee-kee.*

Similar Species: *Boreal* (p. 186), *Northern Saw-whet* (p. 187) and *Short-eared* (p. 185) *owls:* much shorter tails; vertical breast streaks.

Best Sites: ***MN:*** North Shore of L. Superior; Sax-Zim Bog; northern Aitkin Co. ***WI:*** no consistent sites.

BARRED OWL

Strix varia

Each spring, the memorable sound of courting Barred Owls echoes through our forests: *Who cooks for you? Who cooks for you all?* The escalating laughs, hoots and gargling howls reinforce the bond between pairs. • Barred Owls tend to be more vocal during early evening or early morning when the moon is full and the air is calm. At the height of courtship and when raising young, a pair of Barred Owls may continue their calls well into daylight hours. They are usually most active between midnight and 4:00 AM, when the forest floor rustles with the movements of mice, voles and shrews. • These birds' eyesight in darkness is 100 times keener than that of humans, and they are able to locate prey using sound alone. • Barred Owls have relatively weak talons, so they prey on smaller animals, such as voles. They may also take small birds and even smaller owls.

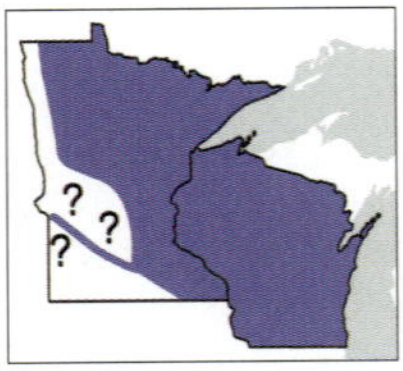

ID: round head; no "ear" tufts; dark eyes; horizontal barring around neck and upper breast; vertical streaking on belly; light-colored bill; mottled, dark gray brown plumage.

Size: *L* 17–24 in; *W* 3½–4 ft.

Status: ***MN:*** uncommon year-round resident throughout the more heavily wooded areas of the state; rare or absent over large areas of south-central and western regions. ***WI:*** fairly common year-round resident.

Habitat: mature deciduous and mixedwood forests, especially in dense stands near swamps, streams and lakes.

Nesting: in a natural tree cavity, broken treetop or abandoned stick nest; adds very little material to the nest; female incubates 2–3 white eggs for 28–33 days; male feeds the female during incubation.

Feeding: nocturnal; swoops down on prey from a perch; eats mostly mice, voles and squirrels; also eats amphibians and smaller birds.

Voice: most characteristic of all the owls; loud, hooting, rhythmic, laughing call is heard mostly in spring but also throughout the year: *Who cooks for you? Who cooks for you all?*

Similar Species: *Great Gray Owl* (p. 183): larger; yellow eyes; well-defined, ringed facial disc; black "chin" patch; lacks horizontal barring on upper breast. *Northern Hawk Owl* (p. 181): yellow eyes; finely barred underparts. *Great Horned Owl* (p. 179): "ear" tufts; light-colored eyes. *Short-eared Owl* (p. 185): yellow eyes; lacks horizontal barring on upper breast.

Best Sites: ***MN:*** wooded river valleys; larger woodland tracts in southern and central regions. ***WI:*** deciduous forests and near wooded river bottoms; White River WA; Wyalusing SP; Crex Meadows WA; Horicon Marsh; Sugar River WA.

GREAT GRAY OWL

Strix nebulosa

With a face like a satellite dish, the Great Gray Owl is able to detect and locate the quietest scurry on the forest floor. It can hear even the faint sounds of a tiny rodent moving around under 20 inches of snow. The Great Gray's facial disc funnels sound into its asymmetrically placed ears, enabling it, through triangulation, to pinpoint the precise location of its prey. • This regal owl is highly sought after by birders in our region, but its rare status and secretive lifestyle keep it well hidden. Great Grays occasionally appear in good numbers in the northern parts of our region, usually in years when small mammal populations farther north have crashed. • Even though the Great Gray Owl is the largest North American owl, it is mostly "fluff." Because much of its bulk is made up of insulating plumage, the Great Gray Owl is able to withstand extremely cold winter temperatures.

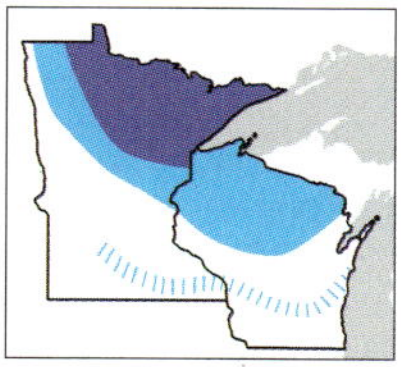

ID: gray brown overall; large, rounded head; no "ear" tufts; long tail; yellow eyes and bill; well-defined, ringed facial disc; black "chin" bordered by white.
Size: *L* 24–33 in; *W* 4½–5 ft.
Status: ***MN:*** rare and local year-round resident in northern regions; accidental elsewhere; occasionally irruptive with hundreds of birds present in the north and a few found into southern regions. ***WI:*** irruptive; rare migrant and winter visitor from late September to early May; very casual breeder.
Habitat: forest clearings, open meadows, spruce or poplar stands adjacent to open fens, bogs or meadows.
Nesting: usually near a spruce bog; in an abandoned hawk, raven or eagle nest; occasionally atop a tall, broken stump; adds little nest material; female incubates 2–4 white eggs for 28–36 days; male feeds the female on the nest.
Feeding: listens and watches from a perch; swoops down to catch voles, mice, shrews, squirrels and hares.
Voice: slow, deep, almost inaudible, resonating series of hoots; also a series of widely spaced, low, rising *wooo* notes.
Similar Species: *Barred Owl* (p. 182): dark eyes; horizontal barring on upper breast. *Great Horned Owl* (p. 179): large "ear" tufts; dark bill. *Snowy Owl* (p. 180): mostly white. *Short-eared Owl* (p. 185): much smaller; black eye sockets; dark bill; black "wrist" crescents.
Best Sites: ***MN:*** Sax-Zim Bog; northern Aitkin Co.; North Shore of L. Superior; Beltrami Island State Forest. ***WI:*** no consistent sites.

LONG-EARED OWL

Asio otus

Long-eared Owls are widespread throughout much of the region, but people often overlook these birds because of their cryptic plumage and reclusive habits. Only at dusk do these owls emerge from their secret hideouts to prey upon the small creatures of the night. Long-eared Owls are most noticeable during the winter months, when they roost in woodlots, hedgerows or isolated tree groves. Concentrations of 10 to 20 birds can occur, and these birds sometimes roost together with Short-eared Owls. • To scare off an intruder, the Long-eared Owl expands its air sacs, puffs its feathers and spreads its wings. To hide from an intruder, it takes the opposite approach—it flattens its feathers and compresses itself into a long, thin, vertical form. • All owls, as well as many other birds, such as herons, gulls, crows and hawks, regurgitate "pellets." A pellet consists of the indigestible parts of the bird's prey compressed into an elongated ball. The feathers, fur and bones that make up the pellets are fascinating to analyze, because they reveal what the bird has eaten.

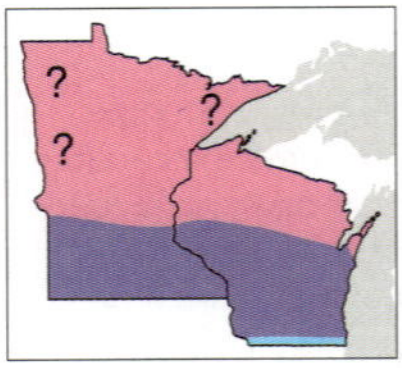

ID: long, relatively close-set "ear" tufts; slim body; vertical belly markings; rusty brown facial disc; mottled brown plumage; yellow eyes; white "eyebrow" and white patch around bill.

Size: *L* 13–16 in; *W* 3–4 ft.

Status: ***MN:*** little is known about migration patterns or breeding range; appears to migrate from early March to mid-April and from mid-September to mid-November; most breeding evidence is from northern regions; in some winters can be found roosting in evergreen groves in the south. ***WI:*** uncommon year-round resident; numbers have diminished in recent years.

Habitat: *Breeding:* dense coniferous, mixed and riparian forests and areas with tall shrubs. *Winter:* woodlots, dense riparian woodlands and hedgerows; isolated tree groves in meadows, fields, cemeteries, farmyards or parks.

Nesting: sometimes in loose colonies; often in an abandoned hawk or crow nest; female incubates 2–6 white eggs for 26–28 days; male feeds the female during incubation.

Feeding: nocturnal; flies low, pouncing on prey from the air; eats mostly voles and mice; occasionally takes shrews, moles, small rabbits, small birds and amphibians.

Voice: breeding call is a low, soft, ghostly *quoo-quoo;* alarm call is *weck-weck-weck;* also issues various shrieks, hisses, whistles, barks, hoots and dovelike coos.

Similar Species: *Great Horned Owl* (p. 179): much larger; "ear" tufts are set farther apart; stout body; rounder face. *Short-eared Owl* (p. 185): lacks long "ear" tufts; nests on the ground. *Eastern Screech-Owl* (p. 178): much shorter, stout body; shorter, wider-set "ear" tufts.

Best Sites: ***MN:*** dense coniferous groves in the south during migration and some winters. ***WI:*** winter roosts in the southern half of the state.

SHORT-EARED OWL

Asio flammeus

Like the Snowy Owl, the Short-eared Owl lacks conspicuous "ear" tufts and fills a niche that has been left unoccupied by forest-dwelling owls. This bird of open country occupies habitats such as wet meadows, marshes and fields. • In spring, pairs perform visually dramatic courtship dances. Courting pairs fly together, and the male claps his wings together on each downstroke as he periodically performs short dives. • Short-eared Owl populations grow and decline in response to dramatic fluctuations in prey availability. Cold weather and decreases in small mammal populations occasionally force large numbers of these owls to become temporary nomads, often sending them to areas well outside their usual breeding range.

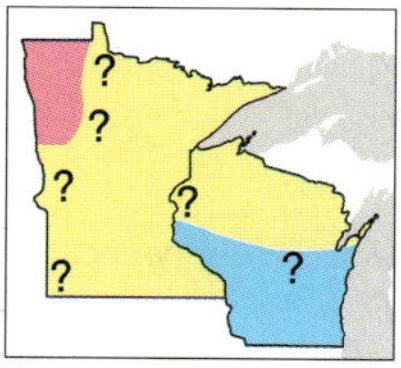

ID: yellow eyes set in black sockets; heavy, vertical streaking on buff belly; straw-colored upperparts; short, inconspicuous "ear" tufts. *In flight:* dark "wrist" crescents; deep wingbeats; long wings.

Size: *L* 13–17 in; *W* 3–4 ft.

Status: ***MN:*** special concern; uncommon to rare migrant from early March to late April and from late September to early December in the west; rare migrant in central and eastern regions; nests irregularly in western regions; occasional in early winter in the south. ***WI:*** special concern; uncommon migrant and winter visitor from early October to early May; rare breeder.

Habitat: open areas, including grasslands, wet meadows, marshes, bogs, fields, airports and forest clearings.

Nesting: on wet ground in an open area; a slight depression is sparsely lined with grass; female incubates 4–7 white eggs for 24–37 days; male feeds the female during incubation.

Feeding: forages while flying low over marshes, wet meadows and tall vegetation; pounces on prey from the air; eats mostly voles and other small rodents; also takes insects, small birds and amphibians.

Voice: generally quiet; produces a soft *toot-toot-toot* during the breeding season; also squeals and barks like a small dog.

Similar Species: *Long-eared Owl* (p. 184) and *Great Horned Owl* (p. 179): long "ear" tufts; rarely hunt during the day. *Barred Owl* (p. 182): dark eyes; horizontal barring on upper breast; nocturnal hunter. *Great Gray Owl* (p. 183): much larger; lacks black eye sockets and dark "wrist" crescents; yellow bill.

Best Sites: ***MN:*** Kittson Co.; Rothsay WMA; Wilkin Co.; Polk Co. ***WI:*** Richard Bong State Recreation Area; Rat River WA; Buena Vista Grasslands; Crex Meadows WA; Bird Sanctuary Park (Douglas County WA); Wood County WA; Horicon Marsh; Killsnake WA.

BOREAL OWL

Aegolius funereus

The Boreal Owl routinely ranks in the top five of the most-desired species to see according to birder surveys across North America, and it is the rarest of the three irruptive northern owl species in our region. Because of the Boreal Owl's preference for remote habitats and its nocturnal habits, ornithologists have yet to uncover many apects of its ecology and behavior. • This small owl is well adapted to snowy forest environments—it is an expert at locating and catching prey that lives beneath the snow. In winter, the Boreal Owl may depart from its secretive, nocturnal summertime activities in dense forest to visit more open woodlands and even suburban gardens. It may occasionally roost at bird feeders and in nest boxes. • This approachable owl was named "Blind One" by native peoples because it was easily captured by hand.

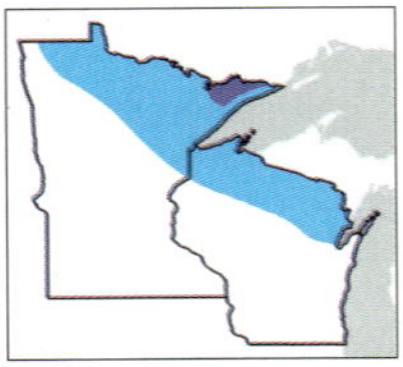

ID: small; rounded head; whitish face with dark border; white spots on black forehead; yellowish bill; vertical, rusty streaks on underparts; white-spotted, brown upperparts; black "eyebrow"; short tail.
Size: *L* 9–12 in; *W* 21½–29 in (female is noticeably larger).
Status: ***MN:*** rare and local year-round resident in the northeast; occasionally irruptive in winter; during irruptions a few individuals may reach central or southern regions. ***WI:*** irruptive; very rare migrant and winter visitor.
Habitat: mature coniferous and mixed forests.

Nesting: in an abandoned woodpecker cavity or natural hollow in a tree; lines the cavity with a few feathers; female incubates 4–6 white eggs for 26–32 days; male feeds the female during incubation.
Feeding: swoops down from a perch to take voles, mice, shrews, flying squirrels and insects; often plunges through the snow to catch prey in winter; may cache food.
Voice: rapid, accelerating, continuous whistle: *whew-whew-whew-whew-whew-whew;* easily imitated.
Similar Species: *Northern Saw-whet Owl* (p. 187): dark bill; white forehead streaking; lacks dark, vertical "eyebrow"; immature has reddish underparts. *Northern Hawk Owl* (p. 181): much longer tail; fine horizontal barring on underparts.
Best Sites: ***MN:*** Lake Co.; Cook Co.
WI: no consistent sites.

NORTHERN SAW-WHET OWL

Aegolius acadicus

The tiny Northern Saw-whet Owl is an opportunistic hunter, taking whatever it can, whenever it can. If temperatures are below freezing and prey is abundant, this small owl may catch more than it can eat in a single sitting. The extra food is stored in trees, where it quickly freezes. When hunting efforts fail, the hungry owl will return to thaw out its frozen cache by "incubating" the food as if it were a clutch of eggs! • The Northern Saw-whet Owl's call, for which it was named, can be difficult to locate because the calling bird rotates its head to mask its location. Saw-whets are usually heard more than they are seen, and from midwinter to early spring their slow, whistled notes are surprisingly common. Some people say it reminds them of the "bleeps" a large truck gives when backing up.

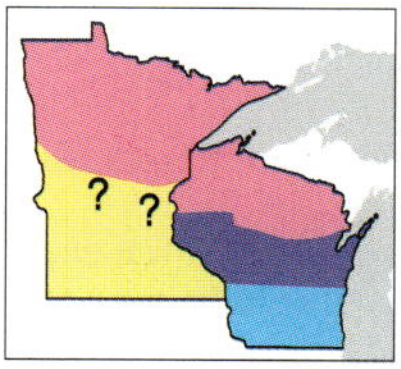

ID: small body; large, rounded head; pale facial disc; dark bill; vertical, rusty streaks on underparts; white-spotted, brown upperparts; white-streaked forehead; short tail. *Immature:* white patch between eyes; rich brown head and breast; buff brown belly.
Size: *L* 7–9 in; *W* 17–22 in.
Status: ***MN:*** little is known about migration patterns; uncommon migrant in March and April and in September; common nocturnal migrant in fall at Duluth; uncommon and local breeder in northern regions; occasionally nests into central regions (Washington Co. and Kandiyohi Co.); occasional in early winter in southern regions as far north as the Twin Cities. ***WI:*** uncommon to common migrant from early September to mid-November and especially from late February to May; uncommon breeder; rare to uncommon winter visitor.
Habitat: pure and mixed coniferous and deciduous forests.
Nesting: in an abandoned woodpecker cavity or natural hollow in a tree; female incubates 5–6 white eggs for 27–29 days; male feeds the female during incubation.
Feeding: swoops down on prey from a perch; eats mostly mice and voles; also eats larger insects, songbirds, shrews, moles and occasionally amphibians; may cache food.
Voice: whistled, evenly spaced notes, repeated about 100 times per minute: *whew-whew-whew-whew;* continuous and easily imitated.
Similar Species: *Boreal Owl* (p. 186): light-colored bill; white spotting on black forehead; dark, vertical "eyebrow"; dark border to facial disc; immature has dark chocolate brown breast. *Northern Hawk Owl* (p. 181): much longer tail; fine, horizontal barring on underparts; white spotting on black forehead.
Best Sites: ***MN:*** Duluth; Cook Co.; Lake Co. ***WI:*** coniferous and deciduous forests and swamps.

COMMON NIGHTHAWK

Chordeiles minor

Each May and June, the male Common Nighthawk flies high above forest clearings, lakeshores and often townsites, gaining elevation in preparation for the climax of his noisy aerial dance. From a great height, the male dives swiftly, then thrusts his wings forward in a final braking action as he strains to pull out of the steep dive. This quick thrust of the wings produces a deep, hollow *vroom* that attracts female nighthawks. • Like other members of the nightjar family, the Common Nighthawk is adapted for catching insects in midair: its gaping mouth is surrounded by feather shafts that funnel insects into its mouth. • Nighthawks are generally less nocturnal than other nightjars, but they still spend most of the daylight hours resting on a tree limb or on the ground. These birds have very short legs and small feet, and sit along the length of a tree branch, rather than across the branch as do most perched birds.

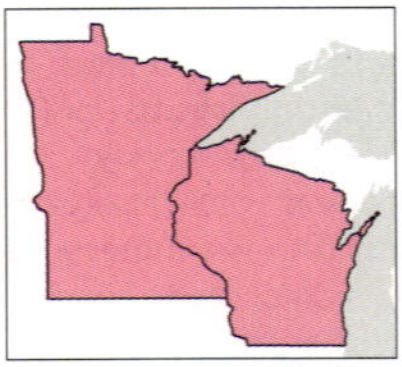

ID: cryptic, mottled plumage; barred underparts. *Male:* white throat. *Female:* buff throat. *In flight:* bold, white "wrist" patches on long, pointed wings; shallowly forked, barred tail; flight is erratic.

Size: *L* $8\frac{1}{2}$–10 in; *W* 24 in.

Status: ***MN:*** common but declining migrant and breeder from mid-April to mid-October. ***WI:*** fairly common to common migrant from early May to early June and from early August to mid-October; fairly common breeder.

Habitat: *Breeding:* in forest openings as well as burns, bogs, rocky outcroppings, gravel rooftops and sometimes fields with sparse cover or bare patches. *In migration:* anywhere large numbers of flying insects can be found; usually roosts in trees, often near water.

Nesting: on bare ground; no nest is built; female incubates 2 well-camouflaged eggs for about 19 days; both adults feed the young.

Feeding: primarily at dawn or dusk; catches insects in flight, often high in the air; may fly around street lights at night to catch prey attracted to the light; eats mosquitoes, blackflies, midges, beetles, flying ants, moths and other flying insects.

Voice: frequently repeated, nasal *peent peent;* also makes a deep, hollow *vroom* with its wings during courtship flight.

Similar Species: *Whip-poor-will* (p. 189): less common; lacks white "wrist" patches; shorter, rounder wings; rounded tail.

Best Sites: ***MN:*** larger urban areas throughout the state, especially Duluth and the Twin Cities area. ***WI:*** various communities, including LaCrosse and Prairie du Chien.

WHIP-POOR-WILL

Caprimulgus vociferus

This nocturnal hunter fills the late evening with the sound of its own name: *whip-poor-will.* Although the Whip-poor-will is heard throughout the open woodlands in our region, this cryptic bird is rarely seen. Because of its camouflaged plumage, sleepy daytime habits and secretive nesting behavior, a hopeful observer must literally stumble upon a Whip-poor-will to see it. • The Whip-poor-will is a member of the nightjar, or "goatsucker," family. During the days of Aristotle, these birds were named "Goatsuckers" because there was a widely believed superstition that they would suck milk from the udders of female goats, causing the goats to go blind! • Within days of hatching, young Whip-poor-wills scurry away from their nest in search of protective cover. For the first 20 days after hatching, until the young are able to fly, the parents feed them regurgitated insects.

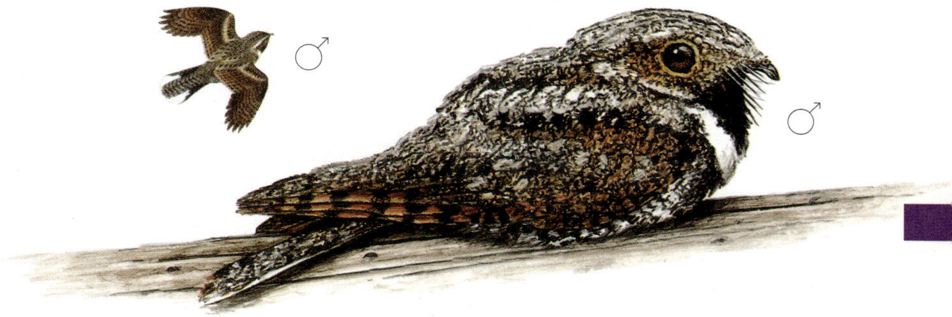

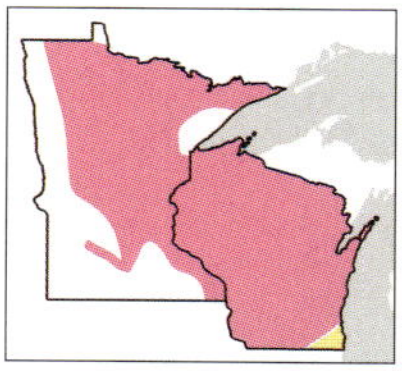

ID: mottled brown gray overall with black flecking; reddish tinge on rounded wings; black throat; long, rounded tail. *Male:* white "necklace"; white outer tail feathers. *Female:* buff "necklace."

Size: *L* 9–10 in; *W* 16–20 in.

Status: ***MN:*** seldom seen migrant from early April to mid-May and from early August to late September; very local breeder in southeastern, central and northwestern regions; casual breeder in northeastern and north-central regions. ***WI:*** fairly common migrant and breeder from mid-April to early October.

Habitat: open, deciduous and pine woodlands; often along forest edges.

Nesting: on the ground, sometimes in leaf or pine needle litter; no nest is built; mostly the female incubates 2 whitish eggs, blotched with brown and gray, for 19–21 days; both adults raise the young.

Feeding: almost entirely nocturnal; catches insects in flight, often high in the air; eats mosquitoes, blackflies, midges, beetles and other flying insects; particularly partial to moths; some grasshoppers are taken and swallowed whole.

Voice: far-carrying and frequently repeated *whip-poor-will,* with emphasis on the *will;* most often uttered at dusk and through the night.

Similar Species: *Common Nighthawk* (p. 188): less rufous in plumage; longer, pointed wings with white "wrist" patches; shallowly forked, barred tail. *Chuck-will's-widow* (p. 360): larger; pale brown to buff throat; whitish "necklace"; darker breast; more reddish overall; much less white on male's tail; different call.

Best Sites: ***MN:*** woodlands along the Mississippi R. and its tributaries in the southeast; mixed woodlands in the northwest. ***WI:*** deciduous forests in White River Marsh, Governor Dodge SP and along or near the Wisconsin, Mississippi and Chippewa Rivers.

CHIMNEY SWIFT

Chaetura pelagica

Chimney Swifts are specialized for high-speed flight—they feed, drink, bathe, collect nesting material and even mate on the wing! They spend much of their time scooping up flying insects high above urban neighborhoods, and only nesting and rest keep these birds off their wings. • Chimney Swifts are most conspicuous as they forage on warm summer evenings and also during fall migration, when huge flocks migrate south alongside large numbers of Common Nighthawks. Chimney Swift populations appear to be declining throughout eastern North America, but the cause is unclear. The answer may lie on their wintering ground in South America. • Chimney Swifts once relied on natural tree cavities and woodpecker excavations for roosting and nesting, but in recent times they have adapted to living in brick chimneys. • The legs of a Chimney Swift are so weak and small that if the bird lands on the ground it may not be able to gain flight again. They do have strong claws, however, which allow them to cling to vertical surfaces. • A Chimney Swift's long pointed wings are either extended while in flight or folded back when at rest, but are never held bent at the joints like a swallow's wings.

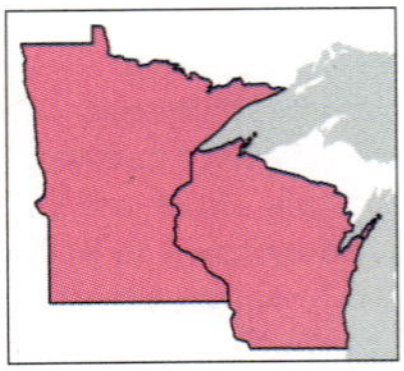

ID: brown overall; slim body; paler on throat, "chin" and "cheeks"; long, thin, pointed wings; squared tail. *In flight:* rapid wingbeats; boomerang-shaped profile; erratic flight pattern.

Size: *L* 5–5½ in; *W* 12–13 in.

Status: ***MN:*** abundant migrant and breeder from mid-April to mid-October. ***WI:*** common migrant and breeder from mid-April to early October.

Habitat: forages over cities and towns; roosts and nests in chimneys; may nest in tree cavities in more remote areas.

Nesting: often colonial; nests deep in the interior of a chimney or tree cavity, or in the attic of an abandoned building; pair fixes a half-saucer nest of short, dead twigs to a vertical wall with saliva; pair incubates 4–5 white eggs for 19–21 days; both adults feed the young.

Feeding: flying insects are swallowed whole during continuous flight.

Voice: rapid, chattering call is given in flight: *chitter-chitter-chitter;* also gives a rapid series of *chip* notes.

Similar Species: *Swallows* (pp. 230–34): broader, shorter wings; smoother flight pattern; most have forked or notched tail.

Best Sites: widespread throughout both states in larger towns and cities.

RUBY-THROATED HUMMINGBIRD

Archilochus colubris

Ruby-throated Hummingbirds span the ecological gap between birds and bees—they feed on the sweet, energy-rich nectar that flowers provide and pollinate the flowers in the process. Many avid gardeners and birders have long understood this interdependence and cultivate native, nectar-producing plants in their yards to attract these delightful birds. Even nongardeners can attract hummingbirds by maintaining a clean sugarwater feeder in a safe location. • Weighing about as much as a nickel, a hummingbird is briefly capable of speeds up to 60 miles per hour. It is also among the few birds that can fly vertically and in reverse. In straight-ahead flight, this tiny bird beats its wings up to 80 times a second, and its heart beats up to 1200 times a minute! • Each year, Ruby-throated Hummingbirds migrate across the Gulf of Mexico—an incredible, nonstop journey of more than 500 miles.

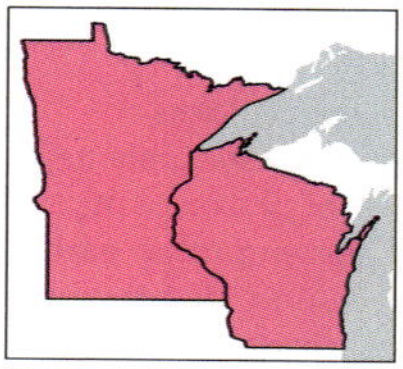

ID: tiny; long bill; iridescent, green back; light underparts; dark tail. *Male:* ruby red throat; black "chin." *Female* and *immature:* fine, dark throat streaking.

Size: *L* 3½–4 in; 4½ in.

Status: ***MN:*** common migrant and breeder from late April to early October; breeds most commonly in northern half of the state; rarely lingers into November.
WI: fairly common migrant and breeder from early May to late September.

Habitat: open, mixed woodlands, wetlands, orchards, tree-lined meadows, flower gardens and backyards with trees and feeders.

Nesting: on a horizontal tree limb; tiny, deep cup nest of plant down and fibers is held together with spider silk; lichens and leaves are pasted on the exterior wall of the nest; female incubates 2 white eggs for 13–16 days; female feeds the young.

Feeding: uses its long bill and tongue to probe blooming flowers and sugar-sweetened water from feeders; also eats small insects and spiders.

Voice: most noticeable is the soft buzzing of the wings while in flight; also produces a loud *chick* and other high squeaks.

Similar Species: *Rufous Hummingbird* (p. 360): male has red on flanks and back; female has red-spotted throat and reddish flanks.

Best Sites: ***MN:*** feeders at homes and resorts near lakes in the north, such as Mille Lacs L., Leech L. and L. Vermilion.
WI: at flowers, especially red-colored ones, and at sugarwater feeders.

BELTED KINGFISHER

Ceryle alcyon

Many of our lakes, rivers, streams, marshes and beaver ponds are closely monitored by the boisterous Belted Kingfisher. Never far from water, this bird is often found uttering its distinctive, rattling call while perched on a bare branch that extends out over a productive pool. With a precise headfirst dive, the Belted Kingfisher can catch fish at depths of up to 2 feet, or snag a frog immersed in only a few inches of water. Kingfishers have even been observed diving into water to elude avian predators. Belted Kingfishers do not concentrate, but are usually encountered as individuals or in small family groups. • During the breeding season, a pair of kingfishers typically takes turns excavating the nest burrow. The birds use their bills to chip away at an exposed sandbank and then kick loose material out of the tunnel with their feet. The female Belted Kingfisher has the traditional female reproductive role for birds but is more colorful than her mate, with an extra red band across her belly.

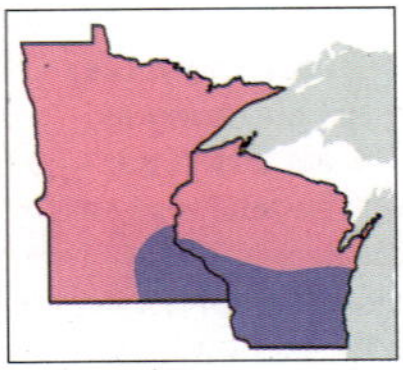

ID: bluish upperparts; shaggy crest; blue gray breast band; white "collar"; long, straight bill; short legs; white underwings; small, white patch near eye. *Male*: no "belt." *Female:* rust-colored "belt" (occasionally incomplete).

Size: *L* 11–14 in; *W* 20 in.

Status: ***MN:*** common migrant and breeder from early March to late November; occasional in winter along open streams, mainly in east-central and southeastern regions. ***WI:*** common migrant and breeder from late March to early November; uncommon winter visitor.

Habitat: rivers, large streams, lakes, marshes and beaver ponds, especially near exposed soil banks, gravel pits or bluffs.

Nesting: in a cavity at the end of an earth burrow, often up to 6 ft long, dug by the pair with their bills and claws; pair incubates 6–7 white eggs for 22–24 days; both adults feed the young.

Feeding: dives headfirst into water, either from a perch or from hovering flight; eats mostly small fish, aquatic invertebrates and tadpoles.

Voice: fast, repetitive, cackling rattle, like a teacup shaking on a saucer.

Similar Species: *Blue Jay* (p. 224): more intense blue color; smaller bill and head.

Best Sites: widespread along lakes, streams and rivers with banks suitable for nesting burrows.

RED-HEADED WOODPECKER

Melanerpes erythrocephalus

The Red-headed Woodpecker lives mostly in deciduous woodlands, urban parks and fields with open groves of large trees. These woodpeckers were once common throughout their range, but their numbers have declined dramatically over the past century. Since the introduction of the European Starling, Red-headed Woodpeckers have been largely outcompeted for nesting cavities. These woodpeckers are also frequent traffic fatalities, often struck by vehicles when they dart from their perches to catch flying insects. • When Alexander Wilson, the "father" of American ornithology, first arrived in North America, the Red-headed Woodpecker was one of the first birds to greet him. Inspired, Wilson wrote of this woodpecker: "His tricolored plumage, so striking…A gay and frolicsome disposition, diving and vociferating around the high dead limbs of some large tree, amusing the passenger with their gambols." • This bird's scientific name *erythrocephalus* means "red head" in Greek.

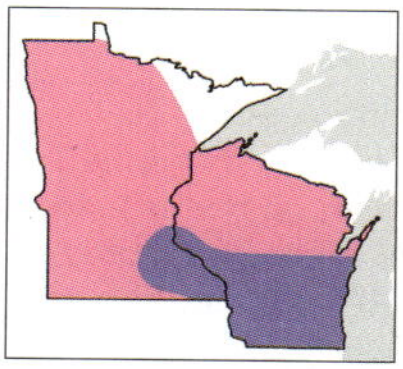

ID: bright red head, "chin," throat and "bib" are bordered with black; black back, wings and tail; white breast, belly, rump, lower back and inner wing patches. *Immature:* brown head, back, wings and tail; slight brown streaking on white underparts.
Size: *L* 9–9½ in; *W* 17 in.
Status: ***MN:*** uncommon migrant and breeder from late March to late October; rare or absent in northeastern and most of the north-central regions; occasional in winter in the southern half of the state except in the southwest. ***WI:*** common migrant from late April to late May and from early September to early October; fairly common breeder; uncommon winter visitor.
Habitat: open deciduous woodlands (especially oak woodlands), urban parks, river edges and roadsides with groves of scattered trees.
Nesting: male excavates a nest cavity in a dead tree or limb; pair incubates 4–5 white eggs for 12–13 days; both adults feed the young.
Feeding: flycatches for insects; hammers dead and decaying wood for grubs; eats mostly insects, earthworms, spiders, nuts, berries, seeds and fruit; may also eat some young birds and eggs.
Voice: loud series of *kweer* or *kwrring* notes; occasionally a chattering *kerr-r-ruck;* also drums softly in short bursts.
Similar Species: adult is distinctive. *Red-bellied Woodpecker* (p. 194): whitish face and underparts; black-and-white-barred back. *Yellow-bellied Sapsucker* (p. 195): large, white wing patch.
Best Sites: ***MN:*** Houston Co.; Big Stone NWR; oak savanna in western and southwestern regions. ***WI:*** deciduous forests and savanna.

RED-BELLIED WOODPECKER

Melanerpes carolinus

Red-bellied Woodpeckers often issue noisy, rolling *churr* calls as they poke around wooded landscapes in search of sustenance. Unlike other woodpeckers, which eat mostly insects, Red-bellies consume large amounts of plant material, seldom excavating wood. When occupying an area together with Red-headed Woodpeckers, Red-bellies will nest in the trunk, below the foliage, and the Red-heads will nest in dead branches among the foliage. • Red-bellied Woodpecker populations are expanding northward and westward. It is a year-round resident in most of its range and does well in suburban areas as well as in more remote wilderness regions. In the southeastern U.S., where they are more common, Red-bellied Woodpeckers are often considered pests because they feed on commercial fruit crops. • The Red-bellied Woodpecker's namesake, its red belly, is only a small reddish area that is difficult to see in the field.

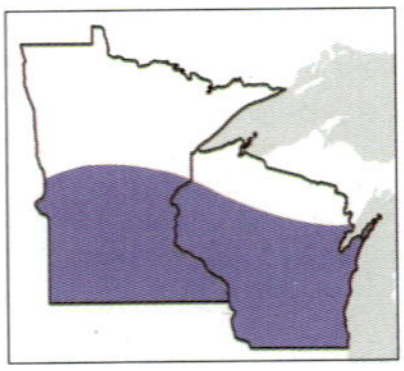

ID: black-and-white-barred back; white patches on rump and topside base of primaries; reddish tinge on belly. *Female:* red nape. *Male:* red nape extends to forehead. *Immature:* dark gray crown; streaked breast.

Size: *L* 9–10½ in; *W* 16 in.

Status: ***MN:*** common year-round resident in southern and central regions; expanding its range into the northwest. ***WI:*** common year-round resident, except in the north where it is uncommon.

Habitat: mature deciduous woodlands; occasionally in wooded residential areas.

Nesting: in a cavity; female selects one of several nest sites excavated by the male; pair may use a natural cavity or the abandoned cavity of another woodpecker; pair incubates 4–5 white eggs for 12–14 days; both adults raise the young.

Feeding: forages in trees, on the ground or occasionally on the wing; eats mostly insects, seeds, nuts and fruit; may also eat tree sap, small amphibians, bird eggs or small fish.

Voice: call is a soft, rolling *churr;* drums in second-long bursts.

Similar Species: *Northern Flicker* (p. 200): yellow underwings; gray crown; brown back with dark barring; black "bib"; large, dark spots on underparts. *Red-headed Woodpecker* (p. 193): all-red head; unbarred, black back and wings; white patch on trailing edge of wing.

Best Sites: ***MN:*** wooded river valleys in the southeast; wooded areas in local and state parks in the southern half of the state. ***WI:*** deciduous forests and wooded river bottoms; residential areas.

YELLOW-BELLIED SAPSUCKER

Sphyrapicus varius

Yellow-bellied Sapsuckers are conspicuous in May, when they perform their courting rituals throughout woodlands in the region. Upon arriving on their breeding grounds, these birds announce themselves with a drumroll. The drumming of sapsuckers differs from that of other woodpeckers in our region—it consists of a loud roll with clearly separated taps at the end, like a motor running out of gas. • Lines of parallel holes freshly drilled in tree bark are a sure sign that sapsuckers are nearby. A pair may drill a number of sites within their forest territory. As the holes fill with sweet, sticky sap, they attract insects, and the sapsuckers then make their rounds, eating both the trapped bugs and the pooled sap. A sapsucker does not actually suck sap—the bird laps it up with a tongue that resembles a paintbrush. • Other species such as hummingbirds, kinglets, warblers and waxwings benefit from the holes made by Yellow-bellied Sapsuckers, especially early in the season when flying insects, fruits and nectar are rare.

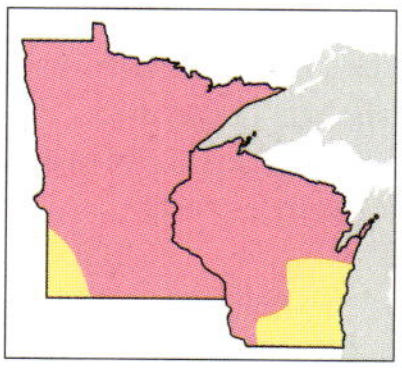

ID: black "bib"; red forecrown; black-and-white face, back, wings and tail; large, white wing patch; yellow wash on lower breast and belly. *Male:* red "chin." *Female:* white "chin." *Immature:* brownish overall, but with large, clearly defined wing patches.

Size: *L* 7–9 in; *W* 16 in.

Status: ***MN:*** common migrant and breeder from late March to late October; uncommon to rare in the southwest; a few linger into early winter in the south. ***WI:*** common migrant and breeder from late March to late October; rare winter visitor.

Habitat: deciduous and mixed forests, especially dry, second-growth woodlands.

Nesting: in a cavity; usually in a live poplar or birch tree with heart rot; often lines the cavity with wood chips; pair incubates 5–6 white eggs for 12–13 days.

Feeding: hammers trees for insects; drills holes in live trees to collect sap and trap insects; also flycatches for insects.

Voice: nasal, catlike *meow;* territorial and courtship hammering has a distinctive, 2-speed quality; soft *vee-ooo* when alarmed.

Similar Species: *Red-headed Woodpecker* (p. 193): juvenile lacks white patch on wing. *Downy Woodpecker* (p. 196) and *Hairy Woodpecker* (p. 197): lack large, white wing patch and red forecrown; red napes; white backs. *Black-backed Woodpecker* (p. 199) and *Three-toed Woodpecker* (p. 198): lack white wing patch; yellow forecrowns; predominantly black heads.

Best Sites: ***MN:*** widespread throughout the state, mainly in wooded river valleys. ***WI:*** deciduous forests and wooded river bottoms in the western and northern regions of the state, such as Wyalusing SP, Brule R. (Douglas Co.) and LaCrosse.

DOWNY WOODPECKER

Picoides pubescens

A regular patron of backyard suet feeders, the small and widely common Downy Woodpecker is often the first woodpecker a novice birder will identify with confidence. Once you become familiar with this bird's dainty appearance, it won't be long before you recognize it by its soft taps and brisk staccato calls that filter through your neighborhood. These encounters are not all confusion free, however, because the closely related Hairy Woodpecker looks remarkably similar. • Like other members of the woodpecker family, the Downy has evolved a number of features that help to cushion the repeated shocks of a lifetime of hammering. These characteristics include a strong bill, strong neck muscles, a flexible, reinforced skull and a brain that is tightly packed in its protective cranium. Another feature that Downies share with other woodpeckers is feathered nostrils, which serve to filter out the sawdust it produces when hammering.

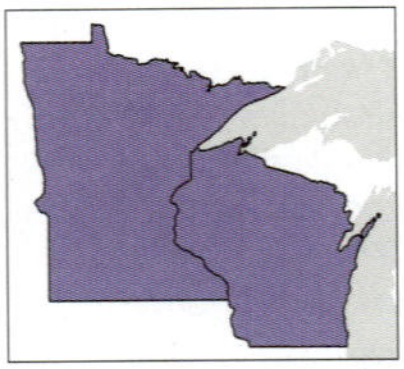

ID: clear white belly and back; white-barred, black wings; black eye line and crown; short, stubby bill; mostly black tail; black-spotted, white outer tail feathers. *Male:* small, red patch on back of head. *Female:* no red patch.

Size: *L* 6–7 in; *W* 12 in.

Status: common year-round resident in both states.

Habitat: all wooded environments, especially deciduous and mixed forests and areas with tall, deciduous shrubs; most common where birch trees are widespread.

Nesting: pair excavates a cavity in a dying or decaying tree trunk or limb and lines it with wood chips; excavation takes more than 2 weeks; pair incubates 4–5 white eggs for 11–13 days; both adults feed the young.

Feeding: forages on trunks and branches, often in saplings and shrubs; chips and probes for insects and their eggs, cocoons and larvae; also eats nuts and seeds; attracted to suet feeders.

Voice: long, unbroken trill; calls are a sharp *pik* or *ki-ki-ki* or whiny *queek queek;* drums more than the Hairy Woodpecker and at a higher pitch, usually on smaller trees and dead branches.

Similar Species: *Hairy Woodpecker* (p. 197): larger; bill is as long as head is wide; no spots on white outer tail feathers. *Yellow-bellied Sapsucker* (p. 195): large, white wing patch; red forecrown; lacks red nape and clean white back. *Black-backed Woodpecker* (p. 199) and *Three-toed Woodpecker* (p. 198): larger; yellow forecrowns; predominantly black heads; black barring on sides.

Best Sites: woods and residential areas.

HAIRY WOODPECKER

Picoides villosus

A second or third look is often required to confirm the identity of the Hairy Woodpecker, because it is so similar in appearance to its smaller cousin, the Downy Woodpecker. A convenient way to learn to distinguish one bird from the other is by watching these woodpeckers at a backyard feeder. It is not uncommon to see both of these birds vying for food, and the Hairy Woodpecker is larger and more aggressive. • The secret to woodpeckers' feeding success is hidden in their skulls. Most woodpeckers have very long tongues—in some cases more than four times the length of the bill—made possible by twin structures that wrap around the perimeter of the skull. These structures store the tongue in much the same way that a measuring tape is stored in its case. Besides being long and maneuverable, the tip of the tongue is sticky with saliva and is finely barbed to help seize reluctant wood-boring insects.

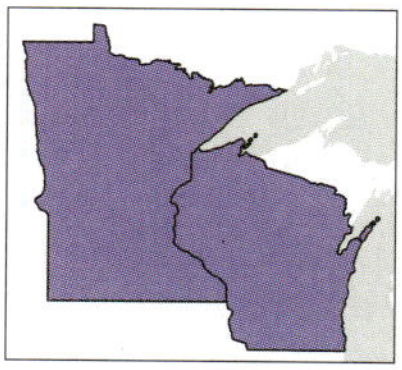

ID: pure white belly; black wings with white spots; black "cheek" and crown; bill is about as long as head is wide; black tail with unspotted, white outer feathers. *Male:* small red patch on back of head. *Female:* no red patch. *Immature:* more indistinct patterning, with brown instead of black.

Size: *L* 8–9½ in; *W* 15 in.

Status: common year-round resident in both states.

Habitat: deciduous and mixed forests, usually in dense, more mature stands with conifers.

Nesting: pair excavates a nest site in a live or decaying tree trunk or limb; excavation takes more than 2 weeks; the cavity is lined with wood chips; pair incubates 4–5 white eggs for 12–14 days; both adults feed the young.

Feeding: forages on tree trunks and branches; chips, hammers and probes bark for insects and their eggs, cocoons and larvae; also eats nuts, fruit and seeds; attracted to feeders with suet, especially in winter.

Voice: loud, sharp call: *peek peek;* long, unbroken trill: *keek-ik-ik-ik-ik-ik;* drums less regularly and at a lower pitch than the Downy Woodpecker, always on tree trunks and large branches.

Similar Species: *Downy Woodpecker* (p. 196): smaller; shorter bill; dark spots on white outer tail feathers. *Yellow-bellied Sapsucker* (p. 195): large, white wing patch; red forecrown; lacks red nape and clean white back. *Black-backed Woodpecker* (p. 199) and *Three-toed Woodpecker* (p. 198): yellow forecrowns; predominantly black heads; black barring on sides.

Best Sites: forests and residential areas.

THREE-TOED WOODPECKER

Picoides tridactylus

The Three-toed Woodpecker is a very rare, quiet visitor to our coniferous forests and is found in areas with standing dead trees infested with wood-boring beetle larvae. Burned-over areas and soggy bogs are also favorite haunts of this elusive bird. • The Three-toed Woodpecker does not drill holes while foraging for food. Instead, it chisels off large flakes of bark from old or dying conifers, exposing the red inner surface of the trunk. Eventually the trees take on a distinct reddish look and are skirted with fragments of bark. • The Three-toed Woodpecker is the only woodpecker found in both North America and Europe and it breeds farther north than any of its relatives. • Both the Three-toed Woodpecker and the Black-backed Woodpecker have three toes on each foot rather than the usual four. The Greek word *tridactylus* means "three toes."

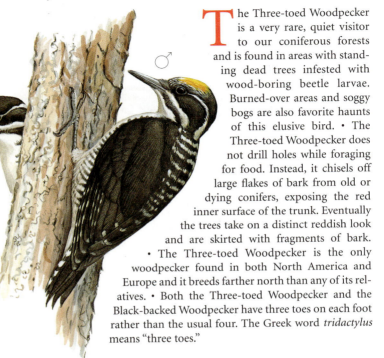

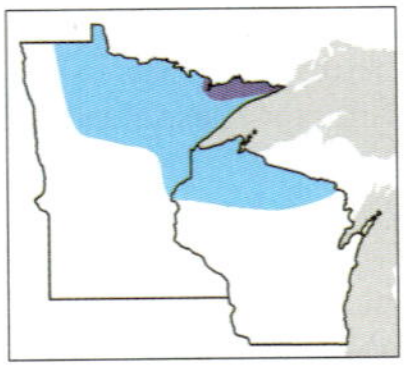

ID: black-and-white barring down center of back; white underparts; black barring on sides; predominantly black head with 2 narrow, white stripes; black tail with black-spotted, white outer tail feathers; 3 toes. *Male:* yellow crown. *Female:* black crown with occasional white spotting.

Size: *L* 8–9 in; *W* 15 in.

Status: ***MN:*** rare and local year-round resident; very rarely moves south to the east-central region in winter. ***WI:*** very rare migrant and winter visitor from late September to mid-April; casual summer visitor.

Habitat: spruce and fir forests, bogs and disturbed areas; coniferous and deciduous forest burns, which traditionally attract this species and the Black-backed Woodpecker in succeeding years owing to beetle destruction.

Nesting: excavates a cavity, usually in a dead or dying conifer trunk; excavation can take up to 12 days; pair incubates 3–4 white eggs for 12–14 days; both adults feed the young.

Feeding: chips away bark to expose larval and adult wood-boring insects; occasionally eats berries and sap.

Voice: call is a low *pik* or *teek;* drumming is a prolonged series of short bursts.

Similar Species: *Black-backed Woodpecker* (p. 199): solid black back; unspotted, white outer tail feathers. *Hairy Woodpecker* (p. 197): clean white back; lacks dark barring on sides. *Yellow-bellied Sapsucker* (p. 195): large, white wing patch; red forecrown; black "bib"; yellow-tinged underparts.

Best Sites: ***MN:*** Cook Co.; Lake Co. ***WI:*** no consistent sites.

BLACK-BACKED WOODPECKER

Picoides arcticus

Black-backed Woodpeckers are found in the northern regions of Minnesota and Wisconsin. This generally quiet woodpecker prefers a secretive life in remote, uninhabited tracts of coniferous forest. Only during the brief courtship season does the male Black-backed Woodpecker advertise his presence by drumming on the top of a broken, standing dead tree or "snag." • This reclusive bird is most active in recently burned forest patches where wood-boring beetles thrive under the charred bark of spruce, pine and fir trees. When it forages on blackened tree trunks, its black-backed form can be difficult to spot, especially from a distance. • In years when food is scarce, this bird often moves beyond its normal breeding range, occasionally showing up in woodlots where it may, over several days or even weeks, totally strip the bark from a dead or dying tree in search of larvae.

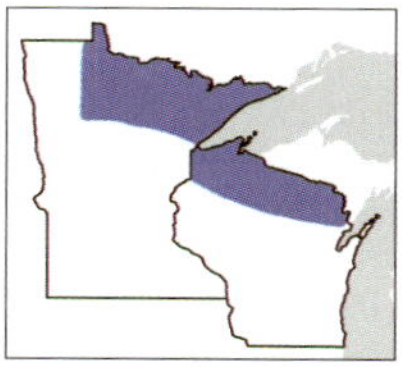

ID: solid black back; white underparts; black barring on sides; predominantly black head with white line below eye; black "mustache" stripe; 3 toes; black tail with pure white outer tail feathers. *Male:* yellow crown. *Female:* black crown.
Size: *L* 9–10 in; *W* 16 in.
Status: ***MN:*** uncommon year-round resident in northeastern and north-central regions; on rare occasions moves into central and southern regions in winter. ***WI:*** uncommon year-round resident in the north; very rare winter visitor elsewhere in the state.
Habitat: coniferous forests, especially burned-over sites with many snags.
Nesting: excavates a cavity in a dead or dying conifer trunk or limb; excavation takes up to 12 days; pair incubates 4 white eggs for 12–14 days; both adults feed the young.
Feeding: chisels away bark flakes to expose larval and adult wood-boring insects; may eat some nuts and fruits.
Voice: call is a low *kik;* drumming is a prolonged series of short bursts.
Similar Species: *Three-toed Woodpecker* (p. 198): white back with black, horizontal barring or spots; black spots on white outer tail feathers. *Hairy Woodpecker* (p. 197): clean white back; lacks dark barring on sides. *Yellow-bellied Sapsucker* (p. 195): black-and-whitish back; large white wing patch; red forecrown; black "bib"; yellow-tinged underparts.
Best Sites: ***MN:*** Superior NF; Red Lake WMA; North Shore of L. Superior in Cook, Lake and St. Louis Counties. ***WI:*** Brule R. (Douglas Co.); forest roads 2174, 2178, 2182, 2183 and 2414 in Forest Co. and Oneida Co.

NORTHERN FLICKER

Colaptes auratus

Northern Flickers are one of the most common woodpeckers in our region. Unlike other woodpeckers, the Northern Flicker spends much of its time on the ground, feeding on ants and other insects. It appears almost robinlike as it hops about in grassy meadows, fields and along forest clearings. • Flickers are often seen bathing in dusty depressions. The dust particles absorb oils and bacteria that are harmful to the birds' feathers. To clean even more thoroughly, flickers will squish captured ants and then preen themselves with the remains (ants produce formic acid, which kills small parasites on the flicker's skin and feathers). • Like many woodpeckers, the Northern Flicker has zygodactyl feet—each foot has two toes facing forward and two toes pointing backward—which allow the bird to move vertically up and down tree trunks. As well, stiff tail feathers help to prop up woodpeckers' bodies while they scale trees and excavate cavities.

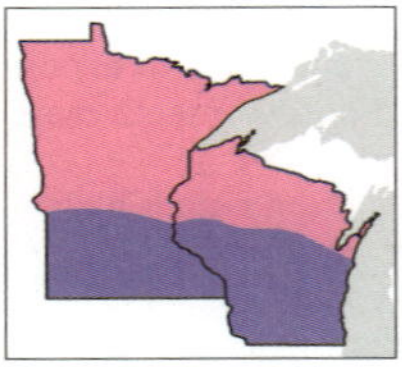

ID: brown, barred back and wings; spotted, buff to whitish underparts; black "bib"; yellow underwings and undertail; white rump; long bill; brownish to buff face; gray crown. *Male:* black "mustache" stripe; red nape crescent. *Female:* no "mustache."

Size: *L* 12½–13 in; *W* 20 in.

Status: ***MN:*** common to abundant migrant and breeder from late February to late November; regular in winter in small numbers in southern regions. ***WI:*** common migrant and breeder from late March to late October; uncommon winter visitor.

Habitat: open deciduous, mixed and coniferous woodlands and forest edges, fields and meadows; swamps in winter.

Nesting: pair excavates a cavity in a dead or dying deciduous tree; excavation lasts about 2 weeks; will also use a nest box; lines the cavity with wood chips; pair incubates 5–8 white eggs for 11–16 days; both adults feed the young.

Feeding: forages on the ground for ants and other terrestrial insects; also eats berries and nuts; probes bark; occasionally flycatches; readily visits feeders for suet, seeds and berries.

Voice: loud, laughing, rapid *kick-kick-kick-kick-kick-kick; woika-woika-woika* issued during courtship.

Similar Species: *Red-bellied Woodpecker* (p. 194): black-and-white pattern on back; more red on head; dark underwings.

Best Sites: deciduous forests and residential areas throughout both states.

PILEATED WOODPECKER

Dryocopus pileatus

With its flaming red crest, swooping flight and maniacal call, this impressive deep-forest dweller can stop hikers in their tracks. Using its powerful, dagger-shaped bill and stubborn determination, the Pileated Woodpecker chisels out uniquely shaped rectangular cavities in its unending search for grubs and ants. These cavities are often the first indication that a breeding pair is resident in an area. • Because they require a large home territory, these magnificent birds are not encountered with much frequency. A pair of breeding Pileated Woodpeckers generally requires more than 100 acres of mature forest in which to settle. • As a primary cavity nester, the Pileated Woodpecker plays an important role in forest ecosystems. Other birds and even mammals depend on the activities of this woodpecker—ducks, small falcons, owls and flying squirrels are frequent nesters in abandoned Pileated Woodpecker cavities. • Not surprisingly, a woodpecker's bill becomes shorter as the bird ages. In Audubon's historic painting of the Pileated Woodpecker, he correctly depicted the bills of the juveniles as slightly longer than those of the adults.

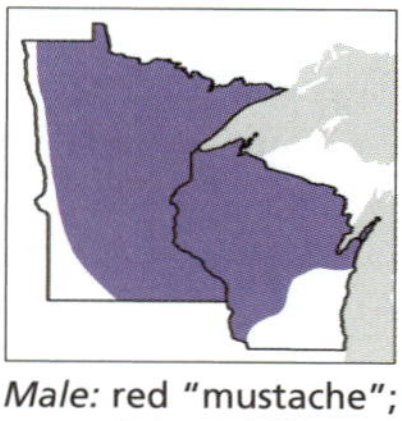

ID: predominantly black; white wing linings; flaming red crest; yellow eyes; stout, dark bill; white stripe runs from bill to shoulder; white "chin." *Male:* red "mustache"; red crest (red extends from bill to nape). *Female:* no red "mustache"; red crest; gray brown forehead.

Size: *L* 16–19 in; *W* 29 in.

Status: ***MN:*** uncommon year-round resident; rare to absent in the southwest and the Red R. valley. ***WI:*** uncommon year-round resident, except in the southeast.

Habitat: extensive tracts of mature deciduous, mixed or coniferous forest; some occur in riparian woodlands or woodlots in suburban and agricultural areas.

Nesting: pair excavates a cavity in a dead or dying tree trunk; excavation can take 3–6 weeks; lines the cavity with wood chips; pair incubates 4 white eggs for 15–18 days; both adults feed the young.

Feeding: hammers the base of rotting trees, creating fist-sized or larger, rectangular holes; eats carpenter ants, wood-boring beetle larvae, berries and nuts.

Voice: loud, fast, rolling *woika-woika-woika-woika;* long series of *kuk* notes; loud resonant drumming; sounds similar to, but louder than, the Northern Flicker.

Similar Species: *Other woodpeckers* (pp. 193–200): much smaller. *American Crow* (p. 226) and *Common Raven* (p. 227): lack white underwings and flaming red crest.

Best Sites: ***MN:*** forested streams, especially in southeastern, east-central and central regions. ***WI:*** deciduous forests and wooded river bottomlands, especially in western and northern areas.

PASSERINES

Passerines are also commonly known as songbirds or perching birds. Although these terms are easier to comprehend, they are not as strictly accurate, because some passerines neither sing nor perch, and many nonpasserines do sing and perch. In a general sense, however, these terms represent passerines adequately: they are among the best singers, and they are typically seen perched on a branch or wire.

Eastern Meadowlark

It is believed that passerines, which all belong to the order Passeriformes, make up the most recent evolutionary group of birds. Theirs is the most numerous of all orders, representing about 45% of the bird species in Minnesota and Wisconsin, and nearly three-fifths of all living birds worldwide.

Passerines are grouped together based on the sum total of many morphological and molecular similarities, including such things as the number of tail and flight feathers and reproductive characteristics. All passerines share the same foot shape: three toes face forward and one faces backward, and no passerines have webbed toes. Also, all passerines have a tendon that runs along the back side of the bird's knee and tightens when the bird perches, giving it a firm grip.

Some of our most common and easily identified birds are passerines, such as the Black-capped Chickadee, American Robin and House Sparrow, but the passerines also include some of the most challenging and frustrating birds to identify, until their distinct songs and call are learned.

Baltimore Oriole

OLIVE-SIDED FLYCATCHER

Contopus cooperi

An early morning hike through a coniferous forest often reveals a most curious and incessant wild call: *quick-three-beers! quick-three-beers!* This interpretation of the male Olive-sided Flycatcher's courtship song may seem silly, but it is surprisingly accurate. Once nesting has begun, this flycatcher quickly changes its tune to an equally enthusiastic, but less memorable, territorial *pip-pip-pip.* Like other "tyrant flycatchers," Olive-sided Flycatchers are fierce defenders of their nests and will harass and chase off squirrels and other predators. • From their perches high among towering conifer spires, Olive-sided Flycatchers have easy access to an abundance of flying insects that inhabit the sunny forest heights. These feisty birds are difficult to spot, so look for a big-headed silhouette perched at the tip of a mature conifer or dead branch. • Like all flycatchers, this olive-vested songbird perches with a distinctive, upright, attentive profile. Its ready-and-waiting stance allows it to quickly launch out and snatch flying insects in midair.

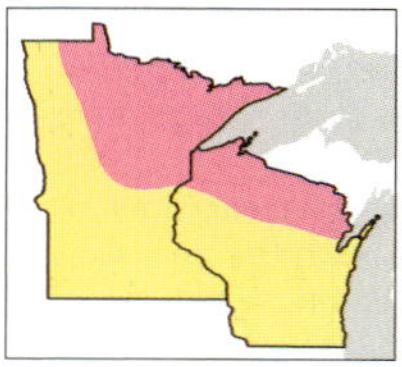

ID: dark olive gray "vest"; light throat and belly; olive gray to olive brown upperparts; white tufts on sides of rump; dark upper mandible; dull yellow orange base to lower mandible; inconspicuous eye ring.

Size: *L* 7–8 in; *W* 13 in.

Status: ***MN:*** uncommon migrant from early May to mid-June and from early August to late September; uncommon breeder in forested areas of northeastern and north-central regions. ***WI:*** uncommon migrant from mid-May to mid-June and from early August to mid-September; uncommon breeder in the north.

Habitat: semi-open mixed and coniferous forests near water; prefers burned areas and wetlands.

Nesting: high in a conifer, usually on a horizontal branch far from the trunk; nest of twigs and plant fibers is bound with spider silk; female incubates 3 white to pinkish buff eggs, with dark spots concentrated at the larger end, for 14–17 days.

Feeding: flycatches insects from a perch.

Voice: song is a chipper and lively *quick-three-beers!,* with the 2nd note highest in pitch; descending *pip-pip-pip* when excited.

Similar Species: *Eastern Wood-Pewee* (p. 204): smaller; lacks white rump tufts; gray breast; 2 faint wing bars. *Eastern Phoebe* (p. 210): lacks white rump tufts; all-dark bill; often wags its tail. *Eastern Kingbird* (p. 213): lacks white rump tufts; all-dark bill; white-tipped tail.

Best Sites: ***MN:*** Chippewa NF; Superior NF; coniferous bogs. ***WI:*** Stone's Bridge–Brule R. (Douglas Co.); forest roads in Forest Co. and Oneida Co.

EASTERN WOOD-PEWEE

Contopus virens

Perched on an exposed tree branch in a suburban park or woodlot edge, the male Eastern Wood-Pewee whistles his plaintive *pee-ah-wee pee-oh* all day long throughout the summer. Some of the keenest suitors will even sing their charms late into the evening, long after most birds have silenced their weary courtship songs. • Like other flycatchers, the Eastern Wood-Pewee loops out from an exposed perch to snatch flying insects in midair, a technique often referred to as "flycatching" or "hawking." • The Eastern Wood-Pewee is less aggressive and showy than most of its close relatives. • Many insects have evolved defense mechanisms to avert potential predators such as the Eastern Wood-Pewee and its flycatching kin. Some insects are camouflaged, while others are distasteful or poisonous and flaunt their foul nature with vivid colors. Interestingly, some insects even mimic their poisonous allies, displaying warning colors even though they are perfectly tasty.

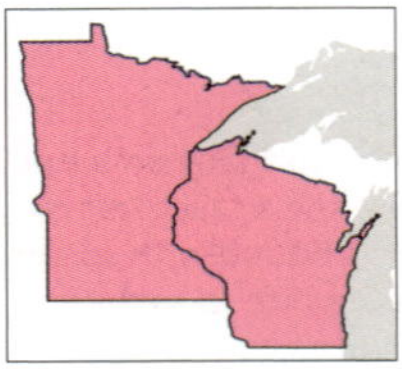

ID: olive gray to olive brown upperparts; 2 narrow, white wing bars; whitish throat; gray breast and sides; whitish or pale yellow belly, flanks and undertail coverts; dark upper mandible; dull yellow orange base to lower mandible; no eye ring.

Size: *L* 6–6½ in; *W* 10 in.

Status: ***MN:*** common migrant and breeder from late April to early October; uncommon migrant and breeder in southwestern and west-central regions. ***WI:*** common migrant and breeder from early May to late September.

Habitat: open mixed and deciduous woodlands with a sparse understory, especially woodland openings and edges; rarely in open coniferous woodlands.

Nesting: on the fork of a horizontal deciduous branch well away from the trunk; open cup nest of grass, plant fibers and lichen is bound with spider silk; female incubates 3 whitish eggs, with dark blotches concentrated at the larger end, for 12–13 days.

Feeding: flycatches insects from a perch; may also glean insects from foliage, especially while hovering.

Voice: a *chip* call; song is a clear, slow, plaintive *pee-ah-wee,* with the 2nd note lower, followed by a downslurred *pee-oh,* given with or without intermittent pauses.

Similar Species: *Olive-sided Flycatcher* (p. 203): larger; white rump tufts; olive gray "vest"; lacks conspicuous, white wing bars. *Eastern Phoebe* (p. 210): lacks conspicuous, white wing bars; all-dark bill; often pumps its tail. *Eastern Kingbird* (p. 213): larger; white-tipped tail; brighter white underparts; all-dark bill. Empidonax *flycatchers* (pp. 205–09): smaller; more conspicuous wing bars; eye rings.

Best Sites: ***MN:*** deciduous forests, especially in central regions. ***WI:*** deciduous forests.

YELLOW-BELLIED FLYCATCHER

Empidonax flaviventris

The somewhat reclusive Yellow-bellied Flycatcher deep within soggy, mosquito-infested bogs, fens and well-shaded coniferous and mixedwood forests. In late spring and early summer, the male spends much of his time singing plain, soft, liquidy *che-lek* songs and occasionally zipping out from inconspicuous perches to help reduce the insect population. Once nesting has begun, the male changes his tune to a slow, rising *per-wee* and focuses his attention on defending his nesting territory and supplying food to his growing young. • Our region offers fine opportunities for birders to develop their *Empidonax* flycatcher identification skills—it boasts a large assemblage of these nearly identical flycatchers. The Yellow-bellied Flycatcher is the most elusive and secretive of this confusing group. It does not habitually perch in the open, but distinguishes itself from other flycatchers by its yellow underparts and by nesting on the ground.

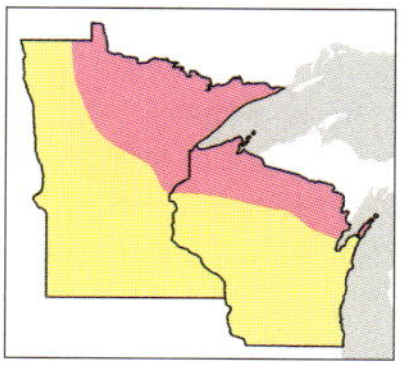

ID: olive green upperparts; yellow underparts; 2 whitish wing bars; yellowish eye ring; white throat; dark upper mandible; pinkish yellow lower mandible; pale olive breast.

Size: *L* 5–6 in; *W* 8 in.

Status: ***MN:*** uncommon migrant from early May to early June and from late July to late September; occasionally common at migration peaks; uncommon breeder in boreal zones of northeastern and north-central regions. ***WI:*** fairly common migrant from mid-May to early June and from late July to early September; uncommon breeder in the north.

Habitat: coniferous bogs and fens and shady spruce and pine forests with a dense shrub understory.

Nesting: on the ground in dense sphagnum moss or among the upturned roots of a fallen tree; small cup nest of moss, rootlets and weeds is lined with grass, sedges and fine rootlets; female incubates 3–4 whitish eggs, lightly spotted with brown, for 12–14 days.

Feeding: flycatches for insects at low to middle levels of the forest; also gleans vegetation for larval and adult invertebrates while hovering.

Voice: song is a soft *che-luk* or *che-lek* (2nd syllable is lower pitched); calls include a chipper *pe-wheep, preee, pur-wee* or *killik*.

Similar Species: *Acadian* (p. 206), *Alder* (p. 207), *Willow* (p. 208) and *Least* (p. 209) *flycatchers:* all lack extensive yellow wash from throat to belly; white eye rings; different songs; all but the Acadian have browner upperparts.

Best Sites: ***MN:*** *Breeding:* wet northern forests, especially boreal bogs; Scenic SP; Boundary Waters Canoe Area Wilderness; L. Vermilion area; County Rd. 18 (Aitkin Co.). *In migration:* woodland edges along streams, especially in state and county parks and national wildlife refuges.
WI: coniferous forests in the north, such as Brule R. (Douglas Co.); forest roads in Oneida, Forest and Vilas Counties.

ACADIAN FLYCATCHER

Empidonax virescens

One of the keys to identifying a flycatcher is to listen for its distinctive song. The Acadian Flycatcher's signature song is a quick, forceful *peet-sa.* • This bird's speedy, aerial courtship chases and the male's hovering flight displays are sights to behold—that is, if you can survive the swarming hordes of bloodsucking mosquitoes deep within the swampy woodlands where these birds are primarily found. • Maple and beech trees provide preferred nesting sites for the Acadian Flycatcher. The nest is built on a horizontal branch up to 20 feet above the ground, and can be quite conspicuous because loose material often dangles from the nest, giving it a sloppy appearance. • Flycatchers are members of the family Tyrannidae, or "Tyrant Flycatchers," so named because of their feisty, aggressive behavior.

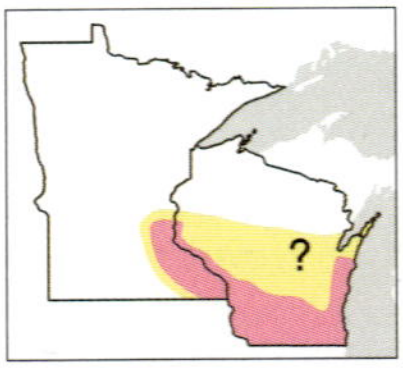

ID: narrow, yellowish eye ring; 2 buff to yellowish wing bars; large bill has dark upper mandible and pinkish yellow lower mandible; white throat; faint olive yellow breast; yellow belly and undertail coverts; olive green upperparts; very long primaries. *Immature:* greenish head and back have buff edges, creating a "scaly" effect; yellow wash on underparts may extend onto throat.

Size: *L* 5½–6 in; *W* 9 in.

Status: ***MN:*** special concern; rare migrant and breeder from mid-May to late August in scattered localities in southeastern, east-central and south-central regions; increasing its range westward and northward. ***WI:*** endangered; uncommon migrant in May and from early August to early September; uncommon breeder.

Habitat: fairly mature deciduous woodlands, riparian woodlands and wooded swamps.

Nesting: low in a beech or maple tree, up to 20 ft above the ground; female builds a loose, sloppy-looking cup nest from bark strips, catkins, fine twigs and grasses held together with spider silk; female incubates 3 creamy white eggs, lightly spotted with brown, for 13–15 days; both adults raise the young.

Feeding: forages primarily by hawking or by gleaning from foliage while hovering; takes insects and insect larvae including wasps, bees, spiders and ants; may also eat berries and small fruits.

Voice: song is a forceful *peet-sa;* call is a softer *peet;* may issue a loud, flickerlike *ti-ti-ti-ti-ti* during the breeding season.

Similar Species: *Alder Flycatcher* (p. 207): song is *fee-bee-o;* narrower, white eye ring is often inconspicuous; browner overall; smaller head relative to its body. *Willow Flycatcher* (p. 208): song is an explosive *fitz-bew;* browner overall; smaller head; very faint eye ring. *Least Flycatcher* (p. 209): song is a clear *che-bek;* prominent, white eye ring; rounded head; shorter wings. *Yellow-bellied Flycatcher* (p. 205): song is a liquid *che-lek;* yellow wash from throat to belly.

Best Sites: ***MN:*** Beaver Creek Valley SP; Murphy-Hanrehan Park Reserve; Nerstrand–Big Woods SP. ***WI:*** Wyalusing SP; Baxter's Hollow; Devil's Lake SP.

ALDER FLYCATCHER

Empidonax alnorum

The Alder Flycatcher is often indistinguishable from other *Empidonax* flycatchers until it opens its small, bicolored beak: with a hearty *fee-bee-o* or *free beer,* it reveals its identity. • This bird is well named because it is often found in alder and willow shrubs. In our region, the Alder Flycatcher frequently competes against the Willow Flycatcher for control over dense, riparian alder and willow thickets. • Many birds have to learn their songs and calls, but Alder Flycatchers instinctively know the simple phrase of their species. Even if a young bird is isolated from the sounds of other Alder Flycatchers, it can produce a perfectly acceptable *fee-bee-o* when it matures. • The Willow Flycatcher is a close relative of the Alder Flycatcher, and until 1973 these two species were grouped together as a single species known as "Traill's Flycatcher."

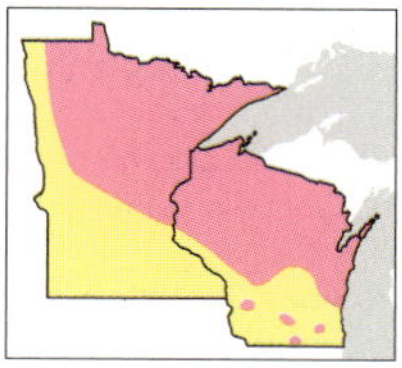

ID: olive brown upperparts; 2 dull white to buff wing bars; faint, whitish eye ring; dark upper mandible; orange lower mandible; long tail; white throat; pale olive breast; pale yellowish belly.

Size: *L* 5½–6 in; *W* 8½ in.

Status: ***MN:*** uncommon migrant from mid-May to early June and from August to early September; may be common at peak migration periods, especially in August and early September; locally common breeder in the northern half of the state. ***WI:*** common migrant from early May to early June and from mid-August to mid-September; fairly common breeder.

Habitat: alder or willow thickets bordering lakes or streams.

Nesting: in a fork in a dense bush or shrub, usually less than 3 ft above the ground; small cup nest is loosely woven of grass and other plant materials; female incubates 3–4 white eggs, with dark spots concentrated around the larger end, for 12–14 days; both adults feed the young.

Feeding: flycatches from a perch for beetles, bees, wasps and other flying insects; also eats berries and occasionally seeds.

Voice: song is a snappy *fee-bee-o* or *free beer;* call is a *wheep* or *peep.*

Similar Species: *Eastern Wood-Pewee* (p. 204): larger; lacks eye ring and conspicuous wing bars. *Willow Flycatcher* (p. 208): song is an explosive *fitz-bew;* mostly found in drier areas. *Least Flycatcher* (p. 209): song is a clear *che-bek;* bolder white eye ring; greener upperparts; pale gray white underparts. *Acadian Flycatcher* (p. 206): song is a forceful *peet-sa;* yellowish eye ring; greener upperparts; yellower underparts. *Yellow-bellied Flycatcher* (p. 205): song is a liquid *che-lek;* yellowish eye ring; greener upperparts; yellower underparts.

Best Sites: ***MN:*** alder thickets, especially in northern regions, including Itasca SP, Scenic SP, Sherburne NWR, Afton SP, Wild River SP and St. Croix SP. ***WI:*** alder shrubbery habitat.

WILLOW FLYCATCHER

Empidonax traillii

Upon arriving in a suitable shrubby area with thick willows and tangled shrubbery, male Willow Flycatchers swing energetically on advantageous perches. They utter their characteristic, sneezing *fitz-bew* call and battle vocally over preferred territories. Early spring is the only time these birds can be safely distinguished from Alder Flycatchers because it is the only time that the two species sing very different songs. • Once the boundaries are drawn and the business of nesting begins, Willow Flycatchers become shy, inconspicuous birds that opt to remain out of sight. Only when an avian intruder violates an established boundary does the resident Willow Flycatcher aggressively reveal itself. After raising their young and fattening themselves up in late summer and early fall, Willow Flycatchers begin their migratory journey to Central and South America.

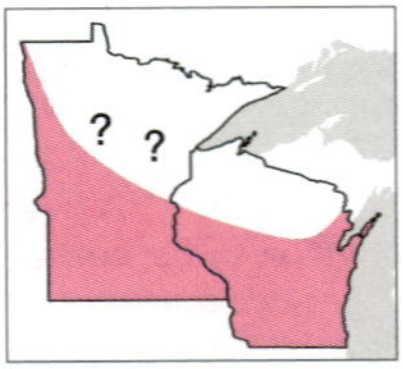

ID: olive brown upperparts; 2 whitish wing bars; indistinct or no eye ring; white throat; yellowish belly; pale olive breast; bicolored bill.

Size: *L* 5½–6 in; *W* 8½ in.

Status: ***MN:*** uncommon to at times common migrant from early May to early June and from August to early September; rare migrant in the north; locally common breeder mainly in the south; a zone of overlap occurs with Alder Flycatcher in central regions. ***WI:*** common migrant from early May to early June and from mid-August to mid-September; fairly common breeder.

Habitat: shrubby areas of hawthorn, apple, red-osier dogwood, willow or other low growth on abandoned farmlands and in riparian corridors.

Nesting: in a fork or on a branch in a dense shrub, usually 3–7 ft above the ground; female builds an open cup nest with grass, bark strips and plant fibers and lines it with down; female incubates 3–4 whitish to pale buff eggs, with brown spots concentrated toward the larger end, for 12–15 days.

Feeding: flycatches insects; also gleans insects from vegetation, usually while hovering.

Voice: song is a quick, sneezy *fitz-bew* that drops off at the end (repeated up to 30 times a minute); call is a quick *whit.*

Similar Species: *Eastern Wood-Pewee* (p. 204): larger; lacks eye ring and conspicuous wing bars. *Alder Flycatcher* (p. 207): song is *fee-bee-o;* usually found in wetter areas. *Least Flycatcher* (p. 209): song is a clear *che-bek;* bolder white eye ring; greener upperparts; pale gray white underparts. *Acadian Flycatcher* (p. 206): song is a forceful *peet-sa;* yellowish eye ring; greener upperparts; yellower underparts. *Yellow-bellied Flycatcher* (p. 205): song is a liquid *che-lek;* yellowish eye ring; greener upperparts; yellower underparts.

Best Sites: ***MN:*** Big Stone NWR; Sherburne NWR; willow groves along streams and wetlands in the south. ***WI:*** young willow habitats.

LEAST FLYCATCHER

Empidonax minimus

This bird might not look like a bully, but the Least Flycatcher is one of the boldest and most pugnacious songbirds of our region's deciduous woodlands. During the nesting season, it is noisy and conspicuous, forcefully repeating its simple, two-part *che-bek* call throughout much of the day. Intense song battles normally eliminate the need for physical aggression, but feather-flying fights are occasionally required to settle disputes over territory and courtship privileges. • Even though it is not as colorful and glamorous as other songbirds, the Least Flycatcher is the most common and widespread *Empidonax* flycatcher in the region. • These birds often fall victim to nest parasitism by the Brown-headed Cowbird, whose hatched young often smother the much smaller Least Flycatcher nestlings.

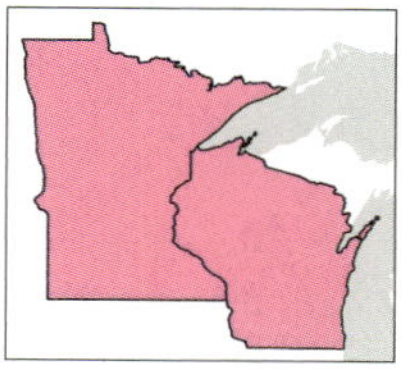

ID: olive brown upperparts; 2 white wing bars; bold, white eye ring; fairly long, narrow tail; mostly dark bill has yellow orange lower base; white throat; gray breast; gray white to yellowish belly and undertail coverts.

Size: *L* 4½–6 in; *W* 7½ in.

Status: ***MN:*** common migrant and breeder from late April to early October. ***WI:*** very common migrant and breeder from early May to early October.

Habitat: open deciduous or mixed woodlands; forest openings and edges; often in second-growth woodlands and occasionally near human habitation.

Nesting: in the crotch or a fork of a small tree or shrub, often against the trunk; female builds a small cup nest of plant fibers and bark and lines it with fine grass, plant down and feathers; female incubates 4 creamy white eggs for 13–15 days; both adults feed the young.

Feeding: flycatches insects; gleans trees and shrubs for insects while hovering; may also eat some fruits and seeds.

Voice: song is a constantly repeated, dry *che-bek che-bek*.

Similar Species: *Eastern Wood-Pewee* (p. 204): larger; lacks eye ring and conspicuous wing bars. *Alder Flycatcher* (p. 207): song is *fee-bee-o;* faint eye ring; different song; usually found in wetter areas. *Willow Flycatcher* (p. 208): song is an explosive *fitz-bew;* lacks eye ring; greener upperparts; yellower underparts. *Acadian Flycatcher* (p. 206) song is a forceful *peet-sa;* yellowish eye ring; greener upperparts; yellower underparts. *Yellow-bellied Flycatcher* (p. 205): song is a liquid *che-lek;* yellowish eye ring; greener upperparts; yellower underparts.

Best Sites: ***MN:*** *Breeding:* deciduous and mixed woodlands, especially in state, county and city parks with open woodlands; Big Stone NWR; Sibley SP; Sherburne NWR; Whitewater SP; Beaver Creek Valley SP; Minnesota River Valley State Recreation Area; Lake Bronson SP. *In migration:* brushy edges of mixed woodlands. ***WI:*** deciduous forests, especially in the northern half of the state.

EASTERN PHOEBE

Sayornis phoebe

Whether you are poking around your summer cottage, a campground picnic shelter or your backyard shed, there is a very good chance you will stumble upon an Eastern Phoebe family and its marvelous mud nest. The Eastern Phoebe's nest building and territorial defense is normally well underway by the time most other songbirds arrive in our region in mid-May. Once limited to nesting on natural cliffs and fallen riparian trees, this adaptive flycatcher has gradually found success in nesting on buildings and bridges, although it prefers sites near water. Too often, people unnecessarily destroy the phoebe's mud nests, though some have caught on to the benefits of having phoebe tenants, because these birds can be effective at controlling pesky insects. • Some other birds pump their tails while perched, but few species can match the zest and frequency of the Eastern Phoebe's tail pumping.

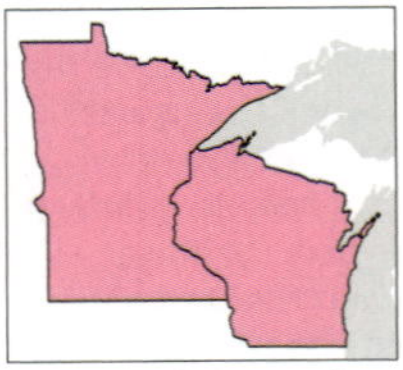

ID: gray brown upperparts; white underparts with gray wash on breast and sides; belly may be washed with yellow in fall; no eye ring; no obvious wing bars; all-black bill; dark legs; frequently pumps its tail.

Size: *L* $6\frac{1}{2}$–7 in; *W* $10\frac{1}{2}$ in.

Status: ***MN:*** common migrant and breeder from mid-March to early November; accidental in early winter. ***WI:*** common migrant and breeder from late March to late October.

Habitat: open deciduous woodlands, forest edges and clearings; usually near water.

Nesting: under the ledge of a building, picnic shelter, culvert, bridge, cliff or well; cup-shaped mud nest is lined with moss, grass, fur and feathers; female incubates 4–5 white eggs, often with a few reddish brown spots, for 14–16 days; both adults feed the young.

Feeding: flycatches beetles, flies, wasps, grasshoppers, mayflies and other insects; occasionally plucks aquatic invertebrates and small fish from the water's surface.

Voice: song is a hearty, snappy *fee-bee,* delivered frequently; call is a sharp *chip.*

Similar Species: *Eastern Wood-Pewee* (p. 204): pale wing bars; bicolored bill; does not pump its tail. *Olive-sided Flycatcher* (p. 203): larger; dark "vest"; white, fluffy patches border rump. Empidonax *flycatchers* (pp. 205–09): most have eye ring and conspicuous wing bars. *Eastern Kingbird* (p. 213): white-tipped tail; black upperparts.

Best Sites: near streams, especially where there are bridges, outbuildings and banks; also residential areas near water.

GREAT CRESTED FLYCATCHER

Myiarchus crinitus

The Great Crested Flycatcher's nesting habits are unusual for a flycatcher: it is a cavity nester, and although it prefers to nest in a natural tree cavity or abandoned woodpecker nest, it will occasionally use a nest box intended for a bluebird. Once in a while, the Great Crested Flycatcher will decorate the entrance of its nest with a shed snakeskin. The purpose of this practice is not fully understood, though it might make any would-be predators think twice! In some instances, this versatile bird has even been known to substitute translucent plastic wrap for genuine reptilian skin. The Great Crested Flycatcher prefers open or semi-open hardwood forests, and is a common summer resident in these parts. • Songbirds such as the Great Crested Flycatcher are often thought of as birds that fly south for the winter. In reality, it would be more correct to say that they fly north for the summer. This flycatcher, as well as many other migrants, are subtropical or tropical birds of Central and South America that visit our country only briefly to raise their young before returning home.

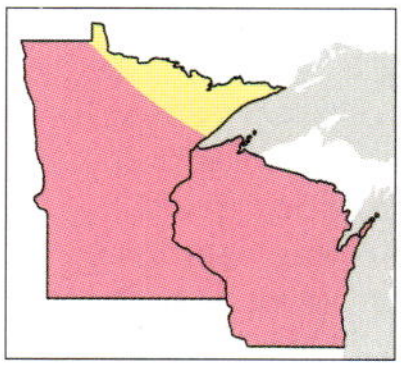

ID: bright yellow belly and undertail coverts; gray throat and upper breast; reddish brown tail; peaked, "crested" head; dark olive brown upperparts; heavy, black bill.
Size: *L* 8–9 in; *W* 13 in.
Status: ***MN:*** uncommon to at times common migrant from late April to late May and from early August to late September; uncommon to common breeder in most areas of the state, but rare or absent from northern portions of northeastern and north-central regions. ***WI:*** common migrant and breeder from early May to late September.
Habitat: deciduous and mixed woodlands and forests, usually near openings or edges.
Nesting: in a tree cavity, nest box or other artificial cavity; nest is lined with grass, bark strips and feathers; may hang a shed snakeskin or plastic wrap at the entrance hole; female incubates 5 creamy white to pale buff eggs, marked with lavender, olive and brown, for 13–15 days.
Feeding: often in the upper branches of deciduous trees, where it flycatches for insects; may also glean caterpillars and occasionally fruit.
Voice: loud, whistled *wheep!* and a rolling *prrrrreet!*
Similar Species: *Yellow-bellied Flycatcher* (p. 205): much smaller; yellow throat; lacks reddish brown tail and large, all-black bill. *Western Kingbird* (p. 212): all-gray head, neck and breast; lacks head crest; darker tail with white outer margins. *Baltimore Oriole* (p. 345): immature is generally browner on head and back, yellower on throat and breast and has pale blue bill and legs.
Best Sites: heavier deciduous forests throughout both states.

WESTERN KINGBIRD

Tyrannus verticalis

More typical of the prairies, the Western Kingbird is an uncommon to rare visitor to our region. In Wisconsin, this bird is seen almost exclusively during migration, especially recently. • Western Kingbirds survey for prey from fence posts, power lines or utility poles. When a kingbird spots an insect, the bird may chase it for up to 50 feet before a capture is made. • Once you have witnessed the kingbird's brave attacks against much larger birds such as crows and hawks, it is easy to understand why this brawler was awarded the name "kingbird." Its scientific name *verticalis* refers to the bird's hidden, red crown patch, which is flared during courtship displays and while in combat with rivals. This red patch, however, is not a good identification mark because it is rarely visible outside the breeding season. • The tumbling, aerial courtship display of the Western Kingbird is a good indication that this bird might be breeding. The male twists and turns as he rises to heights of 65 feet above the ground, then he stalls and tumbles, flipping and twisting as he plummets back to earth.

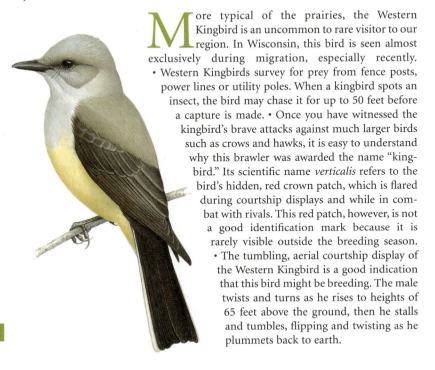

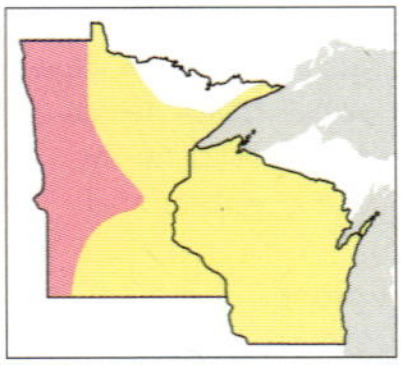

ID: gray head and breast; yellow belly and undertail coverts; black tail; white edge on outer tail feathers; white chin; black bill; ashy gray upperparts; faint, dark gray "mask"; thin, orange red crown (rarely seen).

Size: *L* 8–9 in; *W* 15½ in.

Status: ***MN:*** uncommon migrant from early May to early June and from early August to mid-September; casual fall migrant in the northeast; uncommon breeder in western regions; probably declining. ***WI:*** rare migrant from early May to early June; casual migrant from mid-August to mid-October; very rare breeder (nesting currently nonexistent).

Habitat: open scrubland areas with scattered patches of brush or hedgerows; also along the edges of open fields.

Nesting: in a deciduous tree near the trunk; bulky cup nest of grass, weeds and twigs is lined with fur, plant down and feathers; female incubates 3–5 whitish, heavily blotched eggs for 18–19 days.

Feeding: flycatches insects, including bees, wasps, butterflies, moths, grasshoppers and flies; occasionally eats berries.

Voice: chatty, twittering *whit-ker-whit;* also a short *kit* or extended *kit-kit-keetle-dot.*

Similar Species: *Eastern Kingbird* (p. 213): black upperparts; white underparts; white-tipped tail. *Great Crested Flycatcher* (p. 211): slightly crested head; brownish upperparts; reddish brown tail; yellowish wing bars; lacks white edges to outer tail feathers.

Best Sites: ***MN:*** western tier of counties. ***WI:*** no consistent sites.

EASTERN KINGBIRD

Tyrannus tyrannus

When you think of a tyrant, images of an oppressive dictator or a large carnivorous dinosaur are much more likely to come to mind than a little bird. True as that might be, no one familiar with the pugnacity of the Eastern Kingbird is likely to refute its scientific name, *Tyrannus tyrannus.* This bird is a brawler, and it will fearlessly attack crows, hawks and even humans that pass through its territory. Intruders are often vigorously pursued, pecked and plucked for some distance until the kingbird is satisfied that there is no further threat. In contrast, its butterfly-like courtship flight, which is characterized by short, quivering wingbeats, reveals the gentler side of this bird. • Eastern Kingbirds are common and widespread in our region, so during a drive in the country it is likely you will spot at least one bird sitting on a fenceline or utility wire along a roadside. They are usually encountered as individuals, but loose aggregations of 10 to 15 birds can be found in scattered localities in fall. • Eastern Kingbirds rarely walk or hop on the ground—they prefer to fly, even for very short distances.

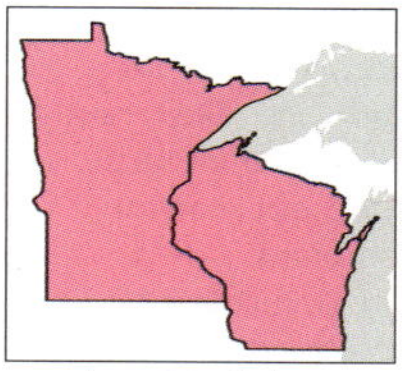

ID: dark gray to black upperparts; white underparts; white-tipped tail; black bill; small head crest; thin, orange red crown (rarely seen); no eye ring; black legs.

Size: *L* 8½ in; *W* 15 in.

Status: ***MN:*** common to at times abundant migrant and breeder from mid-April to late September. ***WI:*** common migrant and breeder from late April to late September.

Habitat: rural fields with scattered trees or hedgerows, clearings in fragmented forests, open roadsides, burned areas and near human settlements.

Nesting: on a horizontal tree or shrub limb; also on a standing stump or an upturned tree root; pair builds a cup nest of weeds, twigs and grass and lines it with root fibers, fine grass and fur; female incubates 3–4 darkly blotched, white to pinkish white eggs for 14–18 days.

Feeding: flycatches aerial insects; infrequently eats berries.

Voice: call is a quick, loud, chattering *kit-kit-kitter-kitter;* also a buzzy *dzee-dzee-dzee.*

Similar Species: *Tree Swallow* (p. 230): dark blue, iridescent back; lacks white-tipped tail; more streamlined body; smaller bill. *Olive-sided Flycatcher* (p. 203): 2 white tufts above rump; lacks white-tipped tail and all-white underparts. *Eastern Wood-Pewee* (p. 204): smaller; bicolored bill; lacks white-tipped tail and all-white underparts.

Best Sites: ***MN:*** agricultural areas, brushy roadsides and forest edges. ***WI:*** near wooded swamps, forests and open fields.

LOGGERHEAD SHRIKE

Lanius ludovicianus

A shrike resembles a Northern Mockingbird in body shape and color, but the Loggerhead's method of hunting is very different. This predatory songbird often perches atop trees and on wires to scan for small prey, which is caught in fast, direct flights or swooping dives. • Like most songbirds, male Loggerhead Shrikes sing to establish their territories and to attract mates. Additionally, males display their hunting prowess by impaling prey on thorns or barbed wire. This behavior may also serve as a means of storing excess food during times of plenty—in spring, you can often see a variety of skewered creatures baking in the sun • Loggerhead Shrike populations have recently declined drastically in many parts of its North American range. Habitat destruction is thought to be the main reason for the population decline. Another cause of Loggerhead mortality is motor vehicles: on their wintering grounds in the southern U.S., shrikes are often traffic fatalities when they fly low across roads to prey on insects attracted to the warm pavement.

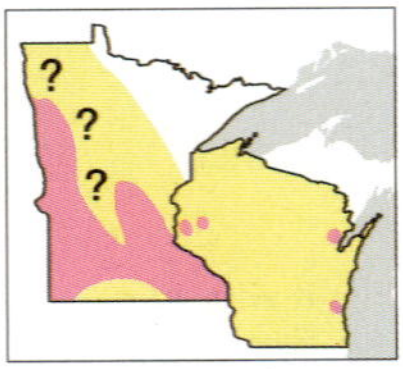

ID: black tail and wings; gray crown and back; white underparts; black "mask" extends above hooked bill onto forehead. *Immature:* brownish gray, barred upperparts. *In flight:* white wing patches; white-edged tail.

Size: *L* 9 in; *W* 12 in.

Status: ***MN:*** threatened; rare to occasionally uncommon migrant from early March to late April and from August to late September in scattered areas of the state; absent over most of the heavily forested portions of north-central and northeastern regions; rare and local breeder; populations may be recovering; a few early winter records. ***WI:*** endangered; uncommon to rare migrant from early April to mid-May and from late July to mid-September; very uncommon to rare breeder.

Habitat: grazed pastures and marginal and abandoned farmlands with scattered hawthorn shrubs, fence posts, barbed wire and nearby wetlands.

Nesting: low in the crotch of a shrub or small tree; prefers thorny hawthorn shrubs; bulky cup nest of twigs and grass is lined with animal hair, feathers, plant down and rootlets; female incubates 5–6 darkly spotted, pale buff to grayish white eggs, for 15–17 days.

Feeding: swoops down on prey from a perch or attacks in pursuit; takes mostly large insects; regularly eats small birds, rodents and shrews; also eats carrion, small snakes and amphibians.

Voice: *Male:* high-pitched, hiccupy *bird-ee bird-ee* in summer; infrequently a harsh *shack-shack* year-round.

Similar Species: *Northern Shrike* (p. 215): usually seen in winter; larger; fine barring on sides and breast; black "mask" does not extend above hooked bill; immature has unbarred, light brown upperparts and strongly, but finely, barred underparts. *Northern Mockingbird* (p. 260): larger; slim bill; no mask; slimmer overall.

Best Sites: ***MN:*** Big Stone NWR; Dakota Co.; Minnesota Valley SP; Felton Prairie SNA. ***WI:*** no consistent sites.

NORTHERN SHRIKE

Lanius excubitor

Like many of our raptors, Northern Shrikes appear in our region each winter in unpredictable and highly variable numbers. During their winter visits, they are typically seen perched like hawks on exposed treetops, from which they survey open and semi-open hunting grounds. Feeders also tempt many shrikes to test their hunting skills on the feeding birds. • The adult Northern Shrike looks somewhat like a gray robin with the bill of a small hawk, and it specializes in catching and killing small birds and rodents. When this bird strikes a large target, it relies on its sharp, hooked bill to dispatch its quarry, although it may use its feet to help. Shrikes are the world's only true carnivorous songbirds and the greatest diversity of shrikes occurs in Africa and Eurasia. • The Northern Shrike's habit of impaling its kills on thorns and barbs has earned it the names "Butcher Bird" and "Nine-Killer." *Lanius* is Latin for "butcher," and *excubitor* is Latin for "watchman" or "sentinel"—"watchful butcher" is an appropriate description of the Northern Shrike's foraging behavior.

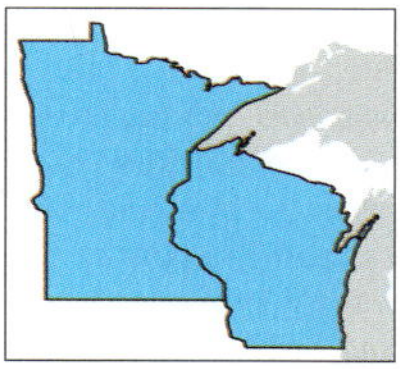

ID: black tail and wings; pale gray upperparts; finely barred, pale underparts; black "mask" does not extend above hooked bill. *Immature:* faint "mask"; light brown upperparts; brown or gray barring on underparts. *In flight:* white wing patches; white-edged tail.

Size: *L* 10 in; *W* 14½ in.

Status: ***MN:*** uncommon migrant and winter visitor from early October to late April; more common in northern and eastern regions. ***WI:*** uncommon migrant and winter visitor from mid-October to early April.

Habitat: open country, including fields, shrubby areas, forest clearings and roadsides.

Nesting: does not nest in our region.

Feeding: swoops down on prey from a perch or chases prey through the air; regularly eats small birds, shrews, rodents and large insects; may also take snakes and frogs; prey may be impaled on a thorn or barb for later consumption.

Voice: usually silent; infrequently gives a long grating laugh: *raa-raa-raa-raa.*

Similar Species: *Loggerhead Shrike* (p. 214): generally absent in winter; black "mask" extends above bill onto forehead; lacks barring on underparts; immature has barred underparts, crown and back. *Northern Mockingbird* (p. 260): slim bill; no "mask"; slimmer overall; paler wings and tail.

Best Sites: ***MN:*** open, brushy WMAs; prairie areas; North Shore of L. Superior; Aitkin Co. ***WI:*** *Winter:* open areas near woods.

WHITE-EYED VIREO

Vireo griseus

Proclaiming its spring arrival, the White-eyed Vireo sings *chick-ticha-wheeyou, chick-ticha-wheeyou-chick* among vibrant, early spring blossoms in local forests. Like most members of the vireo clan, the White-eyed Vireo can be a challenge to spot as it sneaks through dense tangles of branches and foliage in search of insects. • Even more secretive than the bird itself is the location of its precious nest. Intricately woven from grass, twigs, bark, lichens, moss, plant down, leaves and the fibrous paper from a wasp nest, the nest of a White-eyed Vireo is hung between the forking branches of a tree or shrub. • White-eyed Vireos are renowned for their complex vocalizations. A single bird may have a repertoire of a dozen or more songs. This vireo is also an excellent vocal mimic and may incorporate the calls of other bird species in its own songs!

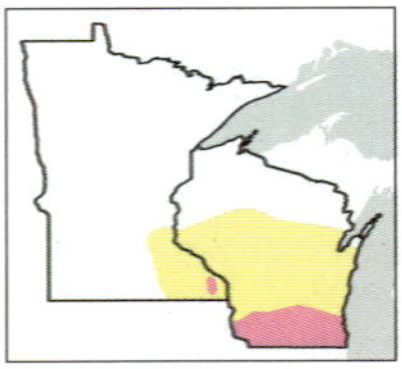

ID: yellow "spectacles"; pale eyes; olive gray upperparts; white underparts; yellow sides and flanks; 2 white wing bars; dark wings and tail.

Size: *L* 5 in; *W* 7½ in.

Status: ***MN:*** casual migrant in May; only 2 fall records, both in October; a few June and July records indicate possible nesting in the state; 1 possible nesting record (1991). ***WI:*** uncommon migrant from late April to early June and from late August to mid-October; very uncommon to rare breeder in southern areas.

Habitat: dense, shrubby undergrowth and thickets in open, swampy, deciduous woodlands, overgrown fields, young second-growth woodlands, woodland clearings and along woodlot edges.

Nesting: in a deciduous shrub or small tree; cup nest hangs from a horizontal fork; pair incubates 4 lightly speckled, white eggs for 13–15 days; both adults feed the young.

Feeding: gleans insects from branches and foliage during very active foraging; often hovers while gleaning.

Voice: loud, snappy, 3–9-note song, usually beginning and ending with "chick": *chick-ticha-wheeyou, chick-ticha-wheeyou-chick!*

Similar Species: *Pine Warbler* (p. 281) and *Yellow-throated Vireo* (p. 218): yellow throat. *Blue-headed Vireo* (p. 219): white "spectacles"; dark eyes; yellow highlights on wings and tail.

Best Sites: ***MN:*** Houston Co. ***WI:*** ***Breeding:*** Governor Dodge SP; Wyalusing SP; Brooklyn WA; Baxter's Hollow; Duck Lake Nature Trail (L. Geneva).

BELL'S VIREO

Vireo bellii

The Bell's Vireo can easily be mistaken for a number of other birds because of its subtle colors and markings—it is among the most nondescript of all vireos. Seldom nesting higher than 6 feet off the ground, these tough-to-spot songsters will boldly sing in close proximity to the nest, with males sometimes singing while incubating the eggs! • The Bell's Vireo eats insects almost exclusively. This bird's strong, slightly curved bill, with a slight hook at the end like the bill of a miniature shrike, reminds us that however gentle these little birds might seem, they are, in fact, successful predators. • Nest parasitism by Brown-headed Cowbirds and the destruction of streamside habitat have caused noticeable declines in Bell's Vireo populations throughout much of its range.

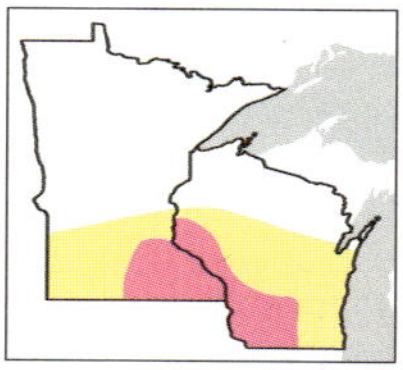

ID: gray to green upperparts; white to yellow underparts; 2 white wing bars (upper bar is usually faint if present); whitish "eyebrow"; whitish eye ring or lores or both. *Eastern (Midwest) form:* olive green above and yellow below.

Size: *L* 4½–5 in; *W* 7 in.

Status: ***MN:*** rare migrant and breeder in May and from July through August, primarily in southeastern and east-central regions. ***WI:*** endangered; uncommon migrant from early May to early June and in September; uncommon breeder.

Habitat: brushy fields and second-growth scrub; also hedgerows between fields, scrub oaks or woodland edges.

Nesting: small hanging cup of woven vegetation is suspended in a fork of a horizontal shrub branch, usually within 6 ft of the ground; pair incubates 3–5 white eggs, with dark dots concentrated at one end, for about 14 days; both adults feed the young.

Feeding: gleans insects from foliage; also catches insects by hawking or hovering; may eat spiders and occasionally berries.

Voice: song is a rapid, nonmusical series of harsh notes, *chu-che-chu-che-chu-che,* increasing in volume and often ending with an upward or downward inflection on the last note.

Similar Species: *Ruby-crowned Kinglet* (p. 247): 2 distinct, white wing bars; bold, broken eye ring; sings 3-part, descending phrases. *Warbling Vireo* (p. 220): longer proportions; sings an extended series of slurred whistles.

Best Sites: ***MN:*** Frontenac SP; Whitewater WMA; McCarthy Lake WMA. ***WI:*** Wyalusing SP; Governor Dodge SP; LaCrosse area; Brooklyn WA; Meridean.

YELLOW-THROATED VIREO

Vireo flavifrons

The Yellow-throated Vireo is usually found in mature deciduous woodlands with little or no understory and particularly likes tall oaks and maples. It prefers to forage high above the forest floor, making it a difficult bird to observe. • An unmated male will sing tirelessly as he searches for nest sites, often placing a few pieces of nest material in several locations. When a female appears, the male dazzles her with his displays and leads her on a tour of potential nest sites within his large territory. If a bond is established, they will mate and build an intricately woven, hanging nest in the forking branches of a deciduous tree. The male is a devoted helper, assisting the female to build the nest, incubate the eggs and rear the young. • The Yellow-throat is North America's most colorful vireo. It is the only vireo with a bright yellow throat and breast and white belly.

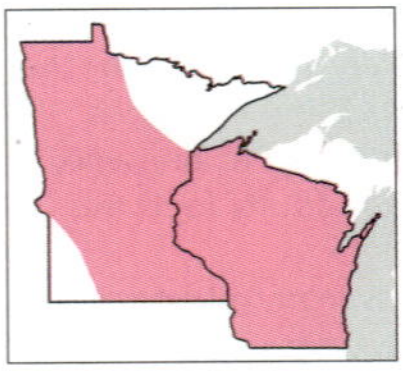

ID: bright yellow "spectacles," "chin," throat and breast; olive upperparts, except for gray rump and dark wings and tail; 2 white wing bars; white belly and undertail coverts.

Size: *L* 5½ in; *W* 9½ in.

Status: ***MN:*** uncommon migrant from late April to early June and from late July to early October; uncommon breeder; rare to absent in the northeast and southwest. ***WI:*** fairly common migrant from late April through May and from late August to late September; fairly common breeder, except in the north where it is uncommon.

Habitat: mature deciduous woodlands with minimal understory.

Nesting: pair builds a hanging cup nest in the fork of a horizontal, deciduous tree branch; pair incubates 4 creamy white to pinkish eggs, with dark spots toward the larger end, for 14–15 days; each parent takes on guardianship of half the fledged young.

Feeding: forages by inspecting branches and foliage in the upper canopy; eats mostly insects, but will also feed on seasonally available berries.

Voice: song is a slowly repeated series of hoarse phrases with long pauses in between: *ahweeo, eeoway, away;* calls include a throaty *heh heh heh.*

Similar Species: *Pine Warbler* (p. 281): olive yellow rump; thinner bill; faint, darkish streaking along sides; yellow belly; faint "spectacles." *White-eyed Vireo* (p. 216): white "chin" and throat; grayer head and back; white eyes. *Blue-headed Vireo* (p. 219): white "spectacles" and throat; yellow highlights in wings and tail.

Best Sites: ***MN:*** Afton SP; Whitewater WMA; Sakatah Lake SP; William O'Brien SP; Sibley SP. ***WI:*** Wyalusing SP; Trempealeau NWR; Governor Dodge SP; Devil's Lake SP; Brooklyn WA; LaCrosse; Tiffany Bottoms.

BLUE-HEADED VIREO

Vireo solitarius

From the canopies of shady woodlands, the purposeful, liquid notes of the Blue-headed Vireo penetrate the dense foliage. This vireo prefers different habitat than many of its relatives, which favor broadleaf trees or immature stands. Though this bird is also found in deciduous habitats, it is the only vireo that commonly occupies coniferous forests. • During courtship, male Blue-headed Vireos fluff out their yellowish flanks and bob ceremoniously to their prospective mates. When mating is complete and the eggs are in the nest, the parents become extremely quiet. Once the young hatch, however, Blue-headed parents will readily scold an intruder long before it gets close to the nest. • The distinctive "spectacles" that frame this bird's eyes provide a good field mark. They are among the boldest of the eye rings seen on our songbirds.

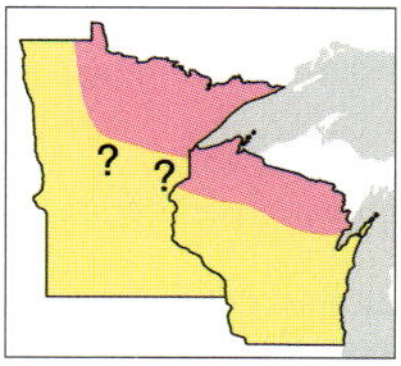

ID: white "spectacles"; blue gray head; 2 white wing bars; olive green upperparts; white underparts; yellow sides and flanks; yellow highlights on dark wings and tail; stout bill; dark legs.

Size: *L* 5–6 in; *W* 9½ in.

Status: ***MN:*** uncommon to occasionally common migrant in May and from late August to October; uncommon breeder. ***WI:*** uncommon migrant; uncommon breeder in the north; isolated nesting elsewhere.

Habitat: primarily remote, mixed coniferous-deciduous forests; also pure coniferous forests and pine plantations.

Nesting: in a horizontal fork in a coniferous tree or tall shrub; hanging, basketlike cup nest is made of grass, roots, plant down, spider silk and cocoons; pair incubates 3–5 whitish eggs, lightly spotted with black and brown, for 12–14 days.

Feeding: gleans branches for insects; frequently hovers to pluck insects from vegetation.

Voice: *churr* call. *Male:* slow, purposeful, slurred, robinlike notes with moderate pauses in between: *chu-wee, taweeto, toowip, cheerio, teeyay.*

Similar Species: *White-eyed Vireo* (p. 216): yellow "spectacles"; light-colored eyes. *Yellow-throated Vireo* (p. 218): yellow "spectacles" and throat.

Best Sites: ***MN:*** William O'Brien SP; Banning SP; Superior NF; Chippewa NF; woodlands throughout the state during migration. ***WI:*** northern mixed deciduous-coniferous forests in Douglas, Bayfield, Vilas, Oneida and Forest Counties.

WARBLING VIREO

Vireo gilvus

The charming Warbling Vireo lacks flashy field marks and is only readily observed when it moves from one leaf-hidden stage to another. • By early May, the Warbling Vireo's wondrous voice fills local parks and backyards. Because this vireo often settles close to urban areas, its bubbly, warbling songs should be familiar to most people. Warbling Vireos prefer mature deciduous trees as foraging and nest sites. In migration, however, they can be found in urban shade trees, second-growth and alder and willow thickets, often with other vireos and warblers. • The hanging nests of vireos are usually much harder to find than the birds themselves. In winter, however, nests are revealed as they swing precariously from bare deciduous branches.

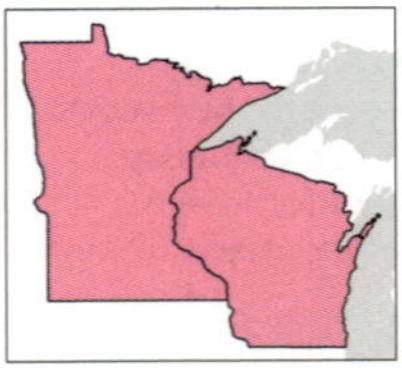

ID: partial, dark eye line borders white "eyebrow"; no wing bars; olive gray upperparts; greenish flanks; white to pale gray underparts; gray crown; blue gray legs and feet.

Size: *L* 5–5½ in; *W* 8½ in.

Status: ***MN:*** common migrant and breeder from late April to late September; uncommon to rare over much of the northwest. ***WI:*** common migrant and breeder from early May to mid-September.

Habitat: open deciduous woodlands; parks and gardens with deciduous trees, especially poplars and maples.

Nesting: in a horizontal fork in a deciduous tree or shrub; hanging, basketlike cup nest is made of grass, roots, plant down, spider silk and a few feathers; pair incubates 4 darkly speckled, white eggs for 12–14 days.

Feeding: gleans foliage for insects; occasionally hovers to glean insects from vegetation.

Voice: *Male:* long, musical warble of slurred whistles.

Similar Species: *Philadelphia Vireo* (p. 221): yellow breast, sides and flanks; full, dark eye line borders white "eyebrow." *Red-eyed Vireo* (p. 222): black eye line extends to bill; blue gray crown; red eyes. *Tennessee Warbler* (p. 268): blue gray "cap" and nape; olive green back; slimmer bill. *Orange-crowned Warbler* (p. 269): yellow overall; slimmer bill.

Best Sites: ***MN:*** Lac Qui Parle SP; deciduous woodlands. ***WI:*** scattered trees and woods, often near water.

PHILADELPHIA VIREO

Vireo philadelphicus

While many similar-looking birds sound quite different, the Philadelphia Vireo and the Red-eyed Vireo are two species that sound very similar but are easy to tell apart once you locate them with your binoculars. Most forest songbirds are initially identified by voice, however, so the Philadelphia Vireo is often overlooked because its song is almost identical to that of the more abundant Red-eyed Vireo. • The Philadelphia Vireo nests in mixed boreal forest, where it fills a niche left unoccupied by the strictly deciduous-dwelling Warbling Vireo. It can also peacefully share habitat with the Red-eyed Vireo. • The Philadelphia Vireo breeds farther north than any other vireo. In migration, it often travels in the company of other warblers and vireos. • This bird bears the name of the city in which the first specimen was collected in 1842.

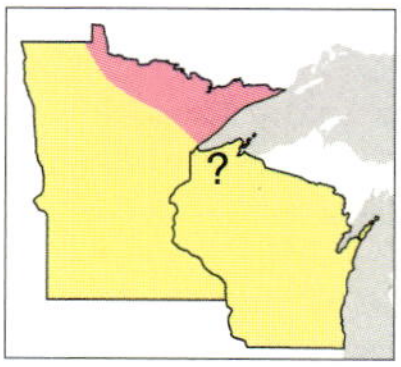

ID: gray "cap"; full, dark eye line borders bold, white "eyebrow"; dark olive green upperparts; pale yellow breast, sides and flanks; white belly (underparts may be completely yellow in fall); robust bill; pale eyes.

Size: *L* $4\frac{1}{2}$–5 in; *W* 8 in.

Status: ***MN:*** uncommon to rare migrant from early May to early June and from mid-August to early October; uncommon to rare breeder. ***WI:*** uncommon migrant in May; fairly common migrant from late August to early October; very casual to accidental breeder.

Habitat: open broadleaf and mixed woodlands with aspen, willow and alder components; second-growth on burns and cutovers; occasionally in gardens and parks.

Nesting: high in a deciduous tree or low in a shrub; basketlike cup nest hangs from a horizontal fork; nest is made of grass, roots, plant down and spider silk; pair incubates 4 white eggs, darkly spotted on the larger end, for about 14 days.

Feeding: gleans vegetation for insects; frequently hovers to glean food from foliage.

Voice: song is similar to that of the Red-eyed Vireo, but is usually slower, slightly higher pitched and not as variable: *Look-up way-up tree-top see-me.*

Similar Species: *Red-eyed Vireo* (p. 222): black-bordered, blue gray "cap"; red eyes; lacks yellow breast; song is very similar. *Warbling Vireo* (p. 220): partial, dark eye line (mostly behind eye); lacks yellow breast. *Tennessee Warbler* (p. 268): blue gray "cap" and nape; olive green back; slimmer bill; lacks yellow breast.

Best Sites: ***MN:*** North Shore of L. Superior; northern Lake Co. and Cook Co.; mixed woodlands in migration. ***WI:*** UW-Madison Arboretum; Wyalusing SP; Heckrodt Wetlands Reserve; Bay Beach Wildlife Sanctuary; High Cliff SP; Wisconsin Pt.; Harrington Beach SP; Milwaukee parks.

RED-EYED VIREO

Vireo olivaceus

The Red-eyed Vireo is the undisputed champion of vocal endurance in our region. In spring and early summer, males sing continuously throughout the day, carrying on long after most songbirds have curtailed their courtship melodies, usually five or six hours after sunrise. One particularly vigorous Red-eyed Vireo male holds the record for the most songs delivered in a single day: approximately 21,000! • The Red-eyed Vireo adopts a particular stance when it hops up and along branches. It tends to be more hunched over than other songbirds, and hops with its body diagonal to the direction of travel. • There is no firm agreement about the reason for this vireo's eye color. Most other vireos, including young Red-eyes, have brown irises. Red eyes are very unusual among songbirds and tend to be more prevalent in nonpasserines, such as accipiters, grebes and some herons. • This vireo is the most common and widespread vireo in our region. Red-eyed Vireos sound a lot like American Robins, and beginning birders are often delighted to discover these nifty birds hiding behind a familiar song.

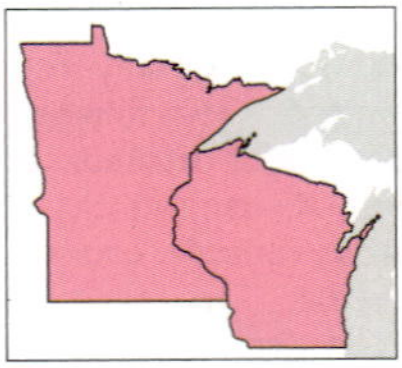

ID: dark eye line; white "eyebrow"; black-bordered, blue gray crown; olive green upperparts; olive "cheek"; white to pale gray underparts; may have yellow wash on sides, flanks and undertail coverts, especially in fall; no wing bars; red eyes (seen only at close range).

Size: *L* 6 in; *W* 10 in.

Status: ***MN:*** common to abundant (at times of peak migration) migrant and breeder from early May to mid-October. ***WI:*** abundant migrant and breeder from early May to mid-October.

Habitat: deciduous woodlands with a shrubby understory; shade trees and shrubbery in urban parks and gardens.

Nesting: in a horizontal fork in a deciduous tree or shrub; hanging, basketlike cup nest is made of grass, roots, spider silk and cocoons; female incubates 4 white eggs, darkly spotted at the larger end, for 11–14 days.

Feeding: gleans foliage for insects, especially caterpillars; often hovers; also eats berries.

Voice: call is a short, scolding *neeah. Male:* song is a continuous, variable, robinlike run of quick, short phrases with distinct pauses in between: *Look-up, way-up, tree-top, see-me, here-I-am!*

Similar Species: *Philadelphia Vireo* (p. 221): yellow breast; lacks black border to blue gray "cap"; song is very similar but slightly higher pitched. *Warbling Vireo* (p. 220): dusky eye line does not extend to bill; lacks black border on gray "cap." *Tennessee Warbler* (p. 268): blue gray "cap" and nape; olive green back; slimmer bill.

Best Sites: deciduous forests throughout both states.

GRAY JAY

Perisoreus canadensis

Few other birds of our region rival the mischievous Gray Jay for curiosity and boldness. Attracted by any foreign sound or potential feeding opportunity, small family groups glide gently and unexpectedly out of spruce, pine and fir stands. Campgrounds and picnic areas are the most common places to find these mooching marauders. • Gray Jays lay their eggs and begin incubation as early as late February. Their nests are well insulated to conserve heat, and early nesting means that young jays will learn how to forage efficiently and store food before the next cold season approaches. • In preparation for winter, Gray Jays often store food. Their specialized salivary glands coat the food with a sticky mucus that helps to preserve it. • This common bird has a number of alternate names: "Whiskey Jack" is derived from the Algonquin name for this bird, *wis-kat-jon;* others affectionately call this bird "Camp Robber" and "Canada Jay."

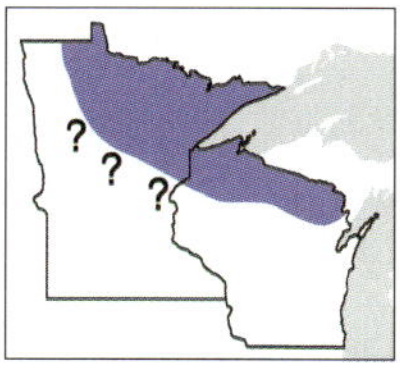

ID: fluffy, pale gray plumage; fairly long tail; white forehead, "cheek," throat and undertail coverts; dark gray nape and upperparts; light gray breast and belly; dark bill. *Immature:* dark sooty gray overall; pale bill with dark tip.

Size: *L* 11–13 in; *W* 18 in.

Status: ***MN:*** uncommon year-round resident; found in central and southern regions only when very irregular fall irruptions occur. ***WI:*** uncommon year-round resident.

Habitat: dense and open coniferous and mixed forests, bogs and fens; also picnic sites and campgrounds.

Nesting: on a branch in a coniferous tree; bulky, well-insulated nest is made of plant fibers, roots, moss, twigs, feathers and fur; female incubates 3–4 pale gray to greenish eggs, marked with brown, greenish or reddish dots, for 17–22 days.

Feeding: searches the ground and vegetation for insects, fruit, seeds, fungi, bird eggs and nestlings, carrion and berries; stores food items at scattered cache sites; will visit feeders in hard times.

Voice: complex vocal repertoire includes a soft, whistled *quee-oo,* a chuckled *cla-cla-cla* and a *churr;* also imitates other birds.

Similar Species: *Northern Shrike* (p. 215) and *Loggerhead Shrike* (p. 214): black "mask"; black-and-white wings and tail; hooked bill. *Northern Mockingbird* (p. 260): darker wings and tail; white patch on wings; white outer tail feathers; longer, slimmer bill.

Best Sites: ***MN:*** Superior NF; St. Louis, Lake and Cook Counties; North Shore of L. Superior during irregular irruptions. ***WI:*** Brule R. (Douglas Co.); forest roads in Vilas, Oneida and Forest Counties.

BLUE JAY

Cyanocitta cristata

The large trees and bushy ornamental shrubs of our suburban neighborhoods and rural communities are perfect habitat for the adaptable Blue Jay. Common wherever backyard feeding stations are maintained with a generous supply of sunflower seeds and peanuts, this jay is one of the most recognizable songbirds. • The Blue Jay embodies all the admirable traits and aggressive qualities of the corvid family, which also includes crows and ravens. Beautiful, resourceful and vocally diverse, the Blue Jay occasionally raids nests and bullies other feeder occupants. • Whether on its own or gathered in a mob, the Blue Jay will rarely hesitate to drive away smaller birds, squirrels or even cats when threatened. It seems there is no predator, not even the Great Horned Owl, that is too formidable for this bird to cajole or harass. • Migrating Blue Jays often form large flocks, sometimes consisting of thousands of birds. In winter, what may appear to be a dozen or so individual "regulars" at a feeder is often, in fact, three or four parties "doing the rounds."

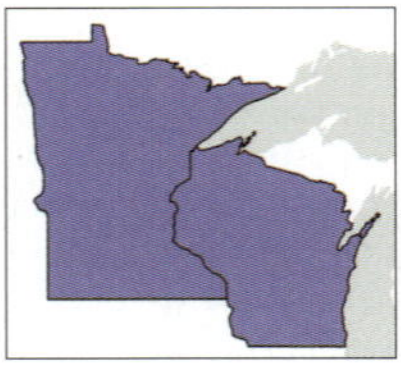

ID: blue crest; black bill; black eye line joins black "necklace"; blue upperparts; white underparts; white bar and flecking on wings; dark bars and white corners on blue tail.
Size: *L* 11–12½ in; *W* 16 in.
Status: ***MN:*** common to abundant migrant in May and from September to October; common to abundant year-round resident. ***WI:*** very common migrant and breeder from mid-April to late October; very common year-round resident.
Habitat: mixed and deciduous forests, agricultural areas, scrubby fields and townsites.
Nesting: in the crotch of a tree or tall shrub; pair builds a bulky stick nest and incubates 4–5 greenish, buff or pale blue eggs, spotted with gray and brown, for 16–18 days.
Feeding: forages on the ground and among vegetation for nuts, berries, eggs, nestlings and birdseed; also eats insects and carrion.
Voice: noisy, screaming *jay-jay-jay;* nasal *queedle queedle queedle-queedle* sounds a little like a muted trumpet; often imitates sounds.
Similar Species: *Belted Kingfisher* (p. 192); larger; unpatterned face; breast band; very different habits. *Eastern Bluebird* (p. 249): smaller; brighter blue on upperparts; no white markings; reddish on breast.
Best Sites: ***MN:*** woodlands and residential areas; Duluth and major river valleys in migration. ***WI:*** forests and residential areas.

BLACK-BILLED MAGPIE

Pica hudsonia

This impressive bird has recently established a foothold in our region. Many westerners are jaded by the omnipresence of magpies, but residents here who see this bird for the first time will be captivated by its beauty and approachability. • The Black-billed Magpie is one of the most exceptional architects among our birds. Its elaborate domed nest is usually located in a tree or cluster of dense shrubs with access to open territory. Constructed of sticks and held together with mud, the domed structure conceals and protects the eggs and young from harsh weather and most predators. The nests are so well built that they may remain abandoned in a tree for years before they are reused, often by nonbuilders such as Great Horned Owls. • The magpie's noisy penchant for mobbing roosting owls occasionally allows observers an entertaining glimpse of both the magpies and their annoyed target. Black-billed Magpies also regularly mob other predators, including domestic cats, coyotes and raptors. Being attacked by a noisy group of birds makes it difficult for the predator to hunt effectively and forces it to withdraw.

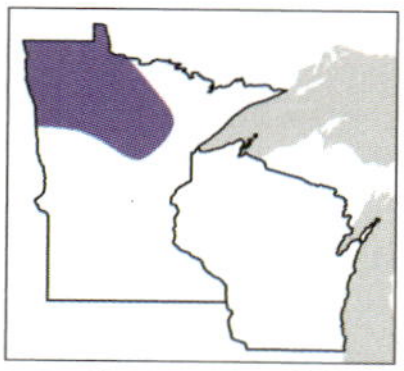

ID: long, black tail; black head, breast and back; rounded, black-and-white wings; black undertail coverts; black bill; white belly; greenish gloss on wings and tail; black legs.

Size: *L* 18–22 in; *W* 25 in.

Status: ***MN:*** uncommon year-round resident in the northwest and as far east as Aitkin Co.; increasing as a breeding species. ***WI:*** very rare to casual migrant and visitor from early April to mid-May and from early October to late November.

Habitat: groves of aspen, willow or alder among open farmlands.

Nesting: in a tree or tall shrub; domed, stick-and-twig nest has an interior cup of mud lined with grass, weeds and hair; female incubates 5–8 greenish gray eggs, heavily spotted with brown, for 16–24 days.

Feeding: forages on the ground for insects, carrion, human food waste, nuts, seeds and berries; may pick insects and ticks off livestock and deer; may eat some eggs and nestlings.

Voice: loud, nasal, frequently repeated *yeck-yeck-yeck;* many other vocalizations.

Similar Species: none.

Best Sites: ***MN:*** Agassiz NWR; Kittson Co.; Roseau Co.; Aitkin Co. ***WI:*** no consistent sites.

AMERICAN CROW

Corvus brachyrhynchos

American Crows are wary and intelligent birds that have flourished despite considerable human effort, over many generations, to reduce their numbers because of the damage they do to crops. These birds are ecological generalists, and much of their strength lies in their ability to adapt to a variety of habitats. • American Crows are common throughout much of our region in both summer and winter. In some places, up to 90,000 crows may roost together on any given winter night. In fall, most group together in flocks numbering in the hundreds or thousands. • Crows are impressive mimics, and some crows in captivity are able to repeat simple spoken words. • The American Crow's cumbersome-sounding scientific name *Corvus brachyrhynchos* is Latin for "raven with the small nose." Aggregations of crows are known as "murders."

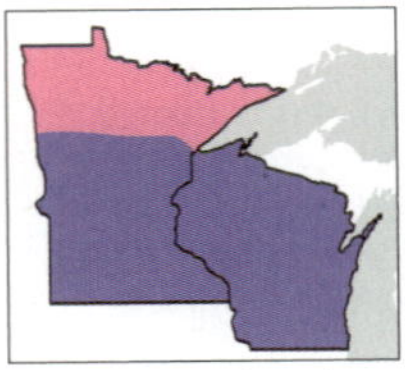

ID: black overall; glossy, purple black plumage; square-shaped tail; black bill and legs; sleek head and throat.

Size: *L* 17–21 in; *W* 3 ft.

Status: ***MN:*** abundant migrant and breeder from early February to late October; common in winter in the south but increasing numbers are occurring in the north. ***WI:*** abundant year-round resident in southern and central regions; common year-round resident in the north.

Habitat: urban areas, agricultural fields and other open areas with scattered woodlands; also among clearings, marshes, lakes and rivers in densely forested areas.

Nesting: in a coniferous or deciduous tree or on a utility pole; large stick-and-branch nest is lined with fur and soft plant materials; female incubates 4–6 gray green to blue green eggs, blotched with brown and gray, for about 18 days.

Feeding: very opportunistic; feeds on small vertebrates, carrion, other birds' eggs and nestlings, berries, seeds, invertebrates and human food waste.

Voice: distinctive, far-carrying, repetitive *caw-caw-caw.*

Similar Species: *Common Raven* (p. 227): larger; wedge-shaped tail; shaggy throat; heavier bill.

Best Sites: ***MN:*** *In migration:* Twin Cities area in the spring. *Winter:* roosts occur in many parts of the south, especially in large metropolitan areas. ***WI:*** woods, open farm fields and residential areas.

COMMON RAVEN

Corvus corax

Whether stealing food from a flock of gulls, harassing a soaring hawk in midair, dining from a roadside carcass or confidently strutting among campers at a park, the Common Raven is worthy of its reputation as a bold and clever bird. It is glorified in native cultures across North America as the avian embodiment of humankind because it exhibits behaviors that many people once thought of as exclusively human. • Ravens maintain loyal, lifelong pair bonds that are reinforced each winter in courtship chases consisting of drag races, barrel rolls, dives and tumbles. • Few birds occupy as large a natural range as the Common Raven. Distributed throughout the Northern Hemisphere, it is found along coastlines, in deserts, on mountaintops and even on arctic tundra. • The Common Raven is the largest passerine, or perching bird.

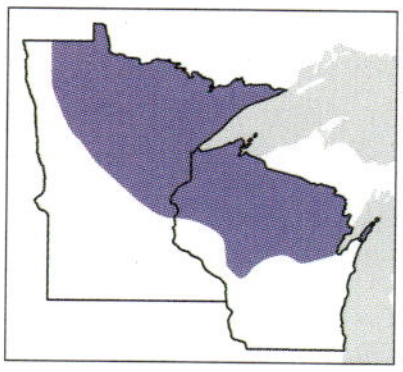

ID: glossy, black plumage; heavy, black bill; wedge-shaped tail; shaggy throat; rounded wings; black legs.

Size: *L* 17–21 in; *W* 3 ft.

Status: ***MN:*** uncommon to occasionally common year-round resident, primarily in boreal zones; may be expanding into central regions; rare migrant along the lower Mississippi R. valley. ***WI:*** common year-round resident in the north; uncommon year-round resident in the central region.

Habitat: coniferous and mixed forests and woodlands; also townsites, campgrounds and landfills.

Nesting: on a ledge, bluff or utility pole or in a tall coniferous tree; large stick-and-branch nest is lined with fur and soft plant materials; female incubates 4–6 greenish eggs, blotched with brown or olive, for 18–21 days.

Feeding: very opportunistic; some birds forage along roadways; feeds on carrion, small vertebrates, other birds' eggs and nestlings, berries, invertebrates and human food waste.

Voice: deep, guttural, far-carrying, repetitive *craww-craww* or *quork quork;* also many other vocalizations.

Similar Species: *American Crow* (p. 226): smaller; square-shaped tail; slim throat; slimmer bill; call is a higher-pitched *caw-caw-caw*.

Best Sites: ***MN:*** *In migration:* Hawk Ridge (Duluth); especially in northeastern forests in Cook, Lake, St. Louis, Carlton and Pine Counties; also Aitkin Co. ***WI:*** northern forests.

HORNED LARK

Eremophila alpestris

The tinkling sounds of Horned Larks flying over pastures and fields are a sure sign that another spring has arrived. Horned Larks are among the earliest arrivals in our region, settling on fields in February, long before the snows are gone. • The male Horned Lark performs an elaborate song-flight courtship display, flying and gliding in circles as high up as 800 feet. After singing his sweet, tinkling song, he closes his wings and plummets downward in a dramatic, high-speed dive that he aborts just before hitting the ground. • In our region, these open-country inhabitants congregate in flocks, sometimes numbering in the thousands, on farm fields. They are often seen in the company of Snow Buntings and Lapland Longspurs, their pale plumage blending in with the surrounding landscape. Horned Larks are also commonly found along the shoulders of gravel roads, where they search for seeds. They are easy to see, but often tough to identify, because they fly off into adjacent fields at the approach of any vehicle.

♂

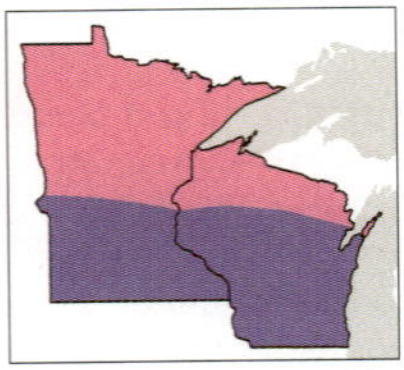

ID: *Male:* small, black "horns" (rarely raised); black line under eye extends from bill to "cheek"; light yellow to white face; dull brown upperparts; black breast band; dark tail with white outer tail feathers; pale throat. *Female:* less distinctively patterned; duller plumage overall.

Size: *L* 7 in; *W* 12 in.

Status: ***MN:*** common to abundant migrant and breeder from mid-January to late November; uncommon to rare in north-central and northeastern regions away from L. Superior; occurs in winter primarily in the south. ***WI:*** common migrant and breeder from early February to early December; fairly common winter visitor.

Habitat: *Breeding:* open areas including pastures, croplands, sparsely vegetated fields, weedy meadows and airfields. *In migration* and *winter:* croplands, roadside ditches and fields.

Nesting: on the ground in a shallow scrape lined with grass, plant fibers and roots; female chooses the nest site and incubates 3–4 pale gray to greenish white eggs, blotched and spotted with brown, for 10–12 days.

Feeding: gleans the ground for seeds; feeds insects to its young during the breeding season.

Voice: call is a tinkling *tsee-titi* or *zoot;* flight song is a long series of tinkling, twittered whistles.

Similar Species: *Sparrows* (pp. 307–24), *Longspurs* (pp. 326–28) and *American Pipit* (p. 263): all lack distinctive facial pattern, "horns" and solid black breast band.

Best Sites: ***MN:*** *In migration* and *winter:* roadsides and open fields; western counties in February and March. ***WI:*** *In migration* and *winter:* roadsides and open fields.

PURPLE MARTIN

Progne subis

Purple Martins once nested in natural tree hollows and cliff crevices, but with today's modern martin "condo" complexes, these birds have all but abandoned natural nest sites. To be successful in attracting these large swallows to your backyard, a martin complex should be placed high on a pole in a large, open area, preferably near water. The condo complex must be designed with correctly sized cavity openings and should be cleaned out each winter. Purple Martins provide an endlessly entertaining summer spectacle, as the martin adults spiral around the house in pursuit of flying insects, and the juveniles perch clumsily at the opening of their apartment cavity. Unfortunately, there is always the chance that aggressive House Sparrows or European Starlings will lay claim to the luxurious digs and chase away any Purple Martins that dare to move in. • The scientific name *Progne* refers to Procne, the daughter of the king of Athens who, according to Greek mythology, was transformed into a swallow.

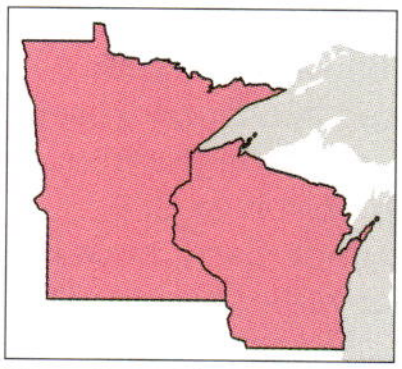

ID: dark blue, glossy body; slightly forked tail; pointed wings; small bill. *Male:* dark underparts. *Female:* sooty gray underparts.

Size: *L* 7–8 in; *W* 18 in.

Status: ***MN:*** common migrant and breeder from early April to early October; numbers have declined drastically in recent years to where it may now be uncommon in many areas. ***WI:*** common migrant and breeder from early April to mid-September.

Habitat: semi-open areas including gardens and fields, often near water.

Nesting: communal; usually in a human-made, apartment-style birdhouse; nest materials include feathers, grass, mud and vegetation; female incubates 4–5 white eggs for 15–18 days.

Feeding: mostly while in flight; usually eats flies, ants, bugs, dragonflies and mosquitoes; may also walk on the ground, taking insects and rarely berries.

Voice: rich, fluty, robinlike *pew-pew,* often heard in flight.

Similar Species: *European Starling* (p. 262): longer bill (yellow in summer); lacks forked tail. *Barn Swallow* (p. 234): deeply forked tail; buff orange to reddish brown throat; whitish to cinnamon underparts. *Tree Swallow* (p. 230): white underparts.

Best Sites: ***MN:*** Mille Lacs L.; Leech L.; Tamarac NWR; larger lakes in Otter Tail Co. ***WI:*** martin "condos" near lakes in various parts of the state, including L. Winnebago, L. Mendota, L. Geneva, Yellowstone L., Green L., Petenwell L. and Rainbow L.

TREE SWALLOW

Tachycineta bicolor

Tree Swallows, our most common summer swallows, are often seen perched beside their fence-post nest boxes. When conditions are favorable, these busy birds may return to their young 10 to 20 times per hour, providing observers with numerous opportunities to watch the birds in action. • Tree Swallows prefer to nest in natural tree hollows or woodpecker cavities in standing dead trees, but where cavities are scarce, nest boxes may be used as temporary sites. Increasingly, landowners, park managers and forestry companies are realizing the value of dead trees as homes for wildlife and are choosing to leave them standing. • In bright spring sunshine, the iridescent back of the Tree Swallow appears dark blue; prior to fall migration, it appears green. Unlike other North American swallows, female Tree Swallows do not acquire their full adult plumage until their second or third year.

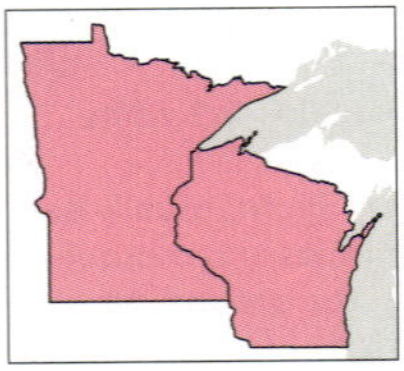

ID: iridescent, dark blue or green head and upperparts; white underparts; no white on "cheek"; dark rump; small bill; long, pointed wings; shallowly forked tail. *Female:* slightly duller. *Immature:* brown upperparts; white underparts.

Size: *L* 5½ in; *W* 14½ in.

Status: ***MN:*** common to abundant migrant and breeder from late March to late October. ***WI:*** abundant migrant and breeder from late March to late October.

Habitat: open areas, such as marshes, lakeshores, field fencelines, townsites and open woodlands.

Nesting: in a tree cavity or nest box lined with weeds, grass and feathers; female incubates 4–6 white eggs for up to 19 days.

Feeding: catches flies, midges, mosquitoes, beetles and ants on the wing; also takes stoneflies, mayflies and caddisflies over water; may eat some berries and seeds.

Voice: alarm call is a metallic, buzzy *klweet*. *Male:* song is a liquid, chattering twitter.

Similar Species: *Purple Martin* (p. 229): female has sooty gray underparts; male is dark blue overall. *Eastern Kingbird* (p. 213): larger; white-tipped tail; longer bill; dark gray to blackish upperparts. *Bank Swallow* (p. 232) and *Northern Rough-winged Swallow* (p. 231): brown upperparts. *Barn Swallow* (p. 234): buff orange to reddish brown throat; deeply forked tail.

Best Sites: ***MN:*** Heron L. (Jackson Co.); near lakes throughout the state. ***WI:*** widespread at nest boxes on fence posts and near swamps and fields.

NORTHERN ROUGH-WINGED SWALLOW

Stelgidopteryx serripennis

The inconspicuous Northern Rough-winged Swallow typically nests in sandy banks along rivers and streams, enjoying its own private piece of waterfront. This swallow is usually seen in single pairs, but it doesn't mind joining a crowd, often gulping down insects in the company of other swallow species. Once in a while, a pair may nest among a large colony of Bank Swallows. The largest concentrations of Northern Rough-wings are seen in the fall, when flocks of 100 or more can be found. • Unlike other swallows in our region, male Northern Rough-wings have curved barbs along the outer edge of their primary wing feathers. The purpose of this saw-toothed edge remains a mystery, but may be used to produce sound during courtship displays. The ornithologist who initially named this bird must have been very impressed with its wings: *Stelgidopteryx* means "scraper wing" and *serripennis* means "saw feather."

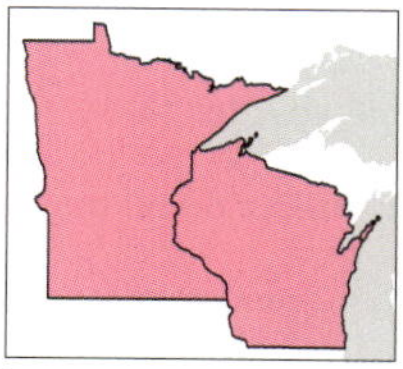

ID: brown upperparts; creamy white underparts; gray brown wash on chest and sides; small bill; dark "cheek"; dark rump. *In flight:* long, pointed wings; notched tail.

Size: *L* 5½ in; *W* 14 in

Status: ***MN:*** common migrant and local breeder from mid-April to early October; uncommon in the northeast. ***WI:*** fairly common migrant from mid-April to mid-May and from early July to mid-September; fairly common breeder in southern and central regions; uncommon breeder in the north.

Habitat: open and semi-open areas, including fields and open woodlands, usually near water.

Nesting: occasionally in small colonies; at the end of a burrow lined with leaves and dry grass; sometimes reuses a kingfisher burrow, rodent burrow or other land crevice; mostly the female incubates 4–8 white eggs for 12–16 days.

Feeding: catches flying insects in midair; occasionally eats insects from the ground; drinks on the wing.

Voice: generally quiet; occasionally a quick, short, squeaky *brrrtt*.

Similar Species: *Bank Swallow* (p. 232): dark breast band. *Tree Swallow* (p. 230): dark, iridescent bluish to greenish upperparts; clean white underparts. *Cliff Swallow* (p. 233): brown-and-blue upperparts; buff forehead and rump patch.

Best Sites: ***MN:*** lakes and streams with suitable banks for nesting burrows; Interstate SP; Fort Snelling SP. ***WI:*** inland lakes and streams; Baxter's Hollow; Devil's Lake SP; Mississippi R. and tributaries.

BANK SWALLOW

Riparia riparia

A colony of Bank Swallows can be a constant flurry of activity as eager parents pop in and out of their earthen burrows with mouthfuls of insects for their insatiable young. Not surprisingly, all this activity tends to attract attention, but few predators are able to catch these swift and agile birds. In summer, these gregarious swallows can be found in colonies that may range in size from 10 to nearly 2000 nests. • Bank Swallows usually excavate their own nest burrows, first using their small bills and later digging with their feet. Most nestlings are safe from predators deep within their nest chamber, which is typically 2 to 3 feet in length. • In medieval Europe, it was believed that swallows spent the winter in the mud at the bottom of swamps because they were not seen at that time of year. In those days, it was beyond imagination that these birds might fly south for the winter.

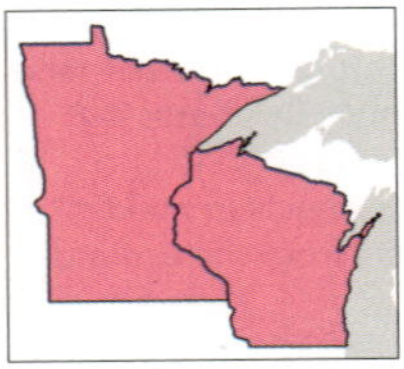

ID: brown upperparts; light underparts; brown breast band; white throat; dark "cheek"; long, pointed wings; shallowly forked tail.

Size: *L* 5½ in; *W* 13 in.

Status: ***MN:*** common migrant and local breeder from mid-April to September; uncommon in northeastern and north-central regions. ***WI:*** common migrant and breeder from mid-April to mid-September.

Habitat: steep banks, lakeshore bluffs and open areas, such as sand or gravel pits.

Nesting: colonial; pair excavates or reuses a long burrow in a steep earthen bank or cliff; the end of the burrow is lined with grass, rootlets, weeds, straw and feathers; pair incubates 4–5 white eggs for 14–16 days.

Feeding: catches flying insects; drinks on the wing.

Voice: twittering chatter: *speed-zeet speed-zeet.*

Similar Species: *Northern Rough-winged Swallow* (p. 231): lacks dark, defined breast band. *Tree Swallow* (p. 230): iridescent, dark bluish to greenish upperparts; lacks dark breast band. *Cliff Swallow* (p. 233): brown-and-blue upperparts; buff forehead and rump; lacks dark breast band.

Best Sites: ***MN:*** *Breeding:* sand and gravel pits throughout the state. ***WI:*** *Breeding:* bluffs along L. Michigan, for example, near Port Washington and Cleveland; inland gravel pits.

CLIFF SWALLOW

Petrochelidon pyrrhonota

If the Cliff Swallow were renamed, it would probably be called "Bridge Swallow," because so many river bridges in eastern North America seem to have a colony living under them. If you stop to inspect the underside of a bridge, you may see hundreds of gourd-shaped mud nests stuck to the pillars and structural beams. Cliff Swallows may also construct their nests under the eaves of houses and other buildings, where they are susceptible to eviction by House Sparrows. • Master mud masons, Cliff Swallows roll mud into balls with their bills and press the pellets together to form their characteristic nests. While nesting, parents peer out of the circular neck of the nest, their gleaming eyes watching the world go by. • Cliff Swallows are brood parasites—females often lay one or more eggs in the temporarily vacant nests of neighboring Cliff Swallows. The owners of the parasitized nests accept the foreign eggs and care for them as if they were their own.

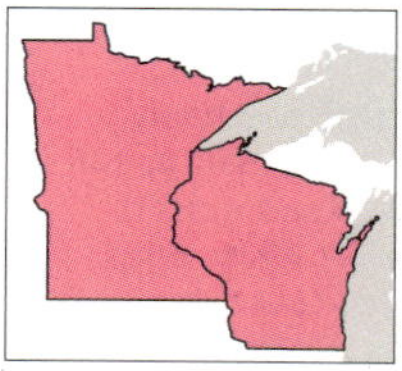

ID: orangy rump; buff forehead; blue gray head and wings; rusty "cheek," nape and throat; buff breast; white belly; spotted undertail coverts; nearly square tail.

Size: *L* 5½ in; *W* 13½ in.

Status: ***MN:*** common to abundant migrant and breeder from mid-April to early October; numbers have increased dramatically in recent years, especially in the northwest. ***WI:*** common migrant and breeder from late April to early October.

Habitat: steep banks, cliffs, bridges and buildings near watercourses.

Nesting: colonial; under a bridge or on a cliff or building; pair builds a gourd-shaped mud nest with a small opening near the bottom; pair incubates 4–5 brown-spotted, white to pinkish eggs for 14–16 days.

Feeding: forages over water, fields and marshes; catches flying insects on the wing; occasionally eats berries; drinks on the wing.

Voice: twittering chatter: *churrr-churrr;* also an alarm call: *nyew.*

Similar Species: *Barn Swallow* (p. 234): deeply forked tail; dark rump; usually has rust-colored underparts and forehead. *Other swallows* (pp. 229–34): lack buff forehead and rump patch.

Best Sites: ***MN:*** bridges over streams,especially in the northwest; also on barns. ***WI:*** bridges over rivers and streams; Wisconsin R. at Necedah–Petenwell L., Prairie du Sac, Sauk City and Spring Green; Mississippi R. at Prairie du Chien and LaCrosse; also on barns.

BARN SWALLOW

Hirundo rustica

Although Barn Swallows do not occur in mass colonies, they are very familiar birds because they usually build their nests on human-made structures. Barn Swallows once nested on cliffs and in the entrances to caves, but their cup-shaped mud nests are now found under house eaves, in barns and boathouses, under bridges or on any other structure that provides shelter from predators and inclement weather. Unfortunately, not everyone appreciates nesting Barn Swallows—the young can be very messy—and nests are often scraped off buildings just as the nesting season begins. However, these graceful birds are natural pest controllers and their close association with urban areas and tolerance for human activity affords us the wondrous opportunity to observe and study the normally secretive reproductive cycle of birds. • The most widely distributed swallow in the world, the Barn Swallow breeds over much of North America, Europe, Asia and Africa, and winters throughout the Southern Hemisphere.

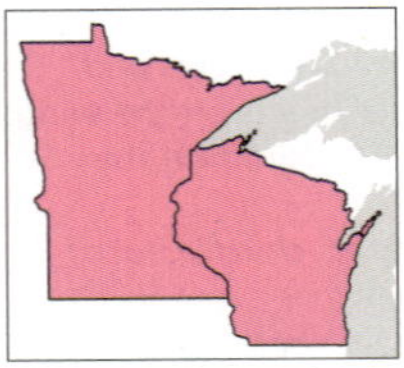

ID: long, deeply forked tail; rufous throat and forehead; blue black upperparts; rust- to buff-colored underparts; long, pointed wings.

Size: *L* 7 in; *W* 15 in.

Status: ***MN:*** common to abundant migrant and breeder from early April to late October, especially in western regions. ***WI:*** common migrant and breeder from mid-April to early October.

Habitat: open rural and urban areas where bridges, culverts and buildings are found near rivers, lakes, marshes or ponds.

Nesting: singly or in small, loose colonies; on a vertical or horizontal building structure under a suitable overhang, on a bridge or in a culvert; half or full cup nest is made of mud and grass or straw; pair incubates 4–7 white eggs, spotted with brown, for 13–17 days.

Feeding: catches flying insects on the wing.

Voice: continuous, twittering chatter: *zip-zip-zip;* also *kvick-kvick.*

Similar Species: *Cliff Swallow* (p. 233): squared tail; buff rump and forehead; pale underparts. *Purple Martin* (p. 229): shallowly forked tail; male is completely blue black; female has sooty gray underparts. *Tree Swallow* (p. 230): clean white underparts; notched tail.

Best Sites: ***MN:*** rural areas throughout the state. ***WI:*** barns, bridges and culverts over steams and lakes statewide.

BLACK-CAPPED CHICKADEE

Poecile atricapilla

In winter, Black-capped Chickadees often join the company of kinglets, nuthatches, creepers, small woodpeckers and sometimes Boreal Chickadees in what appears to be a celebration of life in the forest. At this time of year, these chickadees are common visitors to well-stocked feeders. They can even occasionally be enticed to land on an outstretched hand offering a sunflower seed. In summer, the best place to look for Black-capped Chickadees is wherever there are birch stands—they like to feast on the many insect pests found in these trees. • When foraging, Black-capped Chickadees swing upside down on tree branches, snatching up insects and berries. • Most songbirds have both songs and calls. The chickadee's *swee-tee* song is heard primarily during spring courtship. Its *chick-a-dee-dee-dee* call keeps flocks together and maintains contact between flock members.

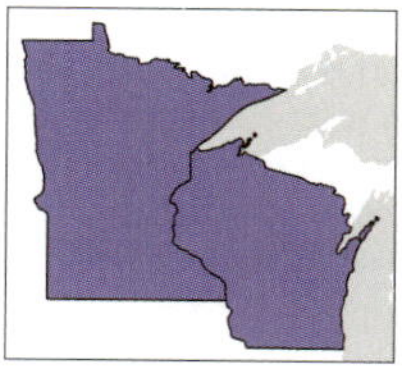

ID: black "cap" and "bib"; white "cheek"; gray back and wings; white underparts; light buff sides and flanks; dark legs; conspicuous white edging on wing feathers.

Size: *L* 5–6 in; *W* 8 in.

Status: ***MN:*** common to at times abundant year-round resident; migrates across the state in spring and fall. ***WI:*** abundant year-round resident and migrant.

Habitat: deciduous and mixed forests, woodlots, riparian woodlands, birch stands, wooded urban parks and backyards with bird feeders.

Nesting: excavates a cavity in a soft, rotting stump or tree; cavity is lined with fur, feathers, moss, grass and cocoons; female incubates 6–8 white eggs, finely dotted with reddish brown, for 12–13 days.

Feeding: gleans vegetation, branches and the ground for small insects and spiders; visits backyard feeders; also eats conifer seeds and invertebrate eggs.

Voice: call is a chipper, whistled *chick-a-dee-dee-dee;* song is a slow, whistled *swee-tee* or *fee-bee.*

Similar Species: *Boreal Chickadee* (p. 236): gray brown "cap," sides and flanks. *Blackpoll Warbler* (p. 285): breeding male has 2 white wing bars, dark streaking on white underparts, orangy legs and longer, paler bill.

Best Sites: urban areas at feeders; wooded wilderness areas.

BOREAL CHICKADEE

Poecile hudsonica

Birders generally love chickadees, and the Boreal Chickadee is especially sought after as the northern representative of this endearing clan. Unlike the more common and familiar Black-capped Chickadee, the Boreal Chickadee prefers the seclusion of coniferous forests, and it tends to be softer spoken. During the nesting season, these birds are so quiet that you would never know they were there at all. • Chickadees burn so much energy that they must replenish their stores daily to survive winter—they have insufficient fat reserves to survive a prolonged stretch of cold weather. Chickadees store food in holes and bark crevices where it will be easy to locate in an emergency. During a cold night, a chickadee enters a state of torpor, which slows the bird's metabolism so that it uses less energy. A chickadee can lower its body temperature at night by as much as 22° F.

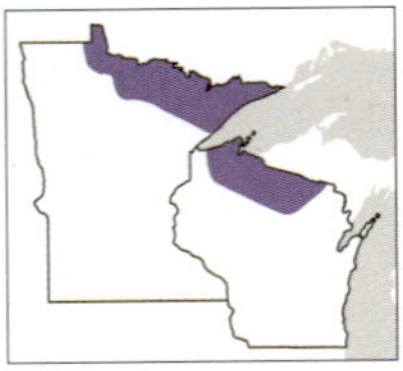

ID: gray brown "cap" and back; rufous flanks; black "chin" and "bib"; whitish to light gray breast and belly; whitish "cheek" patch; gray wings and tail; black bill.

Size: *L* 5–5$\frac{1}{2}$ in; *W* 8 in.

Status: ***MN:*** uncommon year-round resident; casual vagrant in the south in winter. ***WI:*** uncommon year-round resident.

Habitat: spruce, fir and pine forests; occasionally in mixed coniferous forests with a small deciduous component.

Nesting: excavates a cavity in soft, rotting wood or uses a natural cavity or abandoned woodpecker nest in a conifer; female lines the nest with fur, feathers, moss and grass; female incubates 5–8 white eggs, finely dotted with reddish brown, for 11–16 days.

Feeding: gleans vegetation, branches and infrequently the ground for spiders and small, tree-infesting insects (including their pupae and eggs); also eats conifer seeds.

Voice: call is a soft, nasal, wheezy *scick-a day day day,* slower and wheezier than the Black-capped Chickadee.

Similar Species: *Black-capped Chickadee* (p. 235): black "cap"; buffy flanks; more grayish than brownish overall.

Best Sites: ***MN:*** Sax-Zim Bog; North Shore of L. Superior; Superior NF; Lake Co. ***WI:*** northern spruce-fir forests and bogs, such as Pine L. (Forest Co.), Hiles–Three Lakes–Eagle River area (Three Lakes bog on Old A, forest roads 2174, 2178, 2182, 2183, 2414 and Fire Lane Road) and Rolling Stone L.

TUFTED TITMOUSE

Baeolophus bicolor

This bird's amusing feeding antics keep curious observers entertained at bird feeders. Grasping an acorn or sunflower seed with its tiny feet, the dexterous Tufted Titmouse strikes its dainty bill repeatedly against the seed's hard outer coating, exposing the inner core. • A breeding pair of Tufted Titmice will maintain their bond throughout the year, even when joining small, multispecies flocks for the cold winter months. The titmouse family bond is so strong that the young from one breeding season will often stay with their parents long enough to help with nesting and feeding duties the following year. In late winter, mating pairs leave their flocks to search for nesting cavities and soft lining material. If you have titmice living in your area, you might be able to attract nesting pairs by setting out the hair that has accumulated in your hairbrush. There is a good chance that these curious birds will gladly incorporate your offering into the construction of their nest.

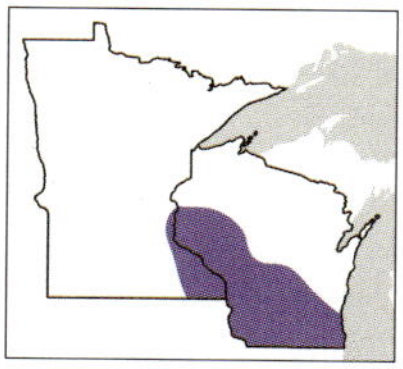

ID: gray crest and upperparts; black forehead; white underparts; buffy flanks.

Size: *L* 6–6½ in; *W* 10 in.

Status: ***MN:*** rare and local year-round resident in the southeast; casual or accidental in other regions. ***WI:*** uncommon year-round resident in southern and central regions; rare in the north.

Habitat: deciduous woodlands, groves and suburban parks with large, mature trees.

Nesting: in a natural cavity or woodpecker cavity lined with soft vegetation and animal hair; female may be fed by the male from courtship to time of hatching; female incubates 5–6 finely dotted, white eggs for 12–14 days; both adults and occasionally a "helper" raise the young.

Feeding: forages on the ground and in trees, often hanging upside down like a chickadee; eats insects supplemented with seeds, nuts and fruits; will eat seeds and suet from feeders.

Voice: noisy, scolding call, like that of a chickadee; song is a whistled *peter peter* or *peter peter peter*.

Similar Species: none.

Best Sites: ***MN:*** Houston Co.; Filmore Co.; Beaver Creek Valley SP; Forestville SP. ***WI:*** Wyalusing SP; near Mazomanie and Sauk City; Madison; LaCrosse; L. Geneva area; Governor Dodge SP.

RED-BREASTED NUTHATCH

Sitta canadensis

The Red-breasted Nuthatch looks a lot like a red rocket as it streaks toward a neighborhood bird feeder from the cover of a coniferous tree. The nuthatch ejects empty shells left behind by other birds and then selects its own meal before jetting off, never lingering longer than it takes to pick up a seed. • The Red-breasted Nuthatch stands out from other songbirds because of its unusual body form and its habit of moving headfirst down tree trunks. Its loud, nasal calls, which are frequently heard in spring, are also distinctive. • Red-breasted Nuthatches tend to make large-scale migrations every three or more years, perhaps owing to cone crop failure on their breeding grounds. • This bird smears the entrance of its nest cavity with pitch from pine or spruce trees. This sticky doormat may inhibit ants and other animals from entering the nest chamber. Invertebrates can be the most serious threat to nesting success because they can transmit fungal infections or parasitize nestlings.

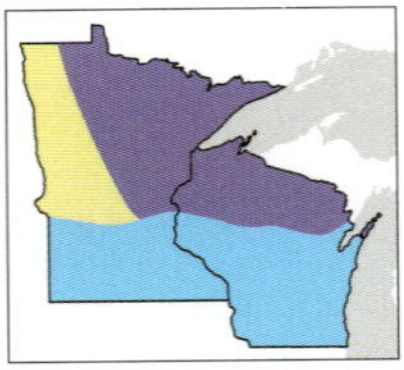

ID: rusty underparts; gray blue upperparts; white "eyebrow"; black eye line; black "cap"; straight bill; short tail; white "cheek." *Male:* deeper rust on breast; black crown. *Female:* light red wash on breast; dark gray crown.

Size: *L* 4½ in; *W* 8½ in.

Status: ***MN:*** common to uncommon year-round resident; widely distributed but local migrant and breeder in the north; uncommon to occasionally common migrant from early April to late May and from mid-August to early November; some birds winter in the south, but numbers fluctuate from year to year. ***WI:*** fairly common migrant from mid-April to late May and from late July to mid-November; fairly common breeder in the north; rare breeder in central regions; fairly common to common winter visitor.

Habitat: *Breeding:* spruce-fir and pine forests; pine plantations. *In migration* and *winter:* mixed woodlands, especially those near bird feeders.

Nesting: excavates a cavity or uses an abandoned woodpecker nest; usually smears the entrance with pitch; nest is made of bark shreds, grass and fur; female incubates 5–6 white eggs, spotted with reddish brown, for about 12 days.

Feeding: forages down trees while probing under loose bark for larval and adult invertebrates; eats pine and spruce seeds in winter; often seen at feeders.

Voice: call is a slow, continually repeated, nasal *eenk eenk eenk,* higher than the White-breasted Nuthatch; also a short *tsip.*

Similar Species: *White-breasted Nuthatch* (p. 239): larger; lacks black eye line and red underparts.

Best Sites: ***MN:*** northern boreal forests year-round; evergreen stands and feeders in the south. ***WI:*** *Breeding:* northern forests. *Winter:* forests and feeders in the south.

WHITE-BREASTED NUTHATCH

Sitta carolinensis

Moving headfirst down a tree trunk, the White-breasted Nuthatch forages for invertebrates, sometimes pausing to survey its surroundings and occasionally issuing a noisy call. Unlike woodpeckers and creepers, nuthatches do not use their tails to brace themselves against tree trunks—nuthatches grasp the tree through foot power alone. • To a novice birder, the sight of a White-breasted Nuthatch calling repeatedly while clinging to the underside of a branch is an odd one. To the bird, however, this gravity-defying act is totally natural, as is their ability to walk headfirst down a tree trunk. • Although White-breasted Nuthatches are regular visitors to backyard feeders, they never stick around longer than it takes to grab a seed and dash. Only an offering of suet can persuade this tiny bird to remain in a single spot for any length of time. • Nuthatches are presumably named for their habit of wedging seeds and nuts into crevices and hacking them open with their bills.

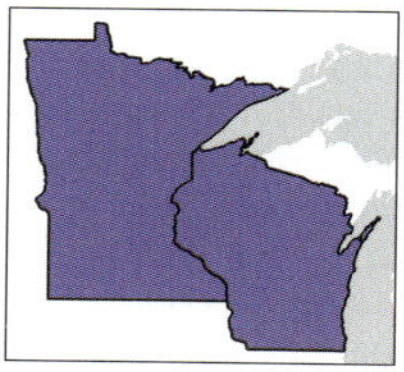

ID: white face and underparts; gray blue back; rusty flanks and undertail coverts; short tail; straight bill; short legs. *Male:* black "cap" and nape. *Female:* dark gray "cap" and black nape.

Size: *L* $5\frac{1}{2}$–6 in; *W* 11 in.

Status: ***MN:*** common year-round resident except in the northeast, where it may be only a spring and fall migrant. ***WI:*** common year-round resident.

Habitat: mixedwood forests, woodlots and backyards.

Nesting: in a natural cavity or abandoned woodpecker nest in a large deciduous tree; female lines the cavity with bark, grass, fur and feathers; female incubates 5–8 white eggs, spotted with reddish brown, for 12–14 days.

Feeding: forages down trees headfirst in search of larval and adult invertebrates; also eats nuts and seeds; regularly visits feeders.

Voice: song is a fast, nasal *yank-hank yank-hank,* lower than the Red-breasted Nuthatch; calls include *ha-ha-ha ha-ha-ha, ank ank* and *ip.*

Similar Species: *Red-breasted Nuthatch* (p. 238): black eye line; rusty underparts. *Black-capped Chickadee* (p. 235): black "bib."

Best Sites: ***MN:*** widely distributed wherever there are woods; at feeders in winter. ***WI:*** at feeders and in woods.

BROWN CREEPER

Certhia americana

The cryptic Brown Creeper is never easy to find, often going unnoticed until a flake of bark suddenly takes the shape of a bird. If a creeper is frightened, it will freeze and flatten itself against a tree trunk, becoming even more difficult to see. • The Brown Creeper feeds by slowly spiraling up a tree trunk, searching for hidden invertebrates. When the creeper reaches the upper branches, it floats down to the base of a neighboring tree to begin another foraging ascent. Its long, stiff tail feathers prop it up against vertical tree trunks as it hitches its way skyward. • Like the call of the Golden-crowned Kinglet, the thin whistle of the Brown Creeper is so high pitched that birders often fail to hear it. To increase the confusion, the creeper's song often takes on the boisterous, warbling quality of a wood-warbler song. • There are many species of creepers in Europe and Asia, but the Brown Creeper is the only member of its family found in North America.

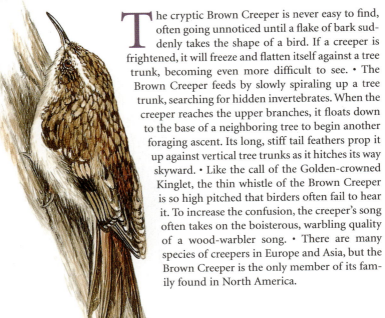

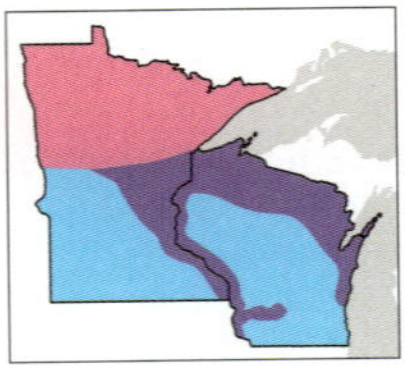

ID: dark brown upperparts are heavily streaked with buffy white; white "eyebrow"; white underparts; downcurved bill; long, pointed tail feathers; rusty rump.
Size: *L* 5–5½ in; *W* 7½ in.
Status: ***MN:*** uncommon to at times common migrant from mid-March to late May and from September through November; uncommon to local breeder in northeastern and north-central regions into portions of east-central and southeastern regions; uncommon in winter in the south, occasionally into northern regions. ***WI:*** fairly common migrant from mid-March to early May and from early September to early November; uncommon breeder in the north; uncommon winter visitor.
Habitat: mature deciduous, coniferous and mixed forests and woodlands, especially in wet areas with large, dead trees; also found near bogs.
Nesting: under loose bark; nest of grass and conifer needles is woven together with spider silk; female incubates 5–6 whitish eggs, dotted with reddish brown, for 14–17 days.
Feeding: hops up tree trunks and large limbs, probing loose bark for adult and larval invertebrates.
Voice: song is a faint, high-pitched *trees-trees-trees see the trees;* call is a high *tseee.*
Similar Species: *Red-breasted Nuthatch* (p. 238) and *White-breasted Nuthatch* (p. 239): gray blue backs; straight or slightly upturned bills. *Woodpeckers* (pp. 193–201): straight bills; all lack brown back streaking.
Best Sites: ***MN:*** wooded areas, especially more mature forests. ***WI:*** wooded areas; may vacate more northerly areas in winter.

CAROLINA WREN

Thryothorus ludovicianus

The energetic and cheerful Carolina Wren can also be shy and retiring, often hiding deep inside dense shubbery. The best opportunity for viewing this large wren is when it sits on a conspicuous perch while unleashing its impressive song. Pairs may perform lively "duets" at any time of day and in any season. The duet often begins with introductory chatter by the female, followed by innumerable, ringing variations of *tea-kettle tea-kettle tea-kettle tea* from her mate. The Carolina Wren's loud and varied repertoire and shy nature mean that this little bird is more often heard than seen. • In years of mild winter weather, Carolina Wren populations remain stable, but a winter of frigid temperatures with ice and snow can greatly reduce their numbers. Fortunately, the effects of such disasters are only temporary and populations recover within a few years.

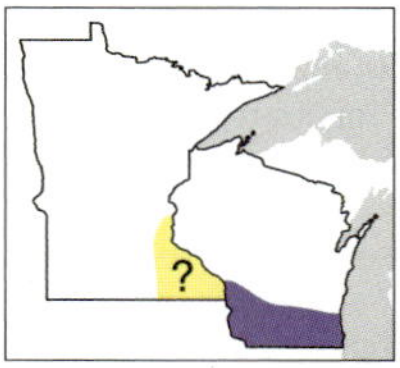

ID: long, prominent, white "eyebrow"; rusty brown upperparts; rich buff-colored underparts; white throat; slightly downcurved bill.

Size: *L* 5½ in; *W* 7½ in.

Status: ***MN:*** very rare and local migrant and summer and winter visitor mainly in southeastern and east-central regions; formerly nested sporadically in the southeast; accidental elsewhere in the state.
WI: rare breeder and winter resident; nonmigratory.

Habitat: dense forest undergrowth, especially shrubby tangles and thickets.

Nesting: in a nest box or natural cavity; both adults fill the cavity with twigs and vegetation and line it with finer materials; nest cup may be domed and may include a snakeskin; female incubates 4–5 brown-blotched, white eggs for 12–16 days; both adults feed the young.

Feeding: usually forages in pairs on the ground and among vegetation; eats mostly insects and other invertebrates; also takes berries, fruits and seeds; will visit feeders for peanuts and suet.

Voice: song is a loud, repetitious *tea-kettle tea-kettle tea-kettle* that may be heard at any time of day or year; female often chatters while male sings.

Similar Species: *House Wren* (p. 242) and *Winter Wren* (p. 243): lack prominent, white "eyebrow." *Marsh Wren* (p. 245): black, triangular back patch is streaked with white; prefers marsh habitat. *Sedge Wren* (p. 244): dark crown and back are streaked with white; pale, indistinct "eyebrow."

Best Sites: ***MN:*** no consistent sites.
WI: Madison area.

HOUSE WREN

Troglodytes aedon

The House Wren's bubbly song and energetic demeanor make it a welcome addition to any neighborhood. A small cavity in a standing dead tree or a custom-made nest box is usually all it takes to attract this joyful bird to most backyards. Sometimes even an empty flowerpot or vacant drainpipe is deemed a suitable nest site, provided there is a local abundance of insect prey. Occasionally, you may find that your nest site offering is packed full of twigs and left abandoned without any nesting birds in sight. Wrens often build numerous nests, which later serve as decoys for their would-be enemies. In such a case, your should just clean out the cavity and hope that another pair of wrens will find your real estate more appealing. • This bird is sometimes called "Jenny Wren."

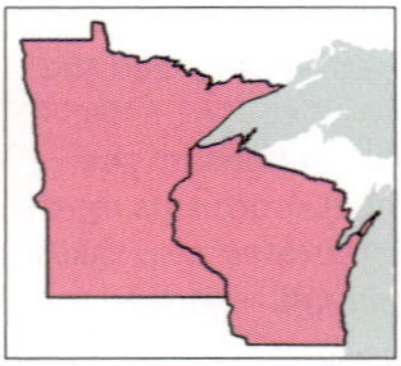

ID: brown upperparts; fine, dark barring on upper wings and lower back; faint, pale "eyebrow" and eye ring; short tail is finely barred with black and held upraised; whitish throat; whitish to buff underparts; faintly barred flanks.

Size: *L* 4½–5 in; *W* 6 in.

Status: ***MN:*** common migrant and breeder from late April to mid-October. ***WI:*** common migrant and breeder from mid-April to mid-October.

Habitat: thickets and shrubby openings in or at the edge of deciduous or mixed woodlands; often in shrubs and thickets near buildings.

Nesting: in a natural cavity or abandoned woodpecker nest; also in a nest box or other artificial cavity; nest of sticks and grass is lined with feathers, fur and other soft materials; female incubates 6–8 white eggs, heavily dotted with reddish brown, for 13–15 days.

Feeding: gleans the ground and vegetation for insects, especially beetles, caterpillars, grasshoppers and spiders.

Voice: call is a harsh, scolding rattle; song is a smooth, running, bubbly warble: *tsi-tsi-tsi-tsi oodle-oodle-oodle-oodle,* lasting about 2–3 seconds.

Similar Species: *Winter Wren* (p. 243): smaller; darker overall; much shorter, stubby tail; prominent, dark barring on flanks. *Sedge Wren* (p. 244): faint, white streaking on dark crown and back.

Best Sites: ***MN:*** residential areas in both urban and rural settings. ***WI:*** *Breeding:* residential areas.

WINTER WREN

Troglodytes troglodytes

Winter Wrens boldly announce their claims to patches of moist coniferous woodland, where they often make their homes in the green moss and gnarled, upturned roots of decomposing tree trunks. • This bird's song is distinguished by its explosive delivery, melodious, bubbly tone and extended duration. Few other singers in our region can sustain their songs for up to 10 music-packed seconds. • The female wren raises the young, while the male brings food to the nest and defends the territory through song. At night, the male sleeps away from his family in an unfinished nest. • The Winter Wren is the only North American wren that is also found across Europe and Asia, where it is a common garden bird known simply as a "Wren."

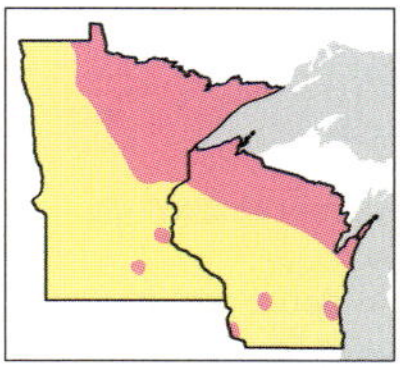

ID: very short, stubby, upraised tail; fine, pale buff "eyebrow"; dark brown upperparts; lighter brown underparts; prominent, dark barring on flanks, wings and tail.

Size: *L* 4 in; *W* $5\frac{1}{2}$ in.

Status: ***MN:*** uncommon migrant from late March to late May and from late August to late October in eastern and central regions; rare migrant in the west; uncommon breeder; occasional in winter in southeastern and east-central regions. ***WI:*** uncommon migrant from early April to early May and from mid-September to late October; uncommon breeder in the north; rare breeder in central regions; rare winter visitor in the south.

Habitat: moist boreal forest, spruce bogs, cedar swamps and mixed forests dominated by mature pine and hemlock; often near water.

Nesting: in a natural cavity, under bark or upturned tree roots or in an abandoned woodpecker cavity; bulky nest is made of twigs, moss, grass and fur; male frequently builds up to 4 "dummy" nests; female incubates 5–7 white eggs, dotted with reddish brown toward the larger end, for 14–16 days.

Feeding: forages on the ground and in trees for beetles, wood-boring insects and other invertebrates.

Voice: *Male:* song is a warbled, tinkling series of quick trills and twitters, often more than 8 seconds long and repeated with undiminished enthusiasm; call is a sharp *chip-chip*.

Similar Species: *House Wren* (p. 242): tail is longer than leg; less conspicuous barring on flanks; paler overall. *Carolina Wren* (p. 241): long, bold, white "eyebrow"; much larger; long tail. *Marsh Wren* (p. 245): white streaking on black back; bold, white "eyebrow." *Sedge Wren* (p. 244): white streaking on black back and crown; longer tail; paler underparts.

Best Sites: ***MN:*** coniferous forests, including Superior NF, Chippewa NF and Boundary Waters Canoe Area Wilderness. ***WI:*** conifer swamps and streams, especially in the north, such as Brule R., Nicolet NF and Chequamegon NF.

SEDGE WREN

Cistothorus platensis

Like most wrens, the Sedge Wren is secretive and difficult to observe. It is the least familiar of all our wrens because it keeps itself well concealed in dense stands of sedges and tall, wet grass. Sedge Wrens are also less loyal to specific sites than other wrens, and may totally disappear from an area after a few years for no apparent reason. • These wrens are feverish nest builders, and construction begins immediately after they settle on a nesting territory. Each energetic male may build several incomplete nests throughout his territory before the females arrive. The decoys or "dummy" nests are not wasted: they often serve as dormitories for young and adult birds later in the season. • This bird used to be known as "Short-billed Marsh Wren."

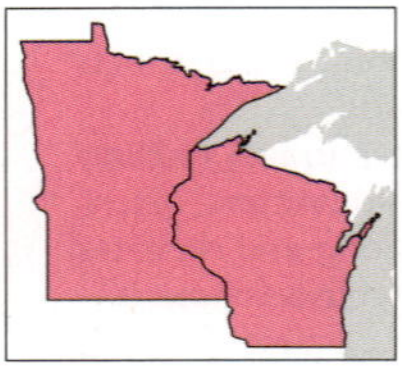

ID: short, narrow tail (often held upraised); faint, pale "eyebrow"; dark crown and back are faintly streaked with white; barring on wing coverts; whitish underparts with buff orange sides, flanks and undertail coverts.

Size: *L* 4–4½ in; *W* 5½ in.

Status: ***MN:*** seldom seen migrant from late April to late May and from early August to mid-October; common breeder in grassy marshes; least common in the northeast. ***WI:*** common migrant and breeder from early May to mid-October.

Habitat: wet sedge meadows, wet grassy fields, marshes, bogs and beaver ponds; often in abandoned, wet fields with low, shrubby willows and alders.

Nesting: usually less than 3 ft from the ground; well-built globe nest with a side entrance is woven from sedges and grasses; female incubates 4–8 unmarked, white eggs for about 14 days.

Feeding: forages low in dense vegetation, where it picks and probes for adult and larval insects and spiders; occasionally catches flying insects.

Voice: song is a few short, staccato notes followed by a rattling trill: *chap-chap-chap-chap, chap, churr-r-r-r-r;* call is a sharp, staccato *chat* or *chep.*

Similar Species: *Marsh Wren* (p. 245): broad, conspicuous, white "eyebrow"; prominent white streaking on black back; unstreaked crown; prefers cattail marshes. *Winter Wren* (p. 243): darker overall; shorter, stubby tail; unstreaked crown. *House Wren* (p. 242): unstreaked, dark brown crown and back.

Best Sites: ***MN:*** Big Stone NWR; Rice Lake NWR; Tamarac NWR; Sherburne NWR; Afton SP; Split Rock Creek SP; Frontenac SP. ***WI:*** Rat River WA; White River Marsh; Horicon Marsh; Killsnake WA; Crex Meadows WA; Richard Bong State Recreation Area; Wood County WA.

MARSH WREN

Cistothorus palustris

Fueled by newly emerged aquatic insects, the Marsh Wren zips about in short bursts through tall stands of cattails and bulrushes. This expert hunter is a reclusive bird that prefers to remain hidden deep within its dense marshland habitat. A patient observer might be rewarded with a brief glimpse of a Marsh Wren, but it is more likely that this bird's distinctive song, reminiscent of an old-fashioned treadle sewing machine, will inform you of its presence. • The Marsh Wren occasionally destroys the nests and eggs of other Marsh Wrens as well as those of other marsh-nesting songbirds such as the Red-winged Blackbird. Other birds are usually prevented from doing the same because the Marsh Wren's globe nest keeps the eggs well hidden, and several "dummy" nests help to divert predators from the real nest. • This bird was formerly known as "Long-billed Marsh Wren."

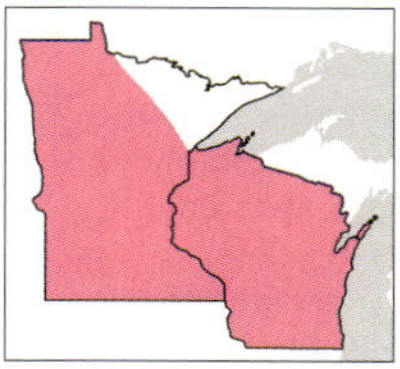

ID: white "chin" and belly; white to light brown upperparts; black triangle on upper back is streaked with white; bold, white "eyebrow"; unstreaked brown crown; long, thin, downcurved bill.

Size: *L* 5 in; *W* 6 in.

Status: ***MN:*** seldom seen migrant from late April to late May and from mid-August to late October; widely distributed breeder in cattail marsh habitat; rare or absent in the northeast; several winter records in the east-central region. ***WI:*** common migrant and breeder from late April to early November.

Habitat: large cattail and bulrush marshes interspersed with open water; occasionally in tall grass–sedge marshes.

Nesting: in a marsh among cattails or tall emergent vegetation; globelike nest is woven from cattails, bulrushes, weeds and grass and lined with cattail down; female incubates 4–6 white to pale brown eggs, heavily dotted with dark brown, for 12–16 days.

Feeding: gleans vegetation and flycatches for adult aquatic invertebrates, especially dragonflies and damselflies.

Voice: *Male:* rapid, rattling, staccato warble sounds like an old-fashioned treadle sewing machine; call is a harsh *chek.*

Similar Species: *Sedge Wren* (p. 244): smaller; streaked crown. *House Wren* (p. 242): faint "eyebrow"; lacks white streaking on black back. *Carolina Wren* (p. 241): larger; black back lacks white streaking; buff underparts.

Best Sites: ***MN:*** Sherburne NWR; Agassiz NWR; wherever cattail marsh habitat exists. ***WI:*** Rat River WA; Horicon Marsh; Trempealeau NWR; White River Marsh; Mead WA; Crex Meadows WA; Powell Marsh; Vernon Marsh; Sensiba WA.

GOLDEN-CROWNED KINGLET

Regulus satrapa

Golden-crowned Kinglets are best seen in spring and fall. As they refuel on insects and berries, kinglets use tree branches as swings and trapezes, flashing their small, regal crowns and constantly flicking their tiny wings. During summer, these dainty forest sprites are often too busy to make an appearance for admiring observers. Not much larger than hummingbirds, Golden-crowned Kinglets can be difficult to spot as they flit and hover among coniferous treetops. • In winter, Golden-crowned Kinglets survive cold winter temperatures by roosting together in groups or in empty squirrel nests. Like chickadees, these birds can lower their body temperatures at night to conserve energy.

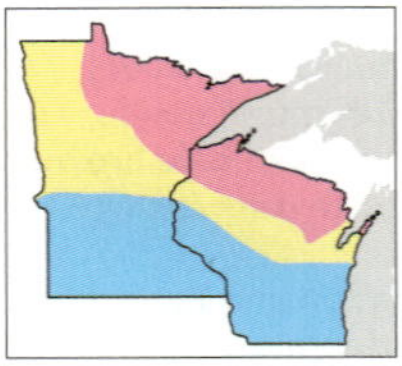

ID: olive back; darker wings and tail; light underparts; dark "cheek"; 2 white wing bars; black eye line; white "eyebrow"; black border around crown. *Male:* reddish orange crown. *Female:* yellow crown.

Size: *L* 4 in; *W* 7 in.

Status: ***MN:*** uncommon migrant from mid-March to mid-May and from early September to early December; occasionally common at peak migration periods; uncommon breeder; uncommon in winter in southeastern and east-central regions; casual in winter in the north. ***WI:*** common migrant from mid-March to early May and from mid-September to mid-November; uncommon breeder; fairly common winter visitor.

Habitat: *Breeding:* mixed and pure mature coniferous forests, especially those dominated by spruce; also conifer plantations. *In migration* and *winter:* coniferous, deciduous and mixed forests and woodlands.

Nesting: usually in a spruce or conifer; hanging nest is made of moss, lichens, twigs and leaves; female incubates 8–9 whitish to pale buff eggs, spotted with gray and brown, for 14–15 days.

Feeding: gleans and hovers among the forest canopy for insects, berries and occasionally sap.

Voice: song is a faint, high-pitched, accelerating *tsee-tsee-tsee-tsee, why do you shilly-shally?;* call is a very high-pitched *tsee tsee tsee.*

Similar Species: *Ruby-crowned Kinglet* (p. 247): bold, broken, white eye ring; crown lacks black border. *Black-capped Chickadee* (p. 235) and *Boreal Chickadee* (p. 236): lack bright, colorful crown.

Best Sites: ***MN:*** *Breeding:* Boundary Waters Canoe Area Wilderness. *In migration:* wooded areas, including Frontenac SP, Superior NF and Itasca SP. ***WI:*** *In migration:* in wooded areas with mixed flocks of migrants.

RUBY-CROWNED KINGLET

Regulus calendula

The loud, rolling song of the Ruby-crowned Kinglet is a familiar tune that echoes through our coniferous forests in early summer, though its loudness and exuberance is somewhat unexpected from such a small bird. The male kinglet erects his brilliant, red crown and sings to impress prospective mates during courtship. Throughout most of the year, however, the crown is impossible to see, even through binoculars—it remains hidden among dull-colored feathers on his head. • While in migration, Ruby-crowned Kinglets are regularly seen flitting among treetops, mingling with a colorful assortment of warblers and vireos. This kinglet might be mistaken for an *Empidonax* flycatcher, but its frequent hovering and energetic wing flicking set it apart from look-alikes. The wing flicking is thought to startle insects into movement, allowing the kinglet to spot them and pounce.

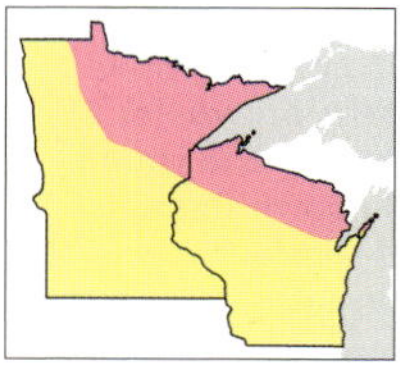

ID: bold, broken eye ring; 2 bold, white wing bars; olive green upperparts; dark wings and tail; whitish to yellowish underparts; short tail; flicks its wings. *Male:* small, red crown (usually hidden). *Female:* lacks red crown.

Size: *L* 4 in; *W* 7½ in.

Status: ***MN:*** common to occasionally abundant migrant from late March to late May and from late August to early November; uncommon to rare breeder in the northeast; accidental in winter in the south. ***WI:*** common migrant from early April to late May and from early September to early November; uncommon breeder.

Habitat: mixed woodlands and pure coniferous forests, especially those dominated by spruce; often found near wet forest openings and edges.

Nesting: usually in a spruce or other conifer; female builds a hanging nest of moss, lichens, twigs and leaves and lines it with feathers, fur and plant down; female incubates 7–8 brown-spotted, whitish to pale buff eggs for 13–14 days.

Feeding: gleans and hovers for insects and spiders; also eats seeds and berries.

Voice: *Male:* song is an accelerating and rising *tea-tea-tea-tew-tew-tew look-at-Me, look-at-Me, look-at-Me.*

Similar Species: *Golden-crowned Kinglet* (p. 246): dark "cheek"; black border around crown; male has orange crown with yellow border; female has yellow crown. *Orange-crowned Warbler* (p. 269): no eye ring or wing bars. Empidonax *flycatchers* (pp. 205–09): complete eye ring or no eye ring at all; larger bills; longer tails; all lack red crown.

Best Sites: *In migration:* with mixed flocks in wooded areas.

BLUE-GRAY GNATCATCHER

Polioptila caerulea

The fidgety Blue-gray Gnatcatcher inhabits woodlands and brushy areas. With its tail held upraised, it issues a scratchy, banjolike twang as it restlessly flits from shrub to shrub, gleaning insects from branches and leaves. • During courtship, the male Blue-gray Gnatcatcher follows his prospective mate around his territory. Once a bond is established, the paired birds become inseparable. Male Blue-gray Gnatcatchers take a greater part in nesting and raising the young than males in closely related species. Like most songbirds, young Blue-gray Gnatcatchers mature quickly and will fly as far as South America within months of hatching. • Although this bird undoubtedly eats gnats, this food item is not a major part of it diet. • The scientific name *Polioptila* means "gray feather," while *caerulea* means "blue."

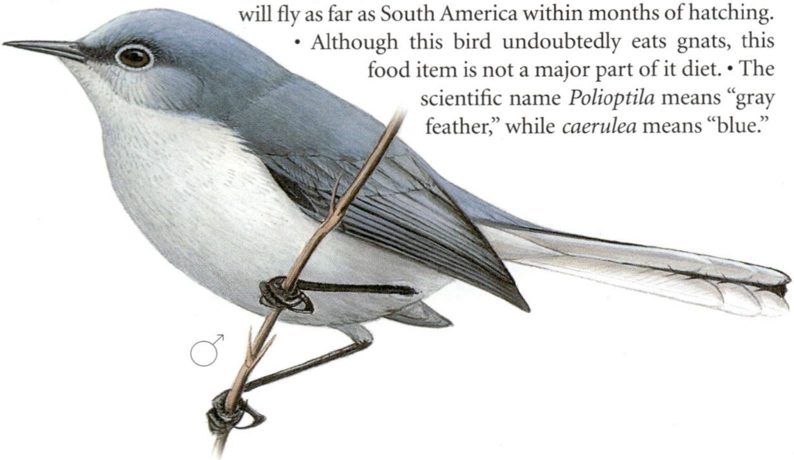

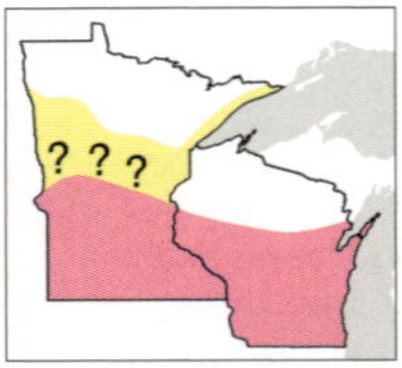

ID: blue gray upperparts; long, thin tail; white eye ring; pale gray underparts; black uppertail with white outer tail feathers; dark legs. *Breeding male:* black forehead. *Immature:* similar to adult; pale bill; brown-washed upperparts. *In flight:* long-tailed and broad-winged; long, fan-shaped tail with flashy white outer feathers.

Size: *L* 4½ in; *W* 6 in.

Status: ***MN:*** uncommon migrant and breeder from late April through August in southeastern and east-central regions; expanding its range into central and southwestern regions; recent pattern of fall vagrancy along the North Shore of L. Superior. ***WI:*** uncommon migrant and breeder from mid-April to mid-September.

Habitat: deciduous woodlands along streams, ponds, lakes and swamps; also in orchards, shrubby tangles along woodland edges and oak savannas.

Nesting: on a branch, usually halfway to the trunk; cup nest of plant fibers and bark chips is decorated with lichens and lined with fine vegetation, hair and feathers; female incubates 3–5 pale bluish white eggs, dotted with reddish brown, for 11–15 days; male feeds the female and young.

Feeding: moves up and down through foliage, flicking its tail constantly, possibly to flush prey into view; eats small insects and spiders.

Voice: calls are thin and high-pitched: single *see* notes, or a short series of "mewing" or chattering notes; can mimic several species.

Similar Species: *Golden-crowned Kinglet* (p. 246) and *Ruby-crowned Kinglet* (p. 247): olive green overall; short tails; wing bars.

Best Sites: ***MN:*** Vasa; Afton SP; William O'Brien SP; Frontenac SP; Whitewater SP; Lake Maria SP; Sibley SP. ***WI:*** Wyalusing SP; Governor Dodge SP; Baxter's Hollow; Devil's Lake SP; Perrot SP; Trempealeau NWR; Hortonville Swamp; Mazomanie Bottoms; White River Marsh.

EASTERN BLUEBIRD

Sialia sialis

Perhaps no other bird is as cherished and admired in rural areas as the lovely Eastern Bluebird. With the colors of the cool sky on its back and the warm setting sun on its breast, the male Eastern Bluebird looks like a piece of pure sky come to life. • When House Sparrows and European Starlings were introduced to North America, Eastern Bluebirds were forced to compete with them for nest sites, and bluebird numbers suffered. The creation of bluebird nest boxes has helped matters—these boxes exclude competing European Starlings because the entrances are too small for them, but perfect for bluebirds. Northern Flickers sometimes chisel out the small openings of bluebird boxes to gain entrance, but will not nest in them because the interior is too small. • Eastern Bluebirds are fond of fields, uncultivated farmlands, and mature woodlots, but an elevated perch is necessary as a base from which to hunt insects.

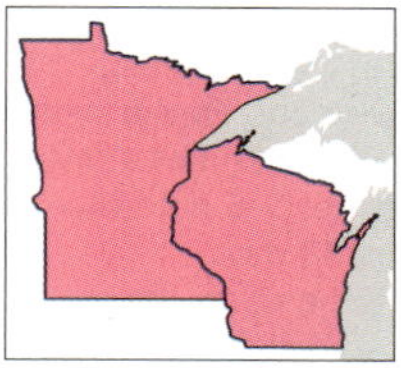

ID: chestnut red "chin," throat, breast and sides; white belly and undertail coverts; dark bill and legs. *Male:* deep blue upperparts. *Female:* thin, white eye ring; gray brown head and back are tinged with blue; blue wings and tail; paler chestnut on underparts.

Size: *L* 7 in; *W* 13 in.

Status: ***MN:*** common to at times abundant migrant and breeder from early March to early November; increasing in recent years; occasional in early winter in southeastern and south-central regions. ***WI:*** common migrant and breeder from early March to late December; rare winter visitor.

Habitat: cropland fencelines, meadows, fallow and abandoned fields, pastures, forest clearings and edges; also golf courses, large lawns and cemeteries.

Nesting: in an abandoned woodpecker cavity, natural cavity or nest box; female builds a cup nest of grass, weed stems and small twigs and lines it with finer materials; mostly the female incubates 4–5 pale blue eggs for 13–16 days.

Feeding: swoops from a perch to pursue flying insects; also forages on the ground for invertebrates.

Voice: song is a rich, warbling *turr, turr-lee, turr-lee;* call is a chittering *pew.*

Similar Species: *Mountain Bluebird* (p. 250): lacks chestnut underparts.

Best Sites: ***MN:*** bluebird nest box trails in most state parks; roadsides in rural areas in the north-central region. ***WI:*** roadsides and nest boxes in rural areas.

MOUNTAIN BLUEBIRD

Sialia currucoides

The Mountain Bluebird is a member of the thrush family, but it shares few of the traits of other members of its clan—it nests in cavities, prefers open habitat and eats predominantly insects. It also frequently hovers while foraging, making this bird more reminiscent of an American Kestrel than a thrush, or even other bluebirds. • The Mountain Bluebird benefits from some human-induced habitat changes, including the clearing of heavily forested areas (though this bird cannot live in an area completely denuded of trees), livestock grazing and the erection of nest boxes. Interestingly, most of what we know about bluebirds is based on the study of nest box populations. • Mountain Bluebirds are the most migratory of the three North American bluebird species, with a breeding range that extends into Alaska, farther north than any other bluebird.

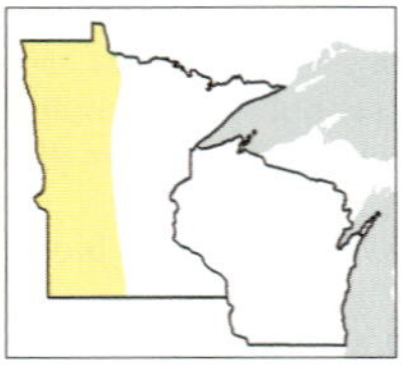

ID: black eyes, bill and legs. *Male:* sky blue body; upperparts are darker than underparts. *Female:* sky blue wings, tail and rump; blue gray back and head; gray brown underparts.

Size: *L* 7 in; *W* 14 in.

Status: ***MN:*** rare spring migrant, mainly in western regions; casual migrant eastward; accidental fall migrant; 6 nesting records (5 involving hybridization with the Eastern Bluebird). ***WI:*** casual migrant and winter visitor.

Habitat: open forests, forests edges, agricultural areas and grasslands.

Nesting: in an abandoned woodpecker cavity, natural cavity or nest box; female builds a cup nest of plant stems, grass, conifer needles and twigs and lines it with fine grass, soft bark and sometimes a few feathers; female incubates 5–6 pale blue to bluish white eggs for 13 days.

Feeding: swoops from a perch for flying and terrestrial insects; also forages on the ground for a variety of invertebrates, such as beetles, ants and bugs.

Voice: call is a low *turr turr*. *Male:* song is a short warble of *chur* notes.

Similar Species: *Blue Jay* (p. 224): prominent crest. *Townsend's Solitaire* (p. 251): peach-colored patches on wings and tail; white outer tail feathers. *Eastern Bluebird* (p. 249): darker blue back; orange breast.

Best Sites: ***MN:*** Kittson Co.; Marshall Co. ***WI:*** no consistent sites.

TOWNSEND'S SOLITAIRE

Myadestes townsendi

In flight, the warm, peachy wing linings of the Townsend's Solitaire shine like sunlight through a bedroom window. This bird makes its home primarily in the western half of the continent and spends the summer in high mountain country. During the summer months, Townsend's Solitaires are true to their name and are seldom seen in groups. In fall, these birds make their way to lower elevations. They are seen in our region as rare spring and fall migrants and winter visitors. During the winter months, both male and female Townsend's Solitaires defend feeding grounds of juniper berries and other fruit-bearing trees—they have the unusual habit of picking fruit off trees while in flight. These birds are conspicuous at this time of year, perched high on treetops watching for intruders, or singing loudly to proclaim possession of their territory. • John James Audubon named this bird in honor of John Kirk Townsend, one of North America's great early ornithologists.

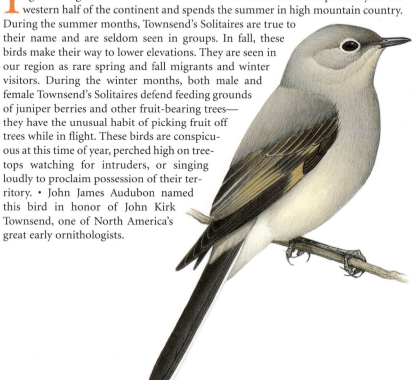

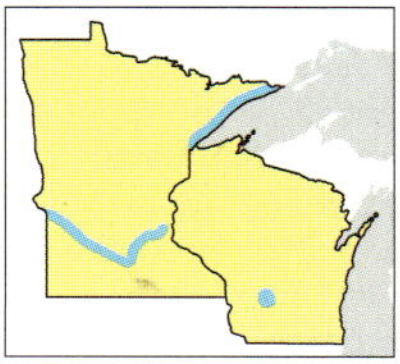

ID: gray body; darker wings and tail; peach-colored wing patches (very evident in flight); white eye ring; white outer tail feathers; long tail. *Immature:* brown body is heavily spotted with buff; pale eye ring.
Size: *L* $8\frac{1}{2}$ in; *W* $14\frac{1}{2}$ in.
Status: ***MN:*** rare spring and fall migrant and occasional winter visitor, most likely along the North Shore of L. Superior. ***WI:*** rare fall migrant and winter visitor; casual spring migrant.

Habitat: coniferous forests, sometimes in mixed coniferous-deciduous woodlands.
Nesting: does not nest in our region.
Feeding: flycatches and gleans vegetation and the ground for invertebrates and berries; plucks berries from trees while in flight.
Voice: call is a harsh *piink*. *Male:* song is a long, bubbly warble.
Similar Species: *Gray Catbird* (p. 259): black "cap"; red undertail coverts. *Eastern Bluebird* (p. 249) and *Mountain Bluebird* (p. 250): blue with varying amounts of orange; no wing bars.
Best Sites: ***MN:*** Grand Marais; Two Harbors; Duluth; Whitewater SP; Minnesota R. valley in winter. ***WI:*** Devil's Lake SP.

VEERY

Catharus fuscescens

Navigating its way across the forest floor, the Veery travels in short, springy hops, flipping leaves and scattering leaf litter in search of worms and grubs. This shy, well-camouflaged bird is always attuned to the sounds of wriggling prey or approaching danger. It is the most terrestrial of the North American thrushes, and is often difficult to find. Listen for the Veery in spring and early summer when its fluty, cascading song is easily detected, especially after other songbirds have called it a day. • When startled by an intruder, the Veery either flushes or faces the threat with its faintly streaked, buffy breast exposed, hoping for concealment. • This bird's name is an imitation of its airy song. The scientific name *fuscescens* is from the Latin word for "dusky," in reference to the Veery's color.

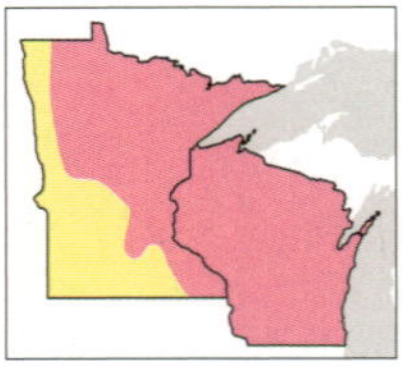

ID: reddish brown or tawny upperparts; very thin, grayish eye ring; faintly streaked, buff throat and upper breast; pale underparts; gray flanks and face patch.

Size: *L* 7 in; *W* 12 in.

Status: ***MN:*** uncommon migrant from late April to late May and from late July to late September, least numerous in southwestern and west-central regions; well-represented breeder in the southeast and most of the north. ***WI:*** common migrant from late April to late May and from mid-August to late September; common breeder in northern and central regions; uncommon breeder in the south.

Habitat: cool, moist deciduous and mixed forests and woodlands with a dense understory of shrubs and ferns; often in disturbed woodlands.

Nesting: on the ground or in a shrub; female builds a bulky nest of leaves, weeds, bark strips and rootlets; female incubates 3–4 pale greenish blue eggs for 10–15 days.

Feeding: gleans the ground and lower vegetation for invertebrates and berries.

Voice: *Male:* song is a fluty, descending *da-vee-ur, vee-ur, vee-ur, veer, veer, veer;* call is a high, whistled *feeyou.*

Similar Species: *Swainson's Thrush* (p. 254): bold eye ring; olive brown upperparts; darker spotting on throat and upper breast. *Hermit Thrush* (p. 255): reddish rump and tail; brownish back; bold eye ring; buff brown flanks; large, dark spots on throat and breast. *Gray-cheeked Thrush* (p. 253): gray brown upperparts; dark breast spots; brownish gray flanks.

Best Sites: ***MN:*** Nerstrand–Big Woods SP; Agassiz NWR; Tamarac NWR; Itasca SP; Frontenac SP; Boundary Waters Canoe Area Wilderness. ***WI:*** deciduous forests and wooded swamps in northern and central regions.

GRAY-CHEEKED THRUSH

Catharus minimus

Few people have ever heard of the Gray-cheeked Thrush, but keen birders find this inconspicuous bird a source of great interest. A champion migrant, this thrush overwinters as far south as Peru and regularly summers in the Arctic. Each spring and fall the Gray-cheeked Thrush migrates through our region to the Hudson Bay Lowlands in Canada—farther north than any other North American thrush—where it nests among willows and stunted black spruce. • In migration, the Gray-cheeked Thrush travels primarily at night, so it is most often seen or heard rustling through shrub-concealed leaf litter in the early morning. The Gray-cheeked Thrush will settle in almost any habitat while migrating, but it does not stay for long. • Until 1995, the Gray-cheeked Thrush and the very similar-looking Bicknell's Thrush *(C. bicknelli)* were classified as a single species.

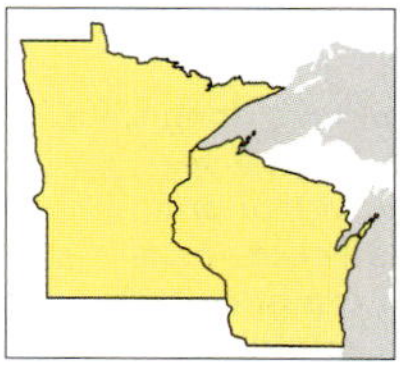

ID: gray brown upperparts; gray face; inconspicuous eye ring may not be visible; heavily spotted breast; pale underparts; gray brown flanks.

Size: *L* 7–8 in; *W* 13 in.

Status: ***MN:*** uncommon migrant from early May to early June and from late August to mid-October; may be locally common at peak migration periods. ***WI:*** fairly common migrant from early May to early June and from late August to mid-October.

Habitat: a variety of forested areas, parks and backyards.

Nesting: does not nest in our region.

Feeding: hops along the ground, picking up insects and other invertebrates; may also feed on berries during migration.

Voice: typically thrushlike in tone, ending with a clear, usually 3-part whistle, with the middle note higher pitched: *wee-o, wee-a, titi wheeee;* call is a downslurred *wee-o.*

Similar Species: *Swainson's Thrush* (p. 254): prominent eye ring; buff "cheek" and upper breast. *Hermit Thrush* (p. 255): reddish tail; olive brown upperparts; lacks gray "cheek." *Veery* (p. 252): reddish brown upperparts; very light breast streaking.

Best Sites: ***MN:*** wooded areas in state parks, national wildlife refuges and local county parks, including Frontenac SP and Minnesota Pt. (Duluth). ***WI:*** Harrington Beach SP; Milwaukee parks; Heckrodt Wetland Reserve; Arboretum and Picnic Pt. (UW-Madison); Wisconsin Pt.; Bay Beach Wildlife Sanctuary.

SWAINSON'S THRUSH

Catharus ustulatus

The upward spiral of this thrush's song lifts the soul of any listener with every rising note. The Swainson's Thrush is an integral part of the morning chorus, and its inspiring song is also heard at dusk. • Most thrushes feed on the ground, but the Swainson's Thrush is also adept at gleaning food from the airy heights of trees, sometimes briefly hover-gleaning like a warbler or vireo. • On its breeding grounds, the Swainson's Thrush is most often seen perched high in a treetop, cast in silhouette against the sky. In migration, this thrush skulks low on the ground under shrubs and tangles, occasionally finding itself in backyards and neighborhood parks. A wary bird, the Swainson's Thrush does not allow many viewing opportunities, and it often gives a sharp warning call from some distance.

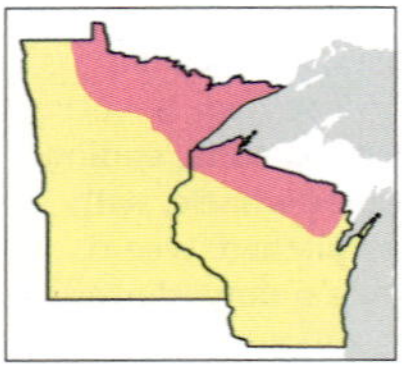

ID: gray brown upperparts; conspicuous buff eye ring; buff wash on "cheek" and upper breast; spots are arranged in streaks on throat and breast; white belly and undertail coverts; brownish gray flanks.

Size: *L* 7 in; *W* 11½ in.

Status: ***MN:*** common migrant from late April to early June and from late July to early October; uncommon breeder. ***WI:*** very common migrant from early May to early June and from early August to late October; uncommon breeder.

Habitat: edges and openings of coniferous and mixed boreal forests; prefers moist areas with spruce and fir.

Nesting: usually in a shrub or small tree; small cup nest is made of grass, moss, leaves, roots and lichens and lined with fur and soft fibers; female incubates 3–4 pale blue eggs, with brown spots toward the larger end, for 12–14 days.

Feeding: gleans vegetation and forages on the ground for invertebrates; also eats berries.

Voice: song is a slow, rolling, rising spiral: *Oh, Aurelia will-ya, will-ya will-yeee;* call is a sharp but pleasant *wick* or *prit.*

Similar Species: *Gray-cheeked Thrush* (p. 253): gray "cheek"; less or no buff wash on breast; lacks conspicuous eye ring. *Hermit Thrush* (p. 255): reddish tail and rump; grayish brown upperparts; darker breast spotting on whiter breast. *Veery* (p. 252): lacks bold eye ring; upperparts are more reddish; faint breast streaking.

Best Sites: ***MN:*** Minnesota R. valley; Frontenac SP; wooded areas in state parks, national wildlife refuges and county parks. ***WI:*** *In migration:* Harrington Beach SP; Milwaukee parks; Bay Beach Wildlife Sanctuary; Heckrodt Wetland Reserve; Arboretum and Picnic Pt. (UW-Madison); Wyalusing SP; Wisconsin Pt.

HERMIT THRUSH

Catharus guttatus

If the beauty of forest birds was gauged by sound rather than appearance, there is no doubt that the Hermit Thrush would be deemed one of the most beautiful birds in our region. • The Hermit Thrush is a ground nester, often hiding its cryptic cup nest in a natural hollow between raised mossy hummocks under the low branches of a spruce or fir. The female incubates the eggs on her own while the male defends the territory. This means that there is less activity around the nest—something that probably benefits the vulnerable eggs. • Though the Hermit Thrush's plumage is quite ordinary, it distinguishes itself when it raises its reddish tail after landing on a perch or when disturbed.

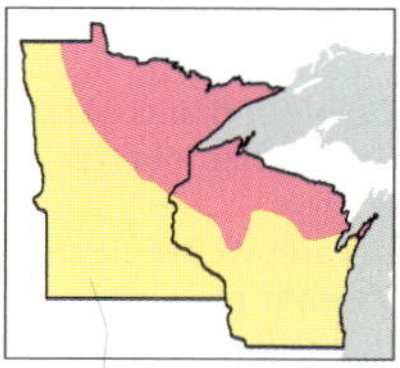

ID: reddish brown tail and rump; grayish brown upperparts; black-spotted throat and breast; pale underparts; gray flanks; whitish eye ring.

Size: *L* 7 in; *W* 11½ in.

Status: ***MN:*** common migrant from late March to mid-May and from early September to early November; common breeder; occasional in winter mainly in the south. ***WI:*** common migrant from late March to early May and from mid-September to early November; common breeder; rare winter visitor in the south.

Habitat: deciduous, mixed or coniferous woodlands; wet coniferous bogs bordered by trees.

Nesting: usually on the ground; occasionally in a small tree or shrub; female builds a bulky cup nest of grass, twigs, moss, ferns and bark strips; female incubates 4 pale blue to greenish blue eggs, sometimes with dark flecks, for 11–13 days.

Feeding: forages on the ground and gleans vegetation for insects and other invertebrates; also eats berries.

Voice: song is a series of beautiful, ethereal, flutelike notes, both rising and falling in pitch; a small questioning note may precede the song; calls include a faint *chuck* and a fluty *treee.*

Similar Species: *Swainson's Thrush* (p. 254): buff "cheek" and wash on breast; grayish brown back and tail. *Veery* (p. 252): lightly streaked upper breast; reddish brown upperparts and tail. *Gray-cheeked Thrush* (p. 253): gray "cheek"; lacks conspicuous eye ring. *Fox Sparrow* (p. 318): stockier build; conical bill; brown breast spots.

Best Sites: ***MN:*** *Breeding:* mixed woodlands in the north. *In migration:* wooded state parks, national wildlife refuges and local parks. ***WI:*** *Breeding:* northern deciduous forests. *In migration:* Harrington Beach SP; Milwaukee parks; Bay Beach Wildlife Sanctuary; Heckrodt Wetland Reserve; Arboretum and Picnic Pt. (UW-Madison); Wyalusing SP; Wisconsin Pt.

WOOD THRUSH

Hylocichla mustelina

The loud, warbled notes of the Wood Thrush once resounded through our woodlands, but forest fragmentation and urban sprawl have eliminated much of this bird's nesting habitat. Broken forests and diminutive woodlots have allowed the invasion of common, open-area predators and parasites, such as raccoons, skunks, crows, jays and cowbirds, which traditionally had little access to nests that were insulated deep within vast stands of hardwood forest. Many tracts of forest that have been urbanized or developed for agriculture now host families of American Robins rather than the once prominent Wood Thrush. • Naturalist and author Henry David Thoreau considered the Wood Thrush's song to be the most beautiful of avian sounds. Male Wood Thrushes can even sing two notes at once!

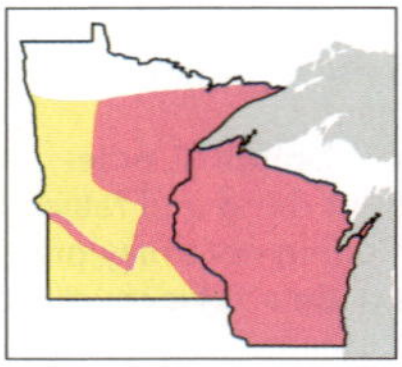

ID: plump body; black spots on white breast, sides and flanks; bold, white eye ring; rusty head and back; brown wings, rump and tail.

Size: *L* 8 in; *W* 13 in.

Status: ***MN:*** uncommon migrant in May in eastern and central regions; most birds leave the state by late July; uncommon breeder in heavily forested areas of southeastern and east-central regions and deciduous forests of northeastern and north-central regions; expanding its range northward and westward; declining in the south. ***WI:*** uncommon migrant and breeder from late April to early October.

Habitat: moist, mature and preferably undisturbed deciduous woodlands and mixed forests.

Nesting: low in the fork of a deciduous tree; female builds a bulky cup nest of grass, twigs, moss, weeds, bark strips and mud and lines it with softer materials; female incubates 3–4 pale greenish blue eggs for 13–14 days.

Feeding: forages on the ground and gleans vegetation for insects and other invertebrates; also eats berries.

Voice: *Male:* bell-like phrases of 3–6 notes, with each note at a different pitch and followed by a trill: *Will you live with me? Way up high in a tree, I'll come right down and...seeee!;* calls include a *pit pit* and *bweebeebeep*.

Similar Species: *Ovenbird* (p. 291): much smaller and browner; black-and-russet crown stripes; streaky spots on underparts. *Other thrushes* (pp. 252–58): smaller spots on underparts; most have colored wash on sides and flanks; all lack bold, white eye ring and rusty "cap" and back.

Best Sites: ***MN:*** William O'Brien SP; Whitewater SP; Frontenac SP; Nerstrand–Big Woods SP; Seven Mile Creek (Nicollet Co.); deciduous woods in Cook Co. and Lake Co. ***WI:*** deciduous forests, including High Cliff SP, Wyalusing SP, Devil's Lake SP and Kettle Moraine State Forest.

AMERICAN ROBIN

Turdus migratorius

American Robins are widely recognized as harbingers of spring, often arriving in our region in early March. Although many American Robins migrate, some overwinter here wherever mountain-ash and other berries are plentiful. These birds may even come to feeders if berries and other fruit are provided. • A hunting robin may appear to be listening for prey, but it is actually looking for movements in the soil—it tilts its head because its eyes are placed on the sides of its head. The robin's habit of stamping is designed to get earthworms to betray their presence by moving. • Robins are occasionally seen hunting with their bills stuffed full of earthworms and grubs, a sign that hungry young birds are somewhere close at hand. Young robins are easily distinguished from their parents by their disheveled appearance and heavily spotted underparts. • The American Robin was named by English colonists after the Robin *(Erithacus rubecula)* of their native land. Both birds look and behave similarly, even though they are only distantly related.

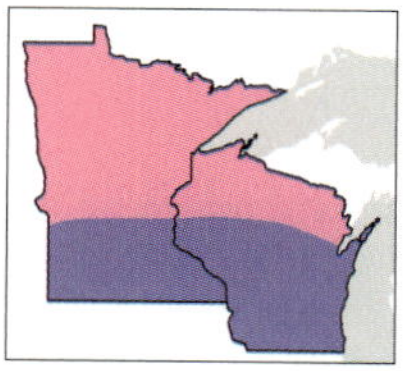

ID: gray brown back; dark head; white throat streaked with black; white undertail coverts; incomplete, white eye ring; black-tipped, yellow bill. *Male:* deep brick red breast; black head. *Female:* light red orange breast; dark gray head. *Immature:* heavily spotted breast.

Size: *L* 10 in; *W* 17 in.

Status: ***MN:*** abundant migrant and breeder from early March to late November; uncommon and local in winter mainly in the south, but can be common at times along the North Shore of L. Superior. ***WI:*** abundant migrant and breeder from early May to mid-November; uncommon winter visitor.

Habitat: residential lawns and gardens, pastures, urban parks, fragmented forests, bogs and river shorelines.

Nesting: in a coniferous or deciduous tree or shrub; sturdy cup nest is built of grass, moss and loose bark and cemented with mud; female incubates 4 light blue eggs for 11–16 days; may raise up to 3 broods each year.

Feeding: forages on the ground and among vegetation for larval and adult insects, earthworms, other invertebrates and berries.

Voice: song is an evenly spaced warble: *cheerily cheer-up cheerio;* call is a rapid *tut-tut-tut.*

Similar Species: *Varied Thrush* (p. 258): black breast band; 2 orange wing bars.

Best Sites: ***MN:*** widespread, especially in river valleys, parks and residential areas. ***WI:*** widespread in residential areas, farms and woods.

VARIED THRUSH

Ixoreus naevius

Varied Thrushes are rare here, so if you find one don't be surprised if fellow birders question your identification skills. Though it is about the size of a robin, this bird's distinctive patterning and coloration mean that it is unlikely to be mistaken for anything but a Varied Thrush. • Varied Thrushes are typically found in western North America, but invariably a few wander off course each fall, making their way into our region. Every year there are five to ten sightings reported in both Minnesota and Wisconsin, usually at backyard feeders with dense coniferous trees to provide shelter for this wayward wanderer. Berries, fruits, seeds, nuts, acorns and suet are some of the offerings that might encourage a lengthy visit from a Varied Thrush—provided that Blue Jays and other backyard regulars don't dominate the wealth of goodies.

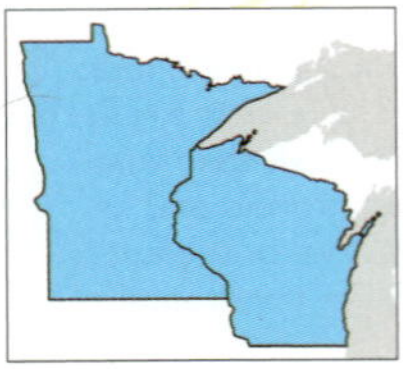

ID: dark upperparts; orange "eyebrow"; orange throat and belly; 2 orange wing bars. *Male:* black breast band; blue black upperparts. *Female:* brown upperparts; faint breast band.

Size: *L* 9 in; *W* 16 in.

Status: ***MN:*** rare migrant and winter visitor from late October to early April. ***WI:*** rare migrant and winter visitor from November to late March.

Habitat: areas with dense coniferous cover near an active feeding station.

Nesting: does not nest in our region.

Feeding: forages on the ground and among vegetation for insects, seeds and berries; takes a variety of foods at feeders, especially suet.

Voice: rarely vocal in our region; male's song is a series of sustained single notes (actually subtle trills) delivered at different pitches, with a lengthy pause between each note; call is a quiet *tuck*.

Similar Species: *American Robin* (p. 257): lacks black breast band and orange "eyebrow," throat and wing bars.

Best Sites: no consistent sites; usually encountered as individuals at feeders in winter.

GRAY CATBIRD

Dumetella carolinensis

Gray Catbirds are most common in summer, when nesting pairs build their loose cup nests deep within impenetrable tangles of shrubs, brambles and thorny thickets. These birds vigorously defend their nesting territories, and their defense tactics are so effective that the nesting success of neighboring warblers and sparrows may increase as a result of the catbird's constant vigilance. Gray Catbirds are less prone to parasitism by Brown-headed Cowbirds because female catbirds are very loyal to their nests. Even if a cowbird sneaks past the watchful female catbird to deposit an egg in the nest, the mother catbird often recognizes the foreign egg and immediately ejects it. • True to its name, this bird's call sounds much like the scratchy mewing of a house cat.

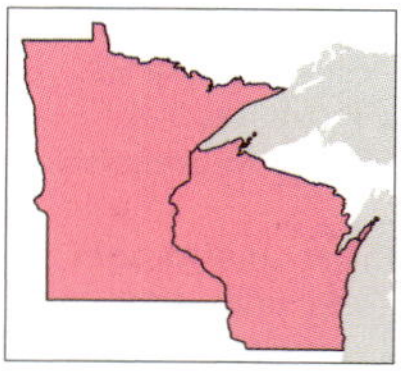

ID: dark gray overall; black crown and forehead; long, dark gray to black tail; chestnut undertail coverts; black eyes, bill and legs; short wings.

Size: *L* 8½–9 in; *W* 11 in.

Status: ***MN:*** common migrant and breeder from early May to mid-October; occasional in early winter mainly in the south. ***WI:*** common migrant and breeder from late April to mid-October; rare winter visitor.

Habitat: dense thickets, brambles, shrubby or brushy areas and hedgerows, often near water.

Nesting: in a dense shrub or thicket; bulky cup nest is loosely built with twigs, leaves and grass and lined with fine material; female incubates 4 greenish blue eggs for 12–15 days.

Feeding: forages on the ground and in vegetation for a wide variety of ants, beetles, grasshoppers, caterpillars, moths and spiders; also eats berries and visits feeders.

Voice: calls include a catlike *meoow* and a harsh *check-check;* song is a variety of warbles, squeaks and mimicked phrases repeated only once and often interspersed with a *mew* call.

Similar Species: *Gray Jay* (p. 223), *Northern Mockingbird* (p. 260) and *Townsend's Solitaire* (p. 251): all lack black crown and chestnut undertail coverts. *Brown Thrasher* (p. 261): rusty brown upperparts; streaked underparts; wing bars; repeats each song phrase twice.

Best Sites: ***MN:*** brushy areas in state and local parks, as well as residential and rural areas. ***WI:*** residential areas and brushy thickets in hedgerows in rural areas.

NORTHERN MOCKINGBIRD

Mimus polyglottos

Northern Mockingbirds are uncommon to rare migrants in our region and seldom breed here. However, after a series of mild winters, some of the spring migrants may remain to nest. Severe winters markedly decrease the number of both residents and migrants. • The Northern Mockingbird thrills people with its impressive vocal repertoire. These birds have been known to sing more than 400 different song types, and they can imitate the vocalizations of other birds, barking dogs and even musical instruments. They replicate sounds so accurately that even computerized auditory analysis is often unable to detect differences between the original source and the mockingbird's imitation.

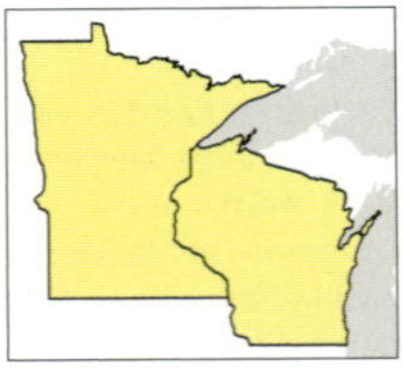

ID: gray upperparts; dark wings; 2 thin, white wing bars; long, dark tail with white outer tail feathers; light gray underparts. *Immature:* paler overall; spotted breast. *In flight:* large, white patch at base of black primaries.

Size: *L* 10 in; *W* 14 in.

Status: ***MN:*** rare but regular, though unpredictable, in all seasons; has occurred in every region; most likely seen in the east; casual in summer with only 3 positive breeding records. ***WI:*** uncommon to rare migrant from early April to late May and in fall; rare breeder; rare winter visitor.

Habitat: hedges, suburban gardens and orchard margins with an abundance of available fruit; hedgerows of multiflora roses are especially important in winter.

Nesting: often in a small shrub or small tree; cup nest is built from twigs, grass, fur and leaves; female incubates 3–4 brown-blotched, bluish gray to greenish eggs for 12–13 days.

Feeding: gleans vegetation and forages on the ground for beetles, ants, wasps and grasshoppers; also eats berries and wild fruit; visits feeders for suet and raisins.

Voice: song is a medley of mimicked phrases, with the phrases often repeated 3 times or more; calls include a harsh *chair* and *chewk*.

Similar Species: *Northern Shrike* (p. 215) and *Loggerhead Shrike* (p. 214): thicker, hooked bill; black mask; immature is stockier and less vocal. *Townsend's Solitaire* (p. 251): prominent eye ring; peach rather than white on wings. *Gray Catbird* (p. 259): gray overall; black crown; chestnut undertail coverts; lacks white outer tail feathers.

Best Sites: no consistent sites.

BROWN THRASHER

Toxostoma rufum

Amid the various chirps and warbles that rise from woodland and lakefront edges in spring and early summer, the song of the male Brown Thrasher stands alone—its lengthy, complex chorus of twice-repeated phrases is unique. This thrasher has the most extensive vocal repertoire of any North American bird, and estimates indicate that it is capable of up to 3000 distinctive combinations of various phrases. • Despite its relatively large size, the Brown Thrasher generally goes unnoticed in its shrubby domain. A typical sighting of this thrasher usually consists of nothing more than a flash of rufous as it zips from one tangle to another. • Because it nests on or close to the ground, this bird's eggs and nestlings are particularly vulnerable to predation by snakes, weasels, skunks and other animals.

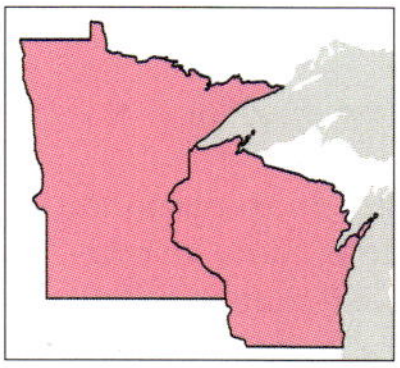

ID: reddish brown upperparts; pale underparts with heavy, brown streaking; long, downcurved bill; yellow orange eyes; long, rufous tail; 2 white wing bars.

Size: *L* 11½ in; *W* 13 in.

Status: ***MN:*** common migrant and breeder from mid-April to mid-October; least numerous in heavily wooded areas of northeastern and north-central regions; occasional in winter in the east. ***WI:*** common migrant and fairly common breeder from mid-April to early October.

Habitat: dense shrubs and thickets, overgrown pastures (especially those with hawthorns), woodland edges and brushy areas; rarely close to human habitation.

Nesting: usually in a low shrub; often on the ground; cup nest made of grass, twigs and leaves is lined with fine vegetation; pair incubates 4 bluish white to pale blue eggs, dotted with reddish brown, for 11–14 days.

Feeding: gleans the ground and vegetation for larval and adult invertebrates; occasionally tosses leaves aside with its bill; also eats seeds and berries.

Voice: sings a large variety of phrases, with each phrase usually repeated twice: *dig-it dig-it, hoe-it hoe-it, pull-it-up pull-it-up;* calls include a loud crackling note, a harsh *shuck,* a soft *churr* and a whistled, 3-note *pit-cher-ee.*

Similar Species: *Hermit Thrush* (p. 255) and *Wood Thrush* (p. 256): spots, not streaks, on underparts; dark eye with pale eye ring; shorter tail; lacks wing bars.

Best Sites: ***MN:*** brushy roadsides and hillsides, mainly in rural areas; also farmsteads. ***WI:*** abandoned fields, farmsteads, scattered brushy areas and fencerows.

EUROPEAN STARLING

Sturnus vulgaris

The European Starling was introduced to North America in 1890 and 1891, when about 100 individuals were released into New York's Central Park as part of the local Shakespeare society's plan to introduce all the birds mentioned in their favorite author's writings. The European Starling quickly established itself in the New York landscape, then spread rapidly across the continent, often at the expense of many native cavity-nesting birds, such as the Tree Swallow, Eastern Bluebird and Red-headed Woodpecker. Despite many concerted efforts to control or even eradicate the European Starling, this species will no doubt continue to assert its claim in the New World. The current population of this species in North America is estimated to be over 200 million birds. • Courting European Starlings are infamous for their ability to reproduce the sounds of other birds such as Killdeers, Red-tailed Hawks, Soras and meadowlarks.

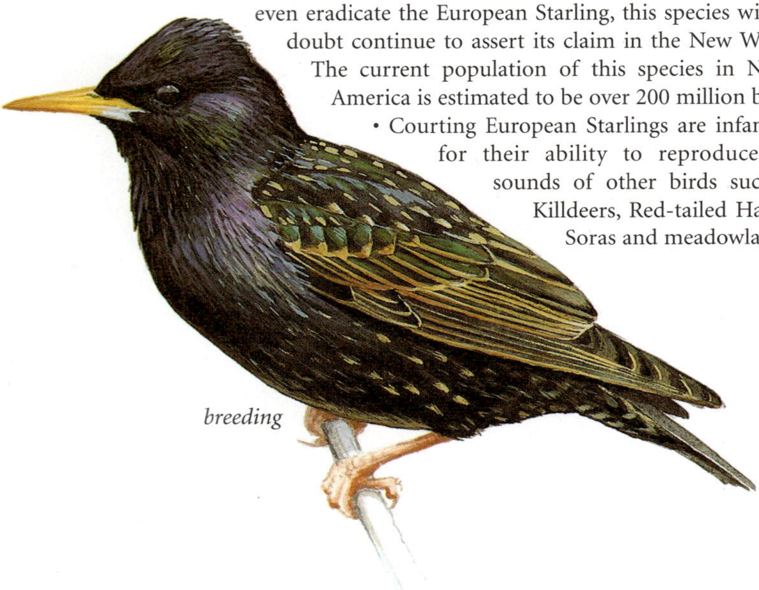

breeding

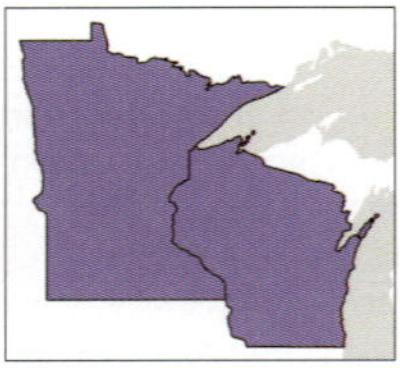

ID: short, squared tail; dark eyes. *Breeding:* blackish, iridescent plumage; yellow bill. *Nonbreeding:* blackish wings; feather tips are heavily spotted with white and buff. *Immature:* gray brown plumage; brown bill. *In flight:* pointed, triangular wings.

Size: *L* 8½ in; *W* 16 in.

Status: ***MN:*** abundant year-round resident, mainly in agricultural and residential areas. ***WI:*** abundant year-round resident.

Habitat: agricultural areas, townsites, woodland and forest edges, landfills and roadsides.

Nesting: in a tree, nest box or other artificial cavity; nest is made of grass, twigs and straw; mostly the female incubates 4–6 bluish to greenish white eggs for 12–14 days.

Feeding: forages mostly on the ground; very diverse diet includes many invertebrates, berries, seeds and human food waste.

Voice: variety of whistles, squeaks and gurgles; imitates other birds throughout the year.

Similar Species: *Rusty Blackbird* (p. 340): longer tail; black bill; lacks spotting; yellow eyes; rusty tinge on upperparts in fall. *Brewer's Blackbird* (p. 341): longer tail; black bill; lacks spotting; male has yellow eyes; female is brown overall. *Brown-headed Cowbird* (p. 343): lacks spotting; adult male has longer tail, shorter, dark bill and brown head; immature has streaked underparts, stout bill and longer tail.

Best Sites: widespread throughout both states.

AMERICAN PIPIT

Anthus rubescens

Each spring and fall, agricultural fields and open shorelines serve as refueling stations for American Pipits. Flocks of pipits may go unnoticed to untrained eyes, because their dull brown-and-buff plumage blends in perfectly with the landscape. To keen observers, however, their plain attire, white outer tail feathers and habit of continuously wagging their tails makes them readily identifiable. The best indicator that pipits are near is their telltale, two-syllable call, which is usually given in flight. • Although adults may already be paired up upon arriving on their breeding grounds—a strategy that is thought to save valuable nesting time—a conspicuous courtship display helps each pair establish and defend the boundaries of their exclusive nesting territory. American Pipits nest in the Arctic, so few of us will ever have a chance to view this bird on its nesting grounds. • This bird was formerly known as "Water Pipit" *(A. spinoletta)*.

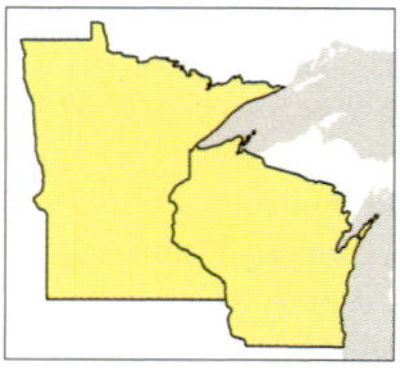

ID: faintly streaked, gray brown upperparts; lightly streaked "necklace" on upper breast; streaked sides and flanks; dark legs; dark tail with white outer tail feathers; buff-colored underparts; slim bill and body.

Size: *L* 6–7 in; *W* 10½ in.

Status: ***MN:*** uncommon to rare migrant from late April to late May; common migrant from mid-September to mid-November. ***WI:*** uncommon migrant from late April to late May and from mid-September to early November.

Habitat: agricultural fields, pastures and the shores of wetlands, lakes and rivers.

Nesting: does not nest in our region.

Feeding: gleans the ground and vegetation for terrestrial and aquatic invertebrates and for seeds.

Voice: familiar flight call is *pip-it pip-it*. *Male:* harsh, sharp *tsip-tsip* or *chiwee*.

Similar Species: *Horned Lark* (p. 228): black "horns"; facial markings. *Sprague's Pipit* (p. 360): lighter back with strong streaking; paler buff breast.

Best Sites: ***MN:*** sewage ponds and the North Shore of L. Superior in fall; sod farms; wet fields. ***WI:*** L. Michigan; L. Superior; edges of flooded fields.

BOHEMIAN WAXWING

Bombycilla garrulus

Descending upon mountain-ash and other ornamental plantings, great flocks of Bohemian Waxwings thrill us with their unpredictable appearances. Bohemian Waxwings nest in the northern forests of Alaska and western Canada, and visit only during winter in search of food. Their faint, quavering whistles attract attentive naturalists who take pleasure in watching the birds descend on berry-filled trees. In most years, Bohemians are only seen in small groups, usually intermingled with overwintering flocks of similar-looking Cedar Waxwings. Their chestnut brown undertail coverts readily distinguish them from their Cedar Waxwing counterparts. • Waxwings get their name from the colorful spots on their secondary feathers. These "waxy" spots are actually colorful enlargements of the feather shafts, whose pigments are derived from the birds' berry-filled diet.

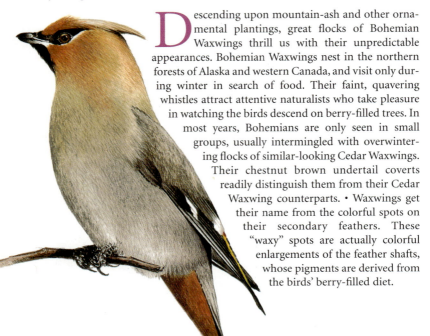

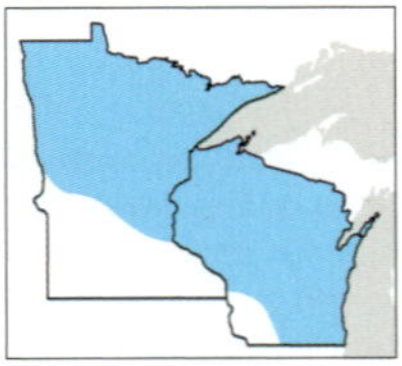

ID: gray and cinnamon crest; black "mask" and throat; soft brownish gray body; yellow terminal tail band; chestnut undertail coverts; small white, red and yellow markings on wings. *Immature:* gray brown upperparts; streaked underparts; pale throat; no "mask"; white wing patches.

Size: *L* 8 in; *W* 14½ in.

Status: ***MN:*** irregular (sometimes abundant, sometimes absent) migrant and winter visitor from late October to mid-April, mainly in the northeast; rare to absent elsewhere; formerly irregular irruptions in winter in northwestern and central regions. ***WI:*** irregular (common to rare) migrant and winter visitor from early November to early April.

Habitat: natural and residential areas with wild berries and fruit.

Nesting: does not nest in our region.

Feeding: gleans vegetation for insects and fruit or catches flying insects on the wing; depends on berries and fruit in winter.

Voice: high-pitched, quavering whistle.

Similar Species: *Cedar Waxwing* (p. 265): smaller; browner overall; slight yellow wash on belly; white undertail coverts; lacks yellow on wings.

Best Sites: ***MN:*** North Shore of L. Superior, such as Duluth and Grand Marais, where mountain-ash trees are present. ***WI:*** residential berry trees in northern and central areas, such as Three Lakes, Eagle River, Ashland, Superior, Wausau, Green Bay and Shawano.

CEDAR WAXWING

Bombycilla cedrorum

Flocks of handsome Cedar Waxwings take turns gorging on berries from bushes or trees in late summer and fall. If a bird's crop is full, it will continue to pluck fruit and pass it down the line of birds as if it were in a bucket brigade, until the fruit is gulped down by a still-hungry bird. Waxwings are able to digest a wide variety of berries, some of which are inedible or even poisonous to humans. If the fruits have fermented, these birds will show definite signs of tipsiness. • Cedar Waxwing pairs perform a wonderful courtship dance: the male first lands slightly away from the female, then tentatively hops toward her and offers her a berry. The female accepts the berry and hops away from the male, then she stops, hops back and offers him the berry. This gentle ritual can last for several minutes. Cedar Waxwings are late nesters, which ensures that berry crops will be ripe when nestlings are ready to be fed.

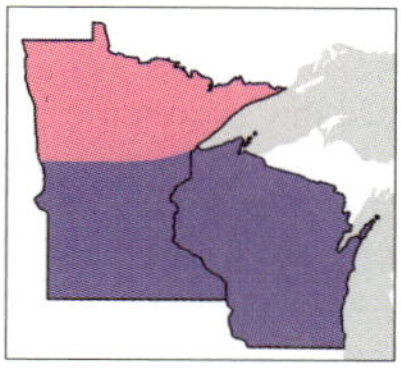

ID: cinnamon crest; brown upperparts; black "mask"; yellow wash on belly; gray rump; yellow terminal tail band; white undertail coverts; small red "drops" on wings. *Immature:* no "mask"; streaked underparts; gray brown body.
Size: *L* 7 in; *W* 12 in.
Status: ***MN:*** common to abundant migrant and breeder from March to November; least numerous in west-central and southwestern regions; common winter visitor, especially in the south. ***WI:*** common migrant and breeder from mid-May to mid-October; uncommon winter visitor.
Habitat: wooded urban parks and gardens, overgrown fields, forest edges, second-growth, riparian and open woodlands.
Nesting: in a coniferous or deciduous tree or shrub; cup nest of twigs, grass, moss and lichens is lined with fine grass; female incubates 3–5 pale gray to bluish gray eggs, with fine dark spotting, for 12–16 days.
Feeding: catches flying insects on the wing or gleans vegetation; also eats large amounts of berries and wild fruit, especially in fall and winter.
Voice: faint, high-pitched, trilled whistle: *tseee-tseee-tseee.*
Similar Species: *Bohemian Waxwing* (p. 264): larger; chestnut undertail coverts; small white, red and yellow markings on wings; immature has chestnut undertail coverts and white wing patches.
Best Sites: ***MN:*** Duluth; North Shore of L. Superior; river valleys and hillsides with cedar groves; wildlife management areas; state, city and county parks. ***WI:*** ***Breeding:*** wooded areas near ponds and streams. *Winter:* berry trees in urban and rural areas.

BLUE-WINGED WARBLER

Vermivora pinus

During the mid-1800s, the Blue-winged Warbler began expanding its range eastward and northward from its home in the central midwestern U.S., finding new breeding territories among overgrown fields and pastures near abandoned human settlements. Eventually it came into contact with the Golden-winged Warbler, a bird with completely different looks but practically identical habitat requirements and breeding biology. Where both species share the same habitat, a distinctive, fertile hybrid known as "Brewster's Warbler" may be produced. This hybrid tends to be more grayish overall, like the Golden-winged Warbler, but retains the thin, black eye line and the touch of yellow on the breast from its Blue-winged parent. In rare instances when two of these hybrids are able to reproduce successfully, a second-generation hybrid known as "Lawrence's Warbler" is the result.

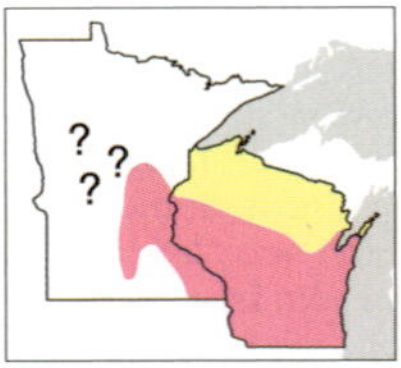

ID: bright yellow head and underparts, except for white to yellowish undertail coverts; olive yellow upperparts; bluish gray wings and tail; black eye line; thin, dark bill; 2 white wing bars; bold, white spots on underside of tail.

Size: *L* 4½–5 in; *W* 7½ in.

Status: ***MN:*** uncommon migrant and breeder from early May to early September; expanding its range to the north and northwest. ***WI:*** uncommon migrant in May and in fall until late September; fairly common breeder in the south and west.

Habitat: second-growth woodlands, willow swamps, shrubby, overgrown fields, pastures, woodland edges and woodland openings.

Nesting: on or near the ground, concealed by vegetation; female builds a narrow, inverted, cone-shaped nest of grass, leaves and bark strips and lines it with soft materials; female incubates 5 white eggs, with fine brown spots toward the larger end, for about 11 days.

Feeding: gleans insects and spiders from the lower branches of trees and shrubs.

Voice: buzzy, 2-note song: *beee-bzzz.*

Similar Species: *Prothonotary Warbler* (p. 289): lacks black eye line and white wing bars. *Pine Warbler* (p. 281): darker; white belly; faint streaking on sides and breast. *Yellow Warbler* (p. 272): yellow wings; lacks black eye line. *Prairie Warbler* (p. 282): black streaking on sides and flanks; darker wings.

Best Sites: ***MN:*** William O'Brien SP; Minnesota River Valley State Recreation Area; Beaver Creek Valley SP; Carver Park Reserve; Frontenac SP; Vasa. ***WI:*** Baxter's Hollow; Governor Dodge SP; Wyalusing SP; LaCrosse area; Mazomanie Bottoms.

GOLDEN-WINGED WARBLER

Vermivora chrysoptera

Unlike people, who are able to build fences around their property, the male Golden-winged Warbler uses song to defend his nesting territory. If song fails to repel rival males, then body language and aggression calls warn intruders to stay away. When a male's claim is seriously challenged, a warning call together with a raised crown and a spread tail may be employed. The last resort is to physically remove the competitor in a high-speed chase or a winged duel. • The battle to maintain breeding territory is not confined within the species—the Golden-winged Warbler may be losing ground to its colonizing relative the Blue-winged Warbler, which seems to be outcompeting the Golden-wing through hybridization.

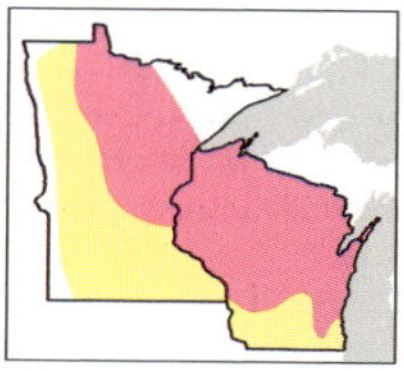

ID: yellow forecrown and wing patch; dark "chin," throat and "mask" over eye are bordered by white; bluish gray upperparts and flanks; white undersides; white spots on underside of tail. *Female* and *immature:* duller overall with gray throat and "mask."

Size: *L* $4\frac{1}{2}$–5 in; *W* $7\frac{1}{2}$ in.

Status: ***MN:*** uncommon migrant from early May to early June and from late July to mid-September in eastern and central regions; rare to casual migrant in the west, but may be increasing; uncommon breeder. ***WI:*** fairly common migrant in May and from early August to mid-September; fairly common breeder.

Habitat: moist, shrubby fields, woodland edges and early-succession forest clearings.

Nesting: on the ground, concealed by vegetation; female builds an open cup nest of grasses, leaves and grapevine bark and lines it with softer materials; female incubates 5 pinkish to pale cream eggs, marked with brown and lilac, for about 11 days.

Feeding: gleans insects and spiders from tree and shrub canopies.

Voice: buzzy song begins with a higher note: *zee-bz-bz-bz;* call is a sweet *chip.*

Similar Species: *Yellow-rumped Warbler* (p. 277): white throat; dark breast patches; yellow sides. *Yellow-throated Warbler* (p. 280): lacks yellow crown; 2 white wing bars; yellow throat. *Black-throated Green Warbler* (p. 278): lacks dark mask; 2 white wing bars; black streaking on sides.

Best Sites: ***MN:*** *Breeding:* deciduous forest edges in the central region. *In migration:* Sherburne NWR; Wild River SP; Banning SP; William O'Brien SP; Kanabec Co.; Frontenac SP. ***WI:*** *Breeding:* forest edges and brushy deciduous areas bordering creeks and swamps in central and northern regions. *In migration:* Milwaukee parks; Harrington Beach SP; Arboretum and Picnic Pt. (UW-Madison); Bay Beach Wildlife Sanctuary; Heckrodt Wetland Reserve.

TENNESSEE WARBLER

Vermivora peregrina

Tennessee Warblers lack the bold, bright features found on other warblers. Even so, they are difficult birds to miss because they have a loud, familiar song and are relatively common in our region. • Migrating Tennessee Warblers often sing their tunes and forage for insects high in the forest canopy. However, inclement weather and the need for food after a long flight often force these birds to lower levels in the forest. • Spruce budworm outbreaks are welcomed by Tennessee Warblers, which thrive on these insects. During times of plenty, these warblers may produce more than seven young in a single brood. • Alexander Wilson discovered this bird along the Cumberland River in Tennessee and named it after that state. It is just a migrant in Tennessee, however, and breeds only in Canada and northeastern Minnesota.

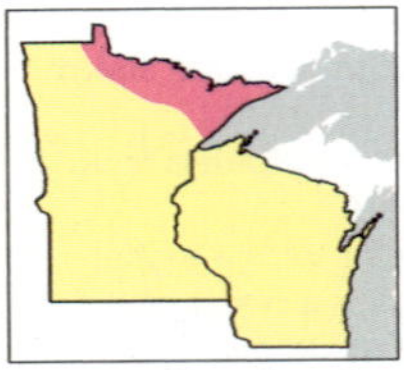

ID: *Breeding male:* blue gray "cap"; olive green back, wings and tail edgings; white "eyebrow"; black eye line; clean white underparts; thin bill. *Breeding female:* yellow wash on breast and "eyebrow"; olive gray "cap." *Nonbreeding:* olive yellow upperparts; yellow "eyebrow"; yellow underparts except for white undertail coverts; male may have white belly.

Size: *L* 4½–5 in; *W* 8 in.

Status: ***MN:*** common to at times abundant migrant from late April to mid-June and from mid-July to late October; rare breeder. ***WI:*** abundant migrant in May and from late July to mid-October; rare nonbreeding summer resident.

Habitat: woodlands or areas with tall shrubs.

Nesting: on the ground or on a raised hummock; female builds a cup nest of grass, moss and roots and lines it with fur; female incubates 5–6 white eggs, marked with brown or purple, for 11–12 days.

Feeding: gleans foliage and buds for small insects, caterpillars and other invertebrates; also eats berries; occasionally visits suet feeders.

Voice: male's song is a loud, sharp, accelerating *ticka-ticka-ticka swit-swit-swit-swit chew-chew-chew-chew-chew;* call is a sweet *chip.*

Similar Species: *Warbling Vireo* (p. 220): stouter overall; thicker bill; much less green on upperparts. *Philadelphia Vireo* (p. 221): stouter overall; thicker bill; yellow breast and sides. *Orange-crowned Warbler* (p. 269): lacks white "eyebrow" and blue gray head.

Best Sites: ***MN:*** state and county parks and national wildlife refuges; Minnesota Pt. (Duluth); widespread during migration. ***WI:*** various parks, preserves and woodlands, such as Harrington Beach SP, Wisconsin Pt., Bay Beach Wildlife Sanctuary, Arboretum and Picnic Pt. (UW-Madison), Milwaukee parks and Wyalusing SP.

ORANGE-CROWNED WARBLER

Vermivora celata

When encountered, the Orange-crowned Warbler usually appears as a blurred olive or grayish yellow bundle flitting nervously among the leaves and branches of low shrubs. Even worse, its drab, olive yellow appearance makes it frustratingly similar to females of other warbler species. Don't be disappointed if you can't see the Orange-crowned Warbler's telltale orange crown, because this bird's most distinguishing characteristic is its lack of field marks: wing bars, eye rings and color patches are all conspicuously absent. • Although this warbler breeds widely over most of the western and northern parts of the continent and eastward across Canada, it is seen in our region only as an early spring and late fall migrant, and can easily be overlooked.

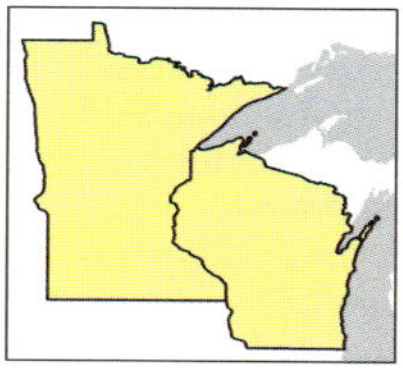

ID: olive yellow to olive gray body; faintly streaked underparts; bright yellow undertail coverts; thin, faint, dark eye line; bright yellow "eyebrow" and broken eye ring; thin bill; faint orange crown patch (rarely seen).
Size: *L* 5 in; *W* 7 in.
Status: ***MN:*** common migrant from late April to late May (a few linger into early June) and from early September to late October. ***WI:*** uncommon migrant from late April to mid-May; fairly common migrant from mid-September to late October.
Habitat: woodlands or areas with tall shrubs.
Nesting: does not nest in our region.
Feeding: gleans foliage for invertebrates, berries, nectar and sap; often hover-gleans.

Voice: song is a faint trill that breaks downward halfway through; call is a sharp *chip*.
Similar Species: *Tennessee Warbler* (p. 268): blue gray head; dark eye line; bold, white "eyebrow"; white underparts including undertail coverts. *Ruby-crowned Kinglet* (p. 247): broken, white eye ring; white wing bars. *Wilson's Warbler* (p. 299): complete, bright yellow eye ring; brighter yellow underparts; pale legs; lacks breast streaks. *Yellow Warbler* (p. 272): brighter head and underparts; reddish breast streaks (faint or absent on female). *Common Yellowthroat* (p. 297): female has darker face and upperparts; lacks breast streaks.
Best Sites: ***MN:*** woodlands across the state, especially Minnesota Pt. (Duluth), Frontenac SP, state and county parks and national wildlife refuges. ***WI:*** Harrington Beach SP; Milwaukee parks; Virmond Park; Bay Beach Wildlife Sanctuary; Arboretum and Picnic Pt. (UW-Madison); Wisconsin Pt.

NASHVILLE WARBLER

Vermivora ruficapilla

The Nashville Warbler has an unusual distribution, with two widely separated summer populations: one in eastern North America and the other in the West. These populations are believed to have been created thousands of years ago when a single core population was split during continental glaciation. • Nashville Warblers are best found in overgrown farmland and second-growth forest as they forage low in trees and thickets, often at the edge of a dry forest or burn area. They have benefited from the clearing of old-growth forests for timber and agriculture. • This warbler was first described near Nashville, Tennessee, but it does not breed in that state. This misnomer is not an isolated incident: the Tennessee, Cape May and Connecticut warblers all bear names that misrepresent their breeding distributions.

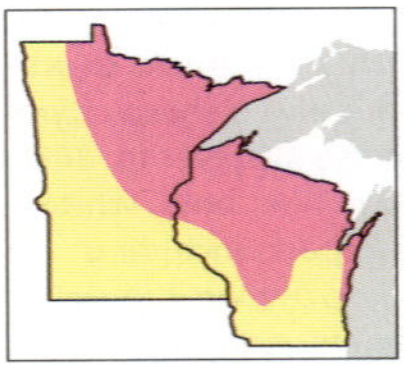

ID: bold, white eye ring; yellow green upperparts; yellow underparts; white between legs. *Male:* blue gray head; may show a small, chestnut red crown. *Female* and *immature:* duller overall; light eye ring; olive gray head; blue gray nape.

Size: *L* 4½–5 in; *W* 7½ in.

Status: ***MN:*** common to occasionally abundant migrant from late April to early June and from late July to mid-October; common breeder in the northeast. ***WI:*** very common migrant from late April through May and from mid-August to mid-October; common breeder in the north; uncommon breeder in central regions.

Habitat: prefers second-growth mixed woodlands; also wet coniferous forests, riparian woodlands, cedar-spruce swamps and moist, shrubby, abandoned fields.

Nesting: on the ground under a fern, sapling or shrubby cover; female builds a cup nest of grass, bark strips, ferns and moss and lines it with conifer needles, fur and fine grasses; female incubates 4–5 white eggs, spotted with reddish brown toward the larger end, for 11–12 days.

Feeding: gleans foliage for insects, such as caterpillars, flies and aphids.

Voice: song begins with a thin, high-pitched *see-it see-it see-it see-it,* followed by a trilling *ti-ti-ti-ti-ti;* call is a metallic *chink.*

Similar Species: *Common Yellowthroat* (p. 297) and *Wilson's Warbler* (p. 299): all-yellow underparts; females lack grayish head and bold, white eye ring. *Connecticut Warbler* (p. 295) and *Mourning Warbler* (p. 296): yellow between legs; females have grayish to brownish "hood."

Best Sites: *In migration:* widespread in woodlands throughout both states.

NORTHERN PARULA

Parula americana

Young Northern Parulas spend the first few weeks of their lives enclosed in a fragile, socklike nest suspended from a tree branch. Once they have grown too large for the nest and their wing feathers are strong enough to allow for a short, awkward flight, the young leave their warm abode, dispersing among the surrounding trees and shrubs. As warm summer nights slip away to be replaced by cooler fall temperatures, newly fledged Northern Parulas migrate to the warmer climes of Central America, but mature birds winter in the U.S. • Northern Parulas are typically found in older forests where the lichens that they use during nesting have had a chance to mature.

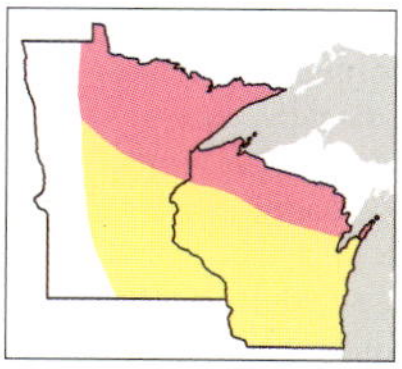

ID: blue gray upperparts; olive patch on back; 2 bold white wing bars; bold, white eye ring is broken by black eye line; yellow "chin," throat and breast; white belly and flanks. *Male:* 1 black and 1 orange breast band.

Size: *L* $4\frac{1}{2}$ in; *W* 7 in.

Status: ***MN:*** uncommon migrant from early May to early June and from late August to mid-October in eastern and central regions; rare migrant in western regions; uncommon breeder. ***WI:*** uncommon migrant in May and from mid-August through September; uncommon breeder.

Habitat: moist coniferous forests, humid riparian woodlands and swampy deciduous woodlands, especially where lichens hang from branches.

Nesting: usually in a conifer; female weaves a small hanging nest into hanging strands of tree lichens; may add lichens to a dense cluster of conifer boughs; pair incubates 4–5 brown-marked, whitish eggs for 12–14 days.

Feeding: forages for insects and other invertebrates by hovering, gleaning or hawking; feeds from the tips of branches and occasionally on the ground.

Voice: song is a rising, buzzy trill ending with an abrupt, lower-pitched *zip*.

Similar Species: *Cerulean Warbler* (p. 286): streaking on breast and sides; lacks white eye ring. *Blue-winged Warbler* (p. 266): yellow underparts. *Yellow-rumped Warbler* (p. 277): yellow rump and crown; lacks yellow throat. *Yellow-throated Warbler* (p. 280): heavy black streaking along sides.

Best Sites: ***MN:*** *Breeding:* Frontenac SP; Itasca SP; Scenic SP; Judge C. R. Magney SP. *In migration:* Mississippi R. valley; St. Croix R. valley. ***WI:*** *Breeding:* Stone's Bridge (Brule R.); Nicolet NF; Chequamegon NF. *In migration:* various parks, preserves and woodlands including Harrington Beach SP, Milwaukee parks, Virmond Park, Bay Beach Wildlife Sanctuary, Arboretum and Picnic Pt. (UW-Madison) and Wisconsin Pt.

YELLOW WARBLER

Dendroica petechia

Yellow Warblers usually arrive here in late April or early May with the first main wave of spring warblers. Flitting from branch to branch among open woodland edges and riparian shrubs, these inquisitive birds seem to be in perpetual motion. • Yellow Warblers are among the most frequent victims of nest parasitism by Brown-headed Cowbirds. Unlike many birds, however, they can recognize the foreign eggs, and many pairs will either abandon their nest or build another nest overtop the old eggs. Some persistent Yellow Warblers build over and over, creating bizarre, multilayered, high-rise nests. • During fall migration, silent, plain-looking Yellow Warblers and other similar-looking warblers can confuse birders who have been lulled into a false sense of familiarity with these birds. Yellow Warblers are unique, however, in having yellow flashes on the sides of their tails.

breeding

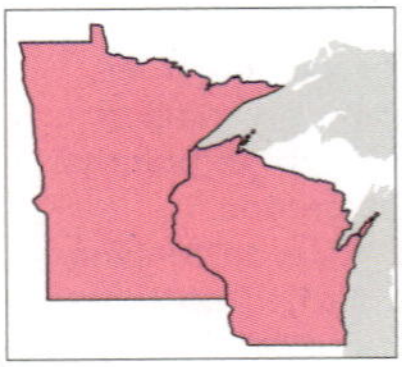

ID: bright yellow body; black bill and eyes; yellow highlights in dark olive tail and wings. *Breeding male:* red breast streaks.

Size: *L* 5 in; *W* 8 in.

Status: ***MN:*** common migrant and breeder from late April to early September. ***WI:*** common migrant and breeder from late April to late August.

Habitat: usually near water in moist, open woodlands with dense, low scrub; also shrubby meadows, willow tangles and riparian woodlands.

Nesting: in a fork in a deciduous tree or small shrub; female builds a compact cup nest of grass, weeds and shredded bark and lines it with plant down and fur; female incubates 4–5 speckled or spotted, greenish white eggs for 11–12 days.

Feeding: gleans foliage and vegetation for invertebrates, especially caterpillars, inchworms, beetles, aphids and cankerworms; occasionally hover-gleans.

Voice: *Male:* song is a fast, frequently repeated *sweet-sweet-sweet summer sweet.*

Similar Species: *Orange-crowned Warbler* (p. 269): darker olive plumage overall; lacks reddish breast streaks. *American Goldfinch* (p. 354): black wings and tail; male often has black forehead. *Wilson's Warbler* (p. 299): shorter, darker tail; male has black "cap"; female has darker crown and upperparts. *Common Yellowthroat* (p. 297): darker face and upperparts; female lacks yellow highlights in wings.

Best Sites: ***MN:*** wooded swamps and marshy areas, especially in parks, preserves and national wildlife refuges, including Beaver Creek Valley SP, Frontenac SP, Flandrau SP, Sherburne SP and Carlos Avery WMA. ***WI:*** Horicon Marsh; Rat River WA; Mead WA; Crex Meadows WA; Vernon Marsh; Mud Lake WA; Trempealeau NWR; almost any swampy area.

CHESTNUT-SIDED WARBLER

Dendroica pensylvanica

When colorful waves of warbler migrants flood across the landscape each May, the Chestnut-sided Warbler is consistently ranked among the most anticipated arrivals. • Chestnut-sided Warblers tend to favor early-succession forests, which have become abundant over the past century. Although clear-cut logging and prescribed forest burns have adversely affected other warbler species, they have created suitable habitat for the Chestnut-sided Warbler in many parts of the region. • Although other warblers lose some of their brighter colors in fall yet still look familiar, the Chestnut-sided Warbler undergoes a complete transformation, looking more like a flycatcher or kinglet in its green-and-gray coat.

breeding

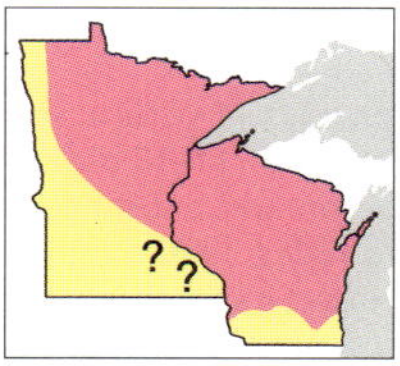

ID: *Breeding:* chestnut sides; white underparts; yellow "cap"; black legs; yellowish wing bars; black "mask." *Male:* bold colors. *Female:* washed-out colors; dark streaking on yellow "cap." *Nonbreeding:* yellow green crown, nape and back; white eye ring; gray face and sides; white underparts.

Size: *L* 5 in; *W* 8 in.

Status: ***MN:*** common migrant from early May to early June and from mid-August to early October; least numerous in western regions; common breeder primarily in the north; absent as a breeder in extreme western and west-central regions. ***WI:*** common migrant in May and from mid-August to early October; common breeder in the north; fairly common breeder in central regions; rare breeder in the south.

Habitat: shrubby, second-growth, deciduous woodlands and abandoned fields and orchards; especially in areas that are regenerating after logging or fire.

Nesting: low in a shrub or sapling; small cup nest is made of bark strips, grass, roots and weed fibers and lined with fine grasses, plant down and fur; female incubates 4 brown-marked, whitish eggs for 11–12 days.

Feeding: gleans trees and shrubs at midlevel for insects.

Voice: loud, clear song: *so pleased, pleased, pleased to MEET-CHA!;* musical *chip* call.

Similar Species: *Bay-breasted Warbler* (p. 284): black face; dark chestnut hindcrown, upper breast and sides; buff belly and undertail coverts; white wing bars. *American Redstart* (p. 288): female has large, yellow patches on wings and tail; more grayish overall. *Flycatchers* (pp. 203–11): less obvious eye rings; perch upright. *Ruby-crowned Kinglet* (p. 247): smaller; buffier underparts; more active.

Best Sites: ***MN:*** *Breeding:* deciduous second-growth shrubby woodlands; Superior NF; Chippewa NF; Frontenac SP. *In migration:* deciduous woodlands, especially with shrubby undergrowth; state, county and city parks, such as Minnesota Pt. (Duluth). ***WI:*** *Breeding:* deciduous forest and shrubby, deciduous second-growth in northern and central regions. *In migration:* Milwaukee parks; Arboretum and Picnic Pt. (UW-Madison); Wyalusing SP; LaCrosse parks; Bay Beach Wildlife Sanctuary; High Cliff SP; Harrington Beach SP.

MAGNOLIA WARBLER

Dendroica magnolia

The Magnolia Warbler is widely regarded as one of the most beautiful wood warblers. Like a customized Cadillac, the Magnolia comes fully loaded with all the fancy features—bold eyebrows, flashy wing bars and tail patches, an elegant "necklace," a bright yellow rump and breast and a dark "mask." It frequently forages along the lower branches of trees and among shrubs, allowing for reliable, close-up observations. In the fall, the Magnolia Warbler loses the dark "mask" and "necklace," but is immediately identifiable by the distinctive white tail flash. • Magnolia Warblers and many other songbirds migrate at night. Unfortunately, many birds are killed each year when they collide with buildings, radio towers and tall smokestacks.

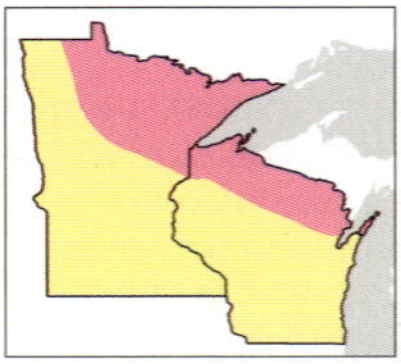

ID: *Breeding male:* yellow underparts with bold black streaks; black "mask"; white "eyebrow"; blue gray crown; dark upperparts; white wing bars often blend into larger patch. *Female* and *nonbreeding male:* duller overall; pale "mask"; 2 distinct white wing bars; streaked olive back.

Size: *L* 4½–5 in; *W* 7½ in.

Status: ***MN:*** uncommon to occasionally common migrant from early May to early June and from early August to early October; most numerous in the east; uncommon breeder. ***WI:*** common migrant in May and from mid-August to early October; uncommon breeder.

Habitat: open coniferous and mixed forests, mostly in natural openings and along edges, often near water; often prefers areas with short balsam fir and white spruce.

Nesting: on a horizontal limb in a conifer; loose cup nest is made of grass, twigs and weeds and is lined with rootlets; female incubates 4 white eggs, marked with olive, brown, gray and lavender, for 11–13 days.

Feeding: gleans vegetation and buds; occasionally flycatches for beetles, flies, wasps, caterpillars and other insects; sometimes eats berries.

Voice: song is a quick, rising *pretty pretty lady* or *wheata wheata wheet-zu;* call is a *clank*.

Similar Species: *Yellow-rumped Warbler* (p. 277): white throat; yellow hindcrown patch; white belly. *Cape May Warbler* (p. 275): chestnut "cheek" patch on yellow face; lacks white tail patches. *Prairie Warbler* (p. 282): dusky jaw stripe; faint yellowish wing bars; immature lacks white tail patches.

Best Sites: ***MN:*** *Breeding:* coniferous forests in Superior NF, Chippewa NF, Boundary Waters Canoe Area Wilderness, North Shore state parks. *In migration:* Frontenac SP; Beaver Creek Valley SP; Afton SP; shrubby woodlands; state, county and city parks. ***WI:*** *Breeding:* coniferous forests in the north. *In migration:* Arboretum and Picnic Pt. (UW-Madison); Wisconsin Pt.; Devil's Lake SP; Bay Beach Wildlife Sanctuary; Milwaukee parks; Virmond Park; Harrington Beach SP; High Cliff SP.

CAPE MAY WARBLER

Dendroica tigrina

Cape May Warblers require mature forests that are at least 50 years old for secure nesting habitat and an abundance of canopy-dwelling insects. This warbler forages and sings at the very top of tall trees. • These small birds are spruce budworm specialists—in years of budworm outbreaks, Cape Mays can successfully fledge more young. The use of pesticides to control budworms and the cutting of old-growth forests may adversely affect populations of this warbler. • The Cape May uses its tubular tongue, unique among wood-warblers, to feed on nectar and fruit juices. • Named after Cape May, New Jersey, where the first scientific specimen was collected in 1811, this bird was not recorded there again for more than 100 years.

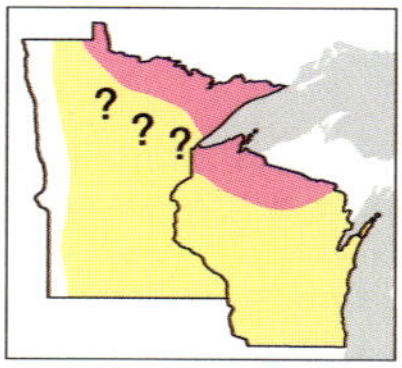

ID: dark streaking on yellow underparts; yellow side "collar"; dark olive green upperparts; yellow rump; clean white undertail coverts. *Breeding male:* chestnut brown "cheek" on yellow face; dark crown; large, white wing patch. *Female:* paler overall; 2 faint, thin, white wing bars; grayish "cheek" and crown.

Size: *L* 5 in; *W* 8 in.

Status: ***MN:*** uncommon migrant in May and from early August through October, mainly in eastern and central regions; rare in western regions; sporadic breeder; strays linger into December. ***WI:*** fairly common migrant in May and from mid-August to mid-October; uncommon breeder.

Habitat: mature coniferous and mixed forests, especially in dense, old-growth stands of white spruce and balsam fir.

Nesting: near the top of a spruce or fir, often near the trunk; female builds a cup nest of moss, weeds and grass and lines it with feathers and fur; female incubates 6–7 whitish eggs, spotted with reddish brown, for about 12 days.

Feeding: gleans treetop branches and foliage for spruce budworms, flies, beetles, moths, wasps and other insects; occasionally hover-gleans.

Voice: song is a very high-pitched, weak *see see see see;* call is a very high-pitched *tsee.*

Similar Species: *Bay-breasted Warbler* (p. 284): male has black face and chestnut throat, upper breast and sides; buff underparts lack black streaking. *Black-throated Green Warbler* (p. 278): black throat or upper breast or both; white lower breast and belly; 2 white wing bars; lacks chestnut "cheek" patch. *Magnolia Warbler* (p. 274): white tail patches; lacks chestnut "cheek" patch and yellow side "collar"; less streaking on underparts.

Best Sites: ***MN:*** *Breeding:* coniferous forests in northern St. Louis, Lake and Cook Counties; Boundary Waters Canoe Area Wilderness; Itasca SP. *In migration:* mixed woodlands in eastern and central regions, such as Frontenac SP. ***WI:*** *Breeding:* northern coniferous forests, such as Brule R. (Douglas Co.). *In migration:* High Cliff SP; Bay Beach Wildlife Sanctuary; Harrington Beach SP; Point Beach State Forest; Wyalusing SP; Arboretum and Picnic Pt. (UW-Madison); Colonial Park Nature Center (Racine); Milwaukee parks.

BLACK-THROATED BLUE WARBLER

Dendroica caerulescens

Dark and handsome, the male Black-throated Blue Warbler is a treasured sight to the eyes of any bird enthusiast or casual admirer. The female looks nothing like her male counterpart, however, appearing more like a vireo or a plain-colored Tennessee Warbler. The males and females are so different in appearance that early naturalists, including John J. Audubon, initially thought that they were two different species. • When foraging, this warbler prefers to work deliberately and methodically over a small area, snatching up insects from branches and foliage. It is generally shy and inconspicuous, foraging secretly in deciduous foliage or within the dense confines of low shrubs and saplings.

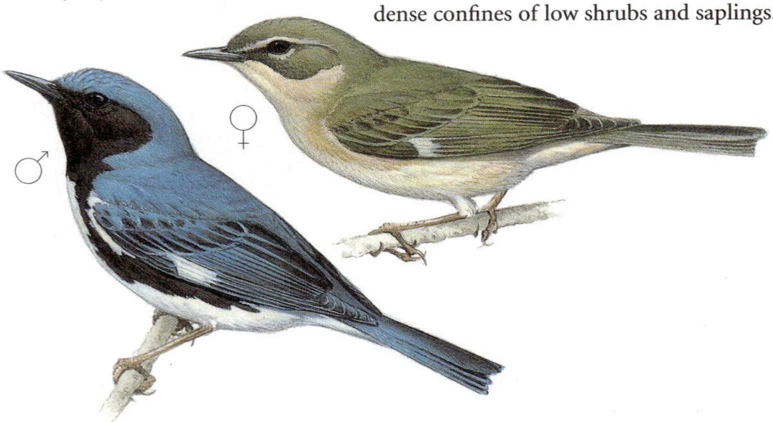

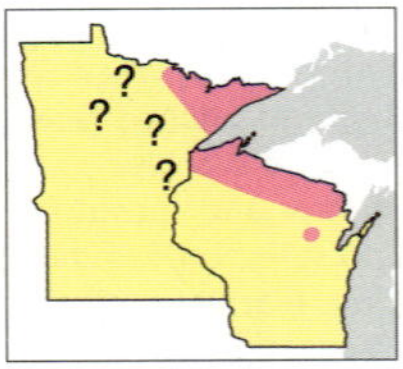

ID: *Male:* black face, throat, upper breast and sides; dark blue upperparts; clean white underparts and wing patch. *Female:* olive brown upperparts; unmarked buff underparts; faint white "eyebrow"; small buff to whitish wing patch (may not be visible).

Size: *L* 5–5½ in; *W* 7½ in.

Status: ***MN:*** rare migrant in May and from late August through October; uncommon and local breeder in Lake Co. and Cook Co. ***WI:*** uncommon migrant in May and from mid-August to early October; uncommon breeder.

Habitat: upland deciduous and mixed forests with a dense understory of deciduous saplings and shrubs; also in second-growth woodlands and brushy clearings.

Nesting: in the fork of a dense shrub or sapling; usually within 3 ft of the ground; female builds an open cup nest of weeds, bark strips and spider silk and lines it with moss, hair and pine needles; female incubates 4 creamy white eggs, blotched with reddish brown and gray toward the larger end, for 12–13 days.

Feeding: thoroughly gleans the understory for caterpillars, moths, spiders and other insects; occasionally eats berries and seeds.

Voice: song is a slow, wheezy *I am soo lay-zeee,* rising slowly throughout; call is a short *tip.*

Similar Species: male is distinctive. *Tennessee Warbler* (p. 268): lighter "cheek"; greener back; lacks white wing patch. *Philadelphia Vireo* (p. 221): stouter bill; lighter "cheek"; more yellowish white below; lacks white wing patch. *Cerulean Warbler* (p. 286): female has 2 white wing bars; broader, yellowish eyebrow.

Best Sites: ***MN:*** Superior Hiking Trail (Lake Co.); Tettegouche SP; George Crosby Manitou SP. ***WI:*** *Breeding:* northern coniferous and mixed forest; forest roads in Oneida, Vilas and Forest Counties. *In migration:* Arboretum and Picnic Pt. (UW-Madison); Harrington Beach SP; Bay Beach Wildlife Sanctuary; Milwaukee parks; Wisconsin Pt.; Heckrodt Wetland Reserve.

YELLOW-RUMPED WARBLER

Dendroica coronata

The Yellow-rumped Warbler is the most abundant and widespread wood-warbler in North America, and you are likeliest to meet one during spring or fall migration. The best time to look for this bird is in the first few hours after dawn, when most Yellow-rumps forage in trees along streams or lakeshores. • Adults are generally quiet when they have eggs or young to guard. When they are noisy and aggressive, it is a good sign that the young have left the nest. • In migration, Yellow-rumps are the least choosy of all warblers, spreading out and using all manner of growth. These birds are generalists and forage in a wide variety of habitats. Yellow-rumps are unique among warblers in their ability to digest the waxes in bayberries, allowing them to winter far to the north, including our region.

"Myrtle Warbler"

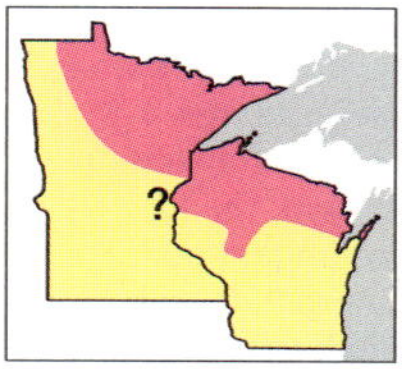

ID: yellow foreshoulder patches and rump; white underparts with dark streaking; faint, white wing bars; thin "eyebrow." *Male:* yellow crown; blue gray upperparts with black streaking; black "cheek" and breast band. *Female:* gray brown upperparts with dark streaking.

Size: *L* 5–6 in; *W* 9 in.

Status: ***MN:*** abundant migrant from late March to early June and from August to early November; common breeder; some linger into late November and December; a few may overwinter in the south.
WI: abundant migrant in April and May and from late August to mid-November; fairly common breeder; rare winter visitor in southern and central regions.

Habitat: coniferous and mixed forests; rarely in pure deciduous woodlands.

Nesting: in the crotch or on a horizontal limb of a conifer; female builds a compact cup nest of grass, bark strips, moss, lichens and spider silk and lines it with feathers and fur; female incubates 4–5 creamy white eggs, with brown and gray markings, for about 12 days.

Feeding: hawks and hovers for beetles, flies, wasps, caterpillars, moths and other insects; also gleans vegetation; sometimes eats berries.

Voice: *Male:* song is a tinkling trill, often given in 2-note phrases that rise or fall at the end (there can be much variation between individuals); call is a sharp *chip* or *check*.

Similar Species: *Magnolia Warbler* (p. 274): yellow underparts; yellow throat; bold white "eyebrow"; white patches on tail; lacks yellow crown. *Chestnut-sided Warbler* (p. 273): chestnut brown sides on otherwise clean white underparts; lacks yellow rump. *Cape May Warbler* (p. 275): heavily streaked yellow throat, breast and sides; lacks yellow crown. *Yellow-throated Warbler* (p. 280): yellow throat; bold white "eyebrow," ear patch and wing bars; lacks yellow crown and rump.

Best Sites: *Breeding:* northern coniferous forests. *In migration:* widespread throughout both states.

BLACK-THROATED GREEN WARBLER

Dendroica virens

Before the first warm rays of dawn brighten the spires of our forests, male Black-throated Green Warblers offer up their distinctive *see-see-see SUZY!* tunes. Unlike other warblers, they continue to sing throughout the summer, although song quality deteriorates later in the season. Not only do males use song to defend their turf, but they also seem to thrive on chasing each other, and even other songbirds, from their territories. • When foraging among the forest canopy, male Black-throated Greens are highly conspicuous as they dart from branch to branch, chipping noisily as they go. Females often prefer to feed at lower levels among the foliage of tall shrubs and sapling trees.

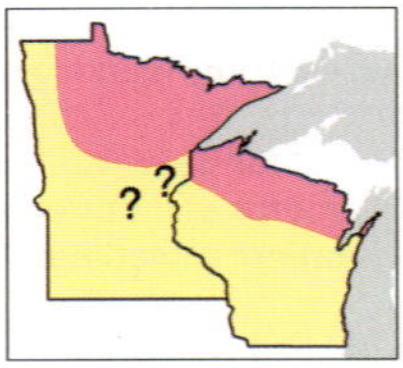

ID: yellow face; may show faint dusky "cheek" or eye line; black upper breast band; streaking along sides; olive crown, back and rump; dark wings and tail; 2 bold white wing bars; white lower breast, belly and undertail coverts. *Male:* black throat. *Female:* yellow throat; thinner wing bars.

Size: *L* 4½–5 in; *W* 7½ in.

Status: ***MN:*** uncommon migrant from late April to early June and from mid-August to mid-October, least numerous in western regions; fairly common but local breeder. ***WI:*** fairly common migrant from late April through May and from mid-August to October; fairly common breeder in the north; rare breeder in the south.

Habitat: coniferous and mixed forests; deciduous woodlands with beech, maple or birch; also cedar swamps, hemlock ravines, second-growth, open parklands and conifer plantations.

Nesting: in a crotch or on a horizontal limb; usually in a conifer; compact cup nest of grass, weeds, twigs, bark, lichens and spider silk is lined with moss, fur, feathers and plant fibers; female incubates 4–5 creamy white to gray eggs, scrawled or spotted with reddish brown, for 12 days.

Feeding: gleans vegetation and buds for beetles, flies, wasps, caterpillars and other insects; sometimes takes berries; frequently hover-gleans.

Voice: fast *see-see-see SUZY!* or *zoo zee zoo zoo zee;* call is a fairly soft *tick.*

Similar Species: *Blackburnian Warbler* (p. 279): female has yellowish underparts and angular, dusky facial patch. *Cape May Warbler* (p. 275): heavily streaked yellow throat, breast and sides. *Pine Warbler* (p. 281): yellowish breast and upper belly; lacks black upper breast band.

Best Sites: ***MN:*** *Breeding:* northern mixed forests; North Shore state parks; Scenic SP. *In migration:* Minnesota Pt. (Duluth); Frontenac SP; Afton SP. ***WI:*** *Breeding:* northern coniferous and mixed forests. *In migration:* Bay Beach Wildlife Sanctuary; Wisconsin Pt.; Wyalusing SP; Devil's Lake SP; Harrington Beach SP; Arboretum and Picnic Pt. (UW-Madison); Milwaukee parks.

BLACKBURNIAN WARBLER

Dendroica fusca

High among towering coniferous spires lives the colorful Blackburnian Warbler, its fiery orange throat ablaze in spring. Widely regarded as one of the most beautiful warblers in our region, the Blackburnian Warbler stays hidden in the upper canopy for much of the summer. • Different species of wood-warblers are able to coexist through a partitioning of foraging niches and feeding strategies. This intricate partitioning reduces competition for food sources and avoids the exhaustion of particular resources. Some warblers inhabit high treetops, a few feed and nest along outer tree branches and others restrict themselves to inner branches and tree trunks. Blackburnians have found their niche predominantly in the outermost branches of the crowns of mature trees.

breeding

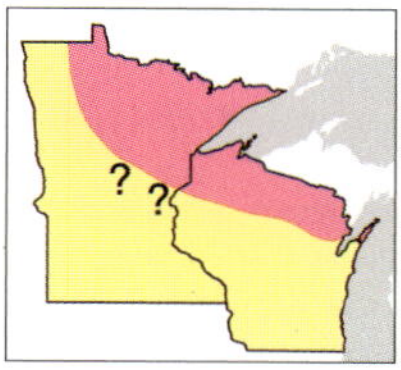

ID: *Breeding male:* fiery, reddish orange upper breast and throat; yellow orange head with black markings; blackish upperparts; large, white wing patch; yellowish to whitish underparts; dark streaking on sides and flanks. *Female:* brown version of male with yellower upper breast and throat.

Size: *L* 5–5½ in; *W* 8½ in.

Status: ***MN:*** uncommon to at times common migrant from early May to early June and from mid-August to late September, best represented in eastern and central regions; fairly common but local breeder. ***WI:*** fairly common migrant in May and from mid-August to early October; fairly common breeder.

Habitat: mature coniferous and mixed forests.

Nesting: high in a mature conifer, often near a branch tip; female builds a cup nest of bark, twigs and plant fibers and lines it with conifer needles, moss and fur; female incubates 3–5 white to greenish white eggs, blotched with reddish brown toward the larger end, for about 13 days.

Feeding: forages on the uppermost branches, gleaning budworms, flies, beetles and other invertebrates; occasionally hover-gleans.

Voice: song is a soft, faint, high-pitched *ptoo-too-too-too tititi zeee* or *see-me see-me see-me see-me;* call is a short *tick.*

Similar Species: *Yellow-throated Warbler* (p. 280): blue gray upperparts; white "eyebrow," ear patch and eye crescent; lacks orange throat. *Prairie Warbler* (p. 282): faint yellowish wingbars; black facial stripes do not form solid angular patch. *Black-throated Green Warbler* (p. 278): olive crown, back and rump.

Best Sites: ***MN:*** *Breeding:* northern coniferous forests; Itasca SP. *In migration:* wooded areas, especially state, county and city parks, including Frontenac SP, Whitewater SP, Minneapolis parks and Minnesota Pt. (Duluth). ***WI:*** *Breeding:* northern coniferous and mixed forests. *In migration:* Arboretum and Picnic Pt. (UW-Madison); Wausau parks; Wisconsin Pt.; High Cliff SP; Bay Beach Wildlife Sanctuary; Harrington Beach SP; Milwaukee parks.

YELLOW-THROATED WARBLER

Dendroica dominica

The striking Yellow-throated Warbler is a breeding bird in the southeastern U.S., but many of these warblers regularly extend their traditional range and migrate into our region, with a few usually nesting. In the 19th century, this bird nested as far north as southern Michigan and northern Ohio, but for unknown reasons it disappeared from this part of its range, retreating southward in the early 20th century. Since the 1940s, the Yellow-throated Warbler has been slowly expanding its breeding range northward, reoccupying its former territory. • Yellow-throats are fond of either dry, upland pine forests or wet, lowland forests, but seem consistent in their preference for the upper canopy. This warbler forages more like a creeper than a warbler, inserting its unusually long bill into cracks and crevices in bark.

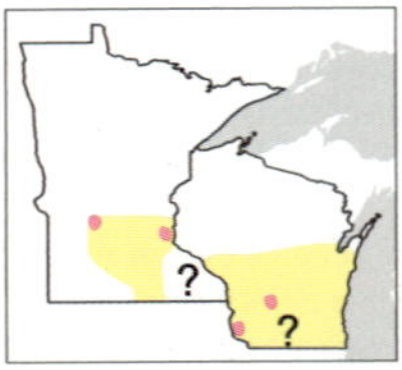

ID: yellow throat and upper breast; triangular black "mask"; black forehead; bold white "eyebrow" and ear patch; white underparts with black streaking on sides; 2 white wing bars; bluish gray upperparts.

Size: *L* 5–5½ in; *W* 8 in.

Status: ***MN:*** casual migrant in May; accidental in the fall; 2 nesting records (1997 and 2001). ***WI:*** endangered; rare spring migrant from late April through May; rare breeder; casual winter visitor.

Habitat: dry, upland pine-oak forests, riparian woodlands and swamps and groves of oak or sycamore; seen at backyard feeders in winter.

Nesting: on a horizontal branch in a deciduous or pine tree, well away from the trunk; female builds a cup nest of fine grasses, weed stems, bark shreds and plant fibers and lines it with plant down and feathers; female incubates 4 pale greenish or grayish white eggs, spotted and blotched with purple, gray and dark red, for about 12 days.

Feeding: primarily insectivorous; gleans insects from tree trunks and foliage by creeping along tree surfaces; often flycatches insects in midair; wintering birds may eat suet from feeders.

Voice: boisterous song is a series of downslurred whistles with a final rising note: *tee-ew tee-ew tee-ew tew-wee;* call is a loud *churp*.

Similar Species: *Magnolia Warbler* (p. 274): black "necklace"; yellow breast, belly and rump; lacks white ear patch. *Blackburnian Warbler* (p. 279): yellow orange to orange red throat, "eyebrow," ear patch and crown stripe; dark brown to blackish upperparts; often shows yellowish underparts. *Yellow-throated Vireo* (p. 218): lacks black and white in face and dark streaking on sides. *Kentucky Warbler* (p. 294): unmarked, all-yellow underparts; yellow "eyebrow"; lacks white ear patch and wing bars.

Best Sites: ***MN:*** Acacia Cemetery (Dakota Co.); Fort Snelling SP; William O'Brien SP; Sibley SP. ***WI:*** Wyalusing SP; Baxter's Hollow.

PINE WARBLER

Dendroica pinus

Pine Warblers are often difficult to observe because they typically forage near the tops of very tall, mature pine trees. They are particularly attracted to stands of long-needled white pine and red pine, and tend to avoid pine trees with shorter needles. The Pine Warbler behaves much like a Brown Creeper when it forages, deliberately probing the furrowed bark or tree trunks in search of hidden insects. • The Pine Warbler's modest appearance is very similar to that of a number of immature and fall-plumaged vireos and warblers, forcing birders to obtain a good, long look before making a positive identification. • The Pine Warbler is peculiar among the wood-warblers in that both its breeding and wintering ranges are located almost entirely within Canada and the U.S.

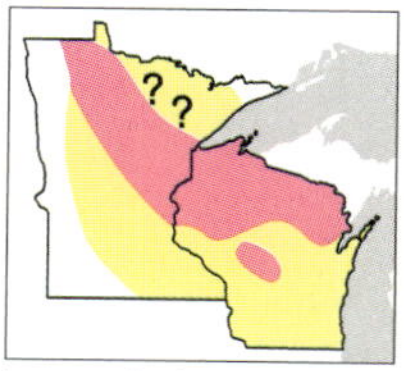

ID: *Male:* olive green head and back; dark grayish wings and tail; whitish to dusky wing bars; yellow throat and breast; faded dark streaking or dusky wash on sides of breast; white undertail coverts and belly; faint yellow, broken eye ring. *Female:* similar to male, but duller, especially in fall.

Size: *L* 5–5½ in; *W* 8½ in.

Status: ***MN:*** uncommon to rare migrant from mid-April to late May; uncommon migrant from mid-August to mid-October, mainly in eastern and central regions; uncommon and local breeder. ***WI:*** uncommon migrant from late April to mid-May and from September to early October; fairly common breeder in the north; uncommon breeder in central regions.

Habitat: prefers open, mature pine woodlands and mature pine plantations for nesting; may be seen in mixed and deciduous woodlands in migration.

Nesting: toward the end of a pine limb; female builds a deep, open cup nest of twigs, bark, weeds, grasses, pine needles and spider silk and lines it with feathers; pair incubates 3–5 whitish eggs, with brown specks toward the larger end, for about 10 days.

Feeding: eats mostly insects, berries and seeds; gleans from the ground or foliage; may hang upside down on branch tips.

Voice: song is a short, musical trill; call note is a sweet *chip*.

Similar Species: *Prairie Warbler* (p. 282): distinctive, dark facial stripes; darker streaking on sides; yellowish wing bars. *Bay-breasted Warbler* (p. 284) and *Blackpoll Warbler* (p. 285): long, thin yellow "eyebrow"; nonbreeding and immature birds have dark streaking on head or back or both. *Yellow-throated Vireo* (p. 218): bright yellow "spectacles"; gray rump; lacks streaking on sides.

Best Sites: ***MN:*** *Breeding:* stands of white pine, especially in cemeteries in the central part of the state. *In migration:* mixed with other migrating warblers in parks, such as Interstate SP, Frontenac SP and St. Croix SP. ***WI:*** *Breeding:* coniferous forests in northern and central regions. *In migration:* watch for it with other warblers during spring warbler movement in various parks and woods.

PRAIRIE WARBLER

Dendroica discolor

Woodland edges and open scrublands host the summer actitivies of the inappropriately named Prairie Warbler. This bird has a preference for early successional areas with such poor soil conditions that the vegetation remains short and scattered. • It is thought the Prairie Warbler was rare over much of its current breeding range in the early 1800s, before North America was widely colonized. As settlers cleared land, the Prairie Warbler gradually occupied what is now its current range. Because this bird uses early successional habitats, which change over time, its breeding locations change as well. A male Prairie Warbler may return each year to a favored nest site until the vegetation in that area grows too tall and dense, at which point he moves to a new area.

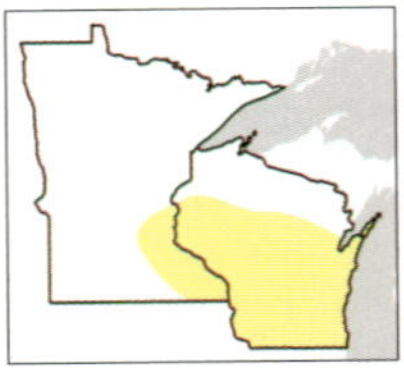

ID: *Male:* bright yellow face and underparts, except for white undertail coverts; dark "cheek" stripe and eye line; black streaking on sides; olive gray upperparts; inconspicuous chestnut streaks on back; 2 faint yellowish wing bars. *Female* and *immature:* similar to male, but duller in color.

Size: *L* $4\frac{1}{2}$–5 in; *W* 7 in.

Status: ***MN:*** rare migrant in spring into early June in east-central and southeastern regions; only 13 records for the state since this bird was first recorded in 1961. ***WI:*** rare migrant in May; casual migrant in September; rare summer resident; no confirmed breeding.

Habitat: dry, open, scrubby sand dunes and rocky pine-oak-juniper scrublands; also found in woodland edges and young pine plantations with deciduous scrub.

Nesting: does not nest in our region.

Feeding: gleans, hover-gleans and occasionally hawks for prey; mainly insectivorous; will also eat berries and tree sap exposed by sapsuckers; caterpillars are a favored item for nestlings.

Voice: buzzy song is an ascending series of *zee* notes; call is sweet *chip*.

Similar Species: *Pine Warbler* (p. 281): lighter streaking on sides; whitish wing bars; lacks distinctive dark streaking on face. *Yellow-throated Warbler* (p. 280): white belly; bold white wing bars, eyebrow and ear patch. *Bay-breasted Warbler* (p. 284) and *Blackpoll Warbler* (p. 285): nonbreeding and immature birds have white bellies and wing bars, as well as lighter upperparts with dark streaking. *Kirtland's Warbler* (p. 360): immature female has brownish upperparts and pale white eye ring.

Best Sites: ***MN:*** no consistent sites. ***WI:*** no consistent sites; may set up territory in woodland edges or pine-oak scrublands.

PALM WARBLER

Dendroica palmarum

The Palm Warbler, which does not forage in palm trees, was apparently named to indicate its subtropical winter range. Based on its summer range, however, it could just as easily have been named "Bog Warbler" because of its preference for northern bogs and fens of sphagnum moss and black spruce. Despite its name, the Palm Warbler nests farther north than all other wood-warblers except the Blackpoll Warbler. • Palm Warblers are unusual in their preference for foraging on the ground or in low shrubs and vegetation. This warbler nests directly on the ground in a bog, usually beneath a young conifer. • The Palm Warbler's incessant tail bobbing is a prominent field mark, particularly in fall, when its distinctive chestnut crown fades to olive brown.

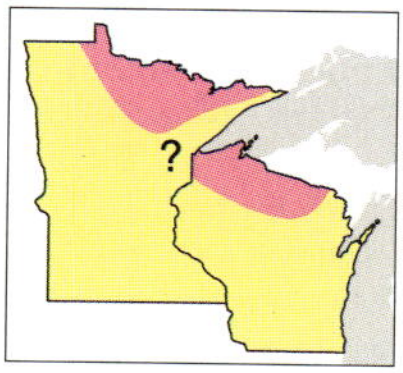

ID: chestnut "cap" (may be inconspicuous in fall); yellow "eyebrow"; yellow throat and undertail coverts; yellow or white breast and belly; dark streaking on breast and sides; olive brown upperparts; may show dull yellowish rump; frequently bobs its tail.

Size: *L* 4–5½ in; *W* 8 in.

Status: ***MN:*** common migrant from late April to late May and mid-August to late October; rare breeder in scattered localities in northeastern and north-central regions. ***WI:*** common migrant from mid-April to mid-May and late August to late October; uncommon breeder.

Habitat: edges of mature bogs with scattered black spruce; less frequently in openings of spruce-tamarack forests with sphagnum moss and shrubs.

Nesting: on the ground or in a low shrub or stunted spruce; often on a sphagnum hummock concealed by grass; female builds a cup nest of grass, weeds and bark and lines it with feathers; female incubates 4–5 brown-marked, creamy white eggs for about 12 days.

Feeding: gleans the ground and vegetation for a wide variety of insects and berries while perched or hovering; occasionally hawks for insects; may take some seeds.

Voice: song is a weak, buzzy trill with a quick finish; call is a sharp *sup* or *check*.

Similar Species: *Yellow-rumped Warbler* (p. 277): white wing bars, throat and undertail coverts; female has bright yellow rump, crown patch and foreshoulder patch. *Prairie Warbler* (p. 282): dark jaw stripe; darker eye line; lacks chestnut crown and dark streaking on breast. *Pine Warbler* (p. 281): faint whitish wing bars; white undertail coverts; lacks chestnut "cap" and bold yellow "eyebrow."

Best Sites: ***MN:*** *In migration:* alongside roads adjoining brushy woodlands and in parks with brushy woodland edges; hundreds may be encountered during peak migration periods. ***WI:*** *Breeding:* coniferous swamps in the north. *In migration:* in warbler flocks, especially during spring warbler flight.

BAY-BREASTED WARBLER

Dendroica castanea

breeding

In summer, the handsome Bay-breasted Warbler can be difficult to spot, because it typically forages deep within stands of old-growth spruce and fir, often on the inner branches of a tree. • Bay-breasted Warblers are invaluable when it comes to long-term suppression of spruce budworm outbreaks. It is estimated that in outbreak years one Bay-breasted Warbler can eat 5000 budworms per acre through the breeding season, and this bird's populations fluctuate from year to year with the cyclical rise and fall of budworm numbers. Although Bay-breasts are insectivorous on their breeding grounds, they switch to an almost all-fruit diet while they winter in Panama and Colombia.

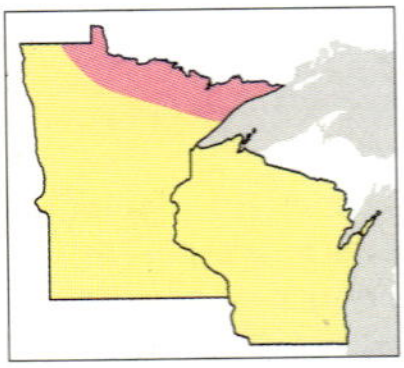

ID: *Breeding male:* black face and "chin"; chestnut crown, throat, sides and flanks; creamy yellow belly, undertail coverts and patch on side of neck; 2 white wing bars. *Breeding female:* paler overall; dusky face; whitish to creamy underparts and neck patch; faint chestnut "cap"; rusty wash on sides and flanks. *Nonbreeding:* yellow olive head and back; dark streaking on crown and back; whiter underparts.

Size: *L* 5–6 in; *W* 9 in.

Status: ***MN:*** uncommon to rare migrant from early May to early June; uncommon to at times common migrant from late July to late October; rare breeder. ***WI:*** common migrant in May and from mid-August to early October; rare summer visitor.

Habitat: mature coniferous and mixed boreal forest; almost exclusively in stands of spruce and fir.

Nesting: usually on a horizontal branch in a conifer; female builds an open cup nest of grass, twigs, moss, roots and lichen and lines it with fine bark strips and fur; female incubates 4–5 whitish eggs, with dark marks toward the larger end, for about 13 days.

Feeding: usually forages at the midlevel of trees; gleans vegetation and branches for spruce budworms, caterpillars and adult invertebrates.

Voice: song is an extremely high-pitched *seee-seese-seese-seee;* call is a high *see*.

Similar Species: *Cape May Warbler* (p. 275): chestnut brown "cheek" on yellow face; dark streaking on mostly yellow underparts; lacks reddish flanks and crown. *Chestnut-sided Warbler* (p. 273): yellow crown; white "cheek" and underparts; nonbreeding has white eye ring, unmarked whitish face and underparts and lacks bold streaking on lime green upperparts. *Blackpoll Warbler* (p. 285): white undertail coverts; nonbreeding and immature have dark streaking on breast and sides and lack chestnut on sides and flanks.

Best Sites: ***MN:*** Frontenac SP; Minnesota Pt. (Duluth); state, county and city parks, wildlife management areas and national wildlife refuges (especially in fall). ***WI:*** Bay Beach Wildlife Sanctuary; Heckrodt Wetland Reserve; Harrington Beach SP; Wyalusing SP; Wisconsin Pt.; Prentice Park (Ashland); Arboretum and Picnic Pt. (UW-Madison); Milwaukee parks.

BLACKPOLL WARBLER

Dendroica striata

The Blackpoll Warbler is the greatest warbler migrant: weighing less than a wet teabag, eastern migrants are known to fly south over the Atlantic, leaving land at Cape Cod and flying for 88 nonstop hours until they reach the northern coast of Venezuela. In a single year a Blackpoll Warbler may fly up to 15,000 miles! In migration, the birds adjust their flying altitude—sometimes flying at altitudes of up to 20,000 feet—to best use shifting prevailing winds in order to reach their destination. This bird is truly an international resident, so conservation of its habitat requires the efforts of several nations. • Blackpoll Warblers in fall plumage are easily confused with very similar-looking Bay-breasted Warblers.

breeding

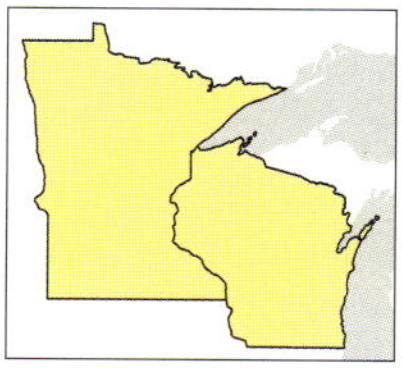

ID: 2 white wing bars; black streaking on white underparts; white undertail coverts. *Breeding male:* black "cap" and "chin" stripe; white "cheek"; black-streaked, olive gray upperparts; white underparts; orange legs. *Breeding female:* streaked, yellow olive head and back; small, dark eye line; pale "eyebrow." *Nonbreeding:* olive yellow head, back, rump, breast and sides; yellow "eyebrow"; dark legs. *Immature:* paler streaking.

Size: *L* 5–5½ in; *W* 9 in.

Status: ***MN:*** uncommon to at times common migrant from early May to early June and from late August to early October. ***WI:*** common migrant from May to early June and from mid-August to early October.

Habitat: coniferous and mixed scrub, open coniferous growth on dry fens and bogs, the backsides of ridged riverbanks and sparsely vegetated beach ridges.

Nesting: does not nest in our region.

Feeding: gleans buds, leaves and branches for aphids, mosquitoes, beetles, wasps, caterpillars and many other insects; often flycatches for insects.

Voice: song is an extremely high-pitched, uniform trill: *tsit tsit tsit;* call is a loud *chip.*

Similar Species: *Black-and-white Warbler* (p. 287): dark legs; black-and-white-striped crown; male has black "chin," throat and "cheek" patch. *Bay-breasted Warbler* (p. 284): chestnut sides and flanks; buff undertail coverts; nonbreeding and immature lack dark streaking on underparts. *Black-capped Chickadee* (p. 235): black "chin" and throat; lacks wing bars and black streaking on underparts.

Best Sites: ***MN:*** Frontenac SP; Minnesota Pt. (Duluth); wooded areas in most state, county and city parks. ***WI:*** Milwaukee parks; Arboretum and Picnic Pt. (UW-Madison); Bay Beach Wildlife Sanctuary; High Cliff SP; Wyalusing SP; Wisconsin Pt.; Harrington Beach SP.

CERULEAN WARBLER

Dendroica cerulea

The Cerulean Warbler leads a mysterious life concealed high in the canopy of mature deciduous forests. The handsome blue-and-white male is particularly difficult to observe as he blends into the sunny summer sky while foraging among treetop foliage. Often the only evidence of a meeting with this largely unobservable canopy-dweller is the sound of the male's buzzy, trilling voice. • Only in the last few decades have ornithologists been able to document this bird's breeding behavior—courtship, mating, nesting and the rearing of young all usually take place high in the canopy, well out of sight of most observers.

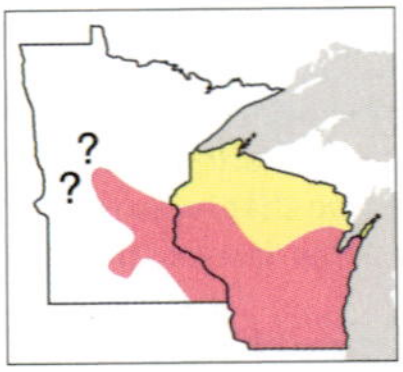

ID: white undertail coverts and wing bars. *Male:* blue upperparts; white throat and underparts; black "necklace" and streaking on sides. *Female:* blue green crown, nape and back; dark eye line; yellow "eyebrow," throat and breast; pale streaking on sides.

Size: *L* 4½–5 in; *W* 7 in.

Status: ***MN:*** special concern; rare to uncommon migrant and breeder from May to August; declining. ***WI:*** threatened; uncommon migrant from late April through May and in fall; locally common breeder in the south; uncommon breeder in central regions; rare breeder in the north.

Habitat: mature deciduous hardwood forests and extensive woodlands with a clear understory; particularly drawn to riparian stands.

Nesting: on the end of a branch high in a deciduous tree; female builds an open cup nest of bark strips, weeds, grass, lichen and spider silk and lines it with fur and moss; female incubates 3–5 brown-spotted, gray to creamy white eggs, for about 12–13 days.

Feeding: insects are gleaned from upper canopy foliage and branches; often hawks for insects.

Voice: song is a rapid, accelerating sequence of buzzy notes leading into a higher trilled note; call is a sharp *chip.*

Similar Species: *Black-throated Blue Warbler* (p. 276): male has black face, "chin" and throat; female has small white wing patch; lacks wing bars. *Blackpoll Warbler* (p. 285) and *Bay-breasted Warbler* (p. 284): similar to female Cerulean but have more yellow than green on mantle. *Pine Warbler* (p. 281): browner; similar to female Cerulean but has more yellow on mantle.

Best Sites: ***MN:*** Beaver Creek Valley SP; Sakatah Lake SP; Seven Mile Creek (Nicollet Co.); Whitewater SP. ***WI:*** ***Breeding:*** along the Mississippi R. north to L. Pepin, including Wyalusing SP, Nelson Dewey SP, LaCrosse area, Perrot SP, Trempealeau NWR, Van Loon WA and Tiffany Bottoms.

BLACK-AND-WHITE WARBLER

Mniotilta varia

The Black-and-white Warbler's foraging behavior stands in sharp contrast to that of most of its kin. Rather than dancing or flitting quickly between twig perches, Black-and-white Warblers behave like creepers and nuthatches—a distantly related group of birds. Birders with frayed nerves and tired eyes from watching flitty warblers will be refreshed by the sight of this bird as it methodically creeps up and down tree trunks, probing bark crevices. • Novice birders can easily identify this unique, two-tone warbler, which retains its standard black-and-white-striped plumage throughout the year.

breeding

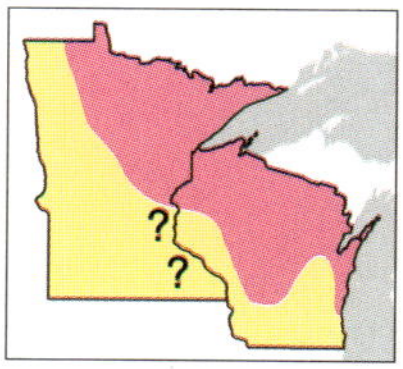

ID: black-and-white-striped crown; dark upperparts with white streaking; 2 white wing bars; white underparts with black streaking on sides, flanks and undertail coverts; black legs. *Breeding male:* black "cheek" and throat. *Breeding female:* gray "cheek"; white throat.

Size: *L* 5 in; *W* 8 in.

Status: ***MN:*** common migrant from late April to late May and from early August to early October; common breeder; may be expanding its breeding range southward. ***WI:*** common migrant from late April through May and from mid-August to early October; common breeder in northern and central regions; rare breeder elsewhere.

Habitat: deciduous or mixed forests, often near water; also cedar swamps and alder and willow thickets bordering beaver ponds.

Nesting: usually on the ground next to a tree, log or large rock; in a shallow scrape, often among a pile of dead leaves; female builds a cup nest of grass, leaves, bark strips, rootlets and pine needles and lines it with fur and fine grasses; female incubates 5 creamy white eggs, with brown flecks toward the larger end, for 10–12 days.

Feeding: gleans insect eggs, larval insects, beetles, spiders and other invertebrates while creeping along tree trunks and branches.

Voice: song is a series of high, thin, 2-syllable notes: *weetsee weetsee weetsee weetsee weetsee weetsee;* call is a sharp *pit* and a soft, high *seat*.

Similar Species: *Blackpoll Warbler* (p. 285): breeding male has solid black "cap" and clean white undertail coverts.

Best Sites: ***MN:*** *Breeding:* mature or second-growth forests; mixed and deciduous wooded swamps in the northeast. *In migration:* widespread in woodlands and thickets. ***WI:*** *Breeding:* cedar swamps and mixed forests in the north. *In migration:* in mixed warbler flocks.

AMERICAN REDSTART

Setophaga ruticilla

American Redstarts are a consistent favorite among birders. These supercharged birds flit from branch to branch in dizzying pursuit of prey. Even when perched, their tails sway rhythmically back and forth. Few birds can rival a mature male redstart for his contrasting black-and-orange plumage, his approachability and his amusing behavior. • A common foraging technique used by the American Redstart is to flash its wings and tail patches to flush prey. If a concealed insect tries to flee, the redstart will give chase. • American Redstarts are typically found in small, rural woodlots and wooded parks in suburban residential areas, wherever there is a dense understory of saplings. • Although Redstarts are common here, their high-pitched, lisping, trilly songs are so variable that identifying one is a challenge to birders of all levels.

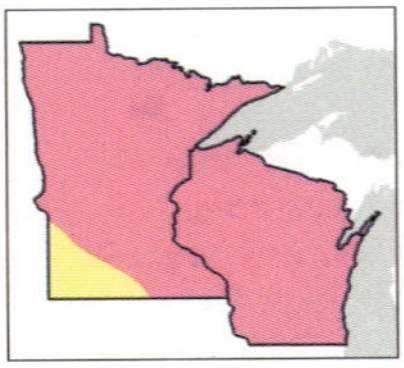

ID: *Male:* black overall; red orange foreshoulder, wing and tail patches; white belly and undertail coverts. *Female:* olive brown upperparts; gray green head; yellow foreshoulder, wing and tail patches; white underparts.
Size: *L* 5 in; $8\frac{1}{2}$ in.
Status: ***MN:*** common migrant and breeder from early May to early October; uncommon in the southwest. ***WI:*** abundant migrant in May and from mid-August to mid-October; common breeder.
Habitat: shrubby woodland edges, open and semi-open deciduous and mixed forests with a regenerating deciduous understory of shrubs and saplings; often near water.
Nesting: in the fork of a shrub or sapling, usually 3–23 ft above the ground; female builds an open cup nest of plant down, bark shreds, grass and rootlets and lines it with feathers; female incubates 4 whitish eggs, marked with brown or gray, for 11–12 days.
Feeding: actively gleans foliage and hawks for insects and spiders on leaves, buds and branches; often hover-gleans.
Voice: song is a highly variable series of *tseet* or *zee* notes, often given at different pitches; call is a sharp, sweet *chip*.
Similar Species: none.
Best Sites: ***MN:*** widespread throughout second-growth woodlands. ***WI:*** widespread throughout the state.

PROTHONOTARY WARBLER

Protonotaria citrea

The Prothonotary Warbler is unusual among the wood-warblers because it nests in cavities. Standing dead trees and stumps riddled with natural cavities and woodpecker excavations provide perfect nesting habitat for this bird, especially if the site is near stagnant, swampy water. Prothonotary Warblers forage for insects along tree trunks and decaying logs, in low, tangled thickets or on debris floating on the water's surface. • A breeding pair of Prothonotary Warblers will often return to the same nest cavity year after year. • This bird acquired its unusual name because its plumage was thought to resemble the yellow hoods worn by prothonotaries, high-ranking clerics in the Roman Catholic Church.

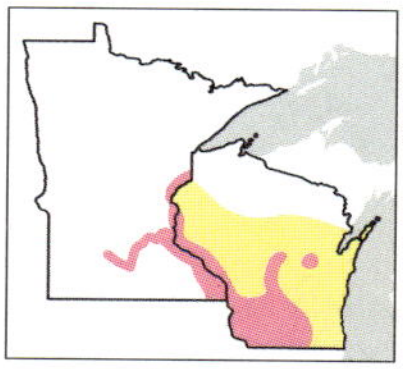

ID: large, dark eye; long bill; unmarked, yellow head; yellow underparts except for white undertail coverts; olive green back; unmarked, bluish gray wings and tail; dark gray legs.

Size: *L* 5½ in; *W* 8½ in.

Status: ***MN:*** seldom seen in migration; usually seen on breeding sites from early May to early August in southeastern and east-central regions, occasionally westward along the Minnesota R. valley; rare vagrant elsewhere in the state. ***WI:*** fairly common to uncommon migrant from late April to May; localized, fairly common breeder along the Mississippi, Wisconsin and St. Croix Rivers; rare elsewhere in southern and central regions.

Habitat: wooded deciduous swamps.

Nesting: cavities in standing dead trees, rotten stumps, birdhouses or abandoned woodpecker nests, from water level to 10 ft above the ground; often returns to the same nest site; mostly the male builds a cup nest of twigs, leaves, moss and plant down and lines it with soft plant material; female incubates 4–6 brown-spotted, creamy to pinkish eggs for 12–14 days.

Feeding: forages for a variety of insects and small mollusks; gleans from vegetation; may hop on floating debris or creep along tree trunks.

Voice: song is a loud, ringing series of *sweet* or *zweet* notes issued on a single pitch; flight-song is *chewee chewee chee chee;* call is a brisk *tink*.

Similar Species: *Blue-winged Warbler* (p. 266): white wing bars; black eye line; yellowish white undertail coverts. *Yellow Warbler* (p. 272): dark wings and tail with yellow highlights; yellow undertail coverts; male has reddish streaking in breast. *Hooded Warbler* (p. 298): female has yellow undertail coverts and yellow olive upperparts.

Best Sites: ***MN:*** Frontenac SP; Minnesota River Valley State Recreation Area; William O'Brien SP; Vermillion R.; Zumbro R.; Cannon R; Root R. ***WI:*** *Breeding:* Mississippi R. at Wyalusing SP, LaCrosse, Van Loon WA, Perrot SP and Trempealeau NWR; St. Croix R.; Wisconsin R.

WORM-EATING WARBLER

Helmitheros vermivorus

Those wishing to see this bird have a challenge ahead of them because Worm-eating Warblers are rare in our region. To make things more difficult, this warbler's subdued colors allow it to blend in with the decomposing twigs, roots and leaves that litter the forest floor. Most of this bird's time is spent on the ground foraging for caterpillars, small terrestrial insects and spiders among dense undergrowth and dead leaves in deciduous forests. • Worm-eating Warblers typically nest near water and on a slope, and are one of a small group of eastern warblers that nest on the ground. Females become completely still if they are approached while on the nest, relying on their striped crown for concealment. • The Worm-eating Warbler is yet another trilling singer. Its trill is faster and more insectlike than the Chipping Sparrow's, and seems loudest in the middle of the trill and weaker at the beginning and end.

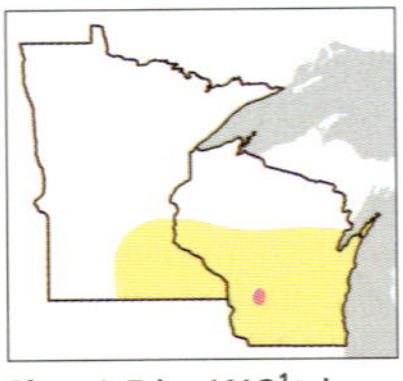

ID: black and buff orange head stripes; brownish olive upperparts; rich buff orange breast; whitish undertail coverts; short tail.

Size: *L* 5 in; *W* 8½ in.

Status: ***MN:*** casual migrant; over 40 records, mostly from late April to late May in southeastern, south-central and east-central regions; no breeding records.
WI: endangered; rare migrant from late April to May and from August through September; rare breeder.

Habitat: steep, deciduous woodland slopes, ravines and swampy woodlands with shrubby understory cover.

Nesting: usually on a hillside or ravine bank, often near water; on the ground hidden under leaf litter; female builds a cup nest of decaying leaves and lines it with fine grass, moss stems and hair; female incubate 3–5 white eggs, speckled with reddish brown, for about 13 days.

Feeding: forages on the ground and in trees and shrubs; eats mostly caterpillars and small insects.

Voice: song is a faster, thinner version of the Chipping Sparrow's chipping trill; call is a buzzy *zeep-zeep*.

Similar Species: *Red-eyed Vireo* (p. 222): gray crown; white "eyebrow"; red eyes; yellow undertail coverts. *Louisiana Waterthrush* (p. 293) and *Northern Waterthrush* (p. 292): darker upperparts; bold white or yellowish "eyebrow"; dark streaking on white breast; lacks striped head.

Best Sites: ***MN:*** no consistent sites.
WI: *Breeding:* Baxter's Hollow; Hemlock Draw; Wyalusing SP (occasional); Tiffany Bottoms (occasional).

OVENBIRD

Seiurus aurocapillus

The Ovenbird's loud and joyous "ode to teachers" is a common sound that echoes through deciduous and mixed forests in spring. Unfortunately, pinpointing the exact location of this resonating call is not always easy. An Ovenbird will rarely expose itself, and even when it does, active searching and patience is necessary to get a good look at it. What may sound like one long-winded Ovenbird may actually be two neighboring males singing and responding on the heels of each other's song. • The name "Ovenbird" refers to this bird's unusual, dome-shaped ground nest. An incubating female nestled within her woven dome usually feels so secure that she will choose to sit tight rather than flee when approached. Nests are so well camouflaged that few people ever find one, even if the nest is located near a public path. A female may have up to three mates to call on for protection and feeding the young.

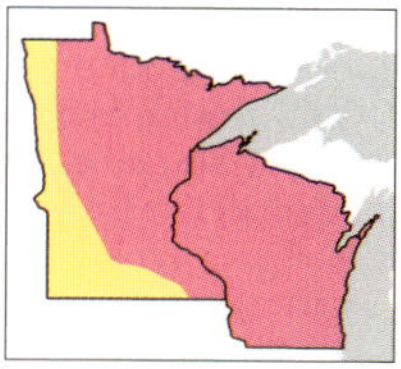

ID: olive brown upperparts; white eye ring; heavy, dark streaking on white breast, sides and flanks; rufous crown bordered with black; pink legs; white undertail coverts; no wing bars.

Size: *L* 6 in; *W* 9½ in.

Status: ***MN:*** common migrant and breeder from late April to early June and from mid-August to mid-October; common breeder in eastern and most of the central regions; uncommon to rare breeder in southwestern, south-central and far western regions. ***WI:*** common migrant in May and from September to mid-October; common to abundant breeder.

Habitat: *Breeding:* undisturbed, mature deciduous, mixed and coniferous forests with a closed canopy and very little understory; often in ravines and riparian areas. *In migration*: dense riparian shrubbery and thickets and a variety of woodlands.

Nesting: on the ground; female builds an oven-shaped, domed nest of grass, weeds, bark, twigs and dead leaves and lines it with animal hair; female incubates 4–5 white eggs, spotted with gray and brown, for 11–13 days.

Feeding: gleans the ground for worms, snails, insects and occasionally seeds.

Voice: song is a loud, distinctive *tea-cher tea-cher tea-CHER tea-CHER,* increasing in speed and volume; night song is an elaborate series of bubbly, warbled notes often ending in *teacher-teacher;* call is a brisk *chip, cheep* or *chock*.

Similar Species: *Northern Waterthrush* (p. 292) and *Louisiana Waterthrush* (p. 293): bold yellowish or white "eyebrow"; darker upperparts; lacks rufous crown. *Thrushes* (pp. 249–58): all are larger and lack rufous crown outlined in black.

Best Sites: ***MN:*** woodlands throughout the state; thickets in migration. ***WI:*** widespread throughout the state.

NORTHERN WATERTHRUSH

Seiurus noveboracensis

Although this bird's long body appears thrushlike, the Northern Waterthrush is actually a wood-warbler. This bird skulks along the shores of deciduous swamps or coniferous bogs, and the fallen logs, shrubby tangles and soggy ground may discourage human visitors. During the relatively bug-free months in spring and fall, birders can typically find migrating Northern Waterthrushes in drier, upland forests or along lofty park trails and boardwalks. Backyards featuring a small garden pond may also attract migrating waterthrushes. • Waterthrushes tip and teeter while walking on logs over water or along shorelines and forest vegetation, a habit similar to that of Spotted Sandpipers and perhaps intended to disturb ground- and water-dwelling insects.

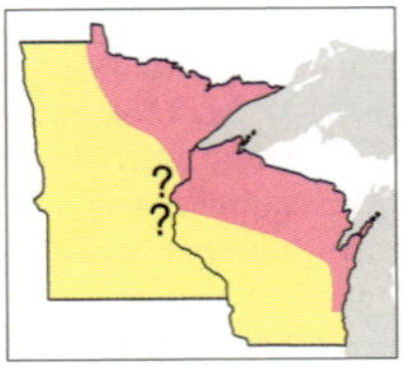

ID: pale yellowish to buff "eyebrow" and underparts; dark streaking on underparts; finely spotted throat; olive brown upperparts; pinkish legs; frequently bobs its tail.

Size: *L* 5–6 in; *W* 9½ in.

Status: ***MN:*** common migrant from late April to early June and from mid-August to early October; uncommon breeder in the northeast. ***WI:*** fairly common migrant from late April to May and from mid-August to early October; uncommon breeder.

Habitat: wooded edges of swamps, lakes, beaver ponds, bogs and rivers; also in moist, wooded ravines and riparian thickets.

Nesting: on the ground, usually near water; female builds a cup nest of moss, leaves, bark shreds, twigs and pine needles and lines it with moss, hair and rootlets; female incubates 4–5 whitish eggs, spotted and blotched with brown and purple gray, for about 13 days.

Feeding: gleans foliage and the ground for invertebrates, frequently tossing aside ground litter with its bill; may also take aquatic invertebrates and small fish from shallow water.

Voice: song is a loud, 3-part *sweet sweet sweet, swee wee wee, chew chew chew chew;* call is a brisk *chip* or *chuck*.

Similar Species: *Louisiana Waterthrush* (p. 293): broader, white "eyebrow"; unspotted, white throat; orange buff wash on flanks. *Ovenbird* (p. 291): rufous crown bordered with black stripe; white eye ring; unspotted throat; lacks pale "eyebrow."

Best Sites: ***MN:*** *Breeding:* wooded swamps in the northeast. *In migration:* wet woods, streamsides and wooded lakeshores in state, county and city parks and wildlife management areas, such as Frontenac SP and Minnesota Pt. (Duluth). ***WI:*** *Breeding:* wooded swamps. *In migration:* Milwaukee parks; Arboretum and Picnic Pt. (UW-Madison); Bay Beach Wildlife Sanctuary; Heckrodt Wetland Reserve.

LOUISIANA WATERTHRUSH

Seiurus motacilla

The Louisiana Waterthrush is often seen sallying along the shorelines of babbling streams and gently swirling pools in search of its next meal. This bird inhabits swamps and sluggish streams throughout much of its North American range, but where its range overlaps with the Northern Waterthrush, it inhabits shorelines near fast-flowing water. Louisiana Waterthrushes have never been recorded in great numbers in our region, partly because little suitable habitat remains for them. • Both the Louisiana Waterthrush and the Northern Waterthrush bob their heads and move their tails up and down as they walk, but the Louisana Waterthrush bobs its tail more slowly and also tends to sway from side to side.

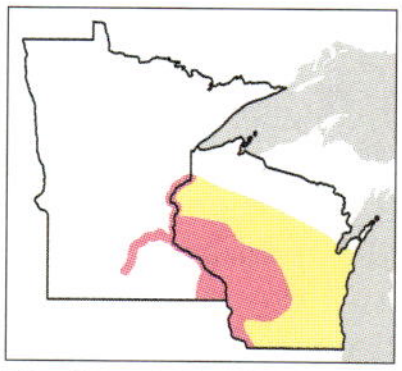

ID: brownish upperparts; long bill; pink legs; white underparts; orange buff wash on flanks; long, dark streaks on breast and sides; bicolored, buff and white "eyebrow"; clean white throat.

Size: *L* 6 in; *W* 10 in.

Status: ***MN:*** special concern; seldom encountered during migration; present from early May to late August; uncommon and local breeder along streams in southeastern and east-central regions and along portions of the Minnesota R. valley south to Blue Earth Co. ***WI:*** uncommon migrant in April and May and from mid-August to early October; uncommon breeder.

Habitat: moist, forested ravines alongside fast-flowing streams; rarely along wooded swamps.

Nesting: concealed within a rocky hollow or within a tangle of tree roots; both adults build a cup nest of leaves, bark strips, twigs and moss and line it with animal hair, ferns and rootlets; female incubates 3–6 creamy white eggs, spotted with brown and purple gray, for about 14 days.

Feeding: terrestrial and aquatic insects and crustaceans are gleaned from rocks and debris in or near shallow water; dead leaves and other debris may be flipped and probed for food; occasionally catches flying insects over water.

Voice: song begins with 3–4 distinctive, shrill, slurred notes followed by a warbling twitter; call is a brisk *chick* or *chink*.

Similar Species: *Northern Waterthrush* (p. 292): yellowish to buff "eyebrow" narrows behind eye; underparts are usually all yellowish or buff (occasionally all white); finely spotted throat; lacks buff orange flanks. *Ovenbird* (p. 291) and *thrushes* (pp. 249–58): lack broad, white "eyebrow."

Best Sites: ***MN:*** *Breeding:* Frontenac SP; Minneopa SP; Beaver Creek Valley SP; Interstate SP; Wild River SP. ***WI:*** *Breeding:* Baxter's Hollow; Wyalusing SP; Kickapoo Valley Reserve.

KENTUCKY WARBLER

Oporornis formosus

Typically found in moist, deciduous woodlands, Kentucky Warblers spend much of their time on the ground, overturning leaves and scurrying through dense thickets in search of insects. These warblers are shy and elusive as they sing their loud springtime songs from secluded perches. As a general rule, male warblers sing most actively in the morning, feeding only intermittently, but quiet down in the afternoon and feed more actively. Once the young hatch, singing becomes rare as both the male and the female spend much of their time feeding the young. Unmated males, however, may continue to sing throughout the summer. The Kentucky Warbler's song may be confused with that of the common Carolina Wren, but the Kentucky Warbler will sing the same song pattern repeatedly, while the Carolina Wren varies its song constantly.

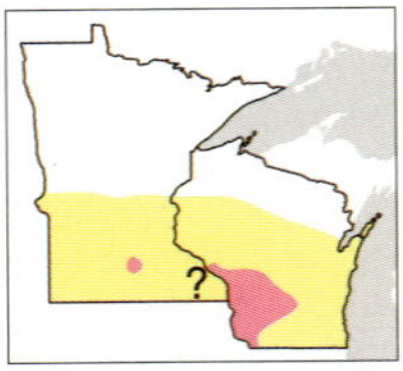

ID: bright yellow "spectacles" and underparts; black crown, "sideburns" and "half mask"; olive green upperparts; pale pinkish legs.

Size: *L* 5–5½ in; *W* 8½ in.

Status: ***MN:*** very rare migrant in May, mainly in southern regions; accidental migrant elsewhere; only 2 fall records; 1 nesting record in Nicollet Co. ***WI:*** threatened; uncommon migrant in May and from mid-August to mid-September; locally common breeder.

Habitat: moist deciduous and mixed woodlands with dense, shrubby cover and herbaceous plant growth including wooded ravines, swamp edges and creek bottomlands.

Nesting: on or close to the ground; both adults build a cup nest of plant material and hair and line it with rootlets and hair; female incubates 4–5 cream-colored eggs, spotted or blotched with reddish brown, for 12–13 days.

Feeding: gleans insects while walking along the ground, flipping over leaf litter or by snatching prey from the undersides of low foliage.

Voice: musical song is a series of 2-syllable notes: *chur-ree chur-ree* (similar to the song of the Carolina Wren); call is a sharp *chick, chuck* or *chip*.

Similar Species: *Canada Warbler* (p. 300): dark, streaky "necklace"; bluish gray upperparts. *Yellow-throated Warbler* (p. 280): bold, white "eyebrow," ear patch and wing bars; white belly and undertail coverts.

Best Sites: ***MN:*** Seven Mile Creek (Nicollet Co.); Minneopa SP; Afton SP; Nerstrand–Big Woods SP. ***WI:*** *Breeding:* Wyalusing SP; along the Wisconsin R. to Sauk Co.; along the Mississippi R. to Trempealeau Co.

CONNECTICUT WARBLER

Oporornis agilis

The elusive nature of the Connecticut Warbler has made it one of the most sought-after birds. Soggy, impenetrable sphagnum bogs, dry jack pine forests and mixed woodlands are all favored habitats for the mysterious and secretive Connecticut Warbler. Some believe that the common denominator between these varied breeding sites is poor drainage, while others feel that a well-developed understory is mandatory. You might hear the boisterous songs of this ground-dwelling warbler on a trip to a northern bog, but pinpointing this bird's location takes patience and good fortune. • Like many other North American birds, the Connecticut Warbler was named for the place where it was first collected, though this bird only visits Connecticut during fall migration.

breeding

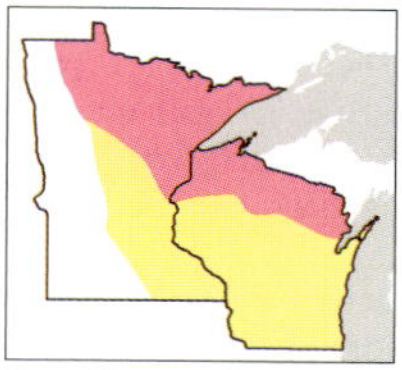

ID: bold, white eye ring; yellow underparts; olive green upperparts; long undertail coverts make tail look short; pink legs; longish bill. *Breeding male:* blue gray "hood." *Female* and *immature:* gray brown "hood"; light gray throat.

Size: *L* 5–6 in; *W* 9 in.

Status: ***MN:*** rare migrant from mid-May to early June and from mid-August to late September primarily in the east and north; casual migrant elsewhere; local breeder in the north as far west as Roseau Co. ***WI:*** uncommon migrant from May to early June and from mid-August to September; uncommon breeder.

Habitat: open pine forests and fairly open spruce bogs and tamarack fens with well-developed understory growth.

Nesting: on the ground on a hummock or in a low shrub; messy nest is made of leaves, weeds, grass, bark strips and moss; female incubates 4–5 creamy white eggs, spotted with black, brown and lilac, for about 12 days.

Feeding: gleans caterpillars, beetles, spiders and other invertebrates from ground leaf litter; occasionally forages among low branches.

Voice: song is a loud, clear, explosive *chip-ity-chipity-chipity chuck* or *per-chipity-chip-ity-chipity choo;* call is a brisk, metallic *cheep* or *peak*.

Similar Species: *Mourning Warbler* (p. 296): no eye ring or thin, incomplete eye ring; shorter undertail coverts; male has blackish breast patch; immature has pale gray to yellow "chin" and throat. *Nashville Warbler* (p. 270): bright yellow throat; shorter, dark legs and bill.

Best Sites: ***MN:*** northern Aitkin Co.; L. Vermilion area; Sax-Zim Bog; Hayes Lake SP. ***WI:*** *Breeding:* Brule R. area; Lyman Lake Bog (Douglas Co.); northern oak–jack pine forests and conifer swamps.

MOURNING WARBLER

Oporornis philadelphia

The Mourning Warbler seldom leaves the protection of its dense, shrubby, often impenetrable habitat, and tends to sing only on its breeding territory. Riparian areas, regenerating clear-cuts and patches of forest that have been recently cleared by fire provide the low shrubs and sapling trees that this warbler relies on for nesting and foraging. Although essentially birds of broadleaf shrubs, Mourning Warblers can sometimes be found deep in boreal conifers, as long as there is some ground cover. Mourning Warblers are best seen during migration, when backyard shrubs and raspberry thickets may attract them. • This bird's dark "hood" and black breast patch reminded pioneering ornithologist Alexander Wilson of someone dressed in mourning.

breeding

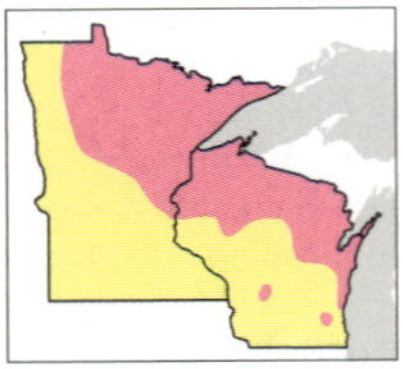

ID: blue gray "hood"; black upper breast patch; yellow underparts; olive green upperparts; short tail; pinkish legs. *Breeding male:* usually no eye ring, but may have broken eye ring. *Female:* gray "hood"; whitish "chin" and throat; may show thin eye ring.

Size: *L* 5–5½ in; *W* 7½ in.

Status: ***MN:*** uncommon migrant from mid-May to early June and from late August to late September; locally common breeder. ***WI:*** fairly common migrant from May to early June and from August to late September; fairly common breeder in the north; uncommon breeder in central and eastern regions.

Habitat: dense and shrubby thickets, tangles and brambles, often in moist areas of forest clearings and along the edges of ponds, lakes and streams.

Nesting: on the ground at the base of a shrub or plant tussock or in a small shrub; bulky nest of leaves, weeds and grass is lined with fur and fine grass; female incubates 3–4 creamy white eggs, spotted or blotched with brown, for about 12 days.

Feeding: forages in dense low shrubs for caterpillars, beetles, spiders and other invertebrates.

Voice: husky, 2-part song is variable and lower-pitched at the end: *churry, churry, churry, churry, chorry, chorry;* call is a loud, low *check*.

Similar Species: *Connecticut Warbler* (p. 295): bold, complete eye ring; lacks black breast patch; long undertail coverts make tail look short; immature has light gray throat. *Nashville Warbler* (p. 270): bright yellow throat; dark legs. *Common Yellowthroat* (p. 297): less obvious "hood"; yellow throat; duller yellow underparts.

Best Sites: ***MN:*** *Breeding:* brushy cutovers and clear-cut areas in the north. *In migration:* thickets; bog or marsh edges; shrubbery in state, county and city parks, wildlife management areas and national wildlife refuges. ***WI:*** *In migration:* Arboretum and Picnic Pt. (UW-Madison); Milwaukee parks; Bay Beach Wildlife Sanctuary; Heckrodt Wetland Reserve; Duck Lake Walk (L. Geneva); Devil's Lake SP.

COMMON YELLOWTHROAT

Geothlypis trichas

This energetic songster of our wetlands is a favorite among birders—the Common Yellowthroat's small size, bright plumage and spunky disposition quickly endear it to all who meet it. • Common Yellowthroats favor cattail marshes and wet, overgrown meadows, shunning the forest habitat preferred by most of their wood-warbler relatives. • In May and June, the male issues his distinctive songs while perched atop a tall cattail or shrub. Observing a male yellowthroat in action will reveal the location of his favorite singing perches, which he visits in rotation. These strategic outposts mark the boundary of his territory, which is fiercely guarded from intrusion by other males.

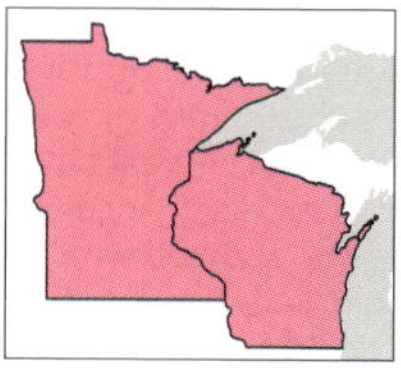

ID: yellow throat, breast and undertail coverts; dingy white belly; olive green to olive brown upperparts; orangy legs. *Breeding male:* broad, black "mask" with white upper border. *Female:* no "mask"; may show faint white eye ring. *Immature:* duller overall.
Size: *L* 5 in.; *W* 7 in.
Status: ***MN:*** common to abundant migrant and breeder from late April to mid-October. ***WI:*** common migrant and breeder from May to mid-October.
Habitat: cattail marshes, riparian willow and alder clumps, sedge wetlands, beaver ponds and wet, overgrown meadows; sometimes on dry, abandoned fields.
Nesting: on or near the ground, often in a small shrub or among emergent aquatic vegetation; female builds a bulky, open cup nest of weeds, grass, sedges and other materials and lines it with hair and soft plant fibers; female incubates 3–5 creamy white eggs, spotted with brown and black, for 12 days.
Feeding: gleans vegetation and hovers for adult and larval insects, including dragonflies, spiders and beetles; occasionally eats seeds.
Voice: song is a clear, oscillating *witchety witchety witchety-witch;* call is a sharp *tcheck* or *tchet.*
Similar Species: male's black "mask" is distinctive. *Kentucky Warbler* (p. 294): yellow "spectacles"; all-yellow underparts; black "half mask." *Yellow Warbler* (p. 272): brighter yellow overall; yellow highlights in wings; all-yellow underparts. *Wilson's Warbler* (p. 299): forehead, "eyebrow" and "cheek" are as bright as the all-yellow underparts; may show dark "cap." *Orange-crowned Warbler* (p. 269): dull olive yellow overall; faint breast streaks. *Nashville Warbler* (p. 270): eye ring; blue gray crown.
Best Sites: ***MN:*** widespread in swamps, marshes, wet thickets and other brushy habitat. ***WI:*** widespread throughout the state.

HOODED WARBLER

Wilsonia citrina

Hooded Warblers are near the northern limit of their range here, so they are rare in most parts of our region. They require extensive mature forests where fallen trees have opened gaps in the canopy, encouraging understory growth. • Different species of wood-warblers can coexist because each species forages exclusively in certain areas. Hooded Warblers also partition between the sexes: males tend to forage in treetops, while the females forage near the ground. • Male Hooded Warblers may return to the same nesting territory year after year. Once the young have left the nest, each parent takes on guardianship of half the fledged young. Hooded Warblers are very territorial and segregate by gender on their wintering grounds—something which is unknown in any other warbler species—with males using mature forests, and females using shrubby and disturbed areas.

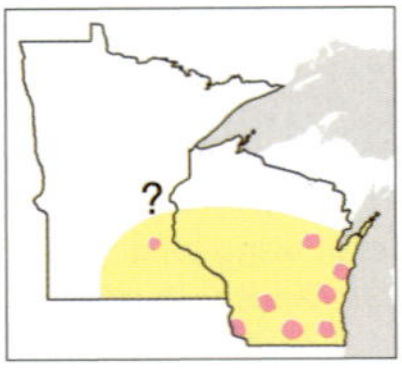

ID: bright yellow underparts; olive green upperparts; white undertail; pinkish legs. *Male:* black "hood"; bright yellow face. *Female:* yellow face and olive crown; may show faint traces of black "hood."

Size: *L* 5½ in; *W* 7 in.

Status: ***MN:*** special concern; very rare and local spring (May) migrant and breeder in southeastern, south-central and east-central regions; accidental elsewhere; only 3 fall records. ***WI:*** threatened; rare to uncommon migrant from late April through May and from mid-August through September; uncommon breeder.

Habitat: clearings with dense, low shrubs in mature, upland deciduous and mixed forests; occasionally in moist ravines or mature white pine plantations with a dense understory of deciduous shrubs.

Nesting: low in a deciduous shrub; mostly the female builds an open cup nest of fine grass, bark strips, dead leaves, animal hair, spider silk and plant down; female incubates 4 creamy white eggs, spotted with brown toward the larger end, for about 12 days.

Feeding: gleans insects and other forest invertebrates from the ground or from shrub branches; may scramble up tree trunks or flycatch.

Voice: clear, whistling song is some variation of *whitta-witta-wit-tee-yo;* call note is a metallic *tink, chink* or *chip.*

Similar Species: *Wilson's Warbler* (p. 299), *Yellow Warbler* (p. 272) and *Common Yellowthroat* (p. 297): females lack white undertail feathers. *Kentucky Warbler* (p. 294): yellow "spectacles"; dark, triangular "half mask."

Best Sites: ***MN:*** Murphy-Hanrehan Park Reserve; Carver Park Reserve. ***WI:*** *Breeding:* Kettle Moraine State Forest (Northern and Southern Units); Baxter's Hollow; Wyalusing SP.

WILSON'S WARBLER

Wilsonia pusilla

You are almost sure to catch sight of the energetic Wilson's Warbler at any of our migration hotspots. This lively bird flickers quickly through tangles of leaves and trees, darting frequently into the air to catch flying insects. Birders often become exhausted while pursuing a Wilson's Warbler, but the bird itself never seems to tire during its lightning-fast performances. • This bird may make brief stopovers in backyard shrubs during spring or fall migration. Though common in migration, the Wilson's Warbler invariably moves farther north to nest, so is rarely found as a breeder in either Minnesota or Wisconsin. • Named after Alexander Wilson, this species epitomizes the energetic devotion that the pioneering ornithologist exhibited in the study of North American birds.

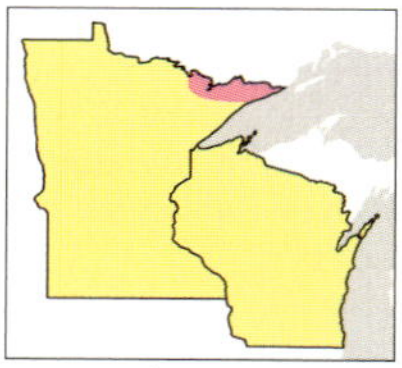

ID: yellow underparts; yellow green upperparts; beady, black eyes; black bill; orange legs. *Male:* black "cap." *Female:* "cap" is very faint or absent.

Size: *L* 4½–5 in; *W* 7 in.

Status: ***MN:*** uncommon to occasionally common migrant from early May to early June and from early August to early October; very rare breeder. ***WI:*** fairly common migrant in May and from mid-August through September; very casual breeder in the north.

Habitat: riparian woodlands, willow and alder thickets, bogs and wet, shrubby meadows; locally in garden shrubbery.

Nesting: on the ground in moss or at the base of a shrub; female builds a nest of moss, grass and leaves and lines it with animal hair and fine grass; female incubates 4–6 brown-marked, creamy white eggs for 10–13 days.

Feeding: hovers, flycatches and gleans vegetation for insects.

Voice: song is a rapid chatter that drops in pitch at the end: *chi chi chi chi chet chet;* call is a flat, low *chet* or *chuck.*

Similar Species: male's black "cap" is distinctive. *Yellow Warbler* (p. 272): male has red breast streaks; brighter yellow upperparts. *Common Yellowthroat* (p. 297): female has darker face. *Kentucky Warbler* (p. 294): yellow "spectacles"; dark, angular "half mask." *Orange-crowned Warbler* (p. 269): dull yellow olive overall; faint breast streaks. *Nashville Warbler* (p. 270): bold, complete eye ring; blue gray crown.

Best Sites: ***MN:*** woodlands, willow and alder thickets and along wooded streams and wet areas in state, county and city parks, wildlife management areas and national wildlfie refuges. ***WI:*** Bay Beach Wildlife Sanctuary; Harrington Beach SP; Milwaukee parks; Arboretum and Picnic Pt. (UW-Madison); High Cliff SP; Devil's Lake SP; LaCrosse parks; Wisconsin Pt.

CANADA WARBLER

Wilsonia canadensis

Male Canada Warblers, with their bold white eye rings, have a wide-eyed, alert appearance. Both sexes are fairly inquisitive and will occasionally pop up from dense shrubs in response to passing hikers. To find nesting Canada Warblers, seek out the wettest and most tangled patches of cover imaginable and then await their staccato, unwarbler-like song. • Canada Warblers live in open defiance of winter: they never stay in one place long enough to experience one! They are one of the last warblers to arrive on their Minnesota and Wisconsin breeding grounds and the first to leave. As the summer nesting season in our region comes to a close, these warblers migrate to South America.

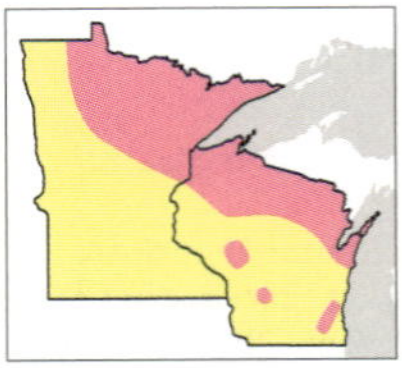

ID: yellow "spectacles"; yellow underparts (except white undertail coverts); blue gray upperparts; pale legs. *Male:* streaky, black "necklace"; dark, angular "half mask." *Female:* blue green back; faint "necklace."

Size: *L* 5–6 in; *W* 8 in.

Status: ***MN:*** uncommon migrant from mid-May to early June and from mid-August to mid-September, most numerous in eastern regions; uncommon breeder. ***WI:*** fairly common migrant in May and early June and from early August to mid-September; fairly common breeder in the north; uncommon breeder in eastern and central regions.

Habitat: wet, low-lying areas of mixed forest with a dense understory, especially riparian willow-alder thickets; also cedar woodlands and swamps.

Nesting: on a mossy hummock or upturned root or stump; female builds a loose, bulky cup nest of leaves, grass, ferns, weeds and bark and lines it with animal hair and soft plant fibers; female incubates 4 brown-spotted, creamy white eggs for 10–14 days.

Feeding: gleans the ground and vegetation for beetles, flies, hairless caterpillars, mosquitoes and other insects; occasionally hovers.

Voice: song begins with 1 sharp *chip* note and continues with a rich, variable warble; call is a loud, quick *chick* or *chip*.

Similar Species: *Kentucky Warbler* (p. 294): yellow undertail coverts; greenish upperparts; half eye ring; lacks black "necklace." *Northern Parula* (p. 271): white wing bars; broken white eye ring; white belly. *Kirtland's Warbler* (p. 360): black streaking on sides and flanks; broken white eye ring; dark streaking on back.

Best Sites: ***MN:*** forest undergrowth and shady thickets; Beaver Creek Vally SP; Whitewater SP; Afton SP; Minneapolis parks; William O'Brien SP; all North Shore state parks. ***WI:*** *In migration:* Governor Dodge SP; Wyalusing SP; Baxter's Hollow; Arboretum and Picnic Pt. (UW-Madison); Milwaukee parks; Duck Lake Walk (L. Geneva); Harrington Beach SP; Bay Beach Wildlife Sanctuary; Heckrodt Wetland Reserve.

YELLOW-BREASTED CHAT

Icteria virens

The unique Yellow-breasted Chat, measuring over 7 inches in length, is almost a warbler-and-a-half. Despite DNA evidence connecting this bird with the wood-warbler family, its odd vocalizations and noisy thrashing behavior suggest a closer relationship to the mimic thrushes such as the Gray Catbird and Northern Mockingbird. Chats typically thrash about in dense undergrowth, and they rarely hold back their strange vocalizations, often drawing attention to themselves. • During courtship, the male advertises for a mate by launching off his perch to hover in the air with head held high and legs dangling, chirping incessantly until he drops back down. This bird has a very localized breeding range in southern Minnesota and Wisconsin, and for the most part is rarely seen here in summer.

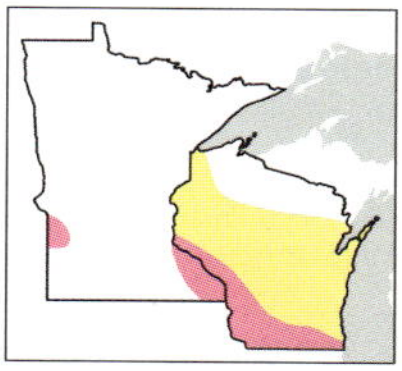

ID: white "spectacles"; white jaw line; heavy, black bill; yellow breast; white undertail coverts; olive green upperparts; long tail; gray black legs. *Male:* black lores. *Female:* gray lores.

Size: *L* 7½ in; *W* 9½ in.

Status: ***MN:*** rare to casual and erratic spring (May) migrant and occasional breeder, mainly in southeastern and west-central regions; accidental elsewhere; present in some years but not in others. ***WI:*** uncommon to rare migrant in May and from mid-August through September; uncommon to rare breeder.

Habitat: riparian thickets, brambles and shrubby tangles.

Nesting: low in a shrub or deciduous sapling; well-concealed, bulky base of leaves and weeds holds an inner woven cup nest made of vine bark and lined with fine grass and plant fibers; female incubates 3–4 creamy white eggs, spotted with brown toward the large end, for about 11 days.

Feeding: gleans insects from low vegetation; eats many berries in fall.

Voice: song is an assorted series of whistles, "laughs," squeaks, grunts, rattles and mews; calls include a *whoit, chack* and *kook*.

Similar Species: none.

Best Sites: ***MN:*** no consistent sites; possibly in brushy thickets along streams in the southeast in areas such as Beaver Creek SP and Lac Qui Parle SP. ***WI:*** *Breeding* and *in migration:* Duck Lake Walk (L. Geneva); Brooklyn WA; Governor Dodge SP; Wyalusing SP.

SUMMER TANAGER

Piranga rubra

Summer Tanagers thrive on a wide variety of insects, but they are best known for their courageous attacks on wasps. These birds snatch flying bees and wasps from menacing swarms, and may even harass the occupants of a wasp nest to the point that the nest is abandoned, leaving the larvae inside free for the picking. A captured bee or wasp is taken to a perch and beaten against it until the insect dies and its stinger falls off. • As is the case with the other red tanagers, the male and female of this species differ so much in appearance that they can be mistaken for different species altogether. The rosy red of the male's plumage makes it one of our more colorful migrants, though the female has her own subtle beauty. Backyard fruit feeders supplied with orange slices or banana are sometimes successful in attracting Summer Tanagers. During early spring and late fall, these birds feed on suet.

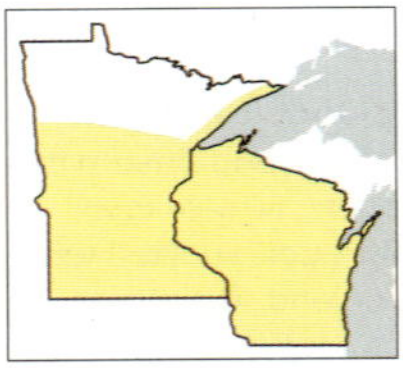

ID: *Male:* rose red overall; pale bill; immature male has patchy, red-and-greenish plumage. *Female:* grayish to greenish yellow upperparts; dusky yellow underparts; may have orange or reddish wash overall.

Size: *L* 7–$7\frac{1}{2}$ in; *W* 12 in.

Status: ***MN:*** rare migrant from late April to late May and from August through October, mainly in southern regions; occurs erratically at Duluth and along the North Shore of L. Superior. ***WI:*** rare migrant from late April to late May and from late August to mid-October; casual winter visitor.

Habitat: pine woodlands, open mixed woodlands (especially those with oak or hickory) or riparian woodlands with cottonwoods.

Nesting: does not nest in our region.

Feeding: gleans insects from the tree canopy; may hover-glean or flycatch insects in midair; eats mainly insects, especially bees and wasps; also eats berries and small fruits; known to raid wasp nests.

Voice: song is a series of 3–5 sweet, clear, whistled phrases, like a faster version of the American Robin's song; call is *pit* or *pit-a-tuck*.

Similar Species: *Scarlet Tanager* (p. 303): smaller bill; male has black tail and black wings; female has darker wings, brighter underparts and uniformly olive upperparts. *Northern Cardinal* (p. 330): red bill; prominent head crest; male has black "mask" and "bib." *Western Tanager* (p. 304): wing bars. *Orchard Oriole* (p. 344) and *Baltimore Oriole* (p. 345): females have sharper bills and wing bars.

Best Sites: ***MN:*** mainly in the south, especially in May at feeders. ***WI:*** at feeders in early spring and late fall; in favorite migratory spots during the main migration period.

SCARLET TANAGER

Piranga olivacea

Each spring, birders eagerly await the sweet, rough-edged song of the lovely Scarlet Tanager. The return of the brilliant red male to wooded ravines and traditional migratory sites is always a much-anticipated event. • During spring migration, you may find yourself in the envious position of observing a Scarlet Tanager at eye level as it forages in the forest understory during cold and rainy weather. At other times, however, this bird can be surprisingly difficult to spot as it darts through the forest canopy in pursuit of insect prey. • The Scarlet Tanager is the only tanager that routinely nests in our region. In Central and South America, however, there are over 200 tanager species representing every color of the rainbow.

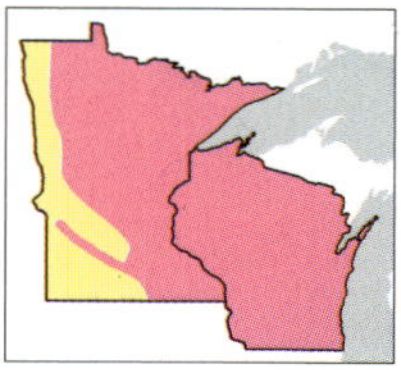

ID: *Breeding male:* bright red overall with black wings and tail; pale bill. *Nonbreeding male:* bright yellow underparts; olive upperparts; black wings and tail. *Female:* uniformly olive upperparts; yellow underparts; grayish brown wings.
Size: *L* 7 in; *W* 11½ in.
Status: ***MN:*** uncommon migrant and breeder from May to early October; uncommon to rare migrant in western regions, especially in the southwest; probably declining. ***WI:*** fairly common migrant and breeder from late April to October.
Habitat: fairly mature, upland deciduous and mixed forests and large woodlands.
Nesting: on a high branch, usually in a deciduous tree, well away from the trunk; female builds a flimsy, shallow cup nest of grass, weeds and twigs and lines it with rootlets and fine grass; female incubates 2–5 pale blue green eggs, with reddish brown to brown spots, for 12–14 days.
Feeding: gleans insects from the tree canopy; may hover-glean or hawk insects in midair; may forage at lower levels during cold weather; also takes some seasonally available berries.
Voice: song is a series of 4–5 sweet, clear, whistled phrases like a slurred version of the American Robin's song; call is a *chip-burrr* or *chip-churrr.*
Similar Species: *Summer Tanager* (p. 302): larger bill; male has red tail and red wings; female has paler wings and is duskier overall, often with orange or reddish tinge. *Northern Cardinal* (p. 330): red bill, wings and tail; prominent head crest; male has black mask and "bib." *Western Tanager* (p. 304): wing bars. *Orchard Oriole* (p. 344) and *Baltimore Oriole* (p. 345): females have sharper bills and wing bars.
Best Sites: ***MN:*** Frontenac SP; Afton SP; William O'Brien SP; mature deciduous woodlands in the southern part of the state. ***WI:*** *Breeding:* deciduous forests. *In migration:* with other songbirds at various migratory stops, including the Arboretum and Picnic Pt. (UW-Madison), High Cliff SP, Wyalusing SP, Milwaukee parks and Harrington Beach SP.

WESTERN TANAGER

Piranga ludoviciana

No other bird in our region can match the tropical splendor of a male Western Tanager. In addition to it being the rarest tanager in our region, the male's golden body, accentuated by black wings and a black tail, makes for a memorable moment when one is seen. Western Tanagers are tropical for most of the year—they fly to our region for only a few short months to raise a new generation on the seasonal explosion of food in our forests. • The song of the male Western Tanager can be difficult to learn, because it closely parallels the phrases of the American Robin's song. This tanager's phrases tend to be hoarser, however, as though the bird has a sore throat. Fortunately, the Western Tanager's hiccupy *pit-a-tik* call, which falls frequently from its treetop perches, is distinctive. • The roots of the tanager family extend deeply into the rainforests of South America, where this group is most diverse. "Tanager" is derived from *tangara,* the Tupi Indian name for this group of birds in the Amazon Basin.

breeding

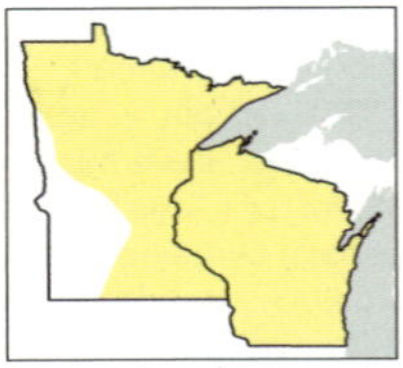

ID: *Breeding male:* yellow underparts, wing bars and rump; black back, wings and tail; often has red on forehead or entire head (variable); light-colored bill. *Breeding female:* olive green overall; lighter underparts; darker upperparts; faint wing bars.

Size: *L* 7 in; *W* $11\frac{1}{2}$ in.

Status: ***MN:*** rare and local spring migrant from late April to early June, mainly in northern and east-central regions; accidental in southwestern and central regions. ***WI:*** very rare spring migrant; casual fall migrant.

Habitat: mature coniferous or mixedwood forests and aspen woodlands.

Nesting: does not nest in our region.

Feeding: gleans vegetation and catches flying insects on the wing; eats wasps, beetles, flies and other insects; also eats caterpillars and fruit.

Voice: call is a hiccupy *pit-a-tik. Male:* song is hoarse and robinlike: *hurry, scurry, scurry, hurry.*

Similar Species: male is distinctive. *Baltimore Oriole* (p. 345): female has thinner bill and darker olive plumage.

Best Sites: no consistent sites; spring sightings are often at a feeder.

SPOTTED TOWHEE

Pipilo maculatus

More commonly found in the western part of the continent, the Spotted Towhee is an exceedingly rare visitor to our region. When seen, it is usually on the ground in a shrubby thicket or in brushy undergrowth, and you might encounter a Spotted Towhee hopping about in the dried leaves that have accumulated underneath a shrub if you are exceptionally lucky. This large sparrow is a noisy forager that scratches at loose leaf litter with both feet. Sometimes its scratching is so noisy that you expect an animal of deer-sized proportions to be the source of all the ruckus. • Until recently, the Spotted Towhee was grouped together with the Eastern Towhee, a spotless, eastern bird more commonly seen in our region, as a single species known as the Rufous-sided Towhee.

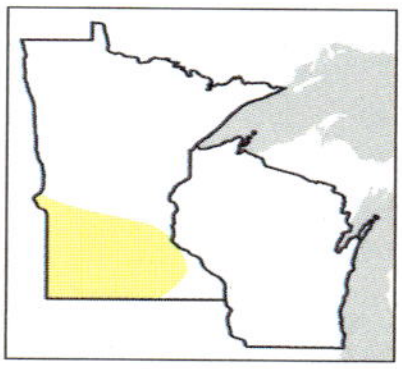

ID: *Male:* black "hood," back, wings and tail; rufous flanks; red eyes; dark, conical bill; white spotting on wings; white outer tail coverts; white belly and undertail. *Female:* somewhat paler overall.

Size: *L* 7–8½ in; *W* 10½ in.

Status: ***MN:*** little is known; records from 16 counties; casual to rare migrant in southwestern and west-central regions; records mainly from fall and spring; a few individuals have overwintered. ***WI:*** casual migrant.

Habitat: riparian shrublands and shrubby fields.

Nesting: does not nest in our region.

Feeding: scratches the ground vigorously for insects and seeds, including caterpillars, moths, beetles, ants and other common invertebrates; periodically visits feeders.

Voice: song is *here here here PLEASE;* call is a raspy or whining *chee.*

Similar Species: *Black-headed Grosbeak* (p. 360): red eyes; much heavier bill; lacks rufous on sides. *Eastern Towhee* (p. 306): all-dark back.

Best Sites: no consistent sites.

EASTERN TOWHEE

Pipilo erythrophthalmus

Eastern Towhees are often heard before they are seen. These noisy foragers rustle about in dense undergrowth, craftily scraping back layers of dry leaves to expose the seeds, berries or insects hidden beneath, though they also take insects and fruit from vegetation above ground. They employ an unusual two-footed technique to uncover food items—a strategy that is especially important in winter when virtually all of their food is taken from the ground. • Although you wouldn't guess it, this colorful bird is a member of the American Sparrow family—a group that is usually drab in color.

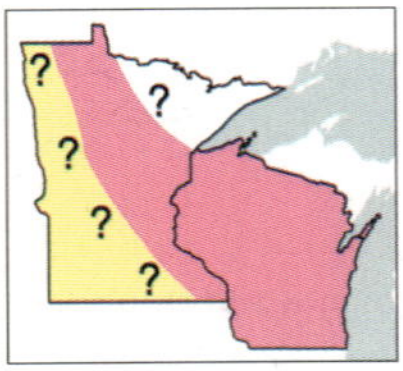

ID: rufous sides and flanks; white outer tail corners; white lower breast and belly; buff undertail coverts; red eyes; dark bill. *Male:* black "hood" and upperparts. *Female:* brown "hood" and upperparts.

Size: *L* 7–$8\frac{1}{2}$ in; *W* $10\frac{1}{2}$ in.

Status: ***MN:*** uncommon migrant and breeder from mid-April to late November in southeastern, central, north-central and northwestern regions; rare to casual elsewhere; rare in winter in east-central and southeastern regions. ***WI:*** fairly common migrant and breeder from mid-April to late October; rare winter visitor in the south.

Habitat: often along woodland edges and in shrubby, abandoned fields.

Nesting: on the ground or low in a dense shrub; female builds a camouflaged cup nest made of twigs, bark strips, grass, weeds, rootlets and animal hair; mostly the female incubates 3–6 creamy white to pale gray eggs, with brown spots toward the larger end, for 12 to 13 days.

Feeding: scratches at leaf litter for insects, seeds and berries; sometimes forages in low shrubs and saplings.

Voice: song is 2 high, whistled notes followed by a trill: *drink your teeeee;* call is a scratchy, slurred *cheweee!* or *chewink!*

Similar Species: *Dark-eyed Junco* (p. 325): much smaller; pale bill; black eyes; white outer tail feathers. *Spotted Towhee* (p. 305): white spots on dark back.

Best Sites: ***MN:*** Sherburne NWR; Houston Co.; William O'Brien SP; Afton SP; Minnesota River Valley State Recreation Area. ***WI:*** upland deciduous forest (mixed oak and jack pine) with open areas.

AMERICAN TREE SPARROW

Spizella arborea

The best time to see the American Tree Sparrow is during the winter and from late March to April, during spring migration. As the small flocks migrate north in spring, they offer bubbly, bright songs between bouts of foraging along the ground or in low, budding shrubs. In fall, they reappear together with Dark-eyed Juncos and spread out over weedy fields, wastelands and roadside thickets. • Although its name suggests a close relationship with trees or forests, the American Tree Sparrow actually prefers treeless fields and semi-open, shrubby habitats. This bird got its name because of a superficial resemblance to the Eurasian Tree Sparrow familiar to early settlers. • With adequate food supplies, the American Tree Sparrow can survive temperatures as cold as –28° F.

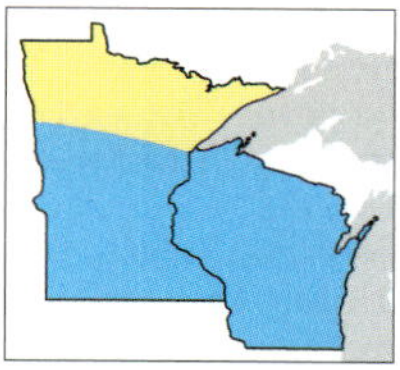

ID: gray underparts; dark, central breast spot; pale rufous "cap"; rufous stripe behind eye; gray face; mottled brown upperparts; notched tail; 2 white wing bars; dark legs; dark upper mandible; yellow lower mandible.
Size: *L* 6–6½ in; *W* 9½ in.
Status: ***MN:*** common to abundant migrant from early March to late May and from mid-September to late November; common to locally abundant winter visitor in the southern half of the state with numbers decreasing in the north. ***WI:*** abundant migrant from mid-March to early May and from early October to mid-December; common winter visitor.
Habitat: brushy thickets, roadside shrubs, semi-open fields and agricultural croplands.
Nesting: does not nest in our region.
Feeding: scratches exposed soil or snow for seeds in winter; eats mostly insects in summer; takes some berries and occasionally visits bird feeders.
Voice: a high, whistled *tseet-tseet* is followed by a short, sweet, musical series of slurred whistles; song may be given in late winter and during spring migration; call is a 3-note *tsee-dle-eat*.
Similar Species: *Chipping Sparrow* (p. 308): clear black eye line; white "eyebrow"; lacks dark breast spot. *Swamp Sparrow* (p. 321): white throat; lacks dark breast spot and white wing bars. *Field Sparrow* (p. 310): white eye ring; orange pink bill; lacks dark breast spot.
Best Sites: ***MN:*** *In migration:* widespread in weedy fields and brushy areas during peak migration periods. *Winter:* at feeders and around brushy farmsteads. ***WI:*** *Winter:* along roadsides and brushy borders; also at feeders.

CHIPPING SPARROW

Spizella passerina

breeding

The Chipping Sparrow and Dark-eyed Junco do not share the same tailor, but they must have attended the same voice lessons, because their songs are very similar. Though the rapid trill of the Chipping Sparrow is slightly faster, drier and less musical than the junco's, even experienced birders can have difficulty identifying this singer. • Chipping Sparrows commonly nest at eye level, so you can easily watch their breeding and nest-building rituals. They are well known for their preference for conifers as a nest site and for hair as a lining material for the nest. By planting conifers in your backyard and offering samples of your pet's hair—or even your own—in backyard baskets in spring, you could attract nesting Chipping Sparrows to your area and contribute to their nesting success.

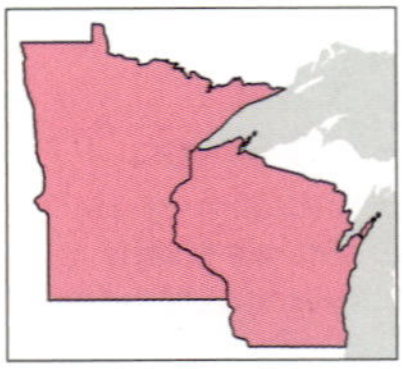

ID: *Breeding:* prominent rufous "cap"; white "eyebrow"; black eye line; light gray, unstreaked underparts; mottled brown upperparts; all-dark bill; 2 faint wing bars; pale legs. *Nonbreeding:* paler crown with dark streaks; brown "eyebrow" and "cheek"; pale lower mandible. *Immature:* gray brown overall with dark brown streaking; pale lower mandible.

Size: *L* 5–6 in; *W* 8½ in.

Status: ***MN:*** common to locally abundant migrant and breeder from late March to early November; most numerous in northern and eastern regions. ***WI:*** common migrant and breeder from early April to late October; very rare winter visitor in the south.

Habitat: open conifers or mixed woodland edges; often in yards and gardens with tree and shrub borders.

Nesting: usually at midlevel in a coniferous tree; female builds a compact cup nest of grass and rootlets, often lined with hair; female incubates 4 pale blue eggs for 11–12 days.

Feeding: gleans seeds while hopping along the ground and from the outer branches of trees or shrubs; prefers seeds from grasses, dandelions and clovers; also eats adult and larval invertebrates; occasionally visits feeders.

Voice: song is a rapid, dry trill of *chip* notes; call is a high-pitched *chip*.

Similar Species: *American Tree Sparrow* (p. 307): dark central breast spot; rufous stripe extends behind eye; lacks bold white "eyebrow." *Swamp Sparrow* (p. 321): lacks white "eyebrow," full, black eye line and white wing bars. *Field Sparrow* (p. 310): lacks bold white "eyebrow"; rufous stripe extends behind eye; white eye ring; gray throat; orange pink bill.

Best Sites: ***MN:*** residential areas and state county and city parks with conifers; along wooded roadsides at peak migration times, especially in the fall.
WI: residential areas with small conifer trees; young conifer stands.

CLAY-COLORED SPARROW

Spizella pallida

For the most part, Clay-colored Sparrows go completely unnoticed because their plumage, habit and voice all contribute to a cryptic lifestyle. Even when males are singing at the top of their "air sacs," they are usually mistaken for buzzing insects. Although subtle in plumage, the Clay-colored Sparrow still possesses an unassuming beauty. • A denizen of brushy, shrubby habitats, populations of this species expanded in the early 20th century as land was cleared by logging and for agricultural purposes. In the last 30 years, however, there have been small but consistent declines in this bird's numbers because of modern agricultural practices and urbanization.

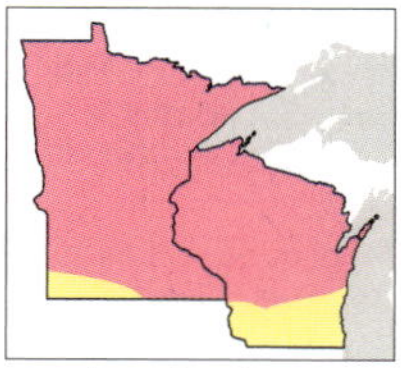

ID: unstreaked, white underparts; buff breast wash; gray nape; light brown "cheek" edged with darker brown; brown crown with dark streak and pale central stripe; pale "eyebrow"; white jaw stripe bordered with brown; white throat; mostly pale bill. *Immature:* dark streaks on buff breast, sides and flanks.

Size: *L* 5–6 in; *W* 7½ in.

Status: ***MN:*** fairly common migrant and breeder from mid-April to mid-October; most common as a breeder in central and northern regions. ***WI:*** fairly common migrant and breeder from late April to mid-October, except in the south and east where it is a rare breeder.

Habitat: brushy open areas along forest and woodland edges; in forest openings, regenerating burn sites, abandoned fields, riparian thickets and young conifer plantations.

Nesting: in a grassy tuft or small shrub; female builds an open cup nest of twigs, grass, weeds and rootlets and lines it with rootlets, fine grass and fur; mostly the female incubates 4 brown-speckled, bluish green eggs for 10–12 days.

Feeding: forages for seeds and insects on the ground and in low vegetation.

Voice: song is a series of 2–5 slow, low-pitched, insectlike buzzes; call is a soft *chip.*

Similar Species: *Chipping Sparrow* (p. 308): breeding adult has prominent rufous "cap," gray "cheek" and underparts, 2 faint, white wing bars and all-dark bill; immature lacks gray nape and buff on sides and flanks, but may look almost identical.

Best Sites: ***MN:*** Big Stone NWR; Afton SP; Tamarac NWR; Itasca SP; Lake Bronson SP. ***WI:*** Crex Meadows WA; old fields and young conifer plantations in the northern two-thirds of the state.

FIELD SPARROW

Spizella pusilla

The pink-billed Field Sparrow frequents overgrown fields, pastures and forest clearings. Deserted farmland may seem unproductive to some people, but to this sparrow it is heaven. For nesting purposes, this bird usually chooses pastures that are scattered with shrubs, herbaceous plants and plenty of tall grass. • The Field Sparrow has learned to recognize when its nest has been parasitized by the Brown-headed Cowbird. Because the unwelcome eggs are usually too large for this small sparrow to eject, the nest is simply abandoned. This sparrow may be so stubborn in refusing to raise young cowbirds that affected pairs may make numerous nesting attempts in a single season. • Some Field Sparrows remain in our region during warm winters, when they are often observed among larger flocks of American Tree Sparrows.

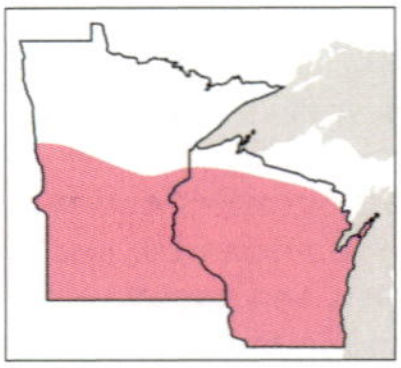

ID: orange pink bill; gray face and throat; rusty crown with gray central stripe; rusty streak behind eye; white eye ring; 2 white wing bars; unstreaked gray underparts; buffy red wash on breast, sides and flanks; pinkish legs.

Size: *L* 5–6 in; *W* 8 in.

Status: ***MN:*** uncommon to occasionally common migrant and breeder from late March to October in central and southern regions; rare to absent over most of the north; a few overwinter in the south. ***WI:*** special concern; common migrant and breeder from late March to late October; uncommon migrant and breeder in the north; rare winter visitor in southern and central regions.

Habitat: abandoned or weedy and overgrown fields and pastures, woodland edges and clearings, extensive shrubby riparian areas and young conifer plantations.

Nesting: on or near the ground, often sheltered by a grass clump, shrub or sapling; female weaves an open cup nest of grass and lines it with animal hair and soft plant material; female incubates 3–5 brown-spotted, whitish to pale bluish white eggs for 10–12 days.

Feeding: forages on the ground; takes mostly insects in summer and seeds in winter.

Voice: song is a series of woeful, musical, down-slurred whistles accelerating into a trill; call is a *chip* or *tsee*.

Similar Species: *American Tree Sparrow* (p. 307): dark central breast spot; dark upper mandible; lacks white eye ring. *Swamp Sparrow* (p. 321): white throat; dark upper mandible; lacks white wing bars and white eye ring. *Chipping Sparrow* (p. 308): all-dark bill; white "eyebrow"; black eye line; lacks buffy red wash on underparts.

Best Sites: ***MN:*** oak savanna areas in state, county and city parks, such as Afton SP and Great River Bluffs SP. ***WI:*** old fields and young forested areas.

VESPER SPARROW

Pooecetes gramineus

For birders who live near grassy fields and agricultural lands with multitudes of confusing little brown sparrows, the Vesper Sparrow offers welcome relief—white outer tail feathers and a chestnut shoulder patch announce its identity whether it is perched or in flight. • The Vesper Sparrow is known for its bold and easily distinguished song, which begins with two sets of double notes: *here-here! there-there!* • More often than not, the Vesper Sparrow builds its nest in a grassy hollow at the base of a small shrub or clump of weeds, which provides camouflage and functions as a windbreak and an umbrella to protect the young. Unfortunately, modern land management practices work against the Vesper Sparrow. Keeping grass short destroys the very habitat this bird prefers, often just as it lays its eggs.

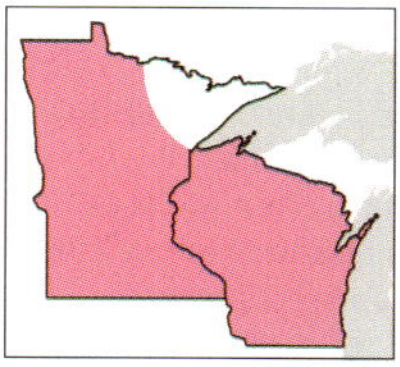

ID: chestnut shoulder patch; white outer tail feathers; pale yellow lores; weak flank streaking; white eye ring; dark upper mandible; paler lower mandible; light-colored legs.

Size: *L* 6 in; *W* 10 in.

Status: ***MN:*** common migrant and breeder from late March to mid-October; rare to absent in the northeast and portions of the north-central region. ***WI:*** special concern; common migrant and breeder from late March to late October.

Habitat: open fields bordered or interspersed with shrubs, semi-open shrublands and grasslands; also in agricultural areas, open, dry conifer plantations and scrubby gravel pits.

Nesting: in a scrape on the ground; often under a canopy of grass or at the base of a shrub; loosely woven cup nest of grass is lined with rootlets, fine grass and hair; mostly the female incubates 3–5 whitish to greenish white eggs, blotched with brown and gray, for 11–13 days.

Feeding: walks and runs along the ground, picking up grasshoppers, beetles, cutworms, other invertebrates and seeds.

Voice: song is 4 characteristic, preliminary notes, with the second higher in pitch, followed by a bubbly trill: *here-here there-there, everybody-down-the-hill.*

Similar Species: *Other sparrows* (pp. 307–24): lack white outer tail feathers and chestnut shoulder patch. *Lark Sparrow* (p. 312): immature has streaking on breast and lacks chestnut shoulder patch. *American Pipit* (p. 263): thinner bill; grayer upperparts lack brown streaking; lacks chestnut shoulder patch. *Lapland Longspur* (p. 326): blackish or buff wash on upper breast; nonbreeding has broad, pale "eyebrow" and reddish edgings to wing feathers.

Best Sites: roadsides, old fields, open grasslands and agricultural areas.

LARK SPARROW

Chondestes grammacus

Though the Lark Sparrow's head pattern is distinctively bold, most sparrows share the same basic pattern in a mixture of less highly contrasting browns and grays. Although these birds are typically seen in open shrubby areas and "edge" habitat, they occasionally venture into meadows, grassy forest openings and wooded areas. • Male Lark Sparrows are renowned for their "turkey walk." Fluffing their chestnut feathers, they lift their beaks to the sky, spread their tails, droop their wings to the ground, and boldly strut back and forth in front of potential mates, all the while bubbling with song. During courtship, the male Lark Sparrow has the interesting behavior of passing a twig to his mate. This gift-giving technique is popular in the bird world, employing either food or nesting material as a request for a mate.

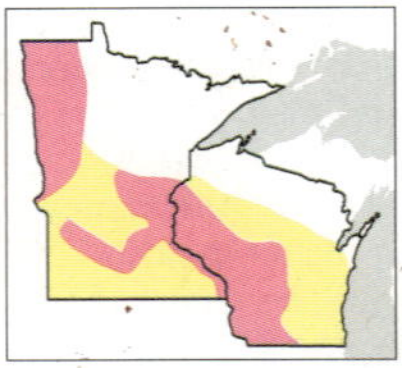

ID: white throat, "eyebrow" and crown stripe and black lines that form distinctive "helmet" on otherwise chestnut red head; unstreaked, pale breast with central spot; black tail with white outer feathers; mottled brown back and wings; light-colored legs.

Size: *L* 6 in; *W* 11 in.

Status: ***MN:*** seldom seen in migration; rare and local breeder in southeastern and east-central regions along the Minnesota R. valley and into west-central and northwestern regions; rare or accidental migrant and breeder elsewhere. ***WI:*** special concern; uncommon migrant from late April to late May in southern, western and central regions; rare migrant from mid-August to mid-September in the south; uncommon breeder.

Habitat: semi-open shrublands, sandhills, prairie and occasionally pastures.

Nesting: on the ground or in a low bush; occasionally reuses an abandoned thrasher nest; female builds a bulky cup nest of grass and twigs and lines it with finer material; female incubates 4–5 white eggs, marked with black, gray and lavender, for 11–12 days.

Feeding: gleans seeds while walking or hopping along the ground; also eats grasshoppers and other invertebrates.

Voice: melodious, variable song that consists of short trills, buzzes, pauses and clear notes.

Similar Species: no other sparrow has the distinctive head pattern.

Best Sites: ***MN:*** Sherburne NWR; Minnesota R. valley; Kellogg-Weaver Dunes SNA. ***WI:*** west of Prairie du Sac; Spring Green Preserve; Meridean area; Grantsburg area.

SAVANNAH SPARROW

Passerculus sandwichensis

The Savannah Sparrow is one of the most common open-country birds in our region. At one time or another, most people have probably seen or heard this sparrow, although they may not have been aware of it. This bird's streaky, dull brown, buff-and-white plumage makes it resemble so many of the other grassland sparrows that it is easily overlooked. • In early spring and summer, male Savannah Sparrows belt out their distinctive, buzzy tunes while perched atop prominent shrubs, tall weeds or strategic fence posts. Later in the summer and throughout early fall, they are most often seen darting across roads, highways and open fields in search of food. However, like most sparrows, Savannahs generally stay out of sight. When danger appears, they take flight only as a last resort, preferring to run swiftly and inconspicuously through the grass like feathered voles.

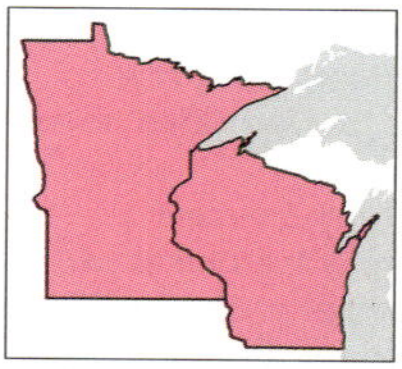

ID: finely streaked breast, sides and flanks; mottled brown upperparts; pale, streaked underparts; yellow lores; light jaw line; pale legs and bill; may show dark breast spot.

Size: *L* 5–6 in; *W* 6½ in.

Status: ***MN:*** common to abundant migrant and breeder from early April to late October. ***WI:*** abundant migrant and breeder from early April to mid-November.

Habitat: agricultural fields (especially hay and alfalfa), moist sedge and grass meadows, pastures.

Nesting: on the ground; in a shallow scrape well concealed by grass or a shrub; female builds an open cup nest woven from and lined with grass; female incubates 3–6 brown-marked, whitish to greenish or pale tan eggs for 10–13 days.

Feeding: gleans insects and seeds while walking or running along the ground; • occasionally scratches.

Voice: song is a high-pitched, clear, buzzy *tea tea teeeeea today;* call is a high, thin *tsit.*

Similar Species: *Vesper Sparrow* (p. 311): white outer tail feathers; chestnut shoulder patch. *Lincoln's Sparrow* (p. 320): buff jaw line; buff wash across breast; broad, gray "eyebrow." *Grasshopper Sparrow* (p. 314): unstreaked breast. *Song Sparrow* (p. 319): triangular "mustache" stripes; pale central crown stripe; rounded tail; lacks yellow lores.

Best Sites: ***MN:*** meadows and grasslands; Felton Prairie SNA; Tamarac NWR; Rice Lake NWR; Rothsay WMA; along grassy roadsides in western and central regions during peak fall (October) migration periods. ***WI:*** widespread in open grasslands, sedge meadows and old fields.

GRASSHOPPER SPARROW

Ammodramus savannarum

The Grasshopper Sparrow is named not for its diet but rather for its buzzy, insectlike song. During courtship flights, males chase females through the air, buzzing at a frequency that is usually inaudible to human ears. The males sing two completely different courtship songs: one ends in a short trill and the other is a prolonged series of high trills that vary in pitch and speed. • The Grasshopper Sparrow is an open-country bird that prefers grassy expanses free of trees and shrubs. Wide, well-drained, grassy ditches occasionally attract nesting Grasshopper Sparrows, so mowing or harvesting these grassy margins early in the nesting season may be detrimental to these birds.

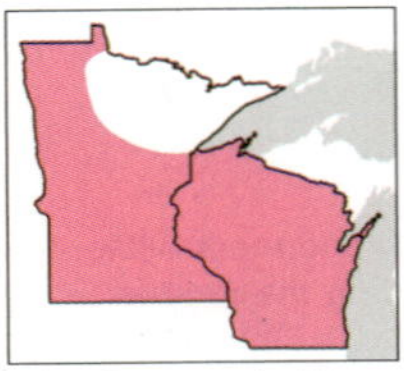

ID: unstreaked, white underparts; buff wash on breast, sides and flanks; flattened head profile; dark crown with pale central stripe; buff "cheek"; mottled brown upperparts; beady, black eyes; sharp tail; pale legs; may show small yellow patch on edge of forewing.

Size: *L* 5–5½ in; *W* 7½ in.

Status: ***MN:*** uncommon migrant and breeder from mid-April through fall; seldom seen in fall migration; rare to absent over most of the north-central and northwestern regions. ***WI:*** special concern; fairly common migrant and breeder from late April to early October in western and central regions; uncommon migrant and breeder in eastern and northern regions.

Habitat: grasslands and grassy fields with little or no shrub or tree cover.

Nesting: in a shallow depression on the ground, usually concealed by grass; female builds a small cup nest of grass and lines it with rootlets, fine grass and hair; female incubates 4–5 creamy white eggs, spotted with gray and reddish brown, for 11–13 days.

Feeding: gleans insects and seeds from the ground and grass; eats a variety of insects, including grasshoppers.

Voice: song is a high, faint, buzzy trill preceded by 1–3 high, thin, whistled notes: *tea-tea-tea zeeeeeeeeee.*

Similar Species: *Le Conte's Sparrow* (p. 316): buff-and-black-striped head with white central crown stripe; gray "cheek"; dark streaking on sides and flanks. *Nelson's Sharp-tailed Sparrow* (p. 317): buff orange face and breast; gray central crown stripe; gray "cheek" and shoulders. *Henslow's Sparrow* (p. 315): similar to immature Grasshopper Sparrow, but with darker breast streaking, rusty wings and small, dark ear and "whisker" marks.

Best Sites: ***MN:*** *Breeding:* extensive grassland or prairie habitat, such as Felton Prairie SNA, Kasota Prairie SNA, Frontenac SP and Sherburne NWR. ***WI:*** Spring Green Preserve; Jersey Flats (Kettle Moraine State Forest–North Unit); open grasslands elsewhere in the state.

HENSLOW'S SPARROW

Ammodramus henslowii

Watch the male Henslow's Sparrow as he throws back his streaky, greenish head while hurling his distinctive, hiccupy song from atop a tall blade of grass. Without the male's lyrical advertisements, the inconspicuous Henslow's Sparrow would be almost impossible to observe as this bird spends most of its time foraging alone along the ground. When disturbed, it may fly a short distance before dropping into cover, but usually it prefers to run through dense, concealing vegetation. • Henslow's Sparrows are known for their unusual habit of singing at night. • Loss of grassland habitat and modern farming practices have led to a decline in Henslow's Sparrow populations to the point that it has become a priority for conservation in many parts of its range.

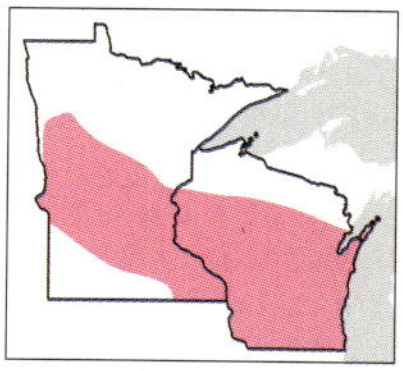

ID: flattened head profile; olive green face, central crown stripe and nape; dark crown and "whisker" stripes; rusty tinge on back, wings and tail; white underparts with dark streaking on buff breast, sides and flanks; thick bill; deeply notched, sharp-edged tail.

Size: *L* 5–5½ in; *W* 6½ in.

Status: ***MN:*** endangered; seldom if ever seen in migration; rare, local and irregular breeder. ***WI:*** threatened; uncommon migrant and breeder from mid-April to mid-October; rare in the north.

Habitat: large, fallow or wild, grassy fields and meadows with a matted ground layer of dead vegetation and scattered shrub or herb perches; often in moist, grassy areas.

Nesting: on the ground at the base of a herbaceous plant or grass clump; mostly the female builds an open cup nest of grass and weeds and lines it with fine grass and hair; female incubates 3–5 whitish to pale greenish white eggs, spotted with gray and reddish brown, for about 11 days.

Feeding: gleans insects and seeds from the ground.

Voice: weak, liquidy, cricketlike *tse-lick* song is distinctive, often given during periods of rain or at night.

Similar Species: *Other sparrows* (pp. 307–24): lack greenish face, central crown strip and nape. *Grasshopper Sparrow* (p. 314): lacks dark "whisker" stripes and prominent streaking on breast and sides. *Savannah Sparrow* (p. 313): lacks buff breast. *Le Conte's Sparrow* (p. 316): buff-and-black-striped head with white central crown stripe; gray "cheek."

Best Sites: ***MN:*** Great River Bluffs SP; Frontenac SP; Afton SP; old fields with mullein. ***WI:*** Jersey Flats (Kettle Moraine State Forest–North Unit); White River Marsh; old fields and open grasslands in the southern two-thirds of the state.

LE CONTE'S SPARROW

Ammodramus leconteii

The Le Conte's Sparrow is difficult to find because of its remote breeding habitat and scattered distribution. These sparrows are secretive, preferring to scurry along the ground under thick cover, and only resorting to flight for short distances before dropping out of sight again. Even singing males typically choose low, concealing perches from which to offer their gentle love ballads. Some skilled birders, however, may follow the buzzy tune to its source to catch a fleeting glimpse of the singer before he dives into tall vegetation and disappears from view. • This bird's namesake, John Le Conte, is best remembered as one of the preeminent American entomologists of the 19th century, though he was interested in all areas of natural history.

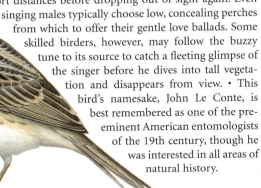

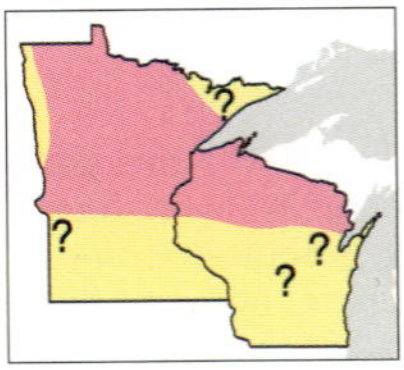

ID: buff orange face; gray "cheek"; black line behind eye; light central crown stripe bordered by black stripes; buff orange upper breast, sides and flanks; dark streaking on sides and flanks; white throat, lower breast and belly; mottled, brown black upperparts; buff streaks on back; pale legs.

Size: *L* $4\frac{1}{2}$–5 in; *W* $6\frac{1}{2}$ in.

Status: ***MN:*** uncommon to rare migrant from mid-April to late May; fairly common migrant from August to late October (especially in early October); uncommon but widespread breeder in central and northern regions, especially the northwest. ***WI:*** special concern; uncommon migrant from mid-April to late May and from mid-September to mid-October; uncommon breeder.

Habitat: grassy meadows with dense vegetation, drier edges of wet sedge and grass meadows, willow and alder flats and forest openings.

Nesting: on or near the ground, concealed by tangled vegetation; female builds an open cup nest woven from grass and rushes and tied to standing plant stems, and lines it with fine grass and hair; female incubates 3–5 grayish white eggs, spotted with gray and brown, for 12–13 days.

Feeding: gleans the ground and low vegetation for insects, spiders and seeds.

Voice: song is a weak, short, raspy, insect-like buzz: *t-t-t-zeeee zee* or *take-it ea-zeee;* alarm call is a high-pitched whistle.

Similar Species: *Nelson's Sharp-tailed Sparrow* (p. 317): gray central crown stripe and nape; white streaks on dark back. *Grasshopper Sparrow* (p. 314): lacks buff orange face and streaking on underparts.

Best Sites: ***MN:*** Hamden Slough NWR; Bluestem Prairie SNA; Rothsay WMA; Rice Lake NWR; sedge meadows, especially in migration in early October. ***WI:*** Crex Meadows WA; Fish Lake WA; Thunder Lake Marsh; Powell Marsh; Comstock Bog-Meadow; sedge meadows and open grasslands in the northern half of the state.

NELSON'S SHARP-TAILED SPARROW

Ammodramus nelsoni

It is hard to find a Nelson's Sharp-tailed Sparrow without getting your feet wet. In its marshland habitat, this small, colorful sparrow resides among dense, concealing stands of cattails and bulrushes, unexpectedly popping out of soggy hiding places and occasionally perching completely exposed at close distances. Sharp-tails are secretive, and prefer to flee danger by scurrying along the ground rather than flushing. • Nelson's Sharp-tailed Sparrows have a very unusual breeding strategy among songbirds: the males rove around the marsh mating with all the available females, which are also promiscuous, and these sparrows do not establish pair bonds or territories. • In 1995, the Sharp-tailed Sparrow was reclassified into two separate species: "Nelson's Sharp-tailed Sparrow" and "Saltmarsh Sharp-tailed Sparrow" *(A. caudacutus)*.

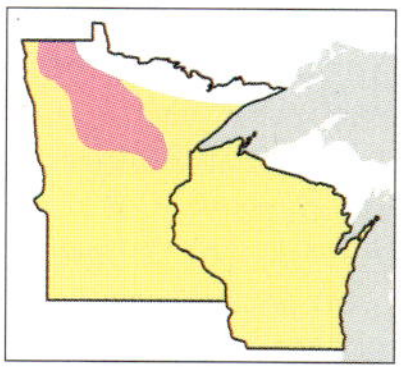

ID: buff orange face, breast, sides and flanks; gray "cheek," central crown stripe and nape; dark line behind eye; indistinct streaking on underparts; brown stripes on gray back; white to light buff throat.
Size: *L* 5–6 in; *W* 7 in.
Status: ***MN:*** special concern; seldom seen in spring migration; rare to uncommon migrant from late August to mid-October mainly in the west; rare breeder. ***WI:*** special concern; rare migrant from late April through May; uncommon migrant from September to mid-October; rare summer resident in the north.
Habitat: wet meadows and marshlands with tall emergent and shoreline vegetation.

Nesting: on the ground or low in upright grass or sedge stems; female builds a bulky cup nest of dry grass and sedges and lines it with fine grass; female incubates 3–5 pale blue green to greenish white eggs, heavily dotted with reddish brown, for 11–12 days.
Feeding: gleans ants, beetles, grasshoppers and other invertebrates from the ground and low vegetation; also eats seeds.
Voice: song is a short, raspy buzz: *ts tse-sheeeee.*
Similar Species: *Le Conte's Sparrow* (p. 316): lacks gray nape and brown stripes on gray back. *Grasshopper Sparrow* (p. 314): lacks streaking on underparts. *Savannah Sparrow* (p. 313): notched tail; heavily streaked underparts.
Best Sites: ***MN:*** McGregor Marsh; Agassiz NWR; Roseau River WMA. ***WI:*** Crex Meadows WA; Fish Lake WA.

FOX SPARROW

Passerella iliaca

Like the Eastern Towhee, the Fox Sparrow eagerly scratches out a living, using both feet to stir up leaves and scrape organic matter along the forest floor. This large sparrow's preference for impenetrable, brushy habitat makes it a difficult species to observe, even though its noisy foraging habits often reveal its whereabouts. The Fox Sparrow is generally agreed to be the best singer among the sparrows and its loud, whistled courtship songs are easily recognized. • Unlike other songbirds, which filter through the region in a series of lingering waves, Fox Sparrows generally appear in our region for only a few short weeks before moving on to their nesting grounds farther north. • The overall reddish brown appearance of this bird inspired taxonomists to name it after the red fox.

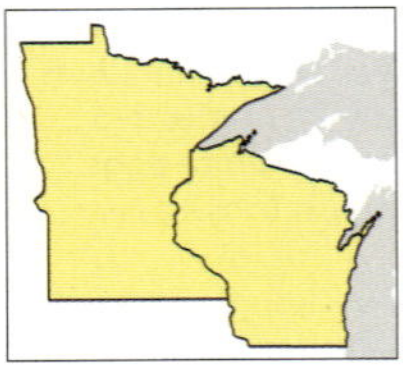

ID: whitish underparts; heavy, reddish brown spotting and streaking; central breast spot; reddish brown wings, rump and tail; gray crown; brown-streaked back; gray "eyebrow" and nape; stubby, conical bill; pale legs.

Size: *L* 6½–7 in; *W* 10½ in.

Status: ***MN:*** common migrant from mid-March to late May and from early September to mid-October; a few overwinter, mainly in east-central and southern regions. ***WI:*** common migrant from mid-March to April and from mid-September to early November; rare winter visitor.

Habitat: riparian thickets and brushy woodland clearings, edges and parklands.

Nesting: does not nest in our region.

Feeding: scratches the ground to uncover seeds, berries and invertebrates; visits backyard feeders in migration and winter.

Voice: song is a long, variable series of melodic whistles: *All I have is what's here dear, won't you won't you take it?;* calls include *chip* and *click* notes.

Similar Species: *Song Sparrow* (p. 319): pale central crown stripe; dark "mustache"; dark brownish (rather than reddish) streaking and upperparts. *Hermit Thrush* (p. 255): longer, thinner bill; light eye ring; dark breast spots; unstreaked olive brown and reddish brown upperparts; lacks heavy streaking on underparts.

Best Sites: ***MN:*** brushy woodlots, plum thickets and brushy edges along back roads. ***WI:*** widespread; joins other sparrows feeding on the ground in yards, woods and sometimes along roadsides.

SONG SPARROW

Melospiza melodia

The Song Sparrow's low-key plumage doesn't prepare you for its symphonic song. This well-named sparrow is known for the complexity, rhythm and emotion of its springtime rhapsodies, although some people will insist that the Fox Sparrow and the Lincoln's Sparrow carry the best tunes. • Young Song Sparrows (and many other songbirds) learn to sing by eavesdropping on their fathers or on rival males. By the time a young male is a few months old, he will have formed the basis for his own courtship tune. • In recent decades, mild winters and an abundance of backyard bird feeders have enticed many Song Sparrows to overwinter. • Most songbirds are lucky if they are able to produce one brood per year. In some years, Song Sparrows in our region will successfully raise three broods.

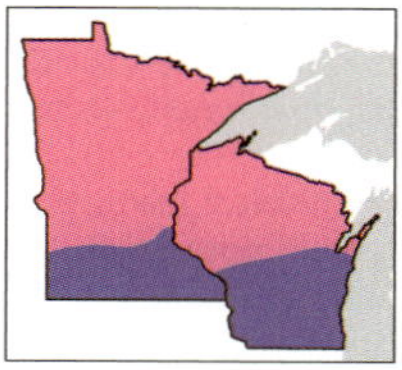

ID: whitish underparts with heavy brown streaking; central breast spot; grayish face; dark line behind eye; dark stripes border white jaw line; dark crown with pale central stripe; mottled brown upperparts; rounded tail tip.

Size: *L* $5\frac{1}{2}$–7 in; *W* $8\frac{1}{2}$ in.

Status: ***MN:*** common migrant and breeder from mid-March to late November; a few overwinter in southeastern and east-central regions. ***WI:*** abundant migrant and breeder from mid-March to early November; uncommon winter visitor.

Habitat: shrubby areas, often near water, including willow shrublands, riparian thickets, forest openings and pastures.

Nesting: usually on the ground or low in a shrub or small tree; female builds an open cup nest of grass, weeds, leaves and bark shreds and lines it with rootlets, fine grass and hair; female incubates 3–5 greenish white eggs, heavily spotted with reddish brown, for 12–14 days; may raise 2–3 broods each summer.

Feeding: gleans the ground, shrubs and trees for cutworms, beetles, grasshoppers, ants, other invertebrates and seeds; also eats wild fruit and visits feeders.

Voice: song is 1–4 bright, distinctive introductory notes, such as *sweet, sweet, sweet,* followed by a buzzy *towee,* then a short, descending trill; calls include a short *tsip* and a nasal *tchep.*

Similar Species: *Fox Sparrow* (p. 318): heavier breast spotting and streaking; reddish rather than dark brownish streaking and upperparts; lacks pale central crown stripe and dark "mustache." *Lincoln's Sparrow* (p. 320): lightly streaked breast with buff wash; buff jaw line. *Savannah Sparrow* (p. 313): lightly streaked breast; yellow lores; notched tail; lacks grayish face and dark triangular "mustache."

Best Sites: ***MN:*** wooded swamps, wet areas, brushy thickets and along roadsides. ***WI:*** residential areas, fields, wooded swamps and along woody, shrubby roadsides.

LINCOLN'S SPARROW

Melospiza lincolnii

There is a certain beauty in the plumage of a Lincoln's Sparrow. In comparison to the scruffier, chunkier Song Sparrow, everything about the Lincoln's Sparrow is refined. • Lincoln's Sparrows seem to be more timid than other sparrows of our region. Males will sit openly on exposed perches and sing their bubbly, wrenlike song, but as soon as they are approached, they slip under the cover of nearby shrubs. When they are not singing their courtship songs, Lincoln's Sparrows remain well hidden in tall grass and dense, bushy growth. Their remote breeding grounds and secretive behavior conspire to keep this species one of the least-known sparrows.

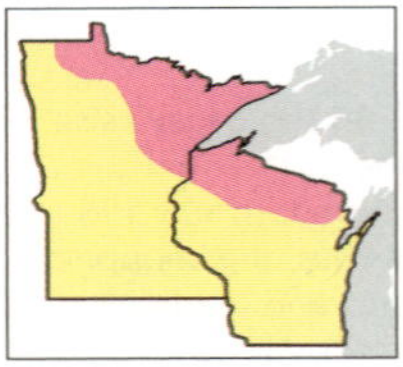

ID: buff breast band, sides and flanks with fine dark streaking; buff jaw stripe; gray "eyebrow," face and "collar"; dark line behind eye; dark reddish "cap" with gray central stripe; white throat and belly; mottled gray brown to reddish brown upperparts; very faint white eye ring.

Size: *L* 5½ in; *W* 7½ in.

Status: ***MN:*** uncommon migrant from mid-April to late May and from late July to early November, most numerous in fall; uncommon breeder. ***WI:*** fairly common migrant from late April through May and from September to mid-November; uncommon breeder.

Habitat: shrubby edges of bogs, swamps, beaver ponds and meadows; also in the shrubby growth of recent forest burns or clearings.

Nesting: on the ground, often on soft moss or concealed beneath a shrub; female builds a well-hidden cup nest of grass and sedges and lines it with fine grass and hair; female incubates 4–5 greenish white to pale green eggs, heavily spotted with reddish brown, for 11–14 days.

Feeding: scratches at the ground to expose invertebrates and seeds; occasionally visits feeders.

Voice: song is a wrenlike musical mixture of buzzes, trills and warbled notes; calls include a buzzy *zeee* and *tsup*.

Similar Species: *Song Sparrow* (p. 319): heavier breast streaking; dark, triangular "mustache"; lacks buff wash on breast, sides and flanks. *Savannah Sparrow* (p. 313): yellow lores; white "eyebrow" and jaw line. *Swamp Sparrow* (p. 321): generally lacks streaking on breast; more contrast between red and gray crown stripes.

Best Sites: ***MN:*** *Breeding:* northern conifer swamps. *In migration:* along brushy roadsides and woodlot edges at peak migration periods. ***WI:*** *Breeding:* northern conifer swamps. *In migration:* in the company of other sparrows at sites such as Bay Beach Sanctuary, Harrington Beach SP, Milwaukee parks, Wisconsin Pt. and the Arboretum and Picnic Pt. (UW-Madison).

SWAMP SPARROW

Melospiza georgiana

Swamp Sparrows are well adapted to life near water. These wetland inhabitants skulk among the emergent vegetation of cattail marshes, foraging for a variety of invertebrates including beetles, caterpillars, spiders, leafhoppers and flies. Like other sparrows, they are unable to swim, but that is no deterrent—many of their meals are snatched directly from the water's surface as they wade through the shallows. • The Swamp Sparrow must keep a lookout for daytime predators such as Northern Harriers, Great Blue Herons and large snakes. At night, the key to survival is finding a secluded, concealing perch that will keep it safe from raccoons, skunks and weasels. • Male Swamp Sparrows are most easily seen in spring, when they sing their familiar trills from the tops of cattails or shoreline shrubs, and both sexes can be seen in fall, often in the company of other sparrows.

breeding

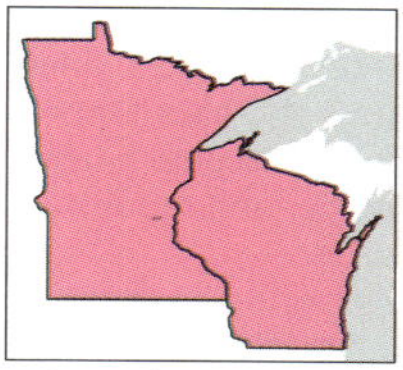

ID: gray face; reddish brown wings; brownish upperparts; dark streaking on back; dull gray breast; white throat and jaw line outlined by black stripes; dark line behind eye. *Breeding:* rusty "cap"; streaked buff sides and flanks. *Nonbreeding:* streaked brown "cap" with gray central crown stripe; more brownish sides.

Size: *L* 5–6 in; *W* 7½ in.

Status: ***MN:*** common migrant and breeder from late March to late November; rare winter visitor in east-central, southeastern and south-central regions. ***WI:*** common migrant and breeder from early April to late October; uncommon to rare winter visitor in southern and central regions.

Habitat: cattail marshes, open wetlands, wet meadows and open, riparian, deciduous thickets.

Nesting: in emergent aquatic vegetation or shoreline bushes; female builds a cup nest of coarse grass and marsh vegetation and lines it with fine grass; nest usually has a partial canopy and a side entrance; female incubates 4–5 greenish white to pale green eggs, heavily marked with reddish brown, for 12–15 days.

Feeding: gleans insects from the ground, vegetation and the water's surface; takes seeds in late summer and fall.

Voice: song is a slow, sharp, metallic trill: *weet-weet-weet-weet;* call is a harsh *chink.*

Similar Species: *Chipping Sparrow* (p. 308): clean white "eyebrow"; full black eye line; uniformly gray underparts; white wing bars. *American Tree Sparrow* (p. 307): dark, central breast spot; white wing bars; 2-tone bill. *Song Sparrow* (p. 319): heavily streaked underparts; lacks gray "collar." *Lincoln's Sparrow* (p. 320): fine breast streaking; less contrast between brown and gray crown stripes.

Best Sites: ***MN:*** cattail marshes and wooded swamps; Carlos Avery WMA. ***WI:*** cattail marshes and wooded swamps.

WHITE-THROATED SPARROW

Zonotrichia albicollis

The handsome White-throated Sparrow is easily identified by its bold white throat and striped crown. Two color morphs are common throughout our region: one has black-and-white stripes on the head; the other has brown-and-tan stripes. White-striped males are more aggressive than tan-striped males, and tan-striped females are more nurturing than white-striped females. These two color morphs are perpetuated because each morph almost always breeds with the opposite color morph. • In spring and fall, White-throated Sparrows can appear anywhere in our region in great abundance. Urban backyards dressed with brushy fenceline tangles and a bird feeder brimming with seeds can attract good numbers of these delightful sparrows.

tan-striped morph

white-striped morph

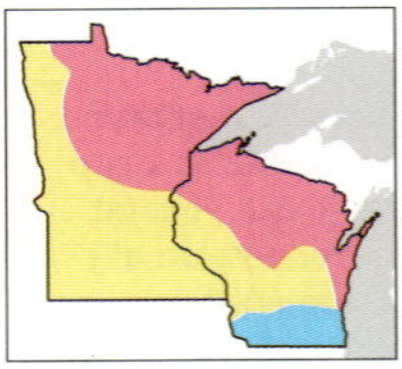

ID: black-and-white (or brown-and-tan) striped head; white throat; gray "cheek"; yellow lores; black eye line; unstreaked, gray underparts; mottled brown upperparts; grayish bill.

Size: *L* 6½–7½ in; *W* 9 in.

Status: ***MN:*** common to at times abundant migrant from mid-April to late May and from mid-August to November; widespread common breeder in north-central and northeastern regions; occasional in winter in the south, mainly in the Twin Cities area and the southeast; rare to accidental in winter farther north. ***WI:*** abundant migrant from mid-April to late May and from late August to early November; common breeder in the north; uncommon breeder in central and eastern regions; uncommon winter visitor.

Habitat: *Breeding:* semi-open coniferous and mixed forests, especially in regenerating clearings and along shrubby forest edges. *In migration:* woodlots, wooded parks and riparian brush.

Nesting: on or near the ground, often concealed by a low shrub or fallen log; female builds an open cup nest of grass, weeds, twigs and conifer needles and lines it with rootlets, fine grass and hair; female incubates 4–5 greenish blue to pale blue eggs, marked with lavender and reddish brown, for 11–14 days.

Feeding: scratches the ground to expose invertebrates, seeds and berries; also gleans insects from vegetation and while in flight; eats seeds from bird feeders in winter.

Voice: variable song is a clear, distinct, whistled *Old Sam Peabody Peabody Peabody;* call is a sharp *chink.*

Similar Species: *White-crowned Sparrow* (p. 324): pinkish bill; gray "collar"; lacks bold white throat and yellow lores. *Swamp Sparrow* (p. 321): smaller; gray and chestnut on crown; streaked underparts; lacks head pattern.

Best Sites: ***MN:*** *Breeding:* coniferous and mixed forests in the northeast. *In migration:* widespread throughout the state. ***WI:*** *Breeding:* open coniferous and mixed forests. *In migration:* widespread throughout the state.

HARRIS'S SPARROW

Zonotrichia querula

An unassuming migrant, the Harris's Sparrow passes through our region in small isolated trickles, frequently mixing with flocks of White-throated Sparrows and White-crowned Sparrows. Occasionally, a few Harris's Sparrows can be seen picking through the seed offerings at backyard feeders. • The Harris's Sparrow breeds in the far north of Canada, where the treeline fades to tundra. Because of the remoteness of its breeding grounds, there is little information about this species' breeding habits, nests and eggs. • John J. Audubon named this sparrow after his friend and amateur naturalist, Edward Harris, with whom he traveled up the Missouri River in 1843.

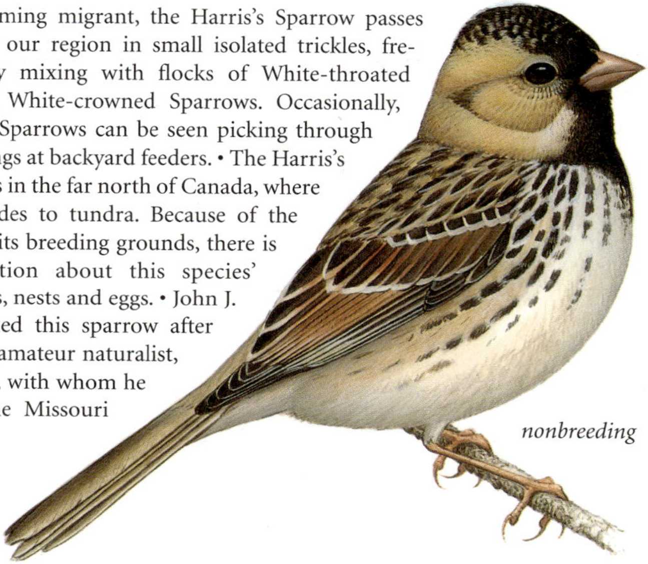

nonbreeding

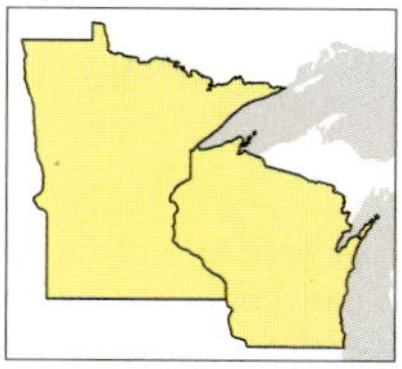

ID: mottled brown-and-black upperparts; white underparts; pink orange bill. *Breeding:* black crown, ear patch, throat and "bib"; gray face; black streaks on sides and flanks; white wing bars. *Nonbreeding:* brown face; brownish sides and flanks; white flecks on black crown.

Size: *L* 7–7½ in; *W* 10½ in.

Status: ***MN:*** common to locally abundant migrant (especially in the fall) from late March to early June and from mid-September to late November, most numerous in the west; occasional in winter in the south, especially in the southwest; casual elsewhere in winter. ***WI:*** uncommon migrant from late April through May and from mid-September to early November, except in the east where it is usually rare; rare winter visitor.

Habitat: brushy roadsides, shrubby vegetation, forest edges and riparian thickets.

Nesting: does not nest in our region.

Feeding: gleans the ground and vegetation for seeds, fresh buds, insects and berries; occasionally takes seeds from bird feeders.

Voice: song is a series of 2–4 long, quavering whistles; each series may be sung at the same or at a different pitch; call is a *jeenk* or *zheenk;* flocks in flight may give a rolling *chug-up chug-up*.

Similar Species: *White-throated Sparrow* (p. 322): grayish bill; yellow lores; black-and-white-striped crown. *White-crowned Sparrow* (p. 324): black-and-white-striped crown; gray "collar"; immature has broad, gray "eyebrow" bordered by brown eye line and crown. *House Sparrow* (p. 356): male is brownish overall; gray crown; broad brown band behind eye; broad, whitish jaw band; dark bill.

Best Sites: ***MN:*** brushy roadsides and woodlot edges and plum thickets; western regions during peak migration periods. *Winter:* at feeders. ***WI:*** *In migration:* in flocks of sparrows feeding at roadsides, shrubby borders and backyard feeders. *Winter:* at feeders.

WHITE-CROWNED SPARROW

Zonotrichia leucophrys

The large, bold, strongly patterned White-crowned Sparrow brightens brushy expanses and suburban parks and gardens with its cheeky song for a few short weeks in spring and fall. Most birders with well-stocked feeders should be especially familiar with this bird—besides being conspicuous in appearance, White-crowned Sparrows are tireless singers, even bursting into song under the light of the moon. • White-crowns breed in the far north, in alpine environments or along the coast of California. This bird has a widespread distribution in North America and populations in different parts of its range vary significantly in behavior and in migratory and nesting habits. • The White-crowned Sparrow is North America's most studied sparrow. Research on this bird has given science tremendous insight into bird physiology, homing behavior and the geographic variability of song dialects.

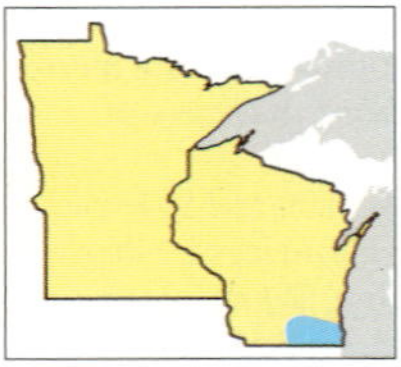

ID: black-and-white-striped head; black eye line; pink orange bill; gray face; unstreaked, gray underparts; pale gray throat; mottled gray brown upperparts; 2 faint white wing bars.

Size: *L* 5½–7 in; *W* 9½ in.

Status: ***MN:*** uncommon to locally common migrant from late April to early June and from early September to late November; occasional in winter mainly in the south. ***WI:*** fairly common migrant from late April to May and from mid-September to early November; rare winter visitor.

Habitat: shrubby, open meadows, bogs, forest edges and clearings, woodlots, brushy tangles and riparian thickets.

Nesting: does not nest in our region.

Feeding: scratches the ground to expose insects and seeds; also eats berries, buds and moss capsules; may take seeds from bird feeders.

Voice: song is a frequently repeated variation of *I gotta go wee-wee now;* call is a high, thin *seet* or sharp *pink.*

Similar Species: *White-throated Sparrow* (p. 322): bold, white throat; grayish bill; yellow lores; browner overall. *Chipping Sparrow* (p. 308): smaller; grayish rump; finer bill. *Golden-crowned Sparrow:* dark bill; golden yellow crown bordered with black.

Best Sites: ***MN:*** *In migration:* along brushy roadsides, in woodlot edges and in plum thickets. *Winter:* singly at feeders. ***WI:*** *In migration:* in flocks of White-throated Sparrows along roadsides, brushy borders and at backyard feeders.

DARK-EYED JUNCO

Junco hyemalis

Each winter, Dark-eyed Juncos congregate in backyards with bird feeders and sheltering conifers, as well as along brushy roadsides. Juncos rarely perch at feeders, preferring to snatch up seeds that are knocked to the ground by other birds. Also known as "Snow Bird," the Dark-eyed Junco is considered a harbinger of winter, even though some are present year-round. • Juncos spend most of their time on the ground, and they are readily flushed from wooded trails and backyard feeders. Their distinctive, white outer tail feathers flash in alarm as they rush for the cover of a nearby tree or shrub. • In 1973, the American Ornithologists' Union grouped five junco species into a single species called the Dark-eyed Junco. Our region is typically home to the subspecies *hyemalis*, the Slate-colored Junco.

"Slate-colored Junco"

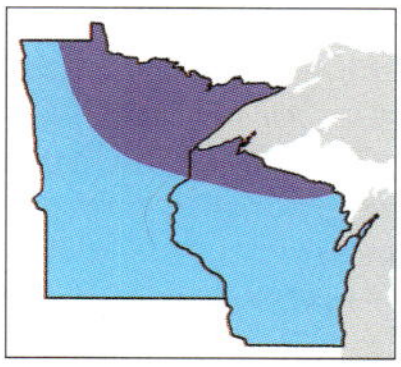

ID: white outer tail feathers; pale bill. *Male:* dark slate gray overall, except for white lower breast, belly and undertail coverts. *Female:* brown rather than gray. *Immature:* brown (like female) streaked with darker brown.

Size: *L* 5½–7 in; *W* 9½ in.

Status: ***MN:*** common to abundant migrant from early March to late May and from late August to early December; uncommon to locally common breeder in northeastern and north-central regions; regular in winter, mainly in southern regions. ***WI:*** abundant migrant from mid-March to early May and from mid-September to mid-November; uncommon breeder in the north; common winter visitor.

Habitat: coniferous and mixed forests, especially in young jack pine stands, burned-over areas and shrubby, regenerating clearings.

Nesting: on the ground, usually concealed by a shrub, tree, root, log or rock; female builds a cup nest of twigs, bark shreds, grass and moss and lines it with fine grass and hair; female incubates 3–5 whitish to bluish white eggs, marked with gray and brown, for 12–13 days.

Feeding: scratches the ground for invertebrates; also eats berries and seeds.

Voice: song is a long, dry trill, very similar to the call of the Chipping Sparrow, but more musical; call is a smacking *chip* note, often given in series.

Similar Species: *Eastern Towhee* (p. 306): larger; female has rufous sides, red eyes and grayish bill. *Sparrows* (pp. 307–24): brownish and streaked; most lack white outer tail feathers.

Best Sites: ***MN:*** *Breeding:* lowland conifers in the northeast. *In migration* and *winter:* backyard feeders and brushy roadsides. ***WI:*** *Breeding:* northern conifer plantations. *In migration* and *winter:* backyard feeders and along roadsides.

LAPLAND LONGSPUR

Calcarius lapponicus

Throughout much of the winter, Lapland Longspurs wheel about in large numbers over the fields of our region. These birds typically appear wherever open fields offer an abundance of seeds or waste grain. Flocks of longspurs can be surprisingly inconspicuous until approached—anyone attempting a closer look at the flock will be awed by the sight of the birds suddenly erupting into the skies, flashing their white outer tail feathers. • In fall, these birds arrive from their breeding grounds looking like mottled, brownish sparrows, and they retain their drab plumage throughout the winter months. When farmers work their fields in spring, Lapland Longspurs have already molted into their bold breeding plumage, which they will wear through the summer.

nonbreeding

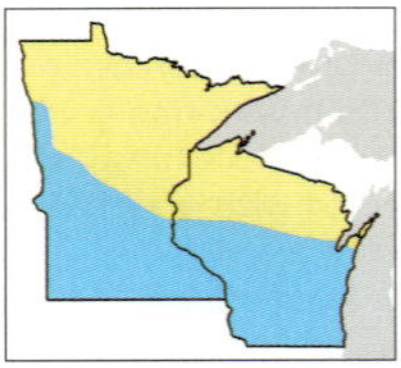

ID: white outer tail feathers; pale yellowish bill. *Breeding male:* black crown, face and "bib"; chestnut nape; broad, white stripe curves from eye to shoulder (may be tinged with buff behind eye). *Breeding female:* mottled brown-and-black upperparts; lightly streaked flanks; narrow, lightly streaked, buff breast band. *Nonbreeding male:* similar to female, but with faint chestnut on nape and diffuse black breast.

Size: *L* 6½ in; *W* 11½ in.

Status: ***MN:*** common to locally abundant migrant from late February to late May and from early September to mid-November; common to uncommon in winter, mainly in the southwest. ***WI:*** common migrant from late September to December and from March to mid-May; uncommon to common winter visitor.

Habitat: pastures, meadows and croplands.

Nesting: does not nest in our region.

Feeding: gleans the ground and snow for seeds and waste grain; eats mainly insects and some seeds in summer.

Voice: flight song is a rapid, slurred warble; musical calls; flight calls include a rattled *tri-di-dit* and a descending *teew*.

Similar Species: *Snow Bunting* (p. 329): black-and-white wing pattern. *Smith's Longspur* (p. 327): buff to buff orange underparts; male has black-and-white face and buff orange nape. *Sparrows* (pp. 307–24): most lack distinctive head pattern and have pale legs.

Best Sites: ***MN:*** North Shore of L. Superior; Rothsay WMA; fields and prairies, often with Snow Buntings, Horned Larks and American Pipits in fall. ***WI:*** along roadsides and adjacent fields, including Arlington ponds, Freedom area and Port Washington area, often with Snow Buntings and Horned Larks.

SMITH'S LONGSPUR

Calcarius pictus

The Smith's Longspur is one of the least-known birds in our region, and few of us could say we've ever seen one! These uncommon and secretive birds may be seen briefly when they retreat south for winter or migrate northward in the spring, but you'll have to look closely through larger flocks of Lapland Longspurs to spot them. • Smith's Longspurs spend their summers far from here, nesting along the coast of Hudson Bay in northern Canada and west into Alaska. These birds have one of the most unusual breeding systems of any songbird. Referred to as polygynandrous, both males and females breed with two or three partners. • This bird's winter range is limited to a few of the south-central states.

breeding

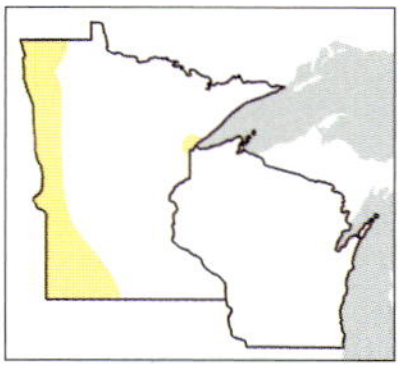

ID: white outer tail feathers; small white shoulder patch (often concealed); mottled brown-and-black upperparts. *Breeding male:* black crown; black-and-white face; buff orange underparts and "collar"; faint streaking on sides and flanks. *Nonbreeding male, female* and *immature:* streaked crown and nape; buff underparts with faint streaking on breast.

Size: *L* 6 in; *W* 11½ in.

Status: ***MN:*** rare migrant; most records are from west-central and southwestern regions and at Duluth. ***WI:*** very casual migrant.

Habitat: prairie and grassland areas, pastures, agricultural fields and airports.

Nesting: does not nest in our region.

Feeding: gleans insects and seeds from the ground and low vegetation.

Voice: song is a warbling *switoo-whidee-deedew, whee-tew;* alarm call is a slow *tick tick tick,* like a watch.

Similar Species: *Lapland Longspur* (p. 326): less white in tail; whitish belly and undertail coverts; often shows black on neck or breast; breeding male has black throat and "bib" and chestnut nape. *Vesper Sparrow* (p. 311): chestnut shoulder patch; white underparts. *American Pipit* (p. 263): thinner bill; streaking on breast; lacks white patch on shoulder.

Best Sites: ***MN:*** Salt L. (Lac Qui Parle Co.); Rothsay WMA; Jeffers Petroglyphs; Duluth. ***WI:*** no consistent sites.

CHESTNUT-COLLARED LONGSPUR

Calcarius ornatus

The Chestnut-collared Longspur is the most colorful of the grassland sparrows—it is gaudily marked in comparison to the dull plumage typical of its neighbors. It is a bird of the prairies, and historically its breeding grounds were located in areas that had been recently grazed by bison or disturbed by fire. These birds prefer uncultivated areas, especially those that have been mowed or grazed. Though seldom seen in our region, your best chance of finding them is on prairie grasslands, pastures and mowed margins or airfields. Chestnut-collared Longspur populations have been adversely affected by the loss of their native short-grass prairie habitat and this bird has disappeared from much of its historical breeding range. • Longspurs are so named because they have an extremely long hind claw.

♂ breeding

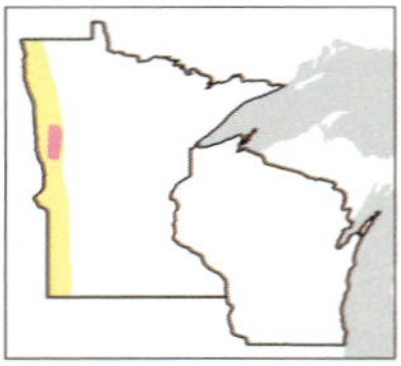

ID: *Breeding male:* chestnut nape; black underparts; yellow throat; black "cap"; white "eyebrow"; mottled brown upperparts; white outer tail feathers; black central and terminal tail feathers; white undertail coverts. *Breeding female:* may show chestnut nape; mottled brown overall; light breast streaks.

Size: *L* 5½–6 in; *W* 10½ in.

Status: ***MN:*** endangered; only 1 breeding area near Felton (Clay Co.); rare to accidental migrant anywhere in the state; may be a casual migrant in far western regions. ***WI:*** accidental migrant.

Habitat: short-grass prairie, grasslands, pastures and mowed areas such as airfields.

Nesting: in a depression or scrape well concealed by grass; female builds a cup nest of woven grass and lines it with finer grasses, feathers and fur; female incubates 3–5 creamy white to pale buff eggs, marked with brown or purple, for 12–13 days.

Feeding: gleans the ground for plant seeds and invertebrates.

Similar Species: breeding male is distinctive. *McCown's Longspur:* female has hint of chestnut on wing. *Vesper Sparrow* (p. 311): chestnut wing patch; more white in face. *Savannah Sparrow* (p. 313): lacks white outer tail feathers.

Best Sites: ***MN:*** Felton Prairie SNA and surrounding grasslands. ***WI:*** no consistent sites.

SNOW BUNTING

Plectrophenax nivalis

In early winter, when flocks of Snow Buntings descend on rural fields, their startling black and white plumage flashes in contrast to the snow-covered backdrop. It may seem strange that Snow Buntings are whiter in summer than in winter, but the darker winter plumage may help these birds absorb heat on clear, cold winter days. • Snow Buntings venture farther north than any other songbird in the world. A single individual, likely misguided and lost, was recorded not far from the North Pole in May 1987. • Snow Buntings are definitely cold-weather songbirds, often bathing in snow in early spring, and burrowing into it during bitter cold snaps to stay warm. In winter, these birds prefer expansive areas, including grain croplands, fields and pastures.

nonbreeding

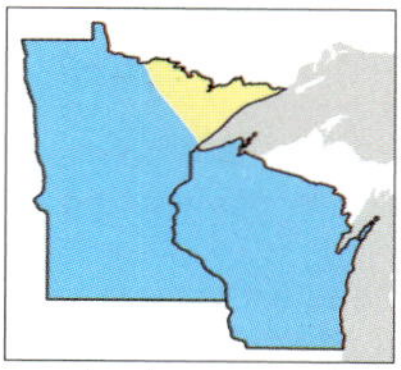

ID: black-and-white wings and tail; white underparts. *Breeding male:* black back; all-white head and rump; black bill. *Breeding female:* streaky, brown-and-whitish crown and back; dark bill. *Nonbreeding male:* yellowish bill; golden brown crown and rump. *Nonbreeding female:* similar to male but with blackish forecrown and dark-streaked golden back.
Size: *L* 6–7½ in; *W* 14 in.
Status: ***MN:*** common to locally abundant migrant and winter visitor from early October to late May, mainly in northern and southwestern regions. ***WI:*** common migrant and winter visitor from late September to late April.
Habitat: fields, feedlots, pastures, grassy meadows, lakeshores and roadsides.
Nesting: does not nest in our region.
Feeding: gleans the ground and snow for seeds and waste grain; also takes insects when available.
Voice: spring song is a high-pitched, musical *chi-chi-churee;* call is a whistled *tew.*
Similar Species: *Lapland Longspur* (p. 326): brownish upperparts; lacks black-and-white wing pattern. *Sparrows* (pp. 307–24): lack white wing and tail patches.
Best Sites: ***MN:*** North Shore of L. Superior (especially in October); Aitkin Co.; Clay Co.; fields and back roads in western regions. ***WI:*** along roadsides and adjacent fields at sites such as Arlington ponds, Freedom area and Port Washington area, often with Lapland Longspurs and Horned Larks.

NORTHERN CARDINAL

Cardinalis cardinalis

The Northern Cardinal is often the first choice for calendars and Christmas cards, and most people can easily recognize this delightful year-round neighbor without the help of a bird identification field guide. These birds prefer the tangled, shrubby edges of woodlands, but they are easily attracted to backyards with feeders and sheltering trees and shrubs. • Northern Cardinals form one of the most faithful pair bonds of the bird world. The male and female remain in close contact year-round, singing to one another through the seasons with soft, bubbly whistles. Females are known to sing while on the nest, and it is believed that she is informing her partner whether or not she and the young need food. Males are highly territorial, and will even challenge their own reflections in windows or hubcaps!

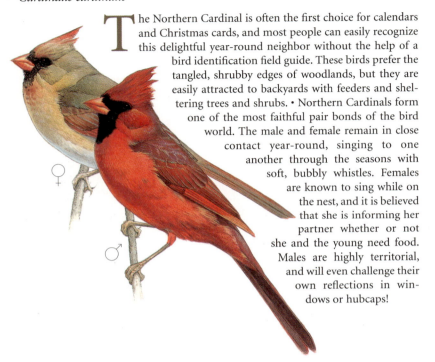

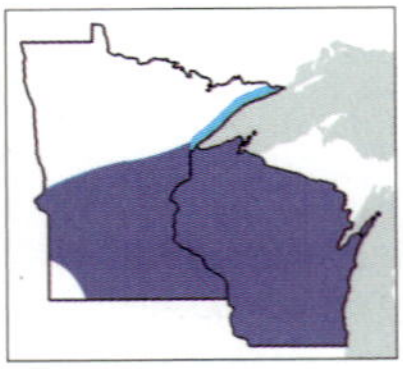

ID: *Male:* red overall; pointed crest; black mask and throat; red, conical bill. *Female:* shaped like male; brown buff to buff olive overall; red bill, crest, wings and tail. *Immature male:* similar to female but with dark bill and crest.

Size: *L* 7½–9 in; *W* 12 in.

Status: ***MN:*** common year-round resident; rare in the far southwest; expanding its range slowly to the northwest and northeast; vagrants occur in winter along the North Shore of L. Superior. ***WI:*** common year-round resident; uncommon in the north.

Habitat: brushy thickets and shrubby tangles along forest and woodland edges, in backyards and in suburban and urban parks.

Nesting: in dense shrubs, thickets, vine tangles or low in a coniferous tree; female builds an open cup nest of twigs, bark shreds, weeds, grass, leaves and rootlets and lines it with hair and fine grass; female incubates 3–4 whitish to bluish or greenish white eggs, marked with gray, brown and purple, for 12–13 days.

Feeding: gleans seeds, insects and berries from low shrubs or while hopping along the ground.

Voice: song is a variable series of clear, bubbly whistled notes: *what cheer! what cheer! birdie-birdie-birdie what cheer!;* call is a metallic *chip.*

Similar Species: *Summer Tanager* (p. 302) and *Scarlet Tanager* (p. 303): lack head crest, black "mask" and throat and red, conical bill; Scarlet Tanager has black wings and tail.

Best Sites: ***MN:*** residential and rural areas, especially near woods. *Winter:* at feeders near woods and brushy areas in southeastern, south-central and east-central regions. ***WI:*** residential and rural areas, especially near woods.

ROSE-BREASTED GROSBEAK

Pheucticus ludovicianus

It's difficult to miss the boisterous, whistled tune of the Rose-breasted Grosbeak. This bird's hurried, robinlike song is easily recognized, and is one of the more common songs heard among our deciduous forests in spring and summer. Although the female lacks the magnificent colors of the male, she shares his talent for beautiful song. • Mating grosbeaks appear pleasantly affectionate toward each other, often touching bills during courtship and after absences. Rose-breasted Grosbeaks usually build their nests low in a tree or tall shrub, but they typically forage high in the canopy where they can be difficult to spot. Luckily for birders, the abundance of berries in fall often draws these birds to ground level.

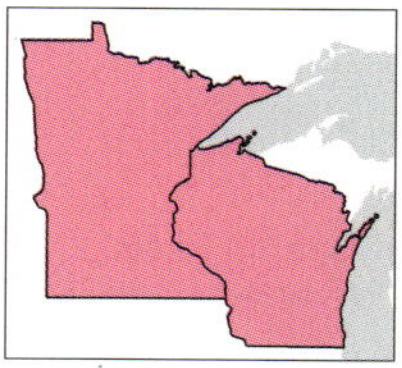

ID: pale, conical bill; dark wings with small, white patches; dark tail. *Male:* black "hood" and back; red breast and inner underwings; white underparts and rump. *Female:* bold, whitish "eyebrow"; thin crown stripe; brown upperparts; buff underparts with dark brown streaking.

Size: *L* 7–8½ in; *W* 12½ in.

Status: ***MN:*** common migrant and breeder from late April to late October; a few linger into December and early January. ***WI:*** common migrant and breeder from May to September.

Habitat: *Breeding:* deciduous and mixed forests with shrubs and second-growth. *In migration:* woodlots, parklands and gardens; may visit feeders in early winter.

Nesting: fairly low in a tree or tall shrub; often near water; mostly the female builds a flimsy cup nest of twigs, bark strips, weeds, grass and leaves and lines it with rootlets and hair; pair incubates 3–5 pale greenish blue eggs, spotted with reddish brown, for 13–14 days.

Feeding: gleans vegetation for insects, seeds, buds, berries and some fruit; occasionally hover-gleans or catches flying insects on the wing; may also visit feeders.

Voice: song is a long, melodious series of whistled notes, much like a fast version of a robin's song; call is a distinctive squeak.

Similar Species: male is distinctive. *Purple Finch* (p. 347): female is much smaller and has heavier streaking on underparts. *Sparrows* (pp. 307–24): smaller; all lack large, conical bill.

Best Sites: ***MN:*** *Breeding:* deciduous woodlands, especially in state, county and city parks. *In migration:* woodlands and brushy areas, especially along streams and rivers. ***WI:*** *Breeding:* deciduous and mixed forests. *In migration:* at feeders with sunflower seeds, often with other songbirds.

BLUE GROSBEAK

Passerina caerulea

Male Blue Grosbeaks owe their spectacular spring plumage not to a fresh molt but, oddly enough, to feather wear. While Blue Grosbeaks are wintering in Mexico and Central America, their brown feather tips slowly wear away, leaving the crystal blue plumage that is seen as they arrive on their breeding grounds. • During the breeding season, Blue Grosbeaks may be spotted in southwestern Minnesota, spreading and flicking their tails and raising their crowns. They are rare migrants elsewhere in the region. • Birders are advised to look carefully for the rusty wing bars that distinguish this bird from the similar-looking, and much more common, Indigo Bunting. Blue Grosbeaks are easy to overlook during country drives—at a distance their striking blue plumage seems black, and many people mistake them for cowbirds.

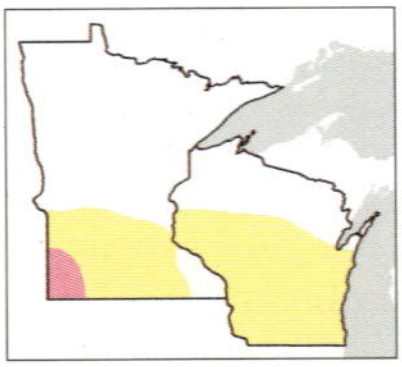

ID: large, pale grayish, conical bill. *Male:* blue overall; 2 rusty wing bars; black around base of bill. *Female:* soft brown plumage overall; whitish throat; rusty wing bars; rump and shoulders faintly washed with blue. *1st-spring male:* similar to female but with blue head.

Size: *L* 6–7½ in; *W* 11 in.

Status: ***MN:*** rare migrant and breeder; known mainly from nesting areas in the extreme southwestern region; accidental elsewhere; may be expanding northward and eastward. ***WI:*** rare migrant in May; casual summer resident.

Habitat: thick brush, riparian thickets, shrubby areas and dense, weedy fields near water.

Nesting: on the ground or in a low bush; female builds cup of grass, leaves, twigs and bark strips and lines it with rootlets, hair and fine grasses; female incubates 3–4 pale blue eggs for 11–13 days.

Feeding: gleans insects while hopping along the ground; occasionally takes seeds; may visit feeders.

Voice: sweet, melodious, warbling song with phrases that rise and fall; call is a loud *chink*.

Similar Species: *Indigo Bunting* (p. 333): smaller body and bill; male lacks wing bars; female has dark brown streaking on breast.

Best Sites: ***MN:*** Blue Mounds SP. ***WI:*** no consistent sites.

INDIGO BUNTING

Passerina cyanea

In the shadow of a towering tree, a male Indigo Bunting can look almost black. If possible, reposition yourself quickly to a place from which you can see the sun strike and enliven this bunting's incomparable indigo plumage. • Raspberry thickets are a favored nesting location for Indigo Buntings. The dense, thorny stems provide the nestlings with protection from many predators, and the berries are a convenient source of food. • The Indigo Bunting employs a clever and comical foraging strategy to reach the grass and weed seeds upon which it feeds. The bird lands midway on a stem and then shuffles slowly toward the seed head, which bends under the bird's weight, giving the bunting easier access to the seeds.

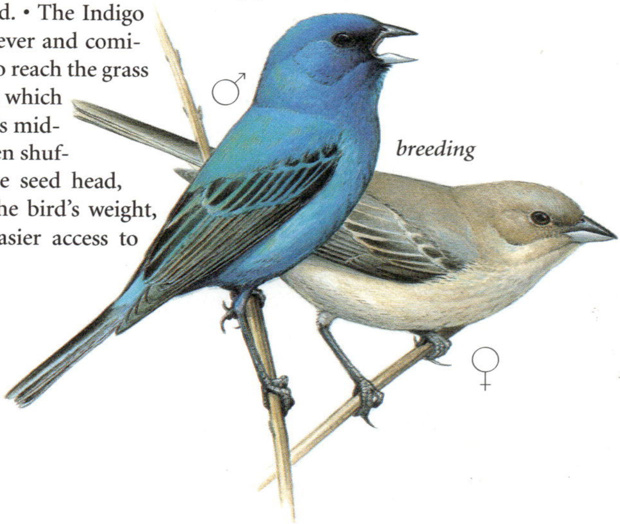

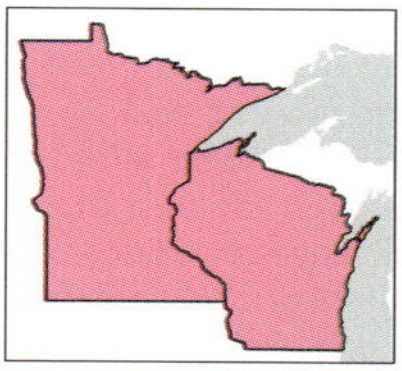

ID: stout, gray, conical bill; beady, black eyes; black legs; no wing bars. *Breeding male:* blue overall; black lores; wings and tail may show some black. *Nonbreeding male:* similar to female, but usually with some blue on wings and tail. *Female:* soft brown overall; brown streaks on breast; whitish throat.

Size: *L* 5½ in; *W* 8 in.

Status: ***MN:*** uncommon to common migrant from May to early June and from late July to mid-October; uncommon to locally common breeder, best represented in eastern and central regions; less common northward, especially in the northeast. ***WI:*** common migrant and breeder from May to mid-October.

Habitat: deciduous forest and woodland edges, regenerating forest clearings, shrubby fields, orchards, abandoned pastures and hedgerows; occasionally along edges of mixed woodlands.

Nesting: usually in an upright fork in a small tree or shrub or within a vine tangle; female builds a cup nest of grass, leaves and bark strips and lines it with rootlets, hair and feathers; female incubates 3–4 white to bluish white eggs for 12–13 days.

Feeding: gleans low vegetation and the ground for insects, especially grasshoppers, beetles, weevils, flies and larvae; also eats berries and the seeds of thistles, dandelions and other native plants.

Voice: song consists of paired warbled whistles: *fire-fire, where-where, here-here, see-it see-it;* call is a quick *spit.*

Similar Species: *Blue Grosbeak* (p. 332): larger overall; larger, more robust bill; 2 rusty wing bars; male has black around base of bill; female lacks streaking on breast. *Mountain Bluebird* (p. 250): larger; slimmer bill; male has pure blue wings and tail.

Best Sites: ***MN:*** brushy woodlands, including Frontenac SP, Sherburne SP, Afton SP, Sibley SP and Itasca SP. ***WI:*** deciduous forests and savanna.

DICKCISSEL

Spiza americana

Dickcissels are an irruptive species and may be common one year and almost totally absent the next. Arriving in suitable nesting habitat before the smaller females, breeding males bravely announce their presence with stuttering, trilled renditions of their own name. Dickcissels are polygynous, and males may mate with up to eight females in a single breeding season. This breeding strategy means that males give no assistance to the females in nesting or brooding. • This "miniature meadowlark" has a special fondness for fields of alfalfa. Though Dickcissels eat mostly insects on their breeding grounds, seeds and grain form the main part of their diet on their South American wintering grounds, making them unpopular with local farmers. Each year large numbers of these birds are killed by pesticides in efforts to reduce crop losses, which may partially explain the Dickcissel's pattern of absence and abundance.

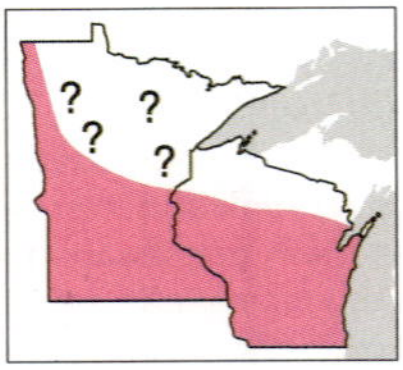

ID: yellow "eyebrow"; gray head, nape and sides of yellow breast; brown upperparts; pale grayish underparts; rufous shoulder patch; dark, conical bill. *Male:* white "chin"; triangular black "bib"; duller colors in nonbreeding plumage. *Female:* duller version of male; white throat.

Size: *L* 6–7 in; *W* 9½ in.

Status: ***MN:*** irruptive; abundant to rare migrant and breeder from mid-May to September; in years of abundance some may reach the Canadian border in northwestern and north-central regions.
WI: special concern; irruptive; uncommon to common migrant and breeder from mid-May to August.

Habitat: abandoned fields, weedy meadows, croplands, grasslands and grassy roadsides.

Nesting: on or near the ground; well concealed among tall, dense vegetation; female builds a bulky, open cup nest of grass, weed stems and leaves and lines it with rootlets, fine grass or hair; female incubates 4 pale blue eggs for 11–13 days.

Feeding: gleans insects and seeds from the ground and low vegetation.

Voice: song consists of 2–3 single notes followed by a trill, often paraphrased as *dick dick dick-cissel;* flight call is a buzzer-like *bzrrrrt*.

Similar Species: *Eastern Meadowlark* (p. 337): much larger; long, pointed bill; yellow "chin" and throat with black "necklace." *American Goldfinch* (p. 354): lacks black "bib"; white or buff yellow bars on dark wings; may show black forecrown.

Best Sites: ***MN:*** alfalfa fields and grasslands in the southern part of the state. ***WI:*** open grasslands and croplands in southern, central and western regions.

BOBOLINK

Dolichonyx oryzivorus

During the nesting season, male and female Bobolinks rarely interact with one another. For the most part, males perform aerial displays and sing their bubbly, tinkling songs from exposed grassy perches while the females carry out the nesting duties. Once the young have hatched, males become scarce, spending much of their time on the ground hunting for insects. Bobolinks once benefited from increased agriculture, but modern practices, such as harvesting hay early in the season, continue to thwart the reproductive efforts of this bird. • At first glimpse, the female Bobolink resembles a sparrow, but the male, with his dark belly and buff-and-black upperparts, is colored like no other bird in our region.

breeding

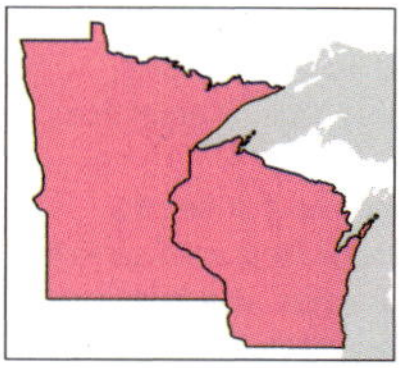

ID: *Breeding male:* black overall; buff nape; white rump and wing patch. *Breeding female:* brown buff overall; yellowish bill; streaked upperparts; pale "eyebrow"; dark eye line; light central crown stripe bordered by dark stripes. *Nonbreeding male:* similar to breeding female, but darker above and rich golden buff below.

Size: *L* 6–8 in; *W* 11½ in.

Status: ***MN:*** common migrant and breeder from late April to early October. ***WI:*** special concern; common migrant and breeder from late April to late October.

Habitat: tall, grassy meadows and ditches, hayfields and some croplands.

Nesting: on the ground, usually in a hay field; well concealed in a shallow depression; female builds a cup nest of grass and weed stems and lines it with fine grass; female incubates 5–6 grayish to light reddish brown eggs, heavily blotched with lavender and brown, for 11–13 days.

Feeding: gleans the ground and low vegetation for adult and larval invertebrates; also eats many seeds.

Voice: song is a series of banjolike twangs: *bobolink bobolink spink spank spink,* often given in flight; also issues a *pink* call in flight.

Similar Species: male is distinctive. *Savannah Sparrow* (p. 313): dark breast streaking; yellow lores. *Vesper Sparrow* (p. 311): breast streaking; white outer tail feathers. *Grasshopper Sparrow* (p. 314): white belly; unstreaked sides and flanks.

Best Sites: ***MN:*** grasslands, prairie areas and sedge meadows, including Afton SP, Felton Prairie SNA, Hamden Slough NWR, Rice Lake SP and Split Rock Creek SP. ***WI:*** open grasslands, sedge meadows and old fields including Rat River WA, Jersey Flats (Kettle Moraine State Forest–North Unit), Crex Meadows WA and Buena Vista Grasslands.

RED-WINGED BLACKBIRD

Agelaius phoeniceus

The sound of the season's first Red-winged Blackbird may be the remedy for a birder's winter blahs. The males get an early start on the season, arriving in our marshes and wetlands a week or so before the females, often in early to mid-March. In the females' absence, the males stake out territories through song and visual displays. The male's bright red shoulders and short, raspy song are his most important tools in the often intricate strategy he employs to defend his territory from rivals. A flashy and richly voiced male who has managed to establish a large and productive territory can attract several mates to his cattail kingdom. • After the male has wooed her, the female starts the busy work of weaving a nest amid the cattails. Cryptic coloration allows her to sit inconspicuously upon her nest, blending in perfectly with the surroundings.

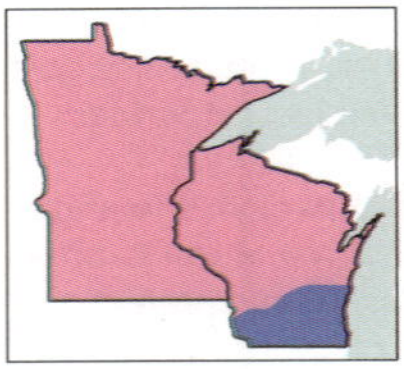

ID: *Male:* all black, except for large, red shoulder patch edged in yellow (occasionally concealed). *Female:* heavily streaked underparts; mottled brown upperparts; faint red shoulder patch; light "eyebrow."

Size: *L* 7–9½ in; *W* 13 in.

Status: ***MN:*** abundant but decreasing migrant and breeder from late February to mid-December; very local and uncommon in winter in southern areas.
WI: abundant migrant and breeder from early March to November; uncommon winter visitor.

Habitat: cattail marshes, wet meadows and ditches, croplands and shoreline shrubs.

Nesting: colonial; in cattails or shoreline bushes; female weaves an open cup nest of dried cattail leaves and grass and lines it with fine grass; female incubates 3–4 darkly marked, pale blue green eggs for 10–12 days.

Feeding: gleans the ground for seeds, waste grain and invertebrates; also gleans vegetation for seeds, insects and berries; occasionally catches insects in flight; may visit feeders.

Voice: song is a loud, raspy *konk-a-ree* or *ogle-reeeee;* calls include a harsh *check* and a high *tseert;* female may give a loud *che-che-che chee chee chee.*

Similar Species: male is distinctive when shoulder patch shows. *Brewer's Blackbird* (p. 341) and *Rusty Blackbird* (p. 340): females lack streaked underparts. *Brown-headed Cowbird* (p. 343): immature is smaller and has stubbier, conical bill.

Best Sites: ***MN:*** widespread in marshlands and agricultural areas with fields and brushy meadows. ***WI:*** *Breeding* and *in migration:* widespread in marshes, swamps and open croplands.

EASTERN MEADOWLARK

Sturnella magna

The Eastern Meadowlark's trademark tune is the voice of rural areas, and it rings throughout spring from fence posts and powerlines, wherever grassy meadows and pastures are found. • The male's bright yellow underparts, black V-shaped "necklace," and white outer tail feathers help attract mates. Females share these colorful attributes for a slightly different purpose: when a predator approaches too close to a nest, the incubating female explodes from the grass in a burst of flashing color. Most predators cannot resist chasing the moving target, and once the female has led the predator away from the nest, she simply folds away her white tail flags, exposes her camouflaged back and disappears into the grass without a trace. • The Eastern Meadowlark is not actually a lark, but a member of the blackbird family.

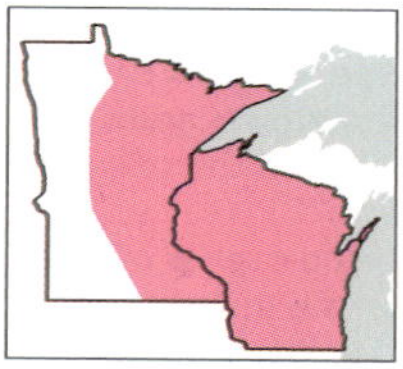

ID: yellow underparts; broad, black breast band; mottled brown upperparts; short, wide tail with white outer tail feathers; long, pinkish legs; yellow lores; long, sharp bill; blackish crown stripes and eye line border pale "eyebrow" and median crown stripe; dark streaking on white sides and flanks.

Size: *L* 9–9½ in; *W* 14 in.

Status: ***MN:*** common migrant and breeder mid-March to late November; uncommon to rare in Lake Co. and Cook Co.; uncommon to rare in central regions; accidental in the west; occasional in winter in the southeast. ***WI:*** special concern; common migrant and breeder from early March to early November; uncommon winter visitor in southern and central regions.

Habitat: grassy meadows and pastures; also in some croplands, weedy fields, grassy roadsides and old orchards.

Nesting: in a depression or scrape on the ground; concealed by dense grass; female builds a domed grass nest, with a side entrance, which is woven into the surrounding vegetation; female incubates 3–7 white eggs, heavily spotted with brown and purple, for about 13–15 days.

Feeding: gleans grasshoppers, crickets, beetles and spiders from the ground and vegetation; extracts grubs and worms by probing its bill into the soil; also eats seeds.

Voice: song is a rich series of 2–8 melodic, clear, slurred whistles: *see-you at school-today* or *this is the year;* gives a rattling flight call and a high, buzzy *dzeart.*

Similar Species: *Western Meadowlark* (p. 338): paler upperparts, especially crown stripes and eye line; yellow on throat extends onto lower "cheek"; different song and call. *Dickcissel* (p. 334): much smaller; solid dark crown; white throat; conical bill; lacks brown streaking on sides and flanks.

Best Sites: ***MN:*** grasslands including Afton SP, Frontenac SP and Sherburne NWR. ***WI:*** open grasslands and croplands.

WESTERN MEADOWLARK

Sturnella neglecta

The brightly colored Western Meadowlark is one of the most abundant and widely distributed birds in the U.S. It is also one of the most popular—the Western Meadowlark is the state bird in six states. • The two meadowlark species are very similar in appearance, so birders must listen for their songs to distinguish one from the other. The song of the Western Meadowlark is more constant, while the Eastern Meadowlark varies its song during bouts of singing. • Meadowlarks' grassy, domed nests are extremely difficult to locate, and are so well concealed that they are often accidentally crushed before they are seen. • Eastern Meadowlarks and Western Meadowlarks may occasionally interbreed where their ranges overlap, but produce infertile offspring.

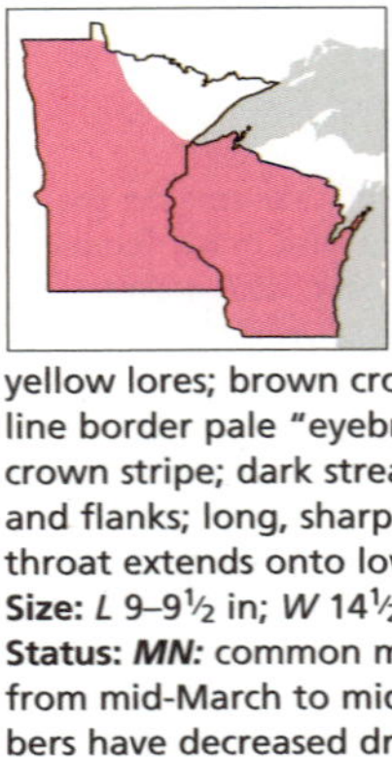

ID: yellow underparts; broad, black breast band; mottled brown upperparts; short, wide tail with white outer tail feathers; long, pinkish legs; yellow lores; brown crown stripes and eye line border pale "eyebrow" and median crown stripe; dark streaking on white sides and flanks; long, sharp bill; yellow on throat extends onto lower "cheek."

Size: *L* 9–9½ in; *W* 14½ in.

Status: ***MN:*** common migrant and breeder from mid-March to mid-November; numbers have decreased dramatically in eastern and central regions; occasional in winter in the southern half of the state. ***WI:*** special concern; common to uncommon migrant and breeder from early March to early November; numbers are decreasing, especially in the eastern half of the state.

Habitat: grassy meadows and pastures; also in some croplands, weedy fields and grassy roadsides.

Nesting: in a depression or scrape on the ground; concealed by dense grass or rarely low shrubs; female builds a domed grass nest, with a side entrance, which is woven into the surrounding vegetation; female incubates 3–7 white eggs, heavily spotted with brown and purple, for 13–15 days.

Feeding: gleans grasshoppers, crickets, beetles, other insects and spiders from the ground and vegetation; extracts grubs and worms by probing its bill into the soil; also eats seeds.

Voice: song is a rich, melodic series of bubbly, flutelike notes; calls include a low, loud *chuck* or *chup,* a rattling flight call and a few clear, whistled notes.

Similar Species: *Eastern Meadowlark* (p. 337): darker upperparts, especially crown stripes and eye line; yellow on throat does not extend onto lower "cheek"; different song and call. *Dickcissel* (p. 334): much smaller; solid dark crown; white throat; lacks brown streaking on sides and flanks.

Best Sites: ***MN:*** grasslands and agricultural areas with brushy and weedy ditches including Split Rock SP, Felton Prairie SNA, Hamden Slough NWR, Rothsay WMA and the Minnesota R. valley. ***WI:*** Buena Vista Grasslands; western counties with an abundance of open grassland and cropland.

YELLOW-HEADED BLACKBIRD

Xanthocephalus xanthocephalus

You might expect a bird as handsome as the Yellow-headed Blackbird to have a song as splendid as its gold-and-black plumage. Unfortunately, a trip to a favored wetland will quickly reveal the surprising truth: when the male arches his golden head backward, his struggles to sing produce only a painful, pathetic, grinding noise. • A large cattail marsh is often highlighted by the presence of male Yellow-headed Blackbirds perched high atop the plants like candle flames. Where Yellow-headed Blackbirds occur together with Red-winged Blackbirds, the larger Yellow-heads dominate, commandeering the center of the wetland and pushing the red-winged competitors to the periphery. Yellow-heads often nest in small colonies of about 30 pairs.

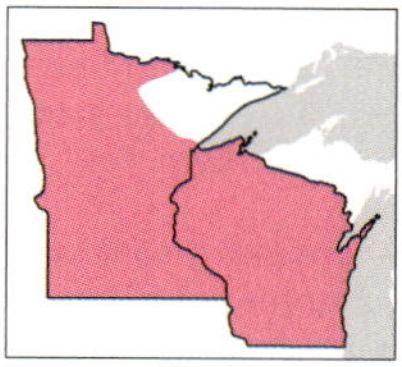

ID: *Male:* yellow head and breast; black body; white wing patches; black lores; long tail; black bill. *Female:* dusky brown overall; yellow breast, throat and "eyebrow"; hints of yellow in face.

Size: *L* 8–11 in; *W* 15 in.

Status: ***MN:*** common migrant and breeder from early April to mid-May and from mid-August to mid-November, mainly in the west; rare in heavily wooded areas of northeastern and north-central regions. ***WI:*** fairly common migrant and breeder from mid-April to mid-October; rare winter visitor in southern and eastern regions.

Habitat: deep, permanent marshes, sloughs, lakeshores and river impoundments where cattails dominate.

Nesting: loosely colonial; female builds a bulky, deep basket of emergent aquatic plants and lines it with dry grass and other vegetation; nest is woven into emergent vegetation over water; female incubates 4 pale green to pale gray eggs, marked with gray or brown, for 11–13 days.

Feeding: gleans the ground for seeds, beetles, snails, waterbugs and dragonflies; also probes into cattail heads for larval invertebrates.

Voice: song is a strained, metallic grating note followed by a descending buzz; call is a deep *krrt* or *ktuk;* low quacks and liquidy clucks may be given during breeding season.

Similar Species: male is distinctive. *Rusty Blackbird* (p. 340) and *Brewer's Blackbird* (p. 341): female lacks yellow throat and face.

Best Sites: ***MN:*** cattail marshes, especially in western areas; Black Rush L. (Lyon Co.); Agassiz NWR; Big Stone NWR; Southwick Marsh WMA (Murray Co.); Tamarac NWR; Swan L. (Nicollet Co.); breeding colonies number in the hundreds of pairs. ***WI:*** cattail marshes with adequate water levels, such as Horicon Marsh, Sensiba WA, Shiocton area, Crex Meadows WA, Trempealeau NWR and Grassy Lake WA.

RUSTY BLACKBIRD

Euphagus carolinus

The Rusty Blackbird owes its name to the rusty color of its fall plumage, but its name could just as well reflect its grating, squeaky song, which sounds very much like a rusty hinge. • The Rusty Blackbird nests in isolated pairs or very small, loose colonies in flooded woodlands and treed, boreal bogs, not in wetlands. • Rusty Blackbirds generally do not travel with grackles and other blackbirds in migration, but instead prefer to keep to themselves. These birds' days are spent foraging along the wooded edges of fields and wetlands, and they will occasionally pick through the manure-laden ground of cattle feedlots. • Rusty Blackbirds are generally less abundant and less aggressive than their relatives, and they usually avoid human-altered environments. Solitary Sandpipers often nest in abandoned Rusty Blackbird nests.

breeding

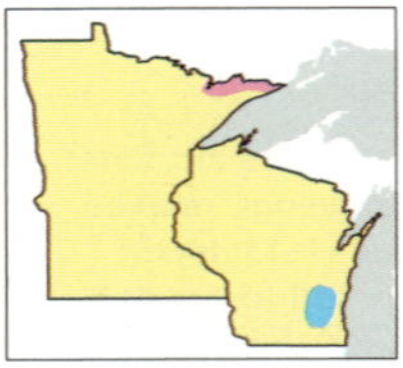

ID: yellow eyes; dark legs; long, sharp bill. *Breeding male:* dark plumage; subtle green gloss on body; subtle bluish or greenish gloss on head. *Breeding female:* paler than male; without gloss. *Nonbreeding male:* rusty wings, back and crown. *Nonbreeding female:* paler than male; buffy underparts; rusty "cheek."

Size: *L* 9 in; *W* 14 in.

Status: ***MN:*** common to at times abundant (especially in fall) migrant from early March to early May and from early September to early December; rare breeder; occasional in winter in the southern half of the state. ***WI:*** common migrant from mid-March through April and from mid-September to early November; very casual breeder; rare winter visitor.

Habitat: *Breeding:* treed bogs, fens, beaver ponds, wet meadows and the shrubby shorelines of lakes, rivers and swamps. *In migration* and *winter:* marshes, open fields, feedlots and woodland edges near water; occasional at feeders in winter.

Nesting: low in a shrub or small conifer; often over or very near water; female builds a bulky nest of twigs, grass and lichens with an inner cup of mud and decaying vegetation and lines it with fine grass; female incubates 4–5 pale blue green eggs, spotted with gray and brown, for about 14 days.

Feeding: walks along shorelines gleaning waterbugs, beetles, dragonflies, snails, grasshoppers and occasionally small fish; also eats waste grain and seeds.

Voice: song is a squeaky, creaking *kush-leeeh ksh-lay;* call is a harsh *chack.*

Similar Species: *Brewer's Blackbird* (p. 341): male has glossier, iridescent plumage, greener body and shows more purple on head; female has dark eyes; nonbreeding birds lack conspicuous rusty highlights. *Common Grackle* (p. 342): longer, keeled tail; larger body and bill; more iridescent. *European Starling* (p. 262): speckled appearance; dark eyes; bill is yellow in summer.

Best Sites: ***MN:*** *In migration:* widespread at peak migration periods, especially near wooded lakes, ponds and mudflats. ***WI:*** *In migration:* wooded swamps and open grasslands.

BREWER'S BLACKBIRD

Euphagus cyanocephalus

The Brewer's Blackbird is the drier-land counterpart to the marsh-loving Rusty Blackbird. This striking bird, with its dark, glossy plumage and piercing yellow eyes, had not been recorded as a breeding species east of western Minnesota before 1914, but since then it has expanded its range rapidly eastward. The Brewer's Blackbird almost always nests in colonies, which often include up to 14 pairs. As fall approaches, the colonies join with other family groups to form large, migrating flocks. • The feathers of this bird show an iridescent quality as reflected rainbows of sunlight move along the feather shafts. As it walks, the Brewer's Blackbird jerks its head back and forth like a chicken, enhancing the glossy effect and distinguishing it from other blackbirds.

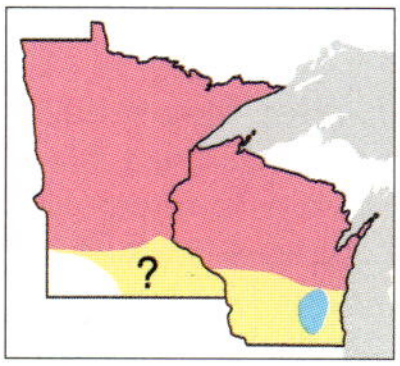

ID: *Male:* iridescent, blue green body and purplish head often look black; yellow eyes; nonbreeding males may show faint rusty feather edgings. *Female:* flat brown plumage; dark eyes.

Size: *L* 8–10 in; *W* 15½ in.

Status: ***MN:*** common migrant and local breeder from mid-March to late November; rare or absent over most of the south. ***WI:*** fairly common migrant and breeder from late March to early October; rare winter visitor.

Habitat: moist, grassy meadows and roadsides with nearby wetlands and patches of trees and shrubs.

Nesting: in small colonies; on the ground or in a shrub or small tree; female builds a bulky, open cup nest of twigs, grass and plant fibers and lines it with rootlets, fine grass and hair; female incubates 4–6 brown-spotted, pale gray to greenish gray eggs for 12–14 days.

Feeding: gleans invertebrates and seeds while walking along shorelines and open areas.

Voice: song is a creaking, 2-note *k-shee;* call is a metallic *chick* or *check*.

Similar Species: *Rusty Blackbird* (p. 340): longer, more slender bill; iridescent plumage has subtler green gloss on body and subtle bluish or greenish gloss on head; female has yellow eyes. *Common Grackle* (p. 342): much longer, keeled tail; larger body and bill. *Brown-headed Cowbird* (p. 343): shorter tail; stubbier, thicker bill; male has dark eyes and brown head; female has paler streaked underparts and very pale throat. *European Starling* (p. 262): speckled appearance; dark eyes; bill is yellow in summer.

Best Sites: ***MN:*** *Breeding:* sedge meadows in association with agricultural lands in central and northwestern regions. *In migration:* large flocks may be encountered in central or northern localities at peak migration periods. ***WI:*** *Breeding* and *in migration:* Crex Meadows WA; Rat River area; Shiocton area; Buena Vista Grasslands. *Winter:* Horicon Marsh.

COMMON GRACKLE

Quiscalus quiscula

The Common Grackle is a poor but spirited singer. Usually while perched in a shrub, a male grackle will slowly take a deep breath to inflate his breast, causing his feathers to spike outward, then close his eyes and give out a loud, strained *tssh-schleek*. Despite his lack of musical talent, the male remains smug and proud, posing with his bill held high. • In fall and sometimes over winter, large and often noisy flocks of Common Grackles gather in rural areas, where they forage for waste grain in open fields. Smaller bands occasionally venture into urban neighborhoods, where they assert their dominance at backyard bird feeders—even bullying Blue Jays will yield feeding rights to these aggressive birds. • The Common Grackle is easily distinguished from Rusty Blackbirds and Brewer's Blackbirds by its long, heavy bill and its lengthy, wedge-shaped tail.

bronze morph

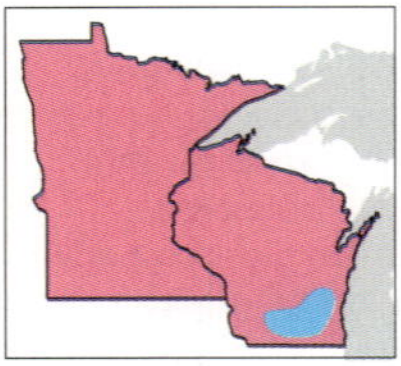

ID: often black-looking, iridescent plumage (purple blue head and breast, bronze back and sides and purple wings and tail); long, keeled tail; yellow eyes; long, heavy bill; female is smaller, duller and browner than male.

Size: *L* 11–13½ in; *W* 17 in.

Status: ***MN:*** abundant migrant and breeder from early March to late November; uncommon and local in heavily wooded areas of north-central and northeastern regions; occasional in winter in the south. ***WI:*** abundant migrant and breeder from early March to early November; uncommon to rare winter visitor.

Habitat: wetlands, fields, wet meadows, riparian woodlands and the edges of coniferous forests and woodlands; also shrubby urban parks and gardens.

Nesting: singly or in small colonies; in dense tree or shrub branches or emergent vegetation; often near water; female builds a bulky open cup nest of twigs, grass, plant fibers and mud and lines it with fine grass or feathers; female incubates 4–5 brown-blotched, pale blue eggs for 12–14 days.

Feeding: slowly struts along the ground, gleaning, snatching and probing for insects, earthworms, seeds, waste grain and fruit; also catches insects in flight and eats small vertebrates; may take some bird eggs.

Voice: song is a series of harsh, strained notes ending with a metallic squeak: *tssh-schleek* or *gri-de-leeek;* call is a quick, loud *swaaaack* or *chaack*.

Similar Species: *Rusty Blackbird* (p. 340) and *Brewer's Blackbird* (p. 341): smaller overall; lack heavy bill and keeled tail. *Red-winged Blackbird* (p. 336): shorter tail; male has red shoulder patch and dark eyes. *European Starling* (p. 262): very short tail; long, thin bill (yellow in summer); speckled appearance; dark eyes.

Best Sites: widespread throughout both states in residential and rural areas.

BROWN-HEADED COWBIRD

Molothrus ater

Historically, Brown-headed Cowbirds followed bison herds across the Great Plains west of Minnesota—they now follow cattle—and their nomadic lifestyle made it impossible for them to construct and tend a nest. Instead, cowbirds engage in "nest parasitism," laying their eggs in the nests of other songbirds. Many of the parasitized songbirds do not recognize that the eggs are not theirs, so they incubate them and raise the cowbirds as their own. Cowbird chicks typically hatch first and develop much more quickly than their nestmates, which are pushed out of the nest or outcompeted for food. • The expansion of ranching, the fragmentation of forests and the development of an extensive network of transportation corridors has significantly increased the Brown-headed Cowbird's range. It now parasitizes more than 140 bird species in North America, including species that probably had no contact with it prior to widespread human settlement.

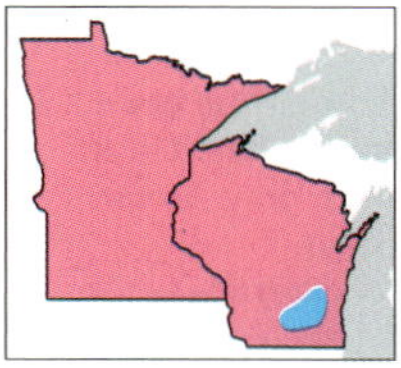

ID: thick, conical bill; short, squared tail; dark eyes. *Male:* iridescent, green blue body plumage (usually looks glossy black); dark brown head. *Female:* brown plumage; faint streaking on light brown underparts; pale throat.

Size: *L* 6–8 in; *W* 12 in.

Status: ***MN:*** common to abundant migrant from early March to early May; uncommon migrant from late July to November; common to abundant breeder; occasional in winter in southern regions. ***WI:*** common migrant and breeder from mid-March to October; uncommon winter visitor.

Habitat: open agricultural and residential areas including fields, woodland edges, utility cutlines, roadsides, fencelines, landfills, campgrounds, picnic areas and areas near cattle.

Nesting: does not build a nest; each female may lay up to 40 eggs a year in the nests of other birds, usually laying 1 egg per nest (larger numbers, up to 8 eggs in a single nest, are probably from several different cowbirds); whitish eggs, marked with gray and brown, hatch after 10–13 days.

Feeding: gleans the ground for seeds, waste grain and invertebrates, especially grasshoppers, beetles and true bugs.

Voice: song is a high, liquidy gurgle: *glug-ahl-whee* or *bubbloozeee;* call is a squeaky, high-pitched *seep, psee* or *wee-tse-tse,* often given in flight; also a fast, chipping *ch-ch-ch-ch-ch-ch.*

Similar Species: *Rusty Blackbird* (p. 340) and *Brewer's Blackbird* (p. 341): longer, slimmer bill; longer tail; lack contrasting brown head and darker body; yellow eyes (except for female Brewer's Blackbird). *Common Grackle* (p. 342): much larger overall; longer, heavier bill; longer, keeled tail.

Best Sites: ***MN:*** widespread, especially in southern and western agricultural areas. ***WI:*** *Breeding* and *in migration:* widespread in residential and rural areas.

ORCHARD ORIOLE

Icterus spurius

Orchards may once have been a favored haunt of this oriole, but since orchards are now heavily sprayed and manicured, it is unlikely that you will ever see this bird in such a locale. Instead, the Orchard Oriole is most commonly found in large shade trees that line roads, paths and streams. • Male Orchard Orioles do not get their adult plumage until their second year, and females and immature males look very similar except that the yearling males have a black "bib." • These orioles are frequent victims of nest parasitism by Brown-headed Cowbirds. In some parts of its breeding range, over half of Orchard Oriole nests are parasitized by cowbirds. • Smaller than all other North American orioles, the Orchard Oriole is one of only two oriole species commonly found in the eastern United States.

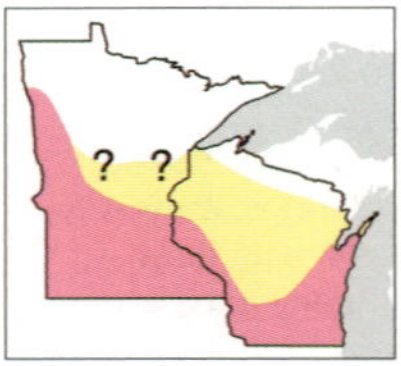

ID: *Male:* black "hood" and tail; chestnut underparts, shoulder and rump; dark wings with white wing bar and feather edgings. *Female* and *immature:* olive upperparts; yellow to olive yellow underparts; faint white wing bars on dusky gray wings.

Size: *L* 6–7 in; *W* 9½ in.

Status: ***MN:*** uncommon migrant and breeder from May through July; seldom seen after the end of July or early August. ***WI:*** special concern; uncommon spring migrant from May to early June; uncommon breeder.

Habitat: open woodlands, suburban parklands, forest edges, hedgerows and groves of shade trees.

Nesting: in the fork of a deciduous tree or shrub; female builds a hanging pouch nest woven from grass and other fine plant fibers; female incubates 4–5 pale bluish white eggs, blotched with gray, brown and purple, for 12–15 days.

Feeding: finds insects and berries while inspecting trees and shrubs; probes flowers for nectar.

Voice: song is a loud, rapid, varied series of whistled notes; call is a quick *chuck*.

Similar Species: *Baltimore Oriole* (p. 345): male has brighter orange plumage with orange on tail; female has orange overtones. *Summer Tanager* (p. 302) and *Scarlet Tanager* (p. 303): females have thicker, pale bills and lack wing bars.

Best Sites: ***MN:*** farmsteads and rural woodlots in southern and western regions; Split Rock Creek SP; Afton SP; Big Stone NWR. ***WI:*** open deciduous forests, farmsteads and savanna along western, eastern and southern sides of the state.

BALTIMORE ORIOLE

Icterus galbula

The male Baltimore Oriole has striking, Halloween-style, black-and-orange plumage that flickers like smoldering embers among our neighborhood treetops. As if his brilliant plumage wasn't enough to secure our admiration, he also sings a rich, flutelike courtship song and will vocalize almost continuously until he finds a mate. • Baltimore Orioles are common in our region. Developing an ear for their whistled *peter peter peter here peter* tune and frequently scanning local deciduous trees will undoubtedly produce enchanting views of this beloved oriole. • This oriole doesn't suffer as much as the Orchard Oriole from nest parasitism by Brown-headed Cowbirds. Female Baltimore Orioles will eject cowbird eggs from the nest and both male and female orioles will react aggressively toward any adult cowbird that approaches their nest. • "Oriole" is derived from Latin and means "golden."

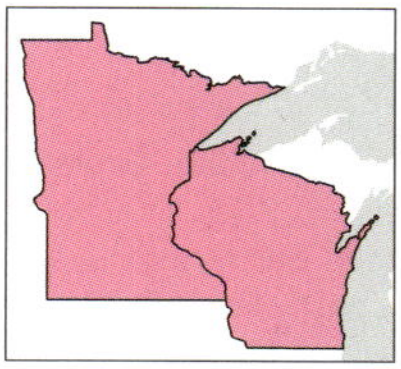

ID: *Male:* black "hood," back, wings and central tail feathers; bright orange underparts, shoulder, rump and outer tail feathers; white wing patch and feather edgings. *Female:* olive brown upperparts (darkest on head); dull yellow orange underparts and rump; white wing bar.
Size: *L* 7–8 in; *W* 11½ in.
Status: ***MN:*** common migrant and breeder from May to early September; uncommon to rare migrant and breeder in the northeast. ***WI:*** common migrant and breeder from May to mid-September.
Habitat: deciduous and mixed forests, particularly riparian woodlands, natural openings, roadsides, orchards, gardens and parklands.
Nesting: high in a deciduous tree, suspended from a branch; female builds a hanging pouch nest of grass, bark shreds, rootlets, plant stems and grapevines and lines it with fine grass, rootlets and fur; may occasionally add string and fishing line; female incubates 4–5 darkly marked, pale gray to bluish white eggs for 12–14 days.
Feeding: gleans canopy vegetation and shrubs for caterpillars, beetles, wasps and other invertebrates; also eats some fruit and nectar; may visit hummingbird feeders and feeding stations that offer orange halves.
Voice: song consists of slow, loud, clear whistles: *peter peter peter here peter;* calls include a 2-note *tea-too* and a rapid chatter: *ch-ch-ch-ch-ch*.
Similar Species: *Orchard Oriole* (p. 344): male has darker chestnut plumage; female is olive yellow and lacks orange overtones. *Summer Tanager* (p. 302) and *Scarlet Tanager* (p. 303): female has thicker, pale bill and lacks wing bars.
Best Sites: ***MN:*** wooded areas, especially where large elms and cottonwoods occur along streams; farmsteads; state, county and city parks. ***WI:*** deciduous forests, farmsteads and residential areas.

PINE GROSBEAK

Pinicola enucleator

The Pine Grosbeak is a large finch that inhabits subarctic and boreal forests across North America. Every so often flocks of these birds find their way south to our region in winter. These erratic winter invasions thrill local naturalists—the Pine Grosbeak's bright colors and exciting flock behavior are certainly a welcome sight. These invasions are not completely understood, but it is thought that cone crop failures or changes to forest ecology caused by logging, forest fires or climatic factors may force these hungry finches southward in search of food. Much of their survival depends on the availability of conifer seeds, so Pine Grosbeaks are always in search of a good crop. • During nesting, adult Pine Grosbeaks develop "gular pouches," throat pouches that allow them to carry food to nestlings.

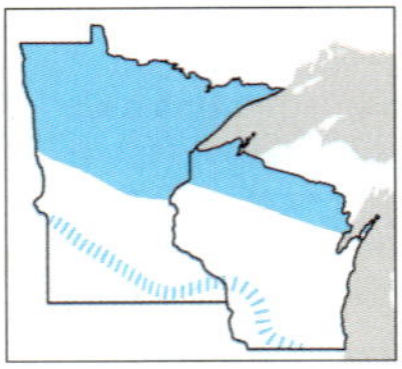

ID: stout, dark, conical bill; 2 white wing bars; black wings and tail. *Male:* rosy red head, upperparts and breast; gray sides, flanks, belly and undertail coverts. *Female* and *immature:* gray overall; yellow or russet wash on head and rump.

Size: *L* 8–10 in; *W* 14½ in.

Status: ***MN:*** uncommon migrant and winter visitor from mid-October to early April, primarily in the north; occasionally moves into central regions in late winter; accidental in the south. ***WI:*** uncommon migrant and winter visitor from early November to late March in the north; rare migrant and winter visitor in the south.

Habitat: conifer plantations and deciduous woodlands with fruiting mountain-ash, crabapple and woody nightshade, as well as backyard feeders.

Nesting: does not nest in our region.

Feeding: gleans buds, berries and seeds from trees; also forages on the ground; visits feeders in winter.

Voice: song is a short, sweet musical warble; call is a 3-note whistle with a higher middle note; short, muffled trill is often given in flight; chatters when feeding in flocks.

Similar Species: *White-winged Crossbill* (p. 350): much smaller; lacks stubby bill and prominent gray coloration. *Red Crossbill* (p. 349): lacks stubby bill and white wing bars. *Evening Grosbeak* (p. 355): female has pale bill, dark "whisker" stripe, tan underparts and broad, white wing patches.

Best Sites: ***MN:*** Hawk Ridge (Duluth); Grand Marais; North Shore of L. Superior; Red Lake WMA; Superior NF. ***WI:*** northern deciduous forests, such as Nicolet NF and Chequamegon NF.

PURPLE FINCH

Carpodacus purpureus

The courtship of Purple Finches is a gentle and appealing ritual. The liquid, warbling song of the male bubbles through conifer boughs, announcing his presence to potential mates. Upon the arrival of an interested female, the colorful male dances lightly around her, beating his wings until he softly lifts into the air. • Flat, table-style feeding stations with nearby tree cover are sure to attract Purple Finches, and erecting one may keep a small flock in your area over winter. • "Purple" *(purpureus)* is simply a false description of this bird's reddish coloration. Roger Tory Peterson said it best when he described the Purple Finch as "a sparrow dipped in raspberry juice." Only the male is brightly colored, however, for the female is a rather drab, unassuming bird by comparison.

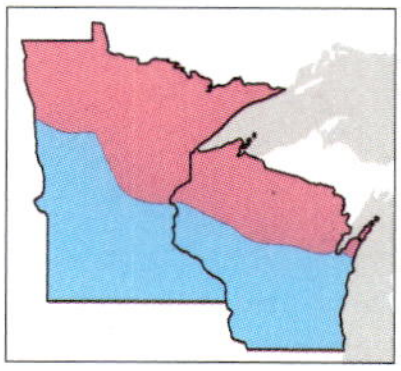

ID: *Male:* pale bill; raspberry red (occasionally yellow to salmon pink) head, throat, breast and nape; brown-and-red-streaked back and flanks; reddish brown "cheek"; red rump; notched tail; light, unstreaked belly and undertail coverts. *Female:* dark brown "cheek" and "jawline"; white "eyebrow" and lower "cheek" stripe; heavily streaked underparts; unstreaked undertail coverts.

Size: *L* 5–6 in; *W* 10 in.

Status: ***MN:*** common migrant from late February to late May and from mid-July to late November in eastern and central regions; uncommon migrant in the west; uncommon to locally common breeder; widespread winter visitor (numbers fluctuate from year to year and region to region). ***WI:*** common to uncommon migrant and winter visitor from mid-September to mid-May; fairly common breeder.

Habitat: *Breeding:* open coniferous and mixed forests. *In migration* and *winter:* coniferous, mixed and deciduous forests, shrubby open areas and feeding stations with nearby tree cover.

Nesting: on a conifer branch, far from the trunk; female builds a cup nest of twigs, grass and rootlets and lines it with moss and hair; female incubates 4–5 pale greenish blue eggs, marked with black and brown, for about 13 days.

Feeding: gleans the ground and vegetation for seeds, buds, berries and insects; readily visits table-style feeding stations.

Voice: song is a bubbly, continuous warble; call is a single metallic *cheep* or *weet*.

Similar Species: *House Finch* (p. 348): squared tail; male lacks reddish "cap"; female lacks distinct "cheek" patch. *Red Crossbill* (p. 349): larger bill with crossed mandibles; male has more red overall and dark "V"s on whitish undertail coverts.

Best Sites: ***MN:*** *In migration:* with flocks of other migrating birds. *Winter:* at feeders in central and southern regions only during irruption years. ***WI:*** varying numbers pass through each year and linger at feeders during winter.

HOUSE FINCH

Carpodacus mexicanus

A native of western North America, the House Finch was brought to eastern parts of the continent as an illegally captured cage bird known as the "Hollywood Finch." In the early 1940s, New York pet shop owners released their birds to avoid prosecution and fines, and it is the descendants of those birds that have colonized our region. The House Finch is now commonly found throughout the continental U.S. and southern Canada and has been introduced in Hawaii. This bird expanded its range into our region in the 1980s, and is now found in most urban areas. • The resourceful House Finch usually gains the upper hand on the more even-tempered Purple Finch, and it is the only bird aggressive and stubborn enough to outcompete the House Sparrow, which also prospers in urban environments. • The male House Finch's plumage varies in color from light yellow to bright red, but females will choose the reddest males with which to breed.

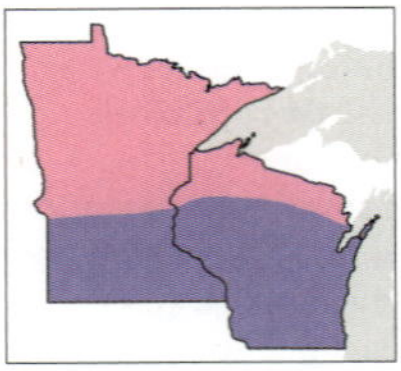

ID: streaked undertail coverts; brown-streaked back; square tail. *Male:* brown "cap"; bright red "eyebrow," forecrown, throat and breast; heavily streaked flanks. *Female:* indistinct facial patterning; heavily streaked underparts.

Size: *L* 5–6 in; *W* 9½ in.

Status: ***MN:*** widespread and common year-round resident; uncommon to rare year-round in the northeast. ***WI:*** common year-round resident; uncommon breeder in the north.

Habitat: urban and some rural areas.

Nesting: in a cavity, building, dense foliage or abandoned bird nest; especially in evergreens and ornamental shrubs near buildings; mostly the female builds an open cup nest of grass, twigs, leaves, hair and feathers, often adding string and other debris; female incubates 4–5 pale blue eggs, dotted with lavender and black, for 12–14 days.

Feeding: gleans vegetation and the ground for seeds; also takes berries, buds and some flower parts; often visits feeders.

Voice: song is a bright, disjointed warble lasting about 3 seconds, often ending with a harsh *jeeer* or *wheer;* flight call is a sweet *cheer,* given singly or in series.

Similar Species: *Purple Finch* (p. 347): notched tail; male has more burgundy red "cap," upper back and flanks; female has distinct "cheek" patch. *Red Crossbill* (p. 349): bill has crossed mandibles; male has more red overall and darker wings.

Best Sites: ***MN:*** in residential areas, especially around feeders, but also in rural areas near farms and along roadsides. ***WI:*** in residential areas in the southern two-thirds of the state.

RED CROSSBILL

Loxia curvirostra

Red Crossbills are the great gypsies of our bird community, wandering through forests in search of pine cones. They may breed at any time of the year if they discover a bumper crop—it's not unusual to hear them singing and see them nest-building in midwinter. Their nomadic ways make them difficult to find, and even during years of plenty there is no guarantee that these birds will surface in our region. Winter is typically the time to see crossbills here, and in some years, large flocks suddenly appear. • The crossbill's oddly shaped bill is an adaptation for prying open conifer cones. While holding the cone with one foot, the crossbill inserts its closed bill between the cone and scales and pries them apart by opening its bill. Once a cone is cracked, the crossbill uses its nimble tongue to extract the soft, energy-rich seeds hidden within.

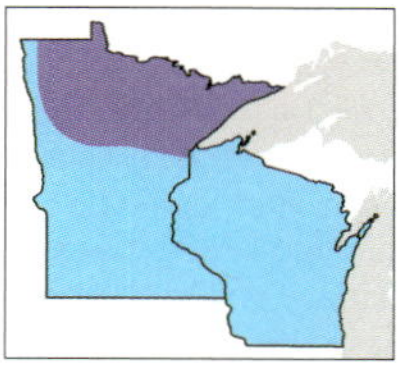

ID: bill has crossed tips. *Male:* dull orange red to brick red plumage; dark wings and tail; always has color on throat. *Female:* olive gray to dusky yellow plumage; plain, dark wings. *Immature:* streaky brown overall.

Size: *L* 5–6½ in; *W* 11 in.

Status: ***MN:*** irruptive; mainly found in the north; may be locally common; occasionally present in summer in the north; only 1 positive breeding record. ***WI:*** irruptive; rare to common migrant and winter visitor from mid-October to mid-May; rare breeder.

Habitat: coniferous forests and plantations; favors red and white pine, but also found in other pine and spruce-fir forests.

Nesting: high on the outer branch of a conifer; female builds an open cup nest of twigs, grass, bark shreds and rootlets and lines it with moss, lichens, rootlets, feathers and hair; female incubates 3–4 pale bluish white to greenish white eggs, dotted with black and purple, for 12–18 days.

Feeding: eats primarily conifer seeds (especially pine); also eats buds, deciduous tree seeds and occasionally insects; often licks road salt or minerals in soil and along roadsides; rarely visits feeders.

Voice: distinctive *jip-jip* call note, often given in flight; song is a varied series of warbles, trills and *chips* (similar to other finches).

Similar Species: *White-winged Crossbill* (p. 350): 2 broad, white wing bars. *Pine Siskin* (p. 353): similar to immature Red Crossbill, but is smaller, lacks crossed bill and has yellow highlights in wing. *Pine Grosbeak* (p. 346): stubby, conical bill; white wing bars. *House Finch* (p. 348) and *Purple Finch* (p. 347): conical bills; less red overall; lighter brownish wings; lack red on lower belly.

Best Sites: ***MN:*** *Winter:* coniferous forests north of L. Superior. ***WI:*** *Winter:* coniferous and mixed forests, especially in the northern part of the state.

WHITE-WINGED CROSSBILL

Loxia leucoptera

People are often amazed by the variety of color and the many different shapes of bird bills. Although the White-winged Crossbill lacks the colorful flair of the tropical toucan or the massive proportions of the hornbill, this bird's well-designed mandibles combine function with artistry. This bill arrangement is shared only by one other bird species in North America, the Red Crossbill. White-winged Crossbills primarily eat spruce and tamarack seeds, and their unusual bills are adapted for prying open conifer cones. • The presence of a foraging group of White-winged Crossbills high in a spruce tree creates an unforgettable shower of cones and crackling chatter. Like many finches, White-winged Crossbills can be abundant one year, then absent the next.

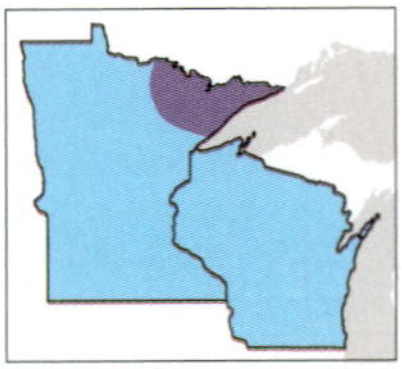

ID: bill has crossed tips; 2 bold, white wing bars. *Male:* pinkish red overall; black wings and tail. *Female:* streaked brown upperparts; dusky yellow underparts slightly streaked with brown; dark wings and tail. *Immature:* streaky brown overall; white wing bars.

Size: *L* 6–7 in; *W* $10\frac{1}{2}$ in.

Status: ***MN:*** irruptive; mainly found in the northern coniferous zone; migration times cannot be easily defined; may nest sporadically in northern coniferous forests; recently nested in Lake Co. ***WI:*** irruptive; rare to fairly common migrant and winter visitor from early November to mid-February.

Habitat: coniferous forests, primarily spruce, fir, tamarack and eastern hemlock; occasionally townsites and deciduous forests.

Nesting: on an outer branch in a conifer; female builds an open cup nest of twigs, grass, bark shreds, leaves and moss and lines it with moss, lichens, rootlets, hair and soft plant down; female incubates 2–4 whitish to pale blue green eggs, spotted with brown and lavender, for 12–14 days.

Feeding: prefers conifer seeds (mostly spruce and tamarack); also eats deciduous tree seeds and occasionally insects; licks salt and minerals from roads when available.

Voice: song is a high-pitched series of warbles, trills and *chips*; call is a series of harsh, questioning *cheat* notes, often given in flight.

Similar Species: *Red Crossbill* (p. 349): lacks white wing bars; male is deeper red (less pinkish). *Pine Siskin* (p. 353): similar to immature White-winged Crossbill but smaller, lacks crossed bill and has yellow highlights in wing. *Pine Grosbeak* (p. 346): stubby, conical bill; thinner wing bars; female is very gray; male has gray sides. *House Finch* (p. 348) and *Purple Finch* (p. 347): conical bills; less red overall; lighter brownish wings.

Best Sites: ***MN:*** Sax-Zim Bog; Aitkin Co.; Grand Marais; Lake Co.; George Crosby Manitou SP. ***WI:*** *Winter:* coniferous and mixed forests, especially in the northern part of the state.

COMMON REDPOLL

Carduelis flammea

A predictably unpredictable winter visitor, the Common Redpoll is seen in varying numbers—it might appear in flocks of hundreds or thousands, or in groups of a dozen or fewer, depending on the year. • Renowned for their effective winter adaptations, redpolls can endure colder temperatures than any other songbird. Because they do not have much body fat, they maintain a high metabolic rate and eat almost constantly to avoid dying from hypothermia—redpolls are continually gleaning waste grain from bare fields or stocking up on seeds at winter feeders. Their focus on food helps make them remarkably fearless of humans. Their highly insulative feathers also help these birds to withstand bitter cold, especially when the feathers are fluffed out to trap layers of warm, insulating air.

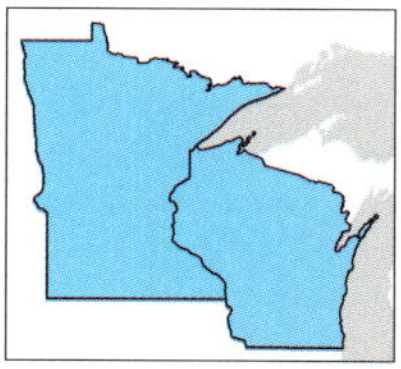

ID: red forecrown; black "chin"; yellowish bill; streaked upperparts, including rump; lightly streaked sides, flanks and undertail coverts; notched tail. *Male:* pinkish red breast (brightest in breeding plumage). *Female:* whitish to pale gray breast.
Size: *L* 5 in; *W* 9 in.
Status: ***MN:*** irruptive; common to at times abundant (at times rare) migrant and winter visitor from early October to late May primarily in the north; can be absent in central and southern regions in nonirruption years. ***WI:*** irruptive; common to rare migrant and winter visitor from early November to mid-April.
Habitat: open fields, meadows, roadsides, utility cutlines, railroads, forest edges and backyards with feeders.
Nesting: does not nest in our region.
Feeding: gleans the ground, snow and vegetation in large flocks for seeds in winter; often visits feeders; takes some insects in summer.
Voice: song is a twittering series of trills; calls are a soft *chit-chit-chit-chit* and a faint *swe-eet;* indistinguishable from the Hoary Redpoll's songs and calls.
Similar Species: *Hoary Redpoll* (p. 352): unstreaked or partly streaked rump; usually has faint or no streaking on sides and flanks; generally paler and plumper overall; bill may look stubbier; lacks streaking on undertail coverts. *Pine Siskin* (p. 353): heavily streaked overall; yellow highlights in wings and tail.
Best Sites: ***MN:*** Cook Co.; Duluth; weedy fields across northern and central regions; at feeders during irruption years. ***WI:*** in weedy fields, especially in the northern two-thirds of the state; at feeders during irruption years.

HOARY REDPOLL

Carduelis hornemanni

Mixed in with the more abundant Common Redpolls, you might see a more lightly colored bird with noticeably less streaking. Could it be an aberrant subspecies of the Common Redpoll, or is it a Hoary Redpoll? If the rump is white or pink with little or no streaking and the bill is small, you've got an unambiguous Hoary. • A bird of northern regions, Hoary Redpolls are well adapted to life in the cold. They have a high level of food intake, in part because they can store food in a special pouch in the esophagus (the esophageal diverticulum), which allows them to carry large quantities of energy-rich seeds. When seed crops fail or icy winds become intolerably cold, however, Hoary Redpolls do not hesitate to move south, where numbers "irrupt" every few years.

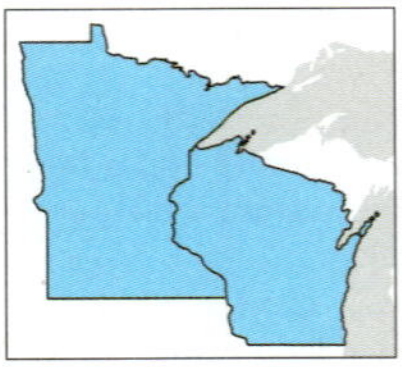

ID: red forecrown; black "chin"; yellowish bill; frosty white plumage overall; lightly streaked upperparts, except for unstreaked rump; unstreaked underparts (flanks may have faint streaking); notched tail. *Male:* pinkish tinged breast. *Female:* white to light gray breast.

Size: *L* 5–5$\frac{1}{2}$ in; *W* 9 in.

Status: ***MN:*** rare migrant and winter visitor from late October to April, mainly in northern regions; casual to accidental in other regions; totally absent from central and southern regions in nonirruption years. ***WI:*** rare migrant and winter visitor from early November to mid-April.

Habitat: open fields, meadows, roadsides, utility cutlines, railroads, forest edges and backyards with feeders.

Nesting: does not nest in our region.

Feeding: gleans the ground, snow and vegetation for seeds and buds; occasionally visits feeders in winter; takes some insects in summer.

Voice: song is a twittering series of trills; calls are a soft *chit-chit-chit-chit* and a faint *swe-eet;* indistinguishable from the Common Redpoll's songs and calls.

Similar Species: *Common Redpoll* (p. 351): streaked rump, sides, flanks and undertail coverts; generally darker and slimmer overall. *Pine Siskin* (p. 353): heavily streaked overall; yellow highlights in wings and tail.

Best Sites: no consistent sites; usually encountered as individuals at feeders or in flocks of Common Redpolls.

PINE SISKIN

Carduelis pinus

You can spend days, weeks and even months in pursuit of Pine Siskins, only to meet with frustration, aching feet and a sore, crimped neck. The best way to meet these birds is to set up a finch feeder filled with black niger seed in your backyard and wait for them to appear. If the feeder is in the right location, you can expect your backyard to be visited by Pine Siskins during migration and in winter. • Tight flocks of these gregarious birds are frequently heard before they are seen. Once you learn to recognize their characteristic, rising *zzzreeeee* calls and boisterous chatter, you can confirm the presence of these finches by simply listening. • Aside from the Pine Siskin's occasional flashes of yellow, its wardrobe is drab and sparrowlike. But for those who get to know it, the bird's behavior reveals a gentle nature that radiates the playfulness and enthusiasm of a goldfinch.

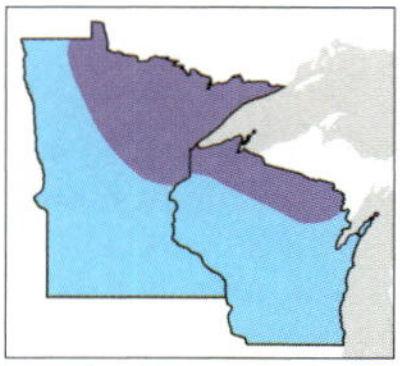

ID: heavily streaked underparts; yellow highlights at base of tail feathers and in wings (easily seen in flight); dull wing bars; darker, heavily streaked upperparts; slightly forked tail; indistinct facial pattern. *Immature:* similar to adult, but overall yellow tint fades through summer.

Size: *L* 5 in; *W* 9 in.

Status: ***MN:*** common to uncommon migrant and breeder in the north; irruptive and sporadic mainly during winter in southeastern and east-central regions where a few may remain to nest during years of abundance; can be an erratic winter visitor and migrant anywhere in the state; most regular in the north. ***WI:*** irruptive; rare to common migrant and winter visitor from mid-September to late May; uncommon breeder in the north.

Habitat: *Breeding:* coniferous and mixed forests; urban and rural ornamental and shade trees. *Winter:* coniferous and mixed forests, forest edges, meadows, roadsides, agricultural fields and backyards with feeders.

Nesting: usually loosely colonial; typically at midheight on an outer branch of a conifer; female builds a loose cup nest of twigs, grass and rootlets and lines it with feathers, hair, rootlets and fine plant fibers; female incubates 3–5 pale blue eggs with dark dots for about 13 days.

Feeding: gleans the ground and vegetation for seeds (especially thistle seeds), buds and some insects; attracted to road salts, mineral licks and ashes; regularly visits feeders.

Voice: song is a variable, bubbly mix of squeaky, metallic, raspy notes, sometimes resembling a jerky laugh; call is a buzzy, rising *zzzreeeee.*

Similar Species: *Common Redpoll* (p. 351) and *Hoary Redpoll* (p. 352): red forecrowns; lack yellow in wings and tails. *Purple Finch* (p. 347) and *House Finch* (p. 348): females have thicker bills and no yellow on wings or tails. *Sparrows* (pp. 307–24): all lack yellow on wings and tails.

Best Sites: ***MN:*** *In migration* and *winter:* at feeders during irruption years; coniferous forests in the northeast. ***WI:*** *In migration* and *winter:* at feeders and in coniferous forests.

AMERICAN GOLDFINCH

Carduelis tristis

breeding

The American Goldfinch is a bright, cheery songbird that is commonly seen in weedy fields, along roadsides and among backyard shrubs throughout summer and fall. Goldfinches seem to delight in perching upon late-summer thistle heads as they search for seeds to feed their newly hatched young. It's hard to miss the familiar, jubilant *po-ta-to-chip* they issue as they flutter over parks and gardens with their distinctive, undulating flight style. • It is enjoyable to observe a flock of goldfinches raining down to ground level to poke and prod the heads of dandelions. These birds can look quite comical as they attempt to step down on the flower stems to reach the crowning seeds. A dandelion-covered lawn always seems a lot less weedy with a flock of glowing goldfinches hopping through it.

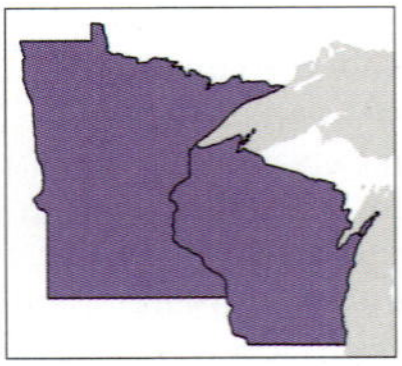

ID: *Breeding male:* black forecrown, black wings and tail; bright yellow body; white wing bars, undertail coverts and tail base; orange bill and legs. *Nonbreeding male:* olive brown back; yellow-tinged head; gray underparts. *Female:* yellow green upperparts and belly; yellow throat and breast.

Size: *L* 5 in; *W* 9 in.

Status: ***MN:*** common to abundant migrant and breeder from early April to late November; least common in north-central and northeastern regions; usually common in winter in southern and central regions but numbers fluctuate widely from year to year, especially farther north. ***WI:*** common migrant and breeder from late April to mid-November; common winter visitor, but numbers can vary.

Habitat: weedy fields, woodland edges, meadows, riparian areas and parks and gardens.

Nesting: in a fork in a deciduous shrub or tree; female builds a compact cup nest of plant fibers, grass and spider silk and lines it with plant down and hair; female incubates 4–6 pale bluish white eggs, occasionally spotted with light brown, for about 12–14 days.

Feeding: gleans vegetation for seeds, primarily thistle, birch and alder, as well as for insects and berries; commonly visits feeders.

Voice: song is a long and varied series of trills, twitters, warbles and hissing notes; calls include *po-ta-to-chip* or *per-chic-or-ee* (often delivered in flight) and a whistled *dear-me, see-me*.

Similar Species: *Evening Grosbeak* (p. 355): much larger; massive bill; lacks black forehead. *Wilson's Warbler* (p. 299): olive upperparts; olive wings without wing bars; thin, dark bill; black "cap" does not extend onto forehead.

Best Sites: ***MN:*** Duluth; at thistle feeders in winter, mainly in the south. ***WI:*** at thistle feeders and in rural areas.

EVENING GROSBEAK

Coccothraustes vespertinus

One chilly winter day, a flock of Evening Grosbeaks descends upon your backyard bird feeder filled with sunflower seeds. You watch the stunning gold-and-black grosbeaks with delight, but you soon come to realize that these birds are both an aesthetic blessing and a financial curse. The birds will eat enormous quantities of expensive birdseed and then suddenly disappear in late winter. Evening Grosbeaks are transient residents in our region, and they are generally encountered every few years in large, wintering flocks. • It is difficult not to notice the massive bill of this seed eater. In French, *gros bec* means "large beak," and any seasoned bird bander will tell you that the Evening Grosbeak's bill can exert an incredible force per unit area—it may be the most powerful of any North American bird.

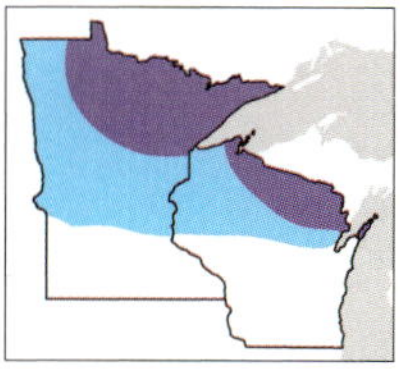

ID: massive, light-colored, conical bill; black wings and tail; broad, white wing patches. *Male:* black crown; bright yellow "eyebrow" and forehead band; dark brown head gradually fades into golden yellow belly and lower back. *Female:* gray head and upper back; yellow-tinged underparts; white undertail coverts.
Size: *L* 7–8½ in; *W* 14 in.
Status: ***MN:*** uncommon year-round resident in northeastern and north-central regions; may be locally common in winter at feeders; erratic breeder; erratic wanderer to central and southern regions but these occurrences have decreased in recent years. ***WI:*** irregular; uncommon to common migrant and winter visitor from mid-October to mid-May; uncommon breeder in the north.
Habitat: *Breeding:* coniferous and mixed forests and woodlands; occasionally in deciduous woodlands, suburban parks and orchards. *Winter:* forests and woodlands; parks and gardens with feeders.
Nesting: on an outer limb in a conifer; female builds a flimsy cup nest of twigs and lines it with rootlets, fine grass, plant fibers, moss and pine needles; female incubates 3–4 pale blue to blue green eggs, blotched with purple, gray and brown, for 11–14 days.
Feeding: gleans the ground and vegetation for seeds, buds and berries; also eats insects and licks mineral-rich soil; often visits feeders for sunflower seeds.
Voice: song is a wandering, halting warble; call is a loud, sharp *clee-ip* or a ringing *peeer.*
Similar Species: *American Goldfinch* (p. 354): much smaller; small bill; smaller wing bars; male has black "cap." *Pine Grosbeak* (p. 346): female is gray overall with black bill and smaller wing bars.
Best Sites: ***MN:*** L. Vermilion; Superior NF. ***WI:*** *In migration* and *winter:* at feeders in northern and central regions.

HOUSE SPARROW

Passer domesticus

For most of us, the House Sparrow is the first bird we meet and recognize in our youth. Although it is one of our most abundant and conspicuous birds, many generations of House Sparrows live out their lives within our backyards with few of us ever knowing much about this omnipresent neighbor. • House Sparrows were introduced to North America in the 1850s around Brooklyn, New York, as part of a plan to control the numbers of insects that were damaging grain and cereal crops. But this sparrow's diet is largely vegetarian, so its impact on crop pests proved to be minimal. Since then, this Eurasian sparrow has managed to colonize most populated areas on the continent, and it has benefited greatly from a close association with humans. Unfortunately, its aggressive behavior has helped it to usurp territory from many native bird species, especially in rural habitats. • House Sparrows are not closely related to the other North American sparrows; they belong to the family of Old World Sparrows or "Weaver Finches."

breeding

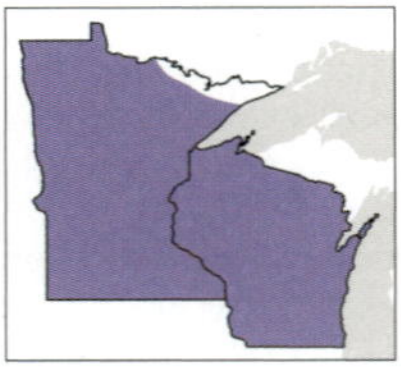

ID: *Breeding male:* gray crown; black "bib" and bill; chestnut nape; light gray "cheek"; white wing bar; dark, mottled upperparts; gray underparts. *Nonbreeding male:* smaller black "bib"; pale bill. *Female:* plain gray brown overall; buffy "eyebrow"; streaked upperparts; indistinct facial patterns; grayish, unstreaked underparts.

Size: *L* 6 in; *W* 9½ in.

Status: ***MN:*** abundant year-round resident; decreasing in abundance northward; absent in Boundary Waters (Cook Co.). ***WI:*** abundant year-round resident.

Habitat: townsites, urban and suburban areas, farmyards and agricultural areas, railroad yards and other developed areas; absent from undeveloped and heavily wooded areas.

Nesting: often communal; in an artificial structure, ornamental shrub or natural cavity; pair builds a large, dome-shaped nest of grass, twigs, plant fibers and litter and often lines it with feathers; pair incubates 4–6 whitish to greenish white eggs, dotted with gray and brown, for 10–13 days.

Feeding: gleans the ground and vegetation for seeds, insects and fruit; frequently visits feeders for seeds.

Voice: song is a familiar, plain *cheep-cheep-cheep-cheep;* call is a short *chill-up*.

Similar Species: female is distinctively drab. *Harris's Sparrow* (p. 323): gray face; black "cap"; pink orange bill.

Best Sites: widespread in residential and agricultural areas, especially around farmsteads.

OCCASIONAL BIRD SPECIES

The following is a selection of 34 of the accidental and casual species (those not seen every year) that occur in Minnesota and Wisconsin. For a full listing of these species, please refer to the checklist (pp. 364–68).

Tricolored Heron

TRICOLORED HERON

Egretta tricolor

MN: casual; occurs mainly in southern and western regions; scattered records from spring and summer of individual birds in 12 counties in different regions; no fall records. **WI:** casual; appears more often in spring, but has occasionally summered in Horicon NWR; rarely appears in fall.

GLOSSY IBIS

Plegadis falcinellus

MN: accidental; 1 record from Heron L. (Jackson Co.) in May 1991. **WI:** accidental; several spring records, including May 2001, plus a fall sighting in October 2002.

WHITE-FACED IBIS

Plegadis chihi

MN: casual; spring migrant summer visitor and occasional fall migrant, mainly in southern and central regions; records are increasing rapidly, especially in the last decade. **WI:** casual, formerly thought to be accidental, but may occur more frequently than Glossy Ibis.

BRANT

Branta bernicla

MN: accidental; a total of 14 records, 9 of them in October or November from various parts of the state and 4 spring records from March and April; 1 summer record from Duluth in June. **WI:** casual; accompanies Canada Goose flocks during spring and fall migration; most recently observed at DePere (November 2002 to January 2003).

EURASIAN WIGEON

Anas penelope

MN: casual; approximately 20 records scattered throughout the state (some may have been hybrids); all but 2 records are from late March to mid-June; 3 fall records in October and November in the Twin Cities area. **WI:** casual; almost always mixed flocks of dabbling ducks with a predominance of American Wigeons; most sightings occur between late March and mid-May.

KING EIDER

Somateria spectabilis

MN: casual; 16 records, mostly from L. Superior in St. Louis, Lake and Cook Counties from mid-October to mid-January; 2 spring records (May 1971 and May 2002). **WI:** casual; most sightings occur during fall and winter on L. Michigan.

BARROW'S GOLDENEYE

Bucephala islandica

MN: casual spring and fall migrant and winter visitor; most records are from late fall, winter and early spring on L. Superior and the Mississippi R. in the Twin Cities area; accidental in other areas in spring and fall. **WI:** casual; occurs in mixed flocks of diving ducks, often predominately Common Goldeneyes; most frequently seen on the two Great Lakes, especially L. Michigan where one has wintered for the past 8 years.

Brant

Whooping Crane

MISSISSIPPI KITE

Ictinia mississippiensis

MN: casual vagrant; has been recorded annually in recent years at Hawk Ridge, Duluth; most records are from early August to late October; 5 mid- to late May records. **WI:** casual; sightings occur during migration periods, especially in spring.

PURPLE GALLINULE

Porphyrio martinica

MN: accidental; 3 records from St. Louis Co. in 1963, Houston Co. in 1967 and Nicollet Co. in 1970. **WI:** accidental; sightings occur in marshy areas.

WHOOPING CRANE

Grus americana

MN: accidental; migrant and breeder throughout prairie areas of the state in the presettlement era of the 19th century; only 3 confirmed records since 1917, at Rice Lake NWR (November 1951), Mahnomen Co. (October 1985) and in Marshall Co. and Polk Co. (October 1990). **WI:** accidental; currently being reintroduced at Necedah NWR, Meadow Valley Wildlife Area and Wood County Wildlife Area in central Wisconsin in a multiyear project that, when completed, will yield a viable population in Wisconsin that winters in Florida.

BLACK-NECKED STILT

Himantopus mexicanus

MN: accidental; 4 records from Hennepin, Stevens, Roseau and Martin Counties in April, May, June and July. **WI:** casual; a rare spring and even rarer fall visitor; a pair nested at Horicon NWR several years ago, successfully fledging 5 young for the first Wisconsin nesting record.

CURLEW SANDPIPER

Calidris ferruginea

MN: accidental; 1 record in May 1994 at Prairie Island. **WI:** accidental; about 10 sightings of individual birds in breeding plumage, mostly in May.

RED PHALAROPE

Phalaropus fulicarius

MN: casual; 11 records, 9 in fall during September, October and November, mainly in northern areas; 2 spring records, both in May, from Moorhead and Duluth. **WI:** casual; most likely to appear in fall on the two Great Lakes, especially L. Michigan; usually seen in nonbreeding plumage.

POMARINE JAEGER

Stercorarius pomarinus

MN: accidental; 15 records, 13 from L. Superior near Duluth, mostly between August and November; 1 May record from Duluth. **WI:** casual; has occurred on both Great Lakes as well as inland; both color morphs have been sighted.

LONG-TAILED JAEGER

Stercorarius longicaudus

MN: accidental; 8 records, 4 from L. Superior (3 Duluth, 1 Cook Co.), and the others from Wadena, Marshall, Jackson and Washington Counties; records are from April, July, August, September, October (2) and November. **WI:** accidental; about an equal number of inland lake sightings as Great Lake sightings, mostly during fall migration (August and September).

BLACK-HEADED GULL

Larus ridibundus

MN: accidental; 7 records, all from Jackson Co. at Heron L., Grover's L. and Spirit L.; records range from April through October. **WI:** casual; often accompanies Bonaparte's Gulls; most sightings are along L. Michigan.

Black-headed Gull

Black-legged Kittiwake

CALIFORNIA GULL

Larus californicus

MN: casual; spring and fall migrant with scattered records from 16 counties, mainly in the western tier of counties; some records from the Twin Cities area and Mille Lacs L. **WI:** casual; has been recorded only a few times, mainly along L. Michigan.

GLAUCOUS-WINGED GULL

Larus glaucescens

MN: accidental; 3 December records, 2 from the Twin Cities area and 1 from Grand Marais on L. Superior. **WI:** accidental; sightings have been mainly during winter and early spring along L. Michigan.

SABINE'S GULL

Xema sabini

MN: casual; mostly a fall vagrant almost anywhere in the state; a high count of 26 birds occurred in Duluth in September 2000. **WI:** casual, though the past several years have yielded flocks of 20 to 30+ birds on L. Superior; occurs on both Great Lakes as well as inland, especially in September and October.

BLACK-LEGGED KITTIWAKE

Rissa tridactyla

MN: casual; primarily a late fall and early winter vagrant, mainly in the north near large lakes; records are increasing along the North Shore of L. Superior; has also been recorded in the Twin Cities area. **WI:** casual; both immature and adult birds have been seen on both Great Lakes as well as inland; most sightings have occurred in fall, with a very few during winter and early spring.

IVORY GULL

Pagophila eburnea

MN: accidental; late fall through early spring vagrant on L. Superior with 1 record from the Twin Cities area on the Mississippi R. **WI:** casual; recorded once inland and several times along L. Michigan.

ARCTIC TERN

Sterna paradisaea

MN: accidental; 13 records, 11 at Duluth in late May and early June and 2 September records. **WI:** casual; accompanies Forster's Terns and Common Terns during late spring and early fall on L. Michigan and L. Superior.

LEAST TERN

Sterna antillarum

MN: casual; 17 records since 1951; primarily found in the southwest as a migrant in May and early June and again in August and September; recent record from Agassiz NWR. **WI:** casual; the rarest tern that frequents the state.

BARN OWL

Tyto alba

MN: accidental; records are from 34 counties; formerly a rare to casual year-round resident in southern regions; declining since the 1950s; last known nesting was in Dakota Co. in 1990 and 1991. **WI:** casual; we are at the northern edge of this bird's breeding range; occasionally a successful nest is discovered in a barn, silo or even the attic of a home.

BURROWING OWL

Athene cunicularia

MN: casual, probably accidental at present; formerly a common local breeder on the prairies in west-central and southwestern regions; numbers have declined drastically in recent years; may become extirpated; 1 bird was sighted in 2002 in Murray Co. which remained at a single site for several weeks in May and June. **WI:** accidental; infrequent sightings during migration, especially in spring.

Sabine's Gull

Black-headed Grosbeak

CHUCK-WILL'S-WIDOW

Caprimulgus carolinensis

MN: accidental; records from Nicollet Co. in 1984 and Sherburne Co. during the summers of 1981 to 1984. **WI:** casual; occasionally (about every 5–10 years) ventures north into the state; often identified by its song.

RUFOUS HUMMINGBIRD

Selasphorus rufus

MN: accidental; first recorded in August 1974 at Grand Rapids; records range from mid-June to late October from 10 different counties in eastern and north-central regions. **WI:** casual; a western species that occasionally wanders in its southward flight in fall; stops at hummingbird feeders for varying lengths of time.

SPRAGUE'S PIPIT

Anthus spragueii

MN: casual; formerly a migrant and breeder in the western tier of counties, but now only a very rare to casual migrant in these areas; last nesting evidence was in Polk Co. in 1988. **WI:** accidental.

KIRTLAND'S WARBLER

Dendroica kirtlandii

MN: accidental; 2 spring records from May 1892 at Minneapolis and from May 1944 at St. Cloud. **WI:** casual; expanding its range into Wisconsin; males have been found infrequently in the past 20+ years in suitable jack pine habitat in some central, northwestern and northern counties; no females have yet been sighted, but there is hope that this bird will eventually breed here.

GREEN-TAILED TOWHEE

Pipilo chlorurus

MN: accidental; 4 records, 2 from Carver Co. and Clay Co. in May and 2 from St. Louis Co. in December. **WI:** casual; occasionally appears at a feeder; most sightings are from late fall through winter with only a few spring records.

LARK BUNTING

Calamospiza melanocorys

MN: casual; formerly a regular migrant and breeder in far western regions, but now rare and sporadic; no nesting records since 1964; last recorded in May 2000, at Stoney Pt.; may occur as a vagrant anywhere in the state, but most likely in the west. **WI:** casual visitor during migration; occurs in open, grassy areas or at residential feeders.

BAIRD'S SPARROW

Ammodramus bairdii

MN: casual; formerly a migrant and breeder in the north; a few records from the northwest, primarily at Felton Prairie, in the late 20th century; 2 singing males were seen in separate locations in Polk Co. during June and July 2002. **WI:** accidental; occurs in prairie habitat; 1 record.

BLACK-HEADED GROSBEAK

Pheucticus melanocephalus

MN: casual; 22 records in 15 counties from April to November; most records are of immature or adult males during migration; recorded in October 2000 at Two Harbors and in May 2002 in Clay Co. **WI:** accidental; most sightings have been individuals at feeders during both migrations and in winter.

LAZULI BUNTING

Passerina amoena

MN: casual; spring and early summer vagrant with 20 records from all regions of the state; recorded in 2001 in Polk Co.; hybrids with the Indigo Bunting have been recorded. **WI:** accidental; highly infrequent sightings, usually at a feeder.

Lark Bunting

SELECT REFERENCES

American Ornithologists' Union. 1998. *Check-list of North American Birds.* 7th ed. (and its supplements). American Ornithologists' Union, Washington, D.C.

Choate, E.A. 1985. *The Dictionary of American Bird Names.* Rev. ed. Harvard Common Press, Cambridge, MA.

Cox, Randall T. 1996. *Birder's Dictionary.* Falcon Publishing, Inc., Helena, MT.

Eckert, Kim R. 2002. *A Birder's Guide to Minnesota.* 4th ed. Gavian Guides, Duluth, MN.

Gromme, Owen J. 1998. *Birds of Wisconsin.* Rev. ed. University of Wisconsin Press, Madison, WI.

Janssen, Robert B. 1987. *Birds in Minnesota.* University of Minnesota Press, Minneapolis, MN.

Kaufman, K. 1996. *Lives of North American Birds.* Houghton Mifflin Co., Boston.

Kaufman, K. 2000. *Birds of North America.* Houghton Mifflin Co., New York.

National Geographic Society. 1999. *Field Guide to the Birds of North America.* 3rd ed. National Geographic Society, Washington, D.C.

Robbins, Samuel D., Jr. 1991. *Wisconsin Birdlife: Population and Distribution Past and Present.* University of Wisconsin Press, Madison, WI.

Sibley, D.A. 2000. *National Audubon Society: The Sibley Guide to Bird Life and Behavior.* Alfred A. Knopf, New York.

Sibley, D.A. 2000. *National Audubon Society: The Sibley Guide to Birds.* Alfred A. Knopf, New York.

Sibley, D.A. 2002. *Sibley's Birding Basics.* Alfred A. Knopf, New York.

Golden Eagle

GLOSSARY

accipiter: a forest hawk (genus *Accipiter*), characterized by a long tail and short, rounded wings; feeds mostly on birds.

brood: *n.* a family of young from one hatching; *v.* to incubate the eggs.

brood parasite: a bird that lays its eggs in other birds' nests.

buteo: a high-soaring hawk (genus *Buteo*), characterized by broad wings and a short, wide tail; feeds mostly on small mammals and other land animals.

cere: on birds of prey, a fleshy area at the base of the bill that contains the nostrils.

clutch: the number of eggs laid by the female at one time.

dabbling: a foraging technique used by some ducks, in which the head and neck are submerged but the body and tail remain on the water's surface; dabbling ducks can usually walk easily on land, can take off without running and have brightly colored speculums.

diurnal: most active during the day.

"eclipse" plumage: a cryptic plumage, similar to that of females, worn by some male ducks in fall when they molt their flight feathers and consequently are unable to fly.

endangered: a species that is facing extirpation or extinction in all or part of its range.

extinct: a species that no longer exists.

extirpated: a species that no longer exists in the wild in a particular region but occurs elsewhere.

flushing: when frightened birds explode into flight in response to a disturbance.

flycatching: a feeding behavior in which the bird leaves a perch, snatches an insect in midair and returns to the same perch; also known as "hawking" or "sallying."

hawking: attempting to capture insects through aerial pursuit.

irruption: a sporadic mass migration of birds into an unusual range.

kettle: a large concentration of hawks, usually seen during migration.

lek: a place where males gather to display for females in the spring.

mantle: the area that includes the back and uppersides of the wings.

molt: the periodic shedding and regrowth of worn feathers (often twice a year).

nocturnal: most active at night.

peep: a sandpiper of the *Calidris* genus.

polyandry: a mating strategy in which one female breeds with many males.

polygyny: a mating strategy in which one male breeds with many females.

precocial: a bird that is relatively well developed at hatching; precocial birds usually have open eyes, extensive down and are fairly mobile.

primaries: the outermost flight feathers of a bird's wing.

raft: a gathering of birds resting on the water.

raptor: a carnivorous (meat-eating) bird; includes eagles, hawks, falcons and owls.

riparian: habitat along rivers or streams.

sexual dimorphism: a difference in plumage, size or other characteristics between males and females of the same species.

special concern: a species that has characteristics that make it particularly sensitive to human activities or disturbance, requires a very specific or unique habitat or whose status is such that it requires careful monitoring.

speculum: a brightly colored patch on the wings of many dabbling ducks.

stage: to gather in one place during migration, usually when birds are flightless or partly flightless during molting.

stoop: a steep dive through the air, usually performed by birds of prey while foraging or during courtship displays.

syrinx: a bird's voice organ.

thistle feeder: a feeder that dispenses thistle (niger) seed; especially attractive to finches.

threatened: a species likely to become endangered in the near future in all or part of its range.

understory: the shrub or thicket layer beneath a canopy of trees.

vagrant: a bird that has wandered outside its normal migration range.

vent: the single opening for excretion of uric acid and other wastes and for sexual reproduction; also known as the "cloaca."

CHECKLIST

The following checklist contains 448 species of birds that have been officially recorded in Minnesota or Wisconsin. Species are grouped by family and listed in taxonomic order in accordance with the A.O.U. *Check-list of North American Birds* (7th ed.) and its supplements.

Casual and accidental species (those that are not seen on a yearly basis) are listed in *italics.* Where a species is regular in one state and accidental or casual in the other, it has been listed as regular. Species that occur in only one of the states have been indicated as such. In addition, the following risk categories are noted: extinct or extirpated (ex), endangered (en), threatened (th) and special concern (sc).

Loons (Gaviidae)
- ❑ Red-throated Loon
- ❑ Pacific Loon
- ❑ Common Loon
- ❑ *Yellow-billed Loon* (MN only)

Grebes (Podicipedidae)
- ❑ Pied-billed Grebe
- ❑ Horned Grebe (th:MN)
- ❑ Red-necked Grebe (en:WI)
- ❑ Eared Grebe
- ❑ Western Grebe
- ❑ Clark's Grebe (MN only)

Pelicans (Pelecanidae)
- ❑ American White Pelican (sc:MN)
- ❑ *Brown Pelican* (WI only)

Cormorants (Phalacrocoracidae)
- ❑ Double-crested Cormorant
- ❑ *Neotropic Cormorant* (MN only)

Darters (Anhingidae)
- ❑ *Anhinga* (WI only)

Frigatebirds (Fregatidae)
- ❑ *Magnificent Frigatebird*

Bitterns & Herons (Ardeidae)
- ❑ American Bittern
- ❑ Least Bittern
- ❑ Great Blue Heron
- ❑ Great Egret (th:WI)
- ❑ Snowy Egret (en:WI)
- ❑ Little Blue Heron
- ❑ *Tricolored Heron*
- ❑ Cattle Egret (sc:WI)
- ❑ Green Heron
- ❑ Black-crowned Night-Heron
- ❑ Yellow-crowned Night-Heron (th:WI)

Ibises & Spoonbills (Threskiornithidae)
- ❑ *White Ibis*
- ❑ *Glossy Ibis*
- ❑ *White-faced Ibis*
- ❑ *Roseate Spoonbill* (WI only)

Storks (Ciconiidae)
- ❑ *Wood Stork* (WI only)

Vultures (Cathartidae)
- ❑ *Black Vulture*
- ❑ Turkey Vulture

Waterfowl (Anatidae)
- ❑ *Black-bellied Whistling-Duck*
- ❑ *Fulvous Whistling-Duck*
- ❑ Greater White-fronted Goose
- ❑ Snow Goose
- ❑ Ross's Goose
- ❑ Canada Goose
- ❑ *Brant*
- ❑ Mute Swan
- ❑ Trumpeter Swan (en:WI; th:MN)
- ❑ Tundra Swan
- ❑ Wood Duck
- ❑ Gadwall
- ❑ *Eurasian Wigeon*
- ❑ American Wigeon (sc:WI)
- ❑ American Black Duck
- ❑ Mallard
- ❑ Blue-winged Teal (sc:WI)
- ❑ Cinnamon Teal
- ❑ Northern Shoveler
- ❑ Northern Pintail
- ❑ *Garganey* (MN only)
- ❑ Green-winged Teal
- ❑ Canvasback
- ❑ Redhead
- ❑ Ring-necked Duck
- ❑ Greater Scaup
- ❑ Lesser Scaup
- ❑ *King Eider*
- ❑ *Common Eider*
- ❑ Harlequin Duck
- ❑ Surf Scoter
- ❑ White-winged Scoter
- ❑ Black Scoter
- ❑ Long-tailed Duck
- ❑ Bufflehead
- ❑ Common Goldeneye
- ❑ *Barrow's Goldeneye*

- ❑ *Smew*
- ❑ Hooded Merganser
- ❑ Common Merganser
- ❑ Red-breasted Merganser
- ❑ *Masked Duck* (WI only)
- ❑ Ruddy Duck

Kites, Hawks & Eagles (Accipetridae)

- ❑ Osprey (th:WI)
- ❑ *Swallow-tailed Kite*
- ❑ *White-tailed Kite*
- ❑ *Mississippi Kite*
- ❑ Bald Eagle (sc:MN)
- ❑ Northern Harrier (sc:WI)
- ❑ Sharp-shinned Hawk
- ❑ Cooper's Hawk
- ❑ Northern Goshawk
- ❑ *Harris's Hawk* (WI only)
- ❑ Red-shouldered Hawk (th:WI; sc:MN)
- ❑ Broad-winged Hawk
- ❑ Swainson's Hawk
- ❑ Red-tailed Hawk
- ❑ *Ferruginous Hawk*
- ❑ Rough-legged Hawk
- ❑ Golden Eagle

Falcons & Caracaras (Falconidae)

- ❑ *Crested Caracara* (MN only)
- ❑ American Kestrel
- ❑ Merlin
- ❑ Gyrfalcon
- ❑ Peregrine Falcon (en:WI; th:MN)
- ❑ Prairie Falcon (MN only)

Grouse & Allies (Phasianidae)

- ❑ Gray Partridge
- ❑ Ring-necked Pheasant
- ❑ Ruffed Grouse
- ❑ Spruce Grouse (th:WI)
- ❑ *Willow Ptarmigan*
- ❑ *Rock Ptarmigan* (MN only)
- ❑ Sharp-tailed Grouse (sc:WI)
- ❑ Greater Prairie-Chicken (th:WI; sc:MN)
- ❑ Wild Turkey

New World Quails (Odontophoridae)

- ❑ Northern Bobwhite

Rails & Coots (Rallidae)

- ❑ Yellow Rail (th:WI; sc:MN)
- ❑ *Black Rail*
- ❑ King Rail (en:MN)
- ❑ Virginia Rail
- ❑ Sora
- ❑ *Purple Gallinule*
- ❑ Common Moorhen (sc:MN)
- ❑ American Coot

Cranes (Gruidae)

- ❑ Sandhill Crane
- ❑ *Whooping Crane*

Plovers (Charadriidae)

- ❑ Black-bellied Plover
- ❑ American Golden-Plover
- ❑ *Snowy Plover*
- ❑ *Wilson's Plover* (MN only)
- ❑ Semipalmated Plover
- ❑ Piping Plover (en)
- ❑ Killdeer

Stilts & Avocets (Recurvirostridae)

- ❑ *Black-necked Stilt*
- ❑ American Avocet

Sandpipers & Allies (Scolopacidae)

- ❑ Greater Yellowlegs
- ❑ Lesser Yellowlegs
- ❑ Solitary Sandpiper
- ❑ Willet
- ❑ Spotted Sandpiper
- ❑ Upland Sandpiper (sc:WI)
- ❑ *Eskimo Curlew*
- ❑ Whimbrel
- ❑ *Long-billed Curlew*
- ❑ Hudsonian Godwit
- ❑ Marbled Godwit (sc:MN)
- ❑ Ruddy Turnstone
- ❑ *Black Turnstone* (WI only)
- ❑ Red Knot
- ❑ Sanderling
- ❑ Semipalmated Sandpiper
- ❑ Western Sandpiper
- ❑ Least Sandpiper
- ❑ White-rumped Sandpiper
- ❑ Baird's Sandpiper
- ❑ Pectoral Sandpiper
- ❑ Purple Sandpiper
- ❑ Dunlin
- ❑ *Curlew Sandpiper*
- ❑ Stilt Sandpiper
- ❑ Buff-breasted Sandpiper
- ❑ *Ruff*
- ❑ Short-billed Dowitcher
- ❑ Long-billed Dowitcher
- ❑ Wilson's Snipe
- ❑ American Woodcock
- ❑ Wilson's Phalarope (th:MN; sc:WI)
- ❑ Red-necked Phalarope
- ❑ *Red Phalarope*

Gulls & Allies (Laridae)

- ❑ *Pomarine Jaeger*
- ❑ Parasitic Jaeger
- ❑ *Long-tailed Jaeger*
- ❑ Laughing Gull
- ❑ Franklin's Gull (sc:MN)
- ❑ Little Gull
- ❑ *Black-headed Gull*
- ❑ Bonaparte's Gull
- ❑ *Mew Gull*
- ❑ Ring-billed Gull
- ❑ *California Gull*
- ❑ Herring Gull
- ❑ Thayer's Gull
- ❑ Iceland Gull
- ❑ Lesser Black-backed Gull

- ❑ *Glaucous-winged Gull*
- ❑ Glaucous Gull
- ❑ Great Black-backed Gull
- ❑ *Sabine's Gull*
- ❑ *Black-legged Kittiwake*
- ❑ *Ross's Gull*
- ❑ *Ivory Gull*
- ❑ Caspian Tern (en:WI)
- ❑ *Royal Tern* (WI only)
- ❑ *Sandwich Tern* (MN only)
- ❑ Common Tern (en:WI; th:MN)
- ❑ *Arctic Tern*
- ❑ Forster's Tern (en:WI; sc:MN)
- ❑ *Least Tern*
- ❑ *Sooty Tern* (WI only)
- ❑ *White-winged Tern* (WI only)
- ❑ Black Tern

Alcids (Alcidae)

- ❑ *Dovekie*
- ❑ *Long-billed Murrelet* (WI only)
- ❑ *Ancient Murrelet*

Pigeons & Doves (Columbidae)

- ❑ Rock Dove
- ❑ *Band-tailed Pigeon*
- ❑ *Eurasian Collared-Dove*
- ❑ *White-winged Dove*
- ❑ Mourning Dove
- ❑ *Passenger Pigeon* (ex)
- ❑ *Common Ground-Dove*

Parakeets, Macaws & Parrots (Psittacidae)

- ❑ *Carolina Parakeet* (WI only) (ex)

Cuckoos & Anis (Cuculidae)

- ❑ Black-billed Cuckoo
- ❑ Yellow-billed Cuckoo
- ❑ *Groove-billed Ani*

Barn Owls (Tytonidae)

- ❑ *Barn Owl* (en:WI)

Owls (Strigidae)

- ❑ Eastern Screech-Owl
- ❑ Great Horned Owl
- ❑ Snowy Owl
- ❑ Northern Hawk Owl
- ❑ *Burrowing Owl* (en:MN)
- ❑ Barred Owl
- ❑ Great Gray Owl
- ❑ Long-eared Owl
- ❑ Short-eared Owl (sc)
- ❑ Boreal Owl
- ❑ Northern Saw-Whet Owl

Nightjars (Caprimulgidae)

- ❑ Common Nighthawk
- ❑ *Common Poorwill* (MN only)
- ❑ *Chuck-will's-widow*
- ❑ Whip-poor-will

Swifts (Apodidae)

- ❑ Chimney Swift
- ❑ *White-throated Swift* (MN only)

Hummingbirds (Trochilidae)

- ❑ *Green Violet-ear* (WI only)
- ❑ *Broad-billed Hummingbird* (WI only)
- ❑ *Magnificent Hummingbird* (MN only)
- ❑ Ruby-throated Hummingbird
- ❑ *Anna's Hummingbird*
- ❑ *Calliope hummingbird* (MN only)
- ❑ *Rufous Hummingbird*

Kingfishers (Alcedinidae)

- ❑ Belted Kingfisher

Woodpeckers (Picidae)

- ❑ *Lewis's Woodpecker*
- ❑ Red-headed Woodpecker
- ❑ Red-bellied Woodpecker
- ❑ *Williamson's Sapsucker* (MN only)
- ❑ Yellow-bellied Sapsucker
- ❑ Downy Woodpecker
- ❑ Hairy Woodpecker
- ❑ Three-toed Woodpecker
- ❑ Black-backed Woodpecker
- ❑ Northern Flicker
- ❑ Pileated Woodpecker

Flycatchers (Tyrannidae)

- ❑ Olive-sided Flycatcher
- ❑ *Western Wood-Pewee*
- ❑ Eastern Wood-Pewee
- ❑ Yellow-bellied Flycatcher
- ❑ Acadian Flycatcher (th:WI; sc:MN)
- ❑ Alder Flycatcher
- ❑ Willow Flycatcher
- ❑ Least Flycatcher
- ❑ *Dusky Flycatcher* (WI only)
- ❑ *Black Phoebe* (MN only)
- ❑ Eastern Phoebe
- ❑ *Say's Phoebe*
- ❑ *Vermilion Flycatcher*
- ❑ *Ash-throated Flycatcher*
- ❑ Great Crested Flycatcher
- ❑ Western Kingbird
- ❑ Eastern Kingbird
- ❑ *Scissor-tailed Flycatcher*
- ❑ *Fork-tailed Flycatcher*

Shrikes (Laniidae)

- ❑ Loggerhead Shrike (en:WI; th:MN)
- ❑ Northern Shrike

Vireos (Vireonidae)

- ❑ White-eyed Vireo
- ❑ Bell's Vireo (th:WI)
- ❑ *Gray Vireo* (WI only)
- ❑ Yellow-throated Vireo
- ❑ Blue-headed Vireo
- ❑ Warbling Vireo

- ❑ Philadelphia Vireo
- ❑ Red-eyed Vireo

Jays & Crows (Corvidae)
- ❑ Gray Jay
- ❑ Blue Jay
- ❑ *Clark's Nutcracker*
- ❑ Black-billed Magpie
- ❑ American Crow
- ❑ Common Raven

Larks (Alaudidae)
- ❑ Horned Lark

Swallows (Hirundinidae)
- ❑ Purple Martin
- ❑ Tree Swallow
- ❑ *Violet-green Swallow* (MN only)
- ❑ Northern Rough-winged Swallow
- ❑ Bank Swallow
- ❑ Cliff Swallow
- ❑ Barn Swallow

Chickadees & Titmice (Paridae)
- ❑ Black-capped Chickadee
- ❑ Boreal Chickadee
- ❑ Tufted Titmouse

Nuthatches (Sittidae)
- ❑ Red-breasted Nuthatch
- ❑ White-breasted Nuthatch
- ❑ *Pygmy Nuthatch* (MN only)
- ❑ *Brown-headed Nuthatch* (WI only)

Creepers (Certhiidae)
- ❑ Brown Creeper

Wrens (Troglodytidae)
- ❑ *Rock Wren* (MN only)
- ❑ Carolina Wren
- ❑ *Bewick's Wren* (en:WI)
- ❑ House Wren
- ❑ Winter Wren
- ❑ Sedge Wren
- ❑ Marsh Wren

Dippers (Cinclidae)
- ❑ *American Dipper* (MN only)

Kinglets (Regulidae)
- ❑ Golden-crowned Kinglet
- ❑ Ruby-crowned Kinglet

Gnatcatchers (Sylviidae)
- ❑ Blue-gray Gnatcatcher

Thrushes (Turdidae)
- ❑ *Northern Wheatear* (MN only)
- ❑ Eastern Bluebird
- ❑ Mountain Bluebird
- ❑ Townsend's Solitaire
- ❑ Veery
- ❑ Gray-cheeked Thrush
- ❑ Swainson's Thrush
- ❑ Hermit Thrush
- ❑ Wood Thrush
- ❑ *Fieldfare* (MN only)
- ❑ American Robin
- ❑ Varied Thrush

Mockingbirds & Thrashers (Mimidae)
- ❑ Gray Catbird
- ❑ Northern Mockingbird
- ❑ *Sage Thrasher*
- ❑ Brown Thrasher
- ❑ *Curve-billed Thrasher*

Starlings (Sturnidae)
- ❑ European Starling

Wagtails & Pipits (Motacillidae)
- ❑ American Pipit
- ❑ *Sprague's Pipit* (MN only) (en)

Waxwings (Bombycillidae)
- ❑ Bohemian Waxwing
- ❑ Cedar Waxwing

Silky-Flycatchers (Ptilogonatidae)
- ❑ *Phainopepla* (WI only)

Wood-Warblers (Parulidae)
- ❑ Blue-winged Warbler
- ❑ Golden-winged Warbler
- ❑ Tennessee Warbler
- ❑ Orange-crowned Warbler
- ❑ Nashville Warbler
- ❑ Northern Parula
- ❑ Yellow Warbler
- ❑ Chestnut-sided Warbler
- ❑ Magnolia Warbler
- ❑ Cape May Warbler
- ❑ Black-throated Blue Warbler
- ❑ Yellow-rumped Warbler
- ❑ *Black-throated Gray Warbler*
- ❑ Black-throated Green Warbler
- ❑ *Townsend's Warbler*
- ❑ *Hermit Warbler*
- ❑ Blackburnian Warbler
- ❑ Yellow-throated Warbler
- ❑ Pine Warbler
- ❑ *Kirtland's Warbler*
- ❑ Prairie Warbler
- ❑ Palm Warbler
- ❑ Bay-breasted Warbler
- ❑ Blackpoll Warbler
- ❑ Cerulean Warbler (th:WI; sc:MN)
- ❑ Black-and-white Warbler
- ❑ American Redstart
- ❑ Prothonotary Warbler
- ❑ Worm-eating Warbler (en:WI)
- ❑ *Swainson's Warbler* (WI only)
- ❑ Ovenbird
- ❑ Northern Waterthrush
- ❑ Louisiana Waterthrush (sc:MN)
- ❑ Kentucky Warbler (th:WI)

- ❑ Connecticut Warbler
- ❑ Mourning Warbler
- ❑ *MacGillivray's Warbler*
- ❑ Common Yellowthroat
- ❑ Hooded Warbler (th:WI; sc:MN)
- ❑ Wilson's Warbler
- ❑ Canada Warbler
- ❑ *Painted Redstart* (MN only)
- ❑ Yellow-breasted Chat

Tanagers (Thraupidae)

- ❑ Summer Tanager
- ❑ Scarlet Tanager
- ❑ Western Tanager

Sparrows & Allies (Emberizidae)

- ❑ *Green-tailed Towhee*
- ❑ Spotted Towhee
- ❑ Eastern Towhee
- ❑ *Rufous-crowned Sparrow* (WI only)
- ❑ American Tree Sparrow
- ❑ Chipping Sparrow
- ❑ Clay-colored Sparrow
- ❑ *Brewer's Sparrow* (MN only)
- ❑ Field Sparrow (sc:WI)
- ❑ Vesper Sparrow (sc:WI)
- ❑ Lark Sparrow (sc:WI)
- ❑ *Black-throated Sparrow*
- ❑ *Lark Bunting*
- ❑ Savannah Sparrow
- ❑ Grasshopper Sparrow (sc:WI)
- ❑ *Baird's Sparrow* (en:MN)
- ❑ Henslow's Sparrow (en:MN; th:WI)
- ❑ Le Conte's Sparrow (sc:WI)
- ❑ Nelson's Sharp-tailed Sparrow (sc)
- ❑ Fox Sparrow
- ❑ Song Sparrow
- ❑ Lincoln's Sparrow
- ❑ Swamp Sparrow
- ❑ White-throated Sparrow
- ❑ Harris's Sparrow
- ❑ White-crowned Sparrow
- ❑ *Golden-crowned Sparrow*
- ❑ Dark-eyed Junco
- ❑ *McCown's Longspur* (MN only)
- ❑ Lapland Longspur
- ❑ Smith's Longspur
- ❑ Chestnut-collared Longspur (en:MN)
- ❑ Snow Bunting

Grosbeaks & Buntings (Cardinalidae)

- ❑ Northern Cardinal
- ❑ Rose-breasted Grosbeak
- ❑ *Black-headed Grosbeak*
- ❑ Blue Grosbeak
- ❑ *Lazuli Bunting*
- ❑ Indigo Bunting
- ❑ *Painted Bunting*
- ❑ Dickcissel (sc:WI)

Blackbirds & Allies (Icteridae)

- ❑ Bobolink (sc:WI)
- ❑ Red-winged Blackbird
- ❑ Eastern Meadowlark (sc:WI)
- ❑ Western Meadowlark (sc:WI)
- ❑ Yellow-headed Blackbird
- ❑ Rusty Blackbird
- ❑ Brewer's Blackbird
- ❑ Common Grackle
- ❑ *Great-tailed Grackle* (MN only)
- ❑ Brown-headed Cowbird
- ❑ Orchard Oriole (sc:WI)
- ❑ *Streak-backed Oriole* (WI only)
- ❑ Baltimore Oriole
- ❑ *Bullock's Oriole*
- ❑ *Scott's Oriole*

Finches (Fringillidae)

- ❑ *Brambling*
- ❑ *Gray-crowned Rosy-Finch*
- ❑ Pine Grosbeak
- ❑ Purple Finch
- ❑ *Cassin's Finch* (MN only)
- ❑ House Finch
- ❑ Red Crossbill
- ❑ White-winged Crossbill
- ❑ Common Redpoll
- ❑ Hoary Redpoll
- ❑ Pine Siskin
- ❑ American Goldfinch
- ❑ Evening Grosbeak

Old World Sparrows (Passeridae)

- ❑ House Sparrow
- ❑ *Eurasian Tree Sparrow*

SCIENTIFIC INDEX

This index references only the primary species accounts.

A

Accipiter
- *cooperii*, 93
- *gentilis*, 94
- *striatus*, 92

Actitis macularia, 132
Aechmophorus
- *clarkii*, 42
- *occidentalis*, 41

Aegolius
- *acadicus*, 187
- *funereus*, 186

Agelaius phoeniceus, 336
Aix sponsa, 63
Ammodramus
- *bairdii*, 360
- *henslowii*, 315
- *leconteii*, 316
- *nelsoni*, 317
- *savannarum*, 314

Anas
- *acuta*, 71
- *americana*, 65
- *clypeata*, 70
- *crecca*, 72
- *cyanoptera*, 69
- *discors*, 68
- *penelope*, 357
- *platyrhynchos*, 67
- *rubripes*, 66
- *strepera*, 64

Anser albifrons, 56
Anthus
- *rubescens*, 263
- *spragueii*, 360

Aquila chrysaetos, 101
Archilochus colubris, 191
Ardea
- *alba*, 48
- *herodias*, 47

Arenaria interpres, 137
Asio
- *flammeus*, 185
- *otus*, 184

Athene cunicularia, 359
Aythya
- *affinis*, 77
- *americana*, 74
- *collaris*, 75
- *marila*, 76
- *valisineria*, 73

B

Baeolophus bicolor, 237
Bartramia longicauda, 133
Bombycilla
- *cedrorum*, 265
- *garrulus*, 264

Bonasa umbellus, 109
Botaurus lentiginosus, 45
Branta
- *bernicla*, 357
- *canadensis*, 59

Bubo virginianus, 179
Bubulcus ibis, 51
Bucephala
- *albeola*, 83
- *clangula*, 84
- *islandica*, 357

Buteo
- *jamaicensis*, 98
- *lagopus*, 100
- *lineatus*, 95
- *platypterus*, 96
- *regalis*, 99
- *swainsoni*, 97

Butorides virescens, 52

C

Calamospiza melanocorys, 360
Calcarius
- *lapponicus*, 326
- *ornatus*, 328
- *pictus*, 327

Calidris
- *alba*, 139
- *alpina*, 147
- *bairdii*, 144
- *canutus*, 138
- *ferruginea*, 358
- *fuscicollis*, 143
- *himantopus*, 148
- *maritima*, 146
- *mauri*, 141
- *melanotos*, 145
- *minutilla*, 142
- *pusilla*, 140

Caprimulgus
- *carolinensis*, 360
- *voiciferus*, 189

Cardinalis cardinalis, 330
Carduelis
- *flammea*, 351
- *hornemanni*, 352
- *pinus*, 353
- *tristis*, 354

Carpodacus
- *mexicanus*, 348
- *purpureus*, 347

Cathartes aura, 55
Catharus
- *fuscescens*, 252
- *guttatus*, 255
- *minimus*, 253
- *ustulatus*, 254

Catoptrophorus semipalmatus, 131
Certhia americana, 240
Ceryle alcyon, 192
Chaetura pelagica, 190
Charadrius
- *melodus*, 125
- *semipalmatus*, 124
- *vociferus*, 126

Chen
- *caerulescens*, 57
- *rossii*, 58

Chlidonias niger, 173
Chondestes grammacus, 312
Chordeiles minor, 188
Circus cyaneus, 91
Cistothorus
- *palustris*, 245
- *platensis*, 244

Clangula hyemalis, 82
Coccothraustes vespertinus, 355
Coccyzus
- *americanus*, 177
- *erythropthalmus*, 176

Colaptes auratus, 200
Colinus virginianus, 114
Columba livia, 174
Contopus
- *cooperi*, 203
- *virens*, 204

Corvus
- *brachyrhynchos*, 226
- *corax*, 227

Coturnicops noveboracensis, 115
Cyanocitta cristata, 224
Cygnus
- *buccinator*, 61
- *columbianus*, 62
- *olor*, 60

D

Dendroica
- *caerulescens*, 276
- *castanea*, 284
- *cerulea*, 286
- *coronata*, 277
- *discolor*, 282
- *dominica*, 280
- *fusca*, 279

kirtlandii, 360
magnolia, 274
palmarum, 283
pensylvanica, 273
petechia, 272
pinus, 281
striata, 285
tigrina, 275
virens, 278
Dolichonyx oryzivorus, 335
Dryocopus pileatus, 201
Dumetella carolinensis, 259

E
Egretta
caerulea, 50
thula, 49
tricolor, 357
Empidonax
alnorum, 207
flaviventris, 205
minimus, 209
traillii, 208
virescens, 206
Eremophila alpestris, 228
Euphagus
carolinus, 340
cyanocephalus, 341

F
Falcipennis canadensis, 110
Falco
columbarius, 103
mexicanus, 106
peregrinus, 105
rusticolus, 104
sparverius, 102
Fulica americana, 120

G
Gallinago delicata, 153
Gallinula chloropus, 119
Gavia
immer, 36
pacifica, 35
stellata, 34
Geothlypis trichas, 297
Grus
americana, 358
canadensis, 121

H
Haliaeetus leucocephalus, 90
Helmitheros vermivorus, 290
Himantopus mexicanus, 358
Hirundo rustica, 234
Histrionicus histrionicus, 78
Hylocichla mustelina, 256

I
Icteria virens, 301
Icterus
galbula, 345
spurius, 344
Ictinia mississippiensis, 358
Ixobrychus exilis, 46
Ixoreus naevius, 258

J
Junco hyemalis, 325

L
Lanius
excubitor, 215
ludovicianus, 214
Larus
argentatus, 164
atricilla, 158
californicus, 359
canus, 162
delawarensis, 163
fuscus, 167
glaucescens, 359
glaucoides, 166
hyperboreus, 168
marinus, 169
minutus, 160
philidelphia, 161
pipixcan, 159
ridibundus, 358
thayeri, 165
Limnodromus
griseus, 151
scolopaceus, 152
Limosa
fedoa, 136
haemastica, 135
Lophodytes cucullatus, 85
Loxia
curvirostra, 349
leucoptera, 350

M
Melanerpes
carolinus, 194
erythrocephalus, 193
Melanitta
fusca, 80
nigra, 81
perspicillata, 79
Meleagris gallopavo, 113
Melospiza
georgiana, 321
lincolnii, 320
melodia, 319
Mergus
merganser, 86
serrator, 87
Mimus polyglottos, 260
Mniotilta varia, 287
Molothrus ater, 343
Myadestes townsendi, 251
Myiarchus crinitus, 211

N
Numenius phaeopus, 134
Nyctanassa violacea, 54
Nyctea scandiaca, 180
Nycticorax nycticorax, 53

O
Oporornis
agilis, 295
formosus, 294
philadelphia, 296
Otus asio, 178
Oxyura jamaicensis, 88

P
Pagophila eburnea, 359
Pandion haliaetus, 89
Parula americana, 271
Passer domesticus, 356
Passerculus sandwichensis, 313
Passerella iliaca, 318
Passerina
amoena, 360
caerulea, 332
cyanea, 333
Pelecanus erythrorhynchos, 43
Perdix perdix, 107
Perisoreus canadensis, 223
Petrochelidon pyrrhonota, 233
Phalacrocorax auritus, 44
Phalaropus
fulicarius, 358
lobatus, 156
tricolor, 155
Phasianus colchicus, 108
Pheucticus
ludovicianus, 331
melanocephalus, 360
Philomachus pugnax, 150
Pica hudsonia, 225
Picoides
arcticus, 199
pubescens, 196
tridactylus, 198
villosus, 197
Pinicola enucleator, 346
Pipilo
chlorurus, 360
erythrophthalamus, 306
maculatus, 305
Piranga
ludoviciana, 304

olivacea, 303
rubra, 302
Plectrophenax nivalis, 329
Plegadis
chihi, 357
falcinellus, 357
Pluvialis
dominica, 123
squatarola, 122
Podiceps
auritus, 38
grisegena, 39
nigricollis, 40
Podilymbus podiceps, 37
Poecile
atricapilla, 235
hudsonica, 236
Polioptila caerulea, 248
Pooecetes gramineus, 311
Porphyrio martinica, 358
Porzana carolina, 118
Progne subis, 229
Protonotaria citrea, 289

Q

Quiscalus quiscula, 342

R

Rallus
elegans, 116
limicola, 117
Recurvirostra americana, 127
Regulus
calendula, 247
satrapa, 246
Riparia riparia, 232
Rissa tridactyla, 359

S

Sayornis phoebe, 210
Scolopax minor, 154
Seiurus
aurocapillus, 291
motacilla, 293
noveboracensis, 292
Selasphorus rufus, 360
Setophaga ruticilla, 288
Sialia
currocoides, 250
sialis, 249
Sitta
canadensis, 238
carolinensis, 239
Somateria spectabilis, 357
Sphyrapicus varius, 195
Spiza americana, 334
Spizella
arborea, 307
pallida, 309
passerina, 308
pusilla, 310
Stelgidopteryx serripennis, 231
Stercorarius
longicaudus, 358
parasiticus, 157
pomarinus, 358
Sterna
antillarum, 359
caspia, 170
forsteri, 172
hirundo, 171
paradisaea, 359
Sternus vulgaris, 262
Strix
nebulosa, 183
varia, 182
Sturnella
magna, 337
neglecta, 338
Surnia ulula, 181

T

Tachycineta bicolor, 230
Thryothorus lucovicianus, 241
Toxostoma rufum, 261
Tringa
flavipes, 129
melanoleuca, 128
solitaria, 130
Troglodytes
aedon, 242
troglodytes, 243
Tryngites subruficollis, 149
Turdus migratorius, 257
Tympanuchus
cupido, 112
phasianellus, 111
Tyrannus tyrannus, 213
Tyrannus verticalis, 212
Tyto alba, 359

V

Vermivora
celata, 269
chrysoptera, 267
peregrina, 268
pinus, 266
ruficapilla, 270
Vireo
bellii, 217
flavifrons, 218
gilvus, 220
griseus, 216
olivaceus, 222
philadelphicus, 221
solitarius, 219

W

Wilsonia
canadensis, 300
citrina, 298
pusilla, 299

X

Xanthocephalus xanthocephalus, 339
Xema sabini, 359

Z

Zenaida macroura, 175
Zonotrichia
albicollis, 322
leucophrys, 324
querula, 323

INDEX OF COMMON NAMES

Page numbers in boldface type refer to the primary species accounts.

A

Avocet, American, **127**

B

Baldpate. *See* Wigeon, American
Bird, Butcher. *See* Shrike, Northern
Bittern
American, **45**, 46, 52, 53
Least, 45, **46**, 52, 116
Blackbird. *See also* Bobolink; Cowbird; Grackle; Meadowlark
Brewer's, 262, 336, 339, 340, **341**, 342, 343
Red-winged, **336**, 342
Rusty, 262, 336, 339, **340**, 341, 342, 343
Yellow-headed, **339**
Blind One. *See* Owl, Boreal
Bluebill. *See* Scaup, Greater
Bluebird
Eastern, 224, **249**, 250, 251
Mountain, 249, **250**, 251, 333
Bobolink, **335**
Bobwhite, Northern, 107, **114**
Brant, 59, 357
Bufflehead, 78, **83**, 85
Bunting
Indigo, 332, **333**
Lark, 360
Lazuli, 360
Snow, 326, **329**

C

Camp Robber. *See* Jay, Gray
Canvasback, **73**, 74
Cardinal, Northern, 302, 303, **330**
Catbird, Gray, 251, **259**, 260
Chat, Yellow-breasted, **301**
Chickadee
Black-capped, **235**, 236, 239, 246, 285
Boreal, 235, **236**, 246
Chuck-will's-widow, 189, 360
Coot, American, 37, 80, 119, **120**
Cormorant, Double-crested, 41, **44**, 59
Cowbird, Brown-headed, 262, 336, 341, **343**
Crane
Sandhill, 47, **121**
Whooping, 48, 121, 358
Creeper, Brown, **240**
Crossbill
Red, 346, 347, 348, **349**, 350
White-winged, 346, 349, **350**
Crow
American, 201, **226**, 227
Rain. *See* Cuckoo, Yellow-billed
Cuckoo
Black-billed, 175, **176**, 177
Yellow-billed, 175, 176, **177**
Curlew. *See also* Whimbrel
Eskimo, 123, 134
Long-billed, 134, 136

D

Dickcissel, **334**, 337, 338
Dove
Mourning, 174, **175**, 176, 177
Rock, 103, **174**, 175
Dowitcher
Long-billed, 135, 136, 138, 151, **152**, 153, 154
Short-billed, 135, 136, 138, **151**,152, 153, 154
Duck. *See also* Bufflehead; Canvasback; Eider; Gadwall; Goldeneye; Mallard;Merganser; Pintail; Redhead; Scaup; Scoter; Shoveler; Teal; Wigeon
American Black, **66**, 67
Harlequin, 63, **78**, 83
Long-tailed, 71, **82**
Ring-necked, 74, **75**, 76, 77
Ruddy, 69, **88**
Wood, **63**
Dunlin, 139, 141, **147**, 148

E

Eagle
Bald, 55, 89, **90**, 101
Golden, 55, 90, **101**
Egret
Cattle, 47, 48, 49, **51**
Great, 47, **48**, 49, 51
Snowy, 47, 48, **49**, 51
Eider, King, 357

F

Falcon. *See also* Gyrfalcon; Kestrel; Merlin
Peregrine, 103, 104, **105**, 106
Prairie, **106**
Finch. *See also* Crossbill; Goldfinch; Grosbeak, Evening; Grosbeak, Pine; Redpoll; Siskin
Hollywood. *See* House F.
House, 347, **348**, 349, 350, 353
Purple, 331, **347**, 348, 349, 350, 353
Flicker, Northern, 194, **200**
Flycatcher. *See also* Kingbird; Phoebe; Wood-Pewee
Acadian, 205, **206**, 207, 208, 209
Alder, 205, 206, **207**, 208, 209
Great Crested, **211**, 212
Least, 205, 206, 207, 208, **209**
Olive-sided, **203**, 204, 210, 213
Willow, 205, 206, 207, **208**, 209
Yellow-bellied, **205**, 206, 207, 208, 209, 211

G

Gadwall, **64**, 65, 66, 71
Gallinule, Purple, 358
Gnatcatcher, Blue-gray, **248**
Godwit
Hudsonian, 131, **135**, 136
Marbled, 131, 135, **136**
Goldeneye
Barrow's, 83, 84, 357
Common, 83, **84**, 86
Golden-Plover, American, 122, **123**
Goldfinch, American, 272, 334, **354**, 355
Goose. *See also* Brant
Canada, 44, 56, **59**
Greater White-fronted, **56**, 59
Ross's, 57, **58**
Snow, 56, **57**, 58, 59, 61, 62
Goshawk, Northern, **94**, 104
Grackle, Common, 340, 341, **342**, 343
Grebe
Clark's, 41, **42**
Eared, 37, 38, 39, **40**, 41
Horned, 37, **38**, 39, 40, 41
Pied-billed, **37**, 38, 39, 40

Red-necked, 38, **39**, 40, 41
Western, 39, **41**, 42
Grosbeak
Black-headed, 305, 360
Blue, **332**, 333
Evening, 346, 354, **355**
Pine, **346**, 349, 350, 355
Rose-breasted, **331**
Grouse. *See also* Bobwhite; Partridge; Pheasant
Ruffed, 107, **109**, 110, 111, 114
Sharp-tailed, 109, 110, **111**, 112
Spruce, 109, **110**, 111
Gull
Black-headed, 158, 159, 160, 161, 358
Bonaparte's, 158, 159, 160, **161**
California, 164, 359
Franklin's, 158, **159**, 160, 161
Glaucous, 163, 164, 165, 166, 167, **168**, 169
Glaucous-winged, 359
Great Black-backed, 164, 166, 167, 168, **169**
Herring, 163, **164**, 165, 166, 167, 168
Iceland, 163, 164, 165, **166**, 167, 168
Ivory, 359
Laughing, **158**, 159, 160
Lesser Black-backed, 163, 164, 165, 166, **167**
Little, 158, 159, **160**, 161
Mew, **162**, 163
Ring-billed, 162, **163**, 164, 165, 166, 167
Sabine's, 159, 160, 161, 359
Thayer's, 163, 164, **165**, 166, 167, 168
Gyrfalcon, 94, **104**, 105, 106

H

Harrier
Hen. *See* Northern H.
Northern, **91**, 100
Hawk. *See also* Goshawk; Harrier
Broad-winged, 95, **96**, 98
Cooper's, 92, **93**, 94, 103
Ferruginous, **99**
Marsh. *See* Harrier, Northern
Pigeon. *See* Merlin
Red-shouldered, **95**, 98
Red-tailed, 91, 95, 97, **98**, 99
Rough-legged, 55, 89, 91, 98, 99, **100**, 101
Sharp-shinned, **92**, 93, 94, 102, 103
Sparrow. *See* Kestrel, American
Swainson's, **97**, 98, 99, 106
Hen
Fool. *See* Grouse, Spruce
Heath. *See* Prairie-Chicken, Greater
Mud. *See* Coot, American
Heron. *See also* Bittern; Egret; Night-Heron
Great Blue, **47**, 53, 121
Green, 45, 46, 47, **52**, 53
Little Blue, 47, 49, **50**
Tricolored, 47, 357
Hummingbird
Ruby-throated, **191**
Rufous, 191, 360
Hun. *See* Partridge, Gray

I

Ibis
Glossy, 357
White-faced, 357

J

Jaeger
Long-tailed, 157, 358
Parasitic, **157**
Pomarine, 157, 358
Jay
Blue, 192, **224**, 250
Canada. *See* Gray J.
Gray, **223**, 259
Junco
Dark-eyed, 306, **325**
Slate-colored. *See* Dark-eyed J.

K

Kestrel, American, 92, 93, **102**, 103
Killdeer, 124, 125, **126**
Kingbird
Eastern, 203, 204, 210, 212, **213**, 230
Western, 211, **212**
Kingfisher, Belted, **192**, 224
Kinglet
Golden-crowned, **246**, 247, 248
Ruby-crowned, 217, 246, **247**, 248, 269, 273
Kite, Mississippi, 358
Kittiwake, Black-legged, 359
Knot, Red, 122, **138**, 139, 150, 151, 152

L

Lark, Horned, **228**, 263
Longspur
Chestnut-collared, **328**
Lapland, 311, **326**, 327, 329
McCown's, 328
Smith's, 326, **327**
Loon
Common, 34, 35, **36**, 41, 44, 86
Pacific, 34, **35**, 36
Red-throated, **34**, 35, 36
Lords and Ladies. *See* Duck, Harlequin

M

Magpie, Black-billed, **225**
Mallard, 64, 66, **67**, 70, 71, 86
Martin, Purple, **229**, 230, 234
Meadowlark
Eastern, 334, **337**, 338
Western, 337, **338**
Merganser
Common, 67, 85, **86**, 87
Hooded, 63, 83, **85**
Red-breasted, 85, 86, **87**
Merlin, 92, 93, 102, **103**, 105, 106, 174
Mockingbird, Northern, 214, 215, 223, 259, **260**
Moorhen, Common, **119**, 120

N

Nighthawk, Common, **188**, 189
Night-Heron
Black-crowned, 45, 46, 47, 52, **53**, 54
Yellow-crowned, 45, 46, 47, 53, **54**
Nine-Killer. *See* Shrike, Northern
Nuthatch
Red-breasted, **238**, 239, 240
White-breasted, 238, **239**, 240

O

Oldsquaw. *See* Duck, Long-tailed
Oriole
Baltimore, 211, 302, 303, 304, 344, **345**
Orchard, 302, 303, **344**, 345
Osprey, **89**, 90
Ovenbird, 256, **291**, 292, 293
Owl. *See also* Screech-Owl
Barn, 359
Barred, 179, **182**, 183, 185
Boreal, 181, **186**, 187
Burrowing, 359

Great Gray, 179, 182, **183**, 185
Great Horned, 178, **179**, 182, 183, 184, 185
Long-eared, 178, 179, **184**, 185
Northern Hawk, **181**, 182, 186, 187
Northern Saw-whet, 178, 181, 186, **187**
Short-eared, 179, 181, 182, 183, 184, **185**
Snowy, **180**, 183
Tengmalm's. *See* Boreal O.

P

Partridge
Gray, **107**, 114
Hungarian. *See* Gray P.
Parula, Northern, **271**, 300
Peep. *See* Dunlin; Knot; Sanderling; Sandpiper, Baird's; Sandpiper, Least; Sandpiper, Pectoral; Sandpiper, Purple; Sandpiper, Semipalmated; Sandpiper, Stilt; Sandpiper, Western; Sandpiper, White-rumped
Pelican, American White, **43**, 57, 58
Phalarope
Red, 155, 156, 358
Red-necked, 155, **156**
Wilson's, **155**, 156
Pheasant, Ring-necked, **108**, 111, 113
Phoebe, Eastern, 203, 204, **210**
Pigeon. *See* Dove, Rock
Pintail, Northern, 64, **71**, 82
Pipit
American, 228, **263**, 311, 327
Sprague's, 263, 360
Water. *See* American P.
Plover. *See also* Golden-Plover; Killdeer
Black-bellied, **122**
Piping, 124, **125**, 126
Semipalmated, **124**, 125, 126
Prairie-Chicken, Greater, 109, 111, **112**

R

Rail. *See also* Sora
Carolina. *See* Sora
King, **116**, 117, 118
Virginia, 115, 116, **117**, 118
Yellow, **115**, 117, 118
Raven, Common, 201, 226, **227**
Redhead, 73, **74**, 75, 76, 77
Redpoll
Common, **351**, 352, 353
Hoary, 351, **352**, 353
Redstart, American, 273, **288**
Reeve. *See* Ruff
Robin, American, **257**, 258
Ruff, 145, 149, **150**

S

Sanderling, 138, **139**, 140, 141, 144, 147
Sandpiper. *See also* Dowitcher; Dunlin; Godwit; Knot; Ruff; Sanderling; Snipe; Turnstone; Whimbrel; Willet; Woodcock; Yellowlegs
Baird's, 140, 141, 143, **144**
Buff-breasted, 123, 133, 138, **149**
Curlew, 138, 143, 148, 358
Least, 139, 140, 141, **142**, 144, 147
Pectoral, 133, 144, **145**, 149
Purple, **146**
Semipalmated, 139, **140**, 141, 142, 144, 147
Solitary, 129, **130**, 132
Spotted, 130, **132**
Stilt, 143, 147, **148**
Upland, **133**, 134, 149
Western, 139, 140, **141**, 142, 144, 147
White-rumped, 140, 141, **143**, 144
Sapsucker, Yellow-bellied, 193, **195**, 196, 197, 198, 199
Scaup
Greater, 74, 75, **76**, 77
Lesser, 74, 75, 76, **77**
Scoter
Black, 79, 80, **81**
Common. *See* Black S.
Surf, 78, **79**, 80, 81
White-winged, 78, 79, **80**, 81
Screech-Owl, Eastern, **178**, 179, 184
Shoveler, Northern, 67, 68, **70**
Shrike
Loggerhead, **214**, 215, 223, 260
Northern, 214, **215**, 223, 260
Siskin, Pine, 349, 350, 351, 352, **353**
Snipe
Common. *See* Wilson's S.
Wilson's, 151, 152, **153**, 154
Snow Bird. *See* Junco, Dark-eyed
Solitaire, Townsend's, 250, **251**, 259, 260
Sora, 115, 117, **118**
Sparrow. *See also* Bunting; Junco; Longspur; Towhee
American Tree, **307**, 308, 310, 321
Baird's, 360
Chipping, 307, **308**, 309, 310, 321, 324
Clay-colored, **309**
Field, 307, 308, **310**
Fox, 255, **318**, 319
Golden-crowned, 324
Grasshopper, 313, **314**, 315, 316, 317, 335
Harris's, **323**, 356
Henslow's, 314, **315**
House, 323, **356**
Lark, 311, **312**
Le Conte's, 314, 315, **316**, 317
Lincoln's, 313, 319, **320**, 321
Nelson's Sharp-tailed, 314, 316, **317**
Saltmarsh Sharp-tailed, 317
Savannah, **313**, 315, 317, 319, 320, 328, 335
Sharp-tailed. *See* Nelson's Sharp-tailed S.
Song, 313, 318, **319**, 320, 321
Swamp, 307, 308, 310, 320, **321**, 322
Vesper, **311**, 313, 327, 328, 335
White-crowned, 322, 323, **324**
White-throated, **322**, 323, 324
Starling, European, 229, **262**, 340, 341, 342
Stilt, Black-necked, 127, 358
Swallow. *See also* Martin
Bank, 230, 231, **232**
Barn, 229, 230, 233, **234**
Cliff, 231, 232, **233**, 234
Northern Rough-winged, 230, **231**, 232
Tree, 213, 229, **230**, 231, 232, 234
Swan
Mute, 57, 58, **60**, 61, 62
Trumpeter, 57, 58, 60, **61**, 62
Tundra, 57, 58, 60, 61, **62**
Swift, Chimney, **190**

T

Tanager
- Scarlet, 302, **303**, 330, 344, 345
- Summer, **302**, 303, 330, 344, 345
- Western, 302, 303, **304**

Teal
- Blue-winged, **68**, 69, 70, 71, 72
- Cinnamon, 68, **69**, 72, 88
- Green-winged, 68, 69, **72**

Tern
- Arctic, 170, 171, 172, 359
- Black, **173**
- Caspian, **170**, 171, 172
- Common, 170, **171**, 172
- Forster's, 170, 171, **172**
- Least, 359

Thrasher, Brown, 259, **261**

Thrush
- Bicknell's, 253
- Gray-cheeked, 252, **253**, 254, 255
- Hermit, 252, 253, 254, **255**, 261, 318
- Swainson's, 252, 253, **254**, 255
- Varied, 257, **258**
- Wood, **256**, 261

Titmouse, Tufted, **237**

Towhee
- Eastern, 305, **306**, 325
- Green-tailed, 360
- Rufous-sided. *See* Spotted T.
- Spotted, **305**, 306

Turkey, Wild, **113**

Turnstone, Ruddy, **137**

V

Veery, **252**, 253, 254, 255

Vireo
- Bell's, **217**
- Blue-headed, 216, 218, **219**
- Philadelphia, 220, **221**, 222, 268, 276
- Red-eyed, 220, 221, **222**, 290
- Traill's. *See* Alder F.
- Warbling, 217, **220**, 221, 222, 268
- White-eyed, **216**, 218, 219
- Yellow-throated, 216, **218**, 219, 280, 281

Vulture
- Black, 55
- Turkey, **55**, 101

W

Warbler. *See also* Chat; Ovenbird; Parula; Redstart; Waterthrush; Yellowthroat
- Bay-breasted, 273, 275, 281, 282, **284**, 285, 286
- Black-and-white, 285, **287**
- Blackburnian, 278, **279**, 280
- Blackpoll, 235, 281, 282, 284, **285**, 286, 287
- Black-throated Blue, **276**, 286
- Black-throated Green, 267, 275, **278**, 279
- Blue-winged, **266**, 271, 289
- Brewster's, 266
- Canada, 294, **300**
- Cape May, 274, **275**, 277, 278, 284
- Cerulean, 271, 276, **286**
- Chestnut-sided, **273**, 277, 284
- Connecticut, 270, **295**, 296
- Golden-winged, **267**
- Hooded, 289, **298**
- Kentucky, 280, **294**, 297, 298, 299, 300
- Kirtland's, 282, 300, 360
- Lawrence's, 266
- Magnolia, **274**, 275, 277, 280
- Mourning, 270, 295, **296**
- Myrtle. *See* Yellow-rumped W.
- Nashville, **270**, 295, 296, 297, 299
- Orange-crowned, 220, 247, 268, **269**, 272, 297, 299
- Palm, **283**
- Pine, 216, 218, 266, 278, **281**, 282, 283, 286
- Prairie, 266, 274, 279, 281, **282**, 283
- Prothonotary, 266, **289**
- Tennessee, 220, 221, 222, **268**, 269, 276
- Wilson's, 269, 270, 272, 297, 298, **299**, 354
- Worm-eating, **290**
- Yellow, 266, 269, **272**, 289, 297, 298, 299
- Yellow-rumped, 267, 271, 274, **277**, 283
- Yellow-throated, 267, 271, 277, 279, **280**, 282, 294

Waterthrush
- Louisiana, 290, 291, 292, **293**
- Northern, 290, 291, **292**, 293

Waxwing
- Bohemian, **264**, 265
- Cedar, 264, **265**

Whimbrel, **134**

Whip-poor-will, 188, **189**

Whiskey Jack. *See* Jay, Gray

Whistler. *See* Goldeneye, Common

Wigeon
- American, 64, **65**, 72
- Eurasian, 65, 357

Willet, 127, 128, 129, **131**, 133

Woodcock, American, 153, **154**

Woodpecker. *See also* Flicker; Sapsucker
- Black-backed, 195, 196, 197, 198, **199**
- Downy, 195, **196**, 197
- Hairy, 195, 196, **197**, 198, 199
- Pileated, **201**
- Red-bellied, 193, **194**, 200
- Red-headed, **193**, 194, 195
- Three-toed, 195, 196, 197, **198**, 199

Wood-Pewee, Eastern, 203, **204**, 207, 208, 209, 210, 213

Wren
- Carolina, **241**, 243, 245
- House, 241, **242**, 243, 244, 245
- Jenny. *See* House W.
- Long-billed Marsh. *See* Marsh W.
- Marsh, 241, 243, 244, **245**
- Sedge, 241, 242, 243, **244**, 245
- Short-billed Marsh. *See* Sedge W.
- Winter, 241, 242, **243**, 244

Y

Yellowlegs
- Greater, **128**, 129, 131, 135, 136, 148, 150
- Lesser, 128, **129**, 130, 148, 150, 155

Yellowthroat, Common, 269, 270, 272, 296, **297**, 298, 299

ABOUT THE AUTHORS

Robert B. Janssen

Bob Janssen has been a birder since he rode his tricycle past a field and saw his first meadowlark at the age of five. A specialist in Minnesota birds, he is the author of *Birds in Minnesota* and for 38 years was the editor of *The Loon,* the journal of the Minnesota Ornithologists' Union. Bob is currently involved in a project to inventory the bird populations in Minnesota's 72 state parks. Using field surveys as well as historical records, the aim of the project is to create a standardized checklist of birds for each park, including the frequency of each bird species at various times of the year. In addition to birding, Bob has taught a course in Spiritual Ecology at the United Theological Seminary of the Twin Cities, and in the spring of 2003 will share his birding knowledge with students at the North House Folk School in Grand Marais.

Daryl D. Tessen

Daryl Tessen is a Wisconsin native and lifetime birder. Though he has concentrated on Wisconsin birds, he is currently involved as a participant and co-leader with birding tours to the western states, including Wyoming, Oregon, Texas and Arizona, and is expanding his birding into the eastern United States. Daryl has been actively involved with the Wisconsin Society for Ornithology for 45 years and was the Western Great Lakes Region editor for *North American Birds* for 24 years. He also edited the second (1976), third (1989) and fourth (2000) editions of *Wisconsin's Favorite Bird Haunts* and has been involved with the North American Breeding Bird Survey since 1967.

Gregory Kennedy

Gregory Kennedy has been an active naturalist since he was very young. He is the author of many books on natural history and has also produced film and television shows on environmental issues and indigenous concerns in Southeast Asia, New Guinea, South and Central America, the high Arctic and elsewhere. He has also been involved in numerous research projects around the world ranging from studies in the upper canopy of tropical and temperate rainforests to deepwater marine investigations.